Redesigning the World Trade Organization for the Twenty-first Century

Studies in International Governance is a research and policy analysis series from the Centre for International Governance Innovation (CIGI) and Wilfrid Laurier University Press. Titles in the series provide timely consideration of emerging trends and current challenges in the broad field of international governance. Representing diverse perspectives on important global issues, the series will be of interest to students and academics while serving also as a reference tool for policy-makers and experts engaged in policy discussion.

Redesigning the World Trade Organization for the Twenty-first Century

Debra P. Steger, editor

The Centre for International Governance Innovation
Centre pour l'innovation dans la gouvernance internationale

Wilfrid Laurier University Press

International Development Research Centre
Ottawa • Cairo • Dakar • Montevideo • Nairobi • New Delhi • Singapore

Wilfrid Laurier University Press acknowledges the financial support of the Government of Canada through its Book Publishing Industry Development Program for its publishing activities. Wilfrid Laurier University Press acknowledges the financial support of the Centre for International Governance Innovation. The Centre for International Governance Innovation gratefully acknowledges support for its work program from the Government of Canada and the Government of Ontario.

Library and Archives Canada Cataloguing in Publication

Redesigning the World Trade Organization for the twenty-first century / Debra P. Steger, editor.
(Studies in international governance series)
Co-published by the International Development Research Centre and the Centre for
    International Governance Innovation.
Includes bibliographical references and index.
Also available in electronic formats.
ISBN 978-1-55458-156-6

1. World Trade Organization. 2. World Trade Organization—Reorganization.
3. World Trade Organization—Management. I. Steger, Debra P., 1952–
II. International Development Research Centre (Canada) III. Centre for
International Governance Innovation IV. Series: Studies in international governance

HF1385.R41 2010   343'.087   C2009-903703-3

Library and Archives Canada Cataloguing in Publication

Redesigning the World Trade Organization for the twenty-first century [electronic resource] /
Debra P. Steger, editor.

(Studies in international governance series)
Co-published by the International Development Research Centre and the Centre for
    International Governance Innovation.
Includes bibliographical references and index.
Also available in printed format.
ISBN 978-1-55458-174-0

1. World Trade Organization. 2. World Trade Organization—Reorganization.
3. World Trade Organization—Management. I. Steger, Debra P., 1952–
II. International Development Research Centre (Canada) III. Centre for
International Governance Innovation IV. Series: Studies in international governance

HF1385.R41 2010a   343'.087

Cover design by Blakeley Words+Pictures. Cover image: Pieter Bruegel, *The Tower of Babel*, courtesy of Das Kunsthistoriche Museum, Vienna. Text design by Catharine Bonas-Taylor.

International Development Research Centre
P.O. Box 8500, Ottawa, ON K1G 3H9, Canada
www.idrc.ca / info@idrc.ca
ISBN 978-1-55250-455-0 (e-book)

This book is printed on FSC recycled paper and is certified Ecologo. It is made from 100% post-consumer fibre, processed chlorine free, and manufactured using biogas energy.

Printed in Canada

Every reasonable effort has been made to acquire permission for copyright material used in this text, and to acknowledge all such indebtedness accurately. Any errors and omissions called to the publisher's attention will be corrected in future printings.

▦ ▦ ▦ Contents

卍 卍 卍 Foreword

Before the end of World War II, an essential element in maintaining the peace and ensuring future economic prosperity was the establishment of three inter-governmental organizations that would work in concert toward economic coop-eration and progress. Two of them, the Bretton Woods institutions—the Interna-tional Monetary Fund (IMF) and the International Bank for Reconstruction and Development (World Bank)—came into being with little delay. The third, the International Trade Organization (ITO), never came into existence, mainly because the Havana Charter was not ratified by the United States Congress.

In place of the ITO, a group of countries negotiated the General Agree-ment on Tariffs and Trade (GATT), which, after a precarious start, was brought into effect by means of a protocol of provisional application that offered few guarantees for its survival. Over time, the GATT managed to expand its mem-bership, carry out successive multilateral trade negotiations to liberalize access to markets, and develop a dispute settlement system. The GATT system of multilateral trade agreements was replaced by the newly created World Trade Organization (WTO) in 1995.

Over time, the GATT/WTO system has gradually improved its relation-ships with the IMF and the World Bank. At the conclusion of the Uruguay Round, ministers agreed to a 'declaration on achieving greater coherence in global economic policy making', in which they called on the WTO to pursue cooperation with the IMF and the bank. This ministerial decision accorded with Article III of the Marrakesh Agreement Establishing the WTO, which set out the basic functions of the WTO. The Ministerial Declaration spurred closer relations between the WTO, the IMF, and the World Bank, and a great deal has been achieved.

The overall structure and internal mechanisms of the WTO, the IMF, and the World Bank are not the same. In some respects, they differ noticeably. These differences in institutional structure, decision-making procedures, and cultures inevitably have repercussions for their ability to cooperate in a coherent manner. For historical reasons, the relationship between the three legs of the original Bretton Woods stool has never fully attained the aims of the post-war planners, nor has it led to cohesive policies and efficient allocation of responsibilities.

The world economy has now suffered a severe jolt, testing the very viability of the international financial system. The financial crisis that erupted in 2008 in the United States, and went on to endanger the global economy, has brought into sharp relief the ineffectiveness and lack of coherence in the international economic system. Governments have reacted both individually and jointly to this deepening crisis, and it has become crystal clear that only their utmost efforts will be enough to overcome the recession as it spreads and threatens overall welfare around the world.

One needs only to read the communiqué of the Group of 20 after its November 2008 Summit Meeting to identify the wide range of problem areas in which governments need to cooperate if their individual stimulus efforts are to succeed.

Trade, finance, credit, and monetary policy inevitably transcend national borders. The world economy is one integrated whole. A given measure taken by any one country will inevitably have repercussions on others. Only effective and coordinated cooperative action, including steps that need to be taken by inter-governmental organizations, will help to provide the necessary equilibrium. The leading international organizations have a crucial role to play at this critical juncture, and prominent among them are the IMF, the World Bank, and the WTO.

In response to the global financial crisis, leaders of the Group of 20 nations have committed themselves to reform the Bretton Woods institutions, in particular the IMF and the World Bank. The President of the World Bank and the Managing Director of the IMF have appointed high-level commissions to look into significant and meaningful reform of those two institutions. What about the WTO? Why is it not on the G20 leaders' radar screen? How can the intricate linkages between international finance and trade be ignored?

The GATT/WTO system is almost exactly as old as the IMF and the World Bank. The WTO also needs institutional reform to put it in step with the demands of the 21st century. All three organizations are woefully outdated. The visions that led to their creation belonged to leaders who had lived through the 1920s, the Great Depression, and the war years.

Today, the world economy is immeasurably more complex, multifaceted, and integrated than it was at the end of World War II. New financial structures, procedures, and interests have multiplied. Many countries have attained independence over this period. Developing countries are now rightfully taking a much greater share in global production, trade, and investment. The rapid economic growth in the emerging economies, in particular, has been stupendous and is bringing with it the rise of a middle class in these countries as well as a host of social, political, and environmental challenges. Multinational corporations are becoming increasingly diverse and powerful. The environment has become a subject of enormous importance for the future of mankind. The world—its problems and challenges—has completely changed since the 1940s when the original Bretton Woods system was conceived.

We are 70 years on and in the middle of a threatening and severe recession. This is the time for action. Governments failed to act in concert in the 1930s, and widespread misery was the outcome of selfish "beggar-thy-neighbour" policies that were designed to respond to each country's own problems, while they hoped that the devil would take the hind-most. As we well know, he took them all one by one.

Today, we are increasingly witnessing governments taking protectionist and nationalistic measures that may very well yield immediate results from their narrow point of view, but whose cumulative effect will be to isolate economies, obstruct the channels of trade and finance, lead to seriously increased disputes in the WTO and other forums, and impede the economic recovery we are all aiming for.

Within its sphere, the WTO is working to analyze these issues and to propose solutions. This is as it should be, but the current financial crisis calls for more. Most particularly, governments have not taken the unpalatable, difficult decisions they should have adopted in the Group of 20: the acceptance by all of a status quo commitment under which no new restrictive trade measures would be imposed.

Parallel to and provoked by the current crisis, the IMF and the World Bank have initiated their own reform processes. World leaders seem determined to redesign the IMF, in particular, to meet the challenges of the current financial crisis. Should the WTO not join them in an equivalent endeavour, not only will it be left behind, it will have missed the first real opportunity since the multilateral trading system was created to become a strong and valid partner in the Bretton Woods triumvirate.

In the past, the GATT/WTO system has shown its capacity to evolve with the times: witness the gradual evolution of the dispute settlement system; the innovative, although ill-fated, Tokyo Round agreements; the initially controversial, and now fully accepted, incorporation of trade in services into the system; and the massive Uruguay Round outcome. Even the Doha Round negotiations, while not concluded, have shown a tendency toward progressive innovation, especially in the areas of trade rules and dispute settlement. There is reason for optimism when it comes to the rules; however, the institutional aspects of the WTO as an organization are often overlooked.

The Sutherland Report on the future of the WTO in 2004 and the Warwick Report in 2007 have contributed perceptive insights into the functioning, objectives, and special characteristics of the multilateral trading system.

Let us never lose sight of the fact that the WTO agreements are 'hard law'. Governments are well aware of the direct and indirect consequences of rules and commitments undertaken in the WTO, and they are understandably cautious and prudent. To cite one example: in several rounds, changes in the dispute settlement system were adopted on a provisional basis, and it was only after they had proved to work in practice that the membership adopted them permanently. Any change in the institutional structure and procedures of the WTO will follow the pattern of the past; it will come at the end of a protracted and complex negotiation conducted by its Members and approved under the rule of consensus.

One aspect of the functioning of the WTO that calls for review is the duration of the multilateral trade negotiations. Initial rounds, such as those held at Annecy and Torquay, lasted a few months. Admittedly, the participation and the subject matter were considerably smaller than has been the case subsequently. The Dillon and Kennedy rounds were somewhat longer. Each successive round has taken longer. The Tokyo Round commenced in 1973 and concluded in 1979, the Uruguay Round took place from 1986 to 1994, and the Doha Round, which commenced in 2001, will hopefully finish in 2009 or 2010. The results of the Doha Round will be applied most likely over a transitional period of five years.

Admittedly, governments must conduct multilateral trade negotiations with care, and detailed preparation and consultation is required. Innumerable factors can cut across the best-laid plans, including the vagaries of internal politics. But unfortunately, the overall aims of a multilateral negotiating round risk losing significant contact with reality when there is a lapse of 10 or 15 years between the date of commencement and the date of implementation of the results. In the modern, fast-changing world we live in, this process has to adapt to meet current realities on an ongoing basis.

Clearly, it is imperative that governments conclude the Doha Round at the earliest possible moment, to avoid repeating errors of the past and to prompt economic recovery. But they also need to strengthen and modernize the multilateral trading system by focusing on reform of the WTO as an institution. In doing so, they must ensure that the WTO, the IMF, and the World Bank are capable of responding effectively, through their respective institutional structures, to the extremely close interconnections between their respective spheres of action.

This book explains why institutional reform of the WTO is so necessary at this critical juncture in world history. It contains thoughtful views from contributors on key aspects of the WTO that need to be redesigned to meet the challenges of the 21st century. Moreover, it includes contributions from researchers in the developing world as well as in developed countries. Rather than simply analyzing the current functioning of the WTO, its problems and challenges, this volume is also a call to action. It lays out proposals that are likely to become a blueprint for reform of the WTO as an institution.

Its contents are abundantly worthy of reflection and subsequent action. I recommend it highly to anyone who is concerned about the future of the global economy.

Julio Lacarte Muró
Montevideo, Uruguay
March 2009

🈂 🈂 🈂 Acknowledgements

This book is the result of a collaborative research project organized by the Emerging Dynamic Global Economies (EDGE) Network together with research institutes and experts around the world. The project was generously funded by Networks of Centres of Excellence Canada (NCE) and the International Development Research Centre (IDRC). Organizational meetings were held in London, England, and in Vancouver, Canada, in 2007. Inspiration and guidance was provided by Professor John H. Jackson, Julio Lacarte Muró, John Weekes, Jane Bradley, Gerhard Erasmus, Gabrielle Marceau, Krista Nadakavukaren-Schefer, Federico Ortino, Seema Sapra, and Peter Van den Bossche at the London meeting. In Vancouver, Padideh Ala'i, Henry Gao, and Julio Lacarte Muró helped to shape the substance and direction of the project. Early drafts of the contributions in this volume were presented and discussed at a workshop called Institutional Reform of the WTO, held at the Centre for International Governance Innovation (CIGI) in Waterloo, Canada, in March 2008.

I am extremely grateful to the contributors who have written and revised many drafts over the course of the past year. Without their hard work and dedication, this book would not have been written. They are Padideh Ala'i, Alberto Alvarez-Jiménez, Ljiljana Biukovic, Yves Bonzon, Thomas Cottier, Carolyn Deere Birkbeck, Manfred Elsig, Gerhard Erasmus, Henry Gao, Pablo Heidrich, Chin Leng Lim, Seema Sapra, Natalia Shpilkovskaya, Diana Tussie, Peter Van den Bossche, and Heng Wang. Thanks are also due to the participants who attended the CIGI workshop and provided their valuable comments on early drafts of the papers. In addition to the authors, the participants included Manmohan Agarwal, Alan Alexandroff, Agata Antkiewicz, Thomas Bernes, Terry Collins-Williams, William Davey, Michael Ewing-Chow, Pieter Jan Kuijper,

Julio Lacarte Muró, John Odell, Sylvia Ostry, Gregory Shaffer, and Robert Wolfe. The workshop was lively, stimulating, and engaging and provided fabulous fodder for the difficult work of revising the papers.

Early versions of some of the papers in this book were published in the Mini-Symposium on Transparency in the WTO in the Journal of International Economic Law, Volume 11 Number 4, December 2008, Oxford University Press. Included in this mini-symposium were articles by Peter Van den Bossche, Yves Bonzon, Padideh Ala'i, and Ljiljana Biukovič, as well as an introduction by me. Henry Gao and Chin Leng Lim also published an early version of their chapter in the same volume of the Journal of International Economic Law. Our appreciation is extended to Professor John Jackson, editor-in-chief, and his co-editors for graciously agreeing to publish the mini-symposium and the article by Professors Gao and Lim in the journal.

The EDGE Network in its life as the Network of Centres of Excellence was a collaborative, interdisciplinary project involving business leaders, scholars, and government officials from across Canada and around the world. Many people deserve recognition for their tireless efforts and dedication to the success of that enterprise—you know who you are. The Board of Directors and, in particular, Donald Campbell, chair of the Board, deserve commendation and praise for their unwavering loyalty and commitment of valuable time and energies to building the Network. This book and the companion volume edited by EDGE Network research leader Jeremy de Beer, *Implementing the World Intellectual Property Organization's Development Agenda*, are the fruits of that labour.

I am deeply indebted to Irena Pawlowski for her indefatigable, dedicated, and loyal assistance in the day-to-day operation of the EDGE Network, including the organization of meetings and workshops, as well as endless administrative, financial, and travel arrangements. David Quayat deserves a special vote of thanks for his remarkable job of tirelessly and persistently editing all the contributions. This book would not have been possible without them.

EDGE Network Research Fellow Alberto Alvarez-Jiménez is to be commended for his diligent, comprehensive research and writing several papers for the project. Natalia Shpilkovskaya also provided industrious and thorough research assistance in the preparation of the papers and bibliography.

The EDGE Network would not exist were it not for the significant funding from the NCE and the IDRC. At the NCE, Jean-Claude Gavrel and Pierre-François Le Fol deserve gratitude for their assistance and support in those critical early years. The wonderful people at IDRC and CIGI have provided ongoing encouragement and assistance for this project, including with the publication and dissemination of this book. In particular, I would like to thank Rohinton Medhora, Robert Robertson, and David O'Brien at IDRC, together with their colleagues Brent Herbert-Copley, Kim Daley, and Bill Carman, for their enthusiastic support of this project. Daniel Schwanen, Agata Antkiewicz, Max Brem, and Jessica Hanson at CIGI have also been very cooperative throughout. Brian Henderson and his team at Wilfrid Laurier University Press deserve recognition and thanks for their meticulous work in bringing this book to fruition.

I also wish to thank the University of Ottawa, and especially Dean Bruce Feldthusen of the Faculty of Common Law, for their continuing support and sustenance of the EDGE Network research projects. From the president to the administrative and financial staff at the University of Ottawa, the EDGE Network has enjoyed tremendous cooperation and assistance since its inception in 2006. For this, I shall always be very grateful.

I dedicate this book with love to my children, Nigel and Alexandra, who bring joy and hope to my life. May we all continue to work together to make your world a better place.

Debra Steger
Faculty of Law
University of Ottawa

꘎ ꘎ ꘎ List of Acronyms

ACP countries	African, Caribbean, and Pacific countries
AD Agreement	Antidumping Agreement
AFTA	ASEAN Free Trade Area Agreement
ASEAN	Association of Southern Eastern Asian Nations
BIS	Bank of International Settlements
CACM	Central American Common Market
CARICOM	Caribbean Community and Common Market
CEMAC	Economic and Monetary Community of Central Africa
CIEL	Centre for International Environmental Law
CIGI	Centre for International Governance Innovation
CITES	Convention on International Trade in Endangered Species of Wild Flora and Fauna
COMESA	Common Market of East and South Africa
CRTA	Committee on Regional Trade Agreements
CTD	Committee on Trade and Development
DDR	Doha Development Round
DG	WTO Director-General
DSB	Dispute Settlement Body
DSM	Dispute Settlement Mechanism
DSU	Understanding on Rules and Procedures Governing the Settlement of Disputes
EC	European Communities
ECJ	European Court of Justice
ECOSOC	United Nations Economic and Social Council
ECOWAS	Economic Community of Western Africa

EDGE Network	Emerging Dynamic Global Economies Network
EPAs	Economic Partnership Agreements
EU	European Union
FAO	Food and Agriculture Organization (UN)
FOGS	Functioning of the GATT System
FTA	free trade agreement
GATS	General Agreement on Trade in Services
GATT	General Agreement on Tariffs and Trade
GPA	Agreement on Government Procurement
GSP	Generalized System of Preferences
IBRD	International Bank for Reconstruction and Development (the World Bank)
ICJ	International Court of Justice
IDRC	International Development Research Centre
IEO	Independent Evaluation Office (IMF)
IGO	inter-governmental organization,
ILO	International Labour Organization
IMF	International Monetary Fund
IMFC	International Monetary and Finance Committee
IO	international organization
ITO	International Trade Organization
LDCs	least developed countries
MERCOSUR	Common Southern Market (Mercado Común del Sur)
MFN	most-favoured-nation
NAFTA	North American Free Trade Agreement (NAFTA)
NGOs	non-governmental organizations
NTBs	non-tariff barriers
OECD	Organization for Economic Co-operation and Development
OTC	Organization for Trade Cooperation
Quad	U.S., EC, Japan, and Canada, a negotiating group in Uruguay Round
RTAs	Regional Trade Agreements
SACU	Southern African Customs Union
SADC	Southern African Development Community
SCM Agreement	Agreement on Subsidies and Countervailing Measures
S&D	special and differential treatment
SDR	Special Drawing Rights
Secretariat	Secretariat of the World Trade Organization

SPS Agreement	Agreement on the Application of Sanitary and Physosanitary Measures
TBT Agreement	Agreement on Technical Barriers to Trade
TNC	Trade Negotiations Committee
TPR	trade policy review
TRPB	Trade Policy Review Body
TPRM	Trade Policy Review Mechanism
TRIPS Agreement	Trade-Related Aspects of Intellectual Property Rights
UNCTAD	United Nations Conference on Trade and Development
UNDP	United Nations Development Program
UNFCCC	United Nations Framework Convention on Climate Change
USTR	United States Trade Representative
VCLT	Vienna Convention on the Law of Treaties
WAEMU	Western Africa Monetary Union
WHO	World Health Organization
WIPO	World Intellectual Property Organization
World Bank	International Bank for Reconstruction and Development
WTO	World Trade Organization
WTO Agreement	Agreement Establishing the World Trade Organization

PART I

Why Institutional Reform Is Necessary

Why Institutional Reform of the WTO Is Necessary

DEBRA STEGER

I. Origins of This Book

This book emanates from an international, collaborative project on institutional reform of the World Trade Organization (WTO), organized by the Emerging Dynamic Global Economies (EDGE) Network and funded by Networks of Centres of Excellence Canada and the International Development Research Centre (IDRC). This project, which commenced in 2007, includes major research institutions and leading researchers in Africa, Asia, Europe, North America, and South America. Inspired by the Report of the Consultative Board to Director-General Supachai Panitchpakdi (the Sutherland Report),[1] it has three major research themes: decision-making and internal management of the WTO; relationship between the WTO and regional trade agreements; and transparency. The contributions in this book were initially presented and discussed at a workshop, 'Institutional Reform of the WTO', held at the Centre for International Governance Innovation (CIGI) in Waterloo, Canada, in March 2008.

In 2003, WTO director-general Supachai Panitchpakdi appointed a consultative board, chaired by former director-general Peter Sutherland, to address institutional challenges facing the WTO in the future. The Sutherland Report was published in 2005, on the tenth anniversary of the WTO, but has met with little response from the Members of the WTO. Among other things, the Sutherland Report expressed serious concern with the spread of preferential trade agreements and recommended that the WTO subject such agreements to meaningful review and effective disciplines. On dialogue with civil society, it suggested that the membership should develop clear objectives for relations with civil society but did not go further to recommend specific avenues for engagement. With respect to decision-making, it recommended that Members take a fresh look at variable geometry as well as approving decisions by a critical mass. It also proposed that the role of the Director-General and Secretariat be strengthened and improved and that a senior officials consultative body be established.[2]

The Sutherland Report was both comprehensive and pragmatic; it addressed serious questions relating to the governance and legitimacy of the WTO as an international organization. It provided an excellent start—it asked the right questions about very important issues and made pragmatic, practical recommendations. If anything, it did not go far enough.

The first Warwick Commission was established in 2007 with a broad mandate to examine the governance of the multilateral trading system and to make recommendations to improve it. It noted that there is waning support for further opening of markets, particularly in industrialized economies, and emphasized that sustaining the WTO is a collective responsibility on the part of all Members.[3] It recommended, inter alia, that consideration be given to the use of a critical mass approach to decision-making. On dispute settlement, it recommended the establishment of a Dispute Settlement ombudsman, the strengthening of transparency mechanisms including acceptance of *amicus curiae* briefs, and consideration of cash compensation as a remedy when compliance is not forthcoming.[4] With respect to preferential trade agreements, the Commission encouraged major industrialized countries to refrain from negotiating such agreements with each other and emphasized the need to clarify WTO disciplines and strengthen review mechanisms for such agreements.[5] Finally, it recommended that 'a process of reflection' be established in the WTO for Members to consider the challenges facing the multilateral system and develop a plan of action to address them.[6]

The Doha Development Round has stalled, with little prospect of real progress being made on the negotiating front in the foreseeable future. This is an appropriate moment to reflect on the WTO as an institution and do some serious thinking about reform of the institutional structures of the WTO.

II. Why Institutional Reform of the WTO Is Necessary

There are a number of reasons that institutional reform of the WTO is important at this time in the history of the multilateral trading system.

We are at a transformational moment in the history of the world. The rapid rise of the emerging economies—China, India, and Brazil—has shifted the global power balance, and the influence of the United States as a hegemonic power is declining. The current architecture of the international system was created in the 1940s by developed countries, led by the United States and Great Britain, for a very different world and time. As originally conceived, there were to be two Bretton Woods organizations: the International Monetary Fund (IMF) and the International Bank for Reconstruction and Development (the World Bank), and the International Trade Organization (ITO). While countries had agreed to establish the ITO, the organization was stillborn because the agreement was not ratified by the U.S. Congress. In its place, 23 countries negotiated the General Agreement on Tariffs and Trade (GATT), which came into effect by means of a protocol of provisional application. In 1955, GATT contracting parties negotiated an agreement to create the Organization for Trade Cooperation (OTC). However, that organization also was not approved by the U.S. Congress. It was not until 1995, as a result of the conclusion of the Uruguay Round, that the World Trade Organization was born.[7]

A major challenge for the next decade will be how the international system responds to the dramatic transformation taking place in the global economic and geopolitical landscape. Will the existing international organizations—the IMF, the World Bank, and the WTO—survive or will they be replaced by other new organizations? Will the large emerging economies seek to develop their own alliances and new organizations or will they work within the existing global system?

The financial crisis has highlighted the need for more international regulation of the global economy, not less. The Washington Consensus is no longer the prevailing ideology in Washington and around the globe. Leaders of the Group of 20 nations, including the major emerging economies, have called for a 'Bretton Woods II' to reform the IMF, in particular, and the World Bank. France and Germany have promoted a stronger regulatory role for the IMF over the global financial system, while Brazil and India have insisted that global power imbalances in the decision-making structures of the international financial organizations must be addressed first before any expansion of its mandate is contemplated. China has recently signalled that it is willing to contribute more money to the IMF, but only if major changes to its governance structures are made.

All three international organizations face major legitimacy and accountability crises because their internal voting and decision-making structures do not reflect the realities of the new power relationships in the global economy. The heads of the IMF and the World Bank recently appointed high-level commissions to recommend reforms to their internal governance structures. The Sutherland Report and the Report of the First Warwick Commission have made recommendations on the future of the WTO, but both reports have been largely ignored by WTO Members. If the international economic organizations are to be relevant, accountable, and effective in the dynamic global economy of the 21st century, significant institutional reforms are needed. Government leaders need to make this a priority.

Unless developing countries are able to actively participate in the design of new governance procedures for the international economic system, the very relevance and legitimacy of these organizations will be at risk. It is a turbulent time in the international system, but in times of stress and uncertainty, ideas for reform can be a powerful beacon to help guide developments in institution building.

This is a particularly difficult time for international negotiations—witness the problems with the Doha Development Round—because new clubs and alliances have not yet been formed. China and India, in particular, are recognized by the United States and the European Union as major economic powers, but they are criticized for not yet using their influence and fulfilling their responsibilities on the world stage. In the Doha Round, for example, China and India are playing a watching, waiting, and learning game, rather than showing leadership in pressing for a conclusion. The real threat to the international community would come if these major developing country powers were to develop their own alliances and institutions and not participate in the established international economic institutions.

International organizations, including the United Nations, the IMF, and the World Bank, have recognized that their governance structures are outdated and are engaged in major reform processes in order to respond to the criticisms about legitimacy, accountability, and decision-making. However, these concerns are not even on the radar screen of Members of the WTO. Why is this so?

A key reason is that the negotiations in the Doha Development Round have been so difficult and protracted. The primary objective of Director-General Pascal Lamy and WTO Members is to conclude the Doha Round of multilateral negotiations. Until that is concluded, no other major issues can be addressed within the organization. However, the longer the current impasse continues, the greater the risk that the WTO will become increasingly outdated and irrelevant to the world community. As the Warwick Commission astutely observed:

> There is evidence that many of the lessons of the 20th century are in danger of being 'unlearned' in the 21st century, especially in relation to the importance of multilateral institutions, and the rules, norms and principles that underpin them. That a malaise afflicts the multilateral trade regime is suggested not only by the impasse in the Doha Development Agenda (DDA) negotiations but also by other symptoms in the contemporary global economy linked to the global trade agenda, including the protests that accompany the ministerial meetings of the WTO; near permanent rumblings of discontent by diverse groups of countries from within the organisation; and growing resort to alternative forms of economic governance, including bilateral and regional PTAs.[8]

Furthermore, a major institutional negotiation in the Uruguay Round led to the establishment of the WTO as an international organization with its own charter[9] and quasi-judicial dispute settlement system.[10] In the transformation from the GATT to the WTO, important new institutions were established, including the WTO itself and the Appellate Body.[11] While the dispute settlement system has functioned effectively and efficiently since 1995, the decision-making processes in the WTO are in need of improvement. When it comes to negotiations and rule-making, the WTO, in many respects, functions much like the old GATT. The new rules for decision-making and amendments, set out in Articles IX and X of the WTO Agreement, are rarely used, and instead, members resort to the familiar GATT practice of decision-making by consensus. The new rule-making procedures in the WTO Agreement have been characterized by commentators as 'cumbersome' and even 'impossible' to use.[12] While there was a recent comprehensive negotiation that led to the establishment of the WTO as an international organization, the Uruguay Round negotiators unfortunately 'did not get the job done'.[13] Much remains to be done to improve and strengthen the governance procedures within the WTO.

The efficiency of the dispute settlement system contrasted with the inefficacy of the decision-making and rule-making system has created an imbalance in the institutional structures of the WTO. The Uruguay Round reforms, including the establishment of the Appellate Body, propelled the dispute settlement system into a judicial model, with compulsory jurisdiction, binding decisions, and arbitral procedures for compliance, setting an example for other international legal systems. The result is a strong, effective dispute settlement mechanism coupled with weak, ineffective, political decision-making procedures. Unlike domestic legal systems, it is almost impossible for decisions of the Appellate Body to be corrected by the legislative bodies—the Ministerial Conference or the General Council. This situation cannot persist indefinitely without damage to the WTO as an institution, especially as pressures increase on the dispute settlement bodies as a result of the inability of Members to negotiate or clarify the rules in the Doha Round.

Because the rule-making procedures of the WTO are so difficult, countries are turning increasingly toward negotiating regional trade agreements. While regional trade regimes have not been shown to provide the same economic benefits as multilateral agreements, there is growing business pressure, especially in the rapidly growing economies of the world, to negotiate new regional arrangements. New regional trade alliances are being forged among developing countries, particularly in Asia and Africa, which have not had a history of regional trade agreements. The United States and the European Union have also embarked on aggressive strategies to negotiate bilateral arrangements with many countries and regional trade agreements around the globe. The explosion of regional trade agreements is causing growing fragmentation of the multilateral trading system and serious erosion of the most-favoured-nation principle.

With the exception of the European Union, the dispute settlement mechanisms of the regional agreements are relatively weak, particularly when compared with the WTO. Thus, while the regional regimes are easier to negotiate and conclude than the WTO is to amend, there is an imbalance between the rule-making and dispute settlement mechanisms of regional agreements. And it is the opposite imbalance from that of the WTO. Although the relationship between the WTO and the regional trade agreements is not clear, we can expect to see more interaction between them in the future. In particular, the strong WTO dispute settlement system will likely be pressed to hear more cases involving possible conflicts or differences between the rules of the WTO and the regional trade agreements.

Looking into the future, a vibrant, relevant WTO would have a mandate to deal with international economic regulation generally, not just trade. The Doha Round is focused on market access: in agriculture, in goods, and in services. Many new issues—competition, investment, technology, environment—are not on the agenda in the current round. As a result, these issues are being negotiated in regional trade agreements and other bilateral agreements. The issues of interest to multinational business, such as rule of law/good governance behind the border, corruption, corporate social responsibility, exchange rates, and immigration, are not even a glimmer in the eye of multilateral trade negotiators. Why not? Partly because the WTO decision-making and rule-making procedures are so cumbersome, if not impossible, to use that governments and private parties have moved to other forums. As a negotiating machine, the WTO is clearly not able to keep pace with the most recent developments in the rapidly changing world economy. It risks becoming irrelevant if its governance structures are not improved to allow for more flexibility in negotiations and rule-making.

Finally, there has been much criticism of the WTO from non-governmental organizations and civil society, challenging its effectiveness, accountability, and legitimacy. These are important concerns that deserve serious consideration by WTO Members. The chapters in this book examine the WTO in light of good governance principles and make recommendations for its strengthening and improvement as an international organization.

The WTO is not sui generis; it is one among international organizations. This is a transformative moment in history for international organizations generally, and the WTO faces effectiveness, legitimacy, and accountability challenges similar to the others. The WTO lacks many of the management structures and rule-making processes that are taken for granted in other international organizations. For example, it does not have an executive body or a management board, a Director-General or Secretariat with real powers to set legislative priorities and propose new rules, a functioning legislative body, formal mechanisms to interact with stakeholders and civil society, or formal structures to approve new rules (other than the consensus of WTO Members acting collectively, as the Contracting Parties did under the GATT 1947). In many ways, it is the 'least developed' of the international organizations. Coherence in the international trading system, among other things, demands that the WTO develop more formalized governance structures to put it on a par with other international organizations, make it more functional and efficient, and render it more accountable to all its Members (including developing countries), stakeholders, and the public.

Notes

1 *The Future of the WTO: Addressing Institutional Challenges in the New Millennium* (Geneva: WTO, 2004).

2 Ibid, at 79–83.

3 The Report of the First Warwick Commission, *The Multilateral Trade Regime: Which Way Forward?* (Coventry, U.K.: University of Warwick, 2007) 22.

4 Ibid, at 36.

5 Ibid, at 53.

6 Ibid, at 56.

7 For the history of this negotiation, see Debra P. Steger, 'The World Trade Organization: A New Constitution for the World Trading System', in Marco Bronckers and Reinhard Quick (eds), *New Directions in International Economic Law: Essays in Honour of John H. Jackson* (The Hague: Kluwer International 2000) 135–54.

8 Above n 3, at 8.

9 Agreement Establishing the World Trade Organization (WTO Agreement), *The Results of the Uruguay Round of Multilateral Trade Negotiations: The Legal Texts* (Geneva: WTO: 1994).

10 Understanding on Rules and Procedures Governing the Settlement of Disputes (DSU), *The Results of the Uruguay Round of Multilateral Trade Negotiations: The Legal Texts* (Geneva: WTO, 1994).

11 For the history of that negotiation, see Steger, above n 7.

12 See Marco C.E.J. Bronckers, 'Better Rules for a New Millennium: A Warning Against Undemocratic Developments in the WTO', 2 Journal of International Economic Law 547 (1999), at 551–52.

13 Comment from Sylvia Ostry at EDGE Network workshop on 'Institutional Reform of the WTO', Waterloo, Canada, March 2008.

Reinvigorating Debate on WTO Reform: The Contours of a Functional and Normative Approach to Analyzing the WTO System

CAROLYN DEERE BIRKBECK[1]

I. Introduction

The debate on institutional reform and governance of the World Trade Organization (WTO) has now been underway for over 15 years.[2] In 1999, only five years after the creation of the WTO, the collapse of the Seattle Ministerial Conference provoked intense demands for reform. By 2003, the failure of the Cancun WTO Ministerial Meeting again sparked debate on WTO reform. Two years later, when Pascal Lamy became WTO Director-General, he proposed that WTO reform should be a key post-Doha priority.[3] In the context of the Doha Round of multilateral trade negotiations stumbling forward in fits and starts, the most prominent focus of discussions of WTO reform has been options for improving the WTO negotiation process.

Throughout the past 10 years there have also been a number of broader debates about the governance of the multilateral trading system and calls for institutional reform at the WTO. Most recently, the onset of the global financial crisis in 2008 reignited more wide-ranging interest in the role of the WTO in global economic management, prompting calls for the WTO to do more to sustain a global open trading system, and in particular to take greater leadership on issues of trade finance, aid for trade, and surveillance of protectionist measures.

In the face of existing and emerging global challenges, both critics and supporters of the WTO pose common questions. Is the WTO as we currently know it fit for its purpose? How can the WTO adapt to changing configurations of economic power in trade, while ensuring the weakest countries are properly and effectively represented? How can the WTO better respond to sustainable development concerns, ranging from poverty reduction, development, and food security, to sustainable fisheries and climate change? Is the WTO's current institutional form appropriate or, are there reforms—incremental, fundamental, or both—that would better equip the WTO to reflect and address both contemporary needs and those likely to emerge in the future?

Amid a growing body of scholarly literature and policy commentary on the governance and institutional reform of the WTO, this chapter proposes a distinctive approach. To set the context, Part II presents a brief overview of key themes in the existing literature, emphasizing the scope of debates on WTO reform. A full review and evaluation of the specific details of proposals offered through the course of these debates is beyond the scope of this chapter. This chapter does, however, highlight the differences among authors regarding what the WTO reform debate is and should be about, including with respect to the feasibility and desirability of a reform agenda. Part III proposes a new five-pronged approach to the question of WTO reform. It argues for (1) analyzing the WTO as a 'system'; (2) disaggregating and analyzing the governance of each of the functions this system serves and should serve; (3) acknowledging the informal nature and dynamism of many practices regarding the governance of these distinctive WTO functions; (4) grounding reform proposals in clear normative principles and priorities, namely to respond to the needs of developing countries and advancing sustainable development; and (5) devoting greater attention to analyzing the political strategies for achieving proposed reforms.

The chapter concludes with some preliminary observations on the reform priorities this approach reveals.[4] It provides indicative examples of how this approach to the WTO reform question yields the prospect of a more broad-ranging reform agenda than many existing studies, and a reinvigorated dialogue on many now 'tired' reform themes.

II. Existing Literature on WTO Reform: The State of Debate

The study of WTO governance is concerned with the set of processes, principles, norms, and institutions through which rules and practices for managing global trade are generated and implemented. The study of institutional reform of the WTO relates to a subset of these concerns—those specifically focused on the 'institutional' aspects of the WTO. Narrowly speaking, these institutional aspects concern only the formal organizational facets of the WTO. More broadly, reference to the institutional aspects of the WTO may also apply to the cultural habits, practices, rules, and procedures that govern how the work of the WTO is supervised, managed, and implemented. Depending on the topic at hand, authors writing on 'WTO reform' sometimes refer explicitly to institutional aspects of that reform.

For some authors, a far wider set of issues falls under the WTO reform umbrella, including proposals for reform in respect of the principles and scope of the WTO's agreements or the substance of particular aspects of WTO nego-tiations (such as those related to the Doha Round). For example, when some analysts write of WTO reform, their emphasis is on limiting the scope of the WTO negotiating agenda (i.e., to ensure it does not cover investment issues), or expanding its scope (i.e., to ensure it covers issues of high importance to developing countries, such as movement of labour or the operationalization of principles, such as special and differential treatment). This chapter inten-tionally focuses tightly on the governance and 'institutional' agenda for WTO reform. That said, it is important to acknowledge that the issues are often entangled: some aspects of round negotiations are directly related to issues that arise in discussions of the governance of the multilateral trading system (e.g., disciplines for regional trading agreements, principles of special and dif-ferential treatment, reform of the dispute settlement system).

The scope of the literature on WTO governance and institutional reform is vast. As noted above, the majority of attention has been on reform of the WTO's negotiation process, as well as its dispute settlement process[5] and the appropriate relationship and balance between the two.[6] Additional recurring areas of interest include (i) the internal governance and management of the WTO Secretariat, its ideal size and budget, as well as the role of the Director-General and the related selection process;[7] (ii) the intersection of WTO rules and other global norms on issues ranging from human rights and the environ-ment to food safety and labour standards;[8] (iii) the WTO's relationship with civil society,[9] industry, and parliaments;[10] (iv) the appropriate role of the WTO in global economic governance and its relationship to other international organizations and agreements;[11] (v) the relationship between WTO agree-ments and the growing number of regional and bilateral trade arrangements; and (vi) the balance between the WTO's judicial and legislative functions.[12]

The prominence of each of these areas of debate on governance and insti-tutional reform has fluctuated over time. In the lead-up to the election of the WTO's Director-General, for instance, debates about the appropriate powers of the Director-General and the election process resurface. Similarly, debates on the 'Green Room' tend to intensify around the time of WTO ministerial conferences and mini-ministerial meetings.

The debate on WTO reform has been punctuated by two major reports,[13] a series of formal submissions from WTO Members, and a suite of proposals from academics and non-governmental organizations (NGOs) covering a diverse range of reform topics. In 1999, the failure of the Seattle Ministerial Conference prompted then Director-General Mike Moore to call on a group of eminent experts for advice about institutional reform, resulting in a report entitled 'The Future of the WTO: Addressing Institutional Challenges in the New Millennium WTO' (the Sutherland Report).

A variety of countries have submitted proposals on aspects of institutional reform, including Canada, Japan, the European Commission, the United Kingdom, and a number of developing countries, such as the Like-Minded Group (LMG) of 15 developing countries (led by India).[14] After the 2003 collapse of the Cancun Ministerial Meeting, Pascal Lamy (at that time the European Union's trade commissioner) famously characterized the WTO as a 'medieval institution' and tabled a European Commission proposal for WTO reform. Then, in 2007, amid concerns about the slow progress of the Doha Round and proliferating regional and bilateral trade agreements, the Warwick Commission, an independent commission of experts chaired by a former Canadian minister for trade and foreign affairs, published its report, 'The Multilateral Trade Regime: Which Way Forward?' (the Warwick Report).

To date, the vast majority of the scholarly literature on the governance and institutional reform of the WTO has emanated from developed countries and is dominated by the analytical perspective of lawyers and economists.[15] The involvement of political scientists and scholars of international relations on the reform agenda has been relatively scarce and recent.[16] Despite the long engagement of developing country scholars on questions of trade and development in the multilateral trading system, their input on debates regarding WTO governance and specific proposals on institutional reform has been similarly tentative, general in nature, and recent compared to the intense engagement of developed country scholars on the topic.[17] The agenda, contours, and themes of the scholarly literature on institutional reform thus remain strongly defined by the preoccupations of developed country scholars, even where they are development-oriented in purpose.

Academic work on WTO reform is supplemented by a vast body of commentary by former WTO insiders (both from governments and the WTO Secretariat), NGOs, civil society groups, and industry associations, as well as governments and parliamentary bodies.[18] Here we find a more consistent interest in what developing countries may have to gain from improvements in the governance and institutional aspects of the WTO. Several intergovernmental organizations have also published documents that include reflections on the purpose and performance of the WTO system and proposals consistent with their respective mandates (e.g., labour, development, public health) and related stakeholder groups.[19]

The remainder of this section highlights several crosscutting themes that underlie the WTO reform debate. Across the spectrum of scholarly and policy analysts, most studies of WTO governance and institutional reform concur that a core purpose, if not the core purpose of the WTO, should be to protect a stable, multilateral, rules-based approach to international trade. For many of these analysts, the WTO's agreements represent the 'rule of law' in the realm of international trade: a global public good that warrants protection in its own right. Beyond that point of consensus (though still not universally shared), the scope of and prescriptions for reform vary as widely as do perspectives on the usefulness, goals, and mandate of the WTO.

The tensions in the WTO reform debate are amply illustrated in the literature on reform of WTO decision-making, rule-making, and negotiating processes. For free trade advocates, this interest is spurred by concerns about the perceived inefficiency of the WTO system in achieving agreements on trade liberalization. These advocates often cite the economic benefits of liberalization, as well as its contribution to peace and political stability, as justification for seeking more efficient ways to conclude new trade deals.[20]

Critics counter that proposals for negotiating process reform that aim simply to achieve trade liberalization faster misunderstand the scope of the WTO's mandate. The WTO is now as much concerned with the regulation of world trade as its liberalization, and the task of negotiating global trade regulations presents different challenges than that of exchanging market access concessions.[21] Furthermore, implementation of agreements may involve distinct political, institutional, and budgetary considerations at the national level. Many who share this line of thinking emphasize that while trade liberalization may well be *a* purpose of the WTO, is it not *the* purpose of the multilateral trading system and should not be pursued as an end in itself. Rather, trade policy—and trade liberalization—should be shaped in light of public policy objectives, such as growth, employment, and sustainable development, set out in WTO agreements. The appropriate speed and efficiency of negotiation processes able to reflect those goals may rightly vary.

Beyond negotiating processes, some scholars advocate fundamental, structural reforms of the WTO. This includes calls for constitutionalizing the WTO—that is, for constructing a constitution for the WTO—to bolster both the strength and legitimacy of the WTO's rules.[22] The varied proposals that fall under this heading are challenged by those concerned that constitutionalization would erode national sovereignty and risk emphasizing economic goals over broader public policy objectives. Some critics call instead for acknowledging the usefulness of and need for greater political contestation rather than more rules at the WTO, and for creating and maintaining spaces within the WTO where political debate can occur within the multilateral trading system.[23]

A further crosscutting area of tension has been the debate on how to boost developing country participation in global trade and make the multilateral trade system more responsive to developing countries. Proposals on these issues extend back to the 1960s when Part IV of the General Agreement on Tariffs and Trade (GATT) was established (which, among other elements, introduced the notion of special and differential treatment for developing countries).[24] The discussion on how to make the WTO work better for developing countries has subsequently greatly expanded, inspiring increased engagement from governments, NGOs, and scholars alike.[25] Here again though, more emphasis has been placed on the immediate and important question of what kinds of trade agreements would best benefit developing countries, rather than on the process of achieving better trade deals or ensuring that the governance of the multilateral system and its institutional features provide the greatest opportunities for the perspectives of developing countries; this question needs to be addressed.

Importantly, the perspectives that development analysts bring to the reform discussion do not always fit neatly within the boundaries of the agendas defined earlier by developed country scholars. There are shared interests in questions of the reform of the WTO's dispute settlement system and in improving rule-making processes. But development-oriented analysts devote greater attention to matters such as understanding and empowering developing countries in the WTO rule-making process, the potential and pitfalls of coalitions among developing countries, and how to operationalize the principle of special and differential treatment. Developing countries and development advocates devote far more attention to the importance of improved trade-related capacity building and technical assistance as part of the institutional reform debate, though there has been surprisingly little attention to the details of how this significant activity should be provided and governed.[26] Developing country analysts and development-oriented analysts also devote greater attention than many developed country counterparts to the interaction between international organizations and regimes, and to the coherence of their work.[27] In particular, many development analysts are concerned with ensuring synergy between the work of the WTO, the International Monetary Fund, and the World Bank, as well as the overseas development assistance that bilateral government donors provide.[28] There is also a high degree of interest in how the interaction of different international regimes, most notably the trade and climate regimes, affects developing countries.[29]

A further crosscutting theme that attracts the attention of WTO critics and supporters alike is that of improving the accountability and transparency of the WTO and expanding opportunities for public participation.[30] Reacting to the anti-globalization backlash against the WTO around the time of the 1999

Seattle Ministerial Conference, many scholars have also taken up questions about the legitimacy of the institution.[31] Some scholars proposed ways to bolster the validity of the WTO, while others argue that only the fundamental transformation of its purpose and processes can boost its legitimacy.[32] Further, some scholars argue that the process of vigorous debate within civil society about the pros and cons of 'constructive engagement' with the WTO and the prospects for reform are in themselves a source of legitimacy for the institution.[33]

The result of debates on accountability and legitimacy has been a suite of reform proposals—some more abstract and others very specific—that aim to embed principles of democratic process, inclusiveness, transparency, and representation in WTO decision-making. These in turn have provoked counter-proposals and rebuttals. Some developing countries, for instance, oppose calls for greater civil society participation in the WTO's formal decision-making due to concerns this would offer greater advantages to better-resourced NGOs in developed countries. Some analysts caution against proposals for a greater role for the private sector and/or civil society in WTO deliberations arguing that the trade-offs with efficiency may be too high and that problems of accountability and transparency should first receive attention at the national level, through enhanced and more participatory national trade policy-making processes.[34]

Civil society organizations have also appealed for constraints on the influence of big business and multinational corporations in the WTO agenda-setting and negotiating process.[35] On the other hand, advocates of greater developing country participation in the trading system often argue that the increased engagement of developing country business interests in national preparations for multilateral negotiations is a vital prerequisite for them to extract greater benefits from the multilateral trading system.[36]

To date, political analysis of the strategies for achieving proposed WTO reforms (and the constraints that frustrate the prospect of such reform efforts) has attracted far less attention than the proposals themselves.[37] This reflects a weakness more broadly in the literature on international regimes and organizations, which has offered greater attention to the emergence, formation, and design than to regime change or organizational change.[38] That said, some scholars and commentators do consider the politics of the WTO reform debate. Some critics question whether the WTO is in fact amenable to the kinds of fundamental institutional redesign advocated by other scholars.

Skeptics of the prospects for the reform of formal decision-making and negotiation processes at the WTO emphasize, for instance, that trade negotiations are necessarily informal and that prospects for restructuring them from the outside are extremely limited.[39] As an alternative, they propose processes of learning and gradual, incremental change as more likely vehicles for change, where players themselves devise more efficient strategies for deal-making. Some analysts also offer strategies for organizing among developing countries.[40]

A compelling case has also been made that the recurring 'crises' of the multilateral trading system—and the reform debates these generate—are used to the advantage of its most powerful Members.[41] More broadly, a number of anti- or alter-globalization critics of the WTO system raise fundamental questions about the accountability of the WTO and the status of national sovereignty in the face of powerful global institutions. They question not only the purpose but also the plausibility of many reform proposals, as well as the underlying economic model underpinning the WTO—one that they argue focuses too much on consumption, economic growth, and control of global economic activity by large corporations. They argue that transforming the global economic system, and the WTO included, to promote equity and environmental sustainability requires 'bottom-up' democratization through the work and growing power of social movements rather than 'institutional tinkering' from above.[42]

III. A New Approach to WTO Governance and Institutional Reform

This section sets forth five elements of a new approach to the question of appropriate institutional reforms at the WTO that responds to the contemporary global challenges and the evolution of the WTO's functions and practices.

A. A 'Systems' Approach

In 1997, John Jackson described the WTO as a set of legal agreements and an institutional framework to administer the implementation of these agreements, settle trade disputes, and provide a forum for ongoing negotiations.[43] In so doing, he reinforced the GATT tradition of seeing the WTO as a legal regime, albeit now with a more formalized institutional structure and stronger dispute settlement mechanism at its heart. Over the past 15 years, however, numerous scholarly efforts have also characterized and analyzed the WTO as an 'international organization'. While the WTO Secretariat may indeed be characterized and analyzed as an 'international organization', this approach has important constraints. In 2006, for instance, a debate on this subject emerged between staff at the WTO Secretariat and the One World Trust regarding the difficulties of applying the literature on the accountability of international organizations to the particular case of the WTO.[44] The Secretariat staff argued that the Member-driven character of WTO decision-making and the legally binding nature of agreements *among* its *Members* are characteristics that make it difficult to discern what exactly one is holding 'the WTO' accountable for and what the WTO is in that context. The Secretariat's argument is that WTO Members rather than the Secretariat are responsible for the content of particular WTO agreements, and that this distinguishes the institution from large international bureaucracies such as the World Bank and IMF, which have a vast array of activities. This example illustrates the challenges of analyzing the WTO as an 'organization'.

Day-to-day language provides a hint of how we might more usefully analyze the WTO. The WTO is frequently referred to coterminously as the 'multilateral trading system'. Rather than examine it as a legal regime or as an 'organization', a promising alternative is to examine it as a system. What then would a systems approach involve? We know that the WTO is indeed a legal regime built on contractual legal obligations between Members, but that it is more than a set of agreements.[45] The WTO is also clearly more than merely a negotiating forum. The WTO also comprises a Secretariat, which is a discrete international organization and bureaucracy with a budget and work program defined by Members[46] that includes responsibilities ranging from the administration of agreements and meetings to the provision of training and technical assistance. Importantly, however, the scope of activities and outcomes for which the WTO Secretariat is directly responsible is smaller than those that WTO Members call on the multilateral trading system to deliver on.

A systems approach acknowledges the composite nature of the WTO and the variety of actors involved in delivering and conducting the various functions and services of the multilateral trading system. While WTO Members conduct most of the formal business of the WTO, the Secretariat provides significant support and conducts important activities. The WTO Appellate Body is, for instance, a distinct but linked international organization with its own budget and working practices. Further, the work of WTO system is animated by interactions among Members (that conduct much of the day-to-day business of the system) and the actions of a host of international agencies, including but not limited to the WTO Secretariat, as well as NGOs (public and private interests), and experts/individuals. This fact is exemplified in the case of the training, technical assistance, and capacity-building function of the WTO system, where some of the work is funded and implemented directly through the Secretariat, but much is implemented through collaborative arrangements with other international organizations and bilateral donors, and also independently by these and non-government actors.[47]

A systems approach to WTO reform acknowledges the range of actors, in addition to the WTO Secretariat and WTO Members, that 'do the work' of the system and explores how they interact to advance that work. This systems approach can then be applied to each of the particular functions the WTO systems serve.

B. A Functional Approach

In addition to its widely discussed negotiation and dispute settlement functions, the WTO system serves a range of additional functions often neglected by scholarly literature, including (i) monitoring and surveillance; (ii) research; (iii) capacity building, technical assistance, and training; (iv) regime maintenance; (v) interaction with other international organizations; and (vi) public outreach and information sharing with a range of non-state stakeholders. A functional approach prompts us to explore how to isolate the appropriate political processes for tackling the distinct functions of the multilateral trading system. The proper formats and processes for negotiation, policy dialogue, problem-solving, monitoring and information exchange, and dispute settlement differ. These may involve various roles for the WTO Secretariat and for its Director-General.

For each of these functions, a series of governance questions can be asked, including about the process through which decisions are made and implemented.[48] How are priorities set and who is involved? Who controls budgetary resources? How is performance monitored, assessed, and evaluated? A 'functional' approach to studying the WTO that examines each of these independently, and the links between them, yields new insights into the challenges and priorities for reform.[49] First, it enables us to see the full range of areas in which governance reforms might generate benefits for sustainable development and developing countries. Second, it provides 'oxygen' to now stale debates on issues such as the appropriate degree of public 'participation' in WTO activities, the scale of the WTO Secretariat, and how effectively developing countries participate in and influence each of the functions of the system. Third, a functional approach extends the scope of reform literature to consider the full range of the WTO's functions. The post-negotiation dimension of the multilateral trading system's activities has a significant impact on Members, especially developing countries. In particular, closer attention to post-agreement bargaining is critical for properly understanding the experience of developing countries in the global trade system and the range of challenges to which proposals for WTO reform should respond. Power politics occur both within global trade talks and in the interpretation and implementation of any resulting agreements.[50] There is also a need for greater attention to negotiation processes that occur outside particular trade rounds, such as negotiations related to accessions, the built-in agenda of the Uruguay Round, and ongoing talks that occur in WTO committees. Each of these aspects involves intense political bargaining over timing, trade-offs, adjustments, and burden sharing.

C. Acknowledge Dynamism

The study of WTO reform must begin with an up-to-date appreciation of how WTO decision-making occurs in practice across the WTO's functions and how this has changed over its first 15 years. The practice of international trade decision-making now differs considerably from that of the early days of the system and, indeed, the prevailing practice at the launch of the Doha Round.[51] Whereas, for instance, proposals on WTO reform in the late 1990s focused on concerns about the exclusive nature of the 'Green Room' and called for formalization of the negotiating process to enhance representation and transparency, the process of negotiations has now evolved and proven far more dynamic than many commentators acknowledge. Power configurations are evolving, and there is constant improvisation with respect to strategies for reaching consensus and closing deals. One of the clearest examples is that in light of the expanding use of coalitions as tools for representation, the infamous Green Room attracts far less criticism than it had previously. That said, there are still important enduring complaints regarding the ability of most of the more than 100 developing country WTO Members to participate effectively in Green Room processes and WTO decision-making, particularly the poorest and weakest among them.[52]

There is also far greater involvement by non-state stakeholders across WTO activities than anticipated in much of the initial scholarship on reform. The participation of developing countries in the Dispute Settlement Understanding has evolved as have its practices with regard to public access to proceedings. The WTO Secretariat's own work is implemented through a variety of formal and informal processes that are dynamic and have evolved over time, and recent analyses have demonstrated how the Secretariat itself may be an actor in its own right, including in WTO negotiations at given moments.[53] The WTO's practices and policies on internal transparency have improved considerably over time.[54] Much has also changed since the early, more abstract discussions of the links between trade and so-called non-trade issues. The WTO system has already been called on to respond to an array of global challenges that have taken it well beyond the initial far tidier world of market access negotiations.

D. Grounding Analysis in Normative Purpose

Reforming the WTO demands clarity as to the objectives and benchmarks against which proposals for institutional reform ought to be tested. Scholarly proposals on WTO reform too often lack a clear articulation of the goals and challenges that proposals seek to address or they focus only on a narrow objective. Proposals for reforms necessary to speed the process for reaching new WTO deals, for instance, neglect broader questions on how to ensure the multilateral trading system advances the ends for which it was established, which include improving economic welfare in all countries, poverty reduction, sustainable development, stability in global trade relations, and a guard against beggar-thy-neighbour trade policies. Yet proposals for WTO reforms are frequently advanced on the basis of ill-defined concerns about weak 'efficiency' or 'performance' without adequate specificity regarding what these concepts mean or the distributional impacts of proposed reforms. Too often scholars write of improving the performance, efficiency, or credibility of the WTO, but it is unclear what they consider the broader normative purpose or benchmarks against which the WTO's performance, efficiency, or credibility should be judged. A sharper focus on such substantive goals would spur recognition that the mandate and purpose of the multilateral trading system are deeply contested both by WTO Members and its diverse stakeholders.

The focus of reform proposals ought not to be limited to helping sustain the WTO per se, but rather on whether reforms help foster progress toward a WTO system that better delivers on the goals set out in its preamble. If sustainable development and improving the plight of developing countries should be, and indeed are, at the heart of political debates about the global trading regime, the discussion of institutional reform and WTO governance should also be motivated by and judged against its ability to address these challenges. Proposals for WTO reform thus need to address two critical political priorities: (1) how to bolster the relative power of developing countries in the system, and (2) how to ensure the system better responds to sustainable development priorities. The challenge for those concerned with WTO reform is to discern how and in what ways proposed reforms address these two inter-linked goals. Of course, not all commentators share the view that these goals should indeed be a core purpose of the system or of reform, and others may prioritize other aspects of the preamble (such as the calls for raising standards of living and ensuring full employment, or expanding the production of and trade in goods and services). There is, however, a clear political and legal rationale for a focus on sustainable development and developing country needs (recognizing that those of particular countries may vary widely) as a benchmark.

In legal terms, the preamble to the Marrakesh Agreement Establishing the WTO (the WTO Agreement) recognizes the importance of sustainable development, calling on governments to conduct their economic and social objectives in trade relations in a way that allows for the optimal use of the world's resources in accordance with the objective of sustainable development, seeking both to protect and preserve the environment and to enhance the means for doing so in a manner consistent with their respective needs and concerns at different levels of economic development.[55]

The WTO's preamble also recognizes that the particular needs of developing countries in the trading system include, *inter alia*, the objective of greater employment. Several of the WTO agreements detail general principles and objectives that emphasize Members' development and public policy objectives, as well as other national goals such as political security.[56] In 2001, WTO Members reaffirmed normative objectives in the Doha Ministerial Declaration, stating their conviction that the open, multilateral trading system and sustainable development 'can and must be mutually supportive' (Para 6, Doha Ministerial Declaration) and making development the stated purpose of the Doha Round. In addition, the Doha Declaration on TRIPS (Trade-Related Aspects of Intellectual Property Rights) and Public Health highlighted that trade policies should not stand in the way of efforts by countries to respond to public health priorities. Several WTO Appellate Body decisions have recognized the importance of non-trade considerations and agreements in their reports on trade disputes.[57]

Those who argue that the WTO ought not to be a 'development institution' or a sustainable development organization or indeed anything more than a forum for commercial bargaining have already been overtaken by political reality. Issues of sustainable development and the concerns of developing countries feature prominently in a number of ongoing trade negotiations. The fact that trade deals are so difficult to reach is in part because governments cannot escape the need to address political issues regarding equity, social, and environment impacts. Many of the obstacles to the conclusion of new trade deals are linked to the real-world need for governments to respond to political demands and tension over development and sustainable development challenges. Negotiations are protracted precisely because the issues before states are complex, demand intensive processes of learning (about challenges, implications, and possible solutions), and require time-consuming efforts to build political support for potential deals in Geneva and among Members.

The call for a WTO that is more friendly to sustainable development and developing countries has moved far beyond early debates that pitted pro-development advocates against the WTO in general or trade liberalization in particular.[58] Indeed, in the years since the WTO was established, the trade and sustainable development debate has evolved considerably[59] as advocates have explored different ways to ensure that the WTO's substantive rules and agreements, and the balance of concessions in the Doha Round, properly incorporate and address sustainable development considerations. However, skeptics argue that the prospect for achieving, implementing, and enforcing truly balanced rules will remain thwarted until fundamental institutional reforms are achieved that address the broad array of decision-making and governance processes at the WTO.

At the launch of the WTO, environmentalists expressed concern about the potential 'scale' effects of liberalized trade on the environment and warned that global trade rules may have a chilling effect on national environmental regulations and undermine global environmental agreements.[60] There is now a more nuanced recognition that some trade rules and flows may help promote more environmentally sustainable outcomes while others may drive or contribute to unsustainable production, distribution, and consumption practices.[61] Although some argued that the prospect of greening the WTO was structurally limited,[62] others now acknowledge that the understanding of trade, environment, and sustainable development issues has evolved considerably and that much progress has been made.[63] Indeed, there is now greater involvement of developing countries and experts in defining a southern agenda for trade and environment.[64] Some developing countries are now proponents of a sustainable development approach to trade policy formulation and to specific aspects of trade negotiations.[65] More generally, the scope of the sustainable development agenda at the WTO has broadened from issues such as eco-labelling requirements and addressing declining global fish stocks, to trade-related dimensions of the effort to stop climate change.[66]

The call to ground analysis in normative principles and priorities is also one for acknowledging the need to enable rather than suppress political contestation at the WTO. Here, several scholars have already called for bringing more politics into WTO negotiations and decision-making as a desirable outcome and for finding more spaces for political contestation to occur.[67] Similarly, the institutional reform agenda is not a technical, legalistic, or bureaucratic matter that can be 'solved' without a thorough consideration of the political demands and concerns driving divergent perspectives and expectations about the end goal(s) of the WTO. These will necessarily affect recommendations on the purposes and strategies for WTO reforms.

Debates that slow current WTO negotiations are not about *whether* sustainable development considerations should be taken into account, but rather *how* they can be taken into account. On the social front, negotiations on non-agricultural market access and services stall because Members have competing national policy considerations to address with regard to poverty alleviation, the creation of good quality work,[68] risks to social cohesion from rapid adjustments, and their own ability to manage the economic and social adjustments. The deadlock on negotiations in agriculture is driven by fundamental concerns about livelihood, food security, and the fate of the 'bottom billion' people in the world in approximately 50 failing states that defy efforts to reduce poverty.[69]

Members have taken up environmental considerations in a discussion of rules on fisheries subsidies and liberalization of trade in environmental goods and services, and there is mounting interest in the relationship between trade rules, the emerging climate regime, and biofuels. Across the range of trade-related environment issues, the challenge is to forge solutions that address social, development, and political considerations and constraints of both developed and developing countries.

The under-representation of developing countries in WTO decision-making and the inadequate response of the WTO system to the varied needs of developing countries remain central challenges in the daily work of the Doha negotiations. Concerns about asymmetric outcomes of the Uruguay Round and the negotiation process have fuelled a broad recognition of the need to improve the accountability and responsiveness of the WTO system to developing country priorities.[70] The addition in the Uruguay Round of a strong regulatory agenda to the WTO's traditional liberalization focus generated significant technical and institutional challenges for developing countries.[71] Developed countries have too rarely fulfilled their promises to take development considerations into account in multilateral negotiations or to translate into meaningful outcomes their commitments to provide technical assistance and promote technology transfer.[72]

The emphasis of WTO Members and the Secretariat on Aid for Trade since 2005 reflects the recognition that capacity building to date has done little to empower developing countries to make effective use of the WTO system. Recognition of the political imperative for greater efforts that assist developing countries has permeated up to key policy-makers, including several Directors-General of the WTO.[73] Core challenges for developing countries that remain inadequately addressed include tariff escalation, disciplines on agricultural subsidies, the failure to understand how these countries trade, and the asymmetric nature of accession negotiations for new developing country Members.[74] In this context, developing countries have maintained their long-standing calls for special and differential treatment.[75] They have added a call for 'policy space' to enable them to balance trade liberalization with targeted measures to promote balanced growth, poverty reduction, and industrialization.[76] In the Doha Round, they make a forceful case for a more development-oriented round and have articulated clear proposals for how this might be achieved.[77] In this endeavour they have been joined by legal scholars,[78] development economists,[79] and NGOs.[80]

In sum, the WTO reform discussion takes place in the context of real-world economic, social, and environmental pressures and political debates over ongoing negotiations. They cannot be isolated from them. The current financial crisis illustrates how quickly the interests and priorities of states can shift, highlighting that processes for dialogue and debate within governance systems are especially important at times when global economic performance weakens.

E. Devising Political Strategy

A final aspect of the proposed approach to WTO reform concerns the politics of reform. First, the power politics that permeate the WTO system will surely also affect the political viability and direction of reform.[81] An important distinction among scholars is between those focused on devising an 'ideal type' of WTO and those focused on politically achievable change in the short and medium term. On both counts, a recurring weakness is that of limited systematic consideration of the political prospects for reform and strategies for making proposed changes happen. There has been careful consideration of the role of the United States in the GATT/WTO system and the prospects of U.S. support for reforms, particularly in Congress.[82]

Recent shifts in the balance of economic power among states in the negotiations, and particularly the rise of countries like India and China, call for a deeper assessment of the political prospects for reform proposals. More broadly, some scholars have noted the importance in general of sustaining political interest in the WTO as a dynamic and relevant international organization. Already, they note the risk that a WTO with a weak legislative function will undermine the credibility and legitimacy of the strong adjudicative function embodied in the dispute settlement mechanism.[83]

IV. Conclusion: Political Challenges, Research Priorities, and Proposals

What should a better multilateral trading system look like? To answer this question, this chapter has argued that scholars need to explore new ways of thinking about the purposes of reform and the way in which the WTO is analyzed. It has argued for analyzing the WTO as a system. This approach enables us to properly account for the range of actors that are involved in the work of the WTO. It also broadens the scope and richness of reform proposals and generates different recommendations than analysis that starts by describing the WTO as either an intergovernmental regime or international organization. Further, this chapter has called for attention to the range of functions that the multilateral trading system serves. Asking questions about the governance of particular WTO functions provides new insights into the challenges of reform and broadens the scope for debate about the system as a whole, not just its negotiation and dispute settlement functions.

This chapter has also argued that a clear point of view on the ends and goals of the trading system is a necessary prerequisite for intelligent discussion of WTO reforms and makes the case that proposals for WTO reform should be grounded in the objectives of sustainable development and empowerment of developing countries in global trade governance. An important challenge—not addressed in detail in this chapter—concerns the kinds of indicators, benchmarks, or questions that can be used to measure how WTO reform proposals and governance (that is, the process by which decisions are made and implemented) contribute to, or constrain, progress in the area of sustainable development. Finally, this chapter has argued that reform proposals should acknowledge and allow the need for a permanent space or spaces for political contestation within the global governance or trade—as well as for greater attention to how reform proposals can be made attractive to WTO Members.

To indicate where this analytical approach could lead, this chapter concludes with examples of some of its implications for the WTO reform debate in relation to four of the functions noted above: monitoring, negotiation, research, and capacity building.

A functional approach to the analysis of needs for WTO reform prompts greater attention to the WTO's monitoring function.[84] The recent financial crisis has already spurred interest in greater surveillance by the WTO Secretariat of protectionist measures by Member States. But a careful examination of the monitoring function in light of the dual objectives of ensuring that it helps advance sustainable development and empower developing countries spurs a deeper and broader reform agenda. How could we reform the trade policy review (TPR) process to better serve as a tool to help governments integrate development considerations into trade decision-making? One option would be for the TPR process to include an assessment of the effects of trade rules in light of development objectives and an identification of national trade-related hurdles that impede their realization. The review process could also perform a stronger role as a catalyst for governments to organize appropriate capacity building. Specific reform proposals could include making the trade policy review process open to the public; involving multi-stakeholder processes at the national level in the development of the national trade policy review reports; inviting recognized international experts as commentators in the trade policy review meetings in Geneva; inviting commentaries from other interested national and international parties (for example, other IGOs [inter-governmental organizations], industry groups, NGOs, academics, etc.); and integrating a new component into the trade policy review process for least developed countries (LDCs) that evaluates the fulfilment by developed countries of their capacity building commitments to LDCs. The adoption of a 'systems' approach leads us to consider that the monitoring function need not, and perhaps cannot, be performed by the WTO Secretariat alone. Instead, the WTO's monitoring function might also be improved by engaging non-state actors through an independent monitoring mechanism.

The approach advocated in this chapter might also lead us to move beyond many of the existing proposals for enhancing the research function of the WTO. To date, there have been several calls for greater research capacity within the WTO Secretariat. A development-oriented and systems approach would instead lead us to favour increased support for independent research and analytical capacity in developing countries at the national and/or regional level in universities, think-tanks, and research centres, as well as in the regional/national headquarters of various UN agencies.[85] (Some initial steps in this direction are already being taken by the WTO Secretariat, albeit amid calls to still boost the WTO's own research capacity.) In addition, a sustainable development perspective would prompt us to call on donors and national governments to support national research and analytical capacity that considers trade objectives in light of domestic development goals.

Regarding the WTO's negotiation function, a systems approach leads us to recognize the prominence of coalitions in negotiations and to consider how there could be stronger financial support to the secretariats of developing country coalitions, drawing on lessons learned from successful experiences (such as those of the coalition of small and vulnerable economies) regarding the effective internal management and operation of coalitions and improving their negotiating capacity.[86] Even the smallest countries with a limited interest in market-access issues at stake in specific WTO negotiations have a long-term interest in understanding and contributing to the development of institutional rules, which they also have obligations to implement and enforce at the national level. Support should thus be given to LDC WTO Members to ensure they have permanent representation in Geneva. This can be accomplished either through mandatory contributions by Members to the WTO's core general budget, or through a voluntary, supplementary contribution scheme. While such measures would not resolve all the questions surrounding the best ways to structure and delineate the scope of WTO negotiations, without representation it is difficult to see how the smallest developing countries can hold the multilateral trading system as a whole accountable to them.

Attention to the specific functions of the WTO system also leads us to consider the engagement of developing countries in decision-making for the system's capacity-building function. Improved capacity building will depend on developing country leadership to push for more effective aid, better articulate their needs, and extract greater value from existing resources. Effective Aid for Trade and capacity building demands that countries organize themselves and stakeholders in order to benefit from both, including through support for multi-stakeholder decision-making processes on trade policy, negotiating priorities, and implementation. On the governance front, the implication is that developing countries need a stronger role in the management of Aid for Trade. Significant steps have been made in this regard to improve the integrated framework for capacity building to developing countries. However, a careful examination of the data on trade-related assistance and Aid for Trade reveals that the majority of assistance flows through bilateral agencies and a diverse range of multilateral agencies beyond those involved in the integrated framework.[87] Developed countries should shift their support from bilateral trade–capacity-building initiatives, often driven by their own mercantilist priorities, to multilateral initiatives that offer great opportunities to delink assistance from developed countries' priorities. The focus of capacity building must be on establishing durable capacity in developing countries and regions rather than supporting a network of international trade consultants. Another shortcoming concerns limited attention to monitoring and evaluation of capacity building and Aid for Trade. This could be boosted through annual independent evaluations and/or peer reviews of trade-related capacity building from the developing country perspective, which takes a sample of countries and reviews that provision of assistance against the priorities established through the Enhanced Integrated Framework, or in other national development strategies (such as the World Bank's Poverty Reduction Strategy Papers). The point here is not simply to evaluate assistance on a project-by-project basis, but to seek metrics or benchmarks for discerning how well assistance helps countries implement trade policies, institutions, and initiatives that advance their development. Further, there should be greater monitoring and public disclosure of regarding the performance of each major donor. Proper acknowledgement of the range of actors and levels at which capacity building is needed takes one away from narrow WTO-centric views of the Secretariat's work on training and technical assistance, but rather sees it in context.

Finally, a functional approach to the question of WTO reform also breathes new life into an often sterile discussion on whether and how to boost 'civil society participation'.[88] The functional approach highlights the ways in which civil society groups already do participate at different levels across the WTO's negotiation, research, capacity-building, and monitoring activities, as well as the opportunities to further enhance these activities.

Notes

1 This chapter is the product of research supported by the Geneva International Academic Network (GIAN) and the Ford Foundation. The author would like to thank Arunabha Ghosh, Ricardo Meléndez-Ortiz, John Odell, Mayur Patel, Richard Steinberg, Robert Wolfe, and Ngaire Woods for their feedback on the paper as well as the participants in a meeting of the Emerging Dynamic Global Economies (EDGE) Network Workshop on WTO Institutional Reform (13–15 March 2008).

2 See generally Pitou van Dijck and Gerrit Faber (eds), *Challenges to the New World Trade Organization* (The Hague: Kluwer Law International, 1996); Anne Krueger (ed), *The WTO as an International Organization* (London: Chicago University Press, 1998); Carolyn Deere Birkbeck and Ricardo Meléndez-Ortiz (eds), *Rebuilding Global Trade: Proposals for a Fairer, More Sustainable Future* (Geneva: GEG and ICTSD, 2009), http://www.globaleconomicgovernance.org/wp-content/uploads/rebuilding -global-trade.pdf (visited 14 April 2009).

3 Pascal Lamy, 'Message from the Director General: A World Trade System for the Benefit of All', http://www.wto.org/english/thewto_e/dg_e/dg_e.htm (visited 9 February 2009).

4 A comprehensive set of recommendations for reform based on this 'systems' approach and normative agenda—and their political feasibility—is available in Carolyn Deere Birkbeck, 'Making Global Trade Governance Work for Developing Countries: Proposals for WTO Reform', Global Economic Governance Programme Working Paper, University College, Oxford (Forthcoming 2009).

5 See, for example, William J. Davey, 'The WTO Dispute Settlement System: The First Ten Years', 8 (1) Journal of International Economic Law 17 (2005); James C. Hecht, 'Operation of WTO Dispute Settlement Panels: Assessing Proposals for Reform', 31 (3) Law & Policy in International Business 657 (2000).

6 See, for example, John Barton, Judith Goldstein, Timothy Josling, and Richard H. Steinberg, *The Evolution of the Trade Regime: Politics, Law, and Economics of the GATT and the WTO* (Princeton: Princeton University Press, 2006); Amrita Narlikar, 'WTO Decision-Making and Developing Countries', TRADE Series Working Paper, South Centre (2001), at 42. Narlikar argues, for instance, that perhaps the 'major and unsustainable discrepancy' in the WTO is the coupling of an automatic and binding system of laws and surveillance with the informal, *ad hoc* practice of bargaining and negotiation.

7 Richard Blackhurst, 'Reforming WTO Decision Making: Lessons from Singapore and Seattle', in Klaus Deutsch and Bernhard Speyer (eds), *The World Trade Organization Millennium Round* (London: Routledge, 2001) 295–310. And see Krueger, above n 2.

8 See, for instance, José Alvarez, 'The WTO as Linkage Machine', 96 (1) The American Journal of International Law 146 (2002); Robert Howse, 'From Politics to Technocracy-and Back Again: The Fate of the Multilateral Trading Regime', 96 (1) The American Journal of International Law 94 (2002); Keith Maskus, 'Regulatory Standards in the WTO: Comparing Intellectual Property Rights with Competition Policy, Environmental Protection, and Core Labor Standards', 1 (2) World Trade Review 135 (2002); Joost

Pauwelyn, *Conflict of Norms in Public International Law: How WTO Law Relates to Other Rules of International Law* (Cambridge: Cambridge University Press, 2003) 556; Joost Pauwelyn, 'The Role of Public International Law in the WTO: How Far Can We Go?', 95 (3) The American Journal of International Law 535 (2001); Ernst-Ulrich Petersmann, 'The Human Rights Approach Advocated by the UN High Commissioner for Human Rights and by the International Labour Organization: Is It Relevant for WTO Law and Policy?', 7 (3) Journal of International Economic Law 605 (2004); Debra P. Steger, 'Afterword: The "Trade and...." Conundrum—A Commentary', 96 (1) The American Journal of International Law 135 (2002); Joel P. Trachtman, 'Institutional Linkage: Transcending "Trade and...."', 96 (1) The American Journal of International Law 77 (2002).

9 On stakeholder engagement, see Steve Charnovitz, 'Non-Governmental Organizations and the Original Trade Regime', 5 Journal of World Trade 111 (1995); Steve Charnovitz, 'Triangulating the World Trade Organization', 96 (1) The American Journal of International Law 28 (2002); Steve Charnovitz, 'Participation of Nongovernmental Organizations in the World Trade Organization', 17 University of Pennsylvania Journal of International Economic Law 331 (1996), at 332; Daniel Esty, 'Non-Governmental Organizations at the World Trade Organization: Cooperation, Competition or Exclusion', 1 Journal of International Economic Law 123 (1998); Robert Housman, 'Democratizing International Trade Decision-Making', 27 Cornell International Law Journal 699 (1994); Christophe Bellmann and Richard Gester, 'Accountability of the World Trade Organization', 30 (6) Journal of World Trade 31 (1996); Lori Wallach and Michelle Sforza, *Whose Trade Organization? Corporate Globalization and the Erosion of Democracy—An Assessment of the World Trade Organization* (Washington, D.C.: Public Citizen, 1999).

10 On parliamentary matters, see Meinhard Hilf, 'How Can Parliamentary Participation in WTO Rule-Making and Democratic Control Be Made More Effective in the WTO?', Presentation given at the University of Hamburg, 19 June 2003; G. Richard Shell, 'The Trade Stakeholders Model and Participation by Non-state Parties in the World Trade Organization', 17 (1) University of Pennsylvania Journal of International Economic Law 359 (1996); Gregory C. Shaffer, 'Parliamentary Oversight of WTO Rule-Making: The Political and Normative Contexts', 7 (3) Journal of International Economic Law 629 (2004). Shaffer also explores the conditions under which greater participation by parliamentarians might be possible. In a panel at the 2007 WTO Public Forum, Harlem Désir, the head of the European Parliament's Trade Committee and an active member of the inter-parliamentary union, emphasized the range of activities the IPU was already undertaking to enhance parliamentary engagement on WTO issues around the world, including informal consultations with the WTO secretariat. Beyond the WTO, concerns about the legitimacy and accountability of global governance have prompted a number of calls for great parliamentary participation in the governance of the global economy. See for instance, Richard Falk and Andrew Strauss, 'Toward Global Parliament', 80 (1) Foreign Affairs 212 (2001).

11 Rorden Wilkinson, 'Peripheralizing Labour: The ILO, WTO and the Completion of the Bretton Woods Project', in Jeffrey Harrod and Robert O'Brien (eds), *Globalized Unions? Theory and Strategies of Organized Labour in the Global Political Economy* (London: Routledge, 2002) 204–20. For the WTO's relationship with WIPO, see Paul Salmon, 'Cooperation Between WIPO and the WTO', 17 St. John's Journal of Legal

Commentary 263 (2003); for the WTO's relationship with the Bretton Woods Institu- .
tions, see Richard Blackhurst, 'The WTO and the Global Economy', 20 (5) The World
Economy 527 (1997); Anne O. Krueger and Sarath Rajapatirana, 'The World Bank
Policies Towards Trade and Trade Policy Reform', 22 (6) The World Economy 717
(1999); Deborah Siegel, 'Legal Aspects of the IMF/WTO Relationship: The Fund's Articles of Agreement and the WTO Agreements', 96 (3) The American Journal of International Law, 561 (2002); David Vines, 'The WTO in Relation to the Fund and the Bank:
Competencies, Agendas and Linkages', in Krueger (ed), above n 4, 59–96. The inter-
section of the WTO's agreements with public health policies has been reviewed in
Carlos Correa (2000), 'Implementing National Public Health Policies in the Framework
of the WTO Agreements', 34 (5) Journal of World Trade 81 (2000); *Globalization and
Access to Drugs: Perspectives on the WTO/TRIPS Agreement, Health Economics and
Drugs* (Geneva: World Health Organization, 1998); WTO/WHO, *WTO Agreements
and Public Health: A Joint Study by the WHO and WTO Secretariat* (Geneva:
WHO/World Trade Organization, 2002); John H. Jackson, 'Fragmentation or Unifica-
tion Among International Institutions: The World Trade Organization', 31 International Law and Politics 823 (1999). The discussion of the appropriate role of the Bank
and IMF has further evolved with the Aid for Trade discussion.

12 Patrick Low, Miguel Rodriguez Mendoza, and Barbara Kotschwar (eds), *Trade Rules in
the Making: Multilateral and Regional Trade Arrangements* (Washington, D.C.: Brookings Institution Press, 1999); Jagdish Bhagwati, *Termites in the Trading System: How Preferential Trade Agreements Undermine Free Trade* (Oxford: Oxford University Press,
2008); Richard Baldwin and Patrick Low, *Multilateralizing Regionalism: Challenges for
the Global Trading System* (Cambridge: Cambridge University Press, 2009).

13 See Consultative Board to the Director-General Supachai Panitchpakdi, *The Future of
the WTO: Addressing Institutional Challenges in the New Millennium* (Geneva: World
Trade Organization, 2004) and The Warwick Commission, *The Multilateral Trade
Regime: Which Way Forward? The Report of the First Warwick Commission* (Warwick:
University of Warwick, 2007) 92. The Warwick Commission report proposed a number of institutional changes at the WTO, including increasing the size of the WTO Secretariat, expanding the powers of the Director-General, and revising the process for
reaching new trade deals.

14 See, for instance, WTO Doc T/GC/M91, General Council—Minutes of Meeting—
Held in the Centre William Rappard on 26 January 2005; WT/MIN (03)/ST/58, Min-
isterial Conference—Fifth Session—Cancún, 10–14 September 2003—Honduras
—Statement by H.E. Mr. Norman García, Secretary of State, Department of Industry
and Commerce; WT/GC/W/477, General Council—Preparatory Process in Geneva
and Negotiating Process at Ministerial Conferences—Communication from Australia,
Canada, Hong Kong, China, New Zealand, Singapore, Switzerland; WT/MIN(01)/
ST/110, Ministerial Conference—Fourth Session—Doha, 9–13 November 2001—
Republic of the Fiji Islands—Statement by H.E. Mr. Isikeli Mataitoga, Ambassador,
Permanent Representative to the WTO; WT/GC/M/57, General Council—Minutes of
Meeting—Held in the Centre William Rappard, 17 and 19 July 2000.

15 See, for example, Krueger above n 2; Sylvia Ostry, 'The World Trading System: In Dire Need of Reform?', 17 Temple International & Comparative Law Journal 109 (2003); Rorden Wilkinson, 'The Contours of Courtship: The WTO and Civil Society', R. Wilkinson and S. Hughes (eds), *Global Governance: Critical Perspectives* (London: Routledge, 2000) 193–200; Patrick Macrory, Arthur Appleton, and Michael G. Plummer, *The World Trade Organization: Legal, Economic and Political Analysis* (New York: Springer Verlag, 2005) 3 vols. Bernard Hoekman and Petros Mavroidis, *The World Trade Organization: Law, Economics and Politics* (Abingdon: Routledge, 2007) 143.

16 Ngaire Woods and Amrita Narlikar, 'Governance and the Limits of Accountability: The WTO, the IMF and the World Bank', 53 (170) International Social Science Journal 569 (2001); Robert Wolfe, 'The World Trade Organisation', in Brian Hocking and Steven McGuire (eds), *Trade Politics: International, Domestic and Regional Perspectives* (London: Routledge, 1999) 207–22.

17 Narlikar, above n 6; Amrita Narlikar, *International Trade and Developing Countries: Bargaining Coalitions in the GATT and WTO* (London: Routledge, 2003) 260; Amrita Narlikar, *The World Trade Organization: A Very Short Introduction* (Oxford: Oxford University Press, 2005) 168; South Centre, 'Institutional Governance and Decision-Making Processes in the WTO', Analytic Note (Geneva: South Centre, 2003) 53.

18 Numerous proposals for WTO reform have also been made by NGOs such as Third World Network, Oxfam, ActionAid, and the International Centre for Trade and Sustainable Development (ICTSD), among others. In November 2000, for instance, U.K.-based NGOs, including ActionAid, CAFOD, Christian Aid, Consumers International, FIELD, Oxfam, RSPB, and the World Development Movement, co-published a discussion paper on 'Recommendations for Ways Forward on Institutional Reform of the World Trade Organisation'.

19 See, for instance, Andrew Cornford, 'Variable Geometry for the WTO: Concept and Precedents', UNCTAD Discussion Paper No. 171 (May 2004), http://www.unctad.org/en/docs/osgdp20045_en.pdf (visited 14 April 2009); UNCTAD, *Positive Agenda for Developing Countries: Issues for Future Trade Negotiations* (Geneva: United Nations, 2000), www.unctad.org/en/docs/itcdtsb10_en.pdf (visited 14 April 2009).

20 The notion that trade liberalization and associated trade rules would be important for peace was a central part of the motivation for creating the GATT system post-WWII. See A. Guinness, 'International Trade and the Making of Peace', 20 (4) International Affairs 495 (1944); Herbert Feis, 'The Geneva Proposal for an International Trade Charter', 2 (1) International Organization 39 (1948); Jacob Viner, 'Conflicts of Principle in Drafting a Trade Charter', 25 (4) Foreign Affairs 612 (1947); C. Wilcox, 'The Promise of the World Trade Charter', 27 (3) Foreign Affairs 486 (1949). In 2008, a statement by Pascal Lamy echoed the enduring commitment of many within the WTO system to the relevance of that ideal, stating that 'there are only advantages in returning to a time in history when the people wanted to create an international system which prevents the repeat of a traumatic situation such as the first world war which they came out of.' Cited in 'Socialist Realism Revealed at WTO', *Tribune de Geneve*, 17 March. 2008.

21 Dani Rodrik, *One Economics, Many Recipes* (Princeton: Princeton University Press, 2007).

22 See, for instance, John O. McGinnis and Mark L. Movsesian, 'The World Trade Constitution', 114 Harvard Law Review 511 (2000), at 523–25; Ernst-Ulrich Petersmann, 'National Constitutions, Foreign Trade Policy, and European Community Law', 3 (1) European Journal of International Law 1 (1992); Christian Joerges and Ernst-Ulrich Petersmann (eds), *Constitutionalism, Multilevel Trade Governance and Social Regulation* (Oxford: Hart Publishers, 2006). For an evaluation of these debates, see Deborah Cass, The Constitutionalization of the *World Trade Organization: Legitimacy, Democracy, and Community in the International Trading System* (Oxford: Oxford University Press, 2005).

23 Robert Howse and Kalypso Nicolaidis, 'Legitimacy and Global Governance: Why a Constitution for the WTO Is a Step Too Far?' in R. Porter, Pierre Sauvé, Arvind Subramaniam, and A. Zampetti (eds), *Equity, Efficiency and Legitimacy: The Multilateral System at the Millennium* (Washington, D.C.: Brookings Institution Press, 2001) 227–63; Steven Charnovitz, 'WTO Cosmopolitics', 34 (2) Journal of International Law and Politics 299 (2003); John H. Dunning, 'The Future of the WTO: A Socio-relational Challenge', 7 (3) Review of International Political Economy 475 (2002); Robert Howse and Kalypso Nicolaidis, 'Enhancing WTO Legitimacy: Constitutionalization or Global Subsidiarity?', 16 (1) Governance 73 (2003); Manfred Elsig, 'The World Trade Organization's Legitimacy Crisis: What Does the Beast Look Like?', 41 (1) Journal of World Trade 75 (2007); Joost Pauwelyn, 'The Sutherland Report: A Missed Opportunity for Genuine Debate on Trade, Globalization and Reforming the WTO', 8 (2) Journal of International Economic Law 329 (2005).

24 Murray Gibbs, 'Special and Differential Treatment in the Context of Globalization', Proceedings of the G15 Symposium on Special and Differential Treatment in the WTO Agreements in New Delhi, India, on 10 December 1998, www.wto.org/english/tratop_e/devel_e/sem01_e/gibbs_e.doc (visited 16 April 2009); Sheila Page and Peter Kleen, *Special and Differential Treatment of Developing Countries in the World Trade Organization* (London: Overseas Development Institute, 2004).

25 Faizel Ismail, *Mainstreaming Development in the WTO: Developing Countries in the Doha Round* (Geneva: FES Geneva and CUTS International, 2007); Joseph Stiglitz and Andrew Charlton, *Fair Trade for All: How Trade Can Promote Development* (Oxford: Oxford University Press, 2005); Rorden Wilkinson and James Scott, 'Developing Country Participation in the GATT: A Reassessment', 7 (2) World Trade Review 473 (2008); Kevin Gallagher (ed), *Putting Development First: The Importance of Policy in the WTO and IFI's* (London: Zed Books, 2005).

26 Carolyn Deere Birkbeck, 'Governing the WTO System: The Capacity-building Function', Global Economic Governance Programme Working Paper 2009/4, University College, Oxford (2009).

27 Gary Sampson (ed), *The Role of the WTO and Global Governance* (Tokyo: United Nations University Press, 2001).

28 Debapriya Bhattacharya, 'Creeping Trade and Phantom Aid: LDCs in the Global Context and Priorities for Reform of Global Governance', Geneva Lectures on Global Economic Governance (29 January 2008, updated February 2009), http://www.globaleconomicgovernance.org/creeping-trade-and-phantom-aid-ldcs-in-the-global-context-and-priorities-for-reform-of-global-governance-geneva-lectures-on-global-economic-governance (visited 16 April 2009).

29 Birkbeck and Meléndez-Ortiz, above n 2.

30 See Bellmann and Gester, above n 9; Wallach and Sforza, above n 9; Woods and Narlikar, above n 16, at 569.

31 Daniel Esty, 'The World Trade Organization's Legitimacy Crisis', 1 (1) World Trade Review 7 (2002); Elsig, 2005, above, n 23; Matthew Eagleton-Pierce, 'Uncovering Symbolic Power: Power Analysis, Southern Countries, and the World Trade Organisation', (Doctoral thesis on file with the University of Oxford, 2007).

32 Some analysts also see accountability as an end in itself, appealing to international human rights norms in that respect. See the work of 3D->Trade-Human Rights-Equitable Economy at http://www.3dthree.org.

33 On this point, some scholars argue that the legitimacy of international institutions is in part derived from conflicts with external agents of change such as social movements. See Balakrishnan Rajagopal, *International Law from Below: Development, Social Movements and Third World Resistance* (Cambridge: Cambridge University Press, 2003).

34 Robert Wolfe with Mark Halle (eds), *Process Matters: Sustainable Development and Domestic Trade Transparency* (Winnipeg: International Institute for Sustainable Development, 2007).

35 Susan Sell, 'Big Business and the New Trade Agreements: The Future of the WTO?', in Richard Stubbs and G. Underhill (eds), *Political Economy and the Changing Global Order* (New York: Oxford University Press, 2000) 174–83; Susan Sell, *Private Power, Public Law: The Globalisation of Intellectual Property Rights* (Cambridge: Cambridge University Press, 2003); Dominic Eagleton, *Under the Influence: Exposing Undue Corporate Influence Over Policymaking at the World Trade Organization* (London: ActionAid, 2006).

36 Sheila Page, *How Developing Countries Trade: The Institutional Constraints* (London: Routledge, 1994) 328.

37 Jane Ford, 'A Social Theory of Trade Regime Change: GATT to WTO', 4 (3) International Studies Review 115 (2002).

38 See, for instance, Ernst B. Haas, *When Knowledge Is Power: Three Models of Change in International Organization* (Berkeley: University of California Press, 1990); Laurence R. Helfer, 'Understanding Change in International Organizations: Globalization and Innovation in the ILO', 59 Vanderbilt Law Review 649 (2006).

39 For a leading proponent of this perspective, see Robert Wolfe, 'Can the Trading System Be Governed: Institutional Implications of the WTO's Suspended Animation', in Alan S. Alexandroff (ed), *Can the World Be Governed? Possibilities for Effective Multilateralism* (Waterloo: Wilfrid Laurier University Press, 2008) 289–352; Robert Wolfe, 'Still Foggy after All These Years: Reform Proposals for the WTO', in Alan Alexandroff (ed), *Trends in World Trade Policy: Essays in Honor of Sylvia Ostry* (Durham: Carolina Academic Press, 2007) 133–54; and Robert Wolfe, 'Decision-making and Transparency in the "medieval" WTO: Does the Sutherland Report Have the Right Prescription?' 8 (3) Journal of International Economic Law 631 (2005).

40 Peter Drahos, for instance, takes up the question of how developing countries can forge more effective coalitions, particularly in the context of forum-shifting by powerful players. See Peter Drahos, 'When the Weak Bargain with the Strong: Negotiations in the World Trade Organization', 8 (1) International Negotiation 79 (2003). See also John Odell, *Negotiating Trade: Developing Countries in the WTO and NAFTA* (Cambridge; Cambridge University Press, 2006).

41 Rorden Wilkinson, *The WTO: Crisis and the Governance of Global Trade* (Oxford: Routledge, 2006) 175.

42 James E. Anderson, 'Why Do Nations Trade (So Little)?', 5(2) Pacific Economic Review 115 (2000); Mark Rupert, *Ideologies of Globalization: Contending Visions of a New World Order* (London: Routledge, 2000) 208; Saskia Sassen, *Globalization and Its Discontents* (New York: New Press, 1998); David Held and Mathias Koenig-Archibungi (eds), *Global Governance and Public Accountability* (Oxford: Blackwells, 2005); Walden Bello, 'Why Reform of the WTO Is the Wrong Agenda' (Focus on Trade 43, December 1999), http://www.tni.org/detail_page.phtml?page=archives_bello_agenda (visited 14 April 2009).

43 See John Jackson, *The Jurisprudence of GATT and the WTO* (Cambridge: Cambridge University Press, 2000) 497; John Jackson, *The World Trading System: Law and Policy of International Economic Relations,* 2nd ed. (Cambridge: MIT Press, 1997) 453.

44 The particular issue was the how the One World Trust's Global Accountability Project (GAP) Framework applied its framework to the WTO. For this case study, see One World Trust, *Global Accountability Profile: WTO* (London: One World Trust, 2006).

45 For a general introduction to the politics, law, and economics of the WTO, see John Barton, Judith Goldstein, Tim Josling, and Richard Steinberg, *The Evolution of the Trade Regime: Politics, Law and the Economics of the GATT and the WTO* (Princeton: Princeton University Press, 2006).

46 While most of the literature approaches the WTO system as a regime (see Barton et al., above n 6; Ford, above n 37), the first major volume on the WTO 'as an international organization' appeared in 1998 (see Krueger, above n 2).

47 See Deere Birkbeck, above n 26.

48 To date, analyses utilizing this functional approach have been completed on the WTO's negotiation, dispute settlement, capacity-building, and monitoring functions. See www.globaleconomicgovernance.org/trade.

49 For the application of this functional approach to another international organization, see Carolyn Deere, 'Reforming Governance to Advance the WIPO Development Agenda', in Jeremy de Beer (ed), *Implementing WIPO's Development Agenda* (Waterloo: Wilfrid Laurier University Press/Centre for International Governance Innovation/International Development Research Centre, 2009).

50 Carolyn Deere, *The Implementation Game: The TRIPS Agreement and the Global Politics of Intellectual Property Reform in Developing Countries* (Oxford: Oxford University Press, 2008).

51 A 2005 study commissioned by the WTO Secretariat provides a factual account of the first decade of the inner workings of the WTO. See Peter Gallagher, *The First Ten Years of the WTO: 1995–2005* (Cambridge: Cambridge University Press, 2005). For more political accounts, see Aileen Kwa, *Power Politics in the WTO*, 2nd ed. (Bangkok: Focus on the Global South, 2003), http://www.focusweb.org/publications/Books/power-politics-in-the-WTO.pdf (visited 15 April 2009); Manfred Elsig, 'The World Trade Organization's Bureaucrats: Runaway Agents or Masters' Servants?', NCCR Trade Regulation Working Paper 19 (March 2007), www.nccr-trade.org/images/stories/publications/IP2/MElsig_NCCRWP_Agency.pdf (visited 4 April 2009).

52 Sonia Rolland, 'Developing Country Coalitions at the WTO: In Search of Legal Support', 48 Harvard International Law Journal 483 (2007); Mayur Patel, 'New Faces in the Green Room: Developing Country Coalitions and Decision-Making in the WTO',

Global Economic Governance Programme Working Paper 2007/33, University College (September 2007).

53 See Elsig, above n 51.

54 Padideh Ala'i, 'From the Periphery to the Center? The Evolving WTO Jurisprudence on Transparency and Good Governance', 11 (4) Journal of International Economic Law 779 (2008).

55 Marrakesh Agreement Establishing the World Trade Organization (WTO Agreement), in WTO, *The Results of the Uruguay Round of Multilateral Trade Negotiations: The Legal Texts* (Geneva: WTO, 2004) 3.

56 Carlos Correa, *Intellectual Property Rights, the WTO and Developing Countries: The TRIPS Agreement and Policy Options* (Penang, Malaysia: Third World Network [TWN], 2000).

57 For examples, see Nathalie Bernasconi-Osterwalder, Daniel Magraw, Maria Julia Oliva, Marcos Orellana, and Elisabeth Tuerk, *Environment and Trade: A Guide to WTO Jurisprudence* (London: Earthscan, 2005).

58 John Audley, *Green Politics and Global Trade: NAFTA and the Future of Environmental Politics* (Washington, D.C.: Georgetown University Press, 1997); Marc Williams and Lucy Ford, 'The World Trade Organisation, Social Movements and Global Environmental Management', 8 (1) Environmental Politics 268 (1999).

59 Jagdish N. Bhagwati and T.N. Srinivasan 'Trade and Environment: Does Environmental Diversity Detract from the Case of Free Trade?' in Jagdish Bhagwati and Robert E. Hudec (eds), *Fair Trade and Harmonization: Prerequisites for Free Trade*, 2nd ed. (Cambridge: MIT Press, 1996) vol 1, 159–226; Halina Ward and Duncan Brack, *Trade, Investment and the Environment* (London: Earthscan, 1999); Graciela Chichilnisky, 'Sustainable Development and North-South Trade', in Lakshman D. Guruswamy and Jeffrey A. McNeely, *Protection of Global Biodiversity: Converging Strategies* (Durham, N.C.: Duke University Press, 1998) 101–17; Patrick Low, *International Trade and the Environment* (Washington, D.C.: World Bank, 2002); Gary Sampson, 'Is There a Need for Restructuring the Collaboration among the WTO and UN Agencies So as to Harness Their Complementarities?', 7 (3) Journal of International Economic Law 717 (2004); Eric Neumayer, 'The WTO and the Environment: Its Past Record Is Better Than Critics Believe, but the Future Outlook Is Bleak', 4 (3) Global Environmental Politics 1 (2004).

60 Ken Conca, 'The WTO and the Undermining of Global Environmental Governance', 7 (3) Review of International Political Economy 484 (2000).

61 Adil Najam, Mark Halle, and Ricardo Meléndez-Ortiz, *Trade and Environment: A Resource Book* (Geneva: IISD/ICTSD, 2007); World Wildlife Federation (WWF), 'Reform of the WTO's Dispute Settlement Mechanism for Sustainable Development', WWF International Discussion Paper (July 1999), http://powerswitch.panda.org/what_we_do/footprint/transforming_markets/news/?3758/Reform-of-the-WTOs-Dispute-Settlement-Mechanism-for-Sustainable-Development-Discussion (visited 14 April 2009).

62 Erik Beukel, 'Greening the World Trade Organization Trading Regime? Towards a Structural Power Model', 4 (2) Journal of International Relations & Development 138 (2001).

63 Daniel Esty, 'Bridging the Trade-Environment Divide', 15 (3) Journal of Economic Perspectives 113 (2001).

64 Adil Najam, Mark Halle, Ricardo Meléndez-Ortiz, *Envisioning a Sustainable Development Agenda for Trade and Environment* (Geneva: IISD/ICTSD, 2007).

65 Chile, for instance, has played a leading role in this respect. See Mario Matus and Eda Rossi, 'Trade and the Environment in the FTAA: A Chilean Perspective', in Carolyn Deere and Daniel Esty (eds), *Greening the Americas: NAFTA's Lessons for the Hemispheric Trade* (Cambridge: MIT Press, 2002) 259, and Carolyn Deere, 'Greening Trade in the Americas: An Agenda for Moving Beyond the North-South Impasse', 38 (1) Journal of World Trade 137 (2004).

66 Carolyn Deere, 'Fisheries Trade and Sustainable Development: Conflict or Compatibility?', 15 The Ocean Yearbook, 345 (2002); Carolyn Deere and Elizabeth Havice, *Fisheries, Trade and Sustainable Development* (Geneva: International Centre for Trade and Sustainable Development, 2006); William M. Reichert, 'Note, Resolving the Trade and Environment Conflict: The WTO and NGO Consultative Relations', 5 Minnesota Journal of Global Trade 219 (1996); Aaditya Mattoo and Arvind Subramanian 'From Doha to the Next Bretton Woods' 88 (1) Foreign Affairs 15 (2009).

67 Pauwelyn, above n 23; Kalypso Nicolaidis and Robert Howse, 'Democracy without Sovereignty: The Global Vocation of Political Ethics' in Tomer Broude and Yuval Shany (eds), *The Shifting Allocation of Authority in International Law: Considering Sovereignty, Supremacy and Subsidiarity* (Oxford: Hart Publishing, 2008) 163–91; and Howse and Nicolaidis, above n 23, 'Legitimacy and Global Governance.'

68 World Commission on the Social Dimension of Globalization, *A Fair Globalization: Creating Opportunities for All* (Geneva: International Labor Organization, 2004); Annie Taylor and Caroline Thomas, *Global Trade and Global Social Issues* (London: Routledge, 1999); United Nations Development Programme (UNDP), *Making Global Trade Work for People* (New York: UNDP, 2003); and UNDP, *Human Development Report 2005—International Cooperation at a Crossroads: Aid, Trade and Security in an Unequal World* (New York: United Nations Development Program, 2005) 372.

69 Paul Collier, *The Bottom Billion: Why the Poorest Countries Are Failing and What Can be Done About It* (Oxford: Oxford University Press, 2007) 224.

70 For historical reviews of the Uruguay Round, see John Croome, *Reshaping the World Trading System: A History of the Uruguay Round*, 2nd ed. (Geneva: World Trade Organization, 1999) 400; Terrance P. Stewart, Susan G. Markel, and Michael T. Kerwin, *The GATT Uruguay Round: A Negotiating History (1986–1992)* (Boston: Kluwer Law and Taxation Publishers, 2003) 342. For historical perspectives on the WTO, see Robert E. Hudec, *The GATT Legal System and World Trade Diplomacy* (New York: Praeger, 1975).

71 Bhagirath Lal Das, *The WTO Agreements: Deficiencies, Imbalances and Required Changes* (London: Zed Books/Third World Network, 1998) 128; Joseph Michael Finger and Philip Schuler, 'Implementation of Uruguay Round Commitments: The Development Challenge', 23 (4) World Economy 511 (1999).

72 Hesham Youssef, *Special and Differential Treatment for Developing Countries in the WTO* (Geneva: South Centre, 1999).

73 See Krueger, above n 2; Mike Moore, 'Efforts to Assist Poor Countries', 8 (4) Presidents & Prime Ministers 30 (1999); Mike Moore, *A World Without Walls: Freedom, Development, Free Trade and Global Governance* (Cambridge: Cambridge University Press, 2003) 304; Zhen Kun Wang, *Africa's Role in Multilateral Trade Negotiations* (Washington, D.C.: World Bank, 1997) 28.

74 See Page above, n 36.

75 Robert Hudec, *Developing Countries in the GATT Legal System* (Aldershot: Trade Policy Research Centre, 1987) 246; Diana Tussie and David Glover (eds), *The Developing Countries in World Trade: Policies and Bargaining Strategies* (Boulder: Lynne Rienner, 1993); Constantine Michalopoulos, *Developing Countries in the WTO* (Basingstoke: Palgrave, 2001) 294.

76 See Das, above n 71; Bhagirath Lal Das, *The Doha Agenda: The New Negotiations on World Trade* (London: Zed Books, 2003) 128. For historical reviews of debates on developing countries in the GATT, see GATT, 'Report of Committee on Trade and Development: Basic Instruments and Selected Documents', 1984–1985, 32nd Supplement #21, L/5913; Alice H. Amsden and Takashi Hikino, 'The Bark Is Worse Than the Bite: New WTO Law and Late Industrialization', 570 Annals of the American Academy of Political and Social Sciences 104 (July 2000); Bela Balassa and Constantine Michalopoulos, 'Liberalizing Trade between Developed and Developing Countries', 20 Journal of World Trade Law 3 (1986); Charles Chukwuma Soludo, Osita Ogbu, and Ha-Joon Chang (eds), *The Politics of Trade and Industrial Policy in Africa: Forced Consensus?* (Ottawa: Africa World Press/IDRC, 2004). On trade, developing countries, and industrialization, see Gallagher, above n 25; Yong-Shik Lee, *Reclaiming Development in the World Trading System* (Cambridge: Cambridge University Press, 2006) 208; Ha-Joon Chang, *Kicking Away the Ladder—Development Strategy in Historical Perspective* (London: Anthem Press, 2002) 187.

77 See Faizel Ismail, 'A Development Perspective on the WTO July 2004 General Council Decision', 8 (2) Journal of International Economic Law 377 (2004). See also Ismail (2007), above n 25; and Dani Rodrik, 'Five Simple Principles for World Trade', *The American Prospect*, 17 January 2000.

78 Joel P. Trachtman, 'Legal Aspects of a Poverty Agenda at the WTO: Trade Law and "Global Apartheid"', 6 (3) Journal of Intellectual Economic Law 3 (2003).

79 Bernard Hoekman, Constantine Michalopoulos, and L. Alan Winters, 'More Favorable and Differential Treatment of Developing Countries: Toward a New Approach in the World Trade Organization', World Bank Policy Research Working Paper No. 3107 (1 August 2003); Bernard Hoekman, *The Political Economy of the World Trading System: The WTO and Beyond*, 2nd ed. (Oxford: Oxford University Press, 2001) 576; Andrew H. Charlton and Joseph E. Stiglitz, 'A Development-friendly Prioritisation of Doha Round Proposals', 28 (3) The World Economy 293 (2005).

80 Oxfam, *Africa and the Doha Round: Fighting to Keep Development Alive* (Oxford: Oxfam, 2005).

81 See Kwa, above n 51; Fatoumata Jawara and Aileen Kwa, *Behind the Scenes at the WTO: The Real World of International Trade Negotiations* (New York: Zed Books, 2003) 224.

82 Gautam Sen, 'The United States and the GATT/WTO System', in Rosemary Foot, Neil MacFarlane, and Michael Mastanduno (eds), *US Hegemony and International Organisations* (Oxford: Oxford University Press, 2003) 115–38.

83 Richard Steinberg and Judith Goldstein, 'Regulatory Shift: The Rise of Judicial Liberalization at the WTO', in Walter Mattli and Ngaire Woods, *The Politics of Global Regulation* (Princeton University Press, 2009) 211–41.

84 For a critical review of the effectiveness of WTO's monitoring and surveillance activities, see Arunabha Ghosh, 'Information Gaps, Information Systems, and the WTO's Trade Policy Review Mechanism', Global Economic Governance Programme Working Paper 2008/40, University College (2008). See also proposals in articles by Robert Wolfe, Félix Pena, and Arunabha Ghosh in Deere Birkbeck and Meléndez-Ortiz, above n 2.

85 Diana Tussie (ed), *The Politics of Trade: The Role of Research in Trade Policy and Negotiation* (Leiden: Martinus Nijhoff, 2009).

86 Mayur Patel, above n 52; Carolyn Deere Birkbeck, Emily Jones, and Ngaire Woods, *Manoeuvring at the Margins: Small States in International Trade Negotiations* (Oxford: Global Economic Governance Programme and London: Commonwealth Secretariat, forthcoming).

87 Deere Birkbeck, above n 2.

88 Peter Van den Bossche, 'NGO Involvement in the WTO: A Comparative Perspective', 11 (4) Journal of International Economic Law 717 (2008); Yves Bonzon, 'Institution-alizing Public Participation in WTO Decision Making: Some Conceptual Hurdles and Avenues', 11 (4) Journal of International Economic Law 751 (2008); Mark Halle, 'Catching up with the Slowest: NGO Accreditation at the WTO', 11 (3) Bridges Monthly 20 (2007).

PART II

Decision-Making in the WTO

A Two-Tier Approach to WTO Decision-Making
THOMAS COTTIER

I. Background

A. Matching Substance–Structure Pairings

Institutions, structures, and procedures are not ends in themselves. They serve and facilitate the attainment of substantive goals. Domestic political processes are shaped by constitutional law with a view to achieving and securing fundamental goals of justice of a given society. To some extent, these goals are equally defined in constitutional law. The situation is no different for international law and organizations. Decision-making processes serve and facilitate the attainment of legitimate outcomes commensurate with the substantive goals of the organization. Indeed, outputs and the legitimacy of outputs are directly related to the decision-making process and institutional rules through which outputs are generated. Thus structures and procedures need to be shaped in a manner conducive to achieving substantive goals. They need to match and be in line with each other. They are mutually dependent. The authority and legitimacy of the institution relies, in other words, on appropriate substance–structure pairings.[1] With the evolution of substance, structures and procedures equally need to change, adapt, and evolve.

The World Trade Organization (WTO) is not immune from needing an appropriate substance–structure pairing. Members need to review the relationship between substance and structure, and assess reform options. Appropriate structures are, as much as trade liberalization, a means to an end: a means to successfully achieve the goals of the organization, depicted in the preambles of the various agreements. In a spirit similar to that of the General

Agreement on Tariffs and Trade (GATT) 1947, Member States recognized in the preamble to the Marrakesh Agreement Establishing the World Trade Organization that relations

> in the field of trade and economic endeavor should be conducted with a view to raising standards of living, ensuring full employment and a large and steadily growing volume of real income and effective demand, and expanding the production of and trade in goods and services, while allowing for the optimal use of the world's resources in accordance with the objective of sustainable development, seeking to protect and preserve the environment and to enhance the means of doing so in a manner consistent with their respective needs and concerns at different levels of economic development.[2]

This preamble recognizes that international trade regulation serves different and partially competing goals. It is required to strike a balance between different objectives and maximize the attainment of them. This requires institutions and processes that can cope with these complexities. The authority of the multilateral trading systems depends on it, and structures and procedures are of key importance.[3] The challenges are well-known. They are constitutional in nature and entail institutional issues within the WTO, as well as horizontal and vertical problems relating to other fields of international and domestic law, respectively.

Within the WTO the relationship between the political and judicial process is at stake. This relationship includes the proper role and function of the Secretariat vis-à-vis the political and judicial. It covers the effectiveness of decision-making, the role of stakeholders, and the relationship between trade rounds and regular activities in the process of law-making. Horizontal issues include the problem of fragmentation and coherence in relation to other international organizations and domains of international law. Vertically, the relationship between WTO and domestic law and the impact of WTO law in trade policy formulation, implementation, and enforcement within Members are predominant concerns. This includes the relationship between WTO law and regional/preferential trade arrangements. The latter are supposed to operate within the bounds of the multilateral framework but increasingly suffer from inflation and non-compliance with WTO rules.

A number of questions must be addressed under the rubric of WTO reform. How can we achieve a better balance between law-making and judicial refinement of WTO law in and by case law? How can we achieve better policy coordination in addressing borderline issues among trade and other fields governed by other institutions, such as culture, human rights, investment protection, finance, monetary affairs, and development assistance? How do we make sure that WTO rules are taken seriously at home, by legislators and domestic courts alike? How can we, in turn, ensure that rule-making responds to the needs for transparency, accountability, and legitimacy? What are the possible legal tools to bring about a proper, well-balanced system? How can the WTO best be structured to cope with these issues and challenges?

It is striking that underlying institutional issues, notwithstanding the significant challenges they pose, have not been addressed by Members. A wide range of studies and reports, containing suggestions and recommendations, has been essentially ignored in trade diplomacy and capitals.[4] Calls by the International Law Association to establish a committee or working group dealing with institutional issues at the WTO have gone without official response.[5] Within the Doha Development Agenda, institutional issues have been discussed only in the context of reforming dispute settlement, an area where reform is least required. Some efforts have been made to address the relationship to preferential agreements and to enhance transparency.[6] Yet disciplines have not been substantially enhanced, and no common will to strengthen conditions for preferential trade has been found.

Overall, the institutional reform taboo may be explained by expediency and concerns that it may further delay, complicate, and impede the conclusion of the current Doha Development Agenda under the 2005 Hong Kong ministerial program.[7] Institutional reform may be seen as a pretext to prolong the current trade round. It may even be seen as a means to filibuster the process. It is not suggested here that institutional change should be undertaken with a view to concluding the Doha Round.[8] The Doha Round can and must be completed within the current institutional rules and procedures. Members cannot change the wheels of a running car.

Instead, it is important to recognize that the main difficulties in concluding the Doha Development Agenda are rooted in complex substantive issues, mainly in agriculture. They relate to classical issues of market access that GATT and the WTO have successfully dealt with previously through a process of claims and responses. Reductions of tariffs and domestic measures entail substantial structural adjustment, which takes time to negotiate and implement. Fifty years of arrears in agricultural reform are difficult to address, and the process is bound to take time. The Doha Round remains less than a decade old.

Negotiations within the current round are focused on agriculture, non-agricultural market access, and services. The July 2008 package was limited to these areas and to certain rules.[9] They will decide the fate of the Doha Agenda. These issues can and must be dealt with under current procedures. In addition, the current agenda on rule-making is relatively modest. It is limited to implementation and marginal improvements of existing agreements in rules, intellectual property, and trade facilitation. Aid for trade is not likely to result in a new legal framework but is likely to work with funding and donor programs within and outside the WTO. More ambitious tasks, in particular negotiations on trade and investment and trade and competition, were not taken up.

The difficulties in concluding the current Doha Development Agenda are often ascribed to outdated modes of negotiations. This is only partly true. While it is not the case for core concerns and the current agenda, it explains why more ambitious plans in the field of rule-making have failed. Some the issues inscribed into the Doha Agenda show structural deficiencies. Reform of the dispute settlement system came to a halt because the issue was addressed in isolation and without linking the debate to the political process of decision-making, which was left untouched.

Negotiations on trade and environment have largely been a disguise for further market access issues. These negotiations have failed, despite an explicit mandate, to take into account services and matters pertaining to technology transfer and intellectual property rights.[10] It is here that the structural limits of present modes of negotiating separately on goods, services, and intellectual property are visible. The WTO has not been able to face complex issues that require the interface of different regulatory areas within the jurisdiction of the Organization. The downsizing of the Doha Agenda in rule-making is attributable in part to structural deficiencies.

These deficiencies need to be addressed with a view to taking up the challenges of a post-Doha agenda.[11] Leftovers, unresolved under the current modes of operation, are likely to be carried over. The future is likely to entail complex issues beyond market access. The challenges of climate change mitigation and adaptation and of the financial crisis will require addressing these problems in their full complexity, possibly involving the reregulation of tariffs, production and process methods, subsidies in industrial and agricultural products, and transfer of technologies. Labour standards and other social issues will likely need to need to be addressed. Additionally, new approaches to the regulation of financial services and cooperation with other international organizations, particularly the International Monetary Fund (IMF), the World Bank (IBRD), and the Bank of International Settlements (BIS). Trade and investment as well as trade and competition are likely to be included. The world will need to see more, not less, positive integration and rule-making in meeting these challenges.

The global recession of 2009 will likely make effective decision-making in both the political and judicial arenas imperative in the coming years. Greater sophistication will be required in dealing with the constitutional, horizontal, and vertical issues that are confronting the WTO. The impetus for institutional reform, however, goes beyond climate change and current events. At its core, institutional reform must deal with profound underlying issues in the context of international trade regulation and international economic relations.[12]

B. The Changing Substance and Context of WTO Law

Long past are the days when the GATT, in light of extensive post–World War II tariff-based protectionism, focused almost exclusively on reducing border protection and enhancing market access for goods traded. True, trade liberalization remains at the heart of the WTO's work. Market access remains of paramount importance, entailing both border and domestic measures. There was never a clear-cut distinction between the two. National treatment, from the very beginning, related to domestic regulation and conditions of competition. Much of the present Doha Development Agenda still belongs to the classical domain of WTO law relating to border measures: non-agriculture market access negotiations, reduction of agricultural tariffs, improvement of disciplines on trade remedies, progressive expansion of national treatment in services under the General Agreement on Trade in Services (GATS), Aid for Trade, Special and Differential Treatment and Graduation, and the Generalized System of Preferences (GSP) focus on market access. The main difficulties in the negotiations are still in these classical areas of multilateral and bilateral negotiations on trade concessions.

Despite the fact that classic areas of concern remain prominent, important changes have taken place. They amount to a parallel of what Wolfgang Friedman, in his time, termed the changing structure of international law when it moved from a law of coexistence to a law of cooperation under the aegis of the post-war United Nations Charter.[13] First, with the progressive reduction of tariffs and the ban on quantitative restrictions on agriculture, the emphasis of regulatory work has shifted to areas pertaining to domestic regulation and securing fair conditions for investment in other fields. Non-tariff barriers addressed in the Agreements on Technical Barriers to Trade and on Sanitary and Phytosanitary Measures, standards on intellectual property in the Agreement on Trade Related Aspects of Intellectual Property (TRIPS Agreement), domestic support in the Agreement on Agriculture, disciplines on subsidies in the Agreement on Subsidies and Countervailing Duties, domestic regulation in GATS, and government procurement all essentially serve as a benchmark for Members' domestic laws.

Much of the work under the GATT since the Tokyo Round, including the Uruguay Round, has been of a legislative or prescriptive nature. Future negotiations are likely to see the realm of rule-making reinforced. Clear distinctions between negative integration (prescribing limits to national sovereignty) and positive integration (prescribing what Members are obliged to do) have been blurred. But the latter is increasing. The challenges of climate change and linkages between trade and issues such as the environment, human rights, investment protection, intellectual property, and the regulation of services, in particular financial services, will further enhance complex rule-making negotiations. These negotiations will need to take into account elements pertaining to different fields, combining goods, services, and intellectual property alike.

Second, the advent of binding dispute settlement has changed the relationship of rule-making and adjudication. While panel decisions could be blocked under GATT 1947, Members are today bound by decisions rendered pursuant to the Dispute Settlement Understanding (DSU). No longer is there a power of veto in dispute settlement. At the same time, decisions taken by dispute settlement are difficult to review in subsequent legislation. While the instruments of authentic interpretation and of revision of treaty provisions formally exist, the tradition of working and negotiating in trade rounds extending on average to a decade practically exclude the possibility of legislative responses to DSU decisions.[14] In fact, the Appellate Body has the last word on interpreting the agreements within the WTO. This results in an imbalance between law-making and adjudication, placing a heavy responsibility on the case law in developing WTO law.

Third, leadership has changed. GATT negotiations in 1947 and successive rounds were launched during the Cold War and led by the United States. The modes of negotiations were developed with a single power dominating the process and others following suit. Eventually, trade negotiations developed into a bipolar framework, with the growth and emergence of post-war Europe negotiating at the table in Geneva with a single voice under a common commercial policy. The core of the Uruguay Round agreement was the product of U.S. and European Communities (EC) bargaining, with the results being eventually multilateralized. Others, such as Japan and large developing countries, played an important but not decisive role.

With the advent of emerging economies, the WTO faces a multipolar world. Since the Cancun Ministerial Meeting, major decisions have required the consent of a number of countries, including Brazil and India. The accession of China to the WTO in 2001 profoundly shifted the negotiating dynamic at the WTO. While China still prefers a discrete voice in multilateral negotiations, it is evident that no major agreement can be achieved without its consent. The future accession of Russia will further change the political economy at the WTO.

Shifts in the club of larger nations are not the only changes that have affected the multipolar world. Medium and small countries have significantly increased their participation and now seek to influence the process through ideas and collation building. Efforts in recent years at building negotiating capacity in smaller Members have paid dividends. Members increasingly operate in a context of flexible, interest-driven coalitions.[15] They may belong to more than one grouping, depending on their interests. It is no coincidence that the WTO has seen a growing number of informal coalitions with coordination going beyond the former formula of groups of friends common in the Uruguay Round.

Fourth, information technology has significantly improved the transparency of WTO work and documentation. Information about the WTO and its activities is broadly accessible and allows for much wider participation of non-governmental organizations.[16] The practical role of non-governmental organizations and academic work has significantly enlarged the constituency of the WTO beyond traditional producer interests. More people than ever before are taking an interest in the work of the WTO, which for many years had been a matter of specialists and government officials working outside the limelight of international diplomacy.

C. Incremental Change and Evolution

While the substance and context has evolved, the formal structure of the WTO has remained largely similar to that of the GATT 1947. The most significant changes have been the evolution of the GATT agreements into a single undertaking under the WTO and the fundamental structural changes undertaken in dispute settlement. The modes of daily business and routine of committees and the General Council have not substantially changed over the years. The mantra of a member-driven organization, a forum of negotiation rather than a multilateral body, still prevails.

The iterative process of round-based negotiations has essentially remained the same since the creation of the GATT in 1947. It is hardly framed by international agreements.[17] The letter of Article XXVIII GATT on tariff negotiations was left behind a long time ago, and the cycles of multilateral trade negotiations developed their own customary procedures and informal conventions. Detailed voting rules, based on one-state one-vote in GATT 1947, were also included in the Marrakesh Agreement but are not applied even when consensus fails. Specific structures of negotiations are established to meet the challenges of a particular round. The work is undertaken in formal and informal committees on the basis of consensus. Problems that are encountered are addressed informally and bilaterally and are discussed in ad hoc processes, guided by the chair of committees and negotiating groups, and the Director-General of the WTO. The Green Room process, with tailor-made participation of usually some 25 ambassadors of interested and hand-picked Members, is critical to bringing about compromise.

The process is flanked by informal talks and coordination among delegations in Geneva and support by the Secretariat and NGOs. The role of trade ministers largely depends on initiatives by Members and the strategies of the Director-General. While mandatory biannual ministerial meetings are held, informal negotiations take place in between meetings, both within the WTO and outside on the initiative of Members. Linkages between agenda items are made based on strategic as opposed to operational considerations. Negotiations are not structured in a manner conducive to interfacing between different areas, such as goods and services or intellectual property. The structure is characterized by organizational fragmentation, and negotiations are essentially conducted in parallel.

Although the basic modus operandi has not changed, the GATT and the WTO have not been static. Changes have taken place over time and incrementally within the bounds of existing structures. To some extent, diplomacy has been able to adjust to new challenges. Bilateral tariff negotiations have been gradually replaced by multilateral approaches applying formula-based tariff reductions and sectoral initiatives based on critical mass. A comparable evolution may be observed in negotiations on services, which increasingly rely on sectoral agreements and critical mass.

Negotiations on rule-making have been conducted within structures originally designed for negotiating market access concessions. Up until the Uruguay Round, this proved largely successful. It brought about substantive disciplines within the GATT and the TRIPS Agreement and successfully created a number of side agreements under the GATT. Importantly, the ability to undertake legislative work in between rounds has been used. The agreements on telecommunication, financial services, and information technology following the conclusion of the Uruguay Round are examples of this legislative work. So too is the revision of the TRIPS Agreement, following the Doha Declaration on Health, and the revision of the Agreement on Government Procurement. Yet the pattern to date does not show constant or ongoing legislative work between trade rounds. The WTO is far from a proper legislative process of deliberation and decision-making comparable to law-making processes in domestic law. Legislative accomplishments between rounds are the exception rather than the rule. And auxiliary instruments have not been used, even in response to dispute settlement.

Most significantly, the major reform of the dispute settlement system was not accompanied by changes to the political processes of the WTO. This has resulted in a new relationship between the political and judicial within the WTO. Dispute settlement has evolved while negotiations have stalled. Some have argued that the resulting imbalance necessitates a return to the former non-binding dispute settlement. The impact on sovereignty and the prerogatives of domestic legislators is not supported by the weak legitimacy of the WTO.[18] Some have argued that what is needed is a strengthened multilateralism and political process. The proper balance should be achieved through an enhanced political process rather than watering down dispute settlement.[19] None of this has happened. Further refining of the DSU, in particular the creation of a professional cadre of panel chairs, a college of standing panellists to draw on, and the ability to remand cases from the Appellate Body to the panel, have not found sufficient support.

A new balance is being sought outside of the WTO. Legislators and domestic courts continue to deny the potential of the direct effect of WTO law and decisions in municipal law and of a more nuanced theory of justiciability, in particular in the United States and the European Union. The imbalance between the political and judicial process within the WTO has facilitated a return to a dualist perspective of international law, delinking international and domestic law.[20] Legalization at the WTO is met with de-legalization of international law in domestic fora.

In conclusion, the structures of the GATT and the WTO were shaped at different times, and for a different agenda. They were shaped for a process of periodic tariff reductions and not law-making over time. They adjusted incrementally, but the framework has reached its limits. New structural elements, combining past experience and success with current and future regulatory challenges, must be developed. The debate, which will be taking place after the completion of the Doha Agenda, calls for preparation and discussion. The suggestion here is to work toward a two-tier approach to negotiations and rule-making, incrementally building on past experience and constitutional thought.

II. Toward a Two-Tier Approach

A. Rounds and Permanent Fora of Negotiations

The tradition and success of negotiating tariff concessions and reducing levels of domestic support show that trade rounds have been able to create necessary momentum and political pressure. The same is likely to apply to concessions exchanged in the field of services, albeit experience with services has been far more limited. Both areas are able to respond to diverging needs of progressive liberalization and individualized levels of commitment. Processes based on specific requests and offers depend on a framework that allows for liberalization in cycles. Absent deadlines or periods of intense pressure, tariff and services negotiations could hardly succeed. They depend on give and take and the possibility to achieve overall package deals with regard to benefits and concessions made in what essentially has remained a mercantilist approach.

It is the shift to negotiating disciplines relating to domestic regulation in WTO law that calls for a review of the negotiating process. These matters differ from individualized concessions. Rules are inherently uniform for all Members, independent of levels of social and economic development and market size. It is much more difficult to accommodate individualized needs in setting international standards. These matters are complex, evolve at different speeds, and induce different levels of interest on the part of Members. It is here that an interest in the variable geometry of rights and obligations and membership to instruments arises. Rule-making in WTO law thus should be shaped differently from the process of claims and response in tariff and non-tariff concessions. Ideally, these matters should be dealt with under the agenda of ongoing and continuous work undertaken in different standing fora of the WTO.

The question that arises is whether a dual approach could work or whether ongoing legislation and rule-making inherently depend on pressure and the outcomes of market access negotiations. Would it have been possible to conclude the TRIPS Agreement, or the basis framework of GATS and the TRIPS Agreement, outside the Uruguay Round? While there were few operational linkages, it is evident that they were essentially dependent on the overall dynamics of the Uruguay Round. Thus it is hardly possible to build a two-tier approach on a complete distinction of concessions, on the one hand, and rule-making on the other hand. Account must be taken of the political importance of each agenda item, and rule-making cannot be dissociated from the dynamics of trade rounds. Negotiations on framework agreements, setting the stage for decades to come, are bound to be undertaken within the momentum and drive of trade rounds.

How then can we combine the momentum of trade rounds, the political pressure needed to achieve outcomes, and the need for ongoing rule-making? How can we ensure that basic principles, rules, rights, and obligations are shared by all Members as the core of multilateralism while allowing for differentiation commensurate with levels of social and economic development, and largely diverging economic interests among Members? How do we avoid divergences further increasing, as some will be bound and contained by disciplines curbing protectionism while others opt out and are eventually left behind? How can we avoid the situation that those assuming fewer obligations are taken seriously? What can we learn from past experience?

The definition and allocation of different regulatory fields to different regulatory levels with possibly diverging modes of decision-making is a major challenge. Some may argue that the task is futile as Members will never be able to agree, particularly in a multipolar world with traditions of liberal democracy no longer able to impose its ideals and tenets. Yet these objections cannot and must not prevent academic discourse on the matter. It is only when a number of viable options are on the table that diplomacy may be able to take the matter up and find ingenious compromises during long nights of negotiations. We have not explored these options. Some suggestions are put forward here to stimulate debate.

B. Constitutional and Secondary Rules

WTO law, in line with the tenets of public international law, operates as a single type of international agreement. Whether it is the Marrakesh Agreement establishing the Organization, the GATT with its profound and fundamental principles of non-discrimination, the framework of GATS, or the detailed rules of the TRIPS Agreement, and whether it is an understanding or an agreement implementing particular disciplines relating to GATT, or a tariff or a services schedule, they all are of the same standing and legal nature.[21] WTO law does not distinguish different and hierarchical sources of law. They all emerge essentially in the same process, and the mutual relationship of the agreements is a horizontal and often unclear one. Likewise, all the WTO instruments enjoy the same status in domestic law forming international agreements of the same type, whether they are dealt with as treaties or as executive agreements.

The time has come to learn from distinctions of primary and secondary sources of law. While primary or constitutional rules setting out basic obligations and the framework for specialized regimes need to be set in an overall bargaining process having the political momentum of a round, the implementation of certain agreed on matters could be left to a secondary process in between rounds. The distinction is firmly established in domestic law with basic distinctions of constitutional law, legislation, executive orders, and administrative regulation. It is well established in EC law with the distinction of primary law and secondary rules, regulations, and directives.

Different sources of law allow the allocation of different modes of decision-making. In international law, the concept of secondary rules is normally used for decisions and acts adopted by the bodies of an international organization. The same is true for the WTO.[22] The concept is used here in a different way. It stands for the proposition of introducing different categories of international agreements within the constitutional framework of a multilateral trading system, without necessarily turning the Organization into a body of supranational law. This approach would allow reducing high-level negotiations to core elements and issues within a package deal, and leaving other issues to subsequent and well-framed negotiations.

Basic agreements set out fundamental rights and obligations of a constitutional nature. They are essential and binding on all Members. Today, they comprise the agreement establishing the WTO, the GATT 1994, GATS, and TRIPS. Tomorrow, it could be limited to a single constitutional WTO Agreement comprising the structure and organization; different sources of law and respective modes of decision-making; basic substantive and procedural obligations, in particular non-discrimination; basic disciplines; exceptions and transparency requirements. Such a single basic agreement would necessarily be binding on all Members of the WTO. Rules on amending the agreement will ensure that it remains a truly multilateral instrument and a single undertaking. Variations among Members, currently pursued by means of largely ineffective special and differential treatment (S&D), could be effected by means of graduation by linking the operation of rules to economic thresholds and indicators of competitiveness of a Member or even of specific industries.[23]

Specific instruments, on the other hand, could be shaped in the form of secondary rules, subject to the constitutional agreement, and not necessarily binding on all Members. Today these instruments comprise Members' schedules and plurilateral agreements. Tomorrow, they could extend to agreements and understandings implementing particular concepts set out in GATT 1994. It is here that the single undertaking could be left behind and variable geometry could take over. Combinations of single undertaking and variable geometry are conceivable.[24] Solutions may be tailor-made, sometimes binding all Members, sometimes not. Under a new WTO Agreement, different categories of instruments could be created and linked to specific procedures and membership requirements, ranging from single undertaking to bilateral, plurilateral, or unilateral obligations.

Importantly, the structures and experience of differentiation are not unknown to the WTO. The examples of negotiations on financial services and telecommunication, mentioned above, demonstrate this point. While these negotiations were perceived as leftover issues, they could have been prospectively designated as a matter to be addressed based on the results achieved in the Uruguay Round. The GATS called for subsequent negotiations on a number of issues, in particular subsidies and safeguards. Efforts might have been more successful if they could have been deliberately pursued on the basis of variable geometry. The elaboration of new rules on access to essential drugs and the amendment of the TRIPS Agreement can be perceived as an exercise in secondary legislation and treaty reform within a given framework. It is worth considering whether it was necessary to undertake the effort as a matter for all Members, or whether it would be sufficient to include those most concerned. Finally, the process of accession follows a route of individualized commitments.

These traditions could form the basis of a new legislative approach, setting out different and distinct avenues of partly shared and partly distinct rights and obligations among Members. It is conceivable to agree on core rights and obligations and leave others to variable geometry. For example, the TRIPS Agreement could have been limited to fundamental rules but have left the elaboration of more specific obligations to a longer-term and better-informed process. It would have offered the possibility of bringing about graduation instead of uniform rules applicable to all countries, independently of levels of social and economic development. In the future, sectoral negotiations in services and in investment and competition could be conducted on such a basis.

A two-tiered approach built on framework agreements and implementing rule-making would enhance the quality of outcomes at the WTO. It would better serve the learning processes of smaller countries and developing countries, many of which have been unable to follow a large and detailed agenda of negotiations. It would allow graduation and the needs of developing countries to be taken into account. In retrospect, a study could be made to determine whether negotiations on GATT side agreements, implementing specific provisions since the Kennedy Round, did not contain elements of secondary legislation. They were bound to stay within the framework of GATT, but were not binding on all Members, and allowed key problems to be addressed by those most affected. The codes may indicate that the idea of secondary legislation does not exclude variable geometry when it comes to follow-up and detailed rules on a particular subject matter. Such an approach could allow for more graduation than the monolithic approach of the Uruguay Round and the Doha Agenda.

C. Linking by Most-Favoured-Nation and Graduation

Fundamental rules in the constitutional framework will offer the basis for linking results achieved in secondary rules. Importantly, the obligation to grant most-favoured-nation treatment applies to all Members, whether or not signatory to a particular rule of secondary order. The basic philosophy of the multilateral system obliges Members to grant most-favoured-nation status to all other Members, irrespective of whether they adhere to a particular instrument of secondary order. The principle implies free-riding, which needs to be addressed in defining the critical mass of membership required.[25]

Secondary rules may leave others aside, while granting rights to all third parties representing smaller trade flows in a particular field. Not committing these countries is tolerable from a point of view of conditions of competition. Yet once outsiders reach competitiveness, mechanisms need to be designed in the constitutional instrument to include them. It is here that the concept of graduation is required. While a Member may not form part of an agreement in the first place, it may eventually be obliged to join if certain conditions are met in real economic terms. Members of the multilateral system, therefore, may be eventually obligated to abide by multilateral rules. This prospect should give them the right to determine whether they want to take part in the negotiations in the first place or be prepared eventually to accept the results.

Such an approach is similar to that of plurilateral agreements, in particular the Government Procurement Agreement, while also combined with graduated commitments. A Member would not be entitled to benefit from rights without eventually joining when a certain threshold of competitiveness is reached. This flows from the logic and experience of a truly multilateral system, as opposed to preferential agreements and bilateralism. The approach of working with thresholds defining obligations to join could overcome the inherent weaknesses of variable geometry witnessed under the Tokyo Round Codes.

D. Allocating Different Modes of Decision-Making

The two-tiered approach is meaningful only if it is linked to differentiation in decision-making. There is no compelling need to apply the same decision-making process to all WTO matters. It should be recalled that fundamental reliance on consensus in dispute settlement—a specific mode of decision-making—no longer applies in the process of assessing rights and obligations between two or more Members.

It is thus conceivable to distinguish modes of decision-making in relation to primary and to secondary rules. Primary rules could continue to operate under a rigid principle of consensus, or alternatively with consensus-minus or weighted voting with a particular quorum required, building on existing WTO provisions. Secondary rules could be subject to alternative means, such as consensus based on critical mass or weighted voting. In some instances, voting on the basis of one-vote one-state could be feasible, for example within an executive committee. The two-tiered approach offers the potential to adopt varied strategies of decision-making with respect to basic obligations and of secondary norms. It also allows the adoption of different variants within these categories. A single approach to decision-making must be rejected. Adopting different modes will facilitate finding future agreement on sensitive issues.

1. Consensus

Consensus is the primary mode of decision-making within the WTO. In fact, consensus is the mode of decision-making in a number of international organizations.[26] Consensus is based on equal representation of Members under the principle of sovereign equality. States see their interests best defended by consensus diplomacy. It has been most suitable for trade rounds and package deals. Of course, consensus does not imply that Members are of equal importance and weight. Consensus implies an informal system of weighted voting, as powerful Members are able to block consensus more easily than small and medium-sized countries. In essence, it allows large players to block decisions in political processes while the same remedy is available to others only at great political cost. It ascribes power that, in reality, does not exist for most. The recourse to the alleged democratic legitimacy of consensus, stressing sovereign equality, therefore is merely formal and does not offer a true and transparent account of power relations.

In WTO decision-making, the crucial question is whether large Members need to retain veto powers in order to work within the Organization. More precisely, the question is whether single large Members need to be in a position to block the adoption of a particular decision. Realists certainly would say so, as control of international organizations is one of the main motivations for hegemonic powers to participate. Debate is needed to determine whether this rationale is suitable in a multipolar world. Blocking decisions today comes at high political cost and may no longer be a tempting option. Successful decision-making requires coalitions, and blocking may thus be limited to such coalitions. Thus the United States and the European Union jointly, or Brazil and India or China jointly, may be able to block proposals, but none of them could do so in their own right. In other words, the system should adopt a consensus-minus rule.

In positive terms, a principle of consensus-minus could become the core feature of a reasonably stable multipolar world. Consensus-minus will be highly contentious, and its use may be limited to issues of secondary legislation discussed above. While trade rounds and negotiations of framework agreements may continue to depend on consensus, consensus-minus may apply failing consensus in matters of implementing framework agreements and work programs adopted. Again, it is possible to modulate consensus rules for primary and secondary rules, or even within these categories. A new balance for the principle of consensus-minus in dispute settlement could thus be found. Both are forms of decision-making operating on a secondary level and are subject to fundamental agreement and consensus on underlying treaties. Furthermore, consensus-minus may be positively formalized by adopting a system of weighted voting.

2. Weighted Voting

The idea of weighted voting reflects past experiences in the WTO and other international organizations that decision-making based on the sovereign equality of states has not transpired in rule-making. Sovereign equality does not sufficiently respond to existing power relations. If formal voting is to be applied and transparency achieved, voting rights should be shaped in a manner that appropriately reflects the relative importance of Members within a multilateral system. The principle was widely applied in international organizations in the post-war architecture beyond Bretton Woods.[27] Weighted voting can be based on a number of criteria such as share of trade, GDP, dependence on foreign trade, and population size. Calculations show that a balanced allocation of voting rights and powers to industrialized, emerging, and developing countries is possible and can be achieved.[28]

In practical terms weighted voting would implement the principle of consensus-minus, as major powers are not able to block the adoption of a decision on their own. And since decision-making in the WTO is generally a matter of coalition building, weighted voting would also give a voice to medium-sized and smaller Members. It is wrong to reject weighted voting simply based on past experience in the Bretton Woods system.[29] There are alternatives available that would render the system reasonably attractive and equitable to all Members alike. Weighted voting can be applied in matters pertaining to primary rules as well as to secondary rules. It also can be used in adopting instruments of limited membership, thus complementing the critical mass approach.

Weighted voting still is generally considered 'outside the box' thinking.[30] Yet this conclusion has been drawn without careful examination of modalities and the potential to modulate the principle for primary and secondary sources. Moreover, political scientists should look into the benefits of the system for governments seeking to balance competing interests. Results adopted on the basis of weighted voting and in a transparent manner allow governments to concede defeat at home and protect themselves from the pressure to block consensus.

3. Critical Mass

Critical mass is an approach to bring about variable geometry on the level of secondary rules to which all Members need not adhere. Members may agree to negotiate a particular legal obligation provided that the main markets, and thus the main partners, are included.[31] The inclusion of key players is a prerequisite while others may abstain. The results of such negotiations are subject to most-favoured-nation, thus all Members of the WTO benefit, even though they do not participate in the agreement and are not subject to its obligations. Past experience with sectoral initiatives in tariff reductions in the Uruguay Round shows that this certainly is a viable avenue for addressing trade concessions. As long as the main markets are included, free-riding by those absent from the agreement is a lesser burden than the risk of failing to achieve agreement under the consensus rule.

The impact of critical mass in rule-making requires careful consideration. There is a risk of creating a variety of asymmetric rights and obligations. It may also encourage parties to abstain, thus avoiding the costs and benefits of locking-in, potentially further widening the gap between those subject and not subject to international disciplines fostering competition. It should be recalled that the main incentive to opt for a single undertaking in the Uruguay Round was to avoid the disadvantages of variable geometry inherent in the code approach of the Kennedy and Tokyo Rounds. The concern could be addressed by defining those areas where critical mass negotiations may take place and those that would be excluded. Again, the two-tiered approach allows different modes of decision-making to be combined and an overall balance to be sought that would render the overall system more flexible.

E. Institutional Issues

Ever since their inception, the GATT and the WTO have worked with flat institutional hierarchies, reflecting their single form of legal undertakings. All Members are represented in the General Council and committees. Unlike most other international organizations, the WTO does not have a formal executive or steering committee with appointed and rotating membership. The steering function is assumed by the informal green room process under the guidance of the Director-General, and by informal conferences of ministers and officials from capitals.[32] This informal mode renders access to negotiations a volatile affair except for the main powers. Small and medium-sized economies, let alone the least developed countries, risk being sidelined.[33] Members are forced to work within a system of flexible coalitions. The system has worked reasonably well, though it has been criticized for lacking transparency and accountability. Members and domestic constituencies face frustration when omitted from the informal inner circles and excluded from negotiations.

Efforts at institutional reform could be built on a two-tiered approach incorporating various modes of decision-making discussed above. Different bodies could operate on different decision-making processes. Some could continue to operate on the basis of consensus, or consensus-minus (as in the Dispute Settlement Body [DSB]). Some could be subject to weighted voting. Others may be suited to operate under a one-member one-vote model. The powers of ministerial meetings, the council, and committees could be shaped accordingly. The two-tiered approach would allow examination of the potential role of a parliamentary assembly and the assignment of specific functions not only of an advisory nature, but also possibly entailing decision-making powers in an effort to enhance the democratic legitimacy of the Organization.[34]

Conceivably, a consultative or executive committee could be created, which includes major powers and represents other Members on the basis of their size, geography, and level of development based on rotating membership fixed for a number of years.[35] The Executive Committee would need to ensure that all pertinent interests and regions have a voice in decision-making. It could be composed of Members reflecting all regions and levels of development, including least-developed Members. Criticism voiced about previous efforts to create a steering body (G-18) and the difficulties in bringing about effective representation need to be taken into account.[36]

The Executive Committee could be responsible for preparing major procedural decisions to be taken by the General Council and ministerial meetings. It could decide on issues relating to the agenda of an ongoing round and work on secondary legislation and housekeeping matters, including the appointment of key Secretariat personnel. Some matters could be allocated to the Executive Committee for final determination, while others may be subject to referendum in the General Council. In other areas, the Executive Committee could be limited to providing advice and consultation. Decision-making would be by consensus, but subject to voting, which on this level would allocate each Member one voice of equal importance. Comparative studies may assist in learning from the experience of other organizations, some of which have shown a much higher level of organization and structure than the WTO.

Finally, institutional reform should also address the status and role of the Secretariat.[37] Again, the two-tiered approach allows functions to be defined in more specific terms. While it may continue to work under established modes in some areas, its role in others may be defined more precisely commensurate with the legal framework and instrument at hand. Both in the process of law-making and that of dispute settlement, its functions could entail limited powers to take initiatives and defend the common concerns of the multilateral trading system.

III. The Way Forward

A. Formal or Incremental Reform?

The GATT and the WTO were built on experience. The 1947 Agreement was modelled after the bilateral trade agreements of the United States of that era. They provided the basis for an incremental evolution both of the negotiating process and of dispute settlement within a broadly defined framework. The latter emerged in practice and was codified for the first time only in 1979. Decision-making and the structures of rounds evolved in diplomacy and do not find expression in binding legal documents. The powers of the Secretariat depend much more on its expertise and skills than statutorily defined functions and tasks. Perhaps the flexibility offered in past and present structures, and the ease of developing customary practices, amounts to the great strength of the WTO. Its success in bringing down tariff and non-tariff barriers may well be assigned to a structure that allows for trial and error.

We are faced with the question whether reform should continue to take place under this philosophy. Is it possible to adjust to the changing structure of international economic law by changing practices under the current WTO agreements? Suggestions to work with an informal directorate, critical mass, restrictions on veto practices in the tradition of a Luxembourg compromise, enhanced recourse to authentic interpretation of existing agreements, enhancing informal initiatives of the Secretariat, building better relations with other international organizations in daily life, all seem to belong to a philosophy building on incremental change.

Or have we reached the limits in the quest for appropriate structure–substance pairings? Do we need formal reform? Should decision-making be formally reviewed? Should an executive body be established? Should the powers and role of the Secretariat be better defined? Should relations to other international organizations be more formally defined? What measures should be taken to further enhance the transparency of the negotiating process? What is necessary to render legislative responses to dispute settlement decisions a viable option, contributing to a better sharing of responsibilities between the political and the judicial process?

Given the difficulties in reaching agreement, the informal avenue is attractive.[38] On the other hand, a deliberate effort to change the rules provides more transparency and is better placed to restore and enhance the legitimacy of the Organization.[39] Debra Steger concludes that

> the WTO needs major surgery in order to respond effectively to the new political realities in the international economic system. The WTO is not the old GATT, and members should abandon the mantras, myths and misunderstandings that are no longer relevant.[40]

The idea of a two-tiered approach allows for a wide range of options to be explored and offers a critical mass for negotiations and compromise. Regardless of whether a formal or informal route is to be pursued, it is important to explore possible options from the outset. Most importantly, the goals of a reform must be defined. Whether such reforms are eventually implemented formally or incrementally is a secondary issue. It may be possible to develop a two-tiered approach within the existing framework. Given the effect of WTO rules on daily life, issues of legitimacy, transparency, and accountability are key to the Organization's future and must be taken into account in designing an appropriate path for reform.

B. Defining the Goals of Reform

Whatever reform routes are chosen, a debate on the goals of reform is imperative in order to secure commonly agreed directions for the multilateral system in a globalizing and multipolar world. It is not simply a matter of redesigning institutions. Legitimacy with regard to transparency and representation in the decision-making process must be prioritized. The goals set forth in the preamble of the WTO remain applicable today in times of globalization. However, they must be bolstered by more specific targets. Answers to substance–structure pairings will depend on specific answers to a host of questions that need to be raised and discussed:

- How can one bring about and secure output legitimacy of rules?
- What is the role of WTO in a world of multilayered governance?
- How can checks and balances against protectionism be attained while allowing for appropriate policy space?
- To what extent should the WTO enjoy enhanced autonomy in supporting these goals?
- How does one properly define the relationship of multilateralism and preferential agreements?
- How does one properly define the relationship with other organizations in a horizontal legal order?
- How does one define the relationship between the WTO and domestic law?
- Should it be entirely left to constitutional law, or is there a shared interest in finding common ground within a doctrine of multilayered governance?
- How does one redefine sovereignty to the benefit of people?[41]

These are basic questions. They need to be asked. People will have different responses, and so they will adopt different but informed attitudes to institutional reform. Although perceptions may differ, a shared understanding that the quest for appropriate substance–structure pairings cannot take place without assessing and defining the fundamental goals of reform is essential.

C. Launching the Debate

The ideas sketched out above merely indicate that there is room to think about alternative options. All of this requires in-depth studies of options and intensive debate. The debate should clearly be delinked from the fate of the Doha

Development Agenda. It is not appropriate to change the rules of the game while gambling is going on. The debate should go past the current round of negotiations, regardless of its outcome. The problems noted above will continue to exist well beyond the current round. A successful conclusion of the Doha round will create the impetus to improve the multilateral system. A failure will create the need to make efforts to save it. The underlying problems remain common to both outcomes.

Further debate on the potential and options for implicit and explicit institutional reform will likely take place in academic circles, which will hopefully inform thinking by governments. At the WTO, it would be feasible to create a standing consultative committee that bridges academia, NGOs, governments, and the Secretariat, essentially assuming the role of a think-tank. In due course, and with a view to preparing post-Doha structures, a standing WTO committee on legal and institutional affairs should be set up, building on the lost traditions of the Committee on the Functioning of GATT (FOG) during the Uruguay Round. The calls of the International Law Association to create such a committee should be taken seriously by capitals. The current state of affairs, the lack of attention and interest paid to issues of decision-making, and structures of decision-making outside the field of dispute settlement is one of the main factors explaining the lack of well-developed options ready for debate.

Notes

1 Thomas Cottier, 'Constitutional Trade Regulation in National and International Law: Structure-Substance Pairings', 8 National Constitutions and International Economic Law 409 (1993), at 411; Thomas Cottier, 'Preparing for Structural Reform in the WTO', 10 Journal of International Economic Law 497 (2007).

2 WTO, *The Results of the Uruguay Round of Multilateral Trade Negotiations: The Legal Texts* (Geneva: WTO, 2004) 4.

3 John H. Jackson, *World Trade and the Law of GATT* (Indianapolis: Bobbs-Merrill, 1969) 788 (stating '[i]n the long run, it may well be the machinery that is most important (i.e., the procedures), rather than the existence of any one or another specific rule of trade conduct.').

4 This is true both for the Sutherland Report and the Warwick Report: Consultative Board to the Director-General Supachai Panitchpakdi, *The Future of the WTO: Addressing Institutional Challenges in the New Millennium* (Geneva: WTO, 2004); Warwick Commission, *The Multilateral Trade Regime: Which Way Forward?*, Report of the First Warwick Commission (Coventry: University of Warwick, 2007).

5 International Law Association, 'Toronto Conference (2006), International Trade Law, Seventh Report of the Committee', at para 38(b), http://www.ila-hq.org/download .cfm/docid/B8DE7062-B7A2-4BA3-92F38D46C61FA203 (visited 11 March 2009).

6 Transparency Mechanism for Regional Trade Agreements, WT/L/671, Adopted on 14 December 2006.

7 See Doha Work Programme, WT/MIN(05)DEC (22 December 2005), Ministerial Conference Sixth Session, Hong Kong, 13–18 December 2005.

8 See also Peter Sutherland, 'The World Trade Organization at Ten Years', 4 World Trade Review 341 (2005), at 353.

9 See World Trade Organization, 'July 2008 Package: Negotiating Texts and Reports', http://www.wto.org/english/tratop_e/dda_e/meet08_texts_e.htm (visited 10 March 2009).

10 Ministerial Declaration, WT/Min(01)/Dec/1, adopted 14 November 2001, at paras. 31–32.

11 See also Joost Pauwelyn, 'New Trade Politics for the 21st Century', 11 Journal of International Economic Law 559 (2008) (stressing the need for reform of the operating system after 60 years).

12 See Debra Steger, 'The Culture of the WTO: Why It Needs to Change', in W.J. Davey and John H. Jackson (eds), *The Future of International Economic Law* (Oxford: Oxford University Press, 2008) 45–57; Debra Steger, 'The Culture of the WTO: Why It Needs to Change', 10 Journal of International Economic Law 483 (2007).

13 Wolfgang Friedman, *The Changing Structure of International Law* (New York: Columbia University Press, 1964) 365–69.

14 For a detailed account, see Claus-Dieter Ehlermann and Lothar Ehring, 'Are WTO Decision-Making Procedures Adequate for Making, Revising, and Implementing Worldwide and Plurilateral? Rules?', in E.U. Petersmann and James Harrison (eds), *Reforming the World Trading System: Legitimacy, Efficiency and Democratic Governance* (Oxford: Oxford University Press, 2005) 497–502; Robert Wolfe, 'Can the Trading System Be Governed? Institutional Implications of the WTO's Suspended Animation', The Centre for International Governance and Innovation, Working Papers No. 30 (September 2007), http://www.cigionline.org (visited 10 March 2008); Andreas Ziegler and Yves Bonzon, 'How to Reform WTO Decision-making? An Analysis of the Current Functioning of the Organization from the Perspectives of Efficiency and Legitimacy', NCCR Working Paper 2007/23 (May 2007).

15 For a survey of WTO coalitions, see Wolfe, ibid, at 46.

16 See Debra P. Steger, 'Mini-Symposium on Transparency in the WTO', 11 Journal of International Economic Law 705 (2008).

17 There is a wide literature on the political functioning of the GATT and the WTO; for a survey, see Thuo Gathii, 'The High Stakes of WTO Reform: Behind the Scenes at the WTO: The Real World of Trade Negotiations', 104 Michigan Law Review 1361 (2006) (reviewing Fatoumata Jawara and Aileen Kwa, *Behind the Scenes at the WTO: The Real World of Trade Negotiations—The Lessons of Cancun* [London: Zed Books, 2004]); Robert Wolfe, 'Informal Political Engagement in the WTO: Are Mini-Ministerials a Good Idea?', in J.M. Curtis and Dan Ciuriak (eds), *Trade Policy Research 2004* (Ottawa: Minister of Public Works and Government Services, 2004) 27–91.

18 In particular see Claude Barfield, *Free Trade, Sovereignty, Democracy* (Washington, D.C.: AEI Press, 2001).

19 See Ehlermann and Ehring, above n 14; Thomas Cottier and Satoko Takenoshita, 'The Balance of Power in WTO Decision-making: Towards Weighted Voting in Legislative Response', 58 Aussenwirtschaft 171 (2003); Thomas Cottier and Satoko Takenoshita, 'Decision-making and the Balance of Powers in WTO Negotiations:

Towards Supplementary Weighted Voting', in Stefan Griller (ed), *At the Crossroads: The World Trading System and the Doha Round* (Vienna: Springer, 2007) 181–231.

20 This in particular can be observed in the case of the European Court of Justice which, unlike U.S. courts, is not legally barred from applying WTO law in a domestic context: see Geert A. Zonnekeyn, *Direct Effect of WTO Law* (London: Cameron May, 2008).

21 Petros C. Mavroidis, 'No Outsourcing of Law? WTO Law as Practiced by WTO Courts', 102 American Journal of International Law 421 (2008), at 427.

22 Ibid, at 429.

23 Thomas Cottier, 'From Progressive Liberalization to Progressive Regulation', 9 Journal of International Economic Law 779 (2006).

24 Pierre Sauvé and Craig Van Grasstek, 'The Consistency of WTO Rules: Can the Single Undertaking Be Squared with Variable Geometry?', 9 Journal of International Economic Law 837 (2006), at 851 ff.

25 Manfred Elsig, 'WTO Decision-Making: Can We Get a Little Help from the Secretariat and the Critical Mass?' in this volume.

26 This is not unique to the WTO; see Erica Gould, 'When Do IO Voting Rules Matter?: A Comparative Analysis of International Organizations' Formal Decision-Making Rules', draft paper November 2007 (on file with author) (summarizing that formal rules are applied to unimportant matters only).

27 See Stephan Zamora, 'Voting in International Economic Organizations', 74 American Journal of International Law 566 (1980); cf. Debbie A. Efraim, *Legal Aspects of International Organization: Sovereign (In)equality in International Organizations*, vol. 34 (New York: Springer, 2000).

28 See Cottier and Takenoshita, 'The Balance of Power in WTO Decision-making', above n 19.

29 Cf. Hector R. Torres, 'Reforming the International Monetary Fund—Why Its Legitimacy Is at Stake', in Davey and Jackson (eds), above n 12, 5–22; Frank J. Garcia, 'Global Justice and the Bretton Woods Institutions', in 'Global Justice and the Bretton Woods Institutions' 10 Journal of International Economic Law 461 (2007); Richard N. Cooper and Edwin M. Truman, 'The IMF Quota Formula: Linchpin of Fund Reform', Policy Briefs in International Economics, No. PB07-1 (February 2007), http://www.iie.com/publications/pb/pb07-1.pdf (visited 10 March 2009).

30 See, for example, Peter Norgaard Pederson, 'The WTO Decision-Making Process and Internal Transparency', 5 World Trade Review 103 (2006), at 131; Sutherland, above n 8.

31 Elsig, WTO Decision-Making.

32 Wolfe, above n 14.

33 Oxfam, 'Institutional Reform of the WTO', Oxfam Great Britain Discussion Paper, March 2000, http://www.oxfam.org.uk/resources/policy/trade/downloads/wto_reform.rtf (visited 10 March 2009).

34 See Markus Krajewski, 'Democratic Governance as an Emerging Principle of International Economic Law', Society of International Economic Law Conference, Geneva, 15–17 July 2008, http://www.sielnet.org/Default.aspx?pageId=160208 (10 March 2009).

35 A consultative board is suggested by Richard Blackhurst and David Hartridge, 'Improving the Capacity of WTO Institutions to Fulfill their Mandate', in Petersmann and Harrison (eds), above n 14, at 454–67; Jeffrey Schott and Jayashree Watal, 'Decisionmaking in the WTO', in Jeffery J. Schott (ed), *The WTO After Seattle* (Washington, D.C.: Institute for International Economics, 2000) 283–91.

36 See Kent Jones, 'Regionalism and the Problem of Representation in the WTO', 19 September 2007 (on file with author) (discussing underlying agency problems).

37 The role of the Secretariat is explored in Manfred Elsig, 'The World Trade Organizations' Bureaucrats: Runaway Agents or Masters' Servants', NCCR Trade Regulation, Working Paper No. 2007/19, online: <http://www.nccr-trade.org/nccr-publications/10.html>; Robert E. Hudec, 'The Role of the GATT Secretariat in the Evolution of the WTO Dispute Settlement Procedure', in J. Bhagwati and M. Hirsch (eds), *The Uruguay Round and Beyond: Essays in Honour of Arthur Dunkel* (New York: Springer, 1998) 101–20. Cf. John Odell, 'Chairing a WTO Negotiation', 8 Journal of International Economic Law 425 (2005).

38 Such as the conclusion reached by Ehlermann and Ehring, above n 14.

39 Pauwelyn, above n 11; Krajewski, above n 34.

40 Steger, above n 12.

41 See John H. Jackson, Sovereignty, the *WTO, and Changing Fundamentals of International Law* (Cambridge: Cambridge University Press, 2006).

WTO Decision-Making: Can We Get a Little Help from the Secretariat and the Critical Mass?

MANFRED ELSIG

I. Introduction

The current design of the international organization system regulating the world economy was conceived by a small group of experts and politicians from the United States and Great Britain in the early 1940s. The mandates and principles guiding the World Bank, the International Monetary Fund, and the envisaged International Trade Organization were inspired by Keynesianism and embraced by British and U.S. economists and high-ranking civil servants. These ideas also resonated well within the political establishments across the transatlantic community.[1] Two explanations, in the form of necessary conditions, for the genesis of the global economic architecture have been advanced: first, the existence of a 'constitutional moment' after the end of World War II; and second, the presence of a liberal hegemonic power to provide for an open and stable trade and monetary regime.[2] Today, the creation of new international organizations is rare despite the opening of a new constitutional moment of liberal orientation after the end of the Cold War.[3] Not only is the establishment of new international organizations costly, but there exists already a multitude of institutions that claim (sometimes competing) regulatory authority over just about all policy issues. Abandoning non-performing international organizations is also difficult.

Thus internal reform is the most likely observed outcome when thinking about reforming international organizations. However, redesigning the rules governing existing international organizations presents a number of challenges. The power of the status quo stands out as a particular problem.[4] First, actors have learned and adapted to decision rules over time, allowing them to navigate the system efficiently given the opportunities and constraints of existing rules.

This leads, in many cases, to the development of a substantial degree of 'loyalty' toward existing rules and resistance to change.[5] Second, from the field of psychology, we also need to take seriously the argument that actors are more likely to defend existing practices and are relatively risk-averse when it comes to new modes of decision-making where outcomes are hard to predict. Thus actors seek a high degree of certainty that post-reform governance models will not lead to pareto-inferior outcomes as measured in procedural and outcome influence. Third, powerful nations hold a veto on the issue of redesign. If they are satisfied with the status quo, the contra-factual case that they will profit from design change is most likely the hardest challenge to be faced in reform activities.

This chapter discusses two reform suggestions related to improving decision-making within the World Trade Organization (WTO). These proposals have been promoted in two recent reports that discuss the future of the WTO. The first (the Sutherland Report) advocates *inter alia* a stronger role for the WTO Secretariat.[6] The second (the Warwick Report) endorses a critical mass approach to decision-making.[7] This chapter explores both proposals further with a view to improving and streamlining decision-making within the WTO. Selected evidence from current and past practices in European Union (EU) decision-making is discussed for the purpose of comparison across IOs (international organizations). The chapter is organized as follows. First, some reflections related to reforming the current system are presented. Second, a more prominent role for the WTO Secretariat in negotiations is discussed as well as new decision-making rules. Third, alternative decision-making approaches leading to variable geometry (in particular 'critical mass') are analyzed. The chapter concludes with a note on challenges that may influence future discussions on reform in the context of the multilateral trading system.

II. Reflections on Reform

A. The Need for Reform

In recent years, international organizations have been subject to intensified scrutiny from an ever-growing number of stakeholders. Many IOs suffer from poor performance and appear insufficiently equipped to deal with 21st-century challenges. The causes of underperformance, however, are not only found within the organizations, but largely emanate from conflicting interests of the members delegating to international organizations. In the case of the WTO, this is borne out by the lack of timely responses to new challenges and general difficulties in finding consensus on further liberalization of markets and designing new rules to govern the world economy.

Early liberal contributions in the international relations literature analyzed various ways international organizations help overcome obstacles to cooperation.[8] However, the nature of cooperation and the urgency of internationally agreed policy responses to the challenges of globalization have changed over time. In today's world, international organizations need to provide services beyond the general functions attributed to them in the past. These functions have included the lowering of transaction costs and information asymmetries as well as the enhancement of compliance. International organizations are increasingly being called on to engage in positive integration and harmonization initiatives that differ from traditional attempts to coordinate policies and find mutually acceptable domestic practices and standards. In addition to increased attention paid to performance, existing power structures behind international organizations have moved farther into the public and scholarly spotlight. In this respect, the institutional capacity of international organizations to control abuses of power by leading states within the system is increasingly being assessed.[9] Alongside this notion of creating accountable international organizations, the broader concept of legitimacy receives continued attention.[10]

The WTO offers one of the most legalized multilateral platforms for dispute settlement. The dispute resolution system has had some success in controlling arbitrary discrimination, but owing to the nature of international politics it is not feasible to eliminate the asymmetry of power completely.[11] Despite its shortcomings, the performance of the new Understanding on Rules and Procedures Governing the Settling of Disputes (DSU) has been widely assessed as positive in overcoming key deficiencies of the General Agreement on Tariffs and Trade (GATT)–type diplomacy in resolving trade disputes.[12] However, the institutional architecture of the WTO's legislative branch, the negotiation platform, has not kept up with the redesign of the litigation apparatus during the Uruguay Round negotiations, resulting in institutional imbalance within the WTO.

B. WTO Reform in Perspective

In approaching WTO reform, four introductory remarks follow to put reform proposals into a wider perspective of institutional change. First, reform projects can take various forms. The most likely reform type is incremental in nature and is characterized by small and modest steps to accommodate some of the pressures from outside and within the system. Examples of this type of incremental change include the modification of informal processes, practices to increase transparency, and granting greater access to a larger group of Members to allow them to participate in restricted deal-breaking negotiation circles (e.g., the Green Room). A number of initiatives to modify informal decision rules followed the failure of the Seattle Ministerial in 1999. These ad hoc measures focused on issues of transparency and participation.[13]

In contrast to incremental reform steps, package deals are more likely to lead to substantial redesign. Big reform steps are usually part of horse-trading deals that lead to (difficult to anticipate) design changes. As the Uruguay Round results indicate, grand institutional redesign is easier to carry through as part of a 'single undertaking'. Against this background, it is interesting to note that WTO Members have excluded negotiations on decision-making rules in the current Doha Round. This reluctance to engage with design change also speaks for WTO Members' lack of interest in tackling governance issues.[14] In the words of a long-time panellist and former ambassador 'the members are like elephants: they are ponderous and are resistant to change'.[15] Governance issues usually do not figure prominently on the agenda at the onset of a trade round. It is not surprising that the reform of the DSU was introduced only in the second half of the Uruguay Round negotiations. In light of the GATT/WTO negotiation history, the hope that the inter-round period will be utilized to work on governance reforms corresponds to turning a blind eye to redesign.

Second, dominating paradigms are difficult to change. Paradigms serve various functions. They are often constructed, advanced, and defended by the powerful insiders of a system and by those who expect to profit from the status quo.[16] As a consequence, impetus for reform needs to develop from outside the inner circles of international organizations. Three paradigms have become central to the WTO: the 'member-driven' nature of the Organization, the consensus principle, and the 'single undertaking'.[17] The perception of many WTO Members is that these paradigms serve their interests and thus they are reluctant to engage in debates over change. In other words, a type of mental 'decision-making trap' has been created.[18] This chapter critically addresses above paradigms and builds an alternative approach that could assist in resolving the current impasse in WTO decision-making.

Third, the WTO is not an institution *sui generis*. Thus this chapter advocates learning from other IOs and suggests a comparative perspective on decision-making. As the WTO is one of the most legalized international organizations, this chapter encourages comparison with the most advanced IO in global governance: the EU.[19] Therefore, when discussing reform proposals, selected lessons from EU integration are introduced into the analysis.

Fourth, there is no such thing as an optimal decision-making system in any polity. Value judgments largely depend on the political theory that underpins the analysis.[20] Whereas some mechanisms might score well on the input side (i.e., access, transparency, and intensive and non-hierarchical deliberation), other decision-making tools might score better on the output side (i.e., delegation, closed negotiations, qualified majority voting). In addition, increasing input legitimacy could improve overall acceptance by stakeholders but might not translate into output legitimacy (e.g., performance). Any detailed reform discussion calls for a dynamic assessment of the potential effects on input and output legitimacy, as well as important trade-offs between the two.

III. Additional Help from the Secretariat

A. The Current Role of the Secretariat

The Warwick Report was largely silent on the function of the WTO Secretariat. In contrast, the Sutherland Report elaborates on the role of the Director-General and the WTO staff in a chapter dedicated to this topic (Chapter IX). The report refers to a type of *malaise*; the Director-General acts more as an international spokesperson and marketing executive than as an important player in the negotiations. In addition, the lack of intellectual input from the Secretariat and the Deputy Directors-General is lamented. Further exploration of the optimal use of advice, expertise, and deal-brokering capacities is suggested. In the view of the Sutherland Report, the WTO system suffers from 'a proliferation of back-seat drivers, each seeking a different destination, with no map and no intention of asking the way'.[21] In conclusion, the report calls for a new institutional voice and the establishment of a true guardian of the treaties by clarifying the poorly defined roles of the Director-General and the WTO Secretariat.[22]

The weak role of the Secretariat in multilateral trade negotiations has to be read in conjunction with the 'member-driven' nature of the WTO. Evidence indicates that the role of the Secretariat in the negotiation processes has decreased over time.[23] Active membership, an increase in the average size of trade missions, more attention paid to trade negotiations, and a greater number of services offered by the Geneva advisory community has weakened the role of the Secretariat in negotiations. At the same time, the reluctance of Members to delegate powers to the Secretariat has not changed. The growing dominance of WTO Members might also be a reflection of increasing attention being paid to controlling international organizations' outcomes more generally. However, 'member-driven' governance creates costs that are often underestimated.[24] These 'sovereignty-related costs' need to be weighed against the benefits of delegating greater responsibility to the Secretariat and potential delegation costs such as the abuse of the Secretariat's autonomy.

B. Strengthening the Secretariat

There are various ways to empower the Secretariat. One option would be to formally increase the role of the Director-General and the Secretariat in managing negotiations to achieve similar standards to those that applied in the pre-Doha era. This would be a move in the direction suggested by the Sutherland Report:

> The Director-General and Secretariat should have the capacity and the standing to be at the centre of negotiations during Ministerial meetings. Deputy Directors-General and divisional Directors should work alongside facilitators throughout the proceedings.[25]

This option could be further enhanced by asking the senior officials to become more involved in the negotiations by chairing certain committees, which was a practice in previous trade rounds.[26]

A more radical approach to strengthening the Secretariat within decision-making would consist of transferring agenda setting prerogatives to the Director-General. What would be the rationale of arming the Director-General with such powers? The Doha Round has become bogged down in a peculiar version of the 'endless cycling' dilemma. In the absence of any clear institutionalized agenda setting, parties constantly table proposals.[27] The current WTO system follows opaque processes leading up to a flow of negotiation texts that eventually form the basis of final negotiations. There is insufficient transparency as to the role of various actors in agenda setting. Most often, texts emerge from discussions in informal negotiation groups. Throughout the process, the chair (a representative of a Member State) with the help of the Secretariat steers the process by tabling 'non-papers' to Members. In these papers, the chair attempts to exclude certain items from the negotiation list and to specify key issues to be resolved. Only toward the end of negotiations, when signals from Members become explicit, will the chair table formal negotiation texts. Thereafter a complex system of bargaining dynamics emerges: additional concessions are exchanged and linkages created, and the pressure to obtain a final result mounts. This is the time when the Director-General is usually asked to provide some compromise formula.

One way to overcome endless cycling within a complex system of decision-making is to streamline decision-making procedures by allocating agenda-setting power to an elected group (e.g., a new form of the Consultative Group of 18) or a supranational actor (e.g., Secretariat, Director-General).[28] This chapter advocates strengthening the role of the Director-General and the Secretariat. WTO Members should grant more responsibility to these supranational actors by delegating agenda-setting powers in the context of the negotiations.

C. Complementing the Secretariat's Powers: Reforming Decision Rules

An additional step to complement shifting agenda-setting prerogatives would be exploring means of moving away from the consensus principle and abandoning the single-package approach. These are difficult 'cultural' hurdles to overcome, as the consensus principle and the single undertaking have received near universal support from WTO Members in recent years.[29] However, reform would not require a giant institutional change, as there are already provisions in the WTO Agreements that allow for certain decisions to be taken—if consensus fails—under different modes of qualified majority voting.[30]

Inspiration for greater delegation of authority to the WTO Secretariat and differentiated decision rules can be found by looking to the experiences of the EU. European Union decision-making in many regulatory fields is characterized by a two-step approach.[31] Translating this mechanism to the WTO, the Secretariat would table proposals based on the input of the WTO Members in the various committees that serve an advisory function. These proposals should not reflect the median of all positions formally and informally communicated, but the Secretariat would balance the vital interests of the Members and represent systemic interests that are supranational in character. As a second step, these proposals would be discussed and deliberated on by the General Council or other specialized committees and accepted or rejected based on a qualified majority voting procedure.

The one-state-one-vote model needs to be revisited, as it does not reflect the fact that states are diverse in size, leadership, and capacity to offer market access to other parties. The current system, with its small group negotiations, already recognizes a hierarchy among states within the international trading system. A qualified majority voting system would only formalize the existing hierarchy and tackle the current 'organized hypocrisy'.[32]

While moving toward a qualified majority voting system could be an objective, it seems obvious not all areas demand the same voting thresholds. Decisions on interpreting provisions of the Customs Valuation Agreement should be treated differently from negotiations on new rules that intrude into national cultural and societal environments. In addition, Members should not engage individually in painstaking regime management issues, such as micromanaging budgets or constraining research activities. They should be encouraged to decide by qualified majority voting to delegate more autonomy to the Secretariat. Delegation could be accompanied by new oversight mechanisms such as reporting requirements or establishing an independent evaluation office.

The history of U.S. trade policy in the late 1920s and early 1930s illustrates the costs of Congress controlling and micromanaging trade policy.[33] This eventually led to pressure to delegate on an ad hoc basis more power from Congress to the president.[34] The internal EU debate on allocating competence between member states and the Community to 'negotiate trade' is also instructive in understanding drivers for change.[35] While qualified majority voting had been the dominant approach in negotiations related to trade in goods since the inception of the Community's trade policy, the modes of decision-making related to other trade issues (i.e., services and intellectual property rights) gradually shifted over time from unanimity to qualified majority voting. Two key factors have led to increased delegation and strengthening of Community competence: the increasing number of EU members and the growing need to provide leadership within the trading system.[36] Today's challenges for the WTO as an organization can be viewed in a similar light.

Finally, to accommodate concerns related to sovereignty transfer, increased delegation to the Secretariat must go hand in hand with additional 'on the spot control' by Members. The suggestion by the Sutherland Report to convene yearly meetings among ministers to resolve certain issues and, if necessary, engage in horse-trading, as happens in the EU during council meetings, would be an additional control mechanism to sell 'more delegation' at home.

IV. Variable Geometry and Critical Mass in the GATT/WTO

The idea of using variable geometry approaches is not new in the GATT/WTO context. In order to discuss different techniques of variable geometry, a distinction is usually suggested between three types of differentiated membership schemes: special and differential treatment for certain groups of developing countries, plurilateral agreements, and critical mass agreements.[37] The focus below will be on the latter two forms of variable geometry. It is argued that the sharp distinction between critical mass (as discussed in the Warwick Report) and plurilateral agreements should be reconsidered. The following section suggests paying more attention to welfare-enhancing effects of cooperation and the consequences of various incentives to free-ride.

A. The Plurilateral Experience

A variable geometry approach received lukewarm approval in the Sutherland Report. In this context, the authors explicitly referred to plurilateral approaches. The report states:

[T]here should be a re-examination of the principle of plurilateral approaches to WTO negotiations. This should pay particularly sensitive attention to the problems that those not choosing to participate might face. Further, the approach should not permit small groups of members to bring into the WTO issues which are strongly and consistently opposed by substantial sections of the rest of the membership.[38]

There have been mixed experiences with so-called plurilateral agreements. These agreements by nature exempt non-members from most-favoured-nation benefits.[39] Two stand out: the Agreement on Government Procurement (GPA) of 1996 and the Agreement on Trade in Civil Aircraft of 1980.[40]

The support for the creation of the plurilateral GPA largely developed within the Organization for Economic Co-operation and Development (OECD). The agreement was first designed as an optional code during the Tokyo Round negotiations.[41] Unlike other codes, however, public procurement was not taken up in the 'single undertaking' exercise of the Uruguay Round. While key developing countries attempted to move the issue onto the multilateral agenda, existing parties to the agreement were skeptical. They feared lack of progress by including all Members and opted for a separate agreement, which led to significant amendments and extensions of the existing agreement.[42] The GPA brought about considerable cooperation and market opening and produced aggregate benefits for the signatories. However, it has not been successful in attracting new members.[43]

More recently, the existing plurilateral public procurement agreement has been supplemented by two multilateral initiatives: first, preparatory work on transparency in procurement practices; and second, multilateral negotiations on public procurement of services. Neither initiative has made much progress.[44] Advancement in the negotiations has been 'hampered by the somewhat schizophrenic manner in which WTO Members have approached the subject, with calls for the development of multilateral disciplines for services procurement sitting alongside existing plurilateral disciplines [...] as well as calls for a set of multilateral rules on transparency and due process in public purchasing.'[45] In August 2004, the council agreed that the issue of transparency 'will not form part of the Doha Work Programme and therefore no work towards negotiations [...] will take place within the WTO during the Doha Round.'[46]

The other plurilateral agreement still in existence is the Agreement on Trade in Civil Aircraft. It was the 'only sector-specific agreement covering a manufactured product that was successfully negotiated in the Tokyo Round.'[47] However, it suffered from disputes related to subsidies in markets largely characterized by oligopolistic structures. Both plurilateral agreements have attracted only a small membership. The sponsors include countries that have highly competitive producers and service providers in the sectors concerned. Owing to the lack of competitiveness of non-participants, these plurilateral agreements do not pose a significant most-favoured-nation concern, nor an issue of free-riding, which will be discussed below.[48]

B. The Warwick Version of Critical Mass and the Tokyo Codes

The Warwick Report has pushed the idea of variable geometry by introducing its version of critical mass decision-making. The authors of the report argue that 'we have a clear precedent from the Tokyo Codes on standards, import licensing, anti-dumping, subsidies and countervailing measures and customs valuation' as 'negotiated outcomes relying on critical mass for their acceptance have been applied on a MFN basis'.[49] They refer to a decision of 29 November 1979 adopted during the Tokyo Codes adoption period.[50] Thus the authors argue that the logic of critical mass was applied during the Tokyo Round negotiations, but they do not elaborate further on the lessons learned. A cautionary reading of automatic most-favoured-nation extension in relation to the Tokyo Codes is warranted.

Whereas GATT membership increased in the 1970s and nearly 100 members were engaged in the Tokyo Round negotiations, only a small group, driven mostly by the United States and the European Community, were actively involved in negotiations of the Tokyo Codes.[51] The negotiations were organized in a manner resembling a top-down pyramid shape.[52] First, negotiations proceeded within bilateral (U.S.–EC) and small-group settings (U.S., EC, Japan, and Canada: also called the Quad). Second, after initial agreement among these groups, the dominant actors attempted to multilateralize the results by offering some concessions to other potential parties to the agreements.[53] The codes, however, were not the priority issue for developing countries.[54] During the Tokyo Round, developing countries were focused on promoting a development agenda and pushed for special treatment in more systematic ways. Toward the end of the negotiations, some developing countries became more engaged in the codes negotiations, but the concessions offered by the key actors were perceived as too vague and as failing to fulfil the objectives of the Tokyo Declaration.[55]

On the process side, developing countries lacked the means to participate and lamented the failure to achieve a multilateral character. As one trade expert noted, 'smaller industrialized countries also complained bitterly about the lack of multilateralism, though they still accepted the results'.[56] The key deals were struck between the United States, the European Community, and Japan. In other words, the critical mass was very small during the negotiations on non-tariff barriers. In total only 17 members signed the *process-verbal*, which represented the formal acceptance of all the results.[57] This of course represented a political and a legal problem of 'how to integrate the Tokyo Round accords into the GATT legal framework in the context of a political process that had left the majority of the GATT membership frustrated and alienated'.[58]

Did the codes extend most-favoured-nation to non-signatories? The Warwick Report suggests that the Tokyo Codes negotiations applied such a logic characterizing a critical mass approach. However, a closer analysis of the negotiating history shows that this is far from clear. The declaration that launched the Tokyo Round and wording from the final negotiations suggest that these codes applied without discrimination to non-members.[59] At the same time, the notion of 'conditional most-favoured-nation' was widely accepted. Non-signatories were, to some degree, denied benefits originating from the codes, including the rights to participate equally in the committees to implement the codes. Winham writes:

> [I]n two cases—the government-procurement and subsidy/countervail codes—the substantive benefits of the agreements were intended to apply only to signatories. For example, the access to government tendering which was extended in the former code was available only to firms in other signatory countries, while on the latter code nations like the United States made the injury test in countervail procedures contingent on the acceptance by other countries of the code's disciplines on subsidies.[60]

Thus the fine line between a plurilateral and a critical mass approach is difficult to draw here. Some codes could be labeled a partial critical mass. As most-favoured-nation extension was far from obvious, the parties were left in limbo as to the exact risks of discriminatory treatment.

C. The Post-Uruguay Round Sector Agreements

The idea of critical mass emerged again during the sector negotiations on trade in services after the Uruguay Round. The sector agreements represented initiatives to liberalize markets.[61] Can we learn any lessons from these agreements that seem to have followed the critical mass approach? Three stand out: the Information Technology Agreement, the Basic Telecom Agreement, and the Financial Services Agreement.[62]

First, there is a north–south pattern of membership (similar to that for the plurilateral agreements and the codes). These agreements offer sector market opening for products of great interest to industries in highly developed countries, and active membership is so far largely limited to OECD countries. In the case of the Information Technology Agreement, there is evidence that Quad interests in particular had been reflected. In this respect, a strong push came from a G7 Ministerial Conference on the global information society.[63] Individual firms and industry associations representing the knowledge and financial services industries lobbied hard for improved market access. In particular, the U.S. government showed great interest in these agreements, particularly the financial services agreement. In contrast, developing countries faced strong domestic political constraints, feared increasing liberalization in vulnerable sectors, and were hampered by their lack of competitiveness. Participation increased because of the differentiated levels of commitments for developing countries and the perception of many Members that they would have to sign the agreements to attract foreign direct investments.

Second, there was an implicit (and in the case of the Information Technology Agreement explicit) understanding that agreements need to attract a sufficient number of producers or service providers in order to function properly.[64] Leading negotiators strategically signalled exemptions if other key actors did not make sufficient commitments. The Basic Telecom Agreement negotiations were deadlocked in 1996, and the U.S. representatives lamented that the offers on the table were still inadequate 'in part because the required "critical mass" of membership (to prevent free-riding) had not been achieved'.[65] In their assessment of the Basic Telecom Agreement, Hoekman and Kostecki further stress, slightly euphemistically, that 'additional time allowed a number of developing countries to improve their offer'.[66] The story has been similar in the financial services negotiations, in which the United States (and other countries) signalled in 1995 that they would not improve their commitments and would take broad most-favoured-nation exemptions based on reciprocity should others not reconsider their offers.

Third, further work following initial successes has been very difficult, calling into question the sustainability of these initiatives over time. With respect to the Information Technology Agreement, various attempts to enlarge product coverage failed. In most sector initiatives, there was a strong push for market opening among leading service providers. However, the momentum generated in the mid-1990s lasted only a short time. In addition, liberalization of financial services sectors was affected by the East Asian financial crises in the second half of the 1990s and has recently made no tangible progress.

D. Critical Mass: Most-Favoured-Nation and the Incentives to Free-ride

The Warwick Report discusses critical mass related to market access and rules, and refers mainly to the post–Uruguay Round sector negotiations.[67] In addition, the report lists certain criteria that should be observed when relying on a critical mass approach. In sum, the Warwick Report demands that results of critical mass negotiations not affect 'the existing balance of rights and obligations' and that the rights acquired by the signatories 'shall be extended to all Members on a non-discriminatory basis, with the obligations falling only on signatories'. Thus the report shares the view that critical mass and non-discrimination (extending most-favoured-nation to non-participants) go hand in hand. The report contains some mixed signals: while an existing but not often used decision-making procedure is promoted, the report attaches onerous conditions for pursuing a type of variable geometry. By explicitly referring to unconditional most-favoured-nation when using critical mass, the report might have even gone beyond the status quo. It remains puzzling why the Warwick Report excluded the potential of plurilateral agreements from its analysis and did not pay more attention to the rich history of codes negotiated during the Tokyo Round and the post–Uruguay Round agreements. In any case, a dogmatic view of most-favoured-nation as advocated in the report's proposals could turn out to be a non-starter as future initiatives will be constrained from the outset.

Instead of using a dichotomous distinction based on most-favoured-nation, greater focus should be placed on the benefits of cooperation and on the free-riding incentives that differ from sector to sector and between market-opening and rule-making.[68] Free-riding not only might affect the outcomes of the negotiations but also exhibits spoiling capacities throughout the negotiations.

What are the free-riding effects related to different regulatory schemes and various liberalization efforts to increase market access in goods and services? There is variance as to the free-rider incentives prevalent in regulatory or market-liberalizing cooperation. The incentive structure for those participating (and abstaining) in critical mass negotiations appears different. If some leading trading nations agree to increase generic standards through a critical mass approach, they will anticipate the effects of the most-favoured-nation extension clause. It is to be expected that parties will negotiate in the shadow of the market power of the non-participants.[69] Participants need to have a sort of safeguard that allows them to take measures against abuse of free-riding (as witnessed in the ITA and financial services cases).[70] If this is not the case, critical mass agreements will likely be limited in scope and effect.[71] Free-rider issues affect the degree of integration and cooperation as witnessed by the existence of various levels of commitments. In other words, Members need to receive some benefits of cooperating beyond existing rules.

These incentives are even more applicable to market-opening strategies, where countries are even more critical about free-riding (e.g., lowering reciprocal tariffs in medical devices or environmental goods if other important exporters abstain from joining the critical mass and continue levying higher tariffs). In these cases, the free-riding effects might be even more direct and transparent than in cases related to rules or generic standards (e.g., health provisions or environmental standards).

What flows from the above is the suggestion to revisit a dogmatic stand on most-favoured-nation extension. To attach too many conditions discourages solutions in the WTO context and further shifts these issues to bilateral or regional trade arrangements. What is important in designing rules for the application of critical mass is creating incentives for non-members to join. There should be no additional strings attached. The general procedures for accession to the WTO have set a bad precedent in this respect as joining the agreement becomes burdensome due to the need to make bilateral deals with all members.

E. The EU Experience with Enhanced Cooperation

The concept of variable geometry has been debated in the field of EU integration studies for quite some time. However, it remains disputed whether variable geometry in the EU context is a temporary deviation from a uniform ideal or has more permanent features.[72] In the former interpretation, variable geometry is perceived as a dynamic approach whereby a handful of members integrates faster. Those engaging in additional cooperation are perceived as 'avant-gardist' or part of 'core Europe' in a multi-speed community.[73] Participation in integration projects (e.g., in the common currency zone) allows for some type of club benefits.[74] The decision on non-participation is related mainly to sovereignty concerns as governments acknowledge the functional logic of further integration, but are constrained by domestic politics. This concept is different from 'Europe à la carte'.[75] In the EU context, the British opt-out from social policy (differentiation in the so-called social protocol in the Maastricht Treaty) comes to mind. This exception seems more a long-term opt-out following the 'à la carte' logic. This type of laggard strategy by some members slows deeper integration efforts by other members.[76]

Overall, there are few empirical cases of differentiated integration in the EU (e.g., Schengen regime, Western European Union, common currency). Nevertheless, debates on how to deal with variable geometry in more systematic ways have increased in recent years. During intergovernmental conferences, EU members have attempted to spell out more clearly the conditions under which variable geometry should proceed.[77] A new concept that came up in the second half of the 1990s has been the mechanism of 'enhanced cooperation'.[78] The Amsterdam Treaty has described the mechanism as a last resort that can be triggered 'when (the Council) has established that the objectives of such cooperation cannot be attained within a reasonable period by the Union as a whole'. The idea was to find an institutional answer to the growing heterogeneity among EU member states in view of enlargement. Existing members anticipated additional pressures for flexibility mechanisms to follow the examples of Schengen and the Euro. The majority of countries aspired to control for future differentiation (and groups cooperating outside the legal system, such as the Schengen regime) by channelling new initiatives through the EU's institutional framework.[79] However, the specific obligations attached to applying 'enhanced cooperation' were hindering its use, such as the last resort condition, the high threshold for initiating the process, and the minimum number of members to be included. Later reforms have redesigned rules to allow for more flexibility to trigger the process to make it more attractive. In addition, more attention has been paid to the relations with non-members and to designing mechanisms to prevent non-members from arbitrarily having an impact on decision-making within the more integrationist group.[80]

What are the potential lessons to be drawn from the EU's experience with variable geometry generally and with 'enhanced cooperation' in particular? There seems to be an implicit understanding that variable geometry is a possible avenue for integration. However, many member states and supranational actors (including the Commission and the European Parliament) seem reluctant to go down this path. There is a widespread perception that 'enhanced cooperation' could create discrimination, and concerns have been voiced in relation to failure to join the avant-gardist camp. There exists an ambiguous attitude of members to let others move ahead, with a tendency to attach excessively stringent rules. However, while new initiatives under 'enhanced cooperation' have not yet materialized, some evidence suggests that the possibility to apply this method may unlock certain negotiations.[81] In other words, the existence of an option for recourse to a flexible instrument to move more quickly among a like-minded group might under certain conditions encourage laggards to move. However, if conditions are too onerous, the threat of moving more quickly within institutional rules might not be credible.[82] This could be instructive in thinking about how to design critical mass in the world trading system. In light of existing 'outside' modes of variable geometry (e.g., bilateral and regional trade agreements), it is even more urgent to consider going down a path of differentiated integration under the auspices of the WTO.

V. Conclusion

This chapter has discussed two reform proposals and has attempted to sketch a new scenario for decision-making in the WTO. Strengthening the Secretariat, combined with a move toward more structured decision-making processes beyond the single package approach and consensual decision-making represent the best way forward for the WTO. Furthermore, empowering the Secretariat by allocating agenda-setting power could assist in overcoming some of the endless cycling problems as witnessed in the Doha Round. In addition, a redesign of procedures and decision rules (e.g., the selective recourse to qualified majority voting, dropping the 'single undertaking') could help mainstream processes.

As to the critical mass approach, the above discussion questions the potential of using this type of variable geometry as approved by the authors of the Warwick Report. This chapter has argued that the conditions advocated by the Warwick Commission might be too onerous in light of the history of variable geometry in the GATT/WTO and the EU. It could be further asked whether not all negotiations (including classical tariff negotiations where a deal needs to be struck between principal suppliers of individual goods and key importers) have followed a version of the critical mass approach.[83] In reflecting on the variance in negotiation processes across the Tokyo Codes, Winham concludes that 'the answer appears to lie not in the negotiation process itself, but rather in the substance of what was being negotiated'.[84] In any case, more systematic research is needed to understand the promises and perils of critical mass decision-making. In addition, more experiments with this approach are needed to test the effects of partial most-favoured-nation exemptions on degrees of integration.

Finally, this chapter suggests combining various reform measures. A stronger supranational actor (e.g., the Secretariat) could play a role in a critical mass approach, not least by representing the interests of the membership as a whole and in particular by assisting those who remain (temporarily) outside.

The time for rethinking WTO decision-making is ripe. In light of the inertia of the status quo, it seems that only a package solution that would allow for some concession-trading could be a potential avenue for change. Such a package, however, as the Uruguay Round has shown, cannot be an institutional reform package alone, but needs to be enhanced with tangible concessions on additional market-opening commitments. For the current round, a reform discussion is too late, but it would become pertinent again should the Doha Round fail. But here lies a paradox. Moving toward a more mature system of decision-making with clearer mandates and committee deadlines will make trade rounds redundant. However, in order to put in place a more elaborate and up-to-date system of decision-making, an institutional design package would need to be adopted in the context of another trade round.

A. More Challenges Ahead?

There are a multitude of factors that explain the current deadlock in WTO negotiations. The lack of leadership is one important factor. The 'liberal transatlantic moment' has lost momentum. The transatlantic partnership has suffered some of its worst crises since the end of World War II. These crises, which developed in the security field, have certainly affected the capacities of the United States and the European Union to manage and drive international trade negotiations. Three additional elements, which are subjects of study and debate in the field of international relations, seem to have affected cooperation incentives in the current Doha Round.

First, an (older) controversy that has divided neo-realists and neo-liberal scholars could be instructive in understanding newer developments in the global trading system: the role of absolute versus relative gains from international cooperation.[85] As we move toward a multipolar trade world, some of the leading actors (the United States and the European Union) are showing signs of reluctance to agree to deals that asymmetrically profit other emerging nations (relative gains concerns). Not only are these types of agreements difficult to sell at home to negatively affected constituencies, but some emerging powers (e.g., China and Brazil) pose certain challenges to the United States (and to some degree to the European Union) with regard to foreign and security policy. There is lack of research on these systemic pressures and their potential effects on different negotiation strategies in the future, including pursuit of greater bilateral agreements.[86] However, there is a real concern that the current financial crisis and the negative spill-over effects on growth figures within the real economy will make parties even more suspicious and lend support to those actors pushing for relative gains.

Second, the relationship between regionalism, bilateralism, and multilateralism continues to affect current trade negotiations. Key trade powers have, over the last decade, redesigned their venue-shopping strategies. In particular, they have created additional platforms to negotiate trade that function as strong alternatives to the multilateral trade arena. These outside options affect, in the words of negotiation theories, the potential zone of agreement. States with strong alternatives will hold out to get a better deal. In addition, export-oriented firms that are pushing for liberalization of markets might be satisfied with bilateral and regional approaches as long as these offer substantial increase in export opportunities. This in turn will lower the support of export industries to counterbalance import-competing industries' voices within the multilateral context.

Third, there is a commitment problem related to the growing power of legalization of some international arrangements. The increase in the binding nature of international trade law has affected the willingness of trading nations to commit to additional liberalization.[87] The argument runs that WTO Members are reluctant to adopt new rules and to agree on additional market liberalization as they (and their domestic interest groups) have learned the lessons of a strong dispute settlement system. In addition, many of the parties have come to realize that changing rules is difficult in a consensus-driven organization and thus the 'shadow of cooperation' increases. As states value future benefits of cooperation, there is an incentive to bargain hard for a good deal, leading to costly stand-offs.[88]

A final observation relates to developing countries. A key challenge remains to assist developing countries (beyond the powerful developing countries) in benefiting more from the multilateral trading system. The history of EU integration has shown that in order to successfully create a common market with rules that in the long run apply to all market actors from various members, rich members need to provide incentives and resources to assist the integration process. The EU has invested considerable financial resources in developing infrastructure and other basic services in its less developed regions. Within the WTO context, the aid-for-trade debate has opened an additional door for developing instruments to assist smaller and weaker parties to further integrate into the world trading system. Financial assistance to address supply-side constraints should go hand in hand with technical assistance to mainstream trade within national development strategies and should be coordinated better among international organizations working in this area. In addition, special and differential treatment for the least developed countries means also finding new and innovative ways to empower weaker states within existing and future governance models.

Notes

1 John Ikenberry, *Liberal Order and Imperial Ambition* (Cambridge, U.K.: Polity, 2006).
2 Charles Kindleberger, *The World in Depression, 1929–39* (Berkeley: University of California Press, 1973); Ikenberry, ibid.
3 See Francis Fukuyama, The End of History and the Last Man (New York: Free Press, 1992). The genesis of the World Trade Organization (WTO) and the International Criminal Court (ICC) stand out. However, the creation of the WTO falls into the category of redesign of a de facto existing international organization.

4 Institutionalist research programs have called the power of the status quo the existing 'stickiness' of institutions.

5 On the concept of loyalty, see Albert Hirschman, *Exit, Voice and Loyalty: Responses to Decline in Firms, Organizations and States* (Cambridge, Mass.: Harvard University Press, 1970).

6 Consultative Board to the Director-General Supachai Panitchpakdi, *The Future of the WTO: Addressing Institutional Challenges in the New Millennium* (Geneva: WTO, 2004).

7 Warwick Commission, *The Multilateral Trade Regime: Which Way Forward?* (Coventry: University of Warwick, 2007).

8 Robert Keohane, After Hegemony: Cooperation and Discord in the World Political Economy (Princeton: Princeton University Press, 1984).

9 Ruth Grant and Robert Keohane, 'Accountability and Abuses of Power in World Politics', 99 American Political Science Review 29 (2005).

10 The input side of a legitimate political system includes participation, deliberation, and mechanisms to hold actors accountable; the output side addresses the contribution toward improving societal problem-solving; Manfred Elsig, 'The World Trade Organization's Legitimacy Crises: What Does the Beast Look Like?', 41 Journal of World Trade 75 (2007).

11 See Grant and Keohane, above n 9; weaker parties might face potential repercussions from more powerful parties if future interaction or collaboration is foreseen. In other words, the prospect of future cooperation reduces incentives to litigate against a big trading partner. There also remains the question whether the losing party will implement (and to what degree) court rulings.

12 It is yet another question to what extent the rules reflect the interests of the powerful actors in the system.

13 Peter Pedersen, 'WTO Decision-Making and Internal Transparency', 5 World Trade Review 103 (2006).

14 This relates to rule-making. Negotiations on modifying the DSU are currently underway. They are not formally part of the Doha negotiations, but the pressure to link negotiations on reforming dispute settlement with other trade issues is present. In order to achieve 'results', linkages will eventually prove pivotal. This is reflected in a public statement by the chairman of the Dispute Settlement Body (DSB) of the Special Session made at a conference held at the Graduate Institute, Geneva: 'The DSB reform needs the round, the round does not need the DSB reform and will not wait for us' (Ambassador Ronald Saborío Soto, 27 February 2008).

15 Discussion, Waterloo Canada, 14 March 2008.

16 John Ruggie, 'International Regimes, Transactions, and Change: Embedded Liberalism in the Postwar Economic Order', 36 International Organization 379 (1982).

17 On mantras and myths, see John Jackson, 'The WTO "Constitution" and Proposed Reforms: Seven "Mantras" Revisited', 4 Journal of International Economic Law 67 (2001); and Debra Steger, 'The Culture of the WTO: Why It Needs Change', 10 Journal of International Economic Law 483 (2007).

18 Fritz Scharpf, 'The Joint-Decision Trap: Lessons from German Federalism and European Integration', 66 Public Administration 239 (1988).

19 On legalization, see Judith Goldstein, Miles Kahler, Robert Keohane, and Anne-Marie Slaughter, 'Introduction: Legalization and World Politics', 54 International Organization 401 (2000); Judith Goldstein and Lisa Martin, 'Legalization, Trade Liberalization, and Domestic Politics: A Cautionary Note', 54 International Organization 603 (2000).

20 Elsig, above n 10.

21 Consultative Board to the Director-General Supachai Panitchpakdi, above n 6, at 77.

22 Article VI of the Marrakesh Agreement Establishing the World Trade Organization reads: '1. There shall be a Secretariat of the WTO (hereinafter referred to as "the Secretariat") headed by a Director-General. 2. The Ministerial Conference shall appoint the Director-General and adopt regulations setting out the powers, duties, conditions of service and term of office of the Director-General. 3. The Director-General shall appoint the members of the staff of the Secretariat and determine their duties and conditions of service in accordance with regulations adopted by the Ministerial Conference. 4. The responsibilities of the Director-General and of the staff of the Secretariat shall be exclusively international in character. In the discharge of their duties, the Director-General and the staff of the Secretariat shall not seek or accept instructions from any government or any other authority external to the WTO. They shall refrain from any action which might adversely reflect on their position as international officials. The Members of the WTO shall respect the international character of the responsibilities of the Director-General and of the staff of the Secretariat and shall not seek to influence them in the discharge of their duties.'

23 Gilbert Winham, *International Trade and the Tokyo Round Negotiation* (Princeton: Princeton University Press, 1986); Manfred Elsig, 'Agency Theory and the WTO: Complex Agency and "Missing Delegation"?', Paper Manuscript (2008); Consultative Board to the Director-General Supachai Panitchpakdi, above n 6.

24 Alexander Thompson, 'Principal Problems: UN Weapons Inspections in Iraq and Beyond', Paper Delivered at the Annual Convention of the International Studies Association, San Diego, 2006.

25 Consultative Board to the Director-General Supachai Panitchpakdi, above n 6, at 82.

26 Elsig, above n 23.

27 William Riker, 'Implications from the Dis-equilibrium of Majority Rule for the Study of Institutions', 74 American Political Science Review 432 (1980); for other functional reasons to empower the Secretariat, see Elsig, above n 23.

28 On the Consultative Group of 18, see Richard Blackhurst and David Hartridge, 'Improving the Capacity of WTO Institutions to Fulfil their Mandate', 7 Journal of International Economic Law 705 (2004).

29 The combination of single package and consensus has led to a type of 'decision-trap' from which it is difficult to escape. In addition, it may have produced the opposite of what was envisaged. Van Grasstek and Sauvé put it as follows: '[P]aradoxically, instead of encouraging bold deals by causing each country to focus on those parts of the package that they most dearly desire, the single undertaking might promote timidity by causing each country to focus on those things that they most fear'; see Craig Van Grasstek and Pierre Sauvé, 'The Consistency of the WTO Rules: Can the Single Undertaking Be Squared with Variable Geometry?', 9 Journal of International Economic Law 837 (2006), at 858.

30 See Steger and Shpilkovskaya, this volume; current voting is based on a one-country one-vote basis.

31 The dominating mode is the co-decision procedure. The commission proposes new regulation (agenda setting) while the European Council and the European Parliament have the right to accept or reject the proposed regulation (co-decision). Regulation is adapted only when both institutions agree.

32 Richard Steinberg, 'In the Shadow of Law or Power? Consensus Based Bargaining in the GATT/WTO', 56 International Organization 339 (2002); some original work has been done on various forms of weighted voting; see Thomas Cottier and Satoko Takenoshita, 'The Balance of Power in WTO Decision-Making: Towards Weighted Voting in Legislative Response', 58 Aussenwirtschaft 171 (2003).

33 See the detailed analysis of the Smoot-Hawley Tariff Act by Elmer Eric Schattschneider, *Politics, Pressures and the Tariff* (New York: Prentice-Hall, 1935).

34 The Reciprocal Trade Agreement Act (RTAA) in 1934 marked the beginning of a system of increased delegation (limited in time) to the executive branch (later called the fast-track procedure and today the trade promotion authority). These mechanisms have increasingly enabled control over the worst forms of protectionist cherry-picking by Congress.

35 Manfred Elsig, *The EU's Common Commercial Policy* (Aldershot: Ashgate Publisher, 2002).

36 Ibid; increased delegation to the Community was a move away from the model of 'shared competence' between member states and the Community. Thus decision rules changed from consensus to qualified majority voting.

37 This chapter does not analyze the first type of approach (special and differential treatment).

38 Consultative Board to the Director-General Supachai Panitchpakdi, above n 6, at 82.

39 The most-favoured-nation (MFN) treatment principle states that parties may not discriminate between trading partners that are members of the GATT/WTO system. Exempting most-favoured-nation means that parties will not give equal treatment to those that have not joined the plurilateral agreement. It is not clear whether the authors of the Sutherland Report deliberately aimed to make a distinction between plurilateral agreements (excluding MFN) and critical mass approaches (with application of most-favoured-nation).

40 Other post–Tokyo Round plurilateral agreements were the International Dairy Agreement and the International Bovine Meat Agreement. Both ended in 1997. 'Countries that had signed the agreements decided that the sectors were better handled under the Agriculture and Sanitary and Phytosanitary agreements. Some aspects of their work had been handicapped by the small number of signatories. For example, some major exporters of dairy products did not sign the Dairy Agreement, and the attempt to cooperate on minimum prices therefore failed—minimum pricing was suspended in 1995 (at http://www.wto.org).' In other words, the absence of an important market actor limited positive integration, as a type of free-riding option (selling at lower prices) stalled cooperation efforts.

41 The GPA is based on the principles of openness, transparency, and non-discrimination, which apply to members' procurement, while the coverage varies from one member to another.

42 Sue Arrowsmith, *Government Procurement and the WTO* (The Hague: Kluwer Law International, 2003).

43 Currently, there are 39 members (including 27 EU member states).

44 Diana Zacharias, 'Art XIII GATS', in Rüdiger Wolfrum, Peter-Tobias Stoll, and Clemens Feinäugle (eds), *WTO-Trade in Services* (Leiden: Martinus Nijhoff Publishers, 2008) 272–86.

45 Pierre Sauvé, 'Completing the GATS Framework: Addressing Uruguay Round Leftovers', 57 Aussenwirtschaft 301 (2002) 305.

46 WTO General Council, Doha Work Programme, WT/L/579, Adopted 4 August 2004, online: http://www.wto.org/english/tratop_e/dda_e/ddadraft_31jul04_e.doc.

47 Bernard Hoekman and Michel Kostecki, The Political Economy of the World Trading System (Oxford: Oxford University Press 2001) 380; the agreement 'eliminates import duties on all aircraft, other than military aircraft, as well as on all other products covered by the agreement—civil aircraft engines and their parts and components, all components and sub-assemblies of civil aircraft, and flight simulators and their parts and components (at http://www.wto.org)'.

48 In the context of the negotiations on the public procurement code during the Tokyo Round, developing countries' concerns related to the lack of opportunities in coverage that could have provided opportunities for low-cost producers, see Winham, above n 23.

49 Few countries signed the codes.

50 See Warwick Commission, above n 7, at 30–31. The decision reads: 'The contracting parties (…) note that existing rights and benefits under the GATT of contracting parties not being parties to these agreements (…) are not affected by these agreements (L/4905).'

51 These were all negotiations on rules (positive integration).

52 Winham, above n 23.

53 This hierarchical negotiation process varied from one code to another. In the negotiations on standards (technical barriers to trade), there was active involvement from a greater number of countries; the negotiation history on subsidies and countervailing duties reads more like a transatlantic story; Winham, above n 23.

54 In the 1970s, in parallel to the GATT negotiations, developing countries invested time and resources to develop an alternative venue for regulating the world economy: the United Nations Conference on Trade and Development (UNCTAD).

55 Ria Kamper, 'The Tokyo Round: Results and Implications for Developing Countries', World Bank Staff Working Paper No. 372 (1980); Winham, above n 23.

56 Kamper, ibid, at 25.

57 Argentina was the only developing country among the signatories, ibid.

58 Winham, above n 23, at 354.

59 Annex 7 of GATT 1979 as agreed in the final negotiations reaffirmed that non-signatories were not affected by these agreements. In addition, they were granted the right to participate with observer status in committee work related to the codes. This was initially resisted by the Quad because of confidentiality and efficiency concerns; Winham, above n 23.

60 Winham, above n 23, at 355. This was confirmed by one of the U.S. negotiators involved in the subsidies and countervailing duties negotiations. The former trade official acknowledged that conditional MFN was used as a key strategic tool throughout the negotiations to pressure important members to join the agreement (Interview, 10 December 2008); see also Kamper, above n 55.

61 This is a form of negative integration. In the current trade round, the concept of critical mass is applied in services negotiations (e.g., group negotiations) and in non-agricultural market access negotiations (e.g., zero-for-zero negotiations for certain products and sectors).

62 It is beyond the scope of this chapter to offer a detailed analysis of these negotiations, but the chapter attempts to focus on key lessons.

63 Hoekman and Kostecki, above n 47.

64 In the case of the ITA, 90 percent of total production of information technology products had to be included under the agreement, ibid.

65 Ibid, at 261.

66 Ibid, at 261.

67 It is noteworthy that all three service sector agreements have been about market opening and not about rules. A partial exception is the reference paper in the telecom agreement, which provides for legal guidelines in relation to sector liberalization.

68 In addition, as trade patterns change and more countries compete in the same markets, the size of critical mass has increased.

69 This is a liberal argument. From a realist perspective, free-riding incentives can be addressed by using sticks to push for the conclusion of agreements and limiting the loopholes; see Lloyd Gruber, Ruling the World: Power Politics and the Rise of Supra-national Institutions (Princeton: Princeton University Press, 2000). See also Steinberg, above n 32.

70 Free-riders will attempt not to engage in the critical mass negotiations as they get a lunch for free. In addition, they are not required to justify their position (absence), which differs from the situation in multilateral negotiations using 'single undertaking'.

71 The sector agreements under the GATS have shown that obstacles to extend coverage and membership are difficult to overcome when automatic MFN extension applies (e.g., financial services agreement.) The leading providers of financial services have shown more enthusiasm for negotiating accession agreements with important new members than for elaborating and extending the sector agreements further.

72 Markus Jachtenfuchs, 'Democracy and Governance in the European Union'. European Integration Online Papers (EIoP) No. 2 (1997), at 5; Alexander Stubb, 'The 1996 Inter-governmental Conference and the Management of Flexible Integration', 4 Journal of European Public Policy 37 (1997).

73 Fritz Scharpf, 'Notes Toward a Theory of Multilevel Governing in Europe', MPIfG Discussion Paper No. 5 (2000), at 24.

74 In the case of the Euro, it is assumed that integration benefits will materialize in the long run, while short-term adjustment costs exist.

75 In the context of the global trading system, this could be labelled 'WTO à la carte'. The Tokyo Codes taking up non-tariff issues were presented as a 'à la carte' integration. Following the Tokyo Round, the view developed within the trade community that this amounted to cherry-picking and thus undermined the global trading system. This debate encouraged the development of the notion of 'single undertaking' not least to attempt to address free-riding.

76 Variation in labour-related standards has further hindered additional integration in the field of services (including labour mobility); see debate on *Bolkestein Directive*.

77 Stubb, above n 72.

78 See Eric Philippart, 'Optimising the Mechanisms for "Enhanced Cooperation" within the EU: Recommendations for the Constitutional Treaty', CEPS Policy Brief No. 33 (2003).

79 Philippe De Schoutheete, 'Closer Cooperation: Political Background and Issues in the Negotiations', in Jörg Monar and Wolfgang Wessels (eds), *The European Union after Amsterdam* (London: Continuum, 2001).

80 See also Philippart, above n 78; *Treaty of Lisbon Report, Joint Study* (Brussels: European Policy Centre, Egmont and CEPS 2007).

81 There is evidence that the variable geometry option has had an impact on integration efforts in relation to taxation or the European arrest warrant; see Philippart, above n 78.

82 There are additional examples of finding constructive ways to design flexibility mechanisms should a group of countries decide to integrate further. These include opt-out or light methods such as 'constructive abstention' in the Common Foreign and Security Policy (CFSP) or the 'opt-out method' of Schengen; for a discussion on the different flexibility mechanisms that developed in the areas of Common Foreign and Security Policy, Economic and Monetary Union, and Freedom, Security and Justice, see *Treaty of Lisbon Report*, above n 80.

83 Winham makes this argument when referring to the Kennedy and the Tokyo Round, above n 23.

84 Ibid, at 369.

85 This notion of absolute and relative gains should not be confused with the concept of absolute and relative advantage as discussed in the classical trade theory literature.

86 See Frank Grundig, 'Patterns of International Cooperation and the Explanatory Power of Relative Gains: An Analysis of Cooperation on Global Climate Change, Ozone Depletion, and International Trade', 50 International Studies Quarterly 781 (2006).

87 Goldstein and Martin, above n 19.

88 James Fearon, 'Bargaining, Enforcement and International Cooperation', 52 International Organization 269 (1998).

Improvements to the WTO Decision-Making Process: Lessons from the International Monetary Fund and the World Bank

ALBERTO ALVAREZ-JIMÉNEZ

I. Introduction

A comparative assessment of the internal governance of the WTO, the International Bank for Reconstruction and Development (the World Bank), and the International Monetary Fund (IMF) is a valuable tool to improve on recommendations to enhance the WTO decision-making process. This is because some of the WTO reform proposals include suggestions similar to what is already in place at both the IMF and the World Bank. However, for this comparative analysis to arrive at meaningful recommendations, it has to take into account two important issues: first, the Bank's and the IMF's organs and decision-making processes are, obviously, related to each organizations' particular mandate and objectives. Care must be taken when suggesting that institutional features of the Bank and the IMF be employed by the WTO. Second, these three organizations have been subject to increasing criticism in recent years and, at the time of this writing, are undergoing important reform processes as a result of the current world financial crisis. Consequently, any recommendations for the WTO based on the institutional history of the IMF and the Bank must be adjusted to current trends in institutional design, marked not only by concerns for efficiency but also for adequate representation of developing and least developed countries.[1]

This chapter illustrates how the history of the World Bank and the IMF, and particularly of the functioning of and inter-relationship between their boards and managements, may assist in improving recommendations to create a consultative body in the WTO and to enhance the position of the WTO Director-General and the WTO Secretariat. This chapter is divided into four parts. Part II analyzes the internal management of the IMF and the role played by each of its decision-making bodies, the relationship between them, and the decision-making processes that have adopted. Part III carries out a similar assessment of the World Bank. Part IV looks at the WTO, and makes recommendations to improve proposals aimed at enhancing WTO decision-making. Finally, Part V presents some general conclusions.

II. Internal Management of the IMF

The IMF was created with the aims of promoting international monetary cooperation, orderly exchange arrangements among its Members, exchange stability, and furnishing Member States with financial assistance for balance of payment difficulties. The IMF pursues these objectives through two main activities that are carried out by all its organs: surveillance and the provision of conditional financial assistance.[2] The former relates to the provision of advice to IMF Members regarding adequate economic policies and the use of peer pressure to persuade Members to pursue such policies. The latter involves providing Members with, subject to conditions related to the adoption of sound economic policies recommended by the IMF, financial assistance to resolve temporary balance of payments difficulties.[3]

Today, the IMF has 185 member countries, which were traditionally divided into two groups: the industrial economies and the developing countries. The former have not drawn on the Fund for decades but dominate the IMF's decision-making process, while the latter do draw on the IMF but do not control decision-making.[4] Until recently, there was a third category of IMF Members: those with broad access to capital markets and that have accumulated large reserves, such as Asian and oil-exporting countries. These Members made infrequent use of the IMF's resources and, therefore, did not need to follow its policy recommendations.[5] The current economic crisis may produce a shift among these emerging markets. Already Hungary, Ukraine, Iceland, Pakistan, Latvia, Serbia, and Belarus have asked the IMF for financial support to cope with the crisis,[6] and negotiations are underway with El Salvador and Turkey.[7] Other European Union countries, such as Romania, Estonia, Bulgaria, and Lithuania, may soon join the growing list of countries seeking IMF assistance.[8]

A recent evaluation of IMF governance carried out by the IMF Independent Evaluation Office (IEO) points out that the strongest feature of such governance is effectiveness, while the weakest aspect is the accountability and voice of developing country Members.[9]

IMF governance occurs within three bodies: the Board of Governors, the Executive Board, and the IMF management. In general terms, the Articles of Agreement approved in Bretton Woods have a clear emphasis on rules rather than on principles. However, reforms introduced at the end of the 1970s reversed this. The result has been an IMF that vests a wide discretion in the Executive Board, guided by principles identified by the IMF's Members.[10] The IMF system of governance has evolved and adapted to the needs of new conditions in the global financial world.[11] However, according to the IEO, the IMF lacks 'clarity on the respective roles of the different governance bodies, and in particular between the Board and Management.'[12]

A. The Board of Governors

The Board of Governors is the highest organ of the IMF, and includes representatives from each IMF Member. The Board of Governors is authorized to delegate some of its powers to the Executive Board, though the Articles of Agreement regard some decisions as non-delegable, such as the allocation or cancellation of special drawing rates, changes to the duration of the basic period of allocation, alteration of the charges of allocation,[13] and amendments the Articles of Agreement and the By-laws.[14]

The Board of Governors is advised by two ministerial committees: the Development Committee; and the International Monetary and Financial Committee (IMFC). The former is a joint committee of the IMF and the Bank that makes suggestions to each organization's boards of governors concerning economic development in emerging countries.

The IMFC is responsible for advising the Board of Governors on inter alia proposals made by the Executive Board to amend the Articles of Agreement, and situations that put the international monetary and financial system at risk. The IMFC is made up of 24 members, usually governors, and its membership reflects the composition of the Executive Board. Each country and group of countries that elect a member of the Executive Board also appoint members to the IMFC. Its mandate is

> supervising the management and adaptation of the international monetary system, including the continuing operation of the adjustment process, and in this connection reviewing developments in global liquidity and the transfer of real resources to developing countries.
>
> … considering proposals by the executive directors to amend the Articles of Agreement; and
>
> … dealing with sudden disturbances that might threaten the [international monetary] system.[15]

The IMFC has played an important role in recent years in major Fund initiatives, and its advisory character has transformed it into a body that, at the ministerial level, endorses decisions made by the Executive Board.[16] At the time of this writing, IMF Members are assessing the issue of putting into operation an already existing council, provided for by the Articles of Agreement, as a political decision-making body that would replace the IMFC. The composition would be similar to that of the Group of 20 and would give some emerging nations a say within the Fund in line with their current economic clout.[17]

B. The Executive Board: Its Structure and Decision-Making Process

The Executive Board allows IMF Members to exercise control over the day-to-day operation of the Fund.[18] The mandate of the Executive Board is to conduct the business of the IMF. This means that the Executive Board is the policy organ of the IMF, oversees all of the Fund's lending operations,[19] and discusses at length all the issues related to the operation of the IMF, from periodic assessments of IMF Members' economies to economic policy topics of particular importance to the global economy. At its inaugural meeting, the Board of Governors virtually delegated all of its powers to the Executive Directors, except the discretion to admit new members and the power to change quotas.

The size of the Executive Board has increased as membership in the IMF has grown.[20] Initially made up of 12 members, the Executive Board now has 24 executive directors. Japan, Germany, France, the United Kingdom, Saudi Arabia, China, Russia, and the United States have representatives on the Executive Board. The other 16 executive directors represent various groupings of IMF Members and vote on behalf of their groups.[21]

Under Section C of the Rules and Regulations of the IMF, the IMF Managing Director has the power to call meetings of the Executive Board. If requested by an executive director, the Managing Director must call a meeting. The agenda of the Executive Board is set by the Managing Director, but any item requested by an executive director must be placed on the agenda. New agenda items can be included on condition of unanimity among executive directors present at the meeting.[22]

The decision-making process at the Executive Board is complex. Decisions by the Executive Board are taken on the basis of proposals tabled either by executive directors or by the IMF Managing Director. The Board operates through standing committees that the Executive Board can create on its own initiative.[23] These committees do not decide on behalf of the Executive Board, but make recommendations to it. Committees and subcommittees of the Executive Board do not engage in formal voting.

These committees allow executive directors to discuss issues in more detail before placing them before the Executive Board as a whole, to deliberate and make recommendations separately from those of IMF management, and to allocate responsibilities with an aim to increasing the Board's efficiency.[24]

In addition to standing committees, the Executive Board operates informally through the creation of ad hoc committees. This practice of informal committees has existed since the IMF's earliest days.[25] The purpose of informal committees is to allow executive directors to express ideas without worrying about speaking on behalf of their constituent Members. This also gives IMF staff the opportunity to canvass the views of executive directors, resulting in the refinement of proposals put to the Executive Board.[26] The ad hoc committee process has proven an invaluable tool in Executive Board decision-making.[27] Moreover, informal committees have also been used as a tool for deeper analysis and reflection when there are major disagreements among Executive Board members.[28] Ad hoc committees have also been set up to discuss particular issues between executive directors and staff when there have been different views between them.[29]

The foregoing discussion of the decision-making processes of the Executive Board and the IMFC demonstrates that both have horizontal and vertical dimensions. The horizontal dimension here refers to the Executive Board operating through standing and ad hoc committees of different composition, which creates input for the Board's deliberations and decisions. The horizontal dimension occurs among IMF Executive Board members, the IMFC, and management.

C. Voting in the IMF

The allocation of voting power has been one of the most criticized features of the IMF governance in recent years. Voting at the Executive Board is weighted according to quota contributions denominated in Special Drawing Rights (SDR). Each member has 250 basic votes and receive an additional vote for each SDR 100,000 of quota.[30] The United States has 16.77 percent of the total voting power in the IMF. Countries with more than 15 percent of the voting power have a de facto veto within the IMF.[31] This includes a veto over changes in the number of members of the Executive Board and amendments to the Articles of Agreement. Measured by the number of seats and compared to its voting power, the European Union is overrepresented on the Executive Board. Like the United States, the aggregated voting power of European Union countries at the IMF is sufficient to give the EU a veto.

The voting majority required to adopt a decision as the Executive Board varies with the type of decision being considered. Generally speaking, a simple majority is required. However, amendments adopted in the 1970s brought about an increase in the number of decisions that require a special majority of either 70 percent or, in some cases, 85 percent. Given that, as was mentioned, the 1970 reforms gave more discretion to the IMF, Members created certain safeguards to prevent abuse of discretion.[32] It was expected that groups of Members—developing countries, the European Members, and the United States—would have enough voting capacity to block decisions affecting their interests.

Recent reforms have introduced changes to the voting rules in order to respond to the significant criticism that the IMF has not given a sufficiently powerful voice to either emerging economies or developing and least developed countries. The process started in 2006, when the Fund increased the quota for China, Korea, Mexico, and Turkey. Under the new formula for the allocation of voting rights, 135 Members increased their voting power.[33] The reforms also included an increase in basic votes for low-income countries.[34]

Although executive directors have the right to call for a vote, current practice considers such a call impolite. This rejection of formal voting is attributable, in part, to the disproportionate voting power held by some Members.[35] Normally, the level of consensus required to adopt a decision is determined by the Managing Director, who ascertains the 'sense of the meeting'.[36] This sense is determined once all executive directors have had the opportunity to speak and to respond to the comments of other executive directors. Based on this discussion, the Managing Director produces a written summary of views in great detail, and the executive directors make comments, which are included in the written summary.[37] Even decisions that require a special majority are typically made by consensus, though Members' voting power does influence decision-making. When adopting the decision, executive directors and the Managing Director know what the final result would have been had a vote been called, and the IMF 'Secretariat keeps an informal record of the count of the vote'.[38]

Final decisions of the Board are carefully drafted and designed to reflect the views of as many executive directors as possible, while achieving effective outcomes.[39] A practice in the summary has developed that enhances the executive directors' role. First, summaries of decisions reflect all views, including minority views;[40] and second, summaries related to the Board's consultations with individual Members are disclosed as public information notices, subject to the Member in question's approval. Once approved, Executive Board decisions are then implemented by IMF staff.[41]

D. The Role of the Managing Director[42]

The Articles of Agreement do not say much about the Managing Director, other than to provide that he or she chairs the Executive Board, is to be selected by the Executive Board, and 'shall be chief of the operating staff of the Fund and shall conduct, under the direction of the Executive Board, the ordinary business of the Fund...'.[43] The Managing Director is in charge of the daily operations of the Fund in the sense that he or she executes the general policies approved by the Board, carries out economic surveillance of IMF Members, and designs the lending operations to countries in difficulty.

IMF Managing Directors have sought to expand the scope of their work beyond daily operations of the IMF. According to the first historian of the IMF, J. Keith Horsefield, 'The principal reason for the strengthening of the staff's position was that it had opportunities for exercising initiative, and took them'[44] during the first two decades of operation. In addition, Managing Directors have been a key actor in ensuring the Fund's effectiveness,[45] and their role has been adjusted in response to challenges in the world economy and to the particular personalities of those who have been appointed.[46]

E. Relations Between the Executive Board and Management

In 1948, the functions of the Executive Board and the Managing Directors were clarified. The Executive Board retained the power to formulate policy and to take decisions on major problems, and the Managing Director and the IMF staff were charged with the duty to study major problems that had to be resolved by the Board and to present conclusions and make recommendations in this regard.[47] The Managing Director and staff have also been responsible for executing Fund policies and handling negotiations with IMF Members.[48]

Over time, the role of the IMF staff has expanded considerably. This has been the result of a number of factors, including the provision of technical assistance and advice to Members and enhanced consultations between Members and the IMF staff in national capitals. Technical assistance has often provided outside of the scrutiny of the Executive Board, which allows IMF staff to gather information that was not otherwise available to the Executive Board.[49] As the relationship between IMF staff and Members evolved, executive directors increasingly found that issues were being resolved by the staff before the Executive Board took action.[50] Consultations between IMF staff and Members provided the opportunity for staff to assist Members in resolving policy difficulties on a regular basis.[51] Often, high-ranking officials or Members would consult in advance with staff about possible IMF reaction to proposed actions at the national level.[52]

Although this has been the general trend, the increase in the relative influence of IMF management and staff has been nuanced and involves a number of factors that must be properly understood. First, the importance of the role of the Managing Director does not mean that the degree of influence held by the Executive Board has not ebbed and flowed over time. Indeed, the relative clout of IMF management has not resulted in the Executive Board becoming a little more than a rubber stamp. Instead, the Executive Board has debated sometimes at great length suggestions by management[53] and has rejected important proposals by IMF staff.[54] On other occasions, the Board has accepted changes in policy recommended by staff, though the scope of the change has not always matched staff recommendations.

In recent years, key activities of the Fund, such as surveillance, which seem to be carried out by management exclusively in its interaction with local authorities, are in fact conducted under precise guidelines approved by the Executive Board.[55] The same can be said of decisions involving the use of Fund resources. Although the negotiations of the program with national authorities are delegated by the Board to management, and the former's involvement takes place at the end of the process, the Board's influence is felt because its adopted policies must be met in order for the program to be approved by the Board.[56]

In sum, although the relations between the Executive Board and the Managing Director are characterized by the pre-eminence of the latter, the former is still an important actor within the Fund's decision-making process.

F. The Steering of the IMF

Although the Managing Director plays a significant role in guiding the organization, the IMF remains an intergovernmental organization. Members play the central role in decision-making within the IMF. In practice, the IMF has been steered by the G10, led by the United States; then by the G5; and today by the G7 (comprising France, Germany, Japan, the United Kingdom, Canada, Italy, and the United States).[57] The Independent Evaluation Office (IEO) of the IMF has criticized the significant influence that large members have on the day-to-day operation of the IMF, with the Asian crisis of the 1990s highlighted as a major example.[58]

The situation is different for borrowing countries. Not only do they not steer the IMF, but the Fund has some degree of power to direct their economic policies. Borrowing countries depend on the Fund's endorsement of their policies to have access to capital markets.[59]

A review of each of the relevant organs of the Fund illustrates that the Board of Governors is, due to its size, unable to provide meaningful political guidance. However, it has addressed this deficiency by creating, first, the Interim Committee and then the IMFC, which evolved from an advisory body to a genuine locus of decision-making.[60] As for the Executive Board, recent analysis has shown that, although it has delegated much of its powers to management, it has retained its character as a decision-making body, particularly in key areas of the operation of the Fund, such as surveillance and the use of the IMF resources.[61]

A historical evaluation of the operation of the governance structure and operation of the Fund reveals some of their shortcomings. The IMF has not always been able to ensure that key Members observe prudent economic policies; voting rights have been slow to reflect contemporary economic realities; and the Fund's contingencies for grave financial crises, such as those of Latin America in the 1980s and Russia and Asia in the 1990s, have been widely criticized. The issue of a democratic deficit has arisen, associated with developing countries' lack of influence within the Fund's decision-making process.[62] Finally, the IMF has been unable to anticipate systemic crises, such as the current crisis caused by the U.S. housing market.[63]

However, the current economic crisis has provided an opportunity for the re-emergence of the IMF as an important actor in the international financial system. In order to allow it to provide financial support to members affected, Japan has loaned the IMF U.S. $100 billion.[64] The IMF is seeking to double its lending base to U.S. $500 billion.[65] In addition, the ongoing crisis seems to have finally added momentum to additional governance reform, including addressing a democratic deficit. A realization within the Fund is emerging that that developing country members and other emerging economies deserve more of a say within the decision-making process and that the time has come for Europe to accept that it is overrepresented in the IMF.[66]

Finally, a meaningful comparative analysis between the IMF and WTO must take into account the ongoing reform process at the Fund and the main criticisms that have been raised regarding the IMF's governance structure and operation. In the IEO's views, the Executive Board should play a supervisory role and should provide strategic guidance and focus less on an executive role so as to enhance accountability within the organization.[67] As for the IMFC, the IEO has recommended its replacement with the council established under the Articles of Agreement, which should decide by consensus and only exceptionally by voting.[68] The IEO has also suggested that the Executive Board focus on supervising management, restricting its executive functions to systemic issues,[69] and that Board committees should always be chaired by an Executive Director.[70]

The IEO has also made recommendations to the functioning of Executive Board committees. In an attempt to enhance the role played by developing country members, one recommendation is to have the council chair rotate, so as to allow representatives from these countries to be appointed to this position.[71] In addition, the IEO is of the view that council members could split their votes to reflect different views in their constituencies.[72] Additionally, it has been suggested that Executive Directors should all be elected, eliminating the current five appointed directors representing the five largest shareholders. Such a move would open the possibility of reducing the representation problem present in some constituencies with a significant number of Members, thereby improving voice and representation.[73] Put together, the IEO's reform proposals seek to achieve a balance between effectiveness, accountability, and voice within the IMF governance.[74]

Likewise, the High-Level Panel on IMF Board Accountability has made important recommendations to improve the accountability of both the Executive Board and the Managing Director. One proposal that was advanced was to create a committee to oversee the performance of the Executive Board. The Executive Board should also create a process for assessing the Management Director's performance, overseen by a Board Committee.[75]

In addition to these reforms, others have emphasized the need for the IMF's to increase its legitimacy by engaging with legislatures. The Executive Board has endorsed such an approach:

> The Working Group encouraged Executive Directors and staff to continue their outreach efforts to and emphasized the importance of an ongoing dialogue with national legislators for the Fund's work. The Working Group agreed that greater interaction between the legislators and the Fund would be particularly beneficial to the Fund, as it would help build understanding of economic reforms and IMF programs, and could provide a useful avenue for informing and receiving comments from legislators about the work of the Fund and its role in the international financial system in general. Directors emphasized that the Fund's outreach should be a two-way dialogue and that it was just as important to listen to legislators. They considered that the focus should be on broader policy or regional issues instead of country issues, given the Fund's mandate to promote global financial stability and growth. Directors recognized that the impact of our outreach will only be evident over time, and will require a prolonged effort.[76]

The reform process and the overall strengthening of the IMF have been expedited in recent months owing to the current financial crisis. The G20 agreed in London on 2 April 2009 to make available for the IMF substantial additional resources to foster growth in developing country and emerging market economies. These new resources are the following: (1) $250 billion immediately available and up to $500 billion; (2) further progress in the implementation of the IMF Flexible Credit Line and its amended lending and conditionality requirements available to IMF members to cope with balance of payments financing difficulties; (3) a new general SDR allocation of $250 billion aimed at increasing global liquidity.[77]

The G20 has also committed itself to press for reforms of both the IMF and the Bank in their governance, mandate, and scope

> to reflect changes in the world economy and the new challenges of globalization, and ... emerging and developing countries, including the poorest, must have greater voice and representation. This must be accompanied by action to increase the credibility and accountability of the institutions.[78]

As to the particular steps related to the reform process, the G20 has agreed to ensure that the Board of Governors provides more strategic direction to the Executive Board and IMF management and to increase the IMF's accountability.[79] Finally, the G20 has determined that the selection process of the IMF Managing Director and senior IMF staff will be carried out in a more transparent way.

Having described the basic overall decision-making structure in the IMF, illustrated some of its most significant weaknesses, and described some of the suggested reforms, this chapter now looks at IMF decision-making in certain specific contexts. This more detailed view will allow consideration of the decision-making processes employed to address specific types of issues.[80]

G. Decision-Making for the Adoption of Specific Decisions

1. Decisions Regarding Reforms to the Articles of Agreement

Amending the Articles of Agreement requires the approval of the Board of Governors. However, the Executive Board and IMF management have also played a role in this process, which is far from surprising given their mandates and their knowledge of both the organization and its Members.

For instance, the second amendment of the Fund's Articles of Agreement was initially discussed by the ad hoc Committee of Twenty, an informal committee of the Board of Governors. The committee's proposals were adopted by the Board of Governors, which in 1974 established the specific areas of the Articles to be amended and ordered the Executive Board to prepare a draft.[81] It is important to mention that, despite the fact that the Committee of Twenty was unable to agree, it kept the process moving by ordering the Executive Board to present proposals. In other words, the Executive Board was used as a *forum* to debate those issues upon which the Committee of Twenty did not reach consensus.[82] When the Executive Board was unable to achieve agreement, it sought further advice from the Interim Committee of the Board of Governors.[83]

Management was also deeply involved in the decision-making process for the second amendment of the Articles of Agreement. Once the Committee of Twenty determined the issues that the second amendment should deal with, management prepared a memorandum for discussion by the Executive Board, which was constantly redrafted during the course of these negotiations.[84] Also worth mentioning is one of the ways in which management acted during these deliberations. It sought to frame the scope of some of the issues to be amended according to the instructions provided by the Committee of Twenty.[85] Subsequently, management acted as a broker by suggesting alternatives in light of deliberations within the Executive Board,[86] which significantly contributed to generating consensus.

2. Decisions Concerning IMF General Policies[87]

Introducing new policies and amending those already in place at the IMF begins with a Governor's initiative or a set of Governors acting together at an annual meeting.[88] When a Governor takes the initiative, he or she has already discussed the issue with his or her own government or group of governments, and the given executive director follows up on the idea. Usually, proposals made by Governors give the Managing Director the opportunity to press for reforms that have already been discussed within the Fund.[89] Once the need for a new policy is established, the work begins for the staff, Managing Director, Executive Directors, and Board of Governors.[90]

Executive Directors can request revisions of any of the policies of the Fund at any time. This is true even if there is no a mandatory review clause inserted in the respective decision or policy,[91] which gives executive directors significant institutional power to shape the IMF's policy. If the issue is raised during meetings of the Executive Board, an informal committee of staff from different departments is created to assess the topic.

If the need for a new policy is identified by staff as a result of the performance of their functions of surveillance or advice, the issue is first examined by a small group of senior officials, usually the Managing Director, the Deputy Managing Director, the General Counsel, the head of the Research Department, and other staff members.[92] If additional study is required, the issue is assigned to a department, which prepares analytical papers that are sent to the Board for informational purposes only.

At this stage of the process of the design of a new policy identified by staff, the Executive Board starts getting involved through informal meetings in which the general policy is discussed and alternatives evaluated. Staff participates in such meetings. While this process is going on, the Managing Director may start exploring the views and reactions of Governors, particularly those in the Group of Ten. Once the Managing Director is sure of the Governors' support, the new policy is put before the Executive Board.[93]

In recent years, the preparation and discussion of policies have involved both the Board and management over a period of several months. Policy proposals are approved by Board consensus.[94]

In sum, the policy amendment and formulation process at the IMF is both top-down and bottom-up. The process is also flexible in the sense that, in the case of bottom-up decision-making, management consults with the Executive Board and the Group of Ten on alternatives to facilitate a decision. Furthermore, the decision-making process is intertwined at three levels of the Fund: G10, Executive Board, and management. Finally, management has been involved in the development of new policies, regardless of who identified the need.

3. Decisions Regarding Budgetary Issues

According to Section 20 of the By-Laws of the IMF, the IMF Managing Director sets the agenda with regard to the IMF budget and has to present the IMF annual administrative budget to the IMF Executive Board for approval. However, the Executive Board analyzes the budget in detail prior to approving it.[95]

Budgetary issues are discussed by the Standing Committee on the Budget, created in 1994 and chaired by the Managing Director.[96] The creation of the standing committee signalled the Executive Board's desire to engage the budget process at an early stage. There have been tensions between management and the Executive Board regarding the precise role of the committee and its terms of reference,[97] with executive directors seeking a more active role and Managing Directors attempting to preserve their power by submitting the budget proposal to the Executive Board for its approval at the final stages of the process of elaboration.[98] Management has ensured that it retains control over the committee not only by holding the chair, but by ensuring that committee membership be restricted to a one-year term.[99]

As can be seen, the decision-making process for budgetary issues is significantly different than the process employed for policy development. Management plays a lead, if not central role in the formulation of the IMF budget. The Executive Board is struggling for a more decisive voice, but its contribution to the Fund's budget-setting process remains marginal.

H. Summary Regarding Decision-Making Processes

From the foregoing discussion, a number of broad observations can be made about IMF decision-making.

1. The Board of Governors, the Executive Board, and IMF management play different roles, depending on the subject matter.

First, the Board of Governors does not decide in full and on its own, as expected, and has delegated its powers to informal committees of the Board, the Interim Committee, and even sometimes the Executive Board, providing it with specific instructions.

Second, the Executive Board does not always play the same role in all decision-making processes. There are occasions in which the Executive Board is the dominant voice (decisions related to the Fund's policies), others in which it functions under the specific guidelines provided by the Board of Governors or the Steering Committee (determinations regarding amendments to the Articles), and finally, others in which the Executive Board has no meaningful voice (budgetary issues).

Third, the Managing Director's role in decision-making is variable. Sometimes this involves following the instructions of G10 countries and at other times this role equals that of the Executive Directors or is at least as influential (decisions regarding changes to the IMF's policies). There are also decision-making processes in which the Managing Director is the dominant player (budgetary determinations and decisions related to Members' policies, among others).

2. IMF management is regularly involved in virtually all decision-making processes and can trigger the adoption of political decisions, such as determinations related to IMF policies.

3. The initiative to trigger decision-making processes resides with a number of actors: the Governor or group of Governors, the Executive Director or a group of Executive Directors, and the Managing Director.

The subject matter of the decision has conditioned the nature of the actor that can trigger the decision-making process. The greater the political character of the decision to be made, the higher the increased involvement of IMF's political organs. The higher the technical nature of the decision, the lower the level of the IMF hierarchy that—as a matter of reality—can trigger the decision-making process.

In sum, IMF decision-making is context-specific. It is sufficiently flexible to meet organizational needs and seems to acknowledge the need to involve different actors depending on the subject of the decision.

III. The Governance of the World Bank

The World Bank provides financial and technical assistance to developing and least developed countries and loans at market interest rates to developing and least developed countries. Its main organs are the Board of Governors, the Board of Directors, and its internal management, headed by the President. Today, the World Bank has 185 Members, which can be divided into two basic categories: non-borrowing Members, namely, industrialized states; and borrowing Members, namely, developing and least developed countries.

Pursuant to Article V(2) of the Articles of Agreement, all the powers of the World Bank are vested in the Board of Governors. Each World Bank Member appoints a representative to the Board of Governors for a five-year term. Decisions by the Board are taken by majority vote. The Board of Governors has delegated most of its powers to the Board of Directors, though it retains the power to admit new members, increase or decrease the bank's capital stock, and to suspend members.[100]

A. The Board of Directors: Its Structure and Decision-Making Process

The World Bank's Board of Directors has three main functions: to approve funding projects for World Bank Members submitted by the Bank President, to determine the general policies that must be followed in the operation of the Bank, and to inform the Board of Governors of the World Bank's activities.[101]

The Board of Directors, originally composed of 12 members, currently has 24 directors. Five members are appointed by the largest shareholders—France, the United Kingdom, the United States, Japan, and Germany. The remaining 19 directors are elected by Members through the formation of constituencies of Member States.[102] The President of the World Bank is selected by the Board of Directors[103] and can attend Board meetings. The President votes at Board meetings only in the event of a tie.

The Board of Directors operates through five standing committees: the Audit Committee, Budget Committee, Personnel Committee, Committee on Development Effectiveness (CODE), and Committee on Governance and Executive Directors' Administrative Matters.[104] Executive directors are members of one of more of these committees in addition to being members of the Steering Committee.[105] The Board's work program is annually determined by the Corporate Secretariat in consultation with the Steering Committee and management.[106] Committees do not adopt decisions on behalf of the Board. However, contrary to IMF practice, they are always chaired by executive directors.[107] In addition, the procedure for the operation of the Bank's committees is more elaborate than at the IMF. Once a committee end its deliberations, a detailed summary identifying their views is prepared by staff. This summary is presented to committee members for comments and is not public. The summary specifies those issues the committee has reached consensus on and those that require further deliberation by the Board.[108]

Membership in committees is determined by the President, who nominates executive directors for the Board to appoint. Committee membership usually comprises eight executive directors, four each from borrowing and non-borrowing bank members.[109] This practice attenuates the voting power within the Board's decision-making process.[110]

Informality is a central feature of the World Bank's decision-making processes. The World Board's unofficial meetings, referred to by various names, help to provide the Board of Directors with advice and guidance.[111]

B. Voting in the World Bank

The World Bank has a system of decision-making based on weighted voting, in which each member country possesses 250 votes plus one additional vote for each share it has in the World Bank's capital stock.[112] North American and European countries have always had significant voting power. In 1947, they cast 74 percent of total votes; in 1971, they cast 61 percent. New members, coming from Africa, Asia, and the Middle East, have increased their voting power from 15 percent in 1947 to 28 percent. Latin American voting power has remained virtually unchanged, at approximately 8.3 percent.[113] This means that the G10, constituting the Bank's major shareholders, has enough of a majority (more than 50 percent of the votes) to adopt decisions within the Board of Governors and has veto power regarding amendments to the Articles of Agreement, although the group lacks the majority to push for such amendments, which require 85 percent of the votes.[114] Although all World Bank Members possess the right to vote, as Foch states, '[n]ot all can make their voice heard and weigh on the decision making'.[115]

Despite the fact that the Board of Directors has a system of weighted voting, the Board decides on the basis of consensus, and few decisions are put to a vote. However, the composition of the Board does determine what issues are brought to the Board and how they are decided.[116] As Griffith-Jones notes, '[i]ndirectly, consensus does reflect the voting power of member countries'.[117] In fact, former Bank officials have accepted that, when their five largest shareholders agree on a particular issue, the Board adopts their position as a decision.[118] Consequently, the G10 has a de facto power to influence the assignment of funds and their conditionality clauses.[119]

C. The President and Management

According to Article V(5) of the Articles of Agreement, the President acts under the direction of the Board of Directors. In practice, however, the President is in charge of the day-to-day operation of the Bank and is the head of management, which, under the guidance of the Board of Directors, is in charge of loans, guarantees, new policies, country assistance strategies, borrowing, and financial determinations.[120]

Given that the World Bank gets its resources from the financial community and not from governments, the President enjoys broad discretion and less political supervision by members.[121] Past Presidents have worked to expand the role of their office, particularly during the Bank's early years. During the World Bank's first 25 years, long-term and short-term borrowing increased and expanded into new areas such as education, agriculture, water, and family planning. This was well beyond the initial conception of lending for electric power and transportation projects: a view still held by some Bank Members.[122]

D. Relations between the Board of Directors and the President

Since its early years, the independence of management from the Board in the day-to-day operations of the World Bank has been a pre-eminent institutional characteristic.[123] Among the factors that have contributed to this significant independence are the expansion of the World Bank's responsibilities and the limited tenure in office of executive directors.[124] As a result, the President has significant power to steer the organization. It is the President who generally sets the agenda for the meetings of Board of Directors and, therefore, determines what issues the Board will decide on and when. Moreover, the President has broad discretion regarding budgetary procedures, procurement, and personnel.[125] Importantly, the President is also vested with the power to make recommendations on policy matters, which may or may not be adopted by the executive directors.[126]

However, the President's power is not without its limits. First, although the President has some control over the Board of Executive Directors' agenda, such control faces some restrictions. When a proposed course of action faces significant opposition by influential executive directors, the President often delays the inclusion of the topic on the agenda of the Board.[127] In this circumstance, it is the Board that has the power, as a matter of reality, to determine when issues will be included on the agenda by the President.

Second, historians of the World Bank have noted that the role of the Board has often been determined by the personality of the President. A strong President tends to result in Boards that feel they must act as a brake on the President.[128] Therefore, Presidents have not been able to reign at will over the Executive Board or Board of Directors.

In sum, the President is certainly the dominant voice in his relationship with the Board, but that voice may be strong or weak depending on a number of circumstances.

E. The Steering of the World Bank

The fact that the President, not the Board of Directors, runs the World Bank has not prevented large shareholders from having significant influence in the day-to-day operations of the Bank.[129] The influence of the United States is important, despite the fact that its contributions and voting power have declined.[130] In total, non-borrowing members possess 62 percent of the votes at the World Bank.[131] On the other hand, developing and least developed countries lack influence because of their lack of collective action and their lack of involvement in the management of the organization. Borrowing countries do not vote against loans, fearing that the reasons justifying such refusals may apply to them in the future.[132]

The functioning of the World Bank illustrates that one of its major institutional weaknesses is its inability to give borrowing countries a more prominent voice in the decision-making process. The World Bank has received broad criticism for this and is in the process of addressing it in its reform process.

There are two types of changes that have been suggested and/or already implemented to enhance the voice and participation of developing countries in the decision-making process of the World Bank: structural and non-structural.[133] The following are the non-structural options recommended by the Development Committee (created by both the IMF and the World Bank):

1. Higher representation of staff from developing countries in the World Bank's senior management;
2. A communications dimension in projects funded by the World Bank;[134]
3. Enhanced Board effectiveness;[135]
4. An increased role in the appointment of the President;
5. Length of executive directors' tenure;[136] and
6. Capacity building in executive directors' offices.

The recommended structural reforms include changing (1) the World Bank's voting structure, (2) the World Bank's capital stock, (3) the composition of the Board of Directors,[137] and (4) special majorities.

Another recommendation that has been made is to establish particular majorities regarding a set of decisions in which the substantial support of developing and transition countries would be required.[138] Also, there has been discussion about certain decisions being taken only if approved by a majority of developing and transition members (double majority).[139]

As with the IMF, the G20 has decided to directly involve the World Bank in finding solutions to the ongoing financial crisis by speeding up the Bank's reform process under the same guiding principles of the reform of the IMF: to update mandates and governance; to increase the voice of developing and emerging members; and to enhance the Bank's accountability.[140] In addition, and to respond to the impact the crisis is having on developing countries, the Bank, supported by the G20, has launched the Global Trade Liquidity Program to provide support to exporters and importers in countries of this character. The initiative has $50 billion available to achieve its objective.[141]

Overall, a review of the history of the operation of the bank yields mixed reviews. To some, the Bank has helped borrowing Members to develop through an outward-looking policy. However, those opposing such a policy criticize the Bank for a lack of results and for its lack of attention to equity and the environment. The World Bank has also changed its focus over the years. Sometimes it had prioritized growth through trade and foreign investment. Today its goal is to fight poverty in developing and the least developed countries. In recent years, and until the current financial crisis, the World Bank has become a less important player for Members. Many middle-income countries did not need the World Bank since they could obtain funding in the financial markets; others simply no longer required its loans.[142] However, the current crisis may well mean a revival of the World Bank, which is actively involved in helping countries in difficult circumstances.[143]

F. Decision-Making for the Adoption of Specific Decisions

1. Decisions Regarding Bank Policies

A change in Bank policy may come from a management initiative. The change is subject to a deep analysis followed by a report authored by a top official. The report is then discussed internally within the Managing Committee. Once the report has been fully debated, and even if there is no consensus on it, it is sent to the Board of Directors for informal discussion at the Board's seminars.[144] Generally, the Board discusses policy papers twice. First, it debates the principles of the policy and then the policy itself.[145]

In recent years, the decision-making process for changes to the Bank's policies has often been triggered by management, in particular by the Operations Policy and Country Services vice-presidency. Management prepares a draft, which is circulated for comments to internal and external experts, clients, and stakeholders, such as NGOs. The outcome of this process is then submitted for additional comments to the responsible units and then to managing directors and ultimately to the Board of Directors.[146]

The Bank President has significant control over the agenda in respect of Bank policies. By the time proposals have arrived for informal discussion before the Board, they have been fully debated by management and have added legitimacy as a result of consultations with outside stakeholders.

2. Decision-Making for Loans to Members

The decision-making process for loans starts when the Bank designs a Country Assistance Strategy (CAS) for a given Member. The strategy details the financial and technical assistance the Bank is willing to grant a Member and the projects that may be carried out to achieve the strategy's objectives. Bank Members participate in the elaboration of their CAS. Members are in charge of preparing projects, but they are nonetheless assisted by the Bank. Once the project is approved by the Member, negotiations about the conditions of the loan start. Operational personnel from the Bank prepare Project Evaluation Documents (PED) and Program Documents (PD), which are submitted to the President, who decides when to submit them to the Board.[147]

Before making a loan, the executive directors, in particular the executive director who was elected by the Member that is the borrower or guarantor of the loan, approve all the documents. Such approvals are understood to mean that the Board—which is the interpreter of the Articles of Agreement—regards the transaction as falling within the sphere of the Articles.[148]

Loan approvals have certain dynamics, though. The Board is reluctant not to approve a loan on the terms negotiated by the President and management, since not approving could be seen as a vote of no confidence in the country seeking the loan, and in management's handling of the loan program. Nonetheless, the Board has instruments to make its voice heard, such as requesting that the President and management not include certain issues in a future loan[149] or requiring information early in the negotiating process between the Bank and a Member seeking a loan.[150] Generally speaking, the Board asks questions, identifies problems, and discourages initiatives that members may not be ready to adopt.[151] But the role of some executive directors in loan approvals may go well beyond this stage and include a role during the negotiations themselves—for example, requiring management to speed up or give priority to certain loans the directors are concerned about.[152]

G. Summary

Some features of the World Bank's decision-making process during its history have been the following:

- A Governor or group of Governors may trigger the decision-making process at the Board of Governors level.
- Some political decisions by the Board of Governors level include interacting with Board of Directors, who, under the guidance of Governors, analyze issues and develop proposals that are sent back to the Governors for deliberation and decision.

- Some decision-making processes, particular those related to loans to Member States, take place at various levels simultaneously: Management, in consultation with the given elected executive director, negotiates with the member concerned.
- Management is usually involved in all decisions and has the power to take the initiative and trigger decision-making processes within the World Bank. In addition, the President can be an important ally of Governors in the political process, leading to the inclusion of their issues within their Board of Governor's agenda.
- Finally, the significance of the influence of the Board of Directors varies, depending on the type of decision at hand. Sometimes, it plays an important role (particularly when it approves an operation but asks that certain issues not be included in future loans). But in others, particularly in cases where major World Bank Members deal directly with the President, it plays a limited role.

IV. Proposals for Reform of the WTO Internal Management in Light of Those of the IMF and the World Bank[153]

Having described some features of the operation of the IMF and the World Bank, this section seeks to use this experience to improve proposals already made to enhance the WTO internal management and its decision-making process. Any WTO Member that relies on the experience of the IMF or World Bank must take account of the current trends in institutional design, characterized not only by concerns for efficiency but also for proper representation of developing and least developed countries.

A. Creation of a WTO Consultative Body

There has been a recommendation to create a consultative body within the WTO decision-making process.[154] Suggestions regarding the mandate and composition vary among authors. On one hand, the Sutherland Report, recommends the creation of a consultative body to be chaired and convened by the WTO Director-General. Ministers or senior officials would participate in this body.[155] Blackhurst and Hartridge share this view and suggest that the body would lack decision-making power.[156] However, Steger and Shpilkovskaya go further and suggest that this body should have advisory, executive, and supervisorial roles.[157] Common ground among these authors is that membership cannot be exclusive and that, on the contrary, it must be fully representative of the whole WTO Membership.

The experience of the IMF's IMFC provides support for the creation of a consultative body within the WTO to improve the effectiveness of its decision-making process. Such experience can be valuable in two ways: first, it illustrates how the body could function to introduce new dynamics to trade negotiations in order to break deadlocks; and, second, the IMFC's experience could guide WTO Members in determining the profile of those individuals appointed to the body.

As to the first, the combination of delegation with instructions from the IMFC to the Executive Board has sometimes made inter-state negotiations in the IMF possible. The ability of the IMF Executive Board to go back to the IMFC to assess progress and agree on new instructions for the former has introduced new dynamism to decision-making processes within the Fund, and it has been a valuable process in overcoming deadlock. A similar interaction could take place between the WTO Ministerial Conference and a WTO consultative body concerning the negotiation of new trade rounds, but also between the consultative body and the Councils of Trade in Goods and Services, and the Council for TRIPS.[158] In effect, WTO councils or committees could also advance issues for further negotiations before the consultative body regarding topics for which consensus is elusive within the councils or committees.

Second, if the WTO body, either consultative or executive, is to play a meaningful role in improving the efficiency of the operation of the WTO decision-making process, the experience of the IMFC regarding its composition could be relevant. The IMFC is made up of IMF governors, namely, finance ministers or heads of central banks. It is the combination of the knowledge and domestic political power of the IMFC's members that has permitted it to become such a significant actor within the IMF's decision-making process. Consequently, the WTO consultative body should be made up of trade ministers capable of making their voices heard within the WTO and their national government. The body would then provide ministerial-level advice to the Ministerial Conference, the General Council, the WTO Director-General, and other WTO political bodies.[159]

As to the mandate, the consultative body could be asked to provide advice regarding mainly issues in a round of negotiations and concerning the implementation of the existing covered agreements. Such a body should have 24 to 30 members and be truly representative of the WTO Membership. Finally, to be able to play a meaningful role within the WTO, the consultative body or its members should be allowed to trigger decision-making processes in particular circumstances.[160] Or, at a minimum, the understanding in creating the body should avoid constraints triggering more formal decision-making and allow the body initiative to evolve through interactions with the Director-General.

B. New Role for the Director-General and the Secretariat

The Sutherland Report, Steger and Shpilkovskaya, and others have proposed enhancing the role of the WTO Director-General (DG) and the Secretariat.[161] Perhaps the only insight that the history of the World Bank and the IMF can offer to WTO Managing Directors is that IMF Managing Directors and World Bank Presidents have been willing to take advantage of the opportunities they have found to increase the institutional relevance of their positions. DGs should behave in a similar way. They have done so recently. For instance, Director-General Panitchpakdi set some precedents that, in addition to seeking the achievement of important objectives of the Organization, had as a side effect the enhancing of the Director-General. Examples of this include the establishment of the consultative board that rendered the Sutherland Report and the creation of an NGO advisory body. The Sutherland Report did not receive the attention it deserved, nor was the NGO Advisory Body well received, even by prominent NGOs, who decided not to participate in it.[162] Nonetheless, these two attempts constitute examples that may have some precedential value and that add to past experiences that show that DGs have some margin of action.

Another potential and more effective way in which the DG and the Secretariat's institutional position within the Organization can be enhanced is by identifying the type of decisions in which their role can be more prominent.[163] This approach is directly drawn from the experience of the IMF and the World Bank, in which the roles of both managements within decision-making processes vary according to the type of decision in question.

However, before attempting to tackle this subject, it is important to link the issue of the enhancement of the DG and the Secretariat to the context of the ongoing reform of the Bretton Woods institutions: any enhancement must take place on the condition that both the DG and the Secretariat act as neutral players and do not openly or covertly favour positions adopted by developed country Members, which has not always been the case. In effect, according to Nordström, the Secretariat has sometimes been perceived by developing countries as advancing developed countries' positions.[164] If the DG and the Secretariat are not seen as neutral players, any attempt to enhance their institutional position will be doomed by developing and least developed countries' opposition.[165]

The WTO Secretariat has the capacity to take make important contributions to the WTO decision-making process and to play a more important role. Indeed, the Secretariat is present in all WTO spheres of action and, consequently, possesses a wide and complete view of the Organization. In effect, the Secretariat participates in all negotiations, in the implementation of each of the covered agreements, and in dispute settlement proceedings at the panel level. In addition, it carries out the trade review of all WTO Members and provides technical assistance to developing and least developed members. Undoubtedly, it is an actor with knowledge of the four corners of the WTO and is in a position to identify needs for change at various levels of the Organization.

Having said this, this chapter turns to identify the type of decision-making processes in which the Secretariat should be given a more active role: those related to internal secondary normativity, secondary soft law, and binding decisions concerning technical issues.

1. The Secretariat and Internal Secondary Normativity

Footer defines this kind of norm as the rules and procedures for meetings of WTO political bodies or other matters of internal procedure.[166] This legal category, in principle, does not create rights and obligations for WTO Members, and therefore, there are factual differences for a distinct decision-making process in which the Secretariat can seize the initiative and play a more active role.

The practice of the Organization reveals that the role of the Secretariat in the design of these rules has been at times more important. Footer specifically refers to the 1995 Technical Note on the Accession Process,[167] which contains a practical guide for WTO Members to carry out accession negotiations as an example of this situation.

2. The Secretariat and Its Initiative Regarding Secondary Soft Law

There should also be some room for the Secretariat to take the initiative regarding non-binding secondary rules, or secondary soft law. As Footer states with great precision, soft law may not be legally binding but may be legally relevant.[168] The notion of soft law requires certain clarification. In her words,

> In the WTO context soft law may be addressed to the membership collectively, or occasionally to individual Members. Primary soft law has a normative content but where it differs from primary hard law is that it has *not* been adopted in treaty form. It may declare new norms—sometimes intended as a precursor to the adoption of a later hard treaty text—or it may elaborate or reaffirm norms previously set forth in binding or non-binding instruments.[169]

This soft law is expressed in the issuing of recommendations and comments by supervisory or monitoring bodies[170] and has in fact already played different roles in the WTO, such as supplementing hard rules or precursors to 'hard law'.[171] The WTO Secretariat could go further in taking the initiative to produce external non-binding regulations, and it is in a privileged position to do so.[172] Given that this kind of norm does not create new rights and obligations, the Secretariat could well be in a position to exert initiative if it sees the need to do so and to be an active participant in the decision-making process.

3. The Secretariat and Binding WTO Law Regarding Technical Issues

It was seen in the first two parts of this chapter that the more technical the issue, the more initiative that managements at both the IMF and the Bank have had to trigger decision-making processes related to the given subject matter. As was illustrated, this situation has its roots in the fact that the Bank's and IMF's staff gain important knowledge of members on the basis of the negotiations for the selection, design, approval, and execution of the Bank's projects or by virtue of the consultations between IMF staff and country authorities regarding their macroeconomic policies.

Could the Secretariat be in a position in which it had privileged access to technical information that could allow it to identify technical issues that require new rules, the fine-tuning of the existing ones, or outright changes? Yes, the Secretariat is usually involved in dealing with complex technical issues such as discussion in relevant WTO political bodies at different levels, ongoing negotiations, trade review reports carried out by the Secretariat,[173] dispute settlement, and implementation of the covered agreements. These channels give the Secretariat privileged information regarding the identification of technical issues that require adjustment, which offers the Secretariat the opportunity to trigger decision-making processes aimed at this result. Thus the Secretariat could start the process within the competent WTO political body and the given process could move up into the hierarchical ladder to the General Council or the Ministerial Conference.[174]

In sum, it can be said that there are areas in which the enhancing of the role of the Secretariat may face less resistance by WTO Members, such as the issuing of internal regulation and secondary soft law, and the fine-tuning or modification of binding rules regarding certain technical issues. The DG and the Secretariat could draw on these gains in institutional relevance to expand their roles to other areas of WTO hard law so as to contribute to increasing the efficiency of the WTO decision-making process. However, there is a precondition for this project to have a chance of success: the Secretariat's neutrality, in the sense that it must be perceived by Members to act in each particular occasion with due consideration for the specific positions adopted by members of all kinds.

Although it is known that the Secretariat can informally take some initiative,[175] the ultimate question is whether the Secretariat has the legal authorization to trigger WTO decision-making processes. To begin with, the functioning of international organizations and their organs would be seriously impaired if they could exclusively carry out those actions they have been explicitly authorized to do. Instead, the authorization can be implicit, and it can be found in Article III.1 of the Marrakesh Agreement Establishing the World Trade Organization, providing for the functions of the WTO to be read in the context of its objectives. Thus, as long as the Secretariat, as expected, is exerting initiative within any of the functions of the WTO and to favour one of its objectives, it is possible to state that the Secretariat has sufficient legal grounds to do so. Obviously, any final determination will rest within the authority of the WTO membership.

V. Conclusion

The chapter has shown that an assessment of the history of the World Bank and the IMF regarding their operations and of the relations between their Boards and managements can offer some lessons to improve on the recommendations to enhance the WTO decision-making process. Such lessons have not been drawn on the basis of a mechanistic comparative approach. On the contrary, the analysis carried out in this chapter has taken into account, first, the particularities of the World Bank's and IMF's mandates and goals; and second, the current trends in international institutional design, marked not only by concerns for efficiency but also for the appropriate representation of developing and least developed countries.

On these bases, this chapter has concluded that the IMF IMFC's experience provides further support for the creation of a consultative body in the WTO as a potential valuable decision-making organ capable of breaking deadlocks in trade negotiations. In addition, the above-mentioned experience also suggests that to achieve this result, the WTO consultative body should be made up of trade ministers.

Finally, the chapter has also illustrated that the IMF's and World Bank's past operation can be useful to give content to the proposal for enhancing the institutional position of the WTO Director-General and the Secretariat. In particular, the experience of the World Bank's and the Fund's management—which has defined their different roles, depending on the type of decision in question—can guide the search for situations in which the strengthening of the WTO Secretariat can take place. These situations are the decision-making process for the adoption of internal procedural norms for some operations of WTO political bodies, secondary non-binding rules, and exceptionally, for binding rules of a technical nature. Regarding this set of determinations, the Secretariat should be recognized as able to exert certain initiatives in triggering decision-making processes within the WTO.

Notes

1 The historical assessment this chapter presents is largely based on the official histories of the IMF and the Bank concerning the evolution of the decision-making bodies of these two international organizations, the development of the relations between such bodies during certain epochs, and how decision-making processes have been conducted as to certain types of determinations at particular times. A complete analysis of all those issues from a full historical perspective and for both the IMF and the Bank goes well beyond the scope of this chapter.

2 Alexander Mountford, 'The Formal Governance Structure of the International Monetary Fund', Independent Evaluation Office. International Monetary Fund. Background Paper BP/08/01. at 6, http://ieo-imf.org/eval/complete/pdf/05212008/BP08_01.pdf (visited 19 February 2009).

3 Ibid, at 6.

4 See Margaret de Vries, 'The Process of Policy Making' in Margaret G. de Vries and J. Keith Hosefield (eds), The International Monetary Fund 1945–1965 (Washington: International Monetary Fund, 1969) vol. 2, 6, and James M. Boughton, Silent Revolution: The International Monetary Fund 1979–1989 (Washington: International Monetary Fund, 2001) 1022.

5 Daniel D. Bradlow, 'The Governance of the IMF: The Need for Comprehensive Reform', at 7 (Presentation given at the meeting of the G24 Technical Committee, September 2006, on file with author).

6 See http://www.imf.org/external/index.htm (visited 21 February 2009).

7 See IMF, 'As Contingency, IMF Aims to Double Its Lendable Resources' 2 February 2009, http://www.imf.org/external/pubs/ft/survey/so/2009/POL020209A.htm (visited 18 February 2009).

8 See Stefan Wagstyl, 'How Not to Annoy Someone from Central or Eastern Europe', Financial Times, 27 February 2009, http://www.ft.com/cms/s/0/5618118a-0507-11 de-8166-000077b07658.html (visited 1 March 2009).

9 See Independent Evaluation Office. International Monetary Fund, 'Governance of the IMF. An Evaluation', 2008, http://www.ieo-imf.org/eval/complete/pdf/05212008/CG_main.pdf (visited 12 February 2009), at 1. [IEO, 'Evaluation IMF Governance'].

10 See Alexander Mountford, 'The Historical Development of IMF Governance', Independent Evaluation Office, International Monetary Fund, Background Paper BP/08/02, http://ieo-imf.org/eval/complete/pdf/05212008/BP08_02.pdf (visited 21 February 2009), at 5.

11 Ibid, at 6.

12 See IEO, 'Evaluation IMF Governance', above n 9, at 1.

13 See Margaret Garritsen de Vries, The International Monetary Fund 1972–1978: Cooperation on Trial (Washington: International Monetary Fund, 1985) vol. 2, 966.

14 See Boughton, above n 4, at 1022.

15 Resolution 54-9, adopted 30 September 1999, as quoted by Mountford, 'Formal IMF Governance', above n 2, at 8.

16 Ibid.

17 Reuters, 'IMF Mulls New Council to Empower Emerging Nations'. 13 February 2009. http://www.reuters.com/article/bondsNews/idUSN1140849920090213?sp=true (visited 21 February 2009).

18 See de Vries, 'Policy Making', above n 4, at 8.

19 See Mountford, 'Formal IMF Governance', above n 2, at 13.

20 See Boughton, above n 4, at 1040–41.

21 Ibid.

22 Section C-6 of the By-Law Rules and Regulations of the IMF. http://www.imf.org/external/pubs/ft/bl/rr03.htm (visited 10 March 2009).

23 See Article XII, Section 2(j) of the IMF Articles of Agreement. http://www.imf.org/external/pubs/ft/aa/aa12.htm#2 (visited 10 March 2009).

24 See Jeff Chelsky, 'The Role and Evolution of Executive Board Standing Committees in IMF Corporate Governance', Independent Evaluation Office of the International Monetary Fund. BP/08/04. (April 2008), at 8. http://www.ieo-imf.org/eval/complete/pdf/05212008/CG_background7.pdf (visited 18 September 2008).

25 See de Vries, 'Policy Making', above n 4, at 17.

26 See Garritsen, *Cooperation on Trial*, above n 13, at 990.

27 See J. Keith Horsefield, *The International Monetary Fund 1945–1965* (Washington, D.C.: International Monetary Fund, 1969) vol. 1, 259.

28 Se ibid, at 311.

29 For a specific situation in which this incidence took place, see Horsefield, above n 27, at 345–46.

30 See online: IMF available at http://www.imf.org/external/np/exr/facts/quotas.htm. For a detailed description of the history of the quota formulas, see http://www.imf.org/external/np/exr/ib/2007/041307.htm.

31 See Peter B. Kenen, 'Reform of the International Monetary Fund', CSR No 29 (Council on Foreign Relations, 2007) http://www.cfr.org/content/publications/attachments/IMF_CSR29.pdf (visited 30 August 2008). See also http://www.imf.org/external/np/sec/memdir/members.htm (visited 28 February 2009).

32 See Mountford, 'Historial IMF Governance', above n 12, at 11–12.

33 See http://www.imf.org/external/about/govrep.htm (visited 15 February 2008).

34 See Mountford, 'Formal IMF Governance', above n 2, at 18.

35 See Joseph Gold, as quoted by Andres Rigo Sureda, 'Informality and Effectiveness in the Operation of the International Bank for Reconstruction and Development', 6 Journal of International Economic Law 565 (2003), at 572.

36 See Garritsen, *Cooperation on Trial*, above n 13, at 988. The Board defined the sense of the meeting as 'a position supported by Executive Directors having sufficient votes to carry the question were a vote to be taken'. Boughton, above n 4, at 1032.

37 See Garritsen, *Cooperation on Trial*, above n 13, at 989.

38 See Mountford, 'Formal IMF Governance', above n 2, at 19.

39 See de Vries, 'Policy Making', above n 4, at 16.

40 See Mountford, 'Formal IMF Governance', above n 2, at 16. However, the IEO states that summings-up are usually vague or contradictory and that minority views are not always detailed. See IEO, 'Evaluation IMF Governance', above n 9, at 14.

41 See de Vries, 'Policy Making', above n 4, at 16.

42 The Managing Director is appointed by the Europeans by virtue of an agreement with the United States, who decided in 1946 that its priority was to appoint the President of the World Bank. See Boughton, above n 4, at 1043.

43 Article XII Section 4(b) of the IMF Articles of Agreement. http://www.imf.org/external/pubs/ft/aa/aa12.htm#2

44 See Horsefield, above n 27, at 472.

45 See IEO, 'Evaluation IMF Governance', above n 9, at 17.

46 See Mountford, 'Formal IMF Governance', above n 2, at 21.

47 See Horsefield, above n 27, at 197.

48 Ibid.

49 Ibid, at 471, and de Vries, 'Policy Making', above n 4, at 11–12.

50 See Horsefield, above n 27, at 472. Sometimes, such negotiations were not endorsed by the Board, which introduced changes. See ibid, at 473.

51 See de Vries, 'Policy Making', above n 4, at 13.

52 Ibid.

53 See Horsefield, above n 27, at 244, 247.

54 For an example, see ibid, at 457–58.

55 See Mountford, 'Formal IMF Governance', above n 2, at 18.

56 Ibid.

57 See Edwin M. Truman, 'Overview on IMF Reform', in Edwin M. Truman (ed), *Reforming the IMF for the 21st Century* (Washington, D.C.: Institute for International Economics, 2006) 31, 85, and Mountford, 'Historical IMF Governance', above n 12, at 8.

58 *See* Independent Evaluation Office, Annual Report 2003 at 13. available at http://www.imf.org/external/np/ieo/2003/ar/Report.pdf.

59 See Bradlow, above n 5, at 13.

60 See Mountford, 'Historical IMF Governance', above n 12, at 18.

61 Ibid, at 18–20.

62 See Mountford, 'Historical IMF Governance', above n 12, at 14.

63 Australia's prime minister criticized the fund for not having anticipated the ongoing financial crisis. See Reuters, 'IMF Mulls New Council to Empower Emerging Nations'.

64 International Monetary Fund, 'IMF Signs $100 Billion Borrowing Agreement with Japan'. 13 February 2009. http://www.imf.org/external/pubs/ft/survey/so/home.aspx (visited 21 February 2009).

65 International Monetary Fund, 'As Contingency, IMF Aims to Double Its Lendable Resources'. 2 February 2009. http://www.imf.org/external/pubs/ft/survey/so/2009/POL020209A.htm (visited 18 February 2009).

66 As to proposals for reform regarding the governance of the IMF, see Edwin M. Truman, 'The G20 and International Institution Reform: Unfinished IMF Reform', http://www.voxeu.org/index.php?q=node/2896 (visited 20 February 20090), and Edwin Truman, 'Globalization Goes into Reverse?, http://www.petersoninstitute.org/realtime/?p=453 (visited 20 February 2009).

67 See IEO, 'Evaluation IMF Governance', above n 9, at 19.

68 Ibid, at 20.

69 Ibid.

70 Ibid, at 21.

71 Ibid, at 20.

72 Ibid, at 19.

73 Ibid, at 21.

74 Concerns for voice are at the forefront of the ongoing reform, and there have been proposals aimed at establishing a double majority for certain types of determinations. According to the High-Level Panel on IMF Board Accountability, double-majority voting 'seeks to balance the interest of the few industrialized countries with large economies and the interest of the more numerous developing countries with smaller economies'. (High-Level Panel on IMF Board Accountability, 'Key Findings & Recommendations', 10 April 2007, at 10. http://www.new-rules.org/docs/imf_board_accountability.pdf [visited 10 March 2008].) According to Woods, by establishing the double majority rule, powerful vote holders would be compelled to try to create coalitions representing more varied types of states and, in particular, borrowing countries. (See Ngaire Woods, 'The Globalizers in Search of a Future: Four reasons Why the IMF and the World Bank Must Change, and Four Ways They Can' [Center for Global Development, 2006], at 5.) This could be done by extending the double majority requirement already existing in the IMF. Today, the decision to expel a Member or to deny it its rights must be adopted by a minimum of 85 percent of voting power and a 60 percent majority of members. (See Ngaire Woods and Domenico Lombardi, 'Effective Representation and the Role of Coalitions within the IMF' [GEG Working Paper 2005/17], at 15. Double majority voting exists in the EU Council of Ministers and the Global Environment Facility in the World Bank. See ibid.)

In consequence, the first majority would be calculated on the basis of weighed votes, but a second majority would be required within the Board. However, Chowla has gone even further in the definition of how the double majority should be designed. He argues that a chair-based majority would not increase developing countries' voices, because developed country executive directors would still dominate the Board, which would not require them to seek higher levels of consensus. See Peter Chowla, 'At Issue: Double Majority Decision Making at the IMF: Implementing Effective Broad Voting Reform', http//brettonwoodsproject.org/doc/wbimfgov/implementingDM.pdf, referred to by the IMF website (visited 25 February 2008). Therefore, he has suggested that the second majority should be a state majority, so that chairs would have the number of votes of the members in their constituency. (See ibid.)

75 See High-Level Panel on IMF Board Accountability, above n 74, at i, ii.

76 International Monetary Fund, 'Report of the Working Group of IMF Executive Directors on Enhancing Communication with National Legislators', 15 January 2004, http//www.imf.org/external/np/ed/2004/ecnl/index.htm (visited 25 February 2008). Likewise, Kahler states that 'legislative engagement can produce strong positive effects on program implementation, offsetting possible costs to negotiate efficiently'. Miles Kahler, *Internal Governance and IMF Performance* in Edwin M. Truman (ed), Reforming The IMF for the 21st Century (Washington, D.C.: Institute for International Economics, 2006) 268.

77 See G20, 'Final Communiqué: The Global Plan for Recovery and Reform', 2 April 2009, paras 18–19, http://www.g20.org/Documents/final-communique.pdf (visited 6 April 2009).

78 Ibid, para 20.

79 Ibid.

80 This is an analysis conducted on the basis of the IMF history and seeks to identify different decision-making processes that can be useful for a comparative assessment with that of the WTO. It is not claimed that today the decisions indicated below are taken through the decision-making process here described.

81 Paramount among them was to amend the IMF provisions on gold, to legalize the position of members with floating rates, and to create a permanent and representative council of governors to supervise the management and adaptation of the international monetary system. See Garritsen, *Cooperation on Trial*, above n 13, at 686.

82 Ibid, at 691.

83 Ibid, at 709–22.

84 Ibid, at 686.

85 Ibid, at 694.

86 Ibid, at 715.

87 Such policies may be related to the creation or amendment of the IMF's loan instruments—facilities—and their most important terms, such as the Poverty Reduction and Growth Facility, Exogenous Shocks Facility, Stand-By Arrangements, the Flexible Credit Line, the Extended Fund Facility, and the emergency assistance for natural disasters. The need to introduce changes may arise due to drastic alterations in external conditions. Examples are the oil shocks of the seventies, the debt crisis of the eighties, the transition process in Eastern and Central Europe during the nineties, and the current world financial crisis. See in this regard International Monetary Fund, 'IMF Lending', http://www.imf.org/external/np/exr/facts/howlend.htm (visited 5 April 2009). Detailed explanations of the IMF policies go beyond the scope of this chapter, since they are specifically related to the operation of the Fund and therefore have not significant value for the comparative exercise carried out here.

88 See Garritsen, *Cooperation on Trial*, above n 13, at 963.

89 Ibid.

90 Ibid, at 965.

91 Ibid, at 989.

92 See de Vries, 'Policy Making', above n 4, at 17.

93 Ibid.

94 See Mountford, 'Formal IMF Governance', above n 2, at 19.

95 See Garritsen, *Cooperation on Trial*, above n 13, at 984.

96 See Chelsky, above n 24, at 17.

97 Ibid, at 11.

98 Ibid, at 34.

99 Ibid, at 23.

100 See Edward S. Mason and Robert E. Asher, *The World Bank since Bretton Woods* (Washington, D.C.: Brookings Institution, 1973) 29.

101 See Arthur Foch, 'The Governance of the World Bank: Analysis and Implications of the Decisional Power of the G10' Documents de Travail du Centre d'Economie de la Sorbonne. Centre de la Recherche Scientifique. 2008. http://halshs.archives-ouvertes.fr/docs/00/23/54/36/PDF/R08007.pdf (visited 15 February 2008), at 13.

102 For a detailed description of the operation of constituencies, see ibid, at 13–14.

103 In practice, the United States appoints the President of the Bank.

104 See World Bank, 'Board of Directors', http://web.worldbank.org/WBSITE/EXTERNAL/ EXTABOUTUS/ORGANIZATION/BODEXT/0,,pagePK:64020055~theSite PK:278036,00.html (visited 7 April 2009).

105 See World Bank, 'Board Work Program', http://web.worldbank.org/WBSITE/ EXTERNAL/EXTABOUTUS/ORGANIZATION/BODEXT/0,,contentMDK:50004944~ menuPK:64020021~pagePK:64020054~piPK:64020408~theSitePK:278036,00.html (visited 7 April 2009).

106 For the content of the annual program, see ibid.

107 See Chelsky, above n 24, at 36.

108 Ibid.

109 See Rigo Sureda, above n 35, at 582.

110 Ibid, at 585.

111 Ibid, at 582.

112 See World Bank, 'Voting Powers', http://web.worldbank.org/WBSITE/EXTERNAL/ EXTABOUTUS/ORGANIZATION/BODEXT/0,,contentMDK:21429866~menuPK: 64020035~pagePK:64020054~piPK:64020408~theSitePK:278036,00.html (visited 7 April 2009).

113 See Mason and Asher, above n 100, at 64.

114 See Foch, above n 101, at 9.

115 Ibid, at 11.

116 See Stephany Griffith-Jones, *Governance of the World Bank*, http:/stephany.acrewoods.net/ _documents/Governance_of_the_World_Ban._Paper_prepared_for_DFID.pdf at 6 (visited 15 February 2008).

117 Ibid.

118 See Foch, above n 101, at 15.

119 Ibid, at 16.

120 For further President's responsibilities and prerogatives, see below Part II.D.

121 However, Foch highlights the Bank's President cannot make decisions without endorsement by the United States, European members, and Japan. See Foch, above n 101, at 17.

122 See Mason and Asher, above n 100, at 101–2.

123 See Devesh Kapur, 'The Changing Anatomy of Governance of the World Bank', in Jonathan R. Pincus and Jeffrey A. Winters (eds), *Reinventing the World Bank* (Ithaca: Cornell University Press, 2002) 55.

124 Ibid.

125 Ibid, at 60.

126 See Rigo Sureda, above n 35, at 567.

127 See Mason and Asher, above n 100, at 93.

128 Ibid, at 94.

129 Woods quotes a British aid official as stating, 'We construct an elaborate mechanism for setting priorities and discipline in the Bank, and then as donors we bypass this mechanism by setting up separate financial incentives to try to get the Bank to do what we want.' Ngaire Woods, 'Power Shift: Do We Need Better Global Economic Institutions?' (Institute for Public Policy Research, 2007), at 21.

130 See Kapur, above n 123, at 63–64. The United States has more than 16 percent of the voting power and retains veto over amendments of the World Bank's Articles of Agreement, which requires 85 percent majority. See Griffith-Jones, above n 116, at 4. Examples of such influence are several. After India's and Pakistan's testing of nuclear weapons,

loans to these countries were curtailed to sectors unrelated to humanitarian issues. After a U.S. president visited India, the Bank changed its position and made a loan for the power sector. See Rigo Sureda, above n 35, at 588.

131 See Griffith-Jones, above n 116, at 4.

132 See Kapur, above n 123, at 67.

133 Development Committee (Joint Ministerial Committee of the Board of Governors of the Bank and the Fund on the Transfer or Real Resources to Developing Countries), 'Voice and Participation of Developing and Transition Countries in Decision Making at the World Bank,' at 1 (2007), http://siteresources.worldbank.org/DEVCOMMINT/ Documentation/21510673/DC2007-0024(E)Voice.pdf (visited 13 February 2008).

134 The Bank believes that this strategy in World Bank–financed projects should involve consultations and communications with local communities, stakeholders, NGOs, and other beneficiaries, which would increase ownership, would allow the identification of key local realities required for successful implementation, and would contribute to governments' accountability to its citizens. See ibid, at 4.

135 The Board of Executive Directors has determined that to improve its effectiveness the following actions must be carried out: enhance the Board's role in strategic priority setting; better design spheres of action between the Board and senior management as to strategy and policy making; improve Board's oversight and following-up and evaluation of implementation of its decisions. Ibid, at 5.

136 Ibid, at 3.

137 Ibid, at 2.

138 Ibid, at 19.

139 Ibid.

140 See G20, above n 77, para 20.

141 See World Bank, 'New Trade Finance Program to Provide up to $50 Billion Boost to Trade in Developing Countries', Press Release No 2009/291/IFC-EXC, 2 April 2009, http://web.worldbank.org/WBSITE/EXTERNAL/NEWS/0,,contentMDK:22127460~ pagePK:64257043~piPK:437376~theSitePK:4607,00.html (visited 6 April 2009).

142 For a review of the operation of the bank, see Jessica Einborn, 'Reforming the World Bank: Creative Destruction', 85 Foreign Affairs 17 (2006).

143 See World Bank, 'Financial Crisis. What the World Bank Is Doing' http://www.worldbank .org/html/extdr/financialcrisis/ (visited 2 March 2009).

144 See Devesh Kapur, John P. Lewis, and Richard Webb, *The World Bank: Its First Half Century* (Washington, D.C.: Brookings Institution, 1997). vol. 1, 336–38.

145 See Rigo Sureda, above n 35, at 581. The Bank's policies relate to the support of economic and social development in areas such as agriculture, infrastructure, urban development, health, education, operation of the judiciary, and the improving of the management of public resources. See World Bank, 'Products & Services', http://web.worldbank.org/WBSITE/EXTERNAL/PROJECTS/0,,contentMDK: 20120721~menuPK:232467~pagePK:41367~piPK:51533~theSitePK:40941,00.html (visited 7 April 2009).

For the purpose of this chapter, it is not necessary to provide additional details regarding the World Bank's policies, since they are intimately related to its mandates and objectives.

146 See World Bank, *A Guide to the World Bank* (Washington, D.C.: World Bank, 2003) 41, and Rigo Sureda, above n 35, at 579.

147 See Foch, above n 101, at 12.

148 See Mason and Asher, above n 100, at 90.

149 For an illustration of this situation, see ibid, at 285–87.

150 Ibid, at 91.

151 Ibid, at 94.

152 Ibid, at 92.

153 This chapter does not provide a description of the internal management of the WTO, since other authors analyze it in this volume.

154 See among others, Richard Blackhurst and David Hartridge, 'Improving the Capacity of the WTO Institutions to Fulfil Their Mandate', 7 Journal of International Economic Law 705 (2004).

155 The Sutherland Report, though, assigned the consultative body a limited role, since it should have neither negotiating nor executive powers. See Report by the Consultative Board to the Director-General Supachai Panitchpakdi, *The Future of the WTO: Addressing Institutional Challenges in the New Millennium* (Geneva: WTO, 2004) para 324.

156 See Blackhurst and Hartridge, above n 154, at 708.

157 See in this volume, Debra P. Steger and Natalia M. Shpilkovskaya, 'Internal Management of the WTO: Room for Improvement'.

158 The Ministerial Conference has adopted decisions that have given instructions to lower WTO political organs, such as councils. See WTO Ministerial Conference, 'Implementation-Related Issues and Concerns', WT/MIN(01)/17 (20 November 2001). See in this regard, Pieter-Jan Kuijper, 'WTO Institutional Aspects', in Daniel Bethlemen, Donald McRae, Rodney Neufeld, and Isabella Van Damme (eds), *The Oxford Handbook of International Trade Law* (Oxford: Oxford University Press, 2009) 79. References to this article allude to its unpublished version.

159 The fact that the WTO consultative body would be made up of trade ministers would not prevent it from convening often, for instance, twice a year. The IMFC meets with such frequency. See International Monetary Fund, 'Governance Structure', http://www.imf.org/external/about/govstruct.htm (visited 7 April 2009).

160 Nonetheless, this is far from suggesting that the Board should have initiative power regarding *any* type of decision.

161 See Sutherland Report, above n 155, para 313, and Steger and Shpilkovskaya, above n 157. Traditionally, GATT/WTO Members have been reluctant to delegate significant powers to the WTO Secretariat. See in this regard, Kuijper, above n 158, at 7. This is not to say that the Secretariat does not perform important functions during the consultations process carried out within WTO political bodies. Hordström highlights how the Secretariat is usually involved even in the case of informal meetings during negotiations, and along with the Director-General, has some control over the process. He also mentions that the Secretariat also plays an advisory role to chairmen of WTO bodies. See Hakan Nordström, 'The World Trade Organization Secretariat in a Changing World', 39 Journal of World Trade 819 (2005), at 844. See also in this regard, and ratifying the Secretariat's informal powers, Mary E. Footer, *An Institutional and Normative Analysis of the World Trade Organization* (Leiden: Martinus Nijhoff Publishers, 2006) 171.

162 See Kuijper, above n 158, at 22.

163 The Secretariat's involvement in WTO decision-making processes is not always the same. As Isabel Fetchtner has shown, in the case of waivers decisions, the Secretariat's participation varies from little relevance, as in the case with the waiver for the

EC-ACP preferences, to active intervention, as was the case of the waivers suspending GATT Article II to allow WTO Members to implement domestically changes to the Harmonized System when their GATT schedules have not yet incorporated such changes. See Isabel Feitchner, 'Law-Making in the WTO: The Law and Politics of the WTO Waiver Power' (Presentation given at the American Society of International Law Research Colloquium, UCLA School of Law, 13 February 2009, on file with the author). This varied degree of intervention within the WTO decision-making process is far from surprising given the multiple mandates the Secretariat has.

164 See Nordström, above n 161, at 835.

165 There are ways in which the Secretariat may exert a wide initiative and display broad levels of neutrality that may appease WTO Members of all kinds. For instance, when exerting its initiative, the Secretariat could table formally or informally proposals based on different alternatives, and not only a single proposal. Such strategy may be seen as one in which the Secretariat increases its institutional role without intruding into the spheres of Members' prerogatives. In addition, the use of proposals by the Secretariat is a tool that enhances its role and preserves the member-driven character of the WTO. Although the following is not an illustration of a case in which the Secretariat exerted initiative in the way suggested here, there is an example in which the design of alternatives by the Secretariat has been used as a tool within a decision-making process. For instance, in the decision-making process that led to the adoption of biennial budgeting, despite the fact that Article VII:1 of the Marrakesh Agreement Establishing the World Trade Organization establishes annual budgeting, the Committee on Budget, Finance and Administration requested the Legal Division to provide the possible instruments to overcome this hurdle. The solution, a decision by the General Council, was one of the options suggested by the division. See Footer, *WTO Institutional Analysis*, above n 161, at 220.

166 Ibid, at 281. This is certainly not to say that this kind of norm is unimportant. It may be well to recall Main's classic statement: 'Substantive law has at first the look of being gradually secreted in the interstices of procedure.' As quoted by Sir Gerald Fitzmaurice, 'Judicial Innovation—Its Uses and Perils—As Exemplified in Some of the Work of the International Court of Justice during Lord McNair's Period of Office', in *Cambridge Essays in International Law: Essays in Honour of Lord McNair* (London: Steven & Sons, 1965) 24 n 1.

167 WTO Secretariat, 'Accession—Procedures for Negotiations under Article XII, Note by the Secretariat', WT/ACC/1, 24 March 1995.

168 See Mary E. Footer, 'The Role of "Soft Law" Norms in Reconciling the Antinomies of WTO Law', (Presentation given at the Inaugural Conference of the Society of International Economic Law, Geneva, July 15–17, 2008, at 4, on file with the author.

169 Ibid, at 7. This without saying that the distinction between hard law and soft law in international organization is clear-cut. As Prosper Weil states:

> The acts accomplished by subjects of international law are so diverse in character that that it is not a simple matter for a jurist to determine what may be called the normativity threshold. i.e. the line of transition between the non-legal and the legal, between what does not constitute a norm and what does.

Prosper Weil, 'Towards Normativity in International Law', 77 American Journal of International Law 413 (1983), at 415. Quoted by Footer, *WTO Institutional Analysis*, above n 161, at 273.

170 See Footer, 'Soft Law', above n 168, at 8.

171 Ibid, at 11–13.

172 Moreover, such a move has an important recent precedent: see WTO Secretariat, 'Recommended Procedures for Implementing the Transparency Obligations of the SPS Agreement (Article 7). Note by the Secretariat', WTO Doc. G/SPS/W/215/Rev 2, 22 April 2008. The non-binding character is evidenced in the following words: 'Members are also encouraged to use the "Procedure to Enhance Transparency of Special and Differential Treatment in Favour of Developing Countries" (G/SPS/33).' See ibid, para 34, http://www.wto.org/english/news_e/news08_e/sps_30may08_e.htm (visited 1 March 2008).

173 See Donald B. Keesing, 'Improving Trade Policy Reviews in the World Trade Organization', 52 Policy Analyses in International Economics, Institute for International Economics 52, 1998.

174 While it is not possible to say that complex political issues may not lie behind the most arcane technical issues in trade policy and regulation, the fact is that the opposite is not true either, and there may be technical trade issues that may not have extreme political sensitivity, which could open the door for some initiative by the Director-General and Secretariat.

175 See Footer, *WTO Institutional Analysis, above* n 161, at 134.

PART III

Internal Management of the WTO

Internal Management of the WTO: Room for Improvement

DEBRA STEGER AND NATALIA SHPILKOVSKAYA[1]

I. Introduction

The focus of this book is on the World Trade Organization (WTO) as an institution. As we know, the WTO faces many challenges. Some commentators believe it faces a legitimacy crisis.[2] While the difficulties of the Uruguay Round and failures of the ministerial conferences in Seattle and Cancun have faded, new obstacles to the effective functioning of the WTO as an institution have emerged. In particular, the rapid rise in the economic and political power of some large developing economies, such as China, India, and Brazil, is having a major impact on the functioning of the WTO. The lack of progress in the Doha Round of multilateral trade negotiations is a sign that all is not well with the decision-making and rule-making machinery of the WTO. The proliferation of regional trade agreements, partly in response to the impasse in the multilateral negotiations, is also diverting precious government resources and attention from the WTO to regional negotiations. A major dilemma, as the Warwick Commission has noted, is that while public support for trade liberalization and trade agreements is waning significantly in developed countries, the developing world is becoming more convinced of the benefits of trade agreements for their domestic economies.[3]

In June 2003, former WTO Director-General Supachai Panitchpakdi appointed a distinguished group of experts to take a long-term view on the future of the WTO as an institution. The report of the Consultative Board, *The Future of the WTO: Addressing Institutional Challenges in the New Millennium* (the Sutherland Report) was released in 2005 on the 10th anniversary of the WTO.[4] Another independent commission, chaired by a former Canadian trade minister, Pierre Pettigrew, was established in 2007 to examine the role of the WTO in the multilateral trading system. The report of the First Warwick Commission, *The Multilateral Trade Regime: Which Way Forward?* (the Warwick Report), was released in December 2007.[5] Both reports identify key institutional problems in the WTO and suggest practical recommendations for reform. Their proposals were carefully chosen to ensure that they were capable of being implemented without new rules or agreements having to be negotiated. Despite the relevant and pragmatic conclusions of these two reports, the Members of the WTO have to date shown no appetite for institutional reform of the Organization.

This chapter focuses on issues related to the internal management of the WTO and provides preliminary proposals for reform of the WTO. The efficiency of an organization and its achievements depend, to a certain extent, on the internal management of the organization. Relevant considerations include whether the bodies of the organization possess enough authority to take the necessary actions and decisions; whether these bodies are equipped to react promptly and appropriately to changing situations; whether there are specific procedures that provide clearly defined processes for rule-making proposals to be considered and approved; and whether the rule-making procedures work in practice, allowing the organization to respond to current realities and power relationships. All these questions are relevant for the evaluation of the internal management of the WTO.

II. Different Visions of the Future of the WTO

The first question that might be asked is whether there is a need to reform the institutional architecture of the WTO.

Where one stands on this question depends on what one believes is the mandate of the WTO. Several experts see the mandate of the WTO as fundamentally focused on trade liberalization.[6] For these people, not surprisingly, the WTO is functioning effectively as it is, as a member-driven organization. In their view, it does not need major institutional reform. It simply needs to get on with the business of negotiating new trade rules. Most Members of the WTO take this view. Other experts believe that the WTO should have a broader mandate in the future as the organization responsible for international economic regulation in the global economy.[7] For these people, the WTO clearly requires major institutional reform to improve its decision- and rule-making machinery if it is to remain relevant and effective in the world of the future.

To those holding the former point of view, the WTO functions much like the old GATT. It is a member-driven organization with trade liberalization as its key purpose and mandate. While there are no formal decision-making structures in the WTO, the time-honoured practice of consensus decision-making has worked effectively in the past, including in the Uruguay Round, and is the only legitimate, effective, and fair means to take decisions in the future. Recognizing the need for diplomacy and politics in rule-making in the WTO, and noting, in particular, the concern with giving developing country Members a greater voice and influence, the experts favouring the current system are generally opposed to the idea of changing the consensus rule in decision-making and tend not to favour the establishment of a management board or other small committees made up of only some of the WTO Members.[8]

Other experts view the mandate of the WTO as extending to international economic regulation generally and are concerned that the WTO does not have the institutional capacity to allow it to function effectively. While not wanting to turn the WTO into a 'world government', proponents of a broader mandate for the WTO emphasize that there is currently an imbalance between the strong, legally binding dispute settlement mechanism, on the one hand, and the comparatively weak, cumbersome, political rule-making and negotiating machinery, on the other.[9]

Marco Bronckers observes that the rule-making and amendment procedures in the WTO make it 'practically impossible' and 'very cumbersome' to clarify or amend existing rules.[10] He worries that

> governments may too easily think that progress can be made in the WTO *through* enforcement; that litigation in the WTO is a faster, more convenient way to resolve difficult issues than an open exchange at the negotiating table. That is worrying because it undermines democratic control over international co-operation and rule-making, and it prevents a more broad-based participation of all stakeholders in the formulation of international rules.[11]

John Jackson notes that there are advantages and disadvantages to the consensus-based decision-making process: 'One downside of requiring full consensus is that it may be a recipe for impasse, stalemate, and paralysis. In other words, the result may be that things do not get done.[12] Concern with the difficulties of decision-making by consensus has led Professor Jackson to propose a 'critical mass' approach, which has been endorsed by the Warwick Commission. Jackson's idea is 'to develop a practice where countries refrain from blocking consensus when a critical mass of countries support a proposed change. This critical mass of countries could be expressed as an overwhelming majority of countries and an overwhelming amount of the trade weight in the world, such as 90 percent of both of these factors. In addition, there could be other factors'.[13]

Thomas Cottier and Satoko Takenoshita go further and suggest supplementing the consensus rule with a weighted-voting system that Members may use in situations when consensus cannot be reached. They take the view that although the current system (one Member, one vote) represents the formal equality of Members, it is imbalanced because it does not take into account the real political and economic power of Members. They propose weighted-voting rules based on a formula with several variables, including contributions to the WTO, gross domestic product, openness of markets, population, and/or basic vote. They consider that this mechanism may be useful in helping to overcome the major difficulties in trade negotiations, in talks between rounds, and in the regular business affairs of the WTO.[14]

Gary Hufbauer has suggested even more radical changes to the voting system in the WTO, favouring a weighted-voting formula. He argues that without this surgical conversion of WTO voting procedures, there is no chance for a successful conclusion of multilateral trade negotiations. He considers that obstruction in decision-making by Members who represent less than 10 percent of world trade is dangerous.[15]

The Warwick Commission considered the idea of a weighted-voting system based on two thresholds: country size (established percentage of global trade or global national income) and a minimum number of Members that voted in support of a decision. While the commission stated that such a combination of thresholds could protect the interests of both big and small countries, it nevertheless decided to refrain from recommending a weighted-voting system. Instead, it decided to support the critical mass approach.[16]

At the root of these differing visions of the WTO are different views of its essential purpose and mandate. For those who believe that the mandate of the WTO is trade liberalization through reciprocal exchanges of concessions, reform of the WTO is not needed. For those who consider that the mandate of the WTO should extend to international economic regulation more generally, institutional reform is an urgent priority.

It is difficult to envision the future of the WTO as an institution without speculating on its future mandate. However, Director-General Supachai Panitchpakdi, in his foreword to the Sutherland Report, emphasized that the purpose of that report was 'to examine the functioning of the institution—the WTO—and to consider how well equipped it is to carry the weight of future responsibilities and demands'.[17]

The assumptions of this chapter are that the WTO is in urgent need of institutional reform.[18] The mandate of the WTO is no longer clear, and '[t]he WTO should be recognized for what it is—an international organization that regulates trade as well as international economic relations generally.[19] In fact,

[t]he WTO needs major surgery in order to respond effectively to the new political realities of the international economic system.... [M]embers should recognize that the mandate of the WTO is not exclusively confined to the liberalization of trade; it includes development as well as a host of other topics that relate to international economic regulation generally. Institutional reform of the WTO is needed to provide it with the architecture and decision making machinery to make it a vibrant, responsive and accountable international organization, relevant to governments, companies and people in the 21st century.[20]

III. Is There a Structural Problem with the Decision-Making Rules in the WTO?

The second question that might be asked is whether the focus of WTO institutional reform should be on the decision-making *rules* themselves or on the *processes* by which the rules are negotiated. The decision-making rules in the WTO were negotiated in the Uruguay Round and are contained in the Marrakesh Agreement Establishing the World Trade Organization (the WTO Agreement).[21] Many experts believe that the key problem with WTO decision-making is that the consensus rule in Article IX:1 is too rigid and, therefore, renders decision-making and rule-making in the WTO 'difficult and susceptible to paralysis'.[22] Some alternative proposals to consensus decision-making have been developed, for example, weighted-voting and different approval methods depending on the types of decisions.[23] More emphasis should be placed on the *processes* by which decisions are made in the WTO. Additionally, formal structures need to be developed within the WTO at the *front end* of the decision- and rule-making system to allow for proposals to be presented to WTO councils and committees for approval under the existing rules in the WTO Agreement.

Before turning to this chapter's proposals, it is worthwhile to describe briefly the decision-making and rule-making framework in the WTO and how the current system functions in practice.

A. Decision-Making Rules of the WTO

The WTO Agreement sets out two methods for decision-making in the WTO: consensus (as the primary rule, continuing the practice under the GATT 1947) and voting (as a secondary rule in circumstances when consensus cannot be reached or the rules specifically provide otherwise). Each Member of the WTO is entitled to one vote, except for the European Community, which has the number of votes equal to the number of its member states that are WTO Members.[24]

The consensus principle emanated from practice under the GATT 1947, although the formal rules in Article XXV:4 of the GATT 1947 called for decisions of the CONTRACTING PARTIES to be taken by majority vote, or in certain cases, by a two-thirds majority of votes. However, as early as 1959, in practice, most decisions were taken by the CONTRACTING PARTIES on the basis of consensus (except for waivers, accessions, and certain amendments).[25] The shift from majority voting to the consensus rule can be explained partly by the increasing number of contracting parties and by the emergence of coalitions based on, for example, geopolitical or economic interests. In addition, there was considerable influence from some other international organizations that preferred the principle of consensus decision-making.

The consensus requirement in the WTO does not require unanimity of all Members. Article XI:1 of the WTO Agreement explicitly clarifies that "[t]he body concerned shall be deemed to have decided by consensus if no Member present at the meeting when the decision is taken formally objects to the proposed decision." Article IX provides that 'where a decision cannot be arrived at by consensus, the matter at issue shall be decided by voting'. However, in the history of the WTO, with the exception of the accession of Ecuador in 1995,[26] no proposal has been made for a decision to be made by voting. For consensus decisions, Rule 16 of the Rules of Procedure for Sessions of the Ministerial Conference and Meetings of the General Council provides that '[a] simple majority of the Members shall constitute a quorum'.[27]

Under Article IX, interpretations of the WTO Agreement and waivers of WTO obligations are to be approved by a three-fourths majority of the Members. Adoption of financial regulations and annual budgets by the General Council, amendments of the Multilateral Trade Agreements contained in Annex 1A and C, and accessions to the WTO shall be taken by a two-thirds majority of Members (respectively, Articles VII:3, X:4 and XII:2 of the WTO Agreement). However, since 15 November 1995, the General Council has sought decisions by consensus on matters related to requests for waivers or accession to the WTO.[28]

There are also exceptional cases in which the majority vote rule does not apply, notably decisions taken by the Dispute Settlement Body;[29] decisions on waivers regarding an 'obligation subject to a transition period or a period for staged implementation that the requesting Member has not performed by the end of the relevant period';[30] and decisions on adding a new plurilateral trade agreement to Annex 4 of the WTO Agreement. In these cases, Members are obliged to follow the consensus rule or other rules set out in the relevant agreement.

The Rules of Procedure for Meetings of the Council for Trade in Goods[31], of the Council for Trade in Services,[32] and of the Council for TRIPS[33] guide decision-making by these bodies. In particular, Rule 33 provides that '[w]here a decision cannot be arrived at by consensus, the matter at issue shall be referred to the General Council for decision'.[34]

Article X of the WTO Agreement establishes a complex set of amending procedures. Pursuant to Article X:1, the general amendment procedure consists of three stages:

1. A WTO Member or a relevant council[35] (within its authority) can propose an amendment to the WTO Agreement or Multilateral Trade Agreements in Annex 1 and submit that proposal to the Ministerial Conference;
2. The Ministerial Conference takes a decision, by consensus, on submitting the proposed amendment to Members for acceptance (if consensus cannot be reached, the Ministerial Conference may take a decision by two-thirds majority of all Members); and
3. Members may accept the proposed amendment by depositing an instrument of acceptance with the Director-General of the WTO within a specified period, after which the amendment will come into force.

There are several qualifications and exceptions to this general procedure, which are specified in paragraphs 2-10 of Article X of the WTO Agreement. The important point to note is that the amendment procedures in Article X make it very difficult, if not impossible, to either amend existing WTO agreements or add new ones. As a result, these rules have, thus far, not been used by Members.

B. Current Practices of Conducting Negotiations in the WTO

Although Articles II and III of the WTO Agreement contemplated new rules, amendments, and even new agreements could be negotiated at any time, WTO Members continue the GATT practice of negotiating new rules only in the context of broad, multilateral trade rounds. Such rounds are formally commenced pursuant to specific terms of reference that are agreed by the Ministerial Conference on the basis of consensus. Under the authority of the General Council, the Trade Negotiations Committee is responsible for supervision of new negotiating rounds and 'establishing appropriate negotiating mechanisms as required and supervising the progress of the negotiations',[36] and is required to report to regular meetings of the General Council.[37] As was the practice under the GATT 1947, informal consultations are a vital mechanism for reaching mutually acceptable solutions among Members.

There is no standard procedure for conducting negotiations in the WTO. Traditionally, the chairs of special sessions and negotiating groups have had the leading role in facilitating negotiations. They facilitate negotiations through convening, as appropriate, meetings of the full negotiating groups or special sessions, as well as informal smaller groups to deal with specific issues. Thus meetings are conducted in several different formats: formal (short, filled with Members' statements that are mostly for the record); informal (more open and sometimes emotional discussions); open-ended (where every Member may come into the negotiation room); small group consultations (Members come by the chair's invitation); and confessionals (private meetings between Members and the chair). Chairs may encourage interested Members to meet in small groups in their individual capacities to work together to narrow issues of contention. Work in small groups is seen as a productive way to build compromises that can lead to consensus. After a common understanding on issues within a small group of key players is found, the number of participants may gradually increase to the level of all WTO Members. This is referred to as the 'concentric circles' approach.

The Director-General may play an active role in stimulating consultations among key Members as a way to facilitate the search for a compromise, using different occasions and variable forums and formats.

It is important to note that the practice of holding meetings in small groups, specifically 'Green Room' meetings, has been criticized for lack of transparency and inclusiveness of all Members in the negotiation process. Some developing countries have complained that trade negotiations are conducted in secret and have requested more 'effective and real participation by all Members'.[38] One of the methods that developing countries have been actively using to get into meetings with limited participation is through informal coalitions of their own. Currently, there are several informal, coalition groups involved in the Doha Round negotiations, including the Group of 20; the Group of 33; NAMA 11; the African Group; the Least-developed Countries Group; the African, Caribbean, and Pacific (ACP) Group; and the Association of South East Asian Nations Group. In small group meetings, the interests of coalitions are represented by their country coordinators, who are expected to inform other members of the coalitions on discussions that occurred at the negotiating table. Thus coalitions of developing countries are a means of managing multilateral trade negotiations and building consensus, as well as increasing transparency and inclusiveness in decision-making. The practice and experience of these informal groups should be taken into account in developing more formalized mechanisms for rule-making and decision-making in the WTO.

C. Is There a Need for Reform of the Rules?

It is clear that the WTO rules on decision-making and amendments are complex. However, they also provide flexibilities, including through fall-backs to majority or enhanced-majority voting, which Members have been reluctant to utilize. Despite all the difficulties, achievement of consensus is still possible. Members have been able to adopt some key decisions based on consensus since 1995. Recent important decisions include the Decision of the General Council on Transparency Mechanism for Regional Trade Agreements;[39] the Ministerial Declaration on Trade in Information Technology Products;[40] the Declaration on the TRIPS Agreement and Public Health;[41] and the Waiver Concerning Kimberley Process Certification Scheme for Rough Diamonds.[42]

Is the problem with WTO decision-making and rule-making to be found in the *rules* in Articles IX and X of the WTO Agreement, or does it lie in the lack of *formal structures* for decision-making and rule-making proposals to move forward in the WTO system? The problem lies in the *front end* (input process) of the WTO system, rather than in the *back end* (approval process).

IV. Improving the Management Processes of the WTO

While it may be very difficult or even impossible to change the decision-making and amendment rules in the WTO, it is worth considering formalizing the informal decision-making processes to make them more effective and inclusive. It is not necessary to modify the decision-making and amendment provisions in Articles IX and X of the WTO Agreement. As indicated previously, these provisions allow for decisions to be made by consensus, but if that is not achievable, in most cases the rules provide for resort to different types of majority voting.

While a great deal of attention has been paid in the academic literature to voting rules, the difficulties with rule-making and decision-making in the WTO may not lie in the rules themselves, but in the culture or attitudes of the WTO Members. It is not the approval of proposals at the *end* of the process that seems to be the problem but rather the lack of formal mechanisms and procedures at the *beginning* of and *during* the process that hampers decision-making. The problems with the rule-making and decision-making apparatus in the WTO lie in its internal governance structures as well as in the attitudes of Members. In order to fulfil its mandate, the WTO must have the necessary structures to enable it to function effectively, efficiently, and accountably.

In comparison to other international organizations or most national governments, the WTO lacks many of the management structures that are taken for granted in most other rule-making systems. For example, it does not have an executive body, a parliament or a legislative body, or a bureaucracy that plays a formative role in setting legislative priorities and in rule-making. Compare, for illustrative purposes, the institutional structure of the European Union, which has a council, a parliament, and a commission that all have specific rule-making authority. The WTO need not emulate the European Union, but it is useful to think of these general institutional functions in developing models for the governance of the WTO.

What reforms should be introduced to make the WTO stronger, more effective, efficient, and accountable to its Members and the world at large?

The notion of "good governance" must be the key guiding principle in any reform of the WTO as an institution. Taking into account conventional wisdom from codes of good governance in the public and private sectors and academic studies of international organizations, as well as the recent governance assessment of the International Monetary Fund (IMF) by the Independent Evaluation Office, the following four dimensions of good governance should be taken into account: effectiveness, efficiency, accountability, and representation.[43]

'Effectiveness' refers to the ability of the organization and its specific bodies to fulfil their functions with quality results in a timely manner. Preconditions for effective governance include clearly defined responsibilities for each element in the organizational structure and coherence in the functioning of the different bodies, including information sharing.[44]

'Efficiency' refers to the optimization of operational costs together with maximum and appropriate utilization of personnel within the organization. Any duplication in the responsibilities assigned to institutional bodies and staff should be avoided.[45]

'Accountability' exists at two levels. First, the staff and management of the organization must be responsible to the Members for carrying out their instructions. Second, the organization must be responsible to the outside world in carrying out its mandate. Accountability must be built into the very operational culture of the organization and be based on clearly defined and established criteria so that the process of assessing performance and results is as objective as possible.[46]

'Representation' refers to the ability of Members to have their views considered and to participate in the decision-making process. It also applies to the ability of other stakeholders (civil society groups, non-governmental organizations, business associations, and parliamentarians) to present their views and to have them considered.[47]

The following proposals to improve and enhance WTO governance structures are made in the light of these four key elements of good governance.

A. A WTO Management Board

Many international organizations, including the International Monetary Fund (IMF), the International Bank for Reconstruction and Development (the World Bank), the World Health Organization, the International Labour Organization, the United Nations Development Program, and the Organization for Economic Cooperation and Development (OECD), have a management board and an executive body or its equivalent. The WTO does not have a formal body analogous to these executive boards, although the idea of such a body was contemplated by the drafters of the Havana Charter for an International Trade Organization (the Havana Charter) and has been discussed at various points in GATT/WTO history, including during the Uruguay Round.[48]

The drafters of the Havana Charter contemplated creating an executive within the Organization that would have had specific functions. In fact, they carefully developed the basic elements for establishing an executive board, including its composition (18 Members selected by the conference), voting rules, and rules of procedure, as well as its potential responsibilities. It is important to note that the drafters planned to give the Executive Board both executive and supervisory functions. In particular, Article 81:1 of the Havana Charter would have enabled the Executive Board to 'be responsible for the execution of the policies of the Organization and … exercise the powers and perform the duties assigned to it by the Conference. It shall supervise the activities of the Commissions and shall take such action upon their recommendations as it may deem appropriate'.[49]

Later, following the creation of the Interim Committee in the IMF, the CONTRACTING PARITES of the GATT 1947 established the Consultative Group of 18, first on a provisional basis in 1975, and then on a permanent basis in 1979.[50] Importantly, the Consultative Group of 18 required rotation of its membership, a process that was carefully followed by the contracting parties. One of the problems in the operation of this group was that it was not very transparent, and documents were not always distributed among all contracting parties. At the same time, according to the reports of the Consultative Group of 18 to the GATT Council, the group made a substantial contribution to the operation of the GATT and the launching of the Uruguay Round negotiations. It was the only forum for the discussion of agricultural policy in 1981–82 and the first to discuss new subjects such as trade in services, intellectual property, and trade-related investment in the GATT 1947. In spite of this, the group was discontinued after 1985.[51]

During the Uruguay Round, the idea of the establishment of a management board was proposed by the United States in the Functioning of the GATT System (FOGS) Negotiating Group.[52] Although this proposal was not ultimately adopted, it is worthwhile to describe some of its elements. The United States proposed the establishment of a management board that would meet at the level of ministers between the biennial plenary meetings of the CONTRACTING PARTIES at the ministerial level and would perform the same functions as what became, in fact, the Ministerial Conference. The management board would have consisted of 18 members whose seats would have been distributed on the basis of the frequency of the Trade Policy Review Mechanism. The management board would have had limited decision-making powers delegated to it by the CONTRACTING PARTIES. It was suggested also that the CONTRACTING PARTIES might assign issues to the management board when achieving consensus proved to be elusive. In addition to the powers assigned to it by the Ministerial Conference, the management board was also

- to serve as a forum for discussion of trade issues of common concern and to resolve issues referred to it by the GATT Council or taken up by the board on its own initiative;
- to assist in the preparation of agendas and other preparations for meetings of the CONTRACTING PARTIES at the ministerial level (including decisions to initiate trade negotiations);
- to take primary responsibility for developing an outline, for consideration by the CONTRACTING PARTIES of a successor organization to the GATT;
- to serve as a nominating committee for the selection of the Director-General and Deputy Directors-General; and
- to guide continuing cooperation between the GATT and the international financial institutions.[53]

In its proposal, the United States suggested creating a management board that would possess delegated authority to take decisions, engage in agenda setting, and carry out general administrative tasks. This proposal, however, was not received positively by other Uruguay Round participants, mainly because of concerns about the limited membership of the proposed management board and its broad functions.

Today, looking at the list of functions of the management board proposed by the United States in 1990, we are reminded of the recent history of the WTO, including difficulties with the preparation of ministerial conferences and with the launching of the Doha Round, as well as the long stalemate and paralysis that occurred in the selection of a Director-General to replace Renato Ruggiero in 1999.

Diversification of the membership and the growing number of different informal groupings for seeking consensus in the WTO demonstrate the need for a management board or an executive body of some type in the Organization. While informal meetings, Green Room meetings, and consultations may contribute, in the end, to positive outcomes, problems still exist with the lack of transparency and legitimacy, especially for those Members that are not included in the small group meetings. The Doha Ministerial Declaration notes Members' recognition of the challenges resulting from the expanding membership and confirms the 'collective responsibility to ensure internal transparency and the effective participation of all Members'.[54]

The idea of a management board has been around since 1947 and continues to be the subject of vigorous debate. While some commentators believe that there is an urgent need for establishment of such a body,[55] others consider it unnecessary or even dangerous.[56]

The idea of a management board or a senior officials' consultative body resurfaced again recently as one of the recommendations in the Sutherland Report. It recommended the establishment of a senior officials' consultative body whose main functions would be to discuss political and economic matters, provide some political guidance, and facilitate the transition of negotiations taking place in the WTO to the Ministerial Conference.[57] Importantly, it would not be vested with executive or negotiating powers. It would be an advisory body to the Director-General without real decision-making power or authority. The consultative body would consist of a maximum of 30 members, who would be capital-based representatives at the level of senior officials or ministers or both. Some Members (major trading nations) would participate in the work of the consultative body on a permanent basis, while others would rotate in a manner similar to the procedure used in the executive boards of the IMF and World Bank. The consultative body, chaired by the Director-General, would meet two to four times per year, and the Director-General would report the results of these meetings to all Members.[58]

The Sutherland Report stressed that the combination of frequency of meetings and participation by countries on a rotating basis should provide the opportunity for all Members to be represented in the consultative body. When necessary, the consultative body would meet wholly or partially at ministerial meetings. Moreover, the Sutherland Report does not exclude the possibility that the consultative body, if represented at the level of ministers, could replace informal 'mini-ministerial' meetings in the WTO. While the Sutherland Report would formalize some senior officials' groups, such as the Evian Group, it would not go so far as to establish a formal limited-membership decision-making and priority-setting body similar to the executive boards of the IMF and the World Bank or as contemplated by the U.S. proposal in the Uruguay Round.[59]

Richard Blackhurst suggests that a formal consultative body with management and decision-making powers is needed in the WTO to deal with what he characterizes as the 'Green Room' problem. He recommends a consultative body that would be a steering committee with 24 members and considers that the largest trading nations would have individual seats with the remaining

Members being divided into groups. Each of these groups would have one seat that would be rotated among the members of the group. Participants would be Geneva-based ambassadors, rather than senior officials from capitals. Meetings of the consultative body would take place only in situations in which the Green Room could not accommodate all Members wishing to participate in the debate. Importantly, in contrast with the World Bank and IMF executive boards, a WTO consultative body would not have authority to take decisions that bind all Members, but it would have powers to consult, debate, and negotiate. The consultative body would prepare recommendations and present them to Members for approval.[60]

A different vision of a management body has been promoted by Matsushita, Schoenbaum, and Mavroidis. They suggest establishing an executive body of the General Council that would have the authority to make decisions. This executive body would comprise permanent members and members who would serve fixed terms on a rotational basis. Selection of the members of the executive body would be based on objective criteria such as countries' level of gross domestic product, share of world trade, and population. In addition, other criteria may be used in to order to ensure appropriate representation of developing countries and geographical balance. This system would provide every Member with an opportunity to be on the executive body.[61]

What role should a management board play in the WTO? What responsibilities should the Ministerial Conference or General Council delegate to a management board? How would it be composed, ensuring representation by all Members as well as accountability, effectiveness, and efficiency?

The WTO would benefit most from a management board vested with consultative, executive, and supervisory functions, similar to the executive board contemplated in the Havana Charter and, to a lesser extent,[62] the proposal of the United States in the Uruguay Round. It would be accountable to the General Council and give instructions to the Director-General. Key principles of good governance should be foremost in its design and functioning. In particular, such a board must be representative, accountable, and transparent in its responsibilities and relations with Members as well as efficient, effective, and transparent in its decision-making functions.

The difficulties encountered by Members in finding mutually acceptable solutions in the Doha Development Round indicate that there is a need for a formal, limited-membership management board that could contribute to finding compromise positions in negotiations. A management board would also be useful when WTO councils or committees fail to achieve consensus on specific proposals. In addition, there is a need for a board that could engage in strategic thinking and help to set priorities to further the mandate of the Organization. The General Council could request the management board to consider specific issues and propose potential solutions. The management board could seek the advice of the Director-General, the Secretariat, and the Members. At the same time, the management board should be able, on its own initiative, to submit advice or make recommendations to the General Council on international economic and trade matters.

The direct involvement of all Members in dealing with administrative matters that relate to the internal functioning of the WTO (for example, budget and planning for meetings) is time-consuming, ineffective, and inefficient. A management board could potentially supervise and work with the Secretariat through the approval and monitoring of administrative guidelines governing staff, introduction and maintenance of an accountability framework for the Director-General and the Secretariat staff, control over expenditure of funds, and adoption of rules concerning preparation by the Secretariat for ministerial conferences. It could also have responsibilities for setting priorities and general direction for the WTO, for example, by setting agendas for ministerial conferences, developing priorities for future negotiations, and assisting in the process of selecting Directors-General, Deputy Directors-General, and Appellate Body Members.

In addition, the General Council could vest the management board with other responsibilities as it deems appropriate. Importantly, the management board should have decision-making powers on matters that fall within its competence. In order to ensure efficiency and effectiveness, its functions should be clearly defined, and overlap in responsibilities with other WTO councils and committees should be avoided to the greatest extent possible.

Composition of the management board would be the most difficult hurdle in establishing such a body. There are two major challenges: (1) determining the number of members on the board; and (2) designing the selection process. The principles of good governance should be taken into account in designing such a board. On the one hand, a smaller board would likely be more effective and efficient in taking decisions and setting priorities than a larger board.[63] On the other hand, a larger board would be more accountable and representative of the Members. The executive boards of the IMF, the World Bank, the World Health Organization, and the United Nations Development Program have 24, 24, 34, and 32 members respectively. Membership of a WTO management board could be in the range of 25 to 30 members. Although it would be difficult to decide how members should be selected to serve on this body, a mechanism could be developed that does take into account the unique history and experience of the WTO, rather than following any particular model.

The General Council should select management board members, and qualification requirements such as knowledge and expertise in trade policy matters should be a prerequisite. In the formula for the selection process for potential members of the management board, a number of principles could be taken into account, including but not limited to equitable geographic representation, representation of different levels of economic development, share of world trade, and regional integration. Existing informal regional groups in the WTO could be formalized and given official representatives on the board. At the same time, representatives sitting on the board would be accountable to specific groups within the Organization. In that way, formal accountability structures could be established vis-à-vis the membership. Most importantly, a rotational scheme would need to be devised so that all WTO Members could have an opportunity to serve on the board at some point. Openness and transparency in all its functions and activities would be required to ensure representativeness and accountability to all the Members.

Establishment of a management board would be an important step toward more effective, efficient, and transparent governance of the WTO. Such a board could serve a number of useful functions, including supervising the general administration of the budget and the Secretariat, planning for ministerial conferences and important meetings, agenda setting for future negotiations, and assistance in the selection of Directors-General, Deputy Directors-General, and Appellate Body Members.

B. Roles of the Director-General and the Secretariat

The roles of the Director-General and the Secretariat are central to the effective and efficient functioning of any international organization. One of the mantras of Members is that the WTO is a 'member-driven' organization. However, as Professor Jackson has noted, this is also one of the reasons that the WTO has not always been efficient and effective, especially in its negotiation and rule-making functions.[64] The Sutherland Report notes that while the Secretariat continues to be highly regarded, 'the mutual confidence between delegations and WTO staff has been less obvious than in the past'.[65] Moreover, Members view the Secretariat's role as exclusively one of support for the Members, and the Members do not usually welcome any demonstration of initiative on the part of the Secretariat.[66]

The Sutherland Report recognizes the importance of enhancing the role of the Director-General and giving the Secretariat the authority to defend the multilateral trading system and to promote its principles. It emphasizes that

> [t]he WTO needs a convincing and persistent institutional voice of its own. If Members are not prepared to defend and promote the principles they subscribe to, then the Secretariat must be free to do so. Indeed, it should be encouraged, even required, to do so.[67]

The report also stresses that 'the membership should also encourage and stimulate a greater intellectual output from the Secretariat'.[68] It calls for the Secretariat to take more of a lead on policy issues and in communicating the WTO's message to the public.[69]

The Sutherland Report also advocates that only the best-qualified candidates with technical competence and experience should be considered for the post of the Director-General. It also suggests that the 'powers and duties' of the Director-General be specifically defined, based on the advice of former Directors-General.[70] Depending on the roles of the Director-General and the Secretariat, the report suggests that proper adjustments may be necessary regarding the number of Deputy Directors-General and the allocation of their responsibilities. For example, if the Secretariat's role is passive and the Director-General is heavily engaged in regular contact with politicians in capitals, then it may be appropriate to appoint a single deputy as a chief executive officer. If the approach is the opposite, then more deputies (two or three) may be necessary.[71]

It is vitally important to strengthen the role and authority of the Director-General and the Secretariat in the WTO. Unlike the secretariats of other international organizations, the WTO Secretariat has had limited capacity and authority to conduct independent research and to make policy proposals to the Members. It is interesting to compare the OECD Secretariat (30 members; annual 340 million Euros budget; 2,500 staff, including about 700 economists, lawyers, and other professionals who provide analysis and research) with the WTO Secretariat (153 Members, 185 million Swiss Francs budget, 625 staff).[72] Only recently have WTO Secretariat staff been allowed to put their names on research papers or to publish independent analytical work. Compared with other international organizations, WTO Members do not encourage serious analytical research and do not generally welcome policy ideas or initiatives from the Secretariat.

WTO Members should encourage and welcome serious research and policy advice, including proposals for negotiations, from the high-quality Secretariat staff. As recommended by the Sutherland Report, the Secretariat should also be encouraged to be the public voice of the WTO to the outside world. However, Members also have an important responsibility to educate and convince their publics of the virtues and values of the multilateral trading system. Steve Charnovitz argues that '[s]elling the benefits of the WTO should be the role of elected officials, cabinet ministers, advocacy organizations, journalists, educators, etc., not the role of international civil servants'.[73]

The WTO Secretariat is probably the leanest secretariat of any international organization, certainly when one takes into consideration the broad responsibilities and functions of the Organization. The total number of Secretariat staff is now approximately 625, which is an insignificant increase from the former GATT Secretariat, which had approximately 500 staff. The number of agreements administered by the Secretariat in the WTO is much larger than those administered under the GATT regime, and the WTO agreements delve far more extensively into areas of domestic regulation than the GATT system did. Moreover, the Secretariat has serviced over 365 disputes that have been brought to the WTO since 1995 and has devoted major resources to providing technical assistance and training for developing and least developed countries. It has accomplished all of this with one of the smallest budgets of any international organization. As Sylvia Ostry has emphasized, the WTO is 'a Mercedes Benz without gas'.[74]

WTO Members clearly need to put gas into the Mercedes, and maybe even buy a newer model than the 1947 edition created for the GATT. More formal powers and responsibilities should be given to the Director-General, including authority to make proposals to the management board and General Council. In order to support the Director-General effectively, the budget and authority of the Secretariat should be enhanced to reflect the tremendous responsibilities and excellent work the Secretariat carries out.

C. Parliamentary Dimension

The WTO is an intergovernmental organization that is driven by its member governments. To enhance the legitimacy and accountability of the WTO, there is a need to establish a parliamentary dimension to the WTO. Clearly, parliaments and legislatures have an important oversight role to play in the national processes of developing negotiating positions as well as approving new international rules. Often, the WTO has been criticized for its lack of transparency and accountability to civil society.[75] However, it is parliamentarians who are the elected and legitimate representatives of their citizens. In order to enhance transparency, accountability, and legitimacy of the WTO, it would be wise to develop a formal parliamentary dimension to the Organization as well as to provide more structured, open relationships with non-governmental organizations and civil society.

Parliamentarians also have a major role in helping their constituents to better understand the work of the WTO, building confidence and support among domestic constituencies for the WTO, and bringing the concerns of their electorates to the WTO. Julio Lacarte, former chair of the WTO Appellate Body and chair of the institutional negotiations in the Uruguay Round has emphasized, 'There is considerable lack of knowledge of the WTO in many parliaments, and this works to the detriment of the Organization.'[76] It is imperative, therefore, to maintain and further develop liaisons between the WTO and parliaments, and to assist parliamentarians in enhancing their awareness and deepening their understanding of the mandate, objectives, and benefits of the WTO.

The parliamentary dimension is addressed in the Sutherland Report. It notes that while this issue is under debate, there is no common position among Members in respect of inter-parliamentary meetings in the WTO. While the European Union supports the idea of conducting such meetings, the United States and some developing countries oppose it. On the basis of these observations, the Sutherland Report makes two recommendations: (1) Members should promote transparency toward their parliamentarians at home; and (2) Parliamentarians should be able to adequately reflect the aim, objectives, and results of WTO negotiations to their constituencies.[77]

The Sutherland Report's modest discussion of the parliamentary dimension of the WTO is disappointing. Steve Charnovitz views it as a 'missed opportunity' either to 'debunk' the opposition to the idea of a parliamentary assembly for the WTO or 'to present a coherent argument against parliamentary involvement'.[78] The report does neither of these things.[79] Unlike non-governmental organizations, parliaments are duly elected by the citizens of their countries and therefore should be viewed as having a legitimate and authoritative voice in WTO affairs.

While the idea of inter-parliamentary meetings in the WTO is still under discussion among Members, the reality is that a parliamentary dimension to the WTO is emerging incrementally through the actions of parliaments of some of its Members. Inspired by the ideas and efforts of William V. Roth (U.S. Senate Finance Committee) and Carlos Westendorp Y Cabeza (head of the Commission for Industry, External Trade, Research and Energy, European Parliament), the first formal meeting of parliamentarians was held in conjunction with the WTO Ministerial Conference in Seattle in 1999. This group called for the 'establishment of a Standing Body of Parliamentarians whereby members of parliaments can exchange views, be informed and monitor WTO negotiations and activities'.[80] The European Parliament supported this initiative: first, in November 1999 and in October 2001, it adopted resolutions with respect to the establishment of a WTO parliamentary assembly with consultative power to achieve greater democratic accountability.[81]

A global parliamentary meeting on international trade took place on 8 and 9 June 2001 in Geneva. The Inter-Parliamentary Union organized it as part of its activities to provide a parliamentary dimension to international cooperation. This parliamentary meeting brought together 182 participants from 71 national parliaments.[82] In the Final Declaration of that meeting, the parliamentarians highlighted the necessity 'to intensify activities in national parliaments to oversee and influence government policy in relation to trade negotiations' and 'to build a parliamentary dimension to international trade negotiations and arrangements'.[83] Significantly, in his speech to that meeting, then WTO Director-General Mike Moore welcomed and supported the initiative. He emphasized:

> This meeting is an important opportunity for members of parliament to commence bridging the gap between the institution like the WTO, which you own and fund, and the people. You have the responsibility in your respective parliaments to act as a relay between the government and the people, and to provide necessary political oversight. To do this, parliamentarians and legislators need to know about the institution they own.... I believe that your involvement can help us promote greater openness, fairness, balance and predictability in international trade.[84]

The next parliamentary meeting, which was jointly organized by the European Parliament and the Inter-Parliamentary Union, took place on 11 November 2001 in Doha, Qatar, on the margins of the fourth WTO Ministerial Conference. More than 100 parliamentarians attended this meeting and discussed possible ways to organize and develop a parliamentary dimension to the WTO.[85] Some legislators favoured a standing body of parliamentarians (formally linked to the WTO or existing separately), while others supported a parliamentary dimension for the WTO through the Inter-Parliamentary Union.[86] Agreement was found in a decision to create a steering group that would present options.[87] Parliamentarians also called on governments to include in the final declaration of the Ministerial Conference the following paragraph: 'Transparency of the WTO should be strengthened by associating Parliaments more closely with the activities of the WTO.'[88] However, this wording was not included in the Ministerial Declaration.

After that meeting, the Post-Doha Steering Committee was established, composed of parliamentarians from 22 countries and officials from 4 international organizations.[89] The Steering Committee met in May and October of 2002 in order to prepare for a parliamentary conference on 17–18 February 2003 in Geneva. This conference brought together more than 500 parliamentarians from 77 countries to discuss multilateral trade issues. During that meeting, legislators stressed the importance of the parliamentary dimension to the WTO and decided to hold a parliamentary conference on the WTO once a year and on the occasion of every WTO Ministerial Conference.[90]

Parliamentarians agreed that the purpose of these conferences would be 'to oversee and promote the effectiveness of WTO activities; maintain dialogue with governmental negotiators and civil society; and facilitate information exchange, sharing of experiences and capacity-building for national parliaments in matters of international trade, in particular, concerning the WTO, and to exert influence on the direction of discussions within the WTO'.[91]

The next Parliamentary Conference on the WTO took place on 9 and 12 September 2003 in Cancún at the fifth WTO Ministerial Conference. It was organized jointly by the European Parliament and the Inter-Parliamentary Union in cooperation with the Mexican Congress. More than 320 legislators from 70 countries and 5 regional parliamentary assemblies attended the Parliamentary Conference. Importantly, the attention of parliamentarians was focused not only on organizational issues, but on some of the key topics of the Doha Round (agriculture negotiations, TRIPS, trade in services).[92]

In 2004, the Parliamentary Conference on the WTO was held from 24 to 26 November in Brussels. Three hundred parliamentarians attended this session from nearly 80 countries. Participants obtained first-hand information on recent developments in the Doha Round and exchanged views on possible parliamentary input to move the negotiation process forward. During this conference, parliamentarians approved the Rules of Procedure of the Parliamentary Conference on the WTO[93] and adopted a declaration in which they 'urge[d] governments and parliaments to engage in a regular dialogue so that the latter can effectively exercise parliamentary oversight of the international trade negotiations and their follow-up'.[94]

From 2005 to 2008, parliamentary conferences on the WTO took place in December 2005 in Hong Kong, China (at the WTO Ministerial Conference),[95] in December 2006,[96] and in September 2008 in Geneva.[97] The documents from these meetings demonstrate parliamentarians' ongoing interest and commitment to the multilateral trading system as well as their intention to play a significant role in overseeing WTO activities and government actions in the field of international trade. Moreover, parliamentarians noted that '[m]ore than ever, the WTO is faced with organizational and institutional challenges. Before long, it will need to engage in institutional reform aimed at improving its functioning, and enhancing its accountability and democratic legitimacy'.[98]

This historical chain of events demonstrates the growing movement toward involvement in the WTO initiated by parliamentarians themselves, aided and abetted by the European Parliament and the Inter-Parliamentary Union. Indeed, the overwhelming success of the Parliamentary Conferences on the WTO reflects the great interest of parliamentarians in the work of the WTO, as well as the need for an international forum that will provide legislators from different countries with an opportunity to exchange views and contribute to WTO decision-making. Adoption of the Rules of Procedure of the Parliamentary Conference on the WTO represents a step toward a regulatory framework for this movement.

The WTO, through successive Directors-General, has also taken important steps in building relationships with parliamentarians. Recent Directors-General of the WTO (Renato Ruggiero, Mike Moore, and Supachai Panitchpakdi) as well as current Director-General, Pascal Lamy, have promoted relationships between parliamentarians and the WTO and have reached out to organize meetings and workshops jointly with parliamentary groups and associations. Among the initiatives that have been undertaken by the WTO are publication of *WTO Policy Issues for Parliamentarians: A Guide to Current Trade Issues for Legislators*;[99] discussions on parliaments and the WTO that took place at the WTO Public Symposium 'Challenges Ahead on the Road to Cancun' on 17 June 2003; and regional and national workshops jointly presented by the WTO and parliamentary associations.[100] Moreover, as a member of the Steering Committee of the Parliamentary Conference on the WTO, the WTO Secretariat is directly involved in the preparation of its conferences and briefing its meetings. It is interesting to note the view of the 12th session of the Conference Steering Committee held on 22–23 June 2006:

> We observe that government negotiators and WTO officials alike show signs of growing openness to the idea of using the Parliamentary Conference on the WTO as a de *facto* parliamentary dimension of this important intergovernmental body. With the constructive engagement of all parties, achievement of this objective *de jure* should also be within reach.[101]

The time has come to build on the experience of the Parliamentary Conference of the WTO, formalize already established relationships between the WTO and parliamentarians, and bring the parliamentary dimension under the framework of the WTO by creating a standing body of parliamentarians formally linked to the WTO.

The main goal of this body would be to provide parliamentarians with a forum in which they would be able to present their views and to have them considered. Such a forum will allow legislators from different countries to exchange views, information, and experience and build capacity in parliaments in the field of international trade; to improve dialogue between governments, parliaments, and civil society; to facilitate parliamentary and civil society awareness on trade issues and the interconnection between trade and sustainable development; to be informed first-hand about negotiations taking place in the WTO and to provide the WTO and its Members with an indication of collective parliamentary opinion.

The administrative and financial implications of the creation of a WTO parliamentary conference are serious concerns. The External Relations Division in the WTO Secretariat, which is currently responsible for relationships with parliamentarians, civil society, and international organizations, is very small,[102] and its budget does not provide the necessary resources for hosting regular meetings of a parliamentary conference.[103] Therefore the human and financial resources needed for the WTO to perform this task would have to be assessed. A parliamentary conference could be organized with the help of ad hoc financial support and contributions from some WTO Members (as in case of the Annual Public Symposium that is funded from extra-budgetary sources),[104] although more secure funding to ensure continuation of outreach meetings with parliamentarians would be desirable. Members could also establish it by means of a new international agreement, along the lines of the Advisory Centre on WTO Law.

When considering the anticipated operational costs of a parliamentary conference, one should consider the tangible benefits from the establishment of a formal relationship between the WTO and parliamentarians. A formal mechanism would enhance dialogue and increase transparency and accountability, thereby improving decision-making effectiveness and efficiency and strengthening overall governance in the WTO. A parliamentary body could act as an appropriate, legitimate interface mechanism between the WTO and civil society, NGOs, and other stakeholder groups. It could also assist in building greater public understanding and support for the multilateral trading system while at the same time conveying the views and interests of its constituents to the WTO.

D. Involvement of Non-State Stakeholders

The role of non-governmental organizations (NGOs) in the WTO has increased over the past decade. The Sutherland Report highlights the expanding role of civil society in promoting more transparent and inclusive global governance, together with the need for a more interactive and effective partnership between state and non-state actors. Such partnerships demonstrate different dimensions. One dimension has been the tension arising from demands of civil society for more substantive participation, governments' irritation about invasion in the fields of governmental responsibilities, and the challenges of international organizations in adjusting their operations to new realities. Another dimension has been the benefits of NGO involvement, including improving public awareness[105] of the importance of trade and its relationship with sustainable development, and the development of additional knowledge and expertise on trade issues.[106]

The Sutherland Report notes that the WTO has enjoyed noticeable progress in building relationships with civil society and working with non-governmental organizations.[107] The General Council adopted special guidelines for the development of communications and improvement of transparency in 1996.[108]

A decision on expedited de-restriction of WTO documents was taken in 2002.[109] WTO documents and explanatory materials are now easily accessible on the website of the Organization. The Director-General and the WTO Secretariat meet on a regular basis with representatives of civil society. Civil society groups and non-governmental organizations may attend plenary sessions of the Ministerial Conferences and public symposiums as well as communicate via online forums on the WTO website.[110]

The Sutherland Report stresses that it is important for the WTO to review its relationships with NGOs. At the same time, it mentions that there are limits to such cooperation. For example, an initiative of NGOs to set up a system of accreditation within the WTO was not approved. The WTO has established, on an ad hoc basis, a registration system for participation in ministerial conferences and public forums. The WTO also does not allow NGOs to participate in meetings as 'observers', contrary to the practice of several other international organizations.[111]

The issue of direct participation of non-governmental organizations in decision-making and meetings in the WTO has been considered, but the Sutherland Report states that many governments believe that this is not in keeping with the character of intergovernmental organizations, including the WTO. The report notes, however, that it is in the interests of both the WTO and individual Members to increase transparency and relationships with civil society. It emphasizes that the primary responsibility lies with individual WTO Members to communicate with their domestic constituencies, including NGOs and civil society groups.[112] On the other hand, the WTO may benefit from additional knowledge and expertise from different stakeholders. Moreover, civil society organizations may be helpful in their ability to influence government positions in negotiations and facilitate implementation of accepted obligations, and this aspect should be taken into account.[113]

As a result of these observations, the Sutherland Report recommends periodic review of the situation with transparency in the Organization and consideration of whether it will be useful to fill the gaps and adopt a framework for reviewing relationships of the WTO and non-governmental organizations and civil society based on several principles:

- Members have primary responsibility for engaging with civil society;
- Members should develop a set of clear objectives for the relationship of the WTO Secretariat with civil society and the public (the dialogue should be constructive on both sides and mutually reinforcing); and
- The necessity of identifying the administrative capacity and financial resources that are needed to support further enhancing external transparency with regard to civil society.[114]

The idea of developing more formal mechanisms for receiving input from non-state stakeholders in the WTO should be explored.[115] In particular, there should be a forum for business and consumer organizations in the WTO as they are key stakeholders in the multilateral trading system. If coherence of international economic policies is ever to be achieved or encouraged with the other international organizations, it must be recognized that more formal mechanisms for cooperation and participation in meetings must be established for other international organizations to have input into the WTO. Moreover, the WTO should open up more meetings to 'observers' as a first step in increasing the openness of meetings to stakeholders and the public.

Other international organizations, such as the International Labour Organization, have included representatives of the private sector and unions in their meetings and deliberations acknowledging their important role as stakeholders in their systems. In the 1947–48 negotiations that led to the Havana Charter and the GATT, representatives of business organizations and unions participated in the meetings.

Comparative analysis of the practice of other international organizations in this respect would be very helpful. The experience of the World Bank in its relationships with NGOs and, in particular, the formation and experience of the World Bank Inspection Panel should be examined to see if there are any useful lessons or models for the WTO.

V. Conclusion

The premise of this chapter is that institutional reform of the decision-making and rule-making processes of the WTO is needed, especially if the WTO is to equip itself for the challenges of the future. Some of the academic commentary to date on the political side of the WTO takes the position that major reform is not needed, that it is working as a government-to-government organization as it should, and that any reform, especially of the consensus principle, could lead to even greater disenfranchisement of the developing countries. Some commentators believe that major institutional reform is needed and focus, in particular, on the consensus principle as causing paralysis and stalemate in the system.

The major problem with rule-making and decision-making in the WTO is not the consensus rule or the decision-making rules in the WTO Agreement. It is not the final phase of adoption of a legislative proposal that causes the delays and blockage in the WTO system but rather the lack of formal mechanisms at the initial and intermediate stages of the legislative or rule-making process and the absence of a management or executive body, analogous to the executive boards of the IMF and World Bank, that leads to the lack of direction and drift in the Organization.

It is time to establish a formal, limited-membership management board within the WTO. Such a board should be specifically designed to be representative of the membership of the WTO, as well as accountable and effective. With a rotational, representative system for selecting members and transparency mechanisms built in, a management board could improve significantly the effectiveness of WTO decision-making.

It is also clear that the roles of the Director-General and the Secretariat of the WTO should be enhanced. In particular, the Secretariat should be permitted and encouraged to take a more proactive role in conducting research and developing proposals for negotiations and rule-making, and the mandate and powers of the Director-General should be formally delineated. The knowledge and technical capacity of the Secretariat should be effectively used and welcomed by Members, as the Secretariat could play a much stronger research and policy development role in negotiations and rule-making.

The WTO has been criticized for its lack of transparency and accountability vis-à-vis NGOs and civil society. Developing a parliamentary dimension to the WTO would go a long way to remedying these deficiencies. Parliaments play an important oversight role before, during, and after negotiations have taken place. Moreover, they are an important link to the domestic constituencies that are stakeholders in a well-functioning WTO system. In order to do their job effectively, parliamentarians need to be informed about the objectives, rules, and procedures of the WTO. The time has come for the idea of a parliamentary dimension to the WTO to be seriously considered.

Finally, the idea of developing more formal mechanisms for receiving input from non-state stakeholders, with an emphasis on business and consumer groups, should be fully explored. In the 1947–48 negotiations that led to the GATT, business organizations, labour unions, and consumer groups had seats in the meetings. They also participate in meetings and decision-making processes of some international organizations, such as the International Labour Organization. Formal relationships need to be built between the WTO and key stakeholders, such as business and consumer interests.

The recent global financial crisis has highlighted the problems with the antiquated machinery of the Bretton Woods system. As originally conceived, there were to be three international organizations responsible for the regulation of the international economy. It is clear that the institutions that emerged from the post–World War II era—the IMF, the World Bank, and the GATT (later the WTO)—were created for a very different time and purpose. The three organizations need to be significantly reformed if they are to remain relevant in the rapidly changing global economy. The WTO is one of these key organizations. Coherence of international economic policies remains a primary goal of the multilateral system, therefore, more effective, clear, cooperative arrangements between the WTO, the IMF, and the World Bank must be established. The global financial crisis offers a unique opportunity for world leaders to redesign and revitalize the international economic organizations, including the WTO, to meet the challenges of the 21st century.

Notes

1 The authors would like to thank Tom Bernes, Terry Collins-Williams, Pieter Jan Kuijper, Julio Lacarte Muró, and Sylvia Ostry for comments on an early draft at the workshop 'WTO Institutional Reform Project' that took place on 13–15 March 2008, at the Centre for International Governance Innovation, Waterloo, Canada. This workshop was organized by the Emerging Dynamic Global Economies (EDGE) Network and funded by the International Development Research Centre (IDRC).

2 See, for example, Debra P. Steger, 'The Struggle for Legitimacy in the WTO', in *Peace Through Trade: Building the WTO* (London: Cameron May, 2004) 287–311.

3 Warwick Commission, *The Multilateral Trade Regime: Which Way Forward? Report of the First Warwick Commission* (Coventry: the University of Warwick, 2007) 11.

4 Consultative Board to the Director-General Supachai Panitchpakdi, *The Future of the WTO: Addressing Institutional Challenges in the New Millennium* (Geneva: World Trade Organization, 2004).

5 Above n 3.

6 Robert Wolfe, Richard Blackhurst, Petros Mavroidis, Robert Lawrence, Allan Sykes, and many trade economists and government officials seem to hold this view.

7 John Jackson, Thomas Cottier, Marco Bronckers, Ernst-Ulrich Petersmann, Deborah Cass, Pieter-Jan Kuijper, and, of course, the authors fit within this group. Interestingly, the experts holding this view are mainly lawyers. See Debra P. Steger, 'The Culture of the WTO: Why It Needs to Change', 10 (3) Journal of International Economic Law 483 (2007).

8 Joost Pauwelyn has a more nuanced point of view. He believes that in order to balance the strong, legalistic, binding dispute settlement system with the member-driven, political system in the WTO, there needs to be strong political input (more voice) into the system. For that reason, he opposes changing the consensus rule in decision-making and the idea of a management board, but he supports greater transparency in the WTO, including allowing participation of NGOs in decision-making. See Joost Pauwelyn, 'The Transformation of World Trade', 104 (1) Michigan Law Review 1 (2005).

9 Claus-Dieter Ehlermann and Lothar Ehring, 'Decision-Making in the World Trade Organization', 8 (1) Journal of International Economic Law 51 (2005); Debra P. Steger, *Peace Through Trade: Building the WTO* (London: Cameron May Ltd., 2004); Marco C. E. J. Bronckers, 'Better Rules for a New Millennium: A Warning Against Undemocratic Developments in the WTO', 2 (4) Journal of International Economic Law 547 (1999).

10 Bronckers, ibid, at 551–52.

11 Ibid, at 550.

12 John H. Jackson, 'The WTO "Constitution" and Proposed Reforms: Seven "Mantras" Revisited', 4 (1) Journal of International Economic Law 67 (2001), at 74–75.

13 Ibid, at 74–75.

14 Thomas Cottier and Satoko Takenoshita, 'Decision-making and the Balance of Powers in WTO Negotiations: Towards Supplementary Weighted Voting', in Stefan Griller (ed), *At the Crossroads: The World Trading System and the Doha Round,* vol. 8 (Vienna: Springer, 2008) 181–223.

15 Gary Clyde Hufbauer, 'Inconsistency Between Diagnosis and Treatment', 8 (2) Journal of International Economic Law 291 (2005), at 296.

16 Warwick Commission, above n 3, at 29–32. See also the chapter by Manfred Elsig in this volume.

17 Consultative Board to the Director-General, above n 4, at 2.

18 Steger, above n 8.

19 Ibid, at 494.

20 Ibid, at 495.

21 The history of the Uruguay Round institutional negotiation is provided in Debra P. Steger, 'The World Trade Organization: A New Constitution for the World Trading System', in Marco Bronckers and Reinhard Quick (eds), *New Directions in International Economic Law: Essays in Honour of John H. Jackson* (The Hague: Kluwer International, 2000) 135–54. See also Pieter-Jan Kuijper, 'WTO Institutional Aspects', in Daniel Bethlehem, Donald McRae, Rodney Neufeld, and Isabelle Van Damme (eds), *The Oxford Handbook of International Trade Law* (Oxford: Oxford University Press, 2009) 79–129.

22 See, for example, Jackson, above n 13, at 74; Ehlermann and Ehring, above n 10, at 65–69; Peter Van den Bossche and Iveta Alexoviãová, 'Effective Global Economic Governance by the World Trade Organization', 8 (3) Journal of International Economic Law 667 (2005), at 671; Mitsuo Matsushita, Thomas J. Schoenbaum, and Petros C. Mavroidis, *The World Trade Organization: Law, Practice and Policy* (Oxford: Oxford University Press, 2003) 14.

23 See, for example, Cottier and Takenoshita, above n 15, at 181; Ehlermann and Ehring, above n 10, at 73.

24 Article IX:1, fn 2 of the WTO Agreement.

25 World Trade Organization, *GATT Analytical Index: Guide to GATT Law and Practice,* 6th ed. (Geneva: World Trade Organization, 1995) 2 vols.

26 General Council, Accession of Ecuador, WT/ACC/ECU/5, Adopted 22 August 1996.

27 *Rules of Procedure for Sessions of the Ministerial Conference and Meetings of the General Council,* WT/L/161, Adopted 25 July 1996. Rule 16 applies for meetings of the Dispute Settlement Body, the Council for Trade in Goods, the Council for Trade in Services, the Council for TRIPS.

28 Statement by the Chairman as Agreed by the General Council on 15 November 1995, Decision-Making Procedures under Articles IX and XII, WT/L/93, 24 November 1995.

29 Article IX:1, fn 3 of the WTO Agreement; Article 2(4) of the Dispute Settlement Understanding.

30 Article IX:3, fn 4 of the WTO Agreement.

31 Rules of Procedure for Meetings of the Council for Trade in Goods, WT/L/79, Adopted 7 August 1995.

32 Rules of Procedure for Meetings of the Council for Trade in Services, S/L/15, Adopted 19 October 1995.

33 Rules of Procedure for Meetings of Council for TRIPS, IP/C/1, Adopted 28 September 1995.

34 Claus-Dieter Ehlermann and Lothar Ehring 'The Authoritative Interpretation Under Article IX:2 of the Agreement Establishing the World Trade Organization: Current Law, Practice and Possible Improvements', 8 (4) Journal of International Economic Law 803 (2005), at 806.

35 The councils are established by Article IV:5) of the WTO Agreement (i.e., the Council for Trade in Goods, the Council for Trade in Services, and the Council for TRIPS).

36 Ministerial Declaration adopted on 14 November 2001, WT/MIN(01)/Dec/1, Adopted 20 November 2001, at para 46.

37 Statement by the Chairman of the General Council, TN/C/1, 4 February 2002.

38 Trade Negotiations Committee, Minutes of the Meeting Held on 26 July 2007, TN/C/M/27, Adopted 30 October 2007.

39 Decision on Transparency Mechanism for Regional Trade Agreements, WT/L/671, Adopted 14 December 2006.

40 Ministerial Declaration on Trade in Information Technology Products, WT/MIN(96)/16, Adopted 13 December 1996.

41 Ministerial Declaration on the TRIPS Agreement and Public Health, WT/MIN(01)/DEC/2, Adopted 14 November 2001.

42 Waiver Concerning Kimberley Process Certification Scheme for Rough Diamonds, WT/L/518, Adopted 27 May 2003.

43 Independent Evaluation Office of the International Monetary Fund, *Governance of the IMF: An Evaluation* (Washington, D.C.: International Monetary Fund, 2008) 4; online: <http://www.ieo-imf.org/eval/complete/pdf/05212008/CG_main.pdf>. See also Leonardo Martinez-Diaz, *Executive Boards in International Organizations: Lessons for Strengthening IMF Governance*, Independent Evaluation Office Background Paper No. BP/08/08 (Washington, D.C.: International Monetary Fund, 2008).

44 Independent Evaluation Office, ibid.

45 Ibid.

46 Ibid.

47 Ibid, at 5.

48 Havana Charter for an International Trade Organization, United Nations Conference on Trade and Employment—Final Act and Related Documents, UN Doc. E/Conf. 2/78 (1948).

49 Ibid, at 46.

50 Originally, it was proposed as a 'management group', but with the insistence of the GATT contracting parties on the limited authority of this group (Consultative Group of 18 shall not adopt binding decisions) the title was changed to the 'Consultative Group'. See Management of GATT: Note by the Secretariat, L/4048, 24 June 1974; Consultative Group of Eighteen: Note by the Director-General, L/4189, 27 June 1975.

51 See, for example, Richard Blackhurst and David Hartridge, 'Improving the Capacity of WTO Institutions to Fulfil Their Mandate', 7 (3) Journal of International Economic Law 705 (2004), at 713–14.

52 Proposal by the United States to Group of Negotiations on Goods, Negotiating Group on the Functioning of the GATT System, MTN.GNG/NG14/W/45, 18 October 1990.

53 Ibid, at 2. It should be noted that the references in the U.S. proposal were to the GATT and the CONTRACTING PARTIES because the idea of establishing the WTO had not as yet been approved by Uruguay Round negotiators. In fact, the United States remained steadfastly opposed to the establishment of an international organization until the very last hour of the Uruguay Round negotiations when it lifted its reservation.

54 Ministerial Declaration, above n 37, at para 10.

55 In particular, David Hartridge states, '[t]he WTO, and the GATT before it, have always needed, and for the past 17 years have lacked, a steering committee or management body. This need grows more urgent as the membership and the difficulty of managing the daily business of the Organization increase. So, a formal consultative body should be established.' See Blackhurst and Hartridge, above n 52, at 711.

56 See, for example, Robert Wolfe, 'Decision-Making and Transparency in the "Medieval" WTO: Does the Sutherland Report Have the Right Prescription?', 8 (3) Journal of International Economic Law 631 (2005), at 641. In particular, Robert Wolfe considers that '[t]he effort to crystallize the informal bodies that are emerging organically might be needlessly divisive without accomplishing much'. Joost Pauwelyn also opposes the idea of a small management body.

57 Consultative Board to the Director-General, above n 4, at paras 321–27.

58 Ibid.

59 Ibid, at paras 325–26.

60 Blackhurst and Hartridge, above n 52, at 708–09.

61 Matsushita, Schoenbaum, and Mavroidis, above n 23, at 15.

62 The proposal of the United States does not implicitly suggest vesting the management board with supervisory functions.

63 Leonardo Martinez-Diaz notes that '[f]or a board to play its role as strategic thinker, it must provide an environment that supports frank and constructive deliberation among board directors. In practice, this means relatively small boards. Corporate governance experts suggest that executive boards should have no more than ten members, with twelve as the absolute maximum'. See Martinez-Diaz, above n 44, at para 16. With respect to the WTO informal process of decision-making, Richard Blackhurst notes that 'once the active participation in a group/committee exceeds a certain number (say 25 or 30), discussions, debates, and negotiations become increasingly cumbersome, inefficient, and ultimately impossible'. See Blackhurst and Hartridge, above n 52, at 707.

64 See Jackson, above n 13, at 72 (where Jackson states, 'A totally member-driven organization is, in many cases, counterproductive, and most certainly inefficient').

65 Consultative Board to the Director-General, above n 4, at para 338.

66 Ibid.

67 Ibid, at para 361.

68 Ibid, at para 365.

69 Ibid, at paras 365–66.

70 Ibid, at paras 342–53.

71 Ibid, at paras 355–56.

72 The information is taken from the respective websites of the OECD and the WTO: http://www.oecd.org/pages/0,3417,en_36734052_36734103_1_1_1_1_1,00.html and http://www.wto.org/english/thewto_e/whatis_e/whatis_e.htm (visited 8 February 2009).

73 Steve Charnovitz believes that the Secretariat cannot debate with civil society and defend the WTO publicly. In his view, it is 'wrong ... for regular WTO staff to serve as a truth squad and respond to critics of the WTO'. See Steve Charnovitz, 'A Close Look at a Few Points', 8 (2) Journal of International Economic Law 311 (2005), at 319.

74 Sylvia Ostry, *The Post-Cold World Trading System: Who's on First* (Chicago: University of Chicago Press, 1997) 202.

75 See, for example, Steve Charnovitz, 'The WTO and Cosmopolitics', 7 (3) Journal of International Economic Law 675 (2004).

76 Julio Lacarte, 'Transparency, Public Debate and Participation by NGOs in the WTO: A WTO Perspective', 7 (3) Journal of International Economic Law 683 (2004), at 686.

77 Consultative Board to the Director-General, above n 4, at paras 201–05.

78 Charnovitz, above n 76, at 316.

79 Ibid.

80 Kobsak Chutikul, 'Options for a Parliamentary Dimension of the WTO' (Discussion paper presented at the Parliamentary Conference on the WTO, Geneva, 17–18 February 2003) 2.

81 Ibid, at 3. See also Erika Mann, 'A Parliamentary Dimension to the WTO—More Than Just a Vision?', 7 (3) Journal of International Economic Law 659 (2004), at 662.

82 Inter-Parliamentary Union, 'WTO Director General Dialogues with MPs at IPU Meeting on International Trade' (9 June 2001), http://www.ipu.org/press-e/gen119.htm (visited 8 February 2009).

83 Inter-Parliamentary Union, Final Declaration of the Parliamentary Meeting on International Trade on 8 and 9 June 2001, http://www.ipu.org/splz-e/trade01dclr.htm (visited 8 February 2009).

84 Inter-Parliamentary Union, Press Release, 119, 'WTO Director General Dialogues with MPs at IPU Meeting on International Trade' (9 June 2001), http://www.ipu.org/press-e/gen119.htm (visited 8 February 2009).

85 Inter-Parliamentary Union, 'Parliamentarians for More Transparency and Accountability of World Trade Negotiations' (12 November 2001), http://www.ipu.org/press-e/Gen124.htm (visited 8 February 2009).

86 Ibid.

87 Ibid.

88 See Final Declaration/Conclusions of the Parliamentary Meeting on the occasion of the fourth WTO Ministerial Conference in Doha, http://www.ipu.org/splz-e/doha.htm (visited 8 February 2009).

89 Belgium, Canada, China, Egypt, Finland, France, Germany, India, Iran (Islamic Republic of), Japan, Kenya, Mauritius, Mexico, Morocco, Namibia, Netherlands, Niger, Nigeria, South Africa, Thailand, Uruguay, United States of America, Inter-Parliamentary Union, European Parliament, Parliamentary Assembly of the Council of Europe, World Trade Organization.

90 Inter-Parliamentary Union, 'Parliaments Have a Special Role in Making the International Trading System More Open, More Equitable, More Predictable and Non-discriminatory' (18 February 2003), http://www.ipu.org/press-e/gen151.htm (visited 8 February 2009).

91 Parliamentary Conference on the WTO, Final Declaration adopted by consensus on 18 February 2003, at para 11, http://www.ipu.org/splz-e/trade03/declaration.pdf (visited 8 February 2009).

92 Inter-Parliamentary Union, Press Release, 'WTO Ministerial Conference: Parliamentarians Committed to Promote Free and Fair Trade That Benefits People Everywhere, Enhances Development and Reduces Poverty' (12 September 2003). See also Parliamentary Conference on the WTO, Final Declaration adopted by consensus on 12 September 2003, http://www.ipu.org/splz-e/cancun/declaration.pdf (visited 8 February 2009).

93 Rules of Procedure of the Parliamentary Conference on the WTO adopted on 26 November 2004 and amended on 12 September 2008, http://www.ipu.org/splz-e/trade08/rules.htm (visited 8 February 2009).

94 Inter-Parliamentary Union and the European Parliament, Joint press release, 195, 'The Parliamentary Conference on the WTO Urges Governments and Parliaments to Engage in a Regular Dialog' (26 November 2006), http://www.ipu.org/press-e/gen195.htm (visited 8 February 2009).

95 Some 400 members of national parliaments representing 65 countries and regional parliamentary assemblies participated in the Parliamentary Conference in Hong Kong in December 2005. Inter-Parliamentary Union, Press Release, 215, 'A Critical Moment for the WTO, Say Parliamentarians' (12 December 2005), http://www.ipu.org/press-e/gen215.htm (visited 8 February 2009).

96 The Parliamentary Conference on the WTO that took place on 1–2 December 2006 brought together some 400 delegates from over 70 countries. Inter-Parliamentary Union, Press Release, 251, 'The Political Cost of Failure Should Perhaps Be Considered as the Most Compelling Reason for Reaching a Deal' (1 December 2006), http://www.ipu.org/press-e/Gen251.htm (visited 8 February 2009).

97 More than 400 parliamentarians from over 80 countries participated in the Parliamentary Conference on the WTO on 12 September 2008. Inter-Parliamentary Union, 'Parliamentarians Urge WTO Negotiators to Close the Deal' (12 September 2008), http://www.ipu.org/press-e/gen309.htm (visited 8 February 2009).

98 Annual 2006 Session of the Parliamentary Conference on the WTO, Declaration adopted by consensus on 2 December 2006, at para 7, http://www.ipu.org/splz-e/trade06/declaration.pdf. See also Annual 2008 Session of the Parliamentary Conference on the WTO, Outcome Document adopted by consensus on 12 September 2008, at paras 8 and 11, http://www.ipu.org/splz-e/trade08/declaration.htm (visited 8 February 2009).

99 World Trade Organization, *WTO Policy Issues for Parliamentarians: A Guide to Current Trade Issues for Legislators* (Geneva: WTO, 2001).

100 For example, in 2003 national workshops for parliamentarians were held in St. Lucia (August), Namibia (November), and Moldova (November), and regional workshops were organized in Cape Town in May (for English-speaking African countries), Trinidad in July (for Caribbean countries), and São Paulo in August (for Latin American countries).

101 Parliamentary Conference on the WTO, Statement of Twelfth Session of the Conference Steering Committee held on 22–23 June 2006, http://www.ipu.org/Splz-e/trade06/statement.pdf (visited 8 February 2009).

102 According to the WTO Directory on March 2008 the External Relations Division consisted of seven people. This division is responsible, in particular, for relations with intergovernmental and non-governmental organizations and parliamentarians, OECD and the UN system, International Trade Center. It coordinates WTO representation at meeting of other organizations.

103 Consultative Board to the Director-General, above n 4, at para 196.

104 Ibid.

105 Importantly, guidelines adopted by the General Council on 18 July 1996 specifically indicate the role of non-governmental organizations: to increase the awareness of the public. See *Guidelines for Arrangements on Relations with Non-governmental Organizations*, WT/L/162, Adopted 23 July 1996.

106 Consultative Board to the Director-General, above n 4, at paras 176–77.

107 The legal basis for building communications between the WTO and non-governmental organizations is Article V:2 of the WTO Agreement, which states: 'The General Council may make appropriate arrangements for consultation and cooperation with non-governmental organizations concerned with matters related to those of the WTO.'

108 Guidelines for Arrangements on Relations with Non-governmental Organizations, WT/L/162, Adopted 23 July 1996.

109 Procedures for the Circulation and De-restriction of WTO Documents, WT/L/452, Adopted 16 May 2002.

110 Consultative Board to the Director-General, above n 4, at paras 183–85.

111 Ibid, at paras 206-10.

112 Ibid, at paras 190-91, 210.

113 Ibid, at paras 193-94.

114 Ibid, at paras 206-12.

115 For more on participation of NGOs in the WTO, see the chapters by Peter Van den Bossche and Yves Bonzon in this volume.

PART IV

Transparency and Domestic Consultation

From the Periphery to the Centre? The Evolving WTO Jurisprudence on Transparency and Good Governance

PADIDEH ALA'I*

1. Introduction

This chapter traces the jurisprudence of Article X of the General Agreement on Tariffs and Trade (GATT) of 1994.[1] Article X is significant because it 'goes to the heart of a country's legal infrastructure, and more precisely to the nature and enforcement of its administrative law regime'.[2] Article X was proposed by the United States in 1947 and was influenced by the contemporaneous enactment of the U.S. Administrative Procedures Act (APA).[3] Article X requires that trade-related measures be promptly published; administered in a uniform, impartial, and reasonable manner; and provide for independent review of administrative action that relates to customs matters.

During the GATT 1947 years,[4] Article X was a silent provision dismissed by panels as 'subsidiary' to other 'substantive' GATT provisions. Since the creation of the World Trade Organization (WTO), Article X has emerged from obscurity and has developed into a provision of fundamental importance as the embodiment of the principles of transparency and due process.[5] The relative prominence of Article X in trade disputes in the WTO is a manifestation of the emerging role of the WTO as a global (supranational) regulatory body.[6] The increased emphasis on Article X also highlights the potential role for the WTO in promoting 'good governance' norms in both the transnational and domestic context.[7]

This chapter will show that WTO Members are increasingly relying on good governance principles, such as transparency and due process in dispute settlement proceedings. These good governance principles, as embodied in Article X, are most often invoked in connection with contentious trade issues, including the administration of anti-dumping or countervailing measures by the U.S. Department of Commerce (DOC).

The growing centrality of Article X also reflects (1) an emerging global consensus regarding good governance values such as transparency, access to information, and participation, which must inform both domestic and global administrative systems; (2) the evolution of the GATT from a system based on tariffs, reciprocal bargaining, and exchange of concessions to one concerned with rule-making; and (3) an attempt by the dispute settlement system to accommodate the emerging role of the WTO as a rule-making body by enforcing its good governance mandate in a manner that avoids political controversy and charges of overreaching by the Members. For example, as discussed below, a panel may expansively interpret a provision of Article X, but then either refuse to address the Article X claim in the name of judicial economy or find that the measure in question does not in fact violate Article X requirements of transparency or due process.[8]

This chapter will first define terms and explore the roots and scope of Article X of GATT 1994. It will then discuss the application of Article X during the GATT 1947 years (1947 to 1994) when, after being a dormant provision for almost 40 years, it was dismissed in the 1980s and early 1990s as merely subsidiary to the more 'substantive' obligations contained in GATT 1947. It will then explore the impact of WTO jurisprudence on the scope and application of Article X's requirements of transparency and due process by analyzing the interpretation and application of Article X by the WTO panels and the Appellate Body from 1995 to the present. This chapter will then review the most prominent Article X cases brought under the Understanding on Rules and Procedures Governing the Settlement of Disputes (DSU),[9] culminating with *European Communities—Selected Customs Matters (EC—Selected Customs Matters)*, in which *all of the claims* were based on alleged violations of Article X.[10] Finally, this chapter will make some observations about the importance of acknowledging the WTO's good governance mandate as we embark on reforming our international economic institutions in light of the current global economic crisis.

II. History of Article X of GATT 1994

Article X was initially proposed by the United States as Article 15 of the draft Charter of the International Trade Organization (ITO),[11] which was subsequently adopted by the GATT 1947 Contracting Parties. At the time of its adoption, no other country expressed an interest in Article X, and it was adopted without any discussion or amendment. The proposed text of Article X generally followed the text of the APA, which was enacted in 1946.[12] At the time of its adoption, the Contracting Parties viewed Article X as creating no new obligations.[13] The text of Article X of GATT 1947 (which remains unchanged under GATT 1994) states:

(1) Laws, regulations, judicial decisions and administrative rulings of general application ... pertaining to the classification or the valuation of products for customs purposes, or to rates of duty, taxes or other charges, or to requirements, restrictions or prohibitions on imports or exports, or on the transfer or payments therefore, or *affecting* their sale, distribution, transportation ... or other use shall be *published promptly* in such manner as to enable governments and traders to become acquainted with them. Agreements affecting international trade policy ... shall also be *published*....

(2) *No* measure of general application ... effecting an advance in a rate of duty ... or imposing a new or *more* burdensome requirement, restriction or prohibition on imports ... shall be *enforced* before such measure has been officially *published*.

(3) (a) Each [Member] shall administer in a *uniform, impartial and reasonable manner* all its law, regulations, decisions and rulings of the kind described in paragraph 1....

(b) Each [Member] shall maintain, or institute as soon as practicable, judicial, arbitral or administrative tribunals or procedures for the purpose ... of the prompt review and correction of administrative action relating to custom matters.... Such tribunals or procedures shall be independent of the agencies entrusted with administrative enforcement....[14]

It has been argued that the motivation of the United States for proposing Article X was to level the playing field for U.S. traders who faced opaque and informal administrative structures in other countries, while U.S. administrative processes had been made more transparent with the enactment of the APA.[15] Article X may have been intended to assist U.S. exporters in the post–World War II world, but its provisions may also be interpreted as expressing the values that led to the enactment of the APA, such as imposing limitations on the exercise of executive discretion through transparency and due process.[16]

From 1947 to 1984 there was no mention of Article X in any adopted GATT panel decisions.[17] By the mid-1980s, faced with diminished competitiveness, the United States became increasingly concerned about the proliferation of non-tariff barriers (NTBs), including non-transparent and ad hoc administration of customs regulations.[18] Early GATT 1947 cases involving Article X were filed by the United States in respect of Japan's non-transparent administration of import quota systems and the extensive use of the informal system of 'administrative guidance' by Japan.[19]

III. Article X and the GATT 1947

Article X was mentioned in only nine adopted GATT 1947 panel decisions.[20] The United States was involved in all of these cases: six as complainant,[21] one as respondent,[22] and two as interested third party.[23] A review of these reports shows that, although the United States and other Contracting Parties to the GATT 1947 recognized that the administration of a measure could give rise to a claim, they preferred to address a measure as being inconsistent with more 'substantive' provisions, such as Article XI:1 of the GATT 1947.[24] Article XI:1 of the GATT 1947 prohibits quotas, import or export licences, or any other measure that in any manner restricts trade. The term 'other measure' can be interpreted broadly to cover a seemingly endless list of NTBs, including *inter alia* import licensing requirements, anti-dumping measures, and health and safety regulations. The breadth of the Article XI:1 obligation allowed GATT panels to find any measure inconsistent with the GATT 1947 without having to refer to the 'administrative' or 'subordinate' claim of Article X.

Three of the nine adopted GATT 1947 cases involving Article X were brought by either the United States or the European Communities (EC) (formerly the European Economic Community) against Japan.[25] At issue in those three cases was the level of transparency required under Article X.[26] In *Japanese Measures on Imports of Leather (Japan—Leather II [US])*, the United States challenged the *administration* of the Japanese quota system on imported leather.[27] The United States argued that the Japanese import leather quota system violated Articles X:1 and X:3 of the GATT 1947 because Japan had failed to publish the total import quotas and certain administrative rulings related to them.[28] Of particular concern was the fact that in administering the leather quotas, Japan had allocated licences so as to channel import trade through Japanese producers and distributors. The United States argued that Japanese producers had 'no incentive to fully utilize the quota amounts allocated to them.'[29] The panel ruled that the Japanese quota system was in violation of Article XI:1 and did not need to address the Article X issue.[30]

The second case involving Article X, *Japan—Restrictions on Imports of Certain Agricultural Products (Japan—Agricultural Products I)*, was decided in 1988. In that dispute, the United States argued that the Japanese quota system for certain agricultural products, in addition to violating Article XI:1, also violated Articles X:1 and X:3. The United States alleged that, in administering the agricultural quota system, Japan had failed to 'publish adequate and timely information on quota volume or value' contrary to Article X:1, which constituted an *unreasonable* administration of the import quota system in violation of Article X:3 (a).[31] Japan responded that there was no requirement to publish information beyond the total amount of the quota to be issued and criteria for application. Japan further argued that any additional disclosure of information as to the identity of the quota holders and other related information was not acceptable as it would only 'cause unnecessary confusion' and induce 'anti-competitive intervention among importers.'[32] The panel found Japan's import quota restrictions inconsistent with Article XI:1 and declined to rule on the Article X claims.[33]

Finally, in *Japan—Trade in Semi-Conductors (Japan—Semi-Conductors)*,[34] the EC invoked Article X in connection with the Third Country Monitoring System that was created by Japan pursuant to a voluntary export restraint arrangement with the United States. At issue was the use of 'administrative guidance' by Japan in implementing the monitoring system, which recorded both the cost and sale prices of semi-conductors that were exported to Europe and 'encouraged' Japanese exporters not to dump in the European market.[35] Although the panel decided that the case did not warrant a decision on the Article X claim, it did recognize the important role 'administrative guidance' played in the promotion and enforcement of governmental policy in Japan.[36] The panel, citing *Japan—Agricultural Products I*, stated that 'the practice of administrative guidance ... was a traditional tool of Japanese government policy based on consensus and peer pressure,'[37] implying that the workings of Japan's system of administrative guidance was *not* meant to be transparent.

Detailed discussion of Article X appears in only two GATT 1947 panel decisions. First, in *Canada—Import, Distribution and Sale of Certain Alcoholic Drinks by Provincial Marketing Agencies (Canada—Provincial Liquor Boards [US])*,[38] the panel concluded that Article X did *not* require Canadian provinces to provide 'information affecting trade available to domestic and foreign suppliers *at the same time*, nor did it require Contracting Parties, to publish trade regulations *in advance* of their entry into force.'[39] Second, in *European Economic Community—Restrictions on Imports of Dessert Apples—Complaint by Chile (EEC—Dessert Apples)*,[40] the panel ruled that the specific act of back-dating quotas on imports of dessert apples by the EEC was inconsistent with the publication requirement of Article X. This is the only adopted GATT 1947 decision to find a violation of Article X. However, the panel also held that the EC's administration of its quota system was not in violation of the 'uniformity' requirement of Article X:3(a). The panel concluded that the requirement of 'uniformity' in administration imposed by Article X:3(a) did not require EC members to have identical administrative procedures with regards to the import of dessert apples. In reaching its conclusion, the panel emphasized the substantive provisions of GATT 1947 by first finding violations of Article XI:1 and Article XIII of GATT 1947 and then only found a violation of Article X with regards to the specific act of back-dating import restrictions from the date of publication to have been a violation of Article X:1.[41]

In the remaining GATT 1947 cases, panels merely dismissed the Article X claims as subsidiary issues that did not need to be addressed.[42] The last adopted GATT 1947 case involving an Article X claim was *United States—Countervailing Duties on Non-Rubber Footwear from Brazil (US—Non-Rubber Footwear)*.[43] The panel dismissed the Article X:3(a) claim as not being within the terms of reference of the panel.[44] Interestingly, this case does foreshadow a line of cases discussed below in which administration of trade remedies by the United States DOC is challenged as being inconsistent, among other things, with the requirements of Article X:3(a).

IV. The Expansion of the WTO Trade Mandate and Its Impact on Article X

Upon creation of the WTO, Article X of the GATT 1947 became Article X of the GATT 1994 and was included as part of Annex 1A of the WTO Agreement without any amendment.[45] Annex 1A also includes other trade agreements that had been negotiated under the auspices of the GATT 1947 on trade in goods.[46] Article X is specifically mentioned in the following Annex 1A agreements: Agreement on Implementation of Article VII of the GATT 1994 (Customs Valuation Agreement),[47] Agreement on Rules of Origin,[48] and Agreement on Safeguards.[49] The other Annex 1A agreements do not mention Article X but do contain provisions addressing transparency and due process in the administration of measures, including the Agreement on the Application of Sanitary and Physosanitary Measures (SPS Agreement);[50] Agreement on Technical Barriers to Trade (TBT Agreement);[51] Agreement on the Implementation of Article VI of the GATT 1994 (Antidumping Agreement);[52] Agreement on Subsidies and Countervailing Measures (SCM Agreement);[53] and the Agreement on Import Licensing Procedures (Licensing Agreement).[54] Outside of trade in goods, the requirements of Article X are replicated throughout the Agreement on Trade in Services (GATS)[55] and the Agreement on Trade Related Aspects of Intellectual Property (TRIPS).[56] In addition, the Trade Policy Review Mechanism (TPRM) monitors 'domestic transparency in government decision-making in the trade policy-making area'.[57] In view of the fact that Article X of GATT is applicable only to trade in goods, this chapter will not discuss in detail the scope of the transparency provisions of GATS, TRIPS, or the TPRM.

The relationship between the transparency and due process obligations of Article X of the GATT 1994 and the provisions of the other Annex 1A agreements is far from clear.[58] The General Interpretative Note to Annex 1A (Interpretative Note) states:

> In the event of conflict between a provision of [GATT] 1994 and a provision of another agreement in Annex 1A to the Agreement Establishing the [WTO], the provision of the other agreement shall prevail to *the extent of the conflict*.[59]

There is no agreement on the interpretation of the term 'conflict' except in cases where provisions directly contradict one another. Such a direct substantive conflict is unlikely to arise in the context of Article X as it is concerned with transparency and due process in the administration of a measure. This absence of clarity gives rise to a number of questions: What is the relationship between Article X and the provisions of other Annex 1A agreements? When a measure falls within the scope of an Annex 1A agreement is it still subject to the transparency and due process requirements of Article X? Are Article X obligations *independent* of the due process requirements of the other Annex 1A agreements? How should the term 'to the extent of the conflict' as stated in the Interpretative Note be construed in relation to Article X?

As the discussion below will show, WTO panels and the Appellate Body have held that the Interpretative Note does not prohibit concurrent application of Article X of GATT 1994 and provisions of other Annex 1A agreements. But, as a general rule, panels and the Appellate Body have tended to focus on more specific provisions of the other Annex 1A agreements. This focus on the relevant provisions of Annex 1A agreements (as opposed to GATT 1994) has not resulted in complete marginalization of Article X requirements of transparency and due process.

V. Interpretation of Article X GATT 1994: Emerging from Obscurity

Since the founding of the WTO, there have been at least 20 cases involving consideration of Article X of the GATT 1994,[60] and almost half of these cases have been brought against the United States and have concerned the administration of safeguard, anti-dumping, and countervailing duty laws. A wide variety of countries at differing levels of economic development have invoked Article X, including Argentina, Australia, Brazil, Chile, Costa Rica, Ecuador, Guatemala, Honduras, India, Indonesia, Korea, Mexico, Thailand, Turkey, and the United States. In contrast to the GATT 1947 days, no WTO Member has referred to their Article X claim as a 'subsidiary' claim.

Some Article X claims brought before WTO panels and the Appellate Body have continued the GATT 1947–era practice of deferring a discussion of the provision in favour of other GATT 1994 violations. However, even in such cases, panels and the Appellate Body have refrained from stating that an Article X claim is a subsidiary issue. As the discussion below will show, even in cases where the panels or the Appellate Body have not found a violation of Article X, they have underscored the importance of Article X obligations and engaged in extensive discussions on the scope and meaning of its provisions. In addition, unlike the GATT 1947 years, WTO panels and the Appellate Body have found national measures to be inconsistent with the provisions of Article X, including *Argentina—Measures Affecting the Export of Bovine Hides and the Import of Finished Leather (Argentina—Hides and Leather)*,[61] *Dominican Republic—Measures Affecting the Importation and Internal Sale of Cigarettes (Dominican Republic—Import and Sales of Cigarettes)*,[62] *EC—Selected Customs Matters*,[63] and *United States—Customs Bond Directive for Merchandise Subject to Anti-Dumping/Countervailing Duties (US—Customs Bond Directive)*.[64]

In the WTO era, Article X of GATT 1994 was first analyzed in 1997 by the Appellate Body in *United States—Restrictions on Imports of Cotton and Man-Made Fibre Underwear (United States—Underwear)*, which stated:

> Article X:2 … may be seen to embody a principle of fundamental importance—that of promoting full disclosure of governmental acts affecting Members and private persons and enterprises, *whether of domestic or foreign nationality*. The relevant policy principle is widely known as the principle of transparency and has obviously due process dimensions. The essential implication is that Members *and other persons affected*, or likely to be affected, by governmental measures imposing restraints, requirements, and other burdens, should have a reasonable opportunity to acquire authentic information about such measures and accordingly to protect and adjust their activities or alternatively to seek modification of such measures….[65]

The Appellate Body's identification of the fundamental importance of Article X lies in sharp contrast to earlier panel discussions of Article X under GATT 1947. The reference to transparency and due process values enshrined in Article X has been widely quoted by subsequent WTO panels. Of particular significance is the Appellate Body's view that Article X's transparency and due process protections extend to administrative actions taken by Members in relation to their own citizens (i.e., internal governance, as well as in relation to foreign traders). Another point highlighted by the Appellate Body in *United States—Underwear* is that Article X, unlike other GATT provisions, is explicitly concerned with the rights and expectations of traders. Finally, the Appellate Body clarified that Article X allows challenges to the administration of measures that are otherwise WTO consistent.

The importance of Article X was also underscored by the Appellate Body in *United States—Import Prohibition of Certain Shrimp and Shrimp Products (US—Shrimp)*.[66] In that case, the Appellate Body held that a U.S. measure prohibiting importation of shrimp or shrimp products fell within the scope of Article XX(g) of the GATT 1994 as a measure that was aimed primarily at the conservation of an exhaustible natural resource, giving effect to restrictions on domestic production or consumption.[67] But the U.S. conservation measure failed the requirements of the chapeau of Article XX because the United States applied the measure in a manner that constituted arbitrary and unjustifiable discrimination between countries where the same conditions prevail.[68] The Appellate Body went on to state:

> Provisions of Article X:3 of the GATT 1994 bear upon this matter. In our view Section 609 [the U.S. restriction on shrimp imports] fall within the [scope of] Article X:1. Inasmuch as there are due process requirements generally for measures that are otherwise imposed in compliance with WTO obligations, it is only reasonable that *rigorous compliance with the fundamental requirements of due process* should be required in the application and administration of a measure which purports to be an exception to the treaty obligations....[69]

The Appellate Body in *US-Shrimp* also goes on to state that the U.S. measure at issue, Section 609, was applied in a manner that was 'contrary to the spirit, if not letter, of Article X:3 [of GATT 1994]'.[70]

A. The Scope of Measures Covered under Article X:1 of the GATT 1994

Article X requires that 'laws, regulations, judicial decisions and administrative rulings of *general application*' (collectively 'measures') be promptly published and administered 'uniformly, impartially and reasonably'.[71] Panels and the Appellate Body, on the whole, have given the term 'general application' a generous interpretation so as not to limit the scope of measures covered under Article X:1. In *European Communities—Regime for the Importation, Sale and Distribution of Bananas (EC—Bananas III)*,[72] the panel and the Appellate Body stated that Article X applies to *both* internal measures and border measures.[73] In *Japan—Measures Affecting Consumer Photographic Film and Paper (Japan— Film)*, the panel held that a measure qualifies under Article X:1 as an administrative ruling of general application even if it is addressed to only a specific company or shipment *if* such a ruling establishes or revises principles applicable in future cases.[74] This reasoning was followed in *Argentina—Hides and Leather*,[75] in which the panel held that a resolution that permitted representatives of the domestic tanning industry to be present during the customs process of export clearance was an administrative measure of general application under Article X:1 even if only one company benefited from it.[76]

In anti-dumping cases, however, panels have been reluctant to find specific dumping determinations 'measures of general application'. In *United States—Anti-Dumping Measures on Certain Hot-Rolled Steel Products from Japan (United States—Hot-Rolled Steel)*,[77] the panel held that a specific anti-dumping ruling in a particular case did not qualify as a measure of general application. Nevertheless, the panel did state that in certain circumstances, the outcome of a single anti-dumping investigation could have 'significant impact on the overall administration of the law' and therefore could be considered a measure of general application within the scope of Article X:1.[78] In 2004, in *Dominican Republic—Import and Sale of Cigarettes,* the panel decided that a survey taken by the Dominican Republic's Central Bank on average prices of cigarettes was an 'administrative ruling of general application' and should have been published because it was '*an essential element* of an administrative ruling' within the scope of Article X:1.[79]

In sum, panels and the Appellate Body have adopted an expansive interpretation of the term 'measures of general application', which includes any specific act of administration that has a 'significant impact' on the overall administration of the law *or* any government action, including a survey, which subsequently forms a basis for an administrative ruling. At the same time, however, panels and the Appellate Body have retained the flexibility to exclude a measure from the scope of Article X:1 if they determine that it does not have a significant impact on the overall administration of a measure.

B. The Scope of Article X:3 of the GATT 1994

Article X:3(a) requires WTO Members to 'administer in a uniform, impartial and reasonable manner all its laws, regulations … and administrative rulings of the kind referred to in Article X:1.' Article X:3(b) and (c) require independent or 'objective and impartial review' of all administrative actions that relate to customs matters.

WTO panels and the Appellate Body have interpreted the term 'applied uniformly' to mean that 'customs laws should not vary, that every exporter and importer should be able to expect treatment of the same kind, in the same manner over time and in different places and with respect to the other persons'.[80] Panels have also stated that 'access to' and 'flow of information' are essential to meeting the due process requirements of Article X:3(a). The panel in *Argentina—Hides and Leather* stated that 'the requirement of reasonableness and impartiality ... both relate to the question of information' and that unless 'access to information' is uniform and reasonable the administration of a measure cannot be impartial.[81] Panels have also emphasized that the three requirements of Article X:3(a) are not cumulative, and that a measure must satisfy *all* three requirements separately.[82] In *Argentina—Hides and Leather*, the panel pointed out that Article X:3(a) applies to the substance of an administrative measure.[83] Panels have also held that the scope of Article X:3(a) is not limited by the most-favoured-nation (MFN) requirement. There is no requirement that Article X:3(a) be applied only in situations where the measure has been applied in an inconsistent manner with respect to the imports from or exports to *two or more* Members.[84]

There has been great reluctance in applying the provisions of Article X:3(a) to specific anti-dumping actions. In *United States—Anti-Dumping Duty on Dynamic Random Access Memory Semiconductors (DRAMS) of One Megabit or Above from Korea (US—DRAMS)*, Korea argued that the due process values of Article X:3(a) renders every action taken by the DOC in administering anti-dumping measures susceptible to scrutiny.[85] Similarly, in *United States— Hot-Rolled Steel*, Japan argued that the scope of Article X:3(a) was broader than the covered agreements because the standards contained in Article X:3 represent in one sense the notion of good faith and in another sense the 'fundamental requirements of due process', and that these principles should be applied to the manner in which the DOC administered the anti-dumping laws.[86]

In *Dominican Republic—Import and Sales of Cigarettes*, the panel defined the term 'reasonable' as 'in accordance with reason, not irrational or absurd, proportionate'.[87] The panel ruled that the administration of the provisions of the Selective Consumption Tax was 'unreasonable' and in violation of Article X:3(a) because it used the 'nearest similar product' to determine the tax rate on imported cigarettes while that was not the criteria that had been stated in the regulation. The Dominican Republic acknowledged the problem with using the nearest similar product and removed the measure while the case was before the panel. Nevertheless, the panel engaged in a relatively extensive discussion of the meaning of the term 'reasonable' in Article X:3(a) and ruled that the Selective Consumption Tax, as it was administered prior to the change, was unreasonable.

C. Protecting the Expectations of Traders

A distinguishing feature of WTO-era Article X jurisprudence has been that the panels have looked toward the expectations of private individual traders who operate in the market place. For example, in *United States—Sunset Reviews of*

Anti-Dumping Measures on Oil Country Tubular Goods from Argentina (US—Oil Country Tubular Goods Sunset Reviews) the panel concentrated on showing the 'real effect' of the DOC's sunset reviews on 'foreign traders operating in the commercial world'.[88] This is unique within the context of the GATT and the WTO where emphasis has been on 'expectations of a competitive relationship' between *the Members* based on a system of reciprocity and mutual concessions.

In *Argentina—Hides and Leather*, the panel addressed the issue of the expectation of traders as follows:

> Article X:3(a) requires an examination of the real effect that a measure might have on traders operating in a commercial world. This, of course, does not require a showing of trade damage, as that is not generally a requirement with respect to violations of GATT 1994. But it can involve an examination of whether there is possible impact on the competitive situation due to alleged partiality, unreasonableness or lack of uniformity in application of custom rules....[89]

The direct and explicit reference to 'expectations of traders' is significant in at least two respects. First, it emphasizes the importance of Article X as private traders ask their governments to focus on the lack of transparency and uniformity in the application of internal or border measures. Second, it underscores the good governance mandate of the WTO as an organization that is expected to protect the expectations of private actors (not only governments) by safeguarding transparency, accountability, and other due process values. This, in turn, demonstrates the evolution of the system away from one based on reciprocal bargaining and mutual concessions among Members to a system that promotes rules of good governance.

D. Relationship of Article X of GATT 1994 and the WTO Agreement

There is a great deal of uncertainty regarding the relationship between the provisions of GATT 1994, including Article X, and other Annex 1A agreements. The Interpretative Note to Annex 1A does not solve this problem as it provides only that, in cases of 'conflict' between the GATT 1994 and other Annex 1A agreements, the provision of the other agreement prevails but only to the 'extent of the conflict'.[90] What does 'conflict' mean when dealing with Article X's relationship to another agreement? As might be expected, the answer to this question is not clear and seems to vary depending on the other agreement at issue.

In *United States—Underwear*, Costa Rica argued that the United States safeguard action against imports of cotton and man-made-fibre underwear was inconsistent with *both* the Agreement on Textiles and Clothing[91] and

Article X:2 of the GATT 1994.[92] The panel held that a transitional safeguard measure was subject to the publication requirements of Article X:2 *as well as* the Agreement on Textiles and Clothing. On appeal, the Appellate Body overturned the Article X:2 violation, but on the ground that Article X:2 does not address whether a Member can give retroactive effect to a safeguard measure. While it did not expressly address the relationship between the provisions of the GATT 1994 and the text of other agreements, the Appellate Body in *United States—Underwear* did clearly imply that both can apply.[93]

The relationship between Licensing Agreement and Article X was addressed in *EC—Bananas III*, in which the panel interpreted the term 'conflict' in the Interpretative Note narrowly to include only those instances where a provision in one agreement prohibits what another agreement explicitly permits or where a Member *cannot* comply with both the requirements of another Annex 1A agreement and Article X.[94] The Appellate Body agreed with the panel that the Interpretative Note allows for the application of *both* Article X:3 and the Licensing Agreement, but ruled that the panel should have applied the Licensing Agreement *first*, as it was the more specific and detailed agreement.[95] If the panel had applied the Licensing Agreement first, the Appellate Body reasoned, 'then there would be no need for it to address … Article X:3(a) of GATT 1994'.[96]

This GATT 1947–like approach of ignoring the requirements of Article X:3 was challenged in *European Communities—Measures Affecting Importation of Certain Poultry Products (EC—Poultry)*.[97] The panel in *EC—Poultry* found that, unlike the *EC—Bananas III* case, even after reviewing the Licensing Agreement, it was obliged to look at Article X:3(a). The panel reasoned that this was appropriate because the Licensing Agreement was relevant only to a portion of the measure at issue, while the scope of Article X was broader.[98]

In contrast to the Licensing Agreement, panels have been reluctant to apply Article X:3(a) to measures falling within the scope of the Antidumping Agreement (AD Agreement). In *United States—Hot-Rolled Steel* the panel stated:

> Where we have found a particular action or category of action is not inconsistent with a specific provision of the AD Agreement, we are faced with the question whether a Member can be found to have violated Article X:3 (a) … we have serious doubts as to whether such a finding would be appropriate.[99]

While this statement does not make Article X:3 explicitly inapplicable to the Antidumping Agreement, it is clear the panel did not find it is appropriate to apply the due process provisions of Article X:3 to the administration of anti-dumping measures in addition to the due process requirements of the Antidumping

Agreement. The applicability of the terms of Article X:3(a) to the administration of U.S. anti-dumping laws was argued forcefully by Korea in *US—DRAMS*:

> WTO Agreements are a unitary whole. The transparency and uniformity obligations of Article X apply to the WTO Agreements, including the [Anti-Dumping Agreement] ... the Member must administer each statute, regulation, and administrative ruling in a way that complies with Article X:3. Thus Article X applies to each and every action of the [DOC]....[100]

In response, the panel expressed reluctance to apply Article X:3(a) to the DOC's actions:

> [W]e have grave doubts as to whether Article X:3 (a) can or should be used in the manner advocated by Korea. As the United States correctly points out ... [Article X:3 (a)] was not intended to function as a mechanism to test the consistency of a Member's particular decision or rulings with the Member's own domestic law and practice; that is a function reserved for each Member's domestic judicial system....[101]

The discomfort of panels in reviewing the administrative structure of a Member is understandable. However, that is what Article X:3(a) allows by giving Members the right to challenge the administration of particular measures.

VI. The *EC—Selected Customs Matters* Dispute

Some 60 years after its inclusion in the GATT 1947, Article X was invoked as the sole legal basis for a trade dispute. In *EC—Selected Customs Matters*,[102] the United States claimed that the EEC system of customs administration 'as a whole' was not administered uniformly as required by Article X:3(a).[103] In its complaint, the United States also pointed to the specific non-uniform application of valuation rules and the administration of customs regulations to imports of liquid crystal display (LCD) monitors and blackout drapery. The United States argued that the lack of any mechanism at the EEC level to address divergences in customs administrations was a violation of the uniformity requirement of Article X:3(a).[104]

The panel agreed that the EC's system of custom administration as a whole is 'complicated and, at times, opaque and confusing'.[105] In fact, the panel further stated:

> We can imagine that the difficulties we encountered in our efforts to understand the EC's system of customs administration would be multiplied for traders in general and small traders in particular who are trying to import into the European Communities.[106]

Nevertheless, the panel dismissed the 'as a whole' challenge as not within the panel's terms of reference.[107] The panel did mention, however, that 'there is nothing in the DSU nor in other WTO agreements that would prevent a complaining Member from challenging a Member's system as a whole or over-all'.[108] The panel did find violations of Article X:3(a) due to non-uniform clas-sification of LDC monitors and blackout drapery linings, and the non-uniform administration of valuation rules by EC members.[109]

On appeal, the Appellate Body held that the EC's system of customs administration could be challenged 'as a whole or overall' under Article X:3(a) and that such a challenge was within the scope of the terms of reference.[110] The Appellate Body went on to hold that the administrative-substantive distinc-tion maintained in *EC—Bananas III* and *EC—Poultry* did not exclude the possibility of allowing challenges to the substance of a measure that leads to inconsistent administration. Specifically, the Appellate Body stated that earlier rulings did 'not exclude … the possibility of challenging under Article X:3(a) the substantive content of a legal instrument that regulates the admin-istration of a legal instrument of the kind described in Article X:1'.[111] Thus a Member *can* challenge the substantive content of a legal instrument if such content determines the administration of that regulation, so long as it can be shown that the substantive measure *necessarily* leads to lack of uniform, impartial, or reasonable administration in violation of Article X:3(a).[112] The Appellate Body held that mere differences in customs laws among EC member states did not necessarily breach the uniformity requirement in Article X:3(a), unless such differences actually lead to non-uniform admin-istration in specific cases.[113]

Having found that the EC system can, in principle, be challenged as a whole, under Article X:3(a), the Appellate Body sidestepped the 'as a whole' challenge by stating that the record did not provide the Appellate Body with enough facts to decide such a claim. Furthermore, the Appellate Body reversed two specific panel findings of inconsistency with Article X:3(a) relating to the administration of customs penalty laws and audit procedures and the tariff classification of blackout drapery, and upheld only the finding that the tariff classification of certain LCD monitors amounted to non-uniform adminis-tration in violation of Article X:3(a) and the panel's dismissal of the claim relating to Article X:3(b).[114] In this landmark case, by further blurring the administrative-substantive distinction, the Appellate Body sanctioned the wider use of Article X and opened the door for future claims, including challenges to the substance of laws as a whole.[115]

VII. The 'Culture' of the WTO DSM and the Future of Article X

The evolution of the jurisprudence of Article X under the WTO has expanded the scope of Article X through interpretation of its provisions and blurring the distinction relied on by earlier panels between a substantive and an administrative measure. The culture of the WTO DSM is such, however, that expansive interpretations of Article X are not necessarily accompanied by application of Article X requirements in specific cases. It is also unclear the extent to which due process requirements of Article X:3(a) are applicable to measures that fall within the scope of various Annex 1A agreements.

Article X:3(a) requirements have not been applied to the Antidumping Agreement, but they have been found to be concurrently applicable with the due process requirements of the Licensing Agreement. Some Members of the WTO view the administration of U.S. trade remedy laws (specifically in the anti-dumping context) to be inconsistent with Article X:3(a) requirements of uniformity, impartiality, and reasonableness.[116] It is, therefore, likely that Article X will continue to be asserted against the United States, the original architect of Article X, as Members emphasize values of fundamental due process, such as transparency and access to information. Panels and the Appellate Body are unlikely to apply Article X to the administration of U.S. trade remedy laws. Instead, panels will likely continue to focus on the specific procedural provisions of the Antidumping Agreement, SCM Agreement, and the Agreement on Safeguards.

Such an approach is consistent with the culture of the DSU. For example, in *EC—Selected Customs Matters,* the Appellate Body expanded the scope of measures that can be challenged under Article X:3(a), but at the same time largely reversed the panel's finding of inconsistency with Article X:3(a) and only affirmed the panel's finding that the non-uniform administration of the tariff classification of LCD monitors by EU members was a violation of Article X:3(a). Similarly, in *Dominican Republic—Import and Sale of Cigarettes,* there is an extensive discussion of the meaning of the term 'reasonable' in Article X:3, even though the measures at issue had already been withdrawn. In *US—DRAMS,* the panel addressed Article X:3 only to conclude that the inconsistency of the measure with the Antidumping Agreement rendered examination of Korea's claims under Article X unnecessary. The seeming discrepancy between the relatively extensive discussions of the requirements of Article X:3(a) and the refusal of the panels to rule on Article X claims is consistent with the culture and practices of the DSM. The practice under the DSU is to avoid making controversial decisions, while incrementally developing the jurisprudence so that future panels and the Appellate Body can accommodate the expansion of the WTO mandate into areas that go beyond the traditional sphere of securing or promoting trade liberalization, and into promoting good governance within Members.[117]

Recent interpretations of the scope of Articles X:1 and X:3(a) have expanded the scope of those provisions. The ruling in *EC—Selected Customs Matters*, that a system as a whole can be challenged under Article X:3(a), will likely encourage Members to bring additional complaints. Specifically, Article X challenges to the EC's system of customs administration are likely to continue given the view expressed by the panel that the EC customs regulations can be opaque and confusing. In addition, *United States—Shrimp* has made the jurisprudence of Article X applicable 'in spirit' if not 'in letter' to the chapeau of Article XX. It is therefore possible that the developing jurisprudence of Article X, and specifically of Article X:3(a), may be used to interpret the application of Article XX measures or to otherwise guide the interpretation of the chapeau of Article XX.

VIII. Conclusion

Article X of the GATT 1994 is the oldest good governance provision at international trade law, and a close study of its history and evolving jurisprudence contributes to an understanding of the emerging role of the WTO as a potential supra-national regulatory body and the final arbiter of appropriate administrative and regulatory structures.[118] The broad language of Article X allows the WTO to review domestic administrative legal regimes based on interpretation of the terms: uniform, impartial, and reasonable. Applying those standards to administrative acts and practices of WTO Members, particularly in the context of claims against administrative systems *as a whole*, could raise serious concerns if seen as interfering in the internal governance of Members. Although such increased reference to fundamental values of transparency and due process may be a sign of an emerging consensus on the elements for good governance, it also has the potential to undermine the utility of such values if they are not addressed or applied in an even-handed manner by panels and the Appellate Body.

The WTO is no longer a system simply based on consensus, reciprocity, and a balancing of concessions. Rather, it is a system based on rules that reflect the reality of the administrative state. The goal of the multilateral trading system is no longer free trade (if it ever was) but rather trade that is regulated in a WTO-consistent manner. As a result, the good governance provisions of the WTO, those addressing transparency and due process, are increasingly central to WTO disputes. Fortunately, the multilateral trading system is very adept at making incremental change. To date, the Appellate Body and panels have been, in most cases, reluctant to find a measure inconsistent with the obligations of Article X:3(a), but have continued to build the jurisprudence of Article X:3(a) through interpretation of its provisions and applauding the values it enshrines.[119]

There is much at stake in how the DSM addresses future transparency claims. There is great discrepancy among Members with regard to their administrative structures and institutional capacity, and the DSM may not be the most appropriate forum to address such differences. It is possible that countries with advanced and complicated regulatory structures may feel more vulnerable to charges of inconsistency with transparency and due process obligations of the WTO. It is therefore important that the WTO acknowledge its good governance mandate through coordination between the transparency-related works of its various committees and the TPRM's mandate to monitor domestic transparency in the trade decision-making area. This coordination could also assist the DSM in interpreting and applying the transparency-related obligations of the WTO Agreements.

In response to the recent financial crisis, there have been calls for reform of the Bretton Woods Institutions, but predictably the focus has been on the IMF and to some extent the World Bank, not on the WTO.[120] This is a mistake. As this article has attempted to show, the role of the WTO goes beyond that of trade liberalization. In fact, the WTO is in a singular position to promote and universalize core values such as transparency and access to information with nation states. For example, a recent study of the World Bank on the efficacy of its anti-corruption efforts in the public sector reform area shows that *direct* approaches to combatting corruption advocated by the World Bank have largely failed and that the most successful examples of combatting corruption have been *indirect* ones that the WTO promotes, such as the removal of ambiguity from laws and regulations and making public announcements of hiring opportunities.[121]

The story of the evolution of Article X demonstrates not only the increasingly prominent role of the WTO in promoting good governance but also the emerging global consensus on core values of good governance, such as transparency or access to information. It is imperative that the WTO's good governance provisions be subjected to greater clarity as we embark on reforming our international economic institutions to meet the enormous challenges posed by the global economic downturn.[122]

Notes

* The author would like to thank Lana Nigro and Lisa Schopler for their assistance with this paper. An earlier version of this paper was delivered at the 4th Global Administrative Law (GAL) Conference in Viterbo, Italy in June 2008.

1 World Trade Organization (WTO), *The Results of the Uruguay Round of Multilateral Trade Negotiations, the Legal Texts* (Geneva: WTO, 2003) 17.

2 Sylvia Ostry, 'China and the WTO: The Transparency Issue', 3 (1) UCLA Journal of International Law and Foreign Affairs (1998), at 2.

3 5 United States Code (USC) paras 551–59.

4 WTO, above n 1, at 423.

5 Transparency is generally defined as 'sharing information or acting in an open manner,' or 'a measure of the degree of which information about official activity is made available to an interested party.' See William Mock, 'On the Centrality of Information Law: A Rational Choice Discussion of Information Law and Transparency', 17 John Marshall Journal of Computer and Information Law (1999), at 1082.

6 In the legal context, the focus of transparency is on procedural due process: publication, access to and flow of information, and independent judicial review. This article is not concerned with the internal governance of the WTO or the external transparency of the WTO as it relates to public (non-state) participation.

7 In this paper 'governance' is defined as the 'process of decision-making and the process by which decisions are implemented'. See United Nations Economic and Social Commission for Asia and the Pacific (ESCAP), 'What Is Good Governance?', http://www.unescap.org/pdd/prs/ProjectActivities/Ongoing/gg/governance.pdf (visited 16 May 2008). The term 'good governance' 'includes five basic characteristics: (1) participation, (2) transparency, (3) responsibility, (4) accountability, and (5) responsiveness: Commission on Human Rights, 'Role of Good Governance in the Promotion of Human Rights', UN Doc. E/CN.4/RES/2000/64 (April 27, 2000). A strong argument can be made that the cumulative effect of the 'good governance' provisions of the WTO, for example requiring notification, publication, participation, responsiveness, and access to information, have potentially far greater impact on domestic governance of states than direct attempts at legal and institutional reform by the World Bank, the International Monetary Fund (IMF), and others. A prominent example of the influence of WTO's transparency and good governance provisions is seen in the case of China, where thousands of pieces of legislation were promulgated in connection with China's accession to the WTO.

8 In such cases, the panels' extensive discussion of Article X provisions may nevertheless set the stage for the future where international review of domestic administrative regimes may be less politically controversial. See below, Part VII.

9 WTO, above n 1, at 354.

10 WTO Appellate Body Report, *European Communities—Selected Customs Matters (EC—Selected Customs Matters)*, WT/DS315/AB/R, adopted 11 December 2006; WTO Panel Report, *European Communities—Selected Customs Matters*, WT/DS315/R, adopted 11 December 2006.

11 Ostry, above n 2, at 3.

12 Article X was also 'partially based on Articles 4 and 6 of the 1923 International Convention Relating to the Simplification of Customs Formalities'. See GATT, *Analytical Index: Guide to GATT Law and Practice*, 6th ed. (WTO & Bernan Press, 1995) vol. I, at 309. See also Padideh Ala'i, 'The Multilateral Trading System and Transparency, in Trends' in Alan S. Alexandroff (ed), *World Trade: Essays in Honor of Sylvia Ostry* (Durham, N.C.: Carolina Academic Press, 2007) at 105, 108–12 (discussing the history and evolution of the U.S. APA and its relationship to Article X of GATT 1947).

13 In fact, a senior Canadian negotiator is quoted as stating at the time of the original enactment of Article X that it contained no additional substantive requirements and should therefore not be of any concern. Sylvia Ostry, 'Article X and the Concept of Transparency in the GATT/WTO', in Alan S. Alexandroff, Sylvia Ostry, and Rafael Gomez (eds), *China and the Long March to Global Trade: The Accession of China to the World Trade Organization* (London: Routledge, 2002) 123–24. See also Ostry, above n 2, at 4.

14 Article X of the GATT (emphasis added).

15 See John H. Jackson, *World Trade and the Law of GATT* (Charlottesville, Va.: Michie Company, 1969) 461–64.

16 See Ala'i, above n 12, at 109–12 (noting that while the APA may have been an attempt to limit executive discretion it also led to the rise of the administrative state with the proliferation of agencies under the executive branch of government).

17 Prior to the formation of the WTO, the GATT dispute settlement panel was driven by consensus that required agreement of all parties for the formation or adoption of panel decisions. The result of this consensus-driven approach was few adopted decisions, and even fewer dealing with controversial issues that may have threatened the legitimacy of the system. This may have included avoiding Article X transparency claims.

18 These issues were addressed more frequently through other mechanisms. For example, in 1977 the United States passed the Foreign Corrupt Practices Act, 15 USC para 78m(b)(2)(B).

19 See, for example, GATT Panel Report, *Japan—Trade in Semi-Conductors (Japan— Semi-Conductors)*, L/6309, adopted 4 May 1988; GATT Panel Report, *Japan—Restrictions on Imports of Certain Agricultural Products (Japan—Agricultural Products I)*, L/6253, adopted 2 March 1988; GATT Panel Report, *Japanese Measures on Imports of Leather (Japan—Leather II (US))*, L/5623, adopted 15 May 1984.

20 GATT Panel Report, *United States—Countervailing Duties on Non-Rubber Footwear from Brazil (US—Non-Rubber Footwear)*, SCM/94, adopted 13 June 1995; GATT Panel Report, *Canada—Import, Distribution and Sale of Certain Alcoholic Drinks by Provincial Marketing Agencies (Canada—Provincial Liquor Boards [US])*, DS17/R, adopted 18 February 1992; GATT Panel Report, *European Economic Community—Regulation on Imports of Parts and Components (EEC—Parts and Components)*, L/6657, adopted 16 May 1990; GATT Panel Report, *Canada—Import Restrictions on Ice Cream and Yoghurt (Canada—Ice Cream and Yoghurt)*, L/6568, adopted 5 December 1989; GATT Panel Report, *European Economic Community—Restrictions on Imports of Apples— Complaint by the United States (EEC—Apples [US])*, L/6513, adopted 22 June 1989; GATT Panel Report, *European Economic Community—Restrictions on Imports of Dessert Apples—Complaint by Chile (EEC—Dessert Apples)*, L/6491, adopted 22 June 1989;

GATT Panel Report, *Republic of Korea—Restrictions on Imports of Beef—Complaint by the United States (Korea—Beef [US])*, L/6503, adopted 7 November 1989; Panel Report, *Japan—Semi-Conductors*, above n 19; Panel Report, *Japan—Agricultural Products I*, above n 19; Panel Report, *Japan—Leather II (US)*, above n 19.

21 Out of the seven cases initiated by the United States three were against Japan. See GATT Panel Report, *Japan—Semi-Conductors*, ibid.; GATT Panel Report, *Japan—Agricultural Products I*, above n 19; GATT Panel Report, *Japan—Leather II (US)*, above n 19. Two were against Canada. See GATT Panel Report, *Canada—Provincial Liquor Boards (US)*, above n 20; GATT Panel Report, *Canada—Ice Cream and Yoghurt*, above n 20. One was against Korea: GATT Panel Report, *Korea—Beef (US)*, above n 20.

22 See Panel Report, *US—Non-Rubber Footwear*, above n 19.

23 Although the United States not an official third party, the measure at issue was related to U.S. actions forcing Japan to limit its exports to the European market. See GATT Panel Report, *Japan—Semi- Conductors*, above n 19, para 4 (acknowledging the special nature of the matter and providing for an adequate opportunity for the United States to participate). See also GATT Panel Report, *EEC—Parts and Components*, above n 20.

24 Article XI:1 of the GATT 1947 states: 'No prohibitions or restrictions other than duties, taxes or other charges, whether made effective through quotas, import or export licenses or other measures, shall be instituted or maintained by any contracting party on the importation of any product of the territory of any other contracting party or on the exportation or sale for export of any product destined for the territory of any other contracting party.'

25 See GATT Panel Report, *Japan—Semi-Conductors*, above n 19; Panel Report, *Japan—Agricultural Products I*, above n 19; Panel Report, *Japan—Leather II (US)*, above n 19.

26 See GATT Panel Report, *Japan—Agricultural Products I*, ibid., para 5.4.1.4 (finding that the practice of 'administrative guidance' is 'a traditional tool of Japanese Government policy based on consensus and peer pressure' and thus finding that under the special circumstances in Japan such administrative guidance could be considered a governmental measure). See also GATT Panel Report, *Japan—Semi-Conductors*, above n 19, para 107 (clarifying the panel's analysis of 'administrative guidance' as a governmental measure in *Japan—Agricultural Products I*).

27 Panel Report, *Japan—Leather II (US)*, above n 19.

28 Ibid, para 16.

29 Ibid, para 28.

30 Ibid, paras 44, 57.

31 GATT Panel Report, *Japan—Agricultural Products I*, above n 19, para 3.1.1. The United States also argued that Japan had failed to meet the requirements of Articles X:1 and 3 'in terms of transparency, specificity and timing of notice given' (para 3.5.1).

32 Ibid, para 3.5.2.

33 Ibid, paras 5.4.2 and 6.2.

34 See Panel Report, *Japan—Semi-Conductors*, above n 19.

35 Ibid, para 35 (outlining the EC argument that Japan's administrative guidance controlled export prices, export volume, production volume, and other aspects related to exports. It was also stated in Japan's Position Paper that 'Japan exercised administrative guidance to achieve production cutbacks').

36 Ibid, paras 35, 53 and 128. In that case, the monitoring system had already been found to be inconsistent with Article XI:1 of the GATT 1947.

37 Ibid, para 107.

38 Panel Report, *Canada—Provincial Liquor Boards (US)*, above n 20.

39 Ibid, para 5.34 (emphasis added).

40 Panel Report, *EEC—Dessert Apples*, above n 20.

41 Ibid, paras 12.29–30 (finding that minimal administrative differences by themselves could not constitute a violation of GATT Article X:3 and that the administration of the quotas was a violation of Article XIII).

42 See Panel Report, *Canada—Ice Cream and Yoghurt*, above n 20; Panel Report, *Korea—Beef (US)*, above n 20.

43 Panel Report, *US—Non-Rubber Footwear*, above n 20.

44 Ibid, para 6.2.

45 Paragraph 1 of the GATT 1994.

46 Under the GATT 1947, contracting parties could pick and choose which agreements they wanted to sign and ratify while still maintaining their membership in the GATT. This changed with the creation of the WTO, where Members are required to sign all of the relevant WTO agreement. The Covered Agreements are the Agreements on Agriculture, Sanitary and Phytosanitary Measures, Textiles and Clothing, Technical Barriers to Trade, Trade-Related Investment Measures, Anti-Dumping, Custom Valuation, Pre-shipment Inspection, Rules of Origin, Import Licensing Agreement, Subsidies and Countervailing Measures, and Safeguards.

47 WTO, above n 1, at 172.

48 Ibid, at 211.

49 Ibid, at 275.

50 Ibid, at 59.

51 Ibid, at 21.

52 Ibid, at 147.

53 Ibid, at 231.

54 Ibid, at 223.

55 Ibid, at 284 (specifically, Article III of the GATS [Transparency] largely follows the language of Article X of the GATT 1994 and requires publication of all relevant measures including international agreements affecting trade in services. In addition, Article III of the GATS requires that WTO Members annually inform the WTO Council for Trade in Services of any changes made to the laws that affect trade in services and the commitments that each Member has made on that agreement. It also requires all Members to 'establish one or more enquiry points to provide specific information to other members'. Article VI of the GATS requires Members to maintain 'judicial, arbitral or administrative tribunals' to review administrative decisions affecting trade in services).

56 Ibid., 321 (Article 63 of the TRIPS [Transparency] requires publication of all intellectual property–related measures and notification to the WTO Council for TRIPS. In addition, Article 63.3 allows Members to object to another Member's specific judicial and administrative rulings in the area of intellectual property and to request detailed written justification for the ruling).

57 Ibid., at 308. Part B of the TPRM states:
'Domestic Transparency—Members recognize the inherent value of domestic transparency of government decision-making on trade policy matters for both Members' economies and the multilateral trading system, and agree to encourage and promote greater transparency within their own systems, acknowledging the implementation of domestic transparency must be on a voluntary basis and take account of each Member's legal and political systems.'

58 This is important not only within the context of Article X, but also the other 'substantive' provisions of the GATT 1994, including Arts. I (most-favoured-nation), II (tariff commitments), III (non-discriminatory application of internal measure), and Article XI:1 (prohibition on quotas and NTBs).

59 WTO, above n 1 at 16.

60 WTO Appellate Body Report, *EC—Selected Customs Matters*, above n 10; Panel Report, *EC—Selected Customs Matters*, above n 10; WTO Appellate Body Report, WTO Panel Report, *United States—Measures Relating to Shrimp from Thailand*, WT/DS343/R, circulated 29 February 2008; WTO Panel Report, *United States—Customs Bond Directive for Merchandise Subject to Anti-Dumping/Countervailing Duties (US—Customs Bond Directive)*, WT/DS345 /R, circulated 29 February 2008; WTO Appellate Body Report, *United States—Customs Bond Directive for Merchandise Subject to Anti-Dumping/Countervailing Duties (US—Customs Bond Directive)*, WT/DS345/AB/R, circulated 16 July 2008; WTO Panel Report, *Turkey—Measures Affecting the Importation of Rice*, WT/DS334/R, adopted 21 September 21 2007; *Mexico—Tax Measures on Soft Drinks and Other Beverages (Mexico—Taxes on Soft Drinks)*, WT/DS308/AB/R, adopted 24 March 2006); WTO Panel Report, *Mexico—Tax Measures on Soft Drinks and Other Beverages (Mexico—Taxes on Soft Drinks)*, WT/DS308/R, adopted 24 March 2006; WTO Appellate Body Report, *Dominican Republic—Measures Affecting the Importation and Internal Sale of Cigarettes (Dominican Republic—Import and Sale of Cigarettes)*, WT/DS302/AB/R, adopted 19 May 2005; WTO Panel Report, *Dominican Republic—Measures Affecting the Importation and Internal Sale of Cigarettes Dominican Republic—Import and Sale of Cigarettes)*, WT/DS302/R, adopted 19 May 2005; WTO Appellate Body Report, *United States—Sunset Reviews of Anti-Dumping Measures on Oil Country Tubular Goods from Argentina (US—Oil Country Tubular Goods Sunset Reviews)*, WT/DS268/AB/R, adopted 17 December 2004; WTO Panel Report, *United States—Sunset Reviews of Anti-Dumping Measures on Oil Country Tubular Goods from Argentina (US—Oil Country Tubular Goods Sunset Reviews)*, WT/DS268/R, adopted 17 December 2004; WTO Appellate Body Report, *United States—Continued Dumping and Subsidy Offset Act of 2000*, WT/DS234/AB/R, adopted 27 January 2003; WTO Panel Report, *United States—Continued Dumping and Subsidy Offset Act of 2000*, WT/DS234/R, adopted 27 January 2003; WTO Panel Report, *Egypt—Definitive Anti-Dumping Measures on Steel Rebar from Turkey*, WT/DS211/R, adopted 1 October 2002; WTO Appellate Body Report, *United States—Anti-Dumping Measures on Certain Hot-Rolled Steel Products from Japan (US—Hot-Rolled Steel)*, WT/DS184/AB/R, adopted 23 August 2001; WTO Panel Report, *United States—Anti-Dumping Measures on Certain Hot-Rolled Steel Products from Japan (US—Hot-Rolled Steel)*, WT/DS184/R, adopted 23 August 2001; WTO Panel Report, *United States—Anti-Dumping Measures on Stainless Steel Plate in Coils and Stainless Steel Sheet and Strip from Korea (US—Stainless*

Steel), WT/DS179/R, adopted 1 February 2001; WTO Panel Report, *Argentina—Measures Affecting the Export of Bovine Hides and the Import of Finished Leather (Argentina—Hides and Leather),* WT/DS155/R, adopted 16 February 2001; WTO Panel Report, *United States—Anti-Dumping Duty on Dynamic Random Access Memory Semiconductors (DRAMS) of One Megabit or Above from Korea (US—DRAMS),* WT/DS99/R, adopted 19 March 1999; WTO Appellate Body Report, *Japan—Measures Affecting Agricultural Products,* WT/DS76/AB/R, adopted 19 March 1999; WTO Panel Report, *Japan—Measures Affecting Agricultural Products,* WT/DS76/R, adopted 19 March 1999; WTO Appellate Body Report, *United States—Import Prohibition of Certain Shrimp and Shrimp Products (US—Shrimp),* WT/DS58AB/R, adopted 6 November 1998; WTO Panel Report, *United States—Import Prohibition of Certain Shrimp and Shrimp Products (US—Shrimp),* WT/DS58/R, adopted 6 November 1998; WTO Appellate Body Report, *European Communities—Measures Affecting Importation of Certain Poultry Products (EC—Poultry),* WT/DS69/AB/R, adopted 23 July 1998; WTO Panel Report, *European Communities—Measures Affecting Importation of Certain Poultry Products (EC—Poultry),* WT/DS69/R, adopted 23 July 1998; WTO Panel Report, *Indonesia—Certain Measures Affecting the Automobile Industry,* WT/DS54/R, WT/DS55/R, WT/DS59/R, WT/DS64/R, adopted 23 July 1998; WTO Panel Report, *Japan—Measures Affecting Consumer Photographic Film and Paper (Japan—Film),* WT/DS44/R, adopted 22 April 1998; WTO Panel Report, *European Communities—Regime for the Importation, Sale and Distribution of Bananas (EC—Bananas III [Mexico]),* WT/DS/27/R/MEX, 25 September 1997; WTO Appellate Body Report, *European Communities—Regime for the Importation, Sale and Distribution of Bananas (EC—Bananas III),* WT/DS/27/AB/R, adopted 25 September 1997; WTO Appellate Body Report, *United States—Restrictions on Imports of Cotton and Man-Made Fibre Underwear (United States—Underwear),* WT/DS24/AB/R, adopted 25 February 1997); WTO Panel Report, *United States—Restrictions on Imports of Cotton and Man-Made Fibre Underwear (United States—Underwear),* WT/DS24/R, adopted 25 February 1997.

61 Panel Report, *Argentina—Hides and Leather,* ibid.

62 Appellate Body Report, *Dominican Republic—Import and Sale of Cigarettes,* above n 60.

63 Appellate Body Report, *EC—Selected Customs Matters,* above n 10.

64 Panel Report, *US—Customs Bond Directive,* above n 60.

65 Appellate Body Report, *US—Underwear,* above n 20, at 20 (emphasis added).

66 Appellate Body Report, *US—Shrimp,* above n 20.

67 Ibid, para 113.

68 Ibid, para 177.

69 Appellate Body Report, *US—Shrimp,* above n 60, para 182.

70 Ibid, para 183.

71 Articles X:1 and X:3(a) of the GATT 1994.

72 Appellate Body Report, *EC—Bananas III,* above n 60; Panel Report, *EC—Bananas III,* above n 60.

73 Panel Report, *EC—Bananas III (Mexico),* above n 60, para 7.206; Appellate Body Report, *EC—Bananas III,* above n 60, para 70. Interestingly, the EC responded that Article X 'only applies to *internal* measures and therefore not applicable in this case' at para 33).

74 Panel Report, *Japan—Film,* above n 60, paras 10.384–10.388.

75 Panel Report, *Argentina—Hides and Leather*, above n 60.

76 Ibid, para 10.5.

77 Panel Report, *US—Hot-Rolled Steel*, above n 59.

78 Ibid, para 7.268.

79 Panel Report, *Dominican Republic—Import and Sale of Cigarettes*, above n 60, paras 7.405–406.

80 Panel Report, *Argentina—Hides and Leather*, above n 60, para 11.83.

81 Ibid, para 11.86.

82 Panel Report, *Dominican Republic—Import and Sale of Cigarettes*, above n 60, para 7.383.

83 Panel Report, *Argentina—Hides and Leather*, above n 60, para 11.71.

84 Ibid, para 11.67.

85 Panel Report, *US—DRAMS*, above n 60.

86 Panel Report, *US—Hot-Rolled Steel*, above n 60, para 7.263.

87 Panel Report, *Dominican Republic—Import and Sale of Cigarettes*, above n 60, para 7.385.

88 Panel Report, *US—Oil Country Tubular Goods Sunset Reviews*, above n 60, para 202–10.

89 Panel Report, *Argentina—Hides and Leather*, above n 60, para 11.77.

90 WTO, above n 1 at 16.

91 Ibid, at 73.

92 Panel Report, *United States—Underwear*, above n 60.

93 Appellate Body Report, *United States—Underwear*, above n 60 (specifically concluding that Article X:2 does not address the issue of whether a Member can give retroactive effect to a safeguard measure).

94 Panel Report, *EC—Bananas III (Mexico)*, above n 60, para 7.159.

95 Appellate Body Report, *EC—Bananas III*, above n 60, para 204.

96 Ibid.

97 Panel Report, *EC—Poultry*, above n 60. In *EC—Poultry*, Brazil had argued that the European Communities' rules relating to imports of frozen poultry were applied in violation of Article X since Brazilian traders cannot know whether a particular shipment is subject to in or out of quota rules (at para 267). The Appellate Body ruled that 'Article X ... does not impose an obligation on Member governments to ensure that exporters are continuously notified by importers as to the treatment of particular impending shipments.' See Appellate Body Report, *EC—Poultry*, above n 60, para 114.

98 The panel held that 'the examination of Article X as well as the [Licensing Agreement] is warranted since ... the [Licensing Agreement] is relevant to only in quota trade and Article X to the total trade'. See Panel Report, *EC—Poultry*, ibid, para 268.

99 Panel Report, *US—Hot-Rolled Steel*, above n 60, para 7.267.

100 Panel Report, *US—DRAMS*, above n 60, para 4.461.

101 Panel Report, *US—Stainless Steel*, above n 60, para 6.50.

102 Panel Report, *EC—Selected Customs Matters*, above n 10.

103 The Appellate Body defined the crux of the U.S. position as 'the European Communities administers its customs laws through 25 separate independent customs authorities and does not provide any institution or mechanism [at the community level] to reconcile the divergences automatically and as a matter of right when they occur.' See Appellate Body Report, *EC—Selected Customs Matters*, above n 10, para 22.

104 The United States also claimed that violation of Article X:3(b) based on the fact that decisions of administrative agencies and customs authorities in one member state does not govern the practice of EC agencies throughout the European Union. Ibid, at para 304.

105 Panel Report, *EC-Selected Customs Matters*, above n 10, para 7.191.

106 Ibid.

107 Ibid, para 8.1

108 Ibid, para 7.44.

109 Ibid (also holding in addition that there was no violation of Article X:3[b]).

110 The Appellate Body stated that the panel was wrong in determining that the claim 'as a whole or overall' was outside the scope of the terms of reference of Article X:3(a) and it could not be ruled on. See generally Appellate Body Report, *EC—Selected Customs Matters*, above n 10.

111 Ibid, para 200.

112 Ibid, para 201.

113 Ibid, para 304.

114 Ibid.

115 This decision may have also expanded the scope of measures more generally by weakening further the mandatory/discretionary distinction which was first formulated under the GATT 1947 and was adhered to in varying degrees in the WTO. The mandatory/discretionary distinction states that only measures that 'mandate' WTO-inconsistent action should be challenged 'as such,' and all discretionary measures that may or may not result in WTO inconsistent administration should be challenged 'as applied'. In *EC—Selected Customs Matters*, the Appellate Body held that Member states can challenge the substance of measures regardless of the mandatory or discretionary substance of the measure. A fuller discussion of this distinction is beyond the scope of this paper. For further discussion of mandatory/discretionary distinction, see, for example, WTO Appellate Body Report, *United States—Anti-dumping Act of 1916*, WT/DS136/R, WT/DS136/AB/R., adopted 26 September 2000; WTO Panel Report, *United States—Section 301-310 of the Trade Act of 1974*, WT/DS152/R, adopted 27 January 2000.

116 Most recently, in 2008 India brought an action against the imposition of anti-dumping duties by United States on imports of shrimp from India, claiming a violation of Article X:3 in addition to the Anti-Dumping Agreement, and Articles XI, XIII, and II of the GATT 1994. The panel, however, on the basis of judicial economic, did not address any of the GATT 1994 claims after having found the measures inconsistent with the Anti-Dumping Agreement. It is noteworthy, however, that India attempted to make both 'as applied' and 'as such' claims under Article X:3(a) with the latter being rejected by the panel for being untimely. See Appellate Body Report, *US—Customs Bond Directive*, above n 60.

117 See Debra P. Steger, 'The Culture of the WTO: Why It Needs to Change', 10 Journal of International Economic Law 483 (2007), at 485–86. Professor Steger writes: 'The mandate and purpose of the WTO is no longer clear. The mandate of the GATT system was continuing the process of trade liberalization.... [T]he preamble to the GATT 1947 reflected these goals. The preamble of the WTO Agreement is broader—it includes the goals of environmental sustainability and development ... but they have not become

part of the accepted theology or culture of the WTO as perceived by its members. So, there is a difference between what the preamble of the WTO says the purpose of the organization is and what its members perceive it to be.'

118 The work of the TPRM and committees in the area of good governance as expressed in Article X must also be studied to get a fuller picture of the good governance mandate of the WTO. Such work is necessary to assist the DSU in its application of Article X.

119 Another example of incremental change has been Article XX of the GATT 1994, where the Appellate Body discussed at great length the need to justify environmental measures under Article XX and elaborated on how Article XX should be read and applied years before they actually found a measure justified under Article XX. In 1999, in the aftermath, of *United States—Shrimp*, I wrote: '[T]he Appellate Body's analysis of Article XX generally and subparagraph (g) in particular ... indicates that although supporters of Article XX interests [environmentalists] may have lost the battle, the prospects look good for winning the war.' See Padideh Ala'i, 'Free Trade or Sustainable Development? An Analysis of the WTO Appellate Body's Shift to a More Balanced Approach to Trade Liberalization', 14 American University International Law Review (1998), at 1170–71.

120 See United Nations General Assembly, 'The First Meeting of the Commission of Experts of the President of the United Nations General Assembly on Reforms of the International Monetary and Financial System, Recommendations for Immediate Action', http://www.un.org/ga/president/63/commission/firstmeeting.pdf (visited 22 January 2009) (listing recommended actions for combatting the global financial crisis, focusing primarily on liquidity and the role of the World Bank and IMF).

121 World Bank, 'Public Sector Reform: What Works and Why?', http://siteresources. worldbank.org/EXTPUBSECREF/Resources/psr_eval.pdf (visited 22 January 2009), at 63. See also Padideh Ala'i, 'The WTO and the Anti-Corruption Movement', Loyola Chicago International Law Review (forthcoming 2009).

122 See The Brookings Institution, 'The G20 Summit: Could the Financial Crisis Push Global Governance Reform?', http://www.brookings.edu/opinions/2008/1024_g20_ summit_linn.aspx?p=1 (visited 22 January 2009) (arguing that a system of global governance is inherently necessary in order to respond effectively to economic challenges in the 21st century).

卍 卍 卍 **8**

Selective Adaptation of WTO Transparency Norms and Local Practices in China and Japan

LJILJANA BIUKOVIÇ*

I. Introduction

This article discusses compliance with World Trade Organization (WTO) transparency measures in the context of China and Japan's implementation of the Agreement on Sanitary and Phytosanitary Measures (SPS Agreement).[1] In brief, it focuses on the importance of Chinese and Japanese local practices, regulatory infrastructure, and local cultural norms related to the principle of transparency and food safety standards as factors in their selective adaptation of WTO norms. It argues that international law can acquire a variety of local meanings that require an understanding of the local history and culture in addition to knowledge of the domestic economy and laws.

This chapter analyzes selective adaptation through an understanding of the dynamics of internalization of international norms through the process of localization.[2] Part II explains the selective adaptation discourse. Part III discusses transparency-related developments at the WTO level, including recent initiatives of the WTO Committee on SPS Measures (SPS Committee) and disputes involving transparency requirements of the SPS Agreement. Parts IV and V analyze China's and Japan's legislative and institutional attempts to comply with Article X of General Agreement on Tariffs and Trade (GATT 1994)[3] in the administration of their laws, regulations, and government orders governing trade in goods in the context of their local culture and practices. The article also examines China's and Japan's efforts at both the WTO level and domestically to enhance transparency by developing legislation, an institutional framework, and processes that govern food safety, animal health, and protection. Part VI connects the conclusions drawn in Parts III, IV, and V with a discussion on transparency within the WTO, focusing on the work of the SPS Committee.

II. The Selective Adaptation Paradigm in the Context of Globalized Trade

Selective adaptation addresses the implementation of international legal norms in the context of local cultural and legal traditions. Underlying selective adaptation is a belief that compliance with WTO rules and norms is dependent *inter alia* on an people's understanding of the international rules and the local norms and practices (the perception factor), the degree of support that members of the local community give to the reception of the international norms (the legitimacy factor), and the extent to which the international norms and the local norms are complementary or capable of coexisting and operating together in non-conflicting and effective ways despite the fact that they might substantively contradict each other (the complementarity factor). Selective adaptation suggests that, due to the globalization of legal rules that regulate the international market, national legal systems are distinguished more by local institutional practices than by differences in the substantive legal norms. Thus another factor, institutional capacity, also affects local implementation of international norms. The institutional capacity factor reveals that compliance with international standards is also a matter of 'structural relationships among regulatory institutions' and

> a function of a particular institutional goal being affected by factors of institutional purpose concerning the institutional goal; the effects of location on understanding of the institutional goal; the effects of institutional orientation as to how the goal is to be pursued; and the extent of institutional cohesion in organizational structure and behavior.[4]

In sum, selective adaptation describes

> a process by which international standards and associated norms are adapted to local conditions, and it invites questions as to whether such adaptation is unified, in which case the international standards and associated norms are accepted relatively conterminously, or is disconnected such that acceptance of international standards is not accompanied by assimilation of the underlying norms.[5]

Thus selective adaptation reveals possibilities for flexible implementation of international standards by identifying degrees of conformity among local and non-local norms. Pitman Potter and Lesley Jacobs argue that the selective adaptation discourse helps to limit the scope of claims that cultural relativism is the cause of non-compliance with international norms, and that the discourse supports an acceptance of normative diversity only where there is an obvious lack of consensus between the international rules and local norms.[6] Selective adaptation does not deny that local legal culture, concepts, and vocabulary are powerful filters applicable to the perception and interpretation of international law.[7] However, it proposes that legal cultures are no longer so isolated as to make it impossible for lawyers and persons educated in one legal tradition to learn and interpret the norms of other legal systems and legal concepts.[8]

III. Development of Transparency Norms and the World Trade System

WTO membership and the acceptance of its rules and disciplines requires serious commitment on the part of states and often leads to legal reforms involving adoption of the Western system of law that is the foundation of the WTO regime.[9] As long as the WTO rules and disciplines are uniformly interpreted and applied by each Member, their adoption certainly leads to the harmonization of trade rules and brings predictability to the legal framework for business. However, uniform interpretation and application of the WTO rules depends not only on the political will of the Members to comply with rules but also on the complexity and efficacy of their domestic legal and political systems, whether they have the financial resources to introduce the reforms necessary to support application of WTO rules, and the ability of the local legal culture to absorb the Western ideas of trade liberalization and the rule of law.[10] One of the ideas central to liberalism and the rule of law is transparency.

Transparency is usually cited as the core principle underpinning the rule of law. It is also cited as a key element of good governance.[11] Businesses considering or involved in commerce abroad embrace the principle of transparency that is embedded in the world trading system. WTO Members accept obligations to comply with its transparency provisions in order to increase competitiveness in the world economy. Undoubtedly, transparent laws, administrative decisions, and procedures encourage foreign investment whereas non-transparent laws and regulations can create barriers to trade, particularly to imports.

Many international organizations emphasize the importance of transparency for the development of a market economy and of society in general and define the principle in terms similar to the provisions of Article X of the GATT 1994. The Organization for Economic Cooperation and Development's (OECD) definition of transparency is two-pronged. The first prong is defined as regulatory transparency or 'the capacity of regulated entities to express views on, identify and understand their obligations under the rule of law'.[12] The second prong of the OECD's definition of transparency requires governments to enhance 'information transparency'. Regulatory transparency protects the rights of private parties to be informed of laws, advised of decisions that concern their rights and interests, and provided with reasoned decisions, and to seek reviews of such decisions.[13] Thus legal reform that leads to regulatory transparency increases openness of the market and reduces business transaction costs. Information transparency includes consultations with interested parties, the electronic dissemination of regulatory materials, the use of plain language in drafting laws and regulations, the exercise of controls on regulatory discretion through transparent procedures, and the establishment of appeal processes.[14]

Robert Wolfe points out that the principle of transparency is relevant to the WTO system in the context of external, internal, and regulatory transparency.[15] External transparency is related to the ability of civil society to see the work of the WTO, while internal transparency reflects the ability of WTO Members, particularly smaller and developing countries, to participate in the work of the Organization.[16] Finally, the principle is relevant in the context of regulatory transparency, or as a tool of good governance, which constitutes 'an important aspect of national administrative law'.[17]

A. WTO and Transparency Provisions

As one of the main pillars of the world trading system, the transparency principle articulated in Article X of the GATT 1994 imposes an obligation on all Members of the WTO to publish all applicable laws and regulations and to administer them as follows:

> 1. Laws, regulations, judicial decisions and administrative rulings of general application, made effective by any contracting party, pertaining to the classification or the valuation of products for customs purposes, or to rates of duty, taxes or other charges, or to requirements, restrictions or prohibitions on imports or exports or on the transfer of payments therefor, or affecting their sale, distribution, transportation, insurance, warehousing inspection, exhibition, processing, mixing or other use, shall be published promptly in such a manner as to enable governments and traders to become acquainted with them. Agreements affecting international trade policy which are in force between the government or a governmental agency of any contracting party and the government or governmental agency of any other contracting party shall also be published....

This far-reaching provision includes the obligation for Members to establish processes for the judicial review of government acts.[18] As Sylvia Ostry explains, this provision puts limits on what Members' bureaucrats can do and how they can do it, and therefore has the capacity for direct impact on the field of administrative law.[19] Ostry traces an interesting evolution from the vaguely defined yet non-controversial principle of Article 38 of the Havana Charter of the International Trade Organization, based on what was primarily the U.S. approach to transparency,[20] to the current far-reaching feature of the WTO's expanded and more integrated world trade system, which requires all acceding Members to undergo deep reforms of domestic administrative or regulatory regimes and institutional infrastructures.[21] The creation of the Trade Policy Review Mechanism (TPRM)[22] as a means of monitoring compliance with the Article X requirements has signalled the increasing importance of transparency in the context of deeper economic integration.

It has been argued that the above-mentioned concepts underpinning transparency are at the core of liberal democracies and open market economies, but not traditional Asian societies.[23] Many authors, including Wolfe, Ostry, and Potter, have questioned the capability of developing countries, especially China, to comply with their transparency obligations due to a lack of institutional capacity, and to the complexity of their constitutional, administrative, and legal systems.[24] Some authors like Potter, Mayeda, and Stein, argue that China's historical and cultural traditions may clash with WTO transparency norms, either because China's local regulatory culture emphasizes the sovereignty of government bureaucracy and the Party rather than the rights of individuals and society to be informed of government decisions and to challenge these decisions[25] or because in China, personal connections rather than transparent, formal administrative processes have been the primary means of securing access to information, including information related to government activities.[26] Consequently, Potter explains, the WTO principle is selectively interpreted and implemented in China.[27] Nevertheless, in order to increase both regulatory and information transparency, many Asian countries have undergone, with varied success, the administrative reforms discussed below.

B. SPS Agreement and Transparency Provisions

Article 7 and Annex B of the SPS Agreement incorporate the transparency principle in recognition of the importance of public control of governmental policies related to public health protection and in order to prevent 'arbitrary or unjustifiable discrimination between Members' and 'a disguised restriction on international trade'. The SPS Agreement fosters intergovernmental regulatory coordination and harmonization of standards and prevents hidden protectionism.[28] This is achieved by allowing governments to impose measures necessary to protect public health in keeping with scientific principles[29] and established international standards,[30] while at the same time requiring that such measures be notified publicly in accordance with the provisions of Annex B.[31] In addition to the transparency principle articulated in Annex B, Article 7 of the SPS Agreement mandates the publication and monitoring of national SPS measures, be they laws, decrees, or general ordinances. Members are required to publish their SPS measures promptly[32] and to establish central enquiry points for answering other Members' questions on their SPS measures.[33] The SPS Agreement has facilitated the establishment of a special body, the SPS Committee, to monitor and coordinate the functioning of the various national SPS regulatory authorities, improve their transparency, and serve as a forum at which disagreements among trading partners might be resolved without formal WTO dispute settlement procedures.[34] Also, Article 4 of Annex B mandates that a Member imposing an SPS measure for which there is no international standard must publish such a measure at an 'early stage', notify other Members through the WTO Secretariat of the products to be covered by the regulation, and allow the other Members to comment on such a measure.

Although the SPS Agreement in general, and its transparency provisions in particular, facilitate the expansion of international regulation at the expense of the regulatory sovereignty of states, only a small portion of WTO case law deals with non-compliance of transparency requirements.[35] However, the relatively limited case law on this subject, as well as the absence of SPS Agreement-related issues in the Doha Round, should not be taken as an indicator that there are no compliance problems with the transparency principle.

Many Members find the SPS Agreement transparency requirements to be burdensome and costly, more so for developing than developed countries.[36] It is easier for developed, liberal market economies than for developing countries to translate the already existing concept of regulatory transparency from administrative law to SPS standard-setting and monitoring procedures. In addition, increased participation by developed countries in international standard setting and in the SPS Committee allows them to exert greater influence in setting these standards and protecting their economic interests. Thus not only transparency standards but also risk assessment standards are culturally influenced, with international standards largely mirroring those of developed countries.[37] Finally, due to their level of economic development, developing countries lack the institutional capacity to establish efficient enquiry points and notification procedures. Article 9 of the SPS Agreement, dealing with technical assistance for developing countries, does little to remedy this problem as it does not impose any obligations on the developed countries to assist the developing ones. In sum, local conditions and practices in developing countries seem to differ significantly from international standards and practices and such differences affect compliance with international standards.

In October 2007, the SPS Committee gave favourable consideration to a proposal by New Zealand for the establishment of a 'mentoring' system aimed at assisting developing country Members in the operation of their SPS National Notification Authorities (NNA) and their National Enquiry Points (NEP).[38] Mentoring involves the development of an informal ad hoc supportive relationship between officials with similar responsibilities so as to provide the opportunity for officials to seek advice and assistance from their counterparts in the NNA and/or NEP. However, this system is voluntary and is not meant to replace other forms of technical assistance.[39] Additional recommendations to improve transparency related to the information that Members share with each other on food safety and animal and plant health were approved on 30 May 2008.[40] These recommendations on transparency include new forms and procedures for countries to submit information and details regarding new on-line databases, where notices filed and other relevant information will be compiled. The recommendations, which took in the latter part of 2008, also encourage Members to notify relevant parties when they adopt international standards.[41] This is a voluntary measure as mandatory notification is required only when a Member's measures do not conform with international standards.

Finally, it is important to note that despite the importance given to the principle of transparency, WTO case law on SPS-related transparency is very limited.[42] China has not yet been involved in any SPS case either as a complainant or a defendant, but Japan's involvement as a defendant has been thoroughly reviewed by legal scholars.[43] The rest of this article analyzes Chinese and Japanese attempts to comply with the WTO and SPS Agreement transparency requirements and recommendations.[44]

It has been often suggested that it is more difficult for developing countries to comply with the SPS Agreement due to their lack of financial resources and expertise.[45] The selective adaptation discourse attempts to explain and predict how local institutions interpret international norms by modifying them to local conditions. Selective adaptation suggests that such modification happens in both developing and developed countries, but that it occurs more often and to a greater degree where there is increased disparity between international and local norms. Japanese and Chinese administrative reforms illustrate this point.

IV. Japan's Selective Adaptation of the WTO and SPS Agreement Transparency Provisions

Until recently, many Japanese government documents and files were not subject to legal scrutiny. Frank Upham argues that Japan should not be considered as a model for the rule of law in the sense of Western (especially U.S.) legal tradition, but rather as a society governed by harmony and consensus in which disputes are resolved often through informal mechanisms.[46] Japanese administrative culture is rooted in the tradition of the 19th-century Prussian law. Thus Japanese perceptions of regulatory transparency and accountability of government should be examined against a historical background in which the basic principle was one of the uncontested political authority of the Emperor's servants.[47] Matsui argues that, as a result of that tradition, many of the Japanese statutes authorizing governmental regulations delegate very broad discretion to administrative agencies.[48] Judicial review is rare. Another marked feature of Japanese administrative culture is that administrative agencies tend to control business activities through administrative guidance, an informal method of control that is not legally binding, hard for the public to ignore, and difficult for the courts to control.[49] For these reasons, very few administrative law cases have been filed in Japan.[50]

In the face of the expanding WTO requirements, and because of the pressure exercised by Japan's major trading partners, this tradition is slowly being altered. Japan's trading partners frequently use the WTO dispute settlement mechanism to deal with issues involving Japanese foreign trade regulations.[51] These complaints have triggered far-reaching political and legal reforms that have affected Japan's internal legal processes and its foreign trade diplomacy.

Invoking the factors of selective adaptation of international treaties and an analysis of local practices and norms reveals important reasons for non-compliance with the WTO transparency rules. Initially, Japan's evolution into a major trading power took place because of its unique legal and political culture of bureaucratic administration of economic activities, utilizing traditional informal mechanisms of economic order rather than formal legal institutions and administrative processes.[52] WTO norms, dispute settlement mechanisms, and its Members' negative attitudes toward Japan's traditional trade diplomacy first caused the Japanese government and important Japanese industries to change their perception of the rule-based WTO trade system.[53] Therefore, in the mid-1990s, Japan made a shift toward the rules-based system of the WTO as a proactive means of advancing its own economic interests.[54] Japan made it a priority to strengthen its position as the second-largest trading power in the WTO and initiated a series of reforms focused on confirming Japan's legitimacy as an important trading partner capable of meeting its WTO obligations.

As discussed above, Japanese non-compliance with the WTO norms was due, in part, to cultural particularities that have played a significant role in the process of the selective adaptation of transparency rules. Japan launched its administrative and regulatory reform process in the late 1990s. The reforms included changes to civil procedures and legal education.[55] As part of this process, the Law Concerning Access to Information Held by Administrative Organs was adopted in 1999 and came into effect in 2001. The law strengthens the regime of rights and obligations relating to the disclosure of information by government administrative agencies with the aim of achieving greater transparency, but remains careful to adapt transparency to Japanese local circumstances (the factor of complementarity). The development of internal regulatory transparency is complementary not only to the goal of compliance with the WTO provisions, but also with what Pekkanen calls the development of Japanese aggressive legalism and enhancement of the country's competitiveness in the world trading system.[56] The statute was patterned on the U.S. Freedom of Information Act.[57] It elaborates rights and obligations with respect to the release of corporate documents and disclosure of information on the operations of the incorporated administrative agencies as a means of ensuring their accountability.[58] However, the statute does not require government agencies to take proactive steps to publish or otherwise make documents publicly available. It only provides the right to request disclosure of information and a corresponding government obligation to respond. Adoption of an information disclosure system does not per se guarantee a more open government.[59]

As a result of the above mentioned reforms, the Office of the Trade and Investment Ombudsperson (OTO)[60] has instituted publication of complaints about government regulations. OTO serves as an administrative mechanism to resolve commercial complaints filed by domestic and foreign companies. The reform was intended to address complaints that Japanese government regulations create obstacles to market access and investment. OTO now systematically publishes statistics on commercial complaints filed in Japan by domestic and foreign individuals, associations, and firms.

In sum, the 2001 statute and the publication of complaints on government regulations and related institutional reforms are steps that have been taken at the administrative level to improve transparency. However, it is clear that full compliance with transparency norms in Japan is still hindered by a number of factors. The WTO Trade Policy Review Body noted in 2002 that some sectors of the Japanese economy, such as agriculture, remained overly protected from foreign competition as a result of a lack of transparency and the country's complex standards, tariff structure, and SPS measures, including quarantine measures.[61] This is particularly relevant considering the fact that Japan is one of the world's largest importers of agricultural goods[62] and that the SPS Agreement's transparency provisions attempt to balance the principles of market access and non-discrimination against the principle of regulatory sovereignty of states and their legitimate concerns about food safety.

In response to its obligations under the SPS Agreement, Japan undertook a number of regulatory reforms and created central institutions required by Annex B of that agreement. For example, Japan's national enquiry point is located at the International Trade Division Economic Affairs Bureau, Ministry of Foreign Affairs (MOFA).[63] However, while detailed information on government institutions, legislation, and procedures dealing with food safety, animal heath, and plant protection is easily accessible in Japanese, the information in English is less complete and must be improved in order to provide foreign governments and businesses with access to information.

The major domestic institutions that have the power to establish sanitary measures in Japan are the Ministry of Health, Labour and Welfare (MHLW) and the Ministry of Agriculture, Forestry and Fisheries (MAFF). The MHLW also oversees food safety administration, while the MAFF oversees animal health. Legislation on food safety—the Food Sanitation Law[64] and the Food Safety Basic Law[65]—is accompanied by relevant ordinances, regulations, procedures, and information and also includes general provisions related to the responsibilities of the state and local governments, businesses, and consumers.[66] It also defines the jurisdiction and responsibilities of the Food Safety Commission (FSC), an independent administrative body responsible for performing risk assessments and responding to food-borne accidents and emergencies.[67] As in the case of food safety, responsibility for animal and plant protection is centralized institutionally,[68] but access by foreign governments and businesses to information remains difficult since the majority of documents are available in only Japanese.

Since the adoption of WTO norms became a priority for the Japanese government and the country's important industries, their internalization has included building an adequate institutional infrastructure and implementing administrative reforms in addition to making very significant changes to legal education. The new approach to legal education is intended to change the attitudes of government bureaucrats, business people, legal practitioners, and scholars, as well as the public, thereby reducing the conflict between international and local norms.[69] In other words, Japan's lack of full compliance and its selective adaptation were the result of a lack of normative consensus, which has now been remedied through far-reaching administrative reforms and reforms in legal education implemented in a system once dominated by a protectionist foreign trade policy. The ambition of the Japanese government and key industries to improve the country's relative economic strength in the global market has led to Japan's improved compliance with international norms and internalization of international norms, such as regulatory transparency.

V. China's Selective Adaptation of the WTO and SPS Agreement Transparency Provisions

It has been argued that China's accession to the WTO triggered significant changes to China's legal system, in particular to its regulatory transparency and administrative law.[70] First, Paragraph I.2.A.1-3 specifies that the WTO Agreement and the Protocol on the Accession of the People's Republic of China is applicable to the entire customs territory of China.[71] Moreover, it mandates the uniform application and administration of all its laws, regulations and other measures at both the national and sub-national levels.[72] Paragraph I.2.C.1-2 of the protocol requires China to comply with Article X of GATT 1994 by publishing all of its laws, regulations, and government orders governing trade and goods services, trade related aspects of intellectual property rights, and foreign exchange in a designated official journal; providing a reasonable period for comment to the appropriate authorities before such measures are implemented; and enforcing only those laws, regulations, and measures affecting trade that are published and readily available to other WTO Members, individuals and enterprises. In addition, China must translate 'into one or more of the official languages of the WTO all laws, regulations and other measures pertaining to or affecting trade in goods, services, TRIPS or the control of forex'.[73] The protocol also requires China to establish mechanisms for administrative and judicial review (Section I.2.D). In other words, the protocol required China to undertake significant administrative and legal reforms in order to bring its regulatory practice into compliance with the WTO norms. Compliance at the sub-national level remains a problem, particularly where regional governments are more independent from the central government.[74]

Ostry identifies at least four new features of the protocol that go beyond the requirements of Article X of GATT: (1) an extension of the coverage (in the Chinese case it includes goods, trade in services, TRIPS, and foreign exchange controls); (2) publication before implementation, including the right to comment on proposed regulations; (3) enforcement of only those laws and regulations that have been published (in contrast to Article X, which requires publication of only those laws and regulations that increase barriers to trade); and (4) creation of a single enquiry point with a time limit for response.[75]

Moreover, Ostry argues, the protocol's judicial review section went beyond the Article X specification when it required China to create independent institutions for the 'prompt review' of 'all administrative actions'.[76]

Many scholars questioned China's capacity to adopt these elaborate transparency and good governance requirements due to its political culture rooted in Confucianism. China's 'patrimonial sovereignty'—which evolved from the idea that the state (or the Party) is a patrimonial sovereign and the administrative agencies and regulators are responsible *for* society but not accountable *to* it—was viewed as a further impediment to compliance with the WTO Agreement.[77] The concept of governance in China had been based on the idea that administrative agencies and regulators are accountable only to their political (and bureaucratic) superiors.[78] There was little room for convergence of the Western ideas of the rule of law and transparency with the culture of a Chinese legal system dominated by the Chinese Communist Party and characterized by a lack of separation of powers among different state institutions.[79] As a consequence, WTO, World Bank, and OECD reports consistently criticized Chinese administrative law for its lack of regulatory transparency and for over-regulating business and insisted on the implementation of broad administrative reforms prior to China's accession to the WTO.[80]

In the course of applying for WTO membership, China embarked on a series of in-depth administrative law reforms. These reforms sought to establish competent and accountable governments at the central, provincial, and municipal levels. Furthermore, the reforms sought to bring about transparent, simplified, and consistent procedures that would enable legal persons to challenge laws, regulations, and decisions, and to enforce their legal rights before administrative agencies. These enforceable rights would include the right to receive remedies for losses caused by incompetent or unlawful administrative actions of various state agencies.[81] In general, these reforms were seen as a positive departure from the Chinese governments' practices of intervention in private business toward reduced supervision of economic activities in general, better governance, and prevention of corruption.[82]

The 2003 Administrative License Law of the People's Republic of China[83] was another measure to improve public access to administrative agencies. This law requires that all government departments publish information relating to laws, regulations, licences, procedures, and complaints via the Internet.[84] Websites of various government departments and agencies multiplied, but the quality of services and depth of the information offered online has proved to be inconsistent, indicating divergent local implementation of the statute.[85] China's Regulations on Government Disclosure of Information approved by the State Council on 17 January 2007 were the first national regulations concerning the government's duty of public disclosure.[86] These important provisions impose a duty on all levels of government (central and local) to inform the public of any rules and decisions made (on health care, education, public finances, etc.), within 20 days of their enactment. However, the regulations confer broad discretion on the government and its agencies to limit access to information when necessary to prevent 'social instability and protect the safety of the state, the public and the economy'. Moreover, the regulations do not apply to Party committees that continue to make decisions with important legal implications in China. Finally, the regulations do not stipulate concrete sanctions for the government officials who fail to comply with the provisions even though there is an indication that such infringements will be investigated and prosecuted.

Bath notes that none of the new administrative statutes adequately address the issue of a private party's right to a remedy for losses caused by unlawful administrative actions or sufficiently simplify the administrative system. Rather, these new administrative statutes focus on a supervisory structure that reinforces the importance of the central government.[87] The priority given by the Chinese government to the regulation of institutional capacity, particularly to its purpose and orientation,[88] may reveal different levels of support for the process of internalization of international norms and standards of transparency. There is little doubt that the Chinese government is concerned about its legitimacy as an important Member of the WTO. Local governments, on the other hand, might question the legitimacy of the international norms that ground local economic and administrative reforms since internalization of such norms ultimately limits the role of local authorities in the making of rules and norms.

Implementation of the SPS Agreement and its related transparency provisions has revealed that the problem with internalization of international norms remains linked to the scope of authority of the central and local authorities.[89] It is noteworthy that food safety, animal health, and plant health in China are overseen by a single ministerial, administrative organ—the General Administration of Quality Supervision, Inspection and Quarantine (AQSIQ).[90] AQSIQ falls directly under the State Council, the highest executive state organ of the PRC chaired by the Premier. It is the main legislative, administrative, and supervisory body in this area[91] and is in charge of national quality; metrology; entry-exit commodity inspection; entry-exit health quarantine; entry-exit animal and plant quarantine; import-export food safety, certification, accreditation, and standardization; as well as the enforcement of administrative law.[92] AQSIQ's laws and implementing regulations are available on its website in Chinese and, for the most part, in English,[93] while its ordinances and notices are available only in Chinese.

At present, the AQSIQ website is the only source of information on the Chinese SPS measures available to foreigners.[94] AQSIQ also oversees China's

National Enquiry Point, established in response to paragraph 3 of Annex B of the SPS Agreement,[95] while China's National Notification Authority (NNA),[96] established in response to paragraph 10 of Annex B, is located at the WTO Notification and Enquiry Center of the Ministry of Commerce (MOFCOM). The Ministry of Commerce is responsible for coordinating the efforts of the ministries and agencies charged with implementation of SPS measures and, together with AQSIQ, drafts and adopts guidelines on notification with respect to SPS measures.[97]

Formulation of national standards for food hygiene is the mandate of the highest central government body, the State Council, and its competent departments.[98] The Standardization Law places food hygiene standards in the category of 'compulsory' national and trade standards.[99] Compulsory standards are standards 'for safeguarding human health and ensuring the safety of the person and of property and those for compulsory executions as prescribed by the laws and administrative rules and regulations'. [100] However, 'local standards formulated by standardization administration departments of provinces, autonomous regions and municipalities directly under the Central Government for the safety and sanitary requirements of industrial products' are also compulsory standards within their respective administrative areas.[101] In other words, local governments are still responsible for standards of locally produced goods.

It can be difficult to access Chinese legislation, procedures, and regulations related to SPS measures and safeguarding food, human, animal, and plant health through government web pages other than AQSIQ. For example, the MOFCOM web page contains links entitled 'E-Government' and 'Your Comment'. However, these links contain no additional information.[102] Another problem is that regulatory measures are sometimes spread over several pieces of legislation, making the legal framework less coherent and transparent. For example, while the main legislation on food safety is the Food Hygiene Law (PRC),[103] provisions governing food control and food hygiene, including provisions related to the import and export of food, can be found in other legislation, such as the Law on Product Quality.[104] The Law on the Entry and Exit of Animals and Plant Quarantine (PRC), with its Implementing Regulations,[105] deals with animal and plant health, but provisions governing animal and plant health can also be found in the Frontier Health and Quarantine Law (PRC),[106] (including its Specific Rules),[107] which governs the prevention of infectious diseases from spreading into and out of the country, the execution of frontier health and quarantine inspections, and the protection of human health.[108]

Finally, in order to enhance transparency and facilitate public access to information related to SPS measures, the MOFCOM website allows the general public to submit enquiries and comments relating to import and export procedures in China online and allows public access online to these enquiries and comments.[109]

In sum, China has made considerable efforts to comply with the SPS Agreement transparency requirements, including publishing regulations and establishing the SPS Notification Authority and enquiry points, and has created a legal framework for the development of SPS measures and standards, the establishment of legal responsibility, including penal provisions for non-compliance, and creation of a network of monitoring and implementing agencies. Although no claims under the SPS Agreement have been brought against China to date, WTO Members have complained about the inadequate compliance by China with international standards, often citing China's non-transparent regulatory measures[110] and problems with its administration of SPS measures at the national and local levels.[111]

Overall, China's implementation of WTO transparency norms caused a major shift in perspective by state elites, with legislative and regulatory reforms accompanying that shift. However, this shift has not yet resulted in full normative consensus or consistency between international and local practices.[112] Analyzed in the context of the factor of complementarity, implementation of the WTO provisions on regulatory transparency might have been seen as desirable not because of an overwhelming acceptance of the underlying values of good governance and the accountability of government to society, but as a means of exercising central government control over local governments and their agencies, since the administrative reforms give the latter the role of implementation only and not that of enactment or interpretation of the relevant administrative rules and standards.[113]

VI. Conclusion

Compliance with WTO provisions on regulatory transparency has become increasingly important as international trade integration has widened and deepened. A number of countries, both developed and developing, face numerous difficulties in complying with the far-reaching WTO requirements. The selective adaptation discourse helps to explain the process of localization of international norms in Japan and China. The selective adaptation paradigm allows us determine the extent to which non-compliance, or less than full compliance, can be attributed to the cultural particularities of states and to what extent other factors, such as lack of political will or institutional shortcomings, are relevant to non-compliance. Non-compliance due to cultural differences could be remedied either by allowing for more flexible compliance, that is, by allowing for the selective localization of international norms or by building normative consensus through broad political, administrative, and cultural reforms. This analysis illustrates that shifts in perception of regulatory transparency norms in China and Japan have had important economic and political consequences internally and externally. Moreover, these shifts have brought about significant administrative law reforms and have contributed to their improved compliance with international norms. Such shifts in perception take place over a relatively long period of time, require a serious commitment on the part of all levels of government, and utilize significant financial resources to build the required institutional capacity. In the meantime, better understanding of local conditions is needed in order to reach normative consensus and to accommodate more flexible approaches to compliance.

The transformation of the world trading system is at the centre of debate between international scholars and national governments. Interdependence of national economies and conflicts of national regulatory policies require greater cooperation and coordination in the creation of, and compliance with, regulatory norms. A selective adaptation paradigm distinguishes a variety of factors of compliance with international treaties and explains compliance with WTO rules as a complex process of implementation of WTO rules through the reference to local conditions.

Selective adaptation calls for an examination of the impact of international norms on local practices. Reference to the factors of perception, complementarity, and legitimacy, in addition to factoring in institutional capacity, enable us to determine the reasons for non-compliance. While cultural relativism could be one of the reasons of non-compliance, it is neither the only one nor the one that justifies non-compliance. Developing an adequate educational program and training interpretative agents could close the cultural gap between international norms and local practices. As selective adaptation analysis applied to China and Japan in this article reveals, factors other than normative consensus, such as lack of political will and institutional capacity, should be taken into consideration when a Member State's capacity to consistently comply with the WTO principles is examined. As argued in this paper, on one hand, China and Japan revised their legislation and administrative regulations to accommodate reception of the WTO transparency rules. However, on the other hand, problems with non-transparent practices of local administrative bodies keep reappearing in both countries, making the complete compliance and incorporation of the WTO standards uncertain in practice.

If the assessment of current Members' performance of their WTO obligations is the starting point of the reform of the world trading system, then selective adaptation offers a valuable insight into the reality of the compliance process. The underlying point of selective adaptation is that normative tensions lead to conflicting and non-uniform reception of international standards by local communities and administrative bodies. This discourse signals that progressive compliance with international regulatory norms is a complex process that takes on a variety of ways in different countries. It is thus increasingly important to understand this process—from the acceptance of the WTO obligations by state parties to their translation into local rules and practices—especially when the WTO membership increases and becomes even more diverse in the socio-historical, economic, and political development of acceding states.

Notes

* The chapter is partially based on a manuscript presented to a workshop held in Lauterpacht Centre, Cambridge, in July 2007 organized by the EDGE Network and the Asia Pacific Dispute Resolution Project of the Institute for Asian Research, University of British Columbia, Canada. The author would like to thank the participants of the workshop for their valuable comments, in particular those of Thomas Cottier, Lesley Jacobs, Ernst Urlich Petersmann, Pitman Potter, and Debra Steger. Some parts of this research appear in 'International, Regional and National Laws Intertwined in Asia' in Ljiljana Biukovic and Pitman B. Potter (eds), *Doing Business in Asia* (Markham, Ont.: Lexis-Nexis, 2008). The research on Chinese and Japanese selective adaptation of the WTO norms was funded by the MCRI grant of the Social Studies and Humanities Research Council of Canada. The author also thanks UBC law students Wenwei Guan, Ph.D. candidate, and Anna Turinov, J.D. 2008, for their valuable research assistance, translation from Mandarin and Japanese to English, respectively, and reports on the implementation of SPS Agreement in China and Japan incorporated into this paper. However, all errors remain the author's own.

1 World Trade Organization, *The Results of the Uruguay Round of Multilateral Trade Negotiations: The Legal Texts* (Cambridge: Cambridge University Press, 2003) 59.

2 Lesley Jacobs and Pitman B. Potter, 'Selective Adaptation and Human Rights to Health in China', 9 (2) Health and Human Rights 113 (2006), at 119.

3 Above n 1, at 423.

4 Pitman B. Potter, 'Selective Adaptation, Institutional Capacity and the Reception of International Law Under Conditions of Globalization', in Ljiljana Biukovic and Pitman B. Potter (eds), *Globalization and Local Adaptation in International Trade Law* (unpublished, manuscript on the file with author).

5 Pitman B. Potter, 'Globalisation and Business Regulation in Local Context', in Ljiljana Biukovic and Pitman B Potter (eds), *Doing Business in Asia* (Markham, Ont.: Lexis/Nexis Canada, forthcoming).

6 Jacobs and Potter, above n 2, at 120. Pitman Potter is the principal investigator of the project that produced the empirical data used in this article.

7 Ljiljana Biukovic, 'Compliance with International Treaties: Selective Adaptation Analysis', Canadian Yearbook of International Law 451 (2006), at 454.

8 Ibid.

9　Sylvia Ostry, 'China and the WTO: Transparency Issue', 3 UCLA Journal of International Law and Foreign Affairs 1 (1998). For further discussion concerning the nature of the WTO normative framework see Biukovic, above n 7.

10　For more on the adoption of the rule of law principle in Asia, see Randall Peerenboom (ed), *Asian Discourses of Rule of Law—Theories and Implementation of Rule of Law in Twelve Asian Countries* (London and New York: RoutledgeCurzon, 2004).

11　Francis Fukuyama, *State-Building: Governance and World Order in the 21st Century* (Ithaca: Cornell University Press, 2004). On the importance of the principle of transparency in the international context, see Abraham Chayes and Antonia Handler Chayes, *The New Sovereignty: Compliance with International Regulatory Agreements* (Cambridge: Harvard University Press, 1995) 62.

12　Organization for Economic Cooperation and Development, 'Flagship Report on Regulatory Quality', PUMA/REG (2001) 10, 21 November 2001, at 41.

13　NERA (National Economic Research Associates) Economic Consulting, 'Regulatory Transparency: International Assessment and Emerging Lessons, A Final Report for the World Bank', 6 June 2005, at 147.

14　OECD, above n 12.

15　Robert Wolfe, 'Regulatory Transparency, Developing Countries and the WTO', 2 World Trade Review 157 (2003), at 158.

16　Ibid.

17　Ibid.

18　Article X of the GATT 1994 states:

> 3. (a) Each contracting party shall administer in a uniform, impartial and reasonable manner all its laws, regulations, decisions and rulings of the kind described in paragraph 1 of this Article.
>
> (b) Each contracting party shall maintain, or institute as soon as practicable, judicial, arbitral or administrative tribunals or procedures for the purpose, inter alia, of the prompt review and correction of administrative action relating to customs matters. Such tribunals or procedures shall be independent of the agencies entrusted with administrative enforcement and their decisions shall be implemented by, and shall govern the practice of, such agencies unless an appeal is lodged with a court or tribunal of superior jurisdiction within the time prescribed for appeals to be lodged by importers; Provided that the central administration of such agency may take steps to obtain a review of the matter in another proceeding if there is good cause to believe that the decision is inconsistent with established principles of law or the actual facts.
>
> (c) The provisions of subparagraph (b) of this paragraph shall not require the elimination or substitution of procedures in force in the territory of a contracting party on the date of this Agreement which in fact provide for an objective and impartial review of administrative action even though such procedures are not fully or formally independent of the agencies entrusted with administrative enforcement. Any contracting party employing such procedures shall, upon request, furnish the CONTRACTING PARTIES with full information thereon in order that they may determine whether such procedures conform to the requirements of this subparagraph.

19　Ostry, above n 9, at 4.

20 Ibid, at 4 and 5. Ostry explains that all 56 delegations at the Havana meeting accepted the U.S. draft of Article 38 even though it was deeply rooted in American administrative law and that Article 38 of the Havana Charter directly incorporated Article 15 of the U.S. State Department document entitled 'Publication and Administration of Trade Regulations—Advance Notice of Restrictive Regulations', which later became incorporated into GATT Article X as 'Publication and Administration of Trade Regulations' without substantive modifications.

21 Ibid, at 9–11. Ostry in particular emphasizes the fact that the WTO expanded international trade rules and disciplines beyond GATT (which focused on tariff barriers controlled by borders) to areas of services, intellectual property, and investment, thus directly influencing domestic regulatory regimes.

22 See WTO, 'Trade Policy Review', http://www.wto.org/english/tratop_e/tpr_e/tpr_e.htm (visited 5 September 2008). The TPRM was created to enable regular monitoring of trade polices and practices of WTO Members and examine the impact of a Member's trade policies and practices on the multilateral trading system.

23 See, for example, Peerenboom, above n 10. See also Randall Peerenboom, *China's Long March Toward Rule of Law* (Cambridge: Cambridge University Press, 2002).

24 Wolfe, above n 15; Pitman B. Potter, 'Globalization and Economic Regulation in China: Selective Adaptation of Globalized Norms and Practices', 1 Washington University Global Studies Law Review 119 (2003); Ostry, above n 7. See also Stanley Lubman, 'Studying Contemporary Chinese Law: Limits, Possibilities, and Strategy', 39 American Journal of Comparative Law 293 (1991).

25 See Potter, ibid.

26 Gregory Stein, 'Acquiring Land Use Rights in Today's China: A Snapshot from on the Ground', 24 UCLA Pacific Basin Law Journal 1 (2006).

27 Potter calls such application 'selective adaptation'. See Potter, above n 4, at 7 and 8.

28 Article 7 of the SPS Agreement. See also Justin Kastner and Douglas Powell, 'The SPS Agreement: Addressing Historical Factors in Trade Dispute Resolution', 19 Agriculture and Human Values 283 (2002), at 284. On the SPS Agreement's major objectives see also Jeffrey L. Dunoff, 'Lotus Eaters: Reflections on the Varietals Dispute, the SPS Agreement, and WTO Dispute Resolution', Institute for International Law and Public Policy Paper Series No. 2006-1 (2006), at 15.

29 Article 2.2 of the SPS Agreement.

30 Article 3.3 of the SPS Agreement.

31 Article 7 of the SPS Agreement.

32 Article 1 of Annex B, of the SPS Agreement.

33 Article 3 of Annex B, of the SPS Agreement.

34 Article 12 of the SPS Agreement.

35 For a detailed overview of the GATT/WTO case law on transparency, see Padideh Alai'i, 'From the Periphery to the Center? The Evolving WTO Jurisprudence on Transparency and Good Governance', which can be found in this volume.

36 Wolfe, above n 15; Michael Friis Jensen, 'Reviewing the SPS Agreement: A Developing Country Perspective', The Royal Veterinary and Agricultural University, Denmark, working paper, January 2002 (Presented at the Centre for Development Research, Copenhagen, on 21 August 2001, on file with author); Kajli Bakhshi, 'SPS Agreement under the WTO: The Indian Experience' (IDF Working Papers, January 2005, on file with the author).

37 See, for example, Dunoff, 'Lotus Eaters' above n 31, at 22–23; Jensen, ibid, at 31. But see also Caroline E. Foster, 'Public Opinion and the Interpretation of the World Trade Organisation's Agreement on Sanitary and Phytosanitary Measures', 11 Journal of International Economic Law 427 (2008). Foster argues that there are significant cultural differences among developing countries that stem from the significance given in different countries to public opinion in decision-making about risks to human health and the environment, as illustrated in the *EC Measures Concerning Meat and Meat Products (EC-Hormones)* case.

38 WTO, Committee on Sanitary and Phytosanitary Measures, 'Proposal for a "Mentoring" System of Assistance Relating to Transparency Provisions of the SPS Agreement', G/SPS/W/217 (20 February 2008), http://www.wto.org/english/tratop_e/sps_e/sps_e.htm#transparency (visited 5 September 2008).

39 Ibid.

40 WTO, 'Members Set to Agree on Regionalization, Improved SPS Transparency' (2 April 2008), http://www.wto.org/english/news_e/news_e.htm (visited 5 September 2008); WTO, 'Decision on SPS Transparency Confirmed' (30 May 2008), http://www.wto.org/english/news_e/news08_e/sps_30may08_e.htm (visited 5 September 2008).

41 Ibid.

42 S. Nuri Erbas, 'Ambiguity, Transparency, and Institutional Strength', IMF Working Paper No. WP/04/115, July 2004, at 3, http://www.imf.org/external/pubs/cat/longres.cfm?sk=17345.0 (visited 5 September 2008). For example, in WTO Panel Report, *Japan—Measures Affecting Agricultural Products (Japan-Agricultural Products II)*, WT/DS76/R, adopted 19 March 1999, the panel devoted only four pages to the evaluation of the Article 7 argument in its 170-page decision. In WTO Appellate Body, *Japan—Measures Affecting Agricultural Products (Japan-Agricultural Products II)*, WT/DS76/AB/R, adopted 19 March 1999, the discussion of Article 7 received less than two pages in the 42-page decision. In WTO Panel Report, *Japan-Measures Affecting the Importation of Apples (Japan—Apples)*, WT/DS245/R, adopted 10 December 2003, Article 7 received less than five pages in a 280-page decision. Finally, in *European Communities—Measures Affecting the Approval and Marketing of Biotech Products (EC—Approval and Marketing of Biotech Products)*, WT/DS291/R, adopted 21 November 2006, the panel devoted less than five pages to the discussion of Article 7 in a report of over 1,000 pages.

43 See, for example, Dunoff, 'Lotus Eaters', above n 31; Saadia M. Pekkanen, *Japan's Aggressive Legalism; Law and Foreign Trade Politics Beyond the WTO* (Stanford: Stanford University Press 2008) 25–30.

44 WTO Members' SPS-related websites, http://www.wto.org/english/tratop_e/sps_e/spslinks_e.htm (visited 5 September 2008). TBT/SPS-Related Chinese sites are available at http://www.tbt-sps.gov.cn/SITES/ENGLISH/Pages/default.aspx (in English) (visited 5 September 2008) and http://www.tbt-sps.gov.cn/Pages/main.aspx (in Chinese) (visited 5 September 2008).

45 See, for example, Wolfe, above n 15.

46 Frank K. Upham, 'Ideology, Experience, and the Rule of Law in Developing Societies', in Meredith Jung-En Woo (ed), *Neoliberalism and Institutional Reform in East Asia: A Comparative Study* (New York: Palgrave, 2007) 35–62 at 49.

47 Shigenori Matsui, 'Business Law in Japan' in Ljiljana Biukovic and Pitman B. Potter (eds), above n 5.

48 Matsui, ibid. Similarly Randall Peerenboom argues that administrative guidance issued
    by an official with a great deal of discretion played an important role in the develop-
    ment of the state in Japan. See Randall Peerenboom, *China Modernizes: Threat to the
    West or Model for the Rest?* (Oxford: Oxford University Press, 2007) 37.
49 Matsui, ibid. Matsui explains that 'it is hard to challenge the administrative guidance
    before the court since it does not have any legally binding power'. See Peerenboom, ibid,
    at 37.
50 Not only is the number of administrative cases small (only about 3,000 per year) but
    in 80 percent of these cases government won. See Matsui, ibid.
51 In particular, the United States has challenged Japanese government control of busi-
    ness as unreasonable, economically harmful, and contrary to international standards.
    See Sadia M. Pekkanen, above n 44.
52 Upham, above n 47, at 51.
53 Pekkanen, above n 44, at 31.
54 Pekkanen argues that this reliance on a rule-based trade diplomacy and the use of
    law and the legal process as a sword is the essence of Japan's aggressive legalism. See
    Pekkanen, above n 44, at 4 and 5.
55 Pekkanen, above n 44, at 10–11.
56 Pekkanen, above n 44, at 5.
57 5 United States Code (USC) section 552.
58 Japan, Ministry of Internal Affairs and Communications, 'Law Concerning Access to
    Information Held by Administrative Organs' (2001), http://www.soumu.go.jp/
    gyoukan/kanri/low0404_2.htm.
59 Lawrence Repeta, 'Local Government Disclosure Systems in Japan', 16 The National
    Bureau of Asian Research (NBR) Executive Insight (1999), at 42, http://www.nbr.org/
    publications/specialreport/pdf/EI16.pdf (visited 5 September 2008).
60 See the Office of the Trade and Investment Ombudsperson (OTO), http://www5.cao.go.jp/
    access/english/oto_main_e.html (visited 5 September 2008). OTO was established in
    1982 and first reformed in 1994 through establishment of the Market Access Ombuds-
    man Council (MAOC) in the Cabinet Office. The Council comprises a group of schol-
    ars and business leaders, including non-Japanese members.
61 Remarks by the chairman of the Trade Policy Review Body (TPRB) about Japan's pro-
    tectionism and the inconsistency of its SPS quarantine measures with Article 7 echoed
    a number of the agriculture-related WTO complaints against Japan by the United
    States, such as in Appellate Body Report, *Japan—Agricultural Products II*, above n 43;
    WTO Appellate Body, *Japan—Measures Affecting the Importation of Apples (Japan—
    Apples)*, WT/DS245/AB/R, adopted 10 December 2003. See also Pekkanen, above n 47
    at 26. Note that the U.S. claim in the *Japan—Apples* case was based on Japan's viola-
    tion of obligations arising out of Article 7 of the SPS Agreement. Annex B was not
    considered by the Appellate Body because the panel found that the United States had
    failed to establish a prima facie case under these provisions: Appellate Body, *Japan—
    Apples, at* para 4. On the other hand, the U.S. complaint that in not having published
    the varietal testing requirement Japan acted inconsistently with its obligations under
    Article 7 of the SPS Agreement and para 1 of Annex B was successful before both panel
    and the Appellate body: Appellate Body, *Japan—Agricultural Products II*, above n 43.

62 WTO, Trade Policy Review, 'Report by the Secretariat: Japan' WT/TPR/S/175/Rev.1, 10 April 2007, para 22 at ix.

63 WTO, Committee on Sanitary and Phytosanitary Measures, National Enquiry Points, G/SPS/ENQ/23, March 27, 2008, http://www.wto.org/english/tratop_e/sps_e.htm# enquiry (visited 5 September 2008). It is noteworthy that the enquiry point does not appear to be available online through the MOFA home page.

64 Shokuhin Eiseiho (Food Sanitation Law), Law No. 223 of 24 December 1947, last amendment Law No. 87 of 26 July 2005, http://www.jetro.go.jp/en/market/regulation (visited 5 September 2008).

65 Shokuhin Anzen Kihanho (Food Safety Basic Law), Law No. 48 of 23 May 2003, last amendment Law No. 50 of 2 June 2006, http://www.fsc.go.jp/enlish/index.html (unofficial translation) (visited 5 September 2008).

66 Ordinances, regulations, procedures, and information on food safety can be also found in English on the MHLW website. Scott McCook, Second Secretary of Embassy of Canada, explained to the author's researcher Anna Turinov that there have been discussions about setting up a consumer affairs agency in Japan, but no concrete action has been taken yet. Notes from interview with Scott McCook of 4 August 2008 (on file with author).

67 Food Safety Basic Law, above n 66, Articles 22–28. Indeed, Scott McCook, Second Secretary of Embassy of Canada, explained that the FCS had been established after the BSE issue emerged. McCook reports that transparency and access to ministries and government agencies does not represent a significant barrier to entry for Canadian exporters to Japan since most information is now available online (in Japanese or English) and because of the willingness of Japanese importers to assist their foreign partners. According to McCook, the remaining difficulty relates to lack of transparency and standardization, and the broad discretion of individual quarantine officers in the categorization of products. See Note from Scott McCook of 4 August 2008, ibid.

68 The Plan Protection States, http://www.maff.go.jp/pps, a facility of the MAFF aimed at protecting Japanese agriculture, is responsible for monitoring plant health and is in charge of the plant quarantine system. See Kachiky Densenbyo Yoboho (the Domestic Animal Infectious Diseases Control Law), Law No. 166 of 31 May 1951, last amendment Law No. 68 of 2 June 2005, http://www.cas.go.jp/jp/seisaku/hourei/data2.html; Kyokenbyo Yoboho (Rabies Prevention Law), Law No. 247 of 26 August 1950, last amendment Law No. 160 of 22 December 1999, http://law.e-gov.go.jp/cgi-bin/ idxsrch.cgi (Japanese text) (visited 5 September 2008); Kansensho no Yobo oyobi Kansensho no Kanja ni tai suru Iryo ni Kankei suru Horitsu (Law Concerning the Prevention of Infections and Medical Care for Patients of Infections), Law No. 114 of 2 October 1998, last amendment Law No. 30 of 2 May 2008, http://law.e-gov.go.jp/ cgi-bin/inxsearch.cgi (Japanese text) (visited 5 September 2008).

69 Pekkanen emphasizes that Japan has fewer lawyers per capita than any other developed country (16,000 qualified lawyers for a population of 120 million in Japan, in comparison to 700,000 to 900,000 U.S. lawyers for a population of 220 million) but that those numbers have been changing rapidly since the legal education reform in the 2000s: see Pekkanen, above n 44, at 10–11. For more on the scope and nature of Japanese legal education reform, particularly in the area of commercial dispute resolution, see Mayumi Saegusa and Julian Dierkes, 'Integrating Alternative Dispute Resolution', in Biukovic and Potter, above n 4.

70 For the most recent discussion on this topic, see Chien-Huei Wu, 'How Does TRIPS Transform Chinese Administrative Law?', 6 Global Jurist Article (2008), at 3–8. For a discussion on the capacity of the WTO to act as the most transformative legal instrument in the history, see Ernst Ulrich Petersmann, 'Multilevel Trade Governance in the WTO Requires Multilevel Constitutionalism', in Christian Joerges and Ernst-Ulrich Petersmann (eds), *Constitutionalism, Multilevel Trade Governance and Social Regulation* (Portland: Hart Publishing: 2006).

71 WT/L/432, 23 November 2001, at 3.

72 Ibid.

73 Report of the Working Party on the Accession of China, WT/MIN(01)/3, 10 November 2001, para 334.

74 For more on the problem of uniform administration of rules in China and the relation between the central and provincial and local governments, see Paulo D. Farah, 'Five Years of China's WTO Membership; EU and US Perspectives on China's Compliance with Transparency Commitments and the Transitional Review Mechanism', 33 Legal Issues of Economic Integration 263 (2006), at 270–78.

75 Ostry, above n 9, at 12.

76 Ibid. Similarly, other authors argued that the requirements (including transparency) of China's accession to the WTO as set out in the protocol go beyond the terms of existing WTO agreements. See Julia Ya Qin, '"WTO-Plus" Obligations and Their Implications for the World Trade Organization Legal System', 37 Journal of World Trade 483 (2003); Karen Halverson, 'China's WTO Accession: Economic, Legal, and Political Implications', 27 Boston College International and Comparative Law Review 319 (2004).

77 Jacobs and Potter, above n 2, at 116–17.

78 Ibid, at 117.

79 Lubman, 'Studying Contemporary Chinese Law', above n 24; Ostry, above n 9.

80 Vivienne Bath, 'Reducing the Role of Government—The Chinese Experiment', 3 (1) Asian Journal of Comparative Law (2008), at 1, http://www.bepress.com/asjcl/vol3/iss1/art9 (visited 5 September 2008).

81 Ibid, at 3. Bath cites enactment of the following legislation related to administrative law in period from 1989 to 2007: Administrative Litigation Law (1989), State Indemnity Law (1994), Administrative Punishments Law (1996), Administrative Supervision Law (1997), Administrative Reconsideration Law (1999), and Administrative Licensing Law (2003).

82 Ibid., at 1. Similarly, Chien-Huei Wu found that the TRIPS transparency provisions resulted in important administrative law reforms. See Chien-Huei Wu, above n 71, at 1.

83 The Administrative Licence Law, promulgated 27 August 2003, effective 1 July 2004, http://www.fdi.gov.cn/pub/FDI_EN/Laws/GeneralLawsandRegulations/BasicLaws/P020060620319981258285.pdf (English text) (visited 5 September 2008).

84 Article 33 of the Administrative Licence Law. See more on the Administrative License Law, above n 82.

85 Chinese web news People's Daily Online reported on 23 March 2007 that 86 percent of Chinese government organs have official websites: 96 percent of the departments of the State Council, 97 percent of provincial government organs, 96.7 percent of municipal government departments, and 87 percent of county-level governments have launched their own websites. In total, 86 percent of government organs have official

websites. It also mentioned that the central government, which launched its website on 1 January 2006 (http://www.gov.cn) has been daily uploading approximately 1,000 pieces of news and information for Chinese and foreign citizens.

86 Regulations of the People's Republic of China on Open Government Information, promulgated 5 April 2007, effective 1 May 2008, http://www.chinaelections.net/Upload-File/2008_5/mc_2723153857356.pdf (visited 8 September 2008) (English text provided by the China Law Center, Yale Law School).

87 Bath, above n 81, at 22.

88 Potter sees institutional purpose as an important factor of institutional capacity since it 'reveals the ways in which the goals of institutions vary with local material and ideological contexts', Potter, 'Selective Adaptation, Institutional Capacity and the Reception of International Law Under Conditions of Globalization' in Biukovic and Potter, above n 4. He identifies institutional orientation as 'the priorities and habitual practices that inform institutional performance' indicating that in Asia this factor may reveal tension between formal and informal modes of operation, where the central government trying to localize more formal (international) modes of information may encounter a resilient local, more informal mode of operation that is based on local social norms and networks.

89 Potter and Jacobs provide two case studies—on the SARS epidemics and treatment of people living with HIV/AIDS in China—to illustrate this problem. See Potter and Jacobs, above n 2.

90 The General Administration of Quality Supervision, Inspection and Quarantine (AQSIQ), http://english.aqsiq.gov.cn/AboutAQSIQ/Mission/ (visited 5 September 2008). The summary of institutional and legal framework is based on the report of a research assistant, Anna Turinov, JD 2008, Faculty of Law, UBC. It is important to note that the AQSIQ supervisory position is different from the position of the related organizations in Japan, where several ministries share supervision.

91 AQSIQ drafts the laws, regulations, binding decrees, ordinances, and notices related to quality supervision, inspection, and quarantine; it organizes implementation of the laws and regulations concerning quality supervision, inspection, and quarantine; and it supervises the administration and enforcement of laws relating to quality supervision, inspection, and quarantine. Ibid.

92 Ibid.

93 Ibid.

94 See WTO, Committee on Sanitary and Phytosanitary Measures, Links to Members' SPS-Related Websites, http://www.wto.org/english/tratop_e/sps_e/spslinks_e.htm (visited 5 September 2008).

95 WTO, Committee on Sanitary and Phytosanitary Measures, 'National Enquiry Points' G/SPS/ENQ/23 (27 March 2008), http://www.wto.org/english/tratop_e/sps_e/sps_e.htm#enquiry (visited 5 September 2008).

96 WTO, Committee on Sanitary and Phytosanitary Measures, 'National Notification Authorities', G/SPS/NNA/13 (27 March 2008), http://www.wto.org/english/tratop_e/sps_e/sps_e.htm#enquiry (visited 5 September 2008).

97 WTO, Committee on SPS Measures, 'Report to the Council for Trade in Goods on China's Transitional Review', G/SPS/38, 1 November 2005, at para 15.

98 China, Standing Committee of the National People's Congress, *Standardization Law* (promulgated 29 December 1988, effective 1 April 1989), Article 12, http://english. aqsiq.gov.cn/LawsandRegulations/ (English text) (visited 5 September 2008).

99 Ibid, Article 18.

100 Ibid, Article 7.

101 Ibid.

102 Ministry of Commerce (PRC), Department of WTO Affairs, http://sms2.mofcom. gov.cn/index.shtml (visited 5 September 2008).

103 China, *Food Hygiene Law* (promulgated by Order No. 59 of the President of the PRC, 30 October 1995, effective 30 October 1995), translated at http://english.aqsiq.gov.cn/ LawsandRegulations/ (visited 5 September 2008).

104 China, *Law on Product Quality* (promulgated by the Standing Committee National People's Congress, 8 July 2000, effective 1 September 2000), translated at http:// english.aqsiq.gov.cn/LawsandRegulations/ (visited 5 September 2008).

105 China, *Law on the Entry and Exit Animal and Plant Quarantine* (promulgated by Order No. 53 of the President of the PRC, 30 October 1991, effective 1 April 1992), translated at http://english.aqsiq.gov.cn/LawsandRegulations/ (visited 5 September 2008).

106 China, *Frontier Health and Quarantine Law* (promulgated by the Standing Committee National People's Congress, 2 December 1986, effective 1 May 1987), translated at http://english.aqsiq.gov.cn/LawsandRegulations/ (visited 5 September 2008).

107 Specific Rules for Enforcing the Frontier Health and Quarantine Law (approved by the State Council, 10 February 1989, issued by the Ministry of Public Health, 6 March 1989), translated in AQSIQ (PRC).

108 Frontier Health and Quarantine Law, Article 1.

109 Ministry of Commerce (PRC), Enquiry Online, http://gzly.mofcom.gov.cn/website/ comment/foreign/english_bbs.jsp (visited 5 September 2008).

110 WTO, Committee on Sanitary and Phytosanitary Measures, 'Report to the Council for Trade in Goods on China's Transitional Review', above n 98. See in particular statements of the European Communities (para 2) and the United States (paras 7 and 11).

111 Ibid, statement of Australia (para 12).

112 Local perception with respect to the principle of transparency has been examined by the research teams of the Asia Pacific Dispute Resolution projects led by Professor Pitman Potter of the University of British Columbia, Canada. In 2005 and 2006 a series of questionnaires were distributed in China, and local business people and legal practitioners were asked various questions about the nature and the functioning of the principle of transparency as applied in China. It is noteworthy that while the majority of respondents revealed their understanding of the importance of access to information and the right to comment, a great number failed to associate the right to information and review with the obligation of the government to provide information, to provide reasoned opinions, and to ensure judicial review of the decision. The importance of private networks seems to be still high. For more on the questionnaires and analysis of the data, see Biukovic, above n 7.

113 Bath's analysis of the first three years of application of the Administrative Licensing Law confirms this point. See Bath, above n 81, at 7. Randall Peerenboom explains that while China readily embarked on market reforms it intentionally resisted advice given by international institutions and experts to speed up with deregulation and to decrease

the role of central government in regulating business. On the contrary, argues Peerenboom, the state in China continued to play a central role in economic reforms and the country pursued adapting basic economic principles to its own circumstances. See Peerenboom, above n 49, at 5-6.

Domestic Politics and the Search for a New Social Purpose of Governance for the WTO: A Proposal for a Declaration on Domestic Consultation

SEEMA SAPRA*

I. Introduction

Clarification and enlargement of the role of non-state actors has been a recurring theme in discussions on World Trade Organization (WTO) institutional reform. The usual emphasis is on an enhanced role for civil society actors, including both value-based international NGOs and private interests, in WTO activities in Geneva.[1] Departing from this focus on Geneva-based participation and on non-governmental organizations (NGOs), this chapter examines whether and why the WTO institutional reform project should also concern itself with the role of non-state actors at the domestic level of trade policy-making.[2]

This chapter is divided into three parts. Part II discusses why a project on WTO institutional reform should be concerned with domestic transparency and participation issues in respect of how trade policy is formulated and implemented. The WTO displays a dysfunction in a lack of congruence between the power structure and the 'social purpose' of the regime. The resulting divergence between power and social purpose leads to current difficulties in negotiating the Doha Round, which are a manifestation of the struggle over defining the social purpose of the WTO. The new social purpose of the global trade regime must derive its content from the social purpose of governance at the domestic level. A new embedded liberal compromise must emerge from within the domestic politics of WTO Members.

Part III of this chapter highlights the reflexive and dynamic linkages between the domestic and the international in the functioning of the WTO. It argues that conceptualizing the WTO as a system of multi-level governance, which includes the domestic sphere as a site of governance, can be useful in designing reform proposals. Reform-oriented changes to processes and institutions at the international level should not have undesirable effects on participation at the domestic level. More proactively, WTO reform proposals must address the domestic origins of the WTO crisis and recommend changes in WTO rules and processes that will stimulate reform of domestic trade policy-making toward more broad-based and inclusive stakeholder participation. Efforts to reform the WTO, and in particular institutional reform proposals that target the role of non-state actors and external transparency, must be based on a holistic understanding of how the WTO works as a multi-level system of trade governance. The centrality of domestic political processes to the WTO's functioning necessitates more transparency and participation by non-state actors in engagement with the WTO at the domestic level.

Part IV discusses potential reform proposals that could lead to improved stakeholder participation at the domestic level. In particular, it is recommended that the Trade Policy Review Mechanism (TPRM) of the WTO include review of a Member's consultation mechanisms for trade policy-making at the domestic level. A declaration on domestic consultation should be adopted by the WTO General Council to provide guidance to the Trade Policy Review Body, as well as to Members in designing domestic consultation procedures. The WTO should also engage in capacity building in domestic consultation procedures for trade policy-making. Some ideas for conceptualizing and evaluating non-state actor capacity, preparedness, and engagement at the domestic level are also discussed.

Before proceeding, a distinction must be drawn between the terms 'non-state actor' and 'NGO' in the sense in which these are used in this chapter. The term 'NGO' is narrower than the term 'non-state actor'. There are two essential characteristics in which NGOs (being a particular type of non-state actor themselves) differ from other non-state actors. First, organizations usually categorized as NGOs have a non-profit or voluntary character. And second, unlike other non-state actors NGOs must have a basic organizational structure and not be ad hoc or spontaneous entities. A useful definition of NGOs offered by Martens is that these are 'formal (professionalized) independent societal organizations whose primary aim is to promote common goods at the national or the international level'.[3] NGOs do not have an international legal personality and are governed (if at all) by relevant national regulation of the state where they are located. Archer points out that the phrase NGO was originally 'an awkwardly negative title coined by the United Nations' and that it described 'a vast range of international and national citizens organizations, trade unions, voluntary associations, research institutes, public policy centers, private government agencies, business and trade associations, foundations and charitable endeavors'.[4]

The term 'non-state actor' is a residual catch-all category that can include all private non-governmental or societal actors and can accommodate the diversity deriving from 'differences in size, duration, range and scope of activities, ideologies, cultural background, organizational culture and legal status'.[5] Thus profit-oriented private actors like businesses are also non-state actors. Similarly, political parties are also non-state actors as their pursuit of political power would disqualify them from being classified as NGOs.[6] The term 'non-state actor' is broad enough to encompass ad hoc movements; individual citizens (whether natural or corporate); parliamentarians; components of the state like parliaments, judges, bureaucrats, journalists, academics, lawyers, and individual producers and consumers who are directly affected by trade policy decisions. This chapter discusses the appropriate role for non-state actors in the global governance of international trade.

II. The Domestic Origins of the WTO Crisis

Any account of the contemporary institutional challenges facing the World Trade Organization cannot help but emphasize the evolving nature of the relationship between the world trade regime and its developing country membership. The difficulties in concluding the Doha Round of trade talks underline the serious crisis that threatens the future relevance of the organization. There is however, no consensus among trade law scholars on how to problematize the WTO.[7]

It is suggested that disagreements about what is going wrong at the WTO and consequentially about what kinds of reforms are required stem in large part from the significant dissonance on the fundamental premises regarding the role, purpose, and objectives of the WTO.[8] Drawing on the theoretical framework of John Ruggie's article on embedded liberalism, this chapter suggests that the 'crisis' at the WTO raises questions about the institution's proper role, purpose, and objective in the globalized political economy.[9] Ruggie's article is famous for having described the post–Bretton Woods global economic regime until the early eighties as a period of 'embedded liberalism'.[10] According to Ruggie, this idea signified 'a grand social bargain whereby all sectors of society agreed to open markets, ... but also to contain and share the social adjustment costs that open markets inevitably produce'.[11] The embedded liberalism compromise ensured that economic liberalization was embedded in social community.[12]

At its core, Ruggie's 1982 article is about 'governance' and its roots (embeddedness) in a particular political, social, and economic context. Ruggie's central idea is his interpretation of what he terms the 'structure of international authority' or his model explaining regime formation and transformation. This chapter focuses on this aspect of Ruggie's analysis that explores how 'governance' via an international regime acquires 'purpose' and thereby 'legitimacy' by virtue of its embeddedness in the political, social, and economic fabric at the level of states, which are traditionally the default and original sites for governance. These ideas about governance, legitimacy, and the emergence of regimes are useful in identifying the reasons that the WTO needs reform. They also call attention to the domestic origins of the WTO's difficulties and the need for creating a new consensus on trade liberalization and regulation within WTO Members.

A. The Theoretical Framework of Embedded Liberalism

The idea of embedded liberalism in Ruggie's article can be conceptualized at two different levels of analysis. First, Ruggie used the term to describe the actual normative substantive bargain that was struck in the Bretton Woods negotiations and that found expression in the rules in the GATT. Thus the phrase 'embedded liberalism' conveys the substance of the agreement about how trade liberalization would be balanced by attention to domestic economic security and stability by governments. The second sense in which Ruggie's article uses the phrase 'embedded liberalism' is to describe the political and social structural origins of the political authority that was projected into the international sphere after the interwar period to set up the international economic regime, and which was based on a particular understanding of 'state-society relations' relevant to the time's social context. Thus the nature of the regime that emerged after World War II was determined by and was rooted in the 'collective reality' of that time concerning the proper scope of political authority in economic relations. In this sense, all viable regimes must necessarily be embedded within a particular social and political context. The failure to establish a particular regime or the disintegration of an existing regime can be explained on account of the incompatibility of its social purpose with the 'collective reality' of its times as to the proper scope of governmental authority.

Ruggie begins with the proposition that the formation and transformation of international regimes represents a 'concrete manifestation of the internationalization of political authority'.[13] He then moves on to consider how the internationalization of political authority takes place. What is the appropriate 'generative grammar' or model that can explain regime formation? Ruggie rejects the explanation provided by the hegemonic stability model on account of its focus on power alone and its failure to consider the social purpose of a regime. The hegemonic stability model is inadequate in that it does not offer any guidance on the 'content' of a particular regime.[14] As Ruggie further explains: 'Whatever its institutional manifestations, internationalized political authority in an international regime represents a fusion of power with legitimate social purpose.'[15]

It is through this combination of power and legitimate social purpose that political authority is *manifested* as well as *legitimated* in a regime. Thus Ruggie accepts the role of power in the establishment of an international regime. However, such exercise of power by itself cannot explain why a regime is established in the sense of being unable to explain what purpose or objectives the regime is expected to serve. How does a regime arrive at its social purpose? In asking this question, Ruggie directs our attention to the original source of legitimized power—domestic politics within states—and to domestic definitions and purposes of state power. Since the original source of power employed by powerful states is located in their domestic politics, it is there we must look to understand the constraints on and the ends of such power and the purposes for which it can be deployed, legitimately or otherwise.[16]

We must examine the contours of political authority within states, for it is there that the social purpose for the deployment of political authority is forged initially. Within the domestic environment of a state, domestic politics (rooted in social and economic structures) determines 'state-society relations' in the economic sphere by a balancing between 'authority' and 'market'.[17] Such balancing defines the 'legitimate social purposes', in pursuit of which state power can be employed in the domestic economy.[18] These understandings of 'state-society relations' at state level form the building blocks for the formulation of social purpose at the international level.

With the internationalization of political authority, the distribution of power between actors in the international system becomes relevant. Depending on the prevailing distribution of power between states, the social purpose of a regime or its 'collective reality' can either be provided by a hegemon unilaterally or arise from a compromise between leading economic powers. Which states get to participate in the internationalization of political authority and in the negotiations about an international regime's social purpose is determined by the extent of power and influence that they enjoy in the given context.

Using this theoretical framework, Ruggie explains the emergence of the post-1945 regime citing three causal factors: (1) a strong U.S. hegemony; (2) a quest for domestic stability shared by all influential states; and (3) the legitimacy resulting from a set of social objectives shared by the leading economic powers. In describing the substantive nature of this regime, Ruggie characterizes it as a new and different kind of liberalism. This 'embedded' liberalism provided a framework that would 'safeguard and even aid the quest for domestic stability without, at the same time, triggering the mutually destructive external consequences that had plagued the interwar period'.[19]

Ruggie's embedded liberalism is multilateral but with its multilateralism 'predicated upon domestic intervention'.[20] The embedded liberalism bargain had both an international and a domestic side. The social purpose of this regime was ultimately derived from the social purpose for governance forged in domestic politics over appropriate *state-society relations* in the regime-giving states.[21] It is in this sense, that for Ruggie 'economic liberalization was embedded in social community'.

Ruggie's interpretation of the internationalization of political authority in a regime is relevant for the topic of WTO institutional reform in several ways. First, it provides an explanation for when regimes are likely to form. Regimes are most likely to form when the concentration of power internationally co-varies positively with the purpose that the regime would advance. This could occur during a period of hegemony, when a single state chooses to advance its preferred social purpose through an international regime. Or it could occur when international power is not concentrated in a single state but is shared by a group of states. This group acting cooperatively and exhibiting a convergence of social purpose can deploy its collective power to establish a regime that advances the common social purpose of governance. Congruence between power and social purpose facilitates and might even be essential for a regime to be established.

Second, Ruggie's analysis provides information on what kinds of regimes are likely to emerge and be sustained. Regimes that advance 'social purposes' considered as 'legitimate' for the exercise of the power that is instrumental in establishing the regime are more likely to exist and subsist.

Third, Ruggie's model can be applied to changes within regimes and to changes of regimes. Regimes are likely to weaken on account of growing divergence between the distribution of power within or surrounding a regime and the social purpose of a regime. However, challenges to the hegemonic exercise of power by the emergence of other powerful states might not threaten a regime if the emerging powers have a shared preference for the social purpose of the regime and continue to support the regime to further that social purpose.

Fourth and most crucially, the above theoretical framework tells us that the social purpose of a regime, which we can call its 'social purpose of governance', *must* derive its meaning, content, and therefore legitimacy from the social purpose of governance at the domestic level. This congruence between the social purpose of governance for a regime and the social purpose of governance for states (who participate in the regime) is an important determinant of 'legitimacy' perceptions about a regime. Because the transfer of legitimate power or political authority to a regime takes place *from* the domestic site for governance (the state) *to* a new site for governance (the international regime), the exercise of such authority at the international level must be responsive to the needs of governance as defined at the domestic level. In the absence of such responsiveness, the regime is likely to face challenges to its legitimacy. This responsiveness is of course a political requirement only in respect of the domestic politics of *regime-givers* (and especially if their domestic politics is democratic). Regimes need not reflect the aspirations of the *regime-takers*, who lack power to reject a regime and are thus excluded from negotiating its social purpose.

B. Historical Externalization of Costs to Developing Countries

To understand the present-day WTO crisis, account must be taken of where developing countries were placed under the embedded liberalism of the GATT. Scholarship on embedded liberalism under the GATT has generally been silent about the terms of participation of developing countries. In the main, Ruggie approaches his topic from the perspective of the developed countries, whom he called the 'regime-makers'. In the final section of his article, under the sub-heading 'Stress, contradiction, and the future', Ruggie asks, 'How enduring is embedded liberalism?'[22]

The future of embedded liberalism, Ruggie argues, depends on stresses in the world political economy produced by the three major modes through which the costs of maintaining the embedded liberalism compromise had, until 1982, been successfully externalized by the regime-makers. These three modes for externalization of adjustment costs were (1) the intertemporal mode, via inflation; (2) the intersectoral mode, 'whereby pressure on domestic and international public authorities is vented into the realm of private markets';[23] and (3) the interstratum mode, whereby 'regime-makers' shift a dispropor-tionate share of adjustment costs onto those who are 'regime-takers'.[24] In his later work, Ruggie elaborated on the externalization of adjustment costs to the developing countries under embedded liberalism:

> The developing countries, of course, never enjoyed the privilege of cushioning the adverse domestic effects of market exposure in the first place. The majority lack the resources, institutional capacity, international support, and, in some instances, the political interest on the part of their ruling elites.[25]

Ruggie has himself declared that the compromise of embedded liberalism has never fully extended to the developing countries.[26]

Ruggie thought it inevitable that the stresses underlying the GATT's embedded liberalism would require 'some manner of renegotiating the forms of domestic and international social accommodation reflected in embedded liberalism'.[27] He regarded inflation as the most serious threat to the future of the post-1945 embedded liberalism regime and as being most 'likely to lead to a direct renegotiation of the modus vivendi that has characterised embedded liberalism'.[28] The exclusion of developing countries from the embedded liberalism compromise by the externalization of its adjustment costs did not, in 1982, strike Ruggie as potentially proving 'fatal' for the future of embedded liberalism.[29] However, as the Doha Round difficulties demonstrate, the future of the WTO regime is today perhaps most seriously threatened by the refusal of the developing countries to continue to bear the adjustment costs of the rapidly unravelling embedded liberalism compromise. Writing in 1982, Ruggie did not foresee the immense structural changes to the international political economy that have occurred in this and the previous decade and the accompanying power shifts in the transition from the GATT to the WTO.

C. Power Shifts at the WTO

In order to describe the unravelling of the embedded liberalism compromise, one must return to the transformations unleashed by the Uruguay Round in the WTO's power structure. The Uruguay Round has been described as a grand North-South bargain: a deal negotiated among the regime-makers later offered to the developing countries with the option to take it or leave it. The regime-makers during the Uruguay Round were essentially the United States, the European Community, Japan, and Canada. Lacking expertise, resources, and influence, developing countries were unable to participate in the Uruguay Round negotiations that lasted nearly a decade and were often conducted through inaccessible informal bilateral processes between the United States and the European Union.[30] However, the Uruguay Round represents a watershed in the evolution of the multilateral trading system. It will be remembered as the round after which developing countries could no longer be ignored in international trade negotiations. In the new regime that the round heralded, developing countries began to move to the centre stage of global trade negotiations, and that process has only further accelerated.

The WTO functions very differently from the GATT. Developing countries are now politically integrated in the WTO regime. The old group of regime-makers has expanded to form the core group in the recently concluded July 2008 mini-ministerial.[31] The old GATT-era power centres have been joined by new power centres in the WTO, especially the emerging economies. Organized coalitions of developing countries have become effective players with significant success in blocking bad deals and in agenda setting. China's accession to the WTO has further shifted the WTO's power structure.

There are many reasons for the power shifts within the WTO. While partly the result of globalization and the geographical diversification of economic growth and prosperity, the power shifts in the WTO have also been facilitated and encouraged by the WTO regime itself.[32] The WTO Agreements have changed the negotiating rules and practices in the global trade regime. The WTO is more democratic. The 'single undertaking' approach and de facto consensus decision-making have worked to empower developing countries in talks. New negotiating practices are more inclusive, with a greater emphasis on transparency, input-legitimacy, and participation by less developed countries. The dispute settlement mechanism, with the reverse consensus rule, allows less powerful WTO Members to enforce compliance by stronger trading partners. The Internet has played an important role in empowering less developed states by significantly improving availability of information and creating greater global connectedness.[33] Internet-enabled transparency in negotiations empowers developing countries and many non-state actors who were excluded from participation in earlier trade rounds.[34]

Increased involvement of civil society and global movements in global trade governance along with other facets of globalization are changing identities and interests. Yet another reason for the empowerment of developing countries in the WTO is a growth in confidence, ability, and expertise among diplomats and officials from developing countries on the substantive and procedural aspects of international trade negotiations. All this has resulted in dramatic changes to the power distribution in the WTO regime. Today, developing countries are certainly no longer mere regime-takers. Indeed, some emerging economies can now be considered part of the regime-givers category. Other developing countries could probably play the role of regime-makers if they are able to cooperate with other countries through effective issue-based coalitions. At the very least, most of the active developing country participants in the Doha Round are now capable of playing the part of regime-blockers.

Another important change that became visible during the Uruguay Round was the growing influence of private power in determining the agenda and outcomes of trade negotiations. The new issues of the Uruguay Round (services, investment, and intellectual property) became central to the U.S. negotiating agenda because of the influence of American business and industry.[35] The influence of private power on government trade policy-making has continued to increase in developed as well as in developing countries. This new shift toward public-private partnership in trade governance has further changed the politics of international trade governance at both the domestic and the international levels.[36]

D. The Unravelling of Embedded Liberalism and the Need for a New Social Purpose of Governance

Recent scholarship has focused on how globalization is putting the embedded liberalism compromise under severe stress in the developed economies. This stress has resulted in increasing opposition to trade liberalization in the domestic politics of these countries. Howse has argued that the agenda that drove the Uruguay Round and then went on to form the core of the WTO treaties 'would prove to be the greatest threat so far to the sustainability of embedded liberalism'.[37] He adds that the WTO rules have had much more ambiguous welfare effects than the GATT rules, and 'the issue of who gains and who loses *within* a given society rears its head and cannot be avoided...'.[38]

Embedded liberalism in developed economies is in trouble. In recent work on embedded liberalism, Ruggie sheds more light on the problem. The problem today for the industrialized countries is that

> embedded liberalism presupposed an *international* world. It presupposed the existence of *national* economies, engaged in *external* transactions, conducted at *arm's length*, which governments could mediate at the *border* by tariffs and exchange rates, among other tools. The globalization of financial markets and production chains, however, challenges each of these premises and threatens to leave behind merely national social bargains.[39]

Howse also quite clearly differentiates between the distinct domestic and international parts to the GATT-era embedded liberalism bargain.[40] He explains that under embedded liberalism

> the function of assuring that trade liberalization commitments worked with, not against, the needs of the domestic polity was understood as in the first instance domestic; ... the law of trade was essentially designed to be *permissive* toward the domestic polity performing those functions (safeguards, etc.).[41]

As both Ruggie and Howse explain, globalization and an expanding trade agenda have encroached on and disturbed the domestic promise of embedded liberalism. Trade liberalization is today increasingly concerned with positive obligations (non-tariff barriers and across-the-border measures instead of tariff reductions), and the autonomy that states enjoyed under the GATT in their domestic regulation is coming under challenge in WTO dispute settlement proceedings. The slide of policy issues and choices, which were previously defined as domestic, into the international arena decreases the potential for input legitimacy and accountability in domestic politics.[42]

The integration of developing economies into the global trade regime has also affected the maintenance of the embedded liberalism compromise in developed economies. As mentioned earlier, Ruggie did not believe that developing countries gained from the old embedded liberalism compromise.[43] Further, as developing countries were excluded from participation in negotiations on the social purpose of the regime, the international component of the embedded liberalism bargain itself externalized the adjustment costs of developed countries to developing countries. Many commentators have pointed out that the trade regime under the GATT exhibited a structural bias toward the industrialized Members.[44]

The power shifts at the WTO mean that developing countries are no longer willing to bear the costs of the old embedded liberalism bargain. Rapidly growing emerging economies are in fact exporting the costs of their own growth to other countries, including developed countries. Having gained significant influence at the WTO, developing countries now need to be included in any new compromise. The Doha Round battles over dismantling the old structural imbalances in the global trading regime and the rising protectionist sentiment in the developed world all point to the demands emanating from capitals for a new embedded liberalism bargain, one that this time includes both the developed and the developing world. Trade policy has entered the mainstream domestic political dialogue, and until a new compromise of embedded liberalism is found, trade policy will continue to remain politicized. [45]

The unravelling of the embedded liberalism compromise at the domestic level is at the heart of the crisis facing the WTO. A new compromise, one better suited to contemporary globalization and the changed global political economy, is needed. Ruggie's work points the way forward. The search for a new compromise to sustain the global trade regime is nothing less than a search for a new social purpose of governance. However, existing differences in the economic, political, and social development levels between industrialized and developing countries make it difficult for the WTO membership to arrive at a consensus on what the *social purpose* of the WTO ought to be.

Ruggie's question—how does a regime arrive at its social purpose?—is extremely important in today's context. This social purpose of governance is initially forged within the domestic political context of states and involves reaching a balance between 'authority' and 'market'. The domestic determination of the appropriate role for government defines the 'legitimate social purposes', in pursuit of which state power can be employed in the domestic economy.[46] In other words, it is through the domestic political process that social compacts are formed or consensus is reached on how far the state ought to interfere with the market in the domestic economy and for what reasons. These domestic understandings of 'state-society relations' then go on to determine the social purpose that an international regime advances. Once the social purpose of governance is forged within individual states, the preferences of different regime-giving states, which could diverge or converge, form the building blocks for determining the social purpose of an international regime.

The challenge for the WTO is to arrive at substantive bargains that help embed trade liberalization in both developed and developing countries. An international regime that fails to align its social purpose with the social purpose of governance as forged in the domestic social and political economies of its influential members runs the risk of dysfunctionality. Such a regime is likely to encounter challenges to its legitimacy and to the legitimacy of the domestic political authority that enforces it. Ruggie's theoretical framework provides that the social purpose of economic governance must first be forged within the domestic context of a state. And this social purpose may differ among states depending on their particular individual circumstances and developmental status. WTO institutional reform, therefore, must include within its scope reform of domestic trade policy-making and capacity building. If a new global compromise of embedded liberalism is going to emerge, it must do so with domestic consensus on trade policy.

III. The WTO System of Multi-level Trade Governance

This section explores how unpacking the governance structure of the WTO takes us back into domestic decision-making and to the importance of partnerships between the private, non-profit, and public sectors if the gains from trade are to be realized. Given the WTO's basic character as a Geneva-based international organization, discussions on its institutional reform, with some justification, tend to dwell on the organizational aspects of the WTO in Geneva. The themes that are usually considered include the role of the Secretariat and the Director-General; adequacy of financial and other resources available in Geneva to carry on WTO activities; the rules of conduct of WTO business including negotiations, ministerial meetings, dispute settlement activities, and regular meetings of various WTO committees and sub-committees; issues of transparency with regard to making documents public; issues of access to the WTO's Geneva-based activities for non-state actors; and the reform of procedural rules for decision-making and the organization of other WTO activities. The focus of the debate on WTO institutional reform has remained its activities, staff, and resources based in Geneva.[47] This, however, neglects the more complex character of the WTO.

The WTO website attempts to answer for the general public the fundamental question—what is the WTO? The answer suggests that the WTO is first and foremost a negotiating forum. This idea is useful in emphasizing the intergovernmental and member-driven nature of the organization. The WTO is, of course, much more than just a negotiating forum. It includes a dispute settlement mechanism, and treaty rules (both substantive and procedural), and a Secretariat with staff and a statesman for a Director-General. The WTO also includes Member delegations convening collectively in their multiple avatars, whether as the Ministerial Conference, the General Council, the Trade Negotiating Committee, the DSB, the Council for Trade in Goods, the Council for Trade in Services, the Council for TRIPS, or as subsidiary committees reporting to the General Council.[48] The WTO is also an international organization with a building in Geneva, its own budget, and full legal personality and capacity necessary to discharge its functions.[49]

The need for greater attention to the domestic context becomes evident once the WTO as a governance system is unpacked. The discussion on WTO institutional reform requires clarity as to how the WTO governs trade. Much has been written about the WTO and its role in global governance.[50] The 'global governance' dilemmas arising from the substantive content of WTO law both in the treaties and in DSU jurisprudence have received considerable attention.[51] However, the structure of the WTO, including the processes through which it makes trade rules, has not been adequately analyzed from the perspective of 'governance'.[52] The Sutherland Report advised that reform efforts should be based on the structure and mandate of the WTO. Understanding the WTO's *political structure* of trade governance could lead to more appropriate suggestions on the role for non-state actors within the WTO. The reform debates need to start their inquiry from the basic theoretical question: how is the WTO system supposed to work?[53]

A useful way of conceptualizing WTO is to understand the procedural, institutional, or political structure of the processes through which the WTO governs trade. The global governance of trade takes place through a series of complex interactions between various actors and processes in what is broadly a two-tier system of decision-making and participation. The member-driven intergovernmental organization that it is, the WTO fits well into the framework of Robert Putnam's logic of two-level games where rule formulation takes place at two levels—first at the national level, where domestic trade policy gets formulated, then at the international level, where global rules are negotiated, and finally again at the domestic level, where internationally agreed rules are implemented and enforced.[54] Instead of a narrow conception of the WTO as an international organization created by treaty rules and based in Geneva with its premises, Secretariat staff and interactions with and among Member State delegations, this chapter adopts a broad conception of the WTO as a member-driven intergovernmental organization with a system of global trade governance that operates at two levels—the international and the domestic. Viewed in this manner, the WTO system of trade governance encompasses a much broader range of actors and processes of participation at both the international and the domestic levels.[55] Conceptualized as a system of multi-level governance, the WTO's structure and design itself make the argument for inclusive non-state stakeholder participation at the domestic level.

The domestic political space of WTO Members is where inter-linkages between governance, development, and trade are negotiated by domestic actors. These inter-linkages lead to the formulation of the national interest in international trade. The conception of international trade negotiations as a two-level game allows recognition of the presence of domestic conflict over identifying the 'national interest'. Assuming an ideal WTO, where the political processes work perfectly in the sense of involving all stakeholders, both at the domestic level and at the intergovernmental level, the law emanating from such a process would be expected to be optimal. This will happen only if domestic politics is robust and inclusive. Getting the politics right at the first level is essential because international trade politics presupposes independent sovereign symmetrical states.

Participation patterns at the domestic level determine negotiation gains for a country at the international level. Similarly, how the WTO functions at the international level can influence domestic processes of participation in trade governance and policy-making. The linkages between the international and domestic levels in two-level negotiating games like the WTO system are complex, dynamic, and reflexive. The interaction works both ways. The dynamic of participation and negotiations at the international level directly feeds into how processes and institutions of participation get structured at the domestic level. And processes at the domestic level significantly determine the international outcome. Ostry has noted that the domestic political processes of the European Union and United States have been the major determinant of the agenda and dynamics of the international process and of outcomes under the GATT and the WTO.[56]

Theories and definitions of modern governance provide more support for the argument that the role of non-state actors in domestic governance of trade is a relevant theme in the project of WTO institutional reform. Modern governance debates have moved away from the idea of government to the idea of governance, and away from the idea of ruling and to the idea of steering.[57] Governance now involves non-hierarchical steering and management of networks of public and private actors. Writing about trade policy consultation processes in Canada, Robert Wolfe comments that, in newer areas of trade policy, it is no longer possible to assume the 'centralized bureaucratic state'.[58] Regulators no longer 'command and control'; instead they 'negotiate and persuade'.[59] According to Wolfe, the unit for policy analysis in trade governance today is no longer the bureaucracy positioned in a hierarchical relationship with respect to other actors. Instead, contemporary trade policy-making involves collaborative horizontal relationships between government agents and non-state actors. Economic actors are often implementation agents for the state. And sometimes economic agents are in the position of principals instructing the government on policy goals.[60]

In his work on governance, Jan Kooiman captures the role for 'governing' interactions between state and non-state actors in modern governance. Governing, according to Kooiman, includes all activities of social, political, and administrative actors that amount to purposeful efforts to guide, steer, control, or manage societies. The patterns that emerge from the governing activities of these actors become governance.[61] Similarly, Yanacopulos emphasizes interactions between state and non-state actors as part and parcel of governance. She describes governance as 'a purposive activity' where state and non-state actors 'attempt to influence other political actors by ways in which they frame and steer issues'.[62] Governance as an 'explanatory framework' explains the 'changing strategic relationship between state and non-state actors in world politics.'[63] A similar emphasis on state and non-state actor interaction is found in the definition of governance adopted by the Commission on Global Governance. According to the commission, governance is

> the sum of the many ways individuals and institutions, public and private, manage their common affairs.... It includes formal institutions and regimes empowered to enforce compliance, as well as informal arrangements that people and institutions either have agreed to or perceive to be in their interest.[64]

The WTO system of trade governance includes space at both the international and domestic levels for state and non-state actors to engage in trade governance through their interactions, struggles, and negotiations.[65] Governance *results* from the sum total of the interactions between all actors at all levels. Interactions and the rules regulating them are as important as institutions and the actors who participate. Global trade governance extends beyond the WTO's formal structure to all activities and interactions between state and non-state actors that have the governing effect of steering trade policy.[66]

The state still remains relevant, though with a shifting role. Governing activity is diffused over various social actors with the state increasingly in the role of facilitator and cooperating partner.[67] Networks of societal actors work in cooperation with and often under the direction of the state.[68] Competition between the public and the private sector is replaced by collaboration.[69] Governance becomes a balancing process.[70] It is no longer static but involves constant coming to grips with governing needs and governing capacities. It needs adaptive capacity.[71] Governance outcomes depend on the quality of governing interactions.[72] The challenge is to make governing interactions productive.[73] Good global trade governance must, therefore, encourage processes and rules that have a positive influence on the context and substance of interactions between state and non-state actors at both the international and domestic levels. The good governance principles of transparency and participation should define the appropriate role for non-state actors within the WTO system.[74]

A deconstruction of how the WTO governs international trade shows that the roadblocks in Geneva often arise on account of imperfect governance at the domestic level.[75] This is yet another reason for the project on WTO institutional reform to discuss institutional changes that would have positive effects for how domestic trade policy gets made. The Sutherland Report notes that Members' objective, long-term interests reside in the development of national capacity and policy ownership.[76] The next section identifies the existence of a capability or governance deficit in domestic trade policy-making.

IV. A Proposal for a Declaration on Domestic Consultation

Thus far, this chapter highlighted the important role of domestic politics in the ongoing WTO crisis. The domestic origins of the WTO crisis, the unravelling of the embedded liberalism compromise, the search for a new social purpose of governance for the WTO regime, an understanding of the WTO's multi-level structure of governance and the changing nature of modern governance all underline the important role for non-state actors in trade policy-making at the domestic level. This chapter recommends that the project on WTO institutional reform adopt as one of its objectives reform of domestic trade policy-making and encouragement of greater transparency and stakeholder participation in domestic engagement with the WTO. Sylvia Ostry and Robert Wolfe have made tentative suggestions that the WTO's Trade Policy Review Mechanism (the TPRM) be expanded to review domestic trade policy consultation processes.[77] This chapter builds on this idea and develops a specific proposal for a WTO declaration on domestic consultation. The proposal is made with the expectation that it will invite discussion and advance the debate on WTO reform. The objective of the declaration will be to invite review of domestic consultation mechanisms in the trade policy reviews undertaken by the WTO and to thereby stimulate reform of domestic trade policy-making.

The General Council of the WTO (or the Ministerial Conference) should adopt a 'Declaration on Domestic Consultation'. This document should call on the Trade Policy Review Body (the TPRB) to undertake, as part of the existing trade policy reviews, the review of Members' consultation procedures in the development and/or implementation of trade policy.[78] The declaration should set out the necessity and benefits of appropriate domestic consultation procedures. It should also include a statement that WTO Members understand the benefits of domestic consultation. Such a declaration will help promote a better understanding of how the WTO works and of how states as well as domestic non-state actors can benefit from the provisions of the WTO agreements.

The declaration should include a broad framework of guidelines on how to design and evaluate domestic stakeholder consultation procedures and institutions. These guidelines should encourage transparency and participation by non-state actors in domestic trade policy matters. The declaration would not create any additional enforceable obligations for Members. The only mandatory feature of the declaration would be the direction to the TPRB to examine domestic consultation procedures in the trade policy reviews it undertakes. The declaration would help promote an understanding among government officials and non-state actors of how to engage the domestic political environment in order to obtain greater benefits from WTO membership. Regular discussion of Members' consultation procedures in trade policy reviews will promote 'social learning' about the challenges of WTO participation among institutions and actors (state and non-state) in developing and developed countries. It is likely that this will lead to the development of improved consultation mechanisms in WTO Member States.

An appraisal of how the TPRM functions demonstrates the potential benefits from more rigorous reviews of the domestic policy-making environment. The TPRM was established on an interim basis in 1989 under the GATT. Its original purpose was to complement reviews that were being regularly produced by the United States Trade Representative (USTR). It is now a permanent part of the WTO, having been incorporated in Annex 3 of the Marrakesh Agreement. The reviews are carried out by the TPRB based on inputs received from WTO Secretariat officials, the Member undergoing review, and other discussants selected and acting in their personal capacity.[79] The reviews examine the policy statement submitted by the Member under review and the report prepared by the WTO Secretariat's Trade Policy Review Division. Secretariat reports typically include detailed chapters that examine the macroeconomic situation and trade policies and practices, as well as trade policy-making institutions.[80]

All this information is published on the WTO website once the review is complete. The TPRM consumes approximately 5 percent of the WTO annual budget.[81]

Trade policy reviews undertaken by the WTO are more in the nature of positive reporting than normative reporting.[82] The reports provide little more than a description of the domestic policy landscape.[83] According to Annex 3, the TPRM is expected to help achieve 'greater transparency in, and understanding of, the trade policies and practices of Members'.[84] This enables collective appreciation and evaluation of Members' policies but is not intended for use in enforcement of commitments and dispute settlement or to impose new policy commitments. Assessments under the TPRM are expected to take into account 'wider economic and developmental needs, policies and objectives' and the external environment of the Member under review, albeit only to the extent relevant.[85]

The primary function of the TPRM is to examine the impact of domestic policies on the multilateral trading system.[86] Therefore, trade policy reviews are not an evaluation of how Members make and implement trade policy. Rather, the reviews *describe* the trade policy of the Member under review. The proposed declaration would introduce this new dimension of evaluation of the policy-making context and process into the trade policy reviews. Members would be encouraged to examine and evaluate whether their consultation procedures are satisfactory, and other Members will have the opportunity to learn about effective consultation and the benefits and downsides of consultation.[87] Currently, Clause B of Annex 3 to the Marrakesh Agreement titled 'Domestic transparency' recognizes the value of domestic transparency in trade policy-making and the need promote greater domestic transparency. The text clarifies that implementation of any initiatives to further domestic transparency would be voluntary and 'take account of each Member's legal and political systems'. However, the declaration would go much further than this limited recognition and would encourage reform of domestic trade politics by encouraging social learning on designing stakeholder consultations.

The potential for social learning stemming from the declaration is evident from the current effects of the TPRM. The WTO website describes the TPRM process as peer reviews that enable outsiders to understand a country's policies but also provide feedback to the Member under review. Francois has found that the TPRM helps promote the credibility of domestic policy reform and an understanding of how such reform is perceived by domestic actors.[88] The TPRM has the potential to assist in generating political support for domestic trade-related reforms. It helps keep policy-making transparent and democratic by exposing policies to domestic actors. These non-state actors include legislators, academics, business media, and the electorate.[89] The 1999 Appraisal Report submitted to the Ministerial Conference by the Trade Policy

Review Body noted the TPRM's contribution to transparency, its role as a catalyst in reconsideration of policies by Members, and its input into policy formulation and identification of technical assistance needs.[90] The report recommended that more attention be given to transparency in government decision-making on trade policy matters in accordance with Paragraph B of Annex 3.[91] While noting that reports submitted under the TPRM often complement one another, the Appraisal Report encourages governments to keep their reports short, WTO-focused, forward-looking, and limited to highlighting 'recent trade policy development, future policy directions and their impact on trade'.[92] This recommendation demonstrates that the scope of the TPRM is circumscribed, no doubt on account of WTO staff and funding scarcities. However, limiting the scope of the TPRM wastes potential opportunities that a more expansive exercise would provide and the benefits of social learning that more detailed Member reports would offer.

A. Designing Domestic Consultations

The proposed declaration could potentially help address the domestic origins of the WTO crisis and enable the creation of a domestic consensus on the new social purpose of governance. The declaration should emphasize the importance of non-state actor participation in trade policy-making and implementation. As stated before, it should include a broad framework to provide guidance both for the design and evaluation of domestic stakeholder consultation procedures and institutions. This framework would enable Members to evaluate their own consultation mechanisms and engage in social learning from others. Some ideas for such a framework are considered here and are based on a review of some recent literature on reform of domestic trade policy-making processes.[93]

The framework should be developed around three basic questions about domestic consultation processes. First, what are or should be the objectives for involving non-state actors in trade policy-making at the domestic level? Second, what kinds of non-state actors should be included in domestic policy-making processes? And third, how should the consultations with non-state actors be structured or what would be appropriate mechanisms for such engagement? Finding answers to these questions will help move the debate from its early 'one-size fits all' mould to a more nuanced discussion based on differentiation between various objectives of engagement, types of non-state actors, and the different roles that these actors perform within the multilevel WTO system of trade governance. Some general comments on consultation as a part of governmental policy-making processes are considered before turning to these questions.

Consultation is a learning process and governments can learn from each other on how to design their own systems. However, models of trade consultation are not necessarily exportable and must be conditioned to particular national conditions.[94] The determinants of consultation characteristics include the constitutional, political, and social circumstances of a state. Thus, the political culture of a state (its democratic character), the territorial distribution of governmental authority (its federal or unitary character), its bureaucratic culture and politics, the characteristics of the national economy, and the particular requirements of trade policy are all factors that determine the appropriate model of trade consultation suited to a state.[95] Domestic capacity among non-state and governmental actors also determines what kinds of consultation processes are feasible and likely. Developed states, with more governmental capacity, are likely to engage in more consultation. Thus the disadvantages that accrue from inadequate consultation arise more often in less developed states.

B. Objectives of Consultations

What are or should be the objectives for involving non-state actors in trade policy-making? The discussion on objectives for non-state actor participation needs to *move on* from the somewhat abstract values of legitimacy, accountability, and democratic deficit toward formulating more concrete objectives and proposals for WTO institutional reform. The Sutherland Report has also called for greater clarity with respect to the objectives for the WTO's engagement with civil society.[96] The report states: '[T]here need to be explicit objectives, with the gains and risks properly assessed....'[97] It clarifies that the objectives for civil society engagement must depend on the WTO's mandate and structure.[98] The objectives for domestic consultation are important because the choice of objectives will determine the selection of which non-state actors with whom to engage. The objectives will also determine the appropriate mechanisms of engagement. The objectives of domestic consultation can be divided into four issue categories addressing various deficits: (1) legitimacy deficit; (2) access deficit; (3) knowledge deficit; and (4) capability or governance deficit.[99]

1. The Legitimacy Deficit

This chapter has discussed how the consensus underpinning trade liberalization has been undermined on account of an expanding and encroaching trade agenda. This is responsible for the reduced political support for the WTO in domestic politics.[100] The legitimacy deficit facing trade policy demands fundamental rethinking of assumptions underlying the purposes of trade diplomacy.[101] The slide of domestic policy into the international sphere, calls for participatory democracy by empowered non-state actors, a decrease in public trust of government institutions, and diminishing capacity of governments to respond to increasingly complex governance problems all create serious legitimacy challenges. Zahrnt notes that actors' preferences are a result of competition between interests and norms. While the logic of consequences dictates interests, the logic of appropriateness makes the norm of participatory governance attractive to domestic actors.[102] A sense of policy ownership among stakeholders is essential to obtain support for implementation of controversial policies.[103]

A key objective for including non-state actors in trade-policy consultations must be to foster a sense of ownership of policy outcomes through participatory processes. In a recent panel discussion at the World Economic Forum in Davos, the panellists emphasized that it is crucial to communicate with domestic constituents on challenges of trade policy if current protectionist sentiments are to be defeated. Consultations can help create a common vocabulary and language for state and non-state actors to discuss important trade policy issues. Consensus-building in the domestic sphere is now an integral part of the job description of domestic trade policy officials. Ostry points out how stronger domestic capability in policy formulation can help legitimize the policy process.[104] Stronger domestic capability requires public-private partnerships to meet trade policy governance needs. Trade policy now needs trade diplomacy directed as much at domestic constituents as at international audiences.[105]

2. The Access Deficit

There is an increasing demand for greater access to domestic trade policy processes by non-state actors. The slide of domestic issues into the international sphere coupled with restricted access at the international level makes access at the national level even more important. Empowerment of non-state actors further feeds demands for access. The Internet has made knowledge more widely available and simultaneously made it easier for actors to network, organize, and lobby. Hocking has recognized the need for a level playing field in consultation processes.[106] If denied adequate access at home, non-state actors can attempt to gain influence through another state's consultation processes using NGO and other community networks. An expanding and encroaching trade agenda increases the range of affected participants. Disaffected domestic constituents have increased pressure for a voice in the decision-making process. Major meetings or negotiations also act as a catalyst for non-state actor demands for consultation.[107]

3. The Knowledge Deficit

Governments rely on the business community for knowledge about how trade policy will affect industry and the economy. Government actors in both the legislative and executive branches have information needs that include evaluation of the effects of WTO agreements, evaluation of domestic regulation needed, evaluation of the effects of the interaction between domestic regulation and international commitments, information on foreign trade barriers, and information on defensive and offensive interests of domestic producers.[108] Effective and beneficial participation in the WTO depends on high-quality research and analysis.[109]

WTO rules and disciplines might not always prescribe the right diagnosis and solutions to development problems. Research is needed on whether proposed WTO rules are consistent with national priorities. Research can identify complementary policies required to address potential negative effects of WTO disciplines. Non-state actors like business can supply relevant information to assess the domestic gains or losses from potential policies. Academics can undertake research while NGOs can provide valuable information on contextual issues such as the impact of trade policies on non-economic interests and values.

4. The Capacity Deficit

In many less developed countries, the domestic processes for preparing policy positions for multilateral trade negotiations are almost non-existent. Engagement with non-state actors at the domestic level, particularly in developing countries, will improve the efficiency and effectiveness of the WTO. Efficiency-directed engagement requires strategies and objectives designed to encourage deeper participation, facilitate negotiations through development of capacity, help identify interests, build new coalitions, and overcome informational asymmetries and agency costs. Efficiency-directed strategies can target information failures, enable domestic issue linkages and trade-offs, enable international negotiations to alter domestic perceptions of costs/benefits and pay-offs, and facilitate direct communication and ties between domestic level participants across national boundaries.[110]

Both human and institutional capacity is necessary to gain from trade.[111] As this chapter has already noted, diminishing government capacity and increasing complexity of policy choices are leading to a less hierarchical trade diplomacy aimed at managing horizontal public-private networks or coalitions as part of governance processes. The implementation of WTO agreements in developing countries is institution-intensive and creates new governance needs.

Government institutions and capabilities need to be upgraded as a result of new WTO commitments.[112] Implementation of WTO rules requires complementary policies and the adaptation of WTO flexibilities to suit local conditions.[113] The capacity to implement and benefit from WTO agreements is determined by the domestic policy reform agenda.[114] The sequence and consistency between domestic reforms and implementation of WTO commitments is an important ingredient of successful development strategies.[115]

All this makes it necessary to involve the private sector in implementing and managing new WTO commitments. Furthermore, benefits from engagement with the WTO need not be limited to economic gains but could deliver governance benefits. Engagement with the WTO could contribute to institution building and improve decision-making in domestic governance. Greater stakeholder participation can improve the quality of trade policy as a component of good development policy by ensuring that other values besides producer interests get their due.[116] Trade policy consultations are a step toward democratization of political systems. Consultations can prevent governments from using trade barriers as a vote-seeking strategy.[117] Consensus building among non-state actors is also important because, in international negotiations, governments are concerned about the capacity of their negotiating partners to deliver domestically on promises made. Therefore, the fourth reason for involvement of non-state actors in domestic trade policy-making is to supply the capacity and governance deficits that all countries face in today's complex policy environment.

C. Selection of Non-State Actors

With what kinds of non-state actors should the domestic trade policy-making process engage? The WTO's multi-level governance system calls for participation by a variety of state and non-state actors at both the international and domestic levels. Since governance must continually adapt to needs and capacities, it would be difficult to identify in advance those non-state actors who should participate in domestic trade policy-making. There is diversity among Members' governance institutions, trade needs, and capacities. Thus, conceptually, the definition of relevant non-state actors should remain open-ended.

The criteria for selecting actors to engage with must be prescribed. All those stakeholders who stand to gain or lose through WTO regulation or whose rights and responsibilities are affected have a legitimate interest in participation.[118] In addition, actors who can contribute to the system also need to be involved. Consultations should also include all relevant actors, because limiting participation can amplify certain interests and voices and lead to policy distortions.[119]

Before turning to modes of engagement, it might be useful to draw up a typology of non-state actors to provide greater clarity and specificity to engagement efforts. Relevant actors include components of the state such as subnational government units; the branches of governments, including individual Members therein; and government officials and bureaucrats from trade and other ministries and regulatory agencies. Actors with egocentric, concentrated, and distributional interests include producers, import-competing and export-oriented special interest groups, business and industry organizations, labour unions, farmers' groups, and individual companies.[120] Actors with dispersed interests include consumers, legislators, political parties, and the general public. Actors with cosmopolitan or idealistic interests include transformational coalitions, value-based NGOs, and civil society organizations and movements. Actors who facilitate trade policy-making are also needed. These include knowledge-oriented actors like universities, academics, research institutes, and think-tanks. Other facilitators include trade practitioners, lawyers, and public opinion shapers like the media. All these actors play important roles within the trade governance system at the domestic level.[121]

A typology of the different kinds of non-state actors can help to understand the different functions and roles they play in the trade policy-making system. The objectives and structure of engagement with a particular variety of non-state actor must be defined with respect to the role that such an actor plays. Different kinds of non-state actors enjoy differentiated access to resources and have their own distinct objectives. A typology of non-state actors can also assist in appreciating the interplay between different domestic constituents.[122] This can help craft more appropriate consultation mechanisms. Thus we need to move away from a one-size-fits-all approach and pay attention to categorizing non-state actors properly so that consultation mechanisms can be crafted with more precision.

D. Choice of Engagement Mechanisms

How should non-state actors be engaged in the domestic trade policy process and what would be appropriate mechanisms or structures? The literature on domestic consultation has articulated a number of approaches to consultation. The choice of a particular mechanism or structure depends on various factors that include the objective of consultation and the type of non-state actors involved. Thus consultations need to be tailored not only to local conditions but also to the target audience. The nature of the issue at stake can also determine what kind of consultation is needed.

1. The 'Wolfe' Model

In his study on domestic trade policy-making in Canada, Wolfe distinguishes between different approaches to engagement with non-state actors.[123] These different approaches, which exhibit different levels of involvement by non-state actors in government policy-making, are canvassed here.

a. The Information Approach

The most superficial approach is the information approach. Under this approach government does little more than make publicly available information on its negotiating positions and the likely direction of policy choices. Wolfe notes that for such a limited interaction, the amount and quality of information provided, and opportunities to use the information become highly relevant.[124] Issues such as to whom information is provided, and how it is made available require greater attention be Members. Websites are a good medium to publish information related to trade policy. Information needs to include trade statistics, discussion papers, briefing papers, newsletters, legislation and negotiation updates, and information about disputes.[125] Information-oriented mechanisms raise normative questions about transparency. Transparency requirements can include prescribed processes for enacting regulations; using plain language in drafting, publication, and codification obligations; ease of access in locating the law; predictability and consistency in implementation; and remedies such as an appeal process.

b. The Basic Consultation Approach

Basic consultations are technical in nature and seek new ideas and views of affected parties. They are useful for providing information, framing issues, and identifying and assessing options, including the acceptability of options to stakeholders. Feedback to participants on consultations is an important factor in determining participant satisfaction about the process. In its domestic consultations on trade policy, Canada has used advisory committees, policy conferences, public meetings, telephone hotlines, websites, and polling and focus groups.[126]

c. The Citizen Engagement Approach

Another step up can be called citizen engagement in trade policy-making.[127] This goes further than consultations and involves in-depth deliberations at policy formulation stages. Its objectives are the determination of goals, values, and principles. Processes of citizen engagement in Canada have included study circles, deliberative polling, citizen juries, public conventions, correspondence, and public debates and dialogue.[128]

d. The Private-Public Partnership Approach

A deeper form of engagement can be described as public-private partnerships with shared decision-making.[129] Such broad multi-stakeholder consultations are useful in exploring compromises on policy issues that are controversial or have asymmetric distributional effects.

e. Political Consultations

Wolfe also identifies political consultation as a distinctive mode of engagement. Political consultation is more about consensus building than about technical detail. It targets groups that reject the premises of free trade and globalization and groups that seek transformational changes in governance models. The need for political consultation points to a role for national parliaments in the oversight of trade policy. Parliamentary committees and hearings are examples of political consultations. Such hearings can also satisfy the information and access needs of parliamentarians.[130]

f. The 'Room-Next-Door' Approach

Another model identified by Wolfe is the room-next-door model, which involves inducting business and other non-state actors including NGOs as part of official delegations to the WTO meetings and conferences.[131]

2. The Need to Tailor Engagement Mechanisms

As stated above, consultation mechanisms need to be tailored to objectives, issues, and actors. Therefore, while ordinary consultations led by government officials can serve technical needs, political issues require a political forum. Mechanisms for gathering commercial intelligence should be kept separate from consultations for other purposes.[132] Consultations can be designed as a manipulative process with the objective of persuading non-state actors to support the government-favoured policy choice. In other cases, consultations can be designed as an argumentative process that attempts to change entrenched understandings of cause and effect.[133] Such consultations are more concerned about framing and defining the problem than in resolving it.

Consultations on some issues and in some situations require only expert participation. The exclusion of the general public in such situations may be justified as a distraction. Detailed technical consultations are an example where access ought to be restricted to knowledge-oriented actors. Consultations on issues like tariff negotiations require engagement structures that are different from those required for negotiations on new trade issues. New trade issues can involve inadequately defined interests or call for social or economic trade-offs.

Therefore, consultations on such unfamiliar issues might require wider citizen engagement and even shared decision-making by state and non-state actors.

Consultations also need to be tailored to the relative size of affected constituencies. Canadian policy-makers have attempted to introduce a flexible consultation system that selects participants according to whether the consultation is aimed at meeting strategic, tactical, or technical needs. Participation at the strategic level of consultation is carried out with ministers and industry CEOs, the tactical level involves senior officials and vice-presidents, and at the technical level the target audience is working-level officials. Horizontal business associations are involved at all three levels. However, academics and NGOs are involved only at the tactical and technical levels, and not at the strategic levels.[134]

Another consideration in tailoring consultations is the choice between formality and informality. Both these approaches can be viewed as complementary, with different situations calling for either formality or informality.[135] While informality can lead to abuses of administrative discretion, it can be useful when sensitive information needs to be communicated or obtained by government officials. Formality has the advantage of transparency and would restrict possible abuse of discretion.

3. The Hocking Approach to Engagement

While Wolfe has highlighted the spectrum of approaches for engagement with non-state actors and the need for flexibility and tailoring, Brian Hocking has described the evolution of domestic trade policy-making in a more structured manner and has identified three different evolutionary models.[136]

a. The Club Model of Domestic Consultation

Domestic consultation involves internal bureaucratic and inter-agency consultation led by the foreign or trade ministries. Sectoral ministries are included in sectoral-specific issues. The objective of this model is policy coordination in a situation of increasing complexity of trade agendas. Bureaucratic and executive consultation can take place either as horizontal or vertical consultation in federal bureaucracies. Hocking has found that such a model essentially operates as a closed bureaucratic system, often marked by turf conflicts. It also demonstrates a tendency to assume a pro-liberalization stance or to view freer trade policy as legitimate.

b. The Adaptive Club Model

The adaptive club model is an intermediate, business-focused model. The objective of consultations is advice and other contributions from the private sector to trade policy making.[137] The principal resource made available is knowledge. This model also partially serves to bring business on board and to ensure acceptance of trade policy at the domestic level.[138] The model is characterized by 'controlled' openness operating within established rules. It is not designed to question free trade goals but does engender debate on relative gains from specific trade policies. Consultation is relatively closed and limited to constituencies most affected by trade policy. The debate is also a limited one with the government still controlling the scope of the discussions and the agenda.

c. The Multi-Stakeholder Approach

The third and most advanced model in Hocking's scale is the multi-stakeholder model with a mix of consultation structures. Participants vary, but civil society representatives are involved. Objectives include generating consensus in favour of trade liberalization in the face of increased public opposition to globalization. The multi-stakeholder model is linked to broader patterns of public diplomacy and includes debate on the objectives and legitimacy of trade liberalization. The multi-stakeholder model is the most advanced, and consultations in Canada and the European Union approximate this model.

The diverse goals and ambitions of participants in the multi-stakeholder consultation process can on occasion create institutional tensions and crises of expectations.[139] NGOs are likely to introduce new issues into the room (primarily legitimacy and 'trade and' issues), while business is more interested in supporting government by providing knowledge, advice, and connections to business interests in other states. This model requires careful management so as to ensure that participants do not get disaffected with the process or introduce into the process conflicting and incompatible expectations.

There is a range of mechanisms for involving non-state actors in domestic trade policy-making. These range from uni-directional information-providing structures to deep public-private partnerships. The mechanisms need to be tailored to objectives, actors, situations, and issues. Hocking's models provide an evolutionary perspective on how policy-makers need to continually respond to new demands of trade policy-making through engagement with non-state actors. The design of domestic consultations mechanisms can be a tricky exercise. However, modern trade policy cannot do without domestic consultations.

V. Conclusion

This chapter has called for the project on WTO institutional reform to extend its scope to reform of the domestic trade policy-making processes. At least two objections to this proposal can be anticipated. First, it could be argued that the WTO institutional reform agenda is already over-crowded with issues and that extending the discussion to the domestic sphere would further burden the project and also dilute its focus. Second, some may argue that any attempt to influence domestic trade policy processes through institutional reform of the WTO would encroach on the sovereignty of Members and, in any event, the WTO can do little to influence domestic political processes and outcomes.

This chapter has advocated for a conceptual inclusion of the domestic sphere into the discussions of WTO institutional reform. The rationale for including the domestic sphere (hopefully) addresses these concerns. This chapter has argued that the domestic context is important because of the domestic origins of the WTO crisis. WTO reform requires a new compromise of embedded liberalism or a new social purpose for governance of the WTO regime. Arriving at this new compromise/purpose will require domestic political engagement. Ruggie's theory of regime formation demonstrates that the legitimacy problems of the WTO arise from a growing discontent in domestic politics. Further, this chapter has shown that how the WTO makes trade policy can be useful in thinking about how to address domestic discontent with the WTO's functioning. The multi-level system of governance at the WTO requires participation by state and non-state actors at both the international and domestic levels. The making of good domestic trade policy is indispensable to the functioning of the WTO. Furthermore, governance is becoming more horizontal and is no longer the exclusive domain of the state. Non-state actors are now part of the governance process.

With the importance of domestic trade policy-making and the importance of non-state actor participation firmly in mind, solutions must be found to the WTO crisis. A declaration on domestic consultation would urge the review of domestic consultation systems by the WTO's Trade Policy Review Mechanism and contribute to social learning on the design and evaluation of consultation systems. Such systems must take account of a number of issues, including the objectives and targets of domestic consultation. The selection of actors for consultation must cater to diversity and need. It should be based on the actors' legitimate interest in trade policy. A typology of non-state actors can help design better mechanisms. And the choice of mechanisms must be tailored to objectives, actors, issues, and national circumstances. A spectrum of approaches is possible. Consultation design can also be viewed from an evolutionary perspective.

Notes

* I would like to thank Professor Debra Steger for inviting me to write this paper. Some of these ideas were presented at an EDGE network workshop in March 2008 at CIGI, Waterloo, and at the Annual Conference of the Society for International Economic Law in July 2008 at Geneva.

1 See Peter Van den Bossche, 'NGO Involvement in the WTO: A Comparative Perspective', 11 Journal of International Economic Law 717 (2008).

2 On the need for WTO institutional reform, see Debra Steger, 'The Culture of the WTO: Why It Needs to Change', 10 (3) Journal of International Economic Law 483 (2007).

3 See Kerstin Martens, 'Mission Impossible? Defining Nongovernmental Organizations', 13 (3) International Journal of Voluntary and Nonprofit Organizations 271 (2002), at 282. In defining NGOs, Martens draws on how the term has evolved in other juridical approaches in international law as well as on sociological perspectives. According to Martens, NGOs must not significantly depend on governments for financial or other support (at 280).

4 Angus Archer, 'Methods of Multilateral Management: The Interrelationships of International Organizations and NGOs', in Toby Trister Gati (ed), *The US, the UN and the Management of Global Change* (New York: UNA-USA, 1983) 303.

5 Thomas Princen and Matthias Finger, 'Introduction', in Thomas Princen and Matthias Finger (eds), *Environmental NGOs in World Politics: Linking the Local and the Global* (London: Routledge, 1994) 6.

6 Martens, above n 3, at 281.

7 See the World Trade Organization, *The Future of the WTO: Addressing Institutional Challenges in the New Millennium* (Geneva: WTO, 2004); Peter Van den Bossche, 'Debating the Future of the World Trade Organization: Divergent Views on the 2005 Sutherland Report', 8 (3) Journal of International Economic Law 759 (2005); Donald McRae, 'Developing Countries and the Future of the WTO', 8 (3) Journal of International Economic Law 603 (2005), at 603 (stating that 'coming to terms with the varied claims of developing country Members of the WTO, or more generally working out the relationship between the rules of the trading system and development' is one of the major challenges facing the WTO).

8 Deborah Cass has described development rather than free trade as the primary goal of the WTO system: see *The Constitutionalization of the World Trade Organization: Legitimacy, Democracy, and Community in the International Trading System* (Oxford: Oxford University Press, 2005) xii. Other experts argue that the WTO is not a development organization: See Pascal Lamy, 'Hong Kong Ministerial Is Last and Best Chance to Conclude the Round by Next Year', 24 September 2005, http://www.wto.org/english/news_e/sppl_e/sppl03_e.htm (where Lamy states: 'The WTO's core role is trade opening, we are not a development agency.')

9 John G. Ruggie, 'International Regimes, Transactions, and Change: Embedded Liberalism in the Postwar Economic Order', 36 (2) International Organization 379 (1982). Also see Andrew T. F. Lang, 'Reconstructing Embedded Liberalism: John Gerard Ruggie and Constructivist Approaches to the Study of the International Trade Regime', 9 (1) Journal of International Economic Law 81 (2006).

10 For Ruggie's more recent work on embedded liberalism, see John G. Ruggie, 'Embedded Liberalism Revisited', in Emanuel Adler and Beverly Crawford (eds), *Progress in*

Postwar International Relations (Columbia University Press, 1995) 201–34; John G. Ruggie (ed), *Multilateralism Matters: The Theory and Praxis of an Institutional Form* (Columbia University Press, 1993); John G. Ruggie, 'At Home Abroad, Abroad at Home: International Liberalisation and Domestic Stability in the New World Economy', 24 (3) Millennium 507 (1994); John G. Ruggie, 'Trade, Protectionism and the Future of Welfare Capitalism', 48 (1) Journal of International Affairs 1 (1994); John G. Ruggie, 'Globalization and the Embedded Liberalism Compromise: The End of an Era?', in Wolfgang Streeck (ed.), *Internationale Wirtshaft, Naionale Demokratie* (Campus Verlag, 1998) 79–98; John G. Ruggie, 'Taking Embedded Liberalism Global: The Corporate Connection', in David Held and Mathias Koenig-Archibugi (eds), *Taming Globalization: Frontiers of Governance* (Wiley-Blackwell, 2003) 93–129.

11 Ruggie, 'Taking Embedded Liberalism Global', ibid, at p. 94.

12 Ibid.

13 Ruggie, 'International Regimes, Transactions, and Change', above n 9, at 380.

14 For an exposition on the hegemonic stability theory, see Robert O. Keohane, 'The Theory of Hegemonic Stability and Changes in International Economic Regimes, 1967–1977', in Ole R. Holsti, Randolph M. Siverson, and Alexander L. George (eds), *Change in the International System* (Boulder, Col.: Westview Press, 1980) 131–62.

15 Ruggie, 'International Regimes, Transactions, and Change', above n 9, at 382.

16 The legitimacy question becomes acute in democracies, while the illegitimate deployment of power (illegitimate from a domestic perspective) by states at the international level is common in authoritarian states.

17 Ruggie, above n 9, at 386.

18 Ibid.

19 Ibid, at 393.

20 Ibid.

21 In Ruggie's words: '[A] new threshold had been crossed in the balance between "market" and "authority" with governments assuming much more direct responsibility for domestic social security and economic stability. The extension of the suffrage and the emergence of working-class political constituencies, parties, and even governments was responsible in part; but demands for social protection were very nearly universal, coming from all sides of the political spectrum and from all ranks of the social hierarchy (with the possible exception of orthodox financial circles).' See ibid, at 388.

22 Ibid, at 413.

23 Ibid.

24 Ibid.

25 See Ruggie, 'Taking Embedded Liberalism Global', above n 10, at 3.

26 Ibid, at 413–14.

27 Ruggie, above n 9 at 413.

28 Ibid, at 415.

29 Ruggie did add that this externalization of adjustment costs 'may prove to be very nearly fatal for some of the poorer developing countries', ibid, at 414.

30 The literature on the Uruguay Round negotiations includes Terence Stewart, *The GATT Uruguay Round: A Negotiating History*, 4 vols. (Boston: Kluwer Law International, 1993); Ernest H. Preeg, *Traders in a Brave New World: The Uruguay Round and the Future of the International Trading System* (University of Chicago Press, 1995);

John Croome, *Reshaping the World Trading System: A History of the Uruguay Round* (Boston: Kluwer Law International, 1999); Jagdish Bhagwati and Mathias Hirsch (eds), *The Uruguay Round and Beyond: Essays in Honour of Arthur Dunkel* (University of Michigan Press, 1998); Bernard Hoekman and Michel Kostecki, *The Political Economy of the World Trading System: From GATT to WTO* (Oxford: Oxford University Press, 1998); Martin Will and L. Alan Winters, *The Uruguay Round: Widening and Deepening the World Trading System* (Washington, D.C.: The World Bank, 1995).

31 India is a member of the new Quad as well as the Group of 7. The core groups have included Australia, Brazil, the European Union, India, Japan, China, and the United States.

32 See Stephen Krasner, 'Structural Causes and Regime Consequences: Regimes as Intervening Variables', 36 International Organization 185 (1982).

33 On the impact of the Internet, see Jurgen Kurtz, 'NGOs, the Internet and International Economic Policy Making: The Failure of the OECD Multilateral Agreement on Investment', 3 Melbourne Journal of International Law 213 (2002); Oren Perez, 'Global Legal Pluralism and Electronic Democracy', in Andrea Rommele, Steven Ward, and Rachel Kay Gibson (eds), *Electronic Democracy: Mobilisation, Organisation and Participation via New ICTs* (New York : Routledge, 2004) 133–52.

34 In earlier rounds, stakeholders and decision-makers in those countries often did not really know what was going on in the closed and inaccessible negotiations under the GATT.

35 Susan Sell has described the political lobbying by multinationals that influenced the U.S. government to insist on the eventual adoption of the TRIPS agreement as part of the Uruguay Round. See Susan K. Sell, *Private Power, Public Law: The Globalization of Intellectual Property Rights* (Cambridge: Cambridge University Press, 2003).

36 See Gregory C. Shaffer, *Defending Interests: Public-Private Partnerships in WTO Litigation* (Washington, D.C.: Brookings Institution Press, 2003).

37 Robert L. Howse, 'From Politics to Technocracy—And Back Again: The Fate of the Multilateral Trading Regime', 96 The American Journal of International Law 94 (2002), at 102.

38 Ibid.

39 Ruggie, 'Taking Embedded Liberalism Global', above n 10, at 94.

40 See Howse, above n 37.

41 Ibid, at 116.

42 See Robert Wolfe and Jesse Helmer, 'Trade Policy Begins at Home: Information and Consultation in the Trade Policy Process', in Mark Halle and Robert Wolfe (eds), *Process Matters: Sustainable Development and Domestic Trade Transparency, International Institute for Sustainable Development* (Winnipeg: International Institute for Sustainable Development, 2007) 7–8.

43 This is because the substantive bargains and norms of embedded liberalism were negotiated by the GATT-era regime-makers and reflected the interests and preferences of the developed states. The social purpose and objectives of the GATT trade regime were based on state-society relations in the developed economies and reflected the social purpose for governance suited to the level of social and economic development of these economies.

44 The most obvious examples of one such structural bias were the exclusion of agricultural and textile trade from the trade liberalization rules of the GATT. The use of voluntary export restraints (VERs) was another.

45 Brian Hocking, 'Changing the Terms of Trade Policy Making: From the 'Club' to the 'Multistakeholder' Model', 3 (1) World Trade Review 3 (2004), at 3.

46 Ruggie, above n 9, at 386.

47 See Consultative Board to the Director-General Supachai Panitchpakdi, *The Future of the WTO: Addressing Institutional Challenges in the New Millennium* (Geneva: WTO, 2005); First Warwick Commission. *The Multilateral Trade Regime: Which Way Forward? The Report of the First Warwick Commission* (Coventry: University of Warwick, 2007).

48 These include the Committee on Trade and Development, the Committee on Balance-of-Payments Restrictions and the Committee on Budget, Finance and Administration.

49 The functions that the WTO system delivers include the negotiation of new rules; monitoring of compliance; administration of the WTO agreements; dispute settlement; delivery of technical assistance and capacity building; research; dissemination of information; and cooperation with other actors such as relevant intergovernmental organizations.

50 See Gary P. Sampson (ed), *The Role of the World Trade Organization in Global Governance* (United Nations University Press, 2001); Gary P. Sampson (ed), *The WTO and Global Governance: Future Directions* (United Nations University Press, 2008); Andrew T. Guzman, 'Global Governance and the WTO', 45 Harvard International Law Journal 303 (2004).

51 See the literature on the relationship of WTO law to public international law, including international environmental law and international human rights law. See, for example, Joost Pauwelyn, *Conflict of Norms in Public International Law—How WTO Law Relates to Other Rules of International Law* (Cambridge University Press, 2003).

52 See Rorden Wilkinson, *The WTO: Crisis and the Governance of Global Trade* (London: Routledge, 2006); Tomer Broude, *International Governance in the WTO: Judicial Boundaries and Political Capitulation* (London: Cameron May, 2004). However, neither of these texts develop a conception of the political structure of trade governance through the WTO. Broude focuses on the judicial structure. The literature on constitutionalization at the WTO also examines governance through the WTO, but again focuses on the substantive content of WTO rules rather than on how those rules get made. See Jeffrey L. Dunoff, 'Why Constitutionalism Now? Text, Context and the Historical Contingency of Ideas', 1 Journal of International Law and International Relations 191 (2005); Thomas Cottier and Maya Hertig, 'The Prospects of 21st Century Constitutionalism', 7 Max Planck Yearbook of United Nations Law 261 (2004); Robert Howse and Kalypso Nicolaidis, 'Enhancing WTO Legitimacy: Constitutionalization or Global Subsidiarity?', 16 (1) Governance 73 (2003); Deborah Z. Cass, *The Constitutionalization of the World Trade Organization: Legitimacy, Democracy, and Community in the International Trading System* (Oxford: Oxford University Press, 2005). On the mandate of the WTO, see Chios Carmody, 'A Theory of WTO Law', 11 Journal of International Economic Law 527 (2008).

53 The discussion of the WTO system in this chapter is limited to its structural aspects. This chapter does not propose a comprehensive theory of WTO trade governance. Its ambition is limited to invoking a simplistic model of the WTO's working structure to offer some commentary conceiving a role for non-state actors.

54 See Robert Putnam, 'Diplomacy and Domestic Politics: The Logic of Two-Level Games', 42 International Organization 427 (1988). Putman explains domestic-international

negotiations as a two-level game: 'The politics of many international negotiations can usefully be conceived as a two-level game. At the national level, domestic groups pursue their interests by pressuring the government to adopt favorable policies, and politicians seek power by constructing coalitions among those groups. At the international level, national governments seek to maximize their own ability to satisfy domestic pressures, while minimizing the adverse consequences of foreign developments. Neither of the two games can be ignored by central decision-makers, so long as their countries remain interdependent, yet sovereign. Each national political leader appears at both game boards. Across the international table sit his foreign counterparts, and at his elbows sit diplomats and other international advisors. Around the domestic table behind him sit party and parliamentary figures, spokespersons for domestic agencies, representatives of key interest groups, and the leader's own political advisors....', at 434. See also Peter Gourevitch, 'The Second Image Reversed: The International Sources of Domestic Politics', 32 International Organization 781 (1978).

55 See Carolyn Deere, 'A Governance Audit of the WTO: Roundtable Discussion on Making Global Trade Governance Work for Development', Global Economic Governance Program, presented at a workshop on Global Governance at New Delhi, 29 April, 2008, http://www.globaleconomicgovernance.org/docs/GEGHEIPublicForum181007.pdf (visited 15 April 2009).

56 Sylvia Ostry, 'Preface' in INTAL-ITD-STA, *The Trade Policy-Making Process—Level One of the Two Level Game: Country Studies in the Western Hemisphere* (Buenos Aires: Inter-American Development Bank, 2002), at ii.

57 B. Guy Peters, 'Governance: A Garbage Can Perspective', in Edgar Grande and Louis W. Paul (eds), *Complex Sovereignty: Reconstituting Political Authority in the Twenty-First Century* (Toronto: University of Toronto Press, 2005) 68–82. Peters points out that the meaning of governance ranges from the extreme traditional view of the centrality of state government with a simple hierarchy to the other extreme view that argues that the state has become ineffective and that governance now takes place without government.

58 Robert Wolfe, 'Transparency and Public Participation in the Canadian Trade Policy Process', in Halle and Wolfe, above n 42, at 23.

59 Ibid.

60 Ibid.

61 See Jan Kooiman (ed), *Modern Governance: New Government—Society Interactions* (New York: Sage, 1993) 2. Also see Jan Kooiman, *Governing as Governance* (New York: Sage, 2003).

62 See Helen Yanacopulos, 'Patterns of Governance: The Rise of Transnational Coalitions of NGOs', 19 (3) Global Society 247 http://www.informaworld.com/smpp/title~content=t713423373~db=all~tab=issueslist~branches=19-v19(2005), at 247. Yanacopulos empirically explores patterns, workings, and mechanics of governance in international development NGO coalitions. Also see James N. Rosenau and Ernst-Otto Czempiel (eds), *Governance without Government: Order and Change in World Politics* (Cambridge University Press, 1992) http://www.informaworld.com/smpp/title~content=t713423373~db=all~tab=issueslist~branches=19-v19.

63 Yanacopulos, ibid.

64 See The Commission on Global Governance, *Our Global Neighborhood: Report of the Commission on Global Governance* (Oxford University Press, 1995) n 31.

65 See Pascal Lamy, 'Harnessing Globalization, Do We Need Cosmopolitics?' (Presentation at the London School of Economics, 1 February 2001), http://old.lse.ac.uk/collections/globalDimensions/lectures/harnessingGlobalisationDoWeNeedCosmopolitics/Default.htm (visited 14 April 2009) (where Pascal Lamy [then EU trade commissioner] preferred to use the term 'cosmopolitics' in place of 'governance', which he defined as the process by which rules are put together, decided upon, and implemented. This system of governance, according to Lamy, provided for inter-connections between governments, markets and civil society).

66 Kooiman, *Modern Governance*, above n 61, at 5.

67 Ibid, at 3.

68 See Peters, above n 57, at 72. See also Susan Strange, *The Retreat of the State: The Diffusion of Power in the World Economy* (Cambridge University Press, 1996).

69 See Wolfe, above n 58, at 24.

70 Kooiman, *Modern Governance*, above n 61, at 2.

71 Peters, above n 57, at 68. Governing requires continuing adaptation of political and administrative activities to changes in the environment. The Commission on Global Governance also cautioned: 'There is no single model or form of global governance, nor is there a single structure or set of structures. It is a broad, dynamic, complex process of interactive decision-making that is constantly evolving and responding to changing circumstances.' (See Commissioner on Global Governance, above n 64.)

72 Kooiman, *Modern Governance*, above n 61, at 5.

73 Ibid, at 4, 13 (stating '[a]n interaction can be considered as a mutually influencing relation between two or more actors or entities').

74 Any discussion of institutional reform of the WTO requires a conception of 'good governance'. The concept of good governance indicates respect for the principles of transparency, accountability, participation, efficacy, efficiency, representativeness, rationality, efficacy, neutrality, clarity, stability, power-sharing, legality, fairness, deliberation, and due process. See Daniel C. Esty, 'Good Governance at the World Trade Organization: Building a Foundation of Administrative Law', 10 (3) Journal of International Economic Law 509 (2007). The European Union recognizes five principles as underpinning good governance: openness, participation, accountability, effectiveness, and coherence. See European Commission, 'European Governance: A White Paper', http://eur-ex.europa.eu/LexUriServ/site/en/com/2001/com2001_0428en01.pdf (visited 2 September 2008).

75 Wolfe, see above n 58.

76 See Consultative Board to the Director-General Supachai Panitchpakdi, above n 47, at para 212.

77 See Sylvia Ostry, 'External Transparency: The Policy Process at the National Level of the Two Level Game' in Mike Moore (ed), *Doha and Beyond: The Future of the Multilateral Trading System* (Cambridge University Press, 2004) 94–114; Wolfe and Helmer, above n 42, at 17.

78 A review of ratification procedures at national levels could also be included in these trade policy reviews. Domestic non-state actors should be allowed to comment on the reviews.

79 The WTO General Council meets as the Trade Policy Review Body. It is supported in its work by the Secretariat's Trade Policies Review Division.

80 The Secretariat report for the latest trade policy review of Japan includes chapters on (1) Economic Environment; (2) Trade Policy Regime: Framework and Objectives; (3) Trade Policies and Practices by Measure; (4) Trade Policies by Sector; and (5) Outlook.

81 General Council, Appraisal Report to the Ministerial Conference, WT/MIN/(99)/2, 8 October 1999.

82 See Joseph F. Francois, 'Trade Policy Transparency and Investor Confidence—The Implications of an Effective Trade Policy Review Mechanism', 9 Review of International Economic 303 (2002).

83 Ibid.

84 Paragraph A(i) of Annex 3 to the Marrakesh Agreement Establishing the World Trade Organization (WTO Agreement) in World Trade Organization, *The Results of the Uruguay Round of the Multilateral Trade Negotiations* (Geneva: WTO, 2004) 380.

85 Ibid, at para A.

86 Ibid.

87 Possible downsides to enhanced domestic consultations have been discussed by Zahrnt. These include possible shifts toward protectionist policy preferences; creation of disincentives for risk-averse governments to cooperate internationally; decreased flexibility for governments in international negotiating forums; greater incentive for governments to appear tough negotiators in the WTO and engage in aggressive gain-claiming. See Valentin Zahrnt, 'Domestic Constituents and the Formulation of WTO Negotiating Positions: What the Delegates Say', 7 World Trade Review 393 (2008).

88 Francois, above n 82.

89 Francois recommends three kinds of improvements to the TPRM: (1) improved organization and retention of data; (2) improved dissemination of information; and (3) technical assistance to use the information provided by the TPRM process. Ibid.

90 Paragraph F of Annex 3 of the WTO Agreement provides for an appraisal of the TPRM by the TPRB five years after the entry into force of the WTO Agreement. The TPRB submitted an appraisal report to the Ministerial Conference in 1999. See WT/MIN/(99)/2, 8 October 1999, at para 4.

91 Ibid, see conclusions of the Appraisal Report.

92 Ibid at para 7.

93 See Ostry, above n 77; Ostry, above n 56; Hocking, above n 45; Wolfe and Helmer, above n 42; Wolfe, above n 58; Zahrnt, above n 87; Yves Bonzon, 'Institutionalizing Public Participation in WTO Decision-making: Some Conceptual Hurdles and Concerns', 11 (4) Journal of International Economic Law 751 (2008).

94 See Hocking, Zahrnt, and Wolfe, ibid.

95 See Hocking, ibid.

96 Consultative Board to the Director-General, above n 47, at para 186.

97 Ibid.

98 The Sutherland Report has identified certain objectives that could drive the WTO's engagement with civil society. The list includes promotion of the image of the WTO as an effective and equitable organization; promotion of the understanding of the principles underlying the WTO, thus leading to a 'more willing acceptance of the value of WTO obligations'; tapping the understandings, knowledge, and expertise of non-state actors like civil society, business, and other stakeholders; assistance from civil society in influencing governments and building caucuses to shift positions and strengthen

commitments to WTO rules; 'create space in the domestic policy-making arena for Member governments to overcome domestic barriers to further liberalization'; enrichment of the debate; and assistance with achieving convergence in difficult areas of policy. See ibid., Chapter V titled 'Transparency and Dialogue with Civil Society'.

99 While the first three items on this deficit list are borrowed from Hocking, the fourth is my own addition.

100 Hocking, above n 45, at 1.

101 Ibid.

102 Zahrnt, above n 87, at 3.

103 See Miguel F. Lengyel, 'Implementing WTO Agreements Lessons from Latin America', 51 id21 insights 7 (November 2005), http://www.id21.org/insights/insights59/insights59.pdf (visited 23 April 2009). Lengyel points out in the Argentinian context that conflicts over implementation of Uruguay Round texts depended on whether key public and private stakeholders perceived a sense of ownership with regard to the reforms. TRIPS rules generated significant local opposition as they were perceived as imposed from the outside.

104 Ostry, above n 56, at iv.

105 Hocking, above n 45.

106 Ibid, at 4.

107 Wolfe, above n 58.

108 Ibid.

109 Lengyel, above n 103.

110 See Putnam, above n 54.

111 Wolfe and Helmer, above n 42, at 2.

112 See Miguel F. Lengyel and Vivianne Ventura-Dias (eds), *Trade Policy Reforms in Latin America: Multilateral Rules and Domestic Institutions* (UK: Palgrave Macmillan, 2004).

113 See Lengyel, above, n 103. He gives the example that Argentina needed to create pest-free and plague-free zones to take advantage of the new market opportunities that the SPS Agreement opened up for agricultural products.

114 See Lengyel, ibid, who notes that Argentina benefited in the case of the SPS Agreement, because a reform process had been already initiated in the late 1980s.

115 Lengyel again gives an example from Argentina. There was a poor fit for the implementation of the WTO-mandated customs valuation changes in Argentina, because the priorities of local customs authorities were different (under-invoicing). See ibid.

116 These other values could be labour rights, human rights, sustainable development objectives, or environmental concerns.

117 See Helen Milner, 'Why the Move to Free Trade? Democracy and Trade Policy in the Developing Countries', 59 International Organization 107 (2005).

118 Wolfe and Helmer, above n 42, at 9.

119 Wolfe, above n 58, at 42.

120 Civil society actors are unlike traditional 'distributional coalitions'. Ostry has called them 'transformational coalitions'. See Ostry, above n 56 at ii.

121 In Canada, consultations have targeted government departments, provinces and municipalities, broad-based industry associations, sectoral industry associations, civil society organizations, individual firms, academics, and citizens. Sub-national officials have also been targeted. See Wolfe, above n 58.

122 For instance, some actors might be in competition with each other. Others must see themselves as allies or collaborators.

123 See Wolfe, above n 58, at 25.

124 Wolfe and Helmer, above n 42, at 8.

125 Ibid.

126 Wolfe, above n 58, at 25.

127 Ibid.

128 Ibid, at 25.

129 Ibid.

130 See Gregory Shaffer, 'Parliamentary Oversight of WTO Rule-Making: The Political, Normative, and Practical Contexts', 7 (3) Journal of International Economic Law 629 (2004).

131 Wolfe, above n 58.

132 Wolfe and Helmer, above n 42, at 12.

133 Wolfe, above n 58, at 24.

134 See ibid, at 31 for Wolfe on the 2006 review of the Canadian system.

135 Wolfe and Helmer, above n 42, at 10.

136 Hocking, above n 45.

137 See International Trade Centre, UN Conference on Trade and Developed, *Business Advocacy in Trade Policy Making: A Developing Country Perspective, the Enterprise Institute* (Geneva: ITC, 2005).

138 The 33 Industry Sectoral Advisory Committees established in the United States in 1974 are a good example of the adaptive club model approach.

139 Business and civil society actors exhibit different objectives, ambitions, expectations, and language, as well as different operational and organizational styles and a lack of familiarity with each other.

Enhancing Business Participation in Trade Policy-Making: Lessons from China

HENG WANG

I. Introduction

Transparency not only helps to dispel unfounded fears and counter misinformation, it constitutes a principal and vital element of the World Trade Organization (WTO). Transparency obligations on WTO Members can be found in Article X of the General Agreement on Tariffs and Trade 1994 (GATT 1994),[1] Article III of the General Agreement on Trade in Services (GATS);[2] and the accession protocols and working party reports of the recently acceded Members, including those of China, Ukraine, and Viet Nam. Transparency obligations require *inter alia* notification, comment, and publication. In the Doha Ministerial Declaration, WTO Members confirmed collective responsibility for ensuring internal transparency and the effective engagement with all Members. The Doha Declaration also undertook to make WTO operations more transparent by disseminating information more effectively and promptly, as well as improving dialogue with the public.[3] Although there is no commonly accepted definition of transparency, and there is dispute as to whether transparency constitutes a norm of international law, transparency is an important element of world trade law.[4]

Significant progress with respect to institutional transparency has been made by the WTO, particularly with non-state actors, which include but are not limited to the following:

- The Marrakesh Agreement Establishing the World Trade Organization (WTO Agreement) states that the General Council may take appropriate arrangements for consultation and cooperation with non-governmental organizations (NGOs) concerned with matters related to those of the WTO.[5]

- In the Annex on Telecommunications included in the GATS, Members recognize the role played by NGOs in ensuring the operations of telecommunications services and commit to making appropriate arrangements for consultations with NGOs on matters arising from the implementation of the annex.[6]
- In 1996, the General Council adopted Guidelines for Arrangements on Relations with Non-governmental Organizations,[7] allowing for the publication of more documents and elaborating on the Secretariat's active role with the NGOs. However, NGOs are prohibited from being directly involved in the work of the WTO or its meetings.[8]
- Every year since 2001, the WTO has hosted a two-day public forum at its headquarters in Geneva,[9] where members of civil society may express their views.
- In 2002, the General Council decided to expedite the de-restriction of WTO documents, and passed the 'Decision of the General Council on the Procedures for the Circulation and Derestriction of WTO Documents'.[10] Many documents are now simultaneously available to the public and to WTO Members.
- The Director-General and staff of the WTO Secretariat now meet with NGO representatives regularly. There are briefings for Geneva-based civil society groups on the meetings of WTO councils and committees, and a good cross-section of NGOs attend plenary sessions of ministerial conferences as well as symposia on WTO issues in Geneva.[11]

It is widely believed that the transparency of the WTO should be further improved. Civil society has been critical of the lack of transparency at the WTO, particularly with respect to negotiations and dispute settlement. Members, other international organizations, and NGOs have criticized the legitimacy and transparency of opaque and informal consensus-building negotiations in working groups, the 'Green Room', and mini-ministerial meetings.[12] A number of developed country Members have submitted views to the General Council on how to improve transparency.[13]

Greater transparency would help to ensure consistency and predictability within the WTO system and would increase public confidence in the WTO. The WTO is not merely the sum of its parts; it has its own image and personality that should be seen to be transparent.[14] Further steps to enhance WTO transparency are still needed. However, greater transparency may have negative consequences, including diminished efficiency and higher costs. Therefore, any push for greater transparency should include efforts to avoid such negative externalities.

The focus on WTO transparency deals with institutional issues, whereas transparency obligations imposed on Members are of critical importance. Without the Members' transparency obligations, the WTO can hardly be sufficiently transparent. This chapter analyzes transparency issues from China's perspective, both as a developing country and a recently acceded WTO Member. The notice-and-comment obligations imposed on China and how these affect or can encourage the involvement of business interests in trade policy will be canvassed. Furthermore, this chapter argues that the extension of WTO-plus comment obligations could be a possible way of enhancing business participation in the world trade system. The notice-and-comment requirements and the participation of businesses in trade policy formulation should be coordinated to enhance public confidence in the WTO.

Part II examines WTO-plus transparency requirements that have been imposed on China. Particular attention will be paid to the public consultation and comment requirements imposed on China in the context of domestic trade measures. China's experience with these requirements, which are not imposed on the WTO's original Members, will be used as a basis of analysis. This part also reviews how businesses participate in China's trade matters. Part III further addresses the involvement of business in the formation of domestic trade policy. After a brief overview of the practices of business participation in trade policy, it discusses why and how businesses participate in trade matters. Businesses can play an important role in the formulation of trade measures. If properly managed, business participation may help to enhance the legitimacy of trade policy-making, tap the expertise and knowledge of the business community, improve debate, balance broader interests, and bring about more equitable decisions. Finally, this chapter puts forward suggestions on enhancing business participation in the trade system.

II. China's Comment Obligations: Rules and Practice

A. Review of China's WTO-Extra Transparency Obligations

China's transparency obligations are set by the WTO Agreement and in the Protocol on the Accession of the People's Republic of China (the Accession Protocol).[15] As a condition to its accession, China agreed to strict transparency requirements, many of which do not apply to other WTO Members:

(a) Only published or readily available laws, regulations, and other measures pertaining to or affecting goods, services, trade-related aspects of intellectual property rights, and the control of foreign exchange (collectively referred to as 'measures') shall be enforced.[16] China also undertook to make available to Members on request these measures before implementation.[17] In emergency situations, trade rules must be made available no later than their entry into force or implementation at the latest when they are implemented or enforced.[18]

(b) The publication of all measures must include the effective date of measures and the products and services affected by the measure, identified by appropriate tariff line and Central Product Classification (CPC) classification.[19]

(c) China is required to publish by classification and service a list of organizations responsible for authorizing, approving, or regulating services activities through the granting of licences or other approvals. Procedures and the conditions for obtaining such licences or approvals must be published.[20]

(d) Measures are to be published in an official journal and all issues of this journal are readily available to individuals and enterprises.[21]

(e) A reasonable period is to be provided for comment to the authorities before implementation of a measure, except for those measures involving national security, specific measures setting foreign exchange rates or monetary policy, and other measures the publication of which would impede law enforcement.[22]

(f) China must afford an opportunity for public consultation and comment on proposed technical standards and regulations, and 'comments [must] be given due consideration regardless of origin'.[23]

(g) One or more enquiry point(s) are to be established where individuals, enterprises, or Members may obtain information about the measures.[24]

(h) The information provided by the enquiry point(s) must include the names of national or sub-national authorities in charge of a measure's implementation.[25] Replies to requests for information are usually to be provided within 30 days following receipt of a request.[26]

(i) Relevant measures are to be translated into one or more of the official WTO languages.[27]

Additional transparency requirements include the following:

(j) The provision of judicial review for measures;[28]

(k) The creation of a mechanism for individuals and enterprises to bring to the attention of national authorities non-uniform implementation of trade regimes.[29] Under China's Regulations on Record-keeping of Regulations and Rules, state administrations, social groups, enterprises, or individuals who believe that a measure is inconsistent with China's WTO obligations can put forward reform suggestions in written form to agencies including the Legislative Affairs Office of the State Council;[30] and

(l) For an eight-year period following accession, China was required to provide additional information to the General Council concerning transparency as part of the WTO's monitoring of China's WTO implementation.[31]

A substantial number of China's transparency obligations impose additional burdens on China in comparison with original Members. The requirements described in (b), (c), (e), (f), (h), (i), (k), and (l) are not or were not applied to original WTO Members. Some of China's transparency obligations resemble those of other Members. Transparency requirements indicated in (a), (d), (g), and (j) above are generally applicable to all Members. However, even these general transparency obligations apply to China more strictly because of the scope of their application: measures relating to or affecting goods, services, trade-related aspects of intellectual property rights, and even foreign exchange control. In addition, unlike original WTO Members, China was required to construct enquiry points to provide information about measures on goods, trade-related aspects of intellectual property rights, and foreign exchange control.

These additional transparency requirements may help others to better understand China's trade policy and to bring predictability to trade with China. They could also lay the foundation for development of broader WTO transparency requirements. These requirements are good for the functioning of the trade regime. Among the WTO-extra transparency obligations listed above, the notice-and-comment obligation is perhaps the most challenging and is representative of the challenges posed in implementing additional transparency obligations.

B. China's Notice and Comment Obligations and Business Participation in China

China's WTO Accession Protocol required it to provide a comment period prior to the adoption of any measure affecting trade in goods and services, trade-related aspects of intellectual property rights, or foreign exchange control.[32] Reference to this general comment obligation is also contained in the Working Party Report on China's WTO accession.[33] The Working Party Report also noted that, on accession, China would need to set minimum time frames for allowing public comment on proposed technical regulations, standards and conformity assessment procedures as provided in the Agreement on Technical Barriers to Trade (TBT Agreement), and relevant decisions and recommendations adopted by the TBT committee.[34] These statements from the Working Party Report created legal obligations for China.[35]

More detailed notice-and-comment requirements can be found in the TBT Agreement and Agreement on the Application of Sanitary and Phytosanitary Measures (SPS Agreement). These comment obligations arise in respect of proposed technical regulations,[36] conformity assessment procedures,[37] and proposed sanitary or phytosanitary regulations.[38] Members must notify other Members of the products to be covered by the proposed measure, together with a brief indication of its objective and rationale.[39] Such notifications must take place at an appropriately early stage, 'when amendments can still be introduced and comments taken into account'.[40] Moreover, Members shall allow 'reasonable time' for other Members to comment, discuss the comments on request, and consider these comments and the discussions results.[41] In case of urgent problems, Members are required to allow other Members to comment, discuss their comments on request, and take these comments and the discussions results into account.[42] However, in urgent situations, a reasonable time frame for comments is not required.

The combined effect of the Accession Protocol and the SPS and TBT agreements require China to allow both other WTO Members and other non-governmental actors to comment on proposed measures. Thus, while some WTO Members are required to take the comments of other Members into account, China is required to do more. China has undertaken to allow a broader array of actors to comment on proposed measures. Additionally, the scope of measures subject to comment is broader for China than for some WTO Members.

The particular requirements of the notice and comment obligations discussed above, and China's implementation of these obligations, are briefly canvassed here.

1. Notice

Notification of TBT and SPS measures in China is made via the websites of the General Administration of Quality Supervision, Inspection and Quarantine of China and the Ministry of Commerce.[43] To obtain information relating to the measures required to be published under paragraph 2(C)1 of the Accession Protocol, individuals, enterprises, and WTO Members may also contact enquiry points and enquiry websites at the Ministry of Commerce and Administration of Quality Supervision, Inspection and Quarantine of China.[44] As for the general comment obligation, an official journal has been appointed for publication. The MOFCOM *Gazette* has been designated as the official journal, and all the major trade-related competent authorities send copies of their newly published documents or drafts to this publication.[45]

Functioning as the *MOFCOM Gazette,* the *China Foreign Trade and Economic Cooperation Gazette* collects and publishes all laws, regulations, and other measures pertaining to or affecting trade in goods and services, trade-related aspects of intellectual property rights, or the control of foreign exchange by China's National People's Congress, State Council, local governments, and government departments. It is the official journal by which the Chinese government makes notification and responds to enquiries by the WTO and its Members, and it is used in WTO trade policy reviews. The texts of regulations pertaining to domestic and foreign trade and international economic cooperation issued by the Ministry of Commerce are the standard texts that have legal effect.

The *Gazette* is edited by General Office of the Ministry of Commerce and is the official journal for understanding China's rules and measures concerning trade and international economic cooperation. One or two issues of the *Gazette* are issued per week, and no more than 80 issues are published annually.[46] An electronic version of the *Gazette* is available at the Ministry of Commerce website.[47] As of 5 May 2008, 426 issues of the *Gazette* have been published.[48] A digital version of the *Gazette* is e-mailed to domestic and overseas users free of charge.[49] The *Gazette* is in Chinese, with the table of contents in English. The published measures in the *Gazette* consist of the following categories: laws and explanation of laws, administrative regulations and other measures of the State Council, and rules and other measures of the Ministry of Commerce, as well as department rules and other measures of government departments and local governments. One important factor in determining what is published is whether a particular measure is trade-related. Pursuant to China's WTO commitment, only trade related measures are to be published in the *Gazette.* How trade related measures and non-trade related measures are distinguished remains an open question.

To better understand Chinese measures, the Legal Affairs Office of the State Council publishes a Chinese-English version of the collection of laws and regulations annually.[50] Some local governments and ministries under the State Council also translate their rules and measures into English.[51] Moreover, a number of websites provide an English version of many Chinese trade rules. These websites are sponsored by different government agencies, including (1) the China Legislative Information Network System Full Text Search System of Legislative Affairs Office of the State Council[52] (including categories of laws and regulations, summary of laws, administrative regulations, legal documents, department rules, and judicial interpretations); (2) the 'Invest in China' website, organized by the Foreign Investment Administration of the Ministry of Commerce and operated by the Investment Promotion Agency of the ministry;[53] and (3) the websites of relevant government departments, such as the website of the Administration of Quality Supervision, Inspection and Quarantine of China.[54] The website of the Chinese Central People's Government also provides some official publications in English.[55]

2. Comment

As noted earlier, China has undertaken two distinct comment obligations. One is the general comment obligation, under which China must allow for a certain period of comment between promulgation and entry into force of trade regulations.[56] The other is the TBT/SPS comment obligation, which requires China to provide a comment period on proposed measures, including standards and technical regulations.

The extent of China's general comment obligation merits analysis. First, China is not required to solicit comments in the process of drafting its trade-related measures. Rather, China's Accession Protocol requires it only to accept comments prior to the implementation of a measure. The relevant authorities have usually passed the measures published in the *Gazette*. Issues concerning laws can be raised through the legal section of the State Council.[57]

The Chinese government appears to have taken into account the notice-and-comment obligation when it drafted the Regulations on Procedures for Formulation of Administrative Regulations,[58] and the Regulations on Procedures of the Rules Formulating.[59] It states that 'pursuant to the notice-and-comment obligation undertaken in the Accession Protocol, the laws, regulations, rules and other measures could not be effective on the publication. Usually there should be a period of time for the public to comment, and for the preparation of implementation.'[60] Therefore, the effective date of administrative regulations is to be specified in the State Council decree that promulgates these regulations.[61] Administrative regulations usually take effect after 30 days from the date of promulgation. However, the following categories of administrative regulations may take effect on the dates of promulgation: (1) administrative regulations that involve national security, the determination of foreign exchange rates, or monetary policies, and (2) those that the implementation of which will be impeded if they are not implemented promptly.[62] Nearly the same requirements exist for rules.[63] Generally, China has confirmed that 'a 30-day period for comment between promulgation and entry into force of all laws, regulations and rules is provided to any individual, enterprise and other WTO Member'.[64]

In contrast, the TBT/SPS Agreement comment obligations require China to accept comments of businesses and other interested parties in the process of drafting measures, before their adoption and promulgation. The Regulations on Procedures for Formulation of Administrative Regulations and the Regulations on Procedures of the Rules Formulating make clear that comments on proposed measures are based on the following: (1) compliance with the TBT Agreement and SPS Agreement requirements that the draft of standards and technical measures shall be published for comments; and (2) the Law on Legislation, which requires that important bills be published for public comment.[65]

An issue that arises is the manner in which comments shall be obtained from businesses and other interested parties. From the Chinese government's perspective, 'China did not make any commitment specifically on ways to solicit public opinions', and that '[p]romulgating drafts of laws, regulations for public comments before implementation is not a necessary process according to China's WTO Commitments or domestic regulations'.[66] No specific stipulation can be found in China's Accession Protocol or Working Party Report with regard to the ways to seek public comment. The manner in which comments are solicited has been stipulated in China's domestic law rather than in the WTO rules. A number of rules in Chinese law govern how interested parties submit their comments on proposed measures. These rules can be found in the Law on Legislation (dealing with the making of laws, administrative regulations, local regulations, autonomous regulations, or special rules),[67] the Regulations on Procedures for Formulation of Administrative Regulations (governing the making of administrative regulations),[68] and the Regulations on Procedures of the Rules Formulating (dealing with the making of rules).[69] The methods by which comments are collected under these provisions are briefly canvassed here.

For laws, comments are collected in various ways in China. The Law on Legislation contains clear provisions for public comment. Article 35 of the Law on Legislation requires that 'an important bill which has been put on the agenda of the Standing Committee may, upon decision of the Caucus of Chairpersons, be presented to the public for comments' and that 'the comments presented by various agencies, organizations and citizens are to be submitted to the working office of the Standing Committee'. When a bill has been placed on the agenda of a session of the Standing Committee of the National People's Congress, relevant special committees and the working office of the Standing Committee may collect comments via inter alia symposia and hearings.[70] In addition, the working office of the Standing Committee distributes draft laws to relevant organizations and experts for comments.[71] Comments are sent to the Legislative Committee, other relevant special committees and, where necessary, distributed among the participants of the current session of the Standing Committee.[72] For local regulations, autonomous regulations, and special rules, comment opportunities exist since the procedure for consideration of such measures is done with reference to the above practices of the National People's Congress.[73]

For administrative regulations, the Law on Legislation provides comment opportunities generally, with detailed provisions articulated by the Regulations on Procedures for Formulation of Administrative Regulations and the Regulations on Procedures of the Rules Formulating. When drafting an administrative regulation, the drafting body shall hear the opinions of relevant agencies, organizations, and citizens through panel discussions, feasibility studies, and hearings.[74] On completion of drafting, the drafting body shall submit opinions from all sides concerning the key issues of the draft regulation to the legislative affairs organization of the State Council for review.[75] The procedures for enacting administrative rules by the State Council and rules of local governments are formulated by the State Council by reference to Chapter Three ('Administrative Regulations') of the Law on Legislation.[76]

The Regulations on Procedures for Formulation of Administrative Regulations and Regulations on Procedures of the Rules Formulating provide for comment opportunities with respect to the formulation of administrative regulations and rules. These comment opportunities are available during the preparation of drafts for examination and during the subsequent review of such drafts. The drafting of administrative regulations is based on 'in-depth investigation and research, summarization of practical experiences, and extensive consultations with organs, organizations and citizens'.[77] Soliciting comments may take place through forums, appraisal meetings, and hearings.[78] Nearly the same procedure exists for the drafting of rules.[79] In the case of rules, written comments may be submitted, as opposed to meetings or hearings.[80] Neither the Regulations on Procedures for Formulation of Administrative Regulations nor Regulations on Procedures of the Rules Formulating contain an exhaustive list of how comments may be received.[81] If government agencies, organizations, or citizens differ on draft rules that have 'direct bearing on the immediate interests' of citizens and legal persons as well as other organizations, the draft should be made open to public and opinions solicited.[82] A public hearing can also be held, with notice of the time and location being provided no less than 30 days before the hearing.[83] Persons participating in a hearing are entitled to raise questions and express their own opinions during the hearing.[84] A written record of comments made at a hearing is required, including the main points and concerns advanced.[85] Drafting authorities are required to take into consideration the opinions provided at a hearing.

When draft rules are submitted for approval, they must include an introductory note that explains how comments were solicited, as well as the underlying rationale of the comments that were provided.[86] Moreover, the explanations of draft regulations for examination shall state, inter alia, the differing opinions from various circles on the main issues in the draft and the circumstances in which comments were solicited from the relevant organs, organizations and citizens.[87]

Drafts for examination are reviewed by the legislative affairs department of the State Council (for draft regulations for examination)[88] and legislative affairs institutions (for draft rules for examination).[89] The opportunity to make comments also exists during this review. The treatment of comments is a review factor for the drafts for examination. When reviewing drafts measures, the legislative affairs department is required to consider whether the drafts have 'correctly handled the opinions' of relevant organs, organizations, and citizens on the drafts for examination.[90] Following the receipt of drafts for examination, the legislative affairs department sends drafts for examination or the main issues that the drafts for examination involve to, inter alia, relevant organizations and experts for comments.[91] On approval of the State Council, drafts for review may be made public for comments.[92] Similar to the aforementioned requirement for drafters of administrative regulations, the department that reviews drafts for examination is also required to solicit comments from the relevant organs, organizations, and citizens at the grassroots level.[93] If draft administrative regulations for examination involve 'major or difficult issues', the legislative affairs department will sponsor forums or appraisal meetings attended by the relevant units and experts to solicit comments and to conduct evaluations.[94] The same requirement applies to draft rules for examination if they involve 'major issues'.[95] In the case of draft administrative regulations for examination having 'direct bearing on the immediate interests' of citizens, legal persons, or other organizations, the legislative affairs department in question may hold hearings to collect comments from relevant departments, organizations, and citizens.[96] If the approval of relevant governments is obtained and certain conditions are met,[97] the draft rules for examination can be made public and hearings may be held.[98] The legislative affairs department studies all comments and, after consulting with the drafting departments, revises the drafts for examination and prepares the drafts of administrative regulations or rules and explanations thereof.[99] In the Regulations on Procedures for Formulation of Administrative Regulations and Regulations on Procedures of the Rules Formulating, there are no clear definitions of terms, including 'major issues', 'major or difficult issues', and 'direct bearing on the immediate interests'. Thus, in some instances the decision to obtain comments may be discretionary.

Under the aforementioned rule-making procedures, ministries or agencies under the State Council are required to solicit comments either in writing or through public means such as symposia or workshops in order to provide an opportunity for interested parties to provide their comments on draft laws and regulations.[100] In recent years, the drafting of over 30 laws and regulations has undergone public scrutiny, particularly through comments made by the media through websites, newspapers, and television.[101] In the first several months of 2008, the standing committee of the National People's Congress and the State Council worked to obtain public comments on the drafting of at least two laws and fifteen regulations.[102]

Businesses may post their comments on government websites. Some measures are pre-published in Chinese. This pre-publication is one of the mechanisms used to disseminate draft rules for consultation with interested parties. Various governmental websites provide the platform of collecting comments, such as the websites of the Central People's Government of China[103] and of the Administration of Quality Supervision, Inspection and Quarantine of China, where a special section for public comments is available.[104] Another example is the China Legislative Information Network System of Legislative Affairs Office of the State Council. It contains two sections where comments for drafted administrative regulations and department rules are solicited.[105] Interested parties may express their opinion as to whether they agree with a specific article of proposed rules and fill in their suggestions for each and every article. Alternatively, they can also provide general comments on the measure.

Another important way for enterprises in China to express their comments on draft bills is through industrial associations. Industrial associations are actively involved in China's trade policy implementation. For example, several industry associations collect and share information, identify and deal with industry problems, discuss trade policy issues affecting their industries, and represent their sectors in relation to the government.[106] These associations include the China Coal Industry Association, China Iron and Steel Association, China National Textiles and Clothing Association, China Machine Industry Federation, China Petroleum and Chemical Industry Association, China Light Industry Federation, China Building Material Industry Association, and the China Nonferrous Metals Society.[107] Recently the draft amendment to Postal Law received 2,395 comments within the first week of being made available for comment.[108] Some international and domestic courier services providers made their suggestions on the earlier draft amendments to the Postal Law to the Office of Legislative Affairs of the State Council. These businesses have expressed their opinions by various means, including contacting the government via Conference of Asia Pacific Express Carriers and China International Freight Forwarders Association.[109]

III. Business Participation in Trade Policy Matters

A. Practices of Business Participation in Trade Policy: A Brief Overview

Businesses can participate in trade policy formulation and implementation either internationally or domestically. Business groups have long advocated for greater access to international trade negotiations. For example, in 1946 the International Chamber of Commerce complained bitterly about the lack of consultation with non-government organizations at the London Preparatory Conference for negotiations on what eventually would become the GATT. The World Federation of Trade Unions protested the prevalence of the 'neo-liberalism' in the draft texts considered at the London Conference.[110]

Businesses actively participate in the formulation of trade policy and rules in developed countries and entities such as the United States, the European Union, and Japan. Multilateral rule-making also attracts the participation of business interests, notably multinational enterprises. Professor Ostry notes that the inclusion of new issues in the Uruguay Round was a U.S. initiative and this policy agenda was largely driven by multinational enterprises in the services and high-technology sectors.[111] These corporations indicated to the United States that without a fundamental rebalancing of the GATT, they would not continue to support a multilateral policy, and would prefer a bilateral or regional track. They also organized business coalitions in support of services and intellectual property in Europe and Japan, as well as some smaller developed countries. This activism paid off, and U.S. multinationals played a key role— perhaps even the key role—in establishing the new global trading system.[112]

Multinational enterprises also played a major role in lobbying for China's membership in the WTO. One important and unintended consequence of the Uruguay Round has been the rise in profile of multinational enterprises, in part due to their role in the Uruguay Round. For skeptics, the Uruguay Round was simply a conspiratorial collusion between U.S. corporations and the U.S. government.[113] U.S. multinationals were conspicuous in their absence in both Seattle and Doha and in supporting fast-track trade bills in Congress. This apathy has profound implications since there is no effective counterbalance to well-developed protectionist lobbies. Trade policy is the most domestic of all policies.[114] Meanwhile, the prominent role of businesses in defining the new trade agenda provided an easy and attractive target as public concern over the growing power of corporations began to mount.[115]

Large firms have interests that extend well beyond the domestic sphere. For example, where a developing country is short of legal and financial resources to pursue a WTO lawsuit, multinational firms may pay a U.S. or European law firm to represent the developing country.[116] Moreover, another open issue is the relationship between NGOs, small and medium-sized enterprises, and multinational enterprises. Multinationals, human rights groups, labour movements, and environmental NGOs have seen trade liberalization and policing of international treaties as an important vehicle for bringing change in certain countries.[117] Some NGOs and multinational enterprises act as enforcers of global regulation and increasingly cooperate to agree on collectively formulated norms (i.e., the United Nations [UN] Global Compact, a partnership between the UN and private companies, or semi-private standardization bodies such as the International Standardisation Organization or the International Accounting Standards Board).[118] The governments of some developing Members have sought assistance from Oxfam in trade negotiations and trade policy development. Oxfam is now supporting cotton producers by helping to establish national and regional producers' organizations and by strengthening their capacity for advocacy and negotiation.[119] In the view of many WTO Members, collaboration with NGOs is a choice to be made by Members, particularly with regard to policy-making.[120] NGOs play an active role in multilateral regulation,[121] but have faced criticism for a lack of accountability in the wake of their growing influence.[122]

B. Business Participation in the World Trade System: Comment Obligations as a Way Forward?

1. Why and How Business Participates in the Trade Matters: Formal Mechanisms in the WTO vs. Domestic Level Mechanisms

Two questions need to be addressed when discussing the participation of business interests in trade policy matters. First, should business interests be allowed to participate in trade policy-making? Second, assuming their participation should be allowed, how should business interests participate in trade policy formulation?

The first question seems largely academic. Businesses have been active players in the world trade regime and are entitled to participate in trade policy formulation in a constructive way. The real challenge of today's international governance is to create the conditions where public and private actors are able to work together, notwithstanding their different constituencies, objectives, cultures, and expertise.[123]

There is a case for businesses to participate in trade policy. First, business participation can help to enhance the legitimacy of trade policy-making. The trade rule-maker should listen to the opinions of those parties who are subject to trade rules. Such participation would in turn increase support for the implementation of trade rules. Second, business participation can help to tap the expertise and knowledge of the business community. Governments may not have or cannot afford to access business expertise, particularly developing Members. Third, business participation can help to improve debate, balance broader interests, and bring about more equitable decisions. Public participation is believed to have good effects on rule-making. Fourth, businesses may help to reach convergence in difficult areas of policy. Businesses would have more confidence and trust in the trading regime if they are involved in its development. The business community knows the economy very well and therefore can be helpful in reaching effective solutions. There are some suggestions that the role and responsibilities of multinational corporations in the trading system are issues that clearly must become part of the new negotiation agenda.[124]

Participation by business interests in trade policy-making is not unproblematic. Businesses may speak only for their own narrow interests and could fail to represent the interests of the general public. The participation of businesses may slow down the process of decision-making. There may be fragmented viewpoints from businesses, a situation that could cost a considerable amount of time and energy to address. However, these disadvantages should not prevent the participation of businesses. To sum up, there is a need for business participation in trade matters. WTO rules affect businesses both directly and indirectly, so the WTO must find effective ways to work with business interests.

To effectively engage businesses, it is necessary to understand the ways in which firms participate in trade matters. Notice-and-comment obligations provide business one avenue of engagement in trade policy. Other avenues include direct input at the WTO level, or consultation mechanisms at the domestic level with WTO Members. But which participation mechanism is better for businesses, including those from developing Members? The primary responsibility for engaging the business community in trade policy matters should rest with the Members at the domestic level for the following reasons:

1. As yet, there is no formalized WTO-level mechanism for direct input by private firms in trade negotiations. The real decision-making activity of the WTO takes place in negotiations and WTO Councils and committees. Businesses and NGOs are not allowed into those meetings. Since the WTO is an intergovernmental organization, it is not easy to find legal authority for direct participation by businesses in WTO decision-making. It is unclear that direct participation by businesses in the WTO could be accomplished without harming the conduct of negotiations.

2. Many developing Members oppose direct involvement by businesses in WTO decision-making. In the view of developing Members, direct participation by businesses would likely be dominated by multinational enterprises from developed Members. The high cost of direct participation in Geneva-based decision-making excludes businesses from the developing world. There is a serious imbalance in the capacities, funding, and expertise of businesses between developing and developed Members. It follows that multinational enterprises from developed Members would lead participation by business interests. Additionally, collaboration between businesses and governments among developing Members tends to be much looser than in similar collaborations among developed Members. This would further disadvantage business in developing Members.

3. It is not clear with whom business would speak in Geneva. Currently, few formally organized meetings provide an opportunity for business interests to address WTO officials and delegations. The WTO Forum, for example, is only a two-day conference for academics and NGOs to present their views. In fact, not many WTO delegations show up at the forum. As a public conference, the WTO Public Forum is not part of the WTO's daily working agenda, and it does not have much to do with the day-to-day workings of the WTO. Businesses have not actively participated in this public forum. Some of them may think that it is not easy to influence WTO decisions in this way. Outside of the WTO public forum, it would also prove difficult to determine how the views of business would be introduced into WTO decision-making. There are insufficient channels for directly influencing the WTO decisions by businesses. Because of this, businesses could not likely participate effectively in the WTO and may prefer instead to observe WTO meetings and other activities. However, with an increasing number of WTO meetings being broadcast online, attending meetings in Geneva is becoming less important.

4. Allowing participation by businesses would create significant logistical challenges. It would be difficult to accommodate 153 Members and a large number of businesses in WTO negotiations. In addition, participation by businesses in WTO decision-making would potentially expand the array of economic, political, social, and other policy areas related to trade, thereby making the negotiations increasingly difficult. It would also be difficult to fairly select qualified, legitimate, accountable, and representative businesses to directly participate in the WTO.

For these reasons, the primary avenue of business participation in trade policy formulation should be at the domestic level. To this end, WTO Members shoulder the primary responsibility for engaging with businesses, while the WTO should make some effort to facilitate such engagement.

2. Extension of WTO-plus Comment Obligations: A Possible Way of Enhancing Business Participation in the World Trade System

Extending the WTO-plus notice and comment obligations to all Members presents a mechanism to enhance business participation in trade matters at the domestic level. As analyzed above, China's notice-and-comment obligations have greatly helped foreign and local businesses participate in trade policy-making. Non-state actors, including foreign businesses, can get directly involved in the drafting of measures concerning or affecting goods, services, trade-related aspects of intellectual property rights, and foreign exchange control in China. This section analyzes how other WTO Members approach notice-and-comment obligations and studies some potential problems that need to be addressed in the extension of the WTO-plus comment obligations.

Aside from China, other countries and regions have adopted comment procedures as a result of or in conformity with WTO commitments, free trade agreements, and domestic laws. Certain recently acceded WTO Members have implemented WTO-plus transparency obligations similar to China or have enacted rules providing public comment procedures on TBT/SPS measures. Generally speaking, recently acceded Members (i.e., Viet Nam and Ukraine) have already implemented more rigorous notice-and-comment rules because of their commitments on WTO accession.

Viet Nam's transparency obligations are similar to those of China. With respect to proposed measures issued by Viet Nam pertaining to or affecting trade in goods, services, and intellectual property, a minimum comment period of 60 days is provided for associations, enterprises, and others to provide comments to appropriate authorities before measures are adopted. Comments received must be taken into account.[125] Viet Nam's new framework Law on Standards and Technical Regulations provides 60 days from the date of notification for public comment, a period that may be shortened in urgent cases, such as risks to public health, safety, environment, or national security.[126]

Ukraine's WTO accession commitments require a minimum comment period of 30 days before all regulations and other measures pertaining to or affecting trade in goods and services and trade-related aspects of intellectual property rights are implemented, except for those involving national emergency or security, or for which the publication would impede law enforcement.[127]

Ukraine's Law on Standards, Technical Regulations and Conformity Assessment Procedures provides an opportunity for public comment.[128] In comparison with Viet Nam and Ukraine, there is no express stipulation for the minimum length of comment period in China's WTO accession agreement.

Comment practices are common among some of the WTO's original Members. Furthermore, notice-and-comment obligations can be found in the North American Free Trade Agreement (NAFTA).[129] NAFTA countries must publish proposed measures (laws, regulations, procedures, and administrative rulings) of general application respecting any matter covered by NAFTA in advance and provide a reasonable opportunity for comment for interested persons, including other NAFTA party states.[130] Article 1803(1) requires each NAFTA country to notify other NAFTA parties of actual or proposed measures that might materially affect the operation of NAFTA or affect that other party's interests. NAFTA countries must, on request, provide other NAFTA countries with information respecting their actual or proposed measures.[131]

Beyond these general notice and comment obligations, NAFTA contains sector- or issue-specific notice-and-comment obligations. These include Article 718 (sanitary and phytosanitary measures) and Article 909 (standards-related measures). There is a notice-and-comment obligation when a party proposes to adopt or modify a technical regulation or a sanitary or phytosanitary measure of general application at the federal level. While similar to the SPS Agreement, NAFTA's notice-and-comment requirements impose greater obligations on NAFTA parties. For example, NAFTA requires a longer notice and comment period, 60 days, than the SPS Agreement.[132] In the case of a technical measure concerning perishable goods, each NAFTA party must endeavour to provide notification at least 30 days prior to the adoption or modification of the measure, but no later than when notification is provided to domestic producers.[133] NAFTA also requires that parties publish and provide the full text of the proposed sanitary or phytosanitary measure.[134] A final difference is that interested persons are allowed to comment, and NAFTA parties must discuss the comments on request and consider the comments and results of discussions.[135] However, these obligations apply only to the state parties to NAFTA.

In general, laws and regulations in Canada (at the federal level and in most provinces) are published in advance with a period provided for interested persons to comment. Since NAFTA, Canada routinely includes at least the general notice-and-comment provisions in its trade agreements (e.g., the free trade agreement between Canada and Peru).[136] The United States has taken a similar approach in its bilateral trade agreements. For instance, Chapter 19 of the United States-Colombia Free Trade Agreement provides an opportunity for comments. To the extent possible, the parties must provide interested persons and other parties 'a reasonable opportunity' to comment on proposed measures.[137] At the administrative level, U.S. federal agencies are required to comply with the notice-and-comment provisions of the Administrative Procedure Act when engaged in the promulgation of rules and regulations of general application. Every state of the United States appears to have a parallel state statute governing state-level agencies. These practices run throughout the U.S. rule-making process.

Notice-and-comment obligations are found outside of the NAFTA zone. In Germany, public discussion of laws and regulations is not only general practice, it is a constitutional imperative. In Japan, there is a 'public comment procedure' available to all natural or juridical persons regardless of nationality.[138] These procedures do not apply to acts of local governments. However, in Japan, most municipalities have established their own public comment procedures modelled after national government rules. Public comment gathering in Japan is conducted largely via the Internet. An e-government portal site has a special column of 'comments' where comments can be posted and reviewed.[139] However, the business community has not always been particularly responsive to these governmental initiatives. For example, a recent request for comments concerning Japan's procedures in dealing with unfair foreign trade practices generated a single response.[140]

While the foregoing demonstrates that notice-and-comment procedures exist at the domestic level among WTO Members, greater work at consistent and uniform comment obligations is required. Existing comment procedures are limited since they are not general international obligations applicable to WTO Members except for those set forth by the TBT and SPS Agreement. Only multilateral obligations can ensure that comment requirements are implemented widely and cannot be withdrawn unilaterally. There is a case for such extension. Such obligations would implement the WTO non-discrimination principle and would avoid dismantling the uniformity of WTO rules. Fair and non-discriminatory trade rules could help to establish more confidence in the WTO. The extension of notice-and-comment requirements may assist in reducing disputes. The fact that notice-and-comment requirements are being imposed on newly acceding WTO Members lends further support to expanding similar obligations to all WTO Members.

If comment obligations are to be extended, certain potential problems arising from the implementation must be addressed. One example of the negative side effects of such requirements is that if a huge number of measures are subject to comment, governments could become overwhelmed by the workload. The comment obligations may delay the response of governments in emergent situations. To minimize the negative effects accompanying the extension of comment requirements, efforts may be needed in the following areas:

1. Exceptions to comment requirements must be provided. These exceptions ought to include emergency situations or times when advanced publication of a measure would impede law enforcement. Generally speaking, these are the exceptions to the notice-and-comment obligations already found in the WTO-plus transparency obligation undertaken by recently acceded Members.

2. The scope of measures subject to comment obligations should be limited. China's notice-and-comment obligations extend to all laws, regulations, and other measures concerning or affecting goods, services, trade-related aspects of intellectual property rights, and foreign exchange controls. Viet Nam's obligation extends to all laws, regulations, decrees, judicial decisions, and administrative rulings of general application pertaining to or affecting customs issues, trade in goods, services, and intellectual property.[141] For Ukraine, all laws, regulations, decrees, judicial decisions, and administrative rulings of general application related to trade are subject to the commitment on advance notice-and-comment for trade regulations.[142] Requiring that notice-and-comment obligations be extended to measures at all governmental levels could be too demanding. To avoid such a burden on Members, measures under the comment obligation should be more restricted to measures at the central/federal and provincial/state level. Measures below the provincial/state level have a smaller scope of application and comparatively lower influence. The negative effect would be comparatively limited, if these measures were to be exempt from the comment requirement. Alternatively, lower-level measures (e.g., at the county and city level) could be subject to a simpler or more lenient comment procedure. This issue may be relevant with regard to WTO-extra transparency requirements.

3. There needs to be consistency in notice-and-comment requirements. For instance, although beyond the requirements on existing WTO Members, the transparency requirements imposed on recently acceded Members is far from uniform. One example is the length of the notice-and-comment period. There is no clear definition of a reasonable time frame for comments.[143] For China, no minimum notice-and-comment period was specified on its accession to the WTO. For Viet Nam, a 'reasonable period' is no less than 60 days,[144] whereas for Ukraine it is no less than 30 days.[145] Shall a minimum length of

comment period be provided? Leaving the term 'reasonable period' in the hands of WTO Members could create room for abuse. While this chapter does not advocate for a particular length of time, it is important that a uniform obligation be imposed on all WTO Members. A minimum comment period of 30 days may help to reduce the potential abuse of rights and guarantee necessary time for comments. Since draft measures for comments are usually written in the language of the Member who proposes it, some time is needed for foreign interested parties to understand it and the proposal and make comments. Another issue is how to determine who should be entitled to offer comments. It is advisable to stipulate that Members, individuals, associations, and enterprises are entitled to provide comments to the appropriate authorities before measures are adopted and implemented.

IV. Conclusion

Businesses could, if rightly engaged, make a positive contribution in enhancing transparency and confidence in the WTO by sharing their expertise and knowledge. Such a process would accommodate a broader array of interests and could assist in helping to achieve consensus in challenging policy issues. There is a real need to promote business participation in formation of trade policy by WTO Members. The question is not whether business participation is needed, but how businesses shall participate. The direct participation of business in the sensitive WTO decision-making may not be compatible with the intergovernmental character of the WTO and may generate objections from developing Members. Currently it is not desirable to have formal mechanisms for business interests to participate in the WTO. Therefore, the primary responsibility for engaging the business community in trade policy matters rest with the Members.

The focus on WTO transparency pertains to institutional issues, whereas transparency obligations imposed on Members are of vital importance. WTO Members generally consider that their efforts at enhancing external transparency will bear little fruit unless they themselves are transparent at home with domestic stakeholders.[146] Extending notice and comment obligations to all WTO Members is a vehicle to achieve greater domestic transparency. It may bring changes as in China's domestic law. On accession, China undertook stringent comment obligations consisting of general and TBT/SPS comment obligations. These obligations have also brought about changes to China's domestic law. Although transparency is regarded as a basic principle for all legislative activities in China since the promulgation of the Law on Legislation in 2000,[147] compliance with China's transparency obligations under the WTO is one of the major reasons for the enactment of the Regulations on Procedures for Formulation of Administrative Regulations and the Regulations on Procedures of the Rules Formulating.[148] Under these domestic laws, foreign and domestic businesses and other interested parties are allowed the chance to comment on certain draft measures and on promulgated trade measures prior to their implementation. Moreover, certain recently acceded Members and developed countries have already adopted advance notice and comment requirements, which have laid a foundation for their extension. Extending a more generalized notice-and-comment requirement to all WTO Members is a logical progression in the movement for greater transparency.

As indicated in the preamble to the WTO Agreement, the needs and concerns at different levels of economic development shall be respected. If there is to be an extension of the comment obligation, certain exceptions or transitional periods for implementing such comment requirements may be necessary. Certain potential problems in implementing such comment obligations must also be addressed. They include clear exceptions to the comment requirements and limiting the scope of measures subject to comment obligations. A more interactive mechanism for business interests, both domestic and foreign, to participate in trade policy-making could be developed. Enhancing trade policy formulation at the domestic level cannot help but enhance the transparency of the WTO.

Notes

1 WTO, *The Results of the Uruguay Round of Multilateral Trade Negotiations: The Legal Texts* (New York: Cambridge University Press, 2004) 17.

2 Ibid, at 284.

3 Ministerial Declaration, WT/MIN(01)/DEC/1, 20 November 2001, at para 10.

4 Carl-Sebastian Zoellner, 'Transparency: An Analysis of an Evolving Fundamental Principle in International Economic Law', 27 Michigan Journal of International Law 579 (2006), at 580.

5 Above n 1, at 7, Article V:2.

6 Annex on of Telecommunications, para 7(b) of the GATS.

7 WT/L/162, Adopted 23 July 1996.

8 Ibid, at para 6.

9 Iana Dreyer, 'WTO Public Forum. To Harness or to Unleash, That Is the Question' (5 October 2007), http://globalconditions.wordpress.com/2007/10/05/wto-public -forum-to-harness-or-to-unleash-that-is-the-question/ (visited 1 March 2008).

10 WT/L/452, Adopted 16 May 2002.

11 Consultative Board to the Director-General Supachai Panitchpakdi, *The Future of the WTO: Addressing Institutional Challenges in the New Millennium* (the Sutherland Report) (Geneva: World Trade Organization, 2004) para 184.

12 Thomas Cottier and Satoko Takenoshita, 'Decision-making and the Balance of Powers in the WTO Negotiation', in Stefan Griller (ed), *At Crossroads: The World Trading System and the Doha Round* (New York and Vienna: Springer, 2008) vol. 8, 184.

13 For example, European Communities Submission to the General Council, 'Improving the Functioning of the WTO System', WT/GC/W/412, 10 October 2000; United States Submission to the General Council and 'External Transparency',WT/GC/W/413 10 October 2000.

14 Above n 11, at para 191.

15 Ministerial Conference Accession of the People's Republic of China (the Accession Protocol), WT/L/432, Adopted 23 November 2001. The Accession Protocol shall include the commitments referred to in paragraph 342 of the Working Party Report. See Part 1, Section 1(2).

16 Ibid, at Part I, Section 2(C)1. Here 'laws, regulations and other measures' refer to laws, regulations, and other measures of the central government as well as local regulations, rules, and other measures issued or applied at the sub-national level. China's local regulations, rules, and other measures of local governments at the sub-national level shall conform to the obligations provided by the WTO Agreement and the Accession Protocol. See ibid., at Part I, Section 2(A)2–3.

17 Ibid, at Part 1, Section 2(C)1.

18 Ibid.

19 Ministerial Conference, Report of the Working Party on the Accession of China (the Working Party Report), WT/MIN(01)/3, 10 November 2001, at para 331. As stated in Part I, Section 1(2) of the Accession Protocol, the Accession Protocol, including the commitments referred to in paragraph 342 of the Working Party Report, is an integral part of the WTO Agreement. Meanwhile, paragraph 342 of the Working Party Report expressly stipulates that the commitments contained in the relevant paragraphs are incorporated in Part 1, Section 1(2) of the Accession Protocol. Paragraph 331 of the Working Party Report is one of the relevant paragraphs mentioned in paragraph 342. Therefore the violation of paragraph 331 of the Working Party Report is a breach of China's obligations under the provisions of Part 1, Section 1(2) of the Accession Protocol (to the extent that it incorporates commitments in paragraph 331 of the Working Party Report). All paragraphs of the Working Party Report quoted in this paper are of the same kind as paragraph 331 of the Working Party Report.

20 Ibid, at para 332.

21 Above n 15, at Part 1, Section 2(C)2.

22 Ibid.

23 Above n 19, at para 178.

24 Ibid, at para 336; above n 15, at Part 1, Section 2(C)3.

25 Above n 19, at para 336.

26 Replies to other Members shall be complete and represent the authoritative view of the Chinese government. Accurate and reliable information shall be provided to individuals and enterprises. See above n 15, at Part 1, Section 2(C)3.

27 Above n 19, at para 334.

28 Above n 15, at Part 1, Section 2(D).

29 Ibid, at Part 1, Section 2(A)4; above n 19, at para 75.

30 General Council, Transitional Review under Section 18.2 of the Protocol of Accession of the People's Republic of China, Information Required in Sections I and III in Annex 1A of the Accession Protocol, Communication from the People's Republic of China, WT/GC/113, 11 December 2007, at 5–6.

31 Above n 15, Part 1, Section 18.

32 Ibid, at Part 1, Section 2(C)2.

33 Above n 19, at para 178.

34 Ibid.

35 Above n 15, at Part 1, Section 1(2).

36 Article 2.9 of the TBT Agreement.

37 Article 5.6 of the TBT Agreement.

38 Annex B, para 5 of the SPS Agreement.

39 Annex B, para 5(b) of the SPS Agreement. Articles 2.9.2 and 5.6.2 of the TBT Agreement.

40 Annex B, para 5(b) of the SPS Agreement. Articles 2.9.2 and 5.6.2 of the TBT Agreement.

41 Articles 2.9.4 and 5.6.4 of the TBT Agreement; Annex B, para 5(b) of the SPS Agreement.

42 Articles 2,10.3 of the TBT Agreement; Annex B, para 6(c) of the SPS Agreement.

43 These websites are http://www.tbt-sps.gov.cn/Pages/main.aspx (in Chinese) and http://www.tbt-sps.gov.cn/sites/english/Pages/default.aspx (in English) (visited 10 April 2009).

44 The WTO/FTA consultation website of the Ministry of Commerce is http://chinawto .mofcom.gov.cn/. These enquiry points and enquiry websites are also responsible for implementing notification obligation to the WTO. See Trade Policy Review Body, 'Trade Policy Review: China, Minutes of Meeting Addendum'. WT/TPR/M/199/Add.1, 28 August 2008, at 155. For more on China's implementation on SPS Agreement transparency provisions, see Ljiljana Biukovi?, 'Selective Adaptation of WTO Transparency Norms And Local Practices in China and Japan', 11 Journal of International Economic Law 803 (2008), at 818–24.

45 Council for Trade in Goods, Report of the Council for Trade in Goods on China's Transitional Review, G/L/844, 7 December 2007, at para 7.34. In the para 330 of Working Party Report, a full list of official journals is provided.

46 See the back cover of *China Foreign Trade and Economic Cooperation Gazette*.

47 The contents in English of the *China Foreign Trade and Economic Cooperation Gazette* are available at http://english.mofcom.gov.cn/static/column/policyrelease/gazette. html/1.

48 Trade Policy Review Body, above n 44, at 155.

49 Ibid.

50 Ibid.

51 Ibid.

52 The website is http://www.chinalaw.gov.cn/article/english/Regulations/Laws/200708/ 20070800037440.shtml.

53 The website is http://www.fdi.gov.cn/pub/FDI_EN/Laws/default_new.jsp?type=530. It provides for searches of Chinese rules and investment cases.

54 The website is http://english.aqsiq.gov.cn/LawsandRegulations/. It publishes the English version of laws and regulations relating to quality supervision, inspection and quarantine.

55 The website is http://www.chinalaw.gov.cn/article/english/ (in English). They cover State Council gazettes, statistical communiqués, white papers, and work reports, among others. More materials in Chinese are provided at http://www.gov.cn/zwgk/index.htm (in Chinese), including documents of the State Council, government gazettes, documents of government departments and local governments, and white papers.

56 Trade Policy Review Body, 'Trade Policy Review: China, Minutes of Meeting', WT/TPR/M/199, 24 July 2008, at para 157.

57 Ibid.

58 Regulations on Procedures for the Formulation of Administrative Regulations, promulgated 16 November 2001, effective 1 January 2002, http://www.gov.cn/english/laws/2005-08/24/content_25827.htm (English text) (visited 25 October 2008).

59 Regulations on Procedures of the Rules Formulating, promulgated 16 November 2001, effective 1 January 2002, http://www.csrc.gov.cn/n575458/n4001948/n4002075/n4002330/4064608.html (English text) (visited 25 October 2008).

60 Office of Legislative Affairs of the State Council, Draft Explanations of the Regulations on Procedures for Formulation of Administrative Regulations, http://www.haolawyer.com/law/view_99187.html (visited 25 October 2008); Office of Legislative Affairs of the State Council, Draft Regulations on Procedures of the Rules Formulating, http://www.lawyee.net/OT_Data/Legislation_Display.asp?ChannelID=7000000&RID=3615 (visited 25 October 2008).

61 Above n 58, at Article 27.

62 Ibid, at Article 29.

63 Above n 59, Article 30 (promulgation date and effective date should be stated) and Article 32 (generally rules become effective after 30 days from the promulgation date with exceptions).

64 See Trade Policy Review Body, above n 44, at 155.

65 See above n 60.

66 See Trade Policy Review Body, above n 44, at 154.

67 Law on Legislation of the People's Republic of China, promulgated 15 March 2000, effective 1 July 2000, http://www.fdi.gov.cn/pub/FDI_EN/Laws/law_en_info.jsp?docid=50981 (English text) (visited October 25, 2008).

68 Administrative regulations are normally entitled 'regulations' and could also be named as 'provisions', 'measures', etc. Rules formulated by the departments of the State Council or the local people's governments cannot be entitled 'regulations'. Above n 58, at Article 4.

69 The rules are usually named as the 'regulations' or 'measures' but not the 'Regulations': see above n 59, at Article 6.

70 Above n 67, at Article 34.

71 Ibid.

72 Ibid, at Article 36.

73 Ibid, at Article 68.

74 Ibid, at Article 58.

75 Ibid, at Article 59.

76 Ibid, at Article 74.

77 Above n 58, at Article 12.

78 Ibid.

79 Above n 59, at Article 14.

80 Ibid.

81 Above n 58, at Article 12.

82 Above n 59, at Article 15.

83 Ibid, at Article 15 (1).

84 Ibid, at Article 15(2).

85 Ibid, at Article 15(3).

86 Ibid, at Article 15(4).

87 Above n 58, at Article 16.

88 Ibid, at Article 17.

89 Above n 59, at Article 18.

90 Ibid, at Article 18(3); above n 58, at Article 17(4).

91 Above n 58, at Article 19 (1); above n 59, at Article 20.

92 Above n 58, at Article 19 (2).

93 Above n 58, at Article 20; above n 59, at Article 21.

94 Above n 58, at Article 21.

95 Above n 59, at Article 22.

96 Above n 58, at Article 22.

97 The conditions are that (1) the draft rules for review have 'direct bearings on the imme-diate interests' of the citizens, legal persons, or other organizations, (2) the above parties concerned are much divided in their opinions, and (3) the drafting units have not published the draft rules for examination or held the symposiums during the drafting work. Above n 59, at Article 23.

98 Ibid, at Article 23.

99 Above n 58, at Article 22; ibid, at Article 25.

100 See Trade Policy Review Body, above n 44, at 155.

101 Ibid.

102 Ibid, at 156.

103 See http://english.gov.cn/ (Central People's Government).

104 See http://www.aqsiq.gov.cn/gzcypt/cazxyj/ (Administration of Quality Supervision, Inspection and Quarantine of China).

105 See http://yijian.chinalaw.gov.cn/lisms/action/loginAction.do?loginfre=loginfre (com-ments for drafted administrative regulations) and http://bmyj.chinalaw.gov.cn/lisms/action/loginAction.do?loginCookie=loginCookie (comments for drafted department rules). Both websites are in Chinese.

106 Trade Policy Review Body, 'Trade Policy Review: Report by the Secretariat-China', WT/TPR/S/199, 16 April 2008, at 32.

107 Ibid, footnote 35.

108 'Over 2000 Pieces of Opinions Received after First Week of Opinion Collection for Postal Law Draft', Xinhua news, http://news.xinhuanet.com/legal/2008-11/07/content_10322583.htm (visited 15 November 2008).

109 Li Xiufeng, 'The Reasons of Professional Associations' Participation in Policy-Mak-ing: Case Study of China International Express Working Committee's Participation in Policy-Making', 5 China-Today Forum (2008) at 51 [in Chinese].

110 Above n 11, at para 179.

111 Sylvia Ostry, 'Globalization: What Does It Mean?', G-78 Annual Conference, Econiche House, Ottawa, October, 1999, at 5, http://www.utoronto.ca/cis/ostry/docs_pdf/G78CONF.pdf (visited 8 February 2008).

112 Ibid.

113 Sylvia Ostry, 'What Are the Necessary Ingredients for the World Trading Order?' in Horst Siebert (ed), *Global Governance: An Architecture for the World Economy* (New York: Springer, 2002) 124–25.

114 Ibid, at 130.

115 Sylvia Ostry, 'Global Integration: Currents and Counter-Currents', Walter Gordon Lecture, Massey College, University of Toronto, 23 May 2001, at 21, http://www.utoronto.ca/cis/ostry/docs_pdf/GlobalIntegration.pdf (visited 11 March 2009).

116 Gregory C. Shaffer, *Defending Interests: Public-Private Partnerships in WTO Litigation* (Washington: Brookings Institution Press, 2003), at 139 and 142.

117 Damian Chalmers, 'Administrative Globalisation and Curbing the Excess of the State', in Christian Joerges and Ernst-Ulrich Petersmann (eds), *Constitutionalism, Multilevel Trade Governance and Social Regulation* (Portland, Oregon: Hart Publishing, 2006) 366.

118 Joost Pauwelyn, 'Non-Traditional Patterns of Global Regulation: Is the WTO "Missing the Boat"?', in Christian Joerges and Ernst-Ulrich Petersmann (eds), *Constitutionalism, Multilevel Trade Governance and Social Regulation* (Portland, Oregon: Hart Publishing, 2006) 203.

119 International Trade Centre, 'Collaborating with an Advocacy NGO', http://www.tradeforum.org/news/fullstory.php/aid/1041 (visited 3 March 2008).

120 General Council, Guidelines for Arrangements on Relations with Non-governmental Organizations, WT/L/162, Adopted on 23 July 1996, at para 6. See also above n 11, at para 190.

121 For example, Oxfam's alleged influence on the failure of the WTO meeting in Cancun as well as its role in the fight against export subsidies of rich countries.

122 See above n 118, at 205.

123 WTO, 'Lamy: Trade Expansion Is Insurance against Financial Turbulences', http://www.wto.org/english/news_e/sppl_e/sppl85_e.htm (visited 13 February 2008).

124 Debra Steger, 'The Culture of the WTO: Why It Needs to Change', 10 Journal of International Economic Law 483 (2007), at 494.

125 Report of the Working Party on the Accession of Viet Nam, WT/ACC/VNM/48, 27 October 2006, at para 518.

126 Ibid, para 309.

127 Report of the Working Party on the Accession of Ukraine to the World Trade Organization, WT/ACC/UKR/152, 25 January 2008, at para 499.

128 Ibid, at para 297.

129 17 December 1992; 32 I.L.M. 289.

130 Article 1802(2) of the NAFTA.

131 Article 1803(2) of the NAFTA.

132 Articles 718.1(a) and 909.1(a) of the NAFTA.

133 Article 909.1 (a) of the NAFTA.

134 Article 718.1 (a) of the NAFTA.

135 Articles 718.1 (d), 718.3(c), 909.1(d), and 909.4(c) of the NAFTA.

136 For instance, Article 1901.2(b) of the Free Trade Agreement Between Canada and the Republic of Peru, May 2008, http://www.international.gc.ca/trade-agreements-accords-commerciaux/agr-acc/andean-andin/can-peru-perou.aspx (visited 14 April 2009).

137 See Article 19.2.2(b) of United States-Colombia Trade Promotion Agreement, 22 November 2006, http://www.ustr.gov/Trade_Agreements/Bilateral/Colombia_FTA/Final_Text/Section_Index.html (visited 15 April 2006).

138 Public Comment Procedure for Formulating, Amending or Repealing a Regulation, Cabinet Decision, 23 March 1999, http://www.soumu.go.jp/gyoukan/kanri/990422.htm (visited 26 July 2008). Administrative Procedure Act, revisions of Act No. 73 of 2005 (Effective 1 April 2006). Administrative Procedure Act (Act No. 88 of 1993), http://www.kl.i.is.nagoya-u.ac.jp/told/h05a08801en.1.0.txt (visited 26 July 2008).

139 The website is http://www.e-gov.go.jp/.

140 Opinion Collection for Unfair Trade Practices Report 2008, http://search.egov.go.jp/servlet/Public?ANKEN_TYPE=3&CLASSNAME=Pcm1020&KID=595207036&OBJCD=&GROUP=&cmbKENSU=10&rdoSEARCH1=0&txtKeyword=%95%73%8C%F6%90%B3%96%66%88%D5%95%F1%8D%90%8F%91&rdoSEARCH2=0&rdoSEARCH3=0&rdoSEARCH4=0& cmbYERST=&txtMonST=&txtDayST=&cmbYERED=&txtMonED=&txtDayED=&hdnParentsCLS=Pc1020&hdnBsSort=&hdnKsSort=0&hdnDispST=1 (visited 28 November 2008).

141 See above n 125, at para 518.

142 See above n 127, at para 499.

143 For standardizing bodies, a period of at least 60 days could be set for submitting comments on the draft standard by interested parties. This period may be shortened in urgent cases. Such a time frame would apply if a standardizing body accepts the Code of Good Practice for the Preparation, Adoption and Application of Standards. See Annex 3, para L of the TBT Agreement.

144 See above n 125, at para 518.

145 See above n 127, at para 499.

146 See above n 11, at para 191.

147 See above n 44, at 155.

148 See above n 60.

PART V

Public Participation

Options for Public Participation in the WTO: Experience from Regional Trade Agreements

YVES BONZON

I. Introduction

Since the early days of the World Trade Organization (WTO), numerous commentators in the political and legal fields have challenged the traditional view according to which inputs from civil society actors in the decision-making process are to be managed at the domestic level and channelled through Members' delegations exclusively.[1] With this in mind, this chapter refers to the concept of *public participation* as including all institutionalized forms of interaction in the decision-making process between organs of an institution and actors that are independent from any government (non-state actors). This approach must be distinguished from other participatory approaches that have been advocated in the WTO context, such as the adoption of international provisions that would regulate public participation at the domestic level,[2] or the creation of a parliamentary body at the WTO level.[3]

Public participation includes two interrelated dimensions that are considered jointly: the *transparency* of an institution's decision-making process and the *engagement* of non-states actors in that process (or *actual participation*).[4] Transparency is a prerequisite for active participation. In cases where the public is entitled to some forms of direct participation, rules must ensure that relevant and timely information is made available in a fair manner in order for active participation to be meaningful. In cases where public participation is more indirect and involves representation, information must allow that representatives are held accountable to the people they represent.[5] Inversely, active participation may be a prerequisite for access to information. Indeed, a dialectic interaction between organs of public authority and the public might sometimes be required to identify the relevant information to be requested.

Current mechanisms of public participation in the WTO are institutionalized by two documents: the Decision of the General Council on the Procedures for the Circulation and De-restriction of WTO Documents,[6] and the Guidelines for Arrangements on Relations with Non-Governmental Organizations.[7] The decision on de-restriction regulates the transparency aspect of public participation, setting the general principle that 'all WTO official documents shall be unrestricted', with some limited exceptions.[8] The guidelines address the WTO's relationship with non-governmental organizations (NGOs) and serve as the basis for current arrangements with civil society. These arrangements include the possibility for non-profit NGOs to attend the plenary meetings of the biannual ministerial conferences; the organization by the WTO Secretariat of symposia, public forums, and other informal meetings where NGOs make presentations to chairpersons of WTO bodies and officials of the WTO Secretariat; and an NGO page on the WTO website where a monthly list of position papers posted by NGOs is compiled.[9]

On the dispute settlement side, panels and the Appellate Body have taken steps of their own to enhance public participation by receiving inputs from non-state actors through the submission of *amicus curiae* briefs.[10] However, under political pressure from a majority of Members, panels have regularly accepted amicus briefs, stressing their discretionary right to accept, consider, or reject any unsolicited submissions but have usually refused to consider them. Finally, with respect to the transparency of the dispute settlement process, some Members have taken the initiative to open to the public sessions of disputes they were involved in.[11]

It can be said in the light of the above that mechanisms of public participation in the WTO are of a rudimentary nature. Indeed, the guidelines are consistent with the strong *state-centred* nature of the WTO by providing that closer consultation and cooperation with NGOs shall occur first and foremost at the national level, and by giving the Secretariat, which is not granted any formal decision-making power in the organization's institutional setting, the primary role in interacting with NGOs.

Many reform proposals in recent years have been calling for the adoption of more structured and formalized mechanisms that would allow for more direct public participation in a fair and effective way. Conceptual models of such mechanisms are to be found at the domestic level of states that have integrated public participation mechanisms in their administrative process, such as provided for in the U.S. Federal Administrative Procedural Act (US FAPA). These mechanisms are usually structured along four parameters (implementation parameters): the *goal* of participation (normative function), the *object* of participation (decisions at stake), the actual *mechanisms* of participation (forms of involvement, which specify in particular whether public participation can be judicially enforced and reviewed), and the *actors* involved (circles of participants).[12]

This chapter compares public participation mechanisms adopted by other international regimes and assesses to what extent these mechanisms could be transposed to the WTO. Since it is argued that all four implementation parameters are interrelated, the goal and the object of public participation are first briefly addressed by focusing on the relationship between the democratic principle and the WTO. Doing so, Part II sets a framework for assessing mechanisms of public participation in other international regimes. Part III turns to the comparative analysis and focuses on public participation mechanisms in selected free trade regimes (the Common Southern Market [Mercado Común del Sur] [MERCOSUR]), the Association of Southern Eastern Asian Nations (ASEAN), and the European Union (EU), and other international regimes. On the basis of the comparative analysis, Part IV considers the further formalization of public participation mechanisms in WTO decision-making and focuses on the possibility of the WTO Panels and Appellate Body performing administrative review of the decision-making processes of those international standard-setting organizations whose rules they may refer to, drawing insights from the *Sardines* case.[13]

II. Public Participation and Democratic Legitimacy

Most proposals for enhancing mechanisms of public participation in the WTO refer to the existence of a 'democratic deficit' in the organization's decision-making process. Focusing on this issue, some commentators argue that as a result of increasingly dealing with the reduction of non-tariff barriers to trade, certain WTO decisions are exerting an impact on individuals that is similar to the impact of decisions reached at the domestic level of states.[14] On this basis, some commentators further argue that traditional 'inter-governmental' decision-making processes no longer provide for sufficient 'legitimization' of such international decisions.[15] In addition, as a consequence of economic globalization, some are drawing attention to the emergence of transnational interests that cannot be sufficiently taken into account in the context of a state-centred system of decision-making at the international level.[16]

In contrast, some authors have denied the existence of a legitimacy deficit in the WTO. These denials are based on arguments that view existing conditions of representation as satisfactory,[17] contest the impact of the regulatory shift,[18] or emphasize the so-called *output* dimension of legitimacy (result-oriented legitimacy), according to which gains of multilateral cooperation compensate for the lack of citizens' representation at the international level.[19]

Regardless of one's stance on the question of a legitimacy deficit in the WTO, two preliminary questions must be addressed when considering the implementation of public participation mechanisms as a means of improving the democratic quality of decision-making. The first question regards the relevance of taking democratic concerns into account at the WTO level (is democratic legitimacy a relevant goal for the WTO?), while the second question relates to the appropriateness of public participation mechanisms to address such democratic concerns.

As regards the first question, an affirmative answer presupposes the existence of convergent democratic values among Members and the recognition that the WTO is meant to perform the constitutional function of promoting and implementing values of democracy at the national as well as the international levels. Some authors have argued that the WTO is implicitly meant to perform such a constitutional function. They take a human rights approach, observing that all WTO Members are parties to treaties and have adopted United Nations resolutions promoting democratic governance and a democratic international order.[20] In addition, others have argued that the procedural requirements imposed on Members by Article X of the General Agreement on Tariffs and Trade (GATT 1947),[21] Article III of the General Agreement on Trade in Services (GATS),[22] and Article 63 of the Agreement on Trade-Related Aspects of Intellectual Property Rights (TRIPS)[23] relating to their domestic decision-making procedures, should be imposed on international decision-making, which would amount to recognizing the existence of constitutional principles at the WTO level.[24]

As regards the appropriateness of public participation mechanisms in enhancing the democratic quality of the WTO decision-making process, proponents of such mechanisms view them as a complement to other sources of democratic legitimization (elections and traditional representative channels) in circumstances where those traditional *input* mechanisms are weak, thus making them particularly appealing at the international level.[25] Some others argue, however, that the deliberative function of public participation can only have a legitimizing effect when a homogenous polity, which is missing at the international level, supports such a process.[26] In response, proponents argue that public participation can contribute to the emergence of such a polity and should be established to compensate for its absence.[27]

Adopting a constitutional perspective as proponents of enhanced public participation does imply that some decisions, because of their *impact*, must be reached according to appropriate procedures that have the potential to legitimize them. In other words, a specific *degree-of-legitimization requirement* is attached to a given type of decision depending on its impact.[28] The normative link between the type of decision and the procedure (institutional setting) for achieving it has been conveniently described by the 'substance-structure pairing' concept,[29] and should be kept in mind when comparing participatory mechanisms in various regimes. From such a 'substance-structure pairing' perspective, the impact of a decision is a combination of its substance and its enforcement mechanisms. Therefore, the following comparative analysis must take into account both elements in order to be meaningful.

III. Comparative Analysis

A. Framework of Analysis

As some commentators have stressed, any comparative analysis of public participation mechanisms runs the risk of proving irrelevant in the light of the dissimilarities between international regimes with regard to their membership, type of goals, and qualities.[30] With this in mind, the following comparative analysis focuses on regimes whose types of decisions (object of public participation) are to some degree similar to those of the WTO from a substantive point of view. Therefore, emphasis is placed on public participation mechanisms in other free trade regimes. In addition, public participation mechanisms of the Codex Alimentarius Commission (Codex) are considered, since the output of this organization is relevant to the WTO by virtue of the WTO rule-referencing practice, as will be explained.[31] Furthermore, public participation mechanisms in selected multilateral environmental agreements are briefly surveyed because of the well-elaborated models they provide.

Moreover, public participation mechanisms in the selected free trade regimes are compared from a normative substance-structure pairing perspective, which means that the degree-of-legitimization requirement of a regime's decisions (focus on substance, or impact) as well as existing institutional features of that regime (focus on structure) are taken into account. On the substance side, the degree-of-legitimization requirement of decisions is assessed by reference to the existence of binding dispute settlement mechanisms at the international level or to domestic courts enforcing them (which would mean that the provisions have direct effect). On the structural side, emphasis is placed on institutional features that might contribute to the legitimization of a regime's decisions, and on which the requirement for enhanced public participation mechanisms might further depend. For instance, public participation will be less required if a regime's decision-making organs include legitimizing bodies like a parliamentary assembly or involve high-ranking political officials.

1. MERCOSUR

On the substantive side, the impact of MERCOSUR law is similar to WTO law. According to the constitutional rules of states parties, MERCOSUR's decisions have no direct effect and must be incorporated into national law before attaining any legal force. As regards dispute settlement mechanisms at the international level, the Article 9 of Olivos Protocol provides for ad hoc arbitration proceedings that can be initiated by any state party involved in a dispute, and Article 17 establishes a review procedure by a permanent review court.[32] The awards of the Permanent Review Court are binding (Article 26), and compensatory measures can be applied to a state party that does not comply with them (Article 31).

On the structural side, MERCOSUR displays a number of peculiarities that, in comparison to the WTO, provide enhanced legitimization of MERCOSUR law.[33] First, meetings of the highest decision-making organ, the Common Market Council, (Consejo del Mercado Comun) are more frequent (twice a year) and the Members' heads of state meet once a year.[34] Second, a MERCOSUR parliament, until 2006 the Joint Parliamentary Group (Comision Parlamentaria Conjunta), has been established to facilitate the integration of MERCOSUR law into the national legal orders of Members (though it is acknowledged that the accomplishments of the parliament have been relatively modest).

Turning to mechanisms of public participation, exchange of information with non-state actors takes place within a social and economic forum established by the organization. This forum is made up of national sections, whose composition is decided autonomously by each state party.[35] The forum serves as a consulting body to the Common Market Council and issues non-binding recommendations that in practice, as noted by some authors, '[have] been reduced to an exchange of opinions on the development of the main aspects of the negotiating agenda'.[36] In addition, institutionalized channels of public participation exist through the MERCOSUR parliament. The parliament's constitutive protocol sets out the general goal of 'guaranteeing the participation of civil society actors in the integration process' and recognizes as a general principle the 'transparency of information and decisions in order to foster trust and enhance the participation of citizens'. Further, the competence of the parliament includes the 'organization of public meetings with civil society and business organizations to address issues relating to the integration process', as well as the possibility to 'receive, examine, and, if appropriate, transmit to the decision-making organs petitions of any individual of the States Parties, natural or juridical person, relating to acts or omissions of MERCOSUR organs'.[37]

2. ASEAN

On the substantive side, the ASEAN Protocol on Enhanced Dispute Settlement Mechanism establishes binding procedures, creates a standing Appellate Body, and allows the use of retaliatory measures (suspension of concessions) in cases of non-compliance with its rulings.[38] The dispute settlement process is driven by the reverse consensus principle and is thus very similar to that of the WTO.

On the structural side, although ASEAN is the framework for a broader integration project calling for the development of a community built on three pillars (political, economic, and socio-cultural), it has not yet established any type of parliament or separate forum for civil society representation. ASEAN's institutions are built on the same hierarchical structure as most other free trade regimes. Its structure can be divided into a 'Track One' and a 'Track Two' approach.[39] Track One is made of the actual decision-making organs, which consist of the ASEAN Summit (where heads of states meet annually) and various ministerial councils. Track Two is made up of the numerous committees and working groups that have powers delegated from Track One organs.

ASEAN has established some formalized patterns of interaction with non-state actors. Meetings organized by Track Two bodies include discussions with think-tank experts, representatives from technical organizations, and other specialists. These meetings ensure the participation of the private sector, which is represented through the ASEAN Chambers of Commerce and Industry (ASEAN-CCI) and other sectoral committees.[40] As one example of formalized mechanisms of interaction with the private sector, the agenda of the Senior Economic Officials Meeting is circulated to the ASEAN-CCI in advance in order to latter's input.[41]

Interaction with some civil society organizations is formalized by a system of accreditation regulated in the 'Guidelines on ASEAN's Relations with Civil Society Organizations (CSOs)'.[42] Its legal basis has been reinforced with the adoption of the 'Charter of the Association of Southeast Asian Nations', which provides in Article 16 that *'associated entities'* are to be listed in its Annex.[43] The ASEAN guidelines set criteria for accreditation and detail the privileges that accreditation entails. Criteria for accreditation mostly relate to the composition of an organization's membership (representation of ASEAN nationals), the compatibility of its goals with those of ASEAN, and its positive contribution to the realization of ASEAN goals. Accreditation entails the privilege of submitting documents to the ASEAN Standing Committee via the ASEAN Secretariat. In addition, accredited organizations can also submit proposals to initiate programs or activities to any appropriate body and attend meetings, at the discretion of the chairman, of any body that deals with matters of direct concern to them. Finally, accredited civil society organizations are allowed access to ASEAN documents on a selective basis, in consultation with the ASEAN Secretariat. Moreover, since 2001, ASEAN has organized the annual ASEAN People's Assembly. It is convened several days ahead of ASEAN summits and adopts a common statement of civil society organizations, which is then read to the heads of state during their summit. This practice was inaugurated in 2005 at the 11th ASEAN Summit in Kuala Lumpur.[44]

More recently, ASEAN Members adopted at their 2007 Summit the 'Blue Print for the ASEAN Economic Community', which devotes a paragraph to the 'involvement of stakeholders' in identifying measures to deepen economic integration in the ASEAN.[45] This paragraph sets the goal of 'creating public awareness' and details a set of actions, including the creation of a regional platform to 'share information in implementing the Community'.

3. European Union

Launched as an economic community, the European integration process has progressively evolved into a political union, thus achieving a high degree of integration in a wide range of policy areas. This explains why the EU institutional structure is elaborate compared to the regimes discussed above. Most importantly, the decision-making structure of the EU goes beyond the strictly member-driven character of other free trade regimes and comprises common institutions with powers independent from the member states: the European Commission, European Council, and the European Parliament. The European Commission initiates the law-making process, whereas the council and the parliament actually pass the laws. In addition, the commission is in charge of implementing EU law on behalf of the European Council. It does so through the 'Comitology' procedure, which must be distinguished from the commission's regular decision-making process, and for which specific rules of transparency and public participation rules apply.[46] Regarding enforcement, rulings of the European Court of Justice have progressively endowed EU law with supranational character, thus granting it direct effect.[47]

The as yet unimplemented European Constitutional Treaty will provide a constitutional basis for transparency and public participation in the European Union. A general 'Right to Transparency' is provided in Article 42, whereas Articles I-50, II-102, and III-399 further specify rights to access documents. In addition, a 'Right to Civil Society Participation' is provided at Article I-47, whose implementation, as authors have noted, would leave many questions open.[48] In practice, most mechanisms of public participation in the European Union relate to the European Commission, which consults interest groups through its directorates-general, the subdivisions that actually draft legislation. Among these mechanisms, EU Members have adopted a legal framework for access to information that grants enforceable rights to individuals.[49] Other institutionalized forms of public participation include the European Economic and Social Committee, which is composed of representatives of various civil society organizations that are nominated by EU member states and must be consulted before decisions are taken on economic and social policies.

In addition to this institutionalized framework of public participation, the European Commission has taken a number of steps to enhance transparency and public participation through *soft law* initiatives. In 2001, it adopted the 'White Paper on European Governance', which articulates principles of good governance relating to transparency (openness, participation, and accountability).[50] On this basis, the commission adopted in 2002 some principles and minimum standards for consulting external parties, which sought to create a common framework to the otherwise decentralized organization of its consultation with non-state actors.[51] As discussed above, these standards address the nature of documents to be provided, 'target groups' to be consulted, time frames for participation, requirements for feedback, and requirements that the results of consultations be published.[52] In practice, dialogue between the directorates-general and interested parties takes many forms, including the release of consultation papers (Green and White Papers), establishment of advisory committees and expert groups, organization of workshops, open hearings and forums, and combinations of these different tools at various phases of policy development. Moreover, online consultation is commonly used. As for the Comitology procedure, it is subject to a specific regime of document disclosure, which involves the 'Register of Comitology', where committees' agendas, draft implementing measures, records of committee meetings, and voting results of opinions delivered by committees are stored.[53] Further, the commission has created the 'Public Register of Commission Expert Groups', which lists both formal and informal groups, providing key information on them, including mention of the lead directorate-general to which they relate, the groups' tasks, and categories of participants. Finally, in 2008, the commission created a voluntary register for interest group representatives.

4. The Codex Alimentarius Commission

Established by the UN Food and Agriculture Organization (FAO) and the World Health Organization (WHO) in 1963, the Codex Alimentarius Commission (Codex Commission) and its subsidiary bodies are pursuing the adoption of international standards on food safety with the goal of 'protecting the health of the consumers and ensuring fair practices in the food trade',[54] thus contributing to the harmonization of the regulations of its 120 member states on the matter.

The elaboration process of standards takes place through several steps that involve two main bodies: the Codex Commission itself, where all member states are officially represented by their delegation, and the Executive Committee.[55] The latter is an organ of limited composition that acts on behalf of the Codex Commission between its sessions.[56] It may make proposals to the commission regarding general orientation, strategic planning, and programming of the work of the commission, and monitors the progress of standards development.

The standards adopted by the Codex Commission are of a voluntary nature.[57] However, the entry into force of the WTO SPS and TBT agreements, with their provisions on rule-referencing, has conferred a particular status on these standards, thereby increasing their authority.[58] This resulted in heightened scrutiny of their elaboration process and in the adoption by the Codex Commission in 1999 of a set of formal principles called the 'Principles Concerning the Participation of International Non-Governmental Organizations in the Work of the Codex Alimentarius Commission' (Principles on NGOs Participation).[59]

These principles provide for an observer status, granted to all international NGOs that have official status at either the FAO or the WHO, or that fulfil a number of criteria. Among these criteria, NGOs must have an international character, be 'representative of the specialized field of interest in which they operate', 'have aims and purposes in conformity with the Statutes of the Codex Alimentarius Commission', and 'have a permanent directing body and Secretariat, authorized representatives and systematic procedures and machinery for communicating with its membership in various countries. Its members shall exercise voting rights in relation to its policies or action or shall have other appropriate mechanisms to express their views.'[60]

NGOs with observer status are granted some privileges and are under certain obligations. Their privileges include an entitlement to send observers to sessions of the Codex Commission, to receive all its working documents and discussion papers in advance of the sessions, to circulate to the commission its views in writing, and to participate in discussions when invited by the chairperson. Among their obligations, NGOs shall 'contribute, as far as possible, and at the request of the Directors-General, to the promotion of a better knowledge and understanding of the Codex Alimentarius Commission and the Joint FAO/WHO Food Standards Programme', and 'send to the Secretary of the Commission on an exchange basis, its reports and publications concerned with matters covering all or part of the Commission's field of activity'.[61]

Whereas meetings of all Codex subsidiary bodies are open to the public,[62] it is important to note that no observer status is provided for meetings of the Codex Commission Executive Committee. A Codex Evaluation recommends filling this gap.[63] However member states, fearing that it would compromise the efficiency of the Executive Committee's proceedings, currently favour solutions that would increase transparency by webcasting the Executive Committee's proceedings.[64]

5. Transparency and Participation Mechanisms in Non-Trade Regimes— Examples of Multilateral Environment Agreements

NGOs' participation in the institutions established under multilateral environment agreements is fairly developed and regulated. As a general matter, most agreements adopted since the 1992 United Nations Conference on Environment and Development in Rio contain a provision prescribing that the Conference of the Parties should 'seek and utilize, where appropriate, the services and cooperation of, and information provided by, competent international organizations and non-governmental bodies' for the implementation of the relevant agreement.[65]

NGOs are usually granted observer status in the meetings of governing bodies under multilateral environment agreements after going through a process of accreditation. This process generally requires fulfilling two conditions.[66] First, NGOs must be 'qualified' in the subject matter of a particular treaty, which means that they either have specific competence or represent a broad constituency with an interest in the matter of the agreement. Second, accreditation must not be objected to by more than one-third of the states party to the convention. Some multilateral environment agreements set additional conditions. For example, the Convention on International Trade in Endangered Species of Wild Flora and Fauna (CITES) requires national NGOs to receive approval from their home government before being accredited and imposes a registration fee on them in order to address capacity problems (with a possibility of waiving the fee).

Some environment agreements allow NGOs to be granted enhanced status, which may entail additional benefits such as permanent observer and adviser status, as well as unconditional and unlimited access to meetings.[67] NGOs with preferential status are usually under enhanced obligations, such as having a global program of activities, a track record of project experience, a positive reputation, and contributing on a regular basis to the further development and application of the policies and technical and scientific tools of the convention at issue. Some NGOs are also charged with Secretariat functions, as in the case of CITES and the Ramsar Convention.

Rules of procedure governing NGOs participation under multilateral environment agreements usually apply to all subsidiary bodies of a regime's institutional structure. Regarding active participation in meetings, NGOs

> may, upon invitation of the President, participate without the right to vote in the proceedings of any meeting in matters of direct concern to the body or agency they represent unless at least one third of the Parties present at the meeting object.[68]

Usually, NGOs can make oral statement at the discretion of the chairman.

Regarding the sharing of information, some rules allow NGOs to submit documents to delegates by means of distribution by the Secretariat. This possibility doesn't imply, however, any formal rights that would create a procedural obligation for states to consider the documents. In addition, the Rules of Procedures of the Ramsar Convention allow the Secretariat to decide whether to issue as official documents those documents submitted by NGOs. The Rules of Procedures under CITES provide for the same possibility under more detailed conditions. As a general matter, secretariats usually have some discretion in synthesizing and integrating reports submitted to them by NGOs.

IV. Conclusion: Comments on the Comparative Analysis and Insights for the WTO

The comparative analysis above provides an overview of existing types of participatory mechanisms in international free trade and other international regimes. First, it can be observed that participation can occur through formal institutions that stand separate from a regime's actual decision-making procedures (the Economic and Social Councils in MERCOSUR and the European Union), or through direct links to decision-makers (access to committees).

With respect to the former, it is generally acknowledged that the advisory function of these councils has little influence on the final outcome of an organization's decisions. In the WTO context, if such an economic and social council were to be created as some commentators have proposed,[69] its Members would have to be entities with an international or regional character. Indeed, it appears that a system of membership based on nominations by each Member State at the national level, as it exists in MERCOSUR and the European Union, would not be achievable in a context that involves 150 Member States. This makes sense from the perspective of implementing mechanisms of public participation as a means to assert interests of a transnational nature.

Attendance by non-state actors at meetings where the substance of decisions is shaped (lower-level bodies) as well as the ability to submit information at these meetings appears to be more effective mechanisms for ensuring transparency and engagement in the decision-making process. In the WTO context, some have advocated for access by non-state actors to meetings of lower-level bodies.[70] In this respect, it can be noted that several WTO bodies have adopted provisions that regulate the granting of observer status to other international organizations.[71] These provisions could serve as templates if Members were to take the step of granting non-state actors access to WTO committees.

It can be observed that participatory opportunities in committees of the regimes surveyed above are often granted on a case-by-case basis at the discretion of the Members or a body's chairman. This leads to focus on one specific type of mechanism: judicial review. The comparative analysis shows that transparency and participation mechanisms are often based on *soft law* commitments, with no judicial review of their enforcement, with the exception of the EU legal framework for access to information.[72]

In the WTO context, judicial review could emerge as a mechanism of public participation in connection with the rule-referencing practice.[73] Reference in some cases to rules adopted by external organizations gives rise to a 'global separation of powers' model, under which WTO Panels and the Appellate Body have the possibility of performing a kind of judicial review, potentially involving requirements of public participation.[74]

Some authors have argued that the absence of such procedural review, which would parallel the one they can perform in relation to national regulatory processes under Article X of the GATT 1994, Article III of the GATS, or Article 63 of the TRIPS Agreement, creates a legitimacy issue.[75] Furthermore, some have argued that by performing such a review, dispute settlement organs, which are mindful of this legitimacy issue, would overcome their present reluctance to apply international standards, which in turn would give rise to increased policy coordination at the WTO that could be beneficial for the protection of social values.[76]

Such patterns of judicial review are discernable in the *European Communities—Trade Description of Sardines (Sardines)*, which offers a glimpse on how this mechanism could be further consolidated.[77] In this case, considering whether the international standard referred to by the claimant was a 'relevant international standard' according to Article 2.4 of the TBT Agreement, the panel held that 'relevance refers to the subject matter at issue, i.e., preserved sardines, and not to the temporal aspect of the international standard or procedural aspect of the adoption of the international standard'.[78] The panel went on, however, to consider the procedural arguments of the defendant. First, it responded to the argument that international standards must be based on consensus according to paragraph 2 of Annex 1 of the TBT Agreement and its explanatory note, concluding that consensus need not be achieved.[79] Second, it dismisses as a mere 'policy statement of preference' a decision of the TBT Committee relied on by the respondent that sets procedural requirements for the international standard-setting process.[80] Finally, it considered the argument of the respondent that the adoption of the standard at issue had violated the standard-setting organization's (in this case the Codex Alimentarius Commission) internal rules of procedure.[81]

It can be observed that the panel in *Sardines* is not impervious to the idea of reviewing the procedural aspects of international standards, since it did consider the procedural arguments of the respondent defendant. It simply concluded that these arguments were ill-founded in facts of the case. Indeed, the panel did take into account the Codex Commission's internal rules of procedure in concluding that they were not violated. As well, the panel seems to conceive that procedural requirements could be set by a committee decision but found that in this particular case the decision at issue does not formally constitute a legal basis. And finally, it considered the standard-setting process in the light of paragraph 2 of Annex 1 of the TBT Agreement but argues that this provision does not require consensus. Therefore, it appears that for dispute settlement bodies to perform a form of judicial review of the standard-setting process that could include requirements of public participation, some criteria would have to be adopted. The Appellate Body, for its part, seems unwilling to go down that path, having relied on the panel's interpretation of the TBT Agreement.[82] Therefore, Members would have to adopt such criteria, possibly in the form of a committee decision that would clearly state its binding character.

Notes

1 Among the early advocates of NGOs' direct involvement in WTO decision-making, see Daniel Esty, 'Non-Governmental Organizations at the World Trade Organization: Cooperation, Competition or Exclusion', 1 Journal of International Economic Law 123 (1998); Steve Charnovitz, 'Participation of Nongovernmental Organizations in the World Trade Organization', 17 University of Pennsylvania Journal of International Economic Law 331 (1996).

2 Some international documents implementing this latter approach have been recently adopted in the environmental field: see United Nations Economic Commission for Europe, Convention on Access to Information, Public Participation in Decision-Making and Access to Justice in Environmental Matters, Adopted June 25 1998 (Aarhus Convention); see also, in the WTO context, a proposal based on provisions of the Trade

Policy Review Mechanisms: Sylvia Ostry, 'What Are the Necessary Ingredients for the World Trading Order?', in Horst Siebert (ed), *Global Governance: An Architecture for the World Economy* (New York : Springer, 2003) 123–47.

3 See articles by Gregory Shaffer, 'Parliamentary Oversight of WTO Rule-Making: The Political, Normative, and Practical Contents', 7 (3) Journal of International Economic Law 629 (2004); David E. Skaggs, 'How Can Parliamentary Participation in WTO Rule-Making and Democratic Control be Made More Effective in the WTO?: A United States Congressional Perspective', 7 (3) Journal of International Economic Law 655 (2004); Erik Mann, 'A Parliamentary Dimension to the WTO—More Than Just a Vision?!', 7 (3) Journal of International Economic Law 659 (2004).

4 See a definition by Francesca Bignani, 'Three Generations of Participation Rights before the European Commission', 68 Law & Contemporary Problems 61 (2004), at 72: 'Transparency allows for scrutiny of public decision-making but leaves influence to existing political and legal mechanisms. Consultation is a specific form of political and, in some countries, judicially enforceable, influence through a formal and routine sequence of objections from interested parties and reasons and justifications from administrators.'

5 See a definition by Eric Stein, 'International Integration and Democracy: No Love at First Sight', 95 American Journal of International Law 489 (2001): 'Transparency entails openness of proceedings and access to official documents. It supports democracy by facilitating access to information that enables citizens to participate in public life, hold public authority accountable to public opinion, counter "a capture" of public institutions by special interests groups, enhance citizens' confidence in public authority, and improve the performance of public officials.'

6 Decision by the General Council, Procedures for the Circulation and De-restriction of WTO Documents, WT/L/452, dated 16 May 2002.

7 Decision by the General Council, Guidelines for Arrangements on Relations with Non-Governmental Organizations, WT/L/162, dated 23 July 1996.

8 These include Members' submissions for a renewable time at their request, the Secretariat's documents for a maximum of 90 days at the request of the body concerned, minutes of meetings of WTO bodies for a maximum of 45 days, and negotiations documents relating to accession and renegotiations of schedules until negotiations are concluded. Moreover, it is important to note that the notion of 'WTO official documents' refers to a categorization system that does not cover certain types of documents, which therefore remain restricted. Among those are informal documents produced by WTO bodies (labelled JOB), background papers issued by the Secretariat, ministerial conferences' preparatory documents, and draft agendas of forthcoming meetings of WTO bodies prepared by the Secretariat. John Jackson, who argues that this situation creates a transparency deficit, calls these undisclosed documents 'non-documents'; see John H. Jackson, *Sovereignty, the WTO and Changing Fundamentals of International Law* (New York: Cambridge University Press, 2006) 119.

9 See WTO, 'Annual Report 2007', at 60, http://www.wto.org/english/res_e/booksp_e/anrep_e/anrep07_e.pdf (visited 4 September 2008). See also Peter Van den Bossche in this volume.

10 The Appellate Body decided in *United States—Import Prohibition of Certain Shrimp and Shrimp Products (US-Shrimp)*, WT/DS58/AB/R, adopted 6 November 1998, that

panels are entitled to accept such briefs as part of their right to seek information in accordance with Article 13 of the Understanding on the Rules and Procedures Governing the Settlement of Disputes (DSU), WTO, *The Results of the Uruguay Round of Multilateral Trade Negotiations, the Legal Texts* (WTO: Geneva, 2003), 354.

11　This practice was initiated in 2005 at the request of the European Union, the United States, and Canada in *United States—Continued Suspension of Obligations in the EC (US—Continued Suspension)*, WT/DS/320, circulated 31 March 2008, and allows the public to watch the proceedings at WTO headquarters in Geneva via a live, closed-circuit broadcast. Other Members have perpetuated it since. Most recent cases whose proceedings were open to the public include *United States—Continued Existence and Application of Zeroing Methodology*, WT/DS/350, and *Australia—Measures Affecting the Importation of Apples from New Zealand*, WT/DS367.

12　On a theoretical framework made of the four 'implementation parameters', see Yves Bonzon, 'Institutionalizing Public Participation in WTO Decision-Making: Some Conceptual Hurdles and Avenues', 11 (4) Journal of International Economic Law 751 (2008).

13　WTO Panel Report, *European Communities—Trade Description of Sardines (Sardines)*, WT/DS231/R, adopted 29 May 2002.

14　A phenomenon described as 'regulatory shift'. Such policy coordination implies the adoption of 'behind the border' measures that take the form of disciplines, often referred to as *harmonization* or *positive integration*, that can potentially conflict with national values, and that at the same time exert a more direct effect on individuals. These disciplines are particularly sensitive in the areas of trade in services, environmental and health protection, sanitary measures, and intellectual property.

15　In practice, such an assessment according to democratic standards of legitimacy can be an issue when domestic courts decide on the possible direct applicability of WTO decisions; see Ernst-Ulrich Petersmann, 'Multilevel Trade Governance in the WTO Requires Multilevel Constitutionalism', in Christian Joerges and Ernst-Ulrich Petersmann (eds), *Constitutionalism, Multilevel Trade Governance and Social Regulation* (Portland: Hart, 2006) 51, and Mattias Kumm, 'The Legitimacy of International Law: A Constitutionalist Framework of Analysis', 15 European Journal of International Law 907 (2004).

16　The 'government-to-government' character of the WTO constitutes the second of John Jackson's seven mantras and, according to the author, should be thought through; see John H. Jackson, 'The WTO "Constitution" and Proposed Reforms: Seven "Mantras" Revisited', 4 Journal of International Economic Law 67 (2001), at 71. Some have referred to WTO Members' way of dealing with environmental matters to justify the claim that a strict member-driven mode of decision-making dominated by executive representation and only allowing participation through individual states' delegations cannot provide for adequate representation of transnational interests; they argue, for example, that members' delegations are unlikely to include experts in environmental matters given the predominance of trade ministers who most of the time act as coordinators in negotiations and tend to make their own ministry's interests prevail; see Ulrike Ehling, 'Environmental Policies and the WTO Committee on Trade and Environment: A Record of Failure?', in Joerges and Petersmann (eds), above n 15, at 437–57. See also Charnovitz, above n 1, who refers to members' handling of certain disputes and mentions cases where the U.S. trade representatives would withhold pro-environment arguments (in the Tuna-Dolphin case) for fear that the EU Commission would turn these arguments against him in subsequent cases. The author also shows how states' delegations can use panel disputes as a lever to influence domestic politics in a manner detrimental to the general interest (at 351).

17 See James Bacchus, 'A Few Thoughts on Legitimacy, Democracy, and the WTO', 7 (3) Journal of International Economic Law 667 (2004).

18 See Rudolf Adlung, 'GATS and Democratic Legitimacy', 59 Aussenwirtschaft 127 (2004).

19 See, for example, Consultative Board to the Director-General Supachai Panitchpakdi, *The Future of the WTO: Addressing Institutional Challenges in the New Millennium* (Geneva: WTO, 2004) in its chapter on sovereignty (Chapter III).

20 See Petersmann, in Joerges and Petersmann (eds), above n 15 (the author refers to the 'cosmopolitan conception of citizens in UN human rights law' at 23). UN Resolutions referred to include Resolution 2004/64 of the UN Commission on Human Rights, 'Promotion of a Democratic and Equitable International Order', E/CN4/2004/127, Adopted on 21 April 2004.

21 WTO, *The Results of the Uruguay Round of Multilateral Trade Negotiations,* 423.

22 Ibid, 284.

23 Ibid, 320.

24 See Steve Charnovitz, 'Transparency and Participation in the World Trade Organization', 56 Rutgers Law *Review* 927 (2004), at 942, who answers affirmatively the question as to 'whether the WTO's requirements for publication, notice and comment, and judicial review at the national level are relevant principles to be applied reflexively to the intergovernmental WTO', arguing further that the basis for the application of administrative law principles to the WTO is to be found in the fact that the WTO is in some respects similar to a domestic agency (at 944). In this context, transparency obligations are of a rather contractual nature, serving first and foremost to ensure the predictability of transactions and Member's compliance with their trade commitments.

25 In this context, it is conceived as an alternative, *process-oriented* approach to legitimacy that improves the acceptance of decisions through fair procedures; see Renaud Dehousse, 'Beyond Representative Democracy: Constitutionalism in a Polycentric Polity', in J. H. H. Weiler and Marlene Wind (eds), *European Constitutionalism Beyond the State* (New York: Cambridge University Press, 2003) 135–56. From that perspective, as the author argues, 'what matters is not that the eventual decision can be formally reduced to the will of the citizenry, but rather that those who so wish be given a chance to express their view' (at 156).

26 See Bignani, above n 4, who argues that public participation entails risks of 'interest capture', which should be checked by an elected body. The author also argues that it can take place only in a polity that shares common traditions of interests' representation, referring to differences, in the European case, between corporatist and pluralist traditions.

27 See Patricia Nanz and Jans Steffek, 'Global Governance, Participation and the Public Sphere', in David Held and Mathias Koenig-Archibugi (eds), *Global Governance and Public Accountability,* 39 (2) Government and Opposition 314 (2004); Rainer Nickel, 'Participatory Transnational Governance', in Joerges and Petersmann (eds), above n 15, at 157–98.

28 On the legitimization requirement's concept, see Markus Krajewski, *Verfassungsperspek-tiven und Legitimation des Rechts der Welthandelsorganisation (WTO)* (Berlin: Duncker & Humblot, 2001) 217. Political scientists have used the concept of 'legalization' to consider the impact of international regimes. See Judith Goldstein Miles Kahler, Robert O. Keohane, and Anne-Marie Slaughter, 'Introduction: Legalization and World Politics', 54 International Organization 385 (2000).

29 See Thomas Cottier, 'Preparing for Structural Reform in the WTO', 10 Journal of International Economic Law 497 (2007), at 503; focusing on the WTO, the author applies the concept in a broad perspective that doesn't solely relate to normative concerns of legitimacy, but also to functional aspects. Further on the substance-structure pairing concept, see Thomas Cottier, 'Constitutional Trade Regulation in National and International Law: Structure-Substance Pairings in the EFTA Experience', in Meinhard Hilf and Ernst-Ulrich Petersmann (eds), *National Constitutions and International Economic Law* (Boston: Kluwer, 1993), 409–42.

30 This is stressed by Philip M. Nichols, 'Realism, Liberalism, Values and the World Trade Organization', 17 Pennsylvania Journal of International Economic Law 851 (1996).

31 According to the rule-referencing practice, the WTO dispute settlement organs may in some cases refer to rules adopted outside the institutional framework of the organization as the basis of their decisions. These rules, such as those adopted by the Codex Alimentarius Commission, become therefore a relevant object of public participation in the WTO context.

32 See MERCOSUR, 'Olivos Protocol for the Settlement of Disputes in MERCOSUR', done at Olivos, 18 February 2002; English translation, http://www.mercosur.int/msweb/portal%20intermediario/es/index.htm (visited 4 September 2008).

33 Institutions of Mercosur are established by the Ouro Preto Protocol ('Additional Protocol to the Treaty of Asuncion, on the Institutional Structure of MERCOSUR') (POP), signed on 17 December 1994 by Argentina, Uruguay, Brazil, and Paraguay.

34 On the influence of heads of state's participation, see H. Moavro, 'Nuevas Articulationes de Los Actores Sociales en el Mercosur: el Caso de los Sindicatos', in Alma Espino (ed), MERCOSUR: *Los Desafı´os de la Integracio´n: Trabajo, Participacio´n y Ambiente* (Montevideo, Uruguay: Red de Apoyo a Organizaciones Sociales del Mercosur 1998).

35 .The forum's internal regulation solely states that there must be parity of representation between labour and business organizations. See Reglamento Interno del Foro Consultivo Economico Social, MERCOSUR/GMC/RES No. 68/96.

36 See Celina Pena and Ricardo Rozemberg, 'MERCOSUR: A Different Approach to Institutional Development', FOCAL Policy Paper FPP-05-06 (2005), at 4.

37 Protocolo Constitutivo del Parlamento del MERCOSUR, MERCOSUR/CPC/CP ACTA No. /05.

38 See ASEAN Protocol on Enhanced Dispute Settlement Mechanism, done at Vientiane, 29 November 2004, http://www.aseansec.org/4924.htm (visited 4 September 2008).

39 See Paul J. Davidson, *ASEAN: The Evolving Legal Framework for Economic Cooperation* (Singapore: Times Academic Press, 2002).

40 Ministerial bodies in charge of trade (implementation of the Common Exterior Preferential Tariff Agreement) that consult with the ASEAN-CCI include the Economic Ministers and Senior Economic Officials Meeting.

41 As regards other civil society organizations, it has been criticized that these are widely excluded from the Track Two policy dialogues and isolated in a 'Track Three' layer, having to rely on Track Two academic think-tanks to find 'entry-points' and to 'bridge the gap' with Track One officials. See Michael Chai, 'Civil Society Making Headway in the Association of Southeast Asian Nations', 7(2) The Social Development Review (2003), http://www.icsw.org/publications/sdr/2003_dec/Commentary3.html (visited 4 September 2008).

42 See ASEAN, 'Guidelines on ASEAN's Relations with Civil Society Organizations (CSOs)', 3 April 2006, http://www.aseansec.org/18362.htm (visited 4 September 2008).

43 See ASEAN, 'Charter of the Association of Southeast Asian Nations', 20 November 2007. Article 16, http://www.aseansec.org/21069.pdf (visited 3 September 2008) (giving competence to the Committee of Permanent Representatives to enact 'rules of procedure and criteria for engagement' upon the recommendation of the secretary-general of ASEAN).

44 The 2007 statement emphasized the need for institutional reforms regarding consultation, including better accreditation procedures in order for ASEAN's engagement with civil society organizations to be on par with business and other groups, and the appointment of a senior office holder to specifically liaise with CSOs as a focal point for the ASEAN Secretariat and member countries. See ASEAN, Civil Society Conference, 'Chairman's Statement', 26–28 October 2007, para 15, http://www.siiaonline.org/?q=news/asean-civil-societyconference-%E2%80%93-october-26-28-2007 (visited 3 September 2008).

45 See ASEAN, 'Declaration on the ASEAN Economic Community Blueprint' ('Communication'), 20 November 2007, at 21, http://www.aseansec.org/21083.pdf (visited 4 September 2008).

46 See Council Decision of 28 June 1999 laying down the procedures for the exercise of implementing powers conferred on the commission (1999/468/EC; OJ L 184/23 of 17.7.1999) (Comitology Decision).

47 The supranational nature of EU law was defined by the European Court of Justice (ECJ), Case 26-62, *Van Gend & Loos v. Netherlands* (1963) ECR 1: 'EC law constitutes a new legal order of international law for the benefit of which the States have limited their sovereign rights, albeit within limited fields, and the subjects of which comprise not only Member States but also their nationals.'

48 See Bignami, above n 4, at 81.

49 See Regulation (EC) No 1049/2001 of the European Parliament and of the Council of 30 May 2001 regarding public access to European Parliament, Council and Commission documents, OJ/L/145/43.

50 COM(2001) 428, July 2001.

51 See Council Decision of 28 June 1999 laying down the procedures for the exercise of implementing powers conferred on the Commission (1999/468/EC; OJ L 184/23 of 17.7.1999) at 16 (Comitology Decision).

52 Regarding time frames, these consultation standards are to be applied at the policy-shaping phase of major proposals and thus do not apply to the formal stages of decision-making as prescribed in the treaty and in other EU legislations. In particular, the exercise of the commission's implementing powers with the assistance of 'Comitology' committees referred to above is excluded.

53 See Register of Comitology of the European Commission: http://ec.europa.eu/ transparency/regcomitology/registre.cfm?CL=en (visited 28 September 2008).

54 See Article 1 (a) of the Statutes of the Codex Alimentarius Commission, World Health Organization (WHO) and the Food and Agricultural Organization (FAO), *Codex Alimentarius Commission Procedural Manual*, 18th ed. (Rome, 2008) 4, ftp://ftp.fao.org/ codex/Publications/ProcManuals/Manual_18e.pdf (visited 9 April 2009).

55 Interestingly, Rule I(4) of the Rules of Procedure of the Codex Commission states that '[e]ach Member of the Commission shall communicate to the Director-General of FAO or of WHO the names of its representative and where possible other members of its delegation before the opening of each session of the Commission', ibid., at 6.

56 See Rule V(2) of the Rules of Procedure of the Codex Commission, ibid, 9.

57 See 'Nature of Standards' of the General Principles of the Codex Alimentarius: 'Codex standards and related texts are not a substitute for, or alternative to national legislation. Every country's laws and administrative procedures contain provisions with which it is essential to comply', ibid, 17.

58 See the Agreement on the Application of Sanitary and Phytosanitary Measures (SPS Agreement), and the Agreement on Technical Barriers to Trade (TBT Agreement), WTO, *The Results of the Uruguay Round of Multilateral Trade Negotiations*, 59 and 121.

59 These principles add to Rule IX(6) of the Rules of Procedures of the Codex Commission, which provides that participation of international non-governmental organizations in the work of the commission shall be governed by applicable regulations of FAO or WHO on relations with international non-governmental organizations, above n 54, at 12.

60 Ibid, at 25.

61 Ibid, at 27–28.

62 Ibid, at 55.

63 See WHO and FAO, 'Evaluation of the Codex Alimentarius and Other FAO and WHO Food Standards Work', 15 November 2002, http://www.codexalimentarius.net/web/ evaluation_en.jsp (visited 18 November 2008).

64 See Thorsten Huller and Matthias Leonard Maier, 'Fixing the Codex?: Global Food-Safety Governance Under Review', in Jeorges and Petersmann, above n 15, 267–300, at 278.

65 For example, Article 7 para. 2(1) of the UN Framework Convention on Climate Change (UNFCCC), done at New York, 9 May 1992, FCCC/INFORMAL/84, http://unfccc.int/ resource/docs/convkp/conveng.pdf (visited 9 April 2009); Article 13 para. 4(i) of the Kyoto Protocol to the UNFCCC (Kyoto Protocol), adopted 11 December 1997, http://unfccc.int/resource/docs/convkp/kpeng.html (visited 9 April 2009); Article 29 para 4(c) of the Cartagena Protocol on Biosafety to the Convention on Biological Diversity (Biosafety Protocol), done at Montreal, on 29 January 2000, http://www.cbd.int/ doc/legal/cartagena-protocol-en.pdf (visited 9 April 2009).

66 For example, Article 7, para 6 of the UNFCCC; Article 13, para 8 of the Kyoto Protocol; Article 29 para 8 of the Biosafety Protocol.

67 Seventh Meeting of the Conference of the Contracting Parties to the Convention on Wetlands, Resolution VII.3: Partnerships with international organizations, San José, Costa Rica, 10–18 May 1999, http://www.ramsar.org/res/key_res_vii.03e.htm (visited 9 April 2009) (defining the category of 'International Partner Organization').

68 Rule 7 of the Rules of Procedures of the UN Framework Convention on Climate Change (UNFCCC).

69 See Steve Charnovitz, 'The WTO and Cosmopolitics', 7 Journal of International Economic Law 675 (2005), at 689.

70 Ibid., at 689. See also a submission paper by the United States issued in 2000 suggesting that some meetings of WTO bodies be opened to observers, with the opportunity for them to make written submissions: General Council, Informal Consultation on External Transparency, Submission from the United States, WT/GC/W/413/Rev., October 2000.

71 See, for example, Committee on Sanitary and Phytosanitary Measures, Consideration of Requests for Observer Status, G/SPS/W/98, 19 February 1999.

72 In accordance with the structure-substance pairing concept referred to above (or the degree of legitimization requirement concept), this latter feature is explained by the supranational character of EU law.

73 Article 2:4 TBT Agreement and Article 3:1 SPS Agreement prescribe that Members should take relevant international standards as a basis for their regulations. By virtue of this 'rule-referencing' practice, rules adopted by external organizations may in some cases constitute a legal basis for dispute settlement decisions. On international standards acquiring legal force by virtue of rule-referencing, see Robert Howse, 'A New Device for Creating International Legal Normativity: The WTO Technical Barriers to Trade Agreement and "International Standards"', in Jeorges and Petersmann (eds), above n 15, 383–96.

74 See Robert B. Stewart, 'U.S. Administrative Law: A Model for Global Administrative Law', IILJ Working Paper Global Administrative Law Series Number 7, New York University (2005), at 40.

75 These authors argue that, as sole conditions set in the agreements for standards to be taken into consideration, the standards-setting body that adopted them must either be listed in the agreements or be open to the participation of all members, without further requirement regarding its composition and mode of functioning. See Harm Schepel, 'The Empire's Drains: Sources of Legal Recognition of Private Standardisation under the TBT Agreement', in Jeorges and Petersmann (eds), above n 15, 397–412, at 409; Joost Pauwelyn, 'Non-traditional Patterns of Global Regulation: Is the WTO 'Missing the Boat'?', in: Jeorges and Petersmann (eds), ibid, 199–227.

76 See Joanne Scott, 'International Trade and Environmental Governance: Relating Rules (and Standards) in the EU and the WTO', 15 European Journal of International Law 307 (2004), at 310 and 330.

77 WT/DS231.

78 WTO Panel Report, ibid, at para 7.71.

79 Ibid, at para 7.89.

80 Ibid, at para 7.91.

81 Ibid, at para 7.95.

82 WTO Appellate Body, above 77, at 227. Deciding that the TBT Agreement does not require consensus in the international standard-setting process, the Appellate Body further makes clear that it is not for them to impose any further procedural requirement: '[Our] conclusion […] is not intended to affect, in any way, the internal requirements that international standard-setting bodies may establish for themselves

for the adoption of standards within their respective operations. In other words, the fact that we find that the TBT Agreement does not require approval by consensus for standards adopted by the international standardization community should not be interpreted to mean that we believe an international standardization body should not require consensus for the adoption of its standards. That is not for us to decide.'

Non-Governmental Organizations and the WTO: Limits to Involvement?

PETER VAN DEN BOSSCHE*

I. Introduction

The importance of non-governmental organizations (NGOs) as international actors has increased sharply over the last decades. Since 1945, when NGOs were explicitly recognized as actors on the international scene by Article 71 of the United Nations Charter, NGOs have become an ever stronger and more vocal force in international policy-making, policy implementation, compliance monitoring, and dispute settlement. The interest and involvement of NGOs in the activities of international organizations have especially intensified since the early 1990s. Currently, a continuously growing number of NGOs participate or aspire to participate in the work of international organizations. Many observers would agree with K. Raustiala that 'this growth of NGO activity may indicate an emerging transformation of the international legal and political system—a decline in the importance of the sovereign state and the state system and an accompanying rise of governance by a dynamic global civil society'.[1]

The most important reason for the empowerment of NGOs on the international plane is the phenomenon of globalization and the growing need to find global solutions for global problems. This has led governments to engage in more negotiation, policy formation, and decision-making at the international level. More often than not, these activities at the international level have significant effects on domestic policy and legislation. In a number of fields, there has, in fact, been a shift in regulatory activity from the national to the international level. Consequently, many NGOs, which were formerly national in focus and organizational structure, have 'internationalized' in order to maintain their ability to participate in the policy debate and affect policy decisions.[2]

The Cardoso Report of 2004, on the relationship between the United Nations and civil society, reports, 'Representative democracy, in which citizens periodically elect their representatives across the full spectrum of political issues, is now supplemented by participatory democracy, in which anyone can enter the debates that most interest them, through advocacy, protest and in other ways.'[3] People are using internationally operating NGOs to express their political views and/or promote their interests. Effective involvement in—and influence over— the policy-making, policy implementation, compliance monitoring, and dispute settlement activities of international organizations is a chief objective—if not the raison d'être—of international NGOs.

International NGOs have been keen to be involved in the activities of the World Trade Organization (WTO). As the primary international organization concerned with trans-border trade, the WTO is at the forefront of the multilateral effort to manage and regulate economic globalization. The law of the WTO governs the trade relations between its 153 Members and plays a crucial role in resolving trade disputes between these Members. Not surprisingly, the WTO has emerged as a prime target for anti-globalization protests. When Mike Moore arrived at the headquarters of the World Trade Organization in the summer 1999 to begin his first day of work as the WTO's new Director-General, he was welcomed by a small but noisy group of demonstrators. One of the demonstrators waved a sign saying, 'Dieu est mort, l'OMC l'a remplacé!' ('God is dead; the WTO has replaced him!'). Another sign said, 'Qui sème la misère récolte la colère!' ('He who sows misery will reap anger'), and a third sign said, 'WTO = World Terror Organization.' This small demonstration was a sign of things to come. A few months later, the WTO Ministerial Conference in Seattle triggered large-scale demonstrations that degenerated into street battles between the police and protestors. Since Seattle, there have been several other mass demonstrations against the WTO, in particular on the occasions of the biannual sessions of the WTO Ministerial Conference. As Guy de Jonquières observed, this 'interest' in the WTO reflects 'growing public awareness—but often imperfect understanding—of its role in promoting, and formulating rules for, global economic integration'.[4]

This chapter examines the nature and the extent of the involvement of NGOs in the activities of the WTO. First, it looks at the arguments for and against NGO involvement in WTO activities. Next, the article discusses the legal basis for the involvement of NGOs in WTO activities and the various forms of involvement provided for. It compares the position of NGOs in the WTO with their position in other international organizations, in particular, the United Nations, the World Intellectual Property Organization (WIPO), and the International Monetary Fund (IMF). Subsequently, the article explores the practice of WTO engagement with NGOs. Finally, it examines and compares the rules and procedures of the WTO, the United Nations, WIPO, and the IMF for the selection/accreditation of the NGOs with which they engage.

II. Arguments For and Against NGO Involvement

While not always wholeheartedly, international organizations have responded positively to the call of NGOs for more involvement and currently allow—to different degrees and in different ways—NGOs to participate in their activities. This has also been the case for the WTO. However, the debate on the desirability of (greater) involvement of NGOs in the work of the WTO is far from settled.

There are four main *arguments in favour* of (greater) NGO involvement in WTO activities (as well as in the activities of most other international organizations). First, NGO participation will enhance the WTO decision-making process because NGOs will provide information, arguments, and perspectives that governments do not bring forward. Many NGOs have a wealth of specialized knowledge, resources, and analytical capacity. As Daniel Esty noted, NGOs can and should function as 'intellectual competitors' to governments in the quest for optimal policies.[5] In fact, governments often lack the resources and very specific expertise necessary to investigate certain issues. NGOs may frequently be able to assist, enhancing the resources and expertise available and enriching the policy debate.

Second, NGO participation will increase the legitimacy of the WTO. In the eyes of many, the WTO is currently a secretive organization in which the governments (of a few major trading nations), unsupervised by parliaments or civil society, set the agenda and push through rules that affect the welfare of people worldwide. WTO decision-making has been described as undemocratic and lacking in transparency. For decision-making to be democratic, it must involve either directly, or through representation, those who will be affected by the decisions taken. Furthermore, decisions must be reached as a result of an open and transparent exchange of rational arguments, which allows those represented to 'watch-dog' the representatives.[6] The legitimacy of the WTO and public confidence in the WTO will increase when NGOs have the opportunity to be heard and to observe the decision-making process. NGOs will contribute to ensuring that decisions result from an open exchange of rational arguments rather than from shady bargaining. Moreover, NGOs can play an important role in disseminating information at the national level, ensuring broader public support and understanding.

Third, transnational interests and concerns may not be adequately represented by any national government. By allowing NGO involvement in WTO discussions, the WTO would hear about important issues that are international in nature.

Finally, civil society participation in the debate at the national level is an option only in those WTO Members with open and democratic processes at the national level. This is not the case for all WTO Members. Hearing NGOs at the WTO can thus compensate for the fact that NGOs are not always heard at the national level in every country.

There are equally four main *arguments against* (greater) involvement of NGOs in the work of the WTO. First, NGO involvement may lead the decision-making process to be captured by special interests.[7] Trade liberalization produces diffuse and hard-to-quantify benefits for the general public, while producing visible harm to specific and well-organized interests. The NGOs seeking access to the WTO are often entities representing special interests, not the interests of the general public. Thus special interests may gain undue influence.

Second, many NGOs lack legitimacy. They are neither accountable to an electorate nor representative in a general way. NGOs typically advocate relatively narrow interests. Unlike governments, they do not balance all of society's interests. It is legitimate to ask questions regarding the actual constituency of an NGO and its financial backing.

Third, most developing-country Members object to greater involvement of NGOs in the WTO because they view most NGOs, and in particular NGOs focusing on environmental or labour issues, as inimical to their interests at their current level of economic development. Moreover, NGOs of industrialized Members tend to be well organized and well financed. It is feared that allowing NGOs a bigger role may therefore further marginalize developing-country Members within the WTO decision-making process. In other words, it may tilt the negotiating balance further to the disadvantage of developing countries.

Finally, WTO decision-making, with its consensus requirement, is already very difficult. NGO involvement will make negotiations and decision-making even more difficult. Further transparency will enable private interest groups to frustrate the negotiating powers of governments in WTO forums. Gary Sampson noted, in this respect, that 'national representatives must on occasion subordinate certain national interests in order to achieve marginally acceptable or sub-optimal compromises that, by definition, require trade-offs. Doubt is expressed whether such a system could continue to work effectively if these trade-offs were open to scrutiny by precisely those special interest groups that would have opposed them'.[8]

The essence of the debate over (greater) NGO involvement in international organizations was captured well by the authors of the Background Paper for the Cardoso Report when they concluded that 'well handled' involvement of NGOs in the policy-deliberation and decision-making processes of international organizations 'enhances the quality of decision-making, increases ownership of the decisions, improves accountability and transparency of the process and enriches outcomes through a variety of views and experiences'.[9] However, 'handled badly, it can confuse choices, hamper the intergovernmental search for common ground, erode the privacy needed for sensitive discussions, over-crowd agendas and present distractions at important meetings'.[10]

The remainder of this chapter will examine how the WTO 'handles' the involvement of NGOs in its activities and will compare this 'handling' with that of other international organizations.

III. Legal Basis for and Forms of NGO Involvement

A. Involvement in the WTO

The Marrakesh Agreement Establishing the World Trade Organization (WTO Agreement)[11] explicitly empowers the WTO to engage with NGOs. Article V:2 of the WTO Agreement provides:

> The General Council may make appropriate arrangements for consultations and cooperation with non-governmental organizations concerned with matters related to those of the WTO.

Such explicit authority to engage with NGOs can also be found in the UN Charter. Article 71 of the UN Charter states:

> The Economic and Social Council may make suitable arrangements for consulta-tion with non-governmental organizations which are concerned with matters within its competence.

The constituent instruments of other international organizations, such as WIPO, the United Nations Conference on Trade and Development (UNCTAD), and the International Labour Organization (ILO) explicitly provide for engagement with NGOs. However, the constituent instruments of two international organ-izations with which the WTO has particularly close links and a shared respon-sibility for coherence in global economic policy-making,[12] namely the IMF and the International Bank for Reconstruction and Development (World Bank), do not provide an explicit legal basis for NGO involvement. While this has not prevented the World Bank and the IMF from engaging with NGOs,[13] it is to be applauded that the WTO was explicitly empowered to engage with NGOs.

The 1948 Havana Charter on the International Trade Organization (ITO) con-tained a provision with wording similar to Article V:2 of the WTO Agreement.[14] The ITO, however, never became operational, and the 1947 General Agreement on Tariffs and Trade (GATT) filled the gap left by the ITO for almost 50 years. The

GATT, by contrast, did not have any provision on cooperation with NGOs. Under the GATT, informal and ad hoc contact existed with NGOs.[15] However, NGOs were denied access to meetings and conferences. That was also the case for the Marrakesh Conference in April 1994, at which the WTO Agreement was signed.[16]

Pursuant to the mandate given to it in Article V:2 of the WTO Agreement, the General Council of the WTO adopted in 1996 the 'Guidelines for Arrangements on Relations with Non-Governmental Organizations' (the 1996 Guidelines).[17] In this one-page document, Members recognized that NGOs can play a role in increasing 'the awareness of the public in respect of WTO activities' and that NGOs are a 'valuable resource' that can 'contribute to the accuracy and richness of the public debate'.[18] In the 1996 Guidelines, it was agreed that interaction with NGOs should be developed through the organization of symposia for NGOs on specific WTO-related issues; informal arrangements to circulate among interested Members' position papers and information that NGOs may wish to make available; the continuation of the practice of the WTO Secretariat of responding to requests for general information and briefings about the WTO; and participation of chairpersons of WTO councils and committees, in their personal capacity, in discussions and meetings with NGOs.[19]

The 1996 Guidelines also made the limits of NGO involvement clear. In the concluding paragraph, the General Council referred to the special character of the WTO, which is both an intergovernmental organization based on a binding treaty of rights and obligations among its Members *and* a forum for negotiations. The General Council then concluded:

> As a result of extensive discussions, there is currently a broadly held view that it would not be possible for NGOs to be directly involved in the work of the WTO or its meetings.[20]

To this, the General Council added:

> Closer consultation and cooperation with NGOs can also be met constructively through appropriate processes at the national level where lies primary responsibility for taking into account the different elements of public interest which are brought to bear on trade policy-making.[21]

While Article V:2 of the WTO Agreement allows the General Council to provide for full-fledged involvement of NGOs in WTO activities, the General Council opted in 1996 to direct the main responsibility for engaging with civil society to the national level. Furthermore, the General Council instructed only the WTO Secretariat to engage with NGOs and effectively barred NGOs from participation in the activities of WTO bodies. While the legal basis in the WTO Agreement is broad enough to allow for this, NGOs do not have consultative status in any WTO bodies.

B. Involvement in the UN ECOSOC

Although Article V:2 of the WTO Agreement and Article 71 of the UN Charter are similarly worded,[22] there is a significant difference in how the United Nations and the WTO approach engagement with NGOs. Unlike the WTO, the United Nations, and in particular the UN Economic and Social Council (ECOSOC), has seized the opportunity to provide for forms of significant involvement of NGOs. Pursuant to the mandate given to ECOSOC in Article 71 of the UN Charter, on 25 July 1996 it adopted Resolution 1996/31 on the 'Consultative Relationship between the United Nations and Non-Governmental Organizations'.[23] This instrument is much more elaborate and provides for notably broader NGO involvement than the 1996 Guidelines. Resolution 1996/31 provides for the granting of 'consultative status' to NGOs. There are three types of such status: general consultative status, special consultative status, and inclusion on the roster.[24] Each type of status corresponds with a different bundle of rights. An NGO in general consultative status

- is informed of the provisional agenda of the Economic and Social Council and may propose to the Council Committee on Non-governmental Organizations (NGO committee) that the committee request the UN secretary-general to place items of special interest on the provisional agenda of the council;[25]
- may orally present to the council introductory statements of an expository nature on items included on the council's agenda at the proposal of the NGO;[26]
- may sit as an observer at public meetings of the council and its subsidiary bodies;[27]
- may submit written statements with a maximum of 2,000 words for circulation to the Members of the council;[28] and
- may make oral statements to the council (at the recommendation of the NGO committee and subject to the approval of the council).[29]

NGOs in special consultative status enjoy some of the same rights granted to NGOs in general consultative status.[30] However, they cannot propose items for the agenda of the council, nor can they make oral statements at meetings of the council.[31] They may, however, speak at meetings of the council's subsidiary bodies that deal with subject matters of specific interest to them.[32] Lastly, NGOs on the roster are informed of the provisional agenda of the council and may attend the meetings of the council and its subsidiary bodies concerned with matters within their field of competence.[33] NGOs on the roster are consulted at the request of the council or its subsidiary bodies.[34] Resolution 1996/31 authorizes NGOs in any type of consultative status to confer with officers of the UN Secretariat, and vice versa.[35] Additionally, the Secretary-General is authorized to offer facilities to NGOs in any type of consultative status, including access to UN grounds; facilities (including conference space) and UN press documentation services; and arrangements for informal discussion on topics of special interest.[36] Even the least-privileged category of NGOs interacting with the council (the category of 'NGOs on the roster') has significantly more 'participation' rights than are granted to NGOs under the 1996 Guidelines of the WTO General Council.

C. Involvement in WIPO

As mentioned above, the constituent instrument of the WIPO explicitly provides—as do the UN Charter and the WTO Agreement—for engagement with NGOs. Article 13(2) of the Convention Establishing the World Intellectual Property Organization, 1967 provides that

> [t]he Organization may, on matters within its competence, make suitable arrangements for consultations and cooperation with international non-governmental organizations and, with the consent of the Governments concerned, with national organizations, governmental or non-governmental.[37]

Article 13(2) of the WIPO Convention provides moreover that the arrangements for consultation and cooperation with NGOs shall be made by the WIPO Director-General after approval by the Coordination Committee, WIPO's executive organ.

NGOs may be involved in WIPO policy deliberations by taking part in meetings of WIPO bodies. To enable NGOs to attend and participate in meetings of WIPO bodies, WIPO may grant to NGOs permanent observer status or may accredit them, on an ad hoc basis, to a particular WIPO body or for a particular event or series of meetings.[38] Other forms of WIPO–NGO relations include NGO meetings with WIPO staff to exchange views and information on particular issues of interest to NGOs. Such meetings are not regular but they take place at least once a year and are usually organized at the request of NGOs.[39] In 2005 WIPO also organized, for the first time, a large interactive meeting with NGOs where more than 500 organizations were invited (permanent and ad hoc observers). The purpose of the meeting was to debrief NGOs about WIPO activities in the preceding year, as well as to listen to the concerns of NGOs and their proposals for further cooperation. However, the meeting did not arouse a lot of interest in the NGO community, with only about 25 organizations actually attending.[40]

WIPO can grant to NGOs an observer status of two types. First, NGOs can become permanent observers. Second, they can be accredited as ad hoc observers to a particular WIPO body (for example, a standing committee) or for an event or series of meetings (for example, for intersessional intergovernmental meetings). There is no difference, with regard to participatory rights, between permanent and ad hoc NGO observers when they are present at a particular meeting. The difference lies only in the scope of meetings they can attend. Naturally, ad hoc observers can attend only those meetings, or meetings of those WIPO bodies, to which they are accredited. By contrast, permanent NGO observers enjoy a standing invitation to many more—although not all—WIPO meetings.[41]

To date, 202 international and 31 national NGOs enjoy permanent observer status with WIPO.[42] To give some examples, international NGOs include the Afro-Asian Book Council, the Association of Commercial Television in Europe, International Anti-Counterfeiting Coalition, Inc., International Association for the Protection of Industrial Property, International Federation of Industrial Property Attorneys, and the International Trademark Association. The national NGOs with permanent observer status include, for example, the American Association for the Advancement of Science and the South African Institute of Intellectual Property Law.[43]

As a matter of practice, NGOs with permanent observer status, whether national or international, are admitted to the following meetings without an additional invitation:

- All WIPO assemblies;
- Diplomatic conferences convened under the auspices of WIPO;
- Intersessional intergovernmental meetings;
- The annual WIPO conference;
- Standing and other committees;
- Working groups.[44]

As reflected in the above list, once an international NGO is admitted to attend, as an observer, the meetings of the Assemblies of the Member States of WIPO, it is also invited to attend, as an observer, meetings of committees, working groups, or other bodies subsidiary to the assemblies, 'if their subject matter seems to be of direct interest to that organization.'[45] For all meetings that NGOs are eligible to attend, WIPO sends out invitations to each and every NGO by mail.

Meetings that remain closed to NGOs with permanent observer status are meetings of the WIPO Coordination Committee and of Executive Committees for Paris and Berne Conventions. Neither can NGOs be accredited to these meetings on an ad hoc basis. Furthermore, regarding NGOs without permanent observer status, ad hoc accreditation is *not* possible for sessions of the assemblies, for diplomatic conferences, or meetings of the WIPO Conference.[46]

WIPO General Rules of Procedure do not contain detailed norms on modalities of NGO participation in WIPO meetings. Its only relevant provision, Rule 24, states:

(1) Observers may take part in debates at the invitation of the Chairman.
(2) They may not submit proposals, amendments or motions.

Rule 24(2) has been interpreted as not precluding NGOs from circulating any other written statements to delegates of Member States. Thus, admitted NGOs have the following rights:

- To attend the meeting;
- To make oral statements (at the invitation of the chairman). Oral statements can also be made on behalf of groups of NGOs. Requests for permission to make an oral statement are usually forwarded to the chairperson in advance of the meeting, and;
- To circulate written statements to representatives of the Member States, before or after the meeting (directly to delegates and not through the Secretariat).[47]

D. Involvement in the IMF

As mentioned above, the constituent instrument of the IMF—the 1944 Articles of Agreement of the International Monetary Fund—does not provide for cooperation with NGOs. Article X of the IMF Articles of Agreement, entitled 'Relations with Other International Organizations', only refers to 'general' and 'public' international organizations. It does not refer to non-governmental organizations. While relations with NGOs are not explicitly provided for in its constituent instrument and the IMF has moreover no biding secondary rules on engagement with NGOs, the IMF does maintain relations with NGOs or—in IMF parlance—civil society organizations.[48] A non-binding policy document—the Guide for Staff Relations with Civil Society Organizations (the Guide)[49]—offers a general framework of good practices.[50]

The IMF started to engage with civil society in the 1980s in response to advocacy at the global level by groups concerned with economic and social justice. Such engagement remains central in IMF–NGO relations.[51] However, until the mid-1990s, the IMF attracted only limited and sporadic attention from NGOs, most prominently in countries implementing adjustment policies with IMF support. The civil society opposition to the IMF intensified in the latter half of the 1990s, particularly in the context of structural adjustment policies, multilateral debt problems, and financial market crises in Asia, Latin America, and Russia.[52] Still, the overall extent of IMF engagement of civil society remains modest today, much less developed than, for example, in the World Bank, as discussed below. Generally, the IMF's position is that it is accountable primarily to the governments of its member countries (as opposed to society at large). For this reason, as explained in the *Guide,* the IMF sees its member governments as primarily responsible for dialogue with civil society organizations. IMF contacts with civil society organizations are deemed a supplement to, and not a substitute for, government dialogue with citizen groups.[53] The IMF does not have a permanent institutional arrangement for consultations with NGOs. All interactions with civil society organizations occur on an ad hoc basis. This entails a considerable difference in practices across countries, departments, and policy settings.[54]

The IMF asserts that it seeks to engage with civil society organizations through information sharing, dialogue, and consultation at both global and national levels.[55] The majority of contacts take place at the IMF headquarters in Washington, D.C., thus Washington-based organizations find themselves in a privileged position.[56] According to the *Guide,* the IMF engages with civil society because such engagement can correct misunderstandings, improve policy content, and enhance the political viability of IMF advice.[57] The IMF acknowledges that although the dialogue with civil society organizations has gradually improved, there remains dissatisfaction on both sides, possibly even a degree of mutual mistrust.[58] Some civil society organizations tend to think that the IMF preaches, does not listen, and does not integrate civil society organization input from the dialogue into its policy-making.[59] As reported in 2001, civil society organizations have frequently characterized the IMF as an unapproachable, secretive, and undemocratic organization that is resistant to public opinion and participation.[60] At the same time, some IMF staff may perceive civil society organizations as generally being interested mainly in pushing their own agenda, often imprecisely defined, and believe that civil society organizations often lack broad support, legitimacy, and accountability.[61]

Principal organs of the IMF are closed to civil society participation. NGOs are not allowed to attend the meetings of the Executive Board, the International Monetary and Finance Committee (IMFC), or the joint IMF–World Bank Development Committee. Only the Board of Governors is a little more open to civil society. Ad hoc accredited civil society organizations can attend and observe the plenary session of the IMF and World Bank Boards of Governors during the IMF–World Bank Annual Meetings. However, as the participatory rights of civil society organizations are very limited at these sessions—they cannot make oral statements, submit written statements, or comment on draft documents—most civil society organizations find little use in attending these sessions. They benefit more from participating in the activities running parallel, and in connection with, these meetings and the IMF–World

Bank spring meetings. For example, in connection with both the annual and the spring meetings, the World Bank and the IMF organize dialogues with civil society. The dialogues serve as a forum for discussion of topical issues by the Bank/IMF officials, government representatives, and civil society. These dialogues provide a place for the many attendees to share information, forge personal relationships, follow up previous information distribution, and return monitoring reports and anecdotal narratives 'from the ground'.[62] During the week of the annual meetings, accredited civil society organizations can additionally participate in the program of seminars. The program includes round-table discussions, seminars, and regional briefings with the participation of senior Bank and IMF officials, private sector representatives, government delegates, and representatives of civil society.

Generally speaking, the IMF meets and consults with civil society organizations on the following occasions:

- during IFM–World Bank annual and spring meetings;
- at ad hoc meetings, conferences, seminars, briefings, and workshops;
- during various IMF missions: Article IV missions, Use of IMF Resources (UFR) missions (especially as they concern longer-term programs of structural reform), External Relations missions, Financial Sector Assessment Program (FSAP) missions, and some technical assistance missions; and
- on invitations extended by the IMF to contribute to reviews of its policies, by attending seminars or by providing comments to papers posted on its website.

Moreover, the resident representative, an IMF staff member based in the member country, can consult with civil society organizations ahead of a mission and feed their information and views into the mission's preparation.

Reportedly, contacts between the IMF and civil society organizations have become, in recent years, more frequent and the discussions more substantive.[63] From 2001 to 2005, the overall number of meetings with civil society organizations ranged between 45 and 75 a year, with an average of 330 civil society organizations involved in these meetings annually.[64] A substantial part of Fund interactions with civil society organizations occur during the IMF–World Bank annual and spring meetings—they account for around 20 percent of all meetings with civil society organizations and involve many civil society organizations. In 2008, the global financial crisis drew as many as 350 civil society organization representatives from over 50 countries to Washington during the IMF–World Bank Annual Meeting.[65]

Most of the remaining interactions take the form of (typically bilateral) meetings organized at the requests of civil society organizations with relevant

IMF headquarters staff and, by far less frequently, with resident representatives.[66] The *Guide* instructs IMF staff to reply promptly to such requests but at the same time states that, in practice, IMF staff cannot meet all civil society organizations that have an interest in IMF activities.[67]

As for the type of civil society organizations that the IMF mostly engages with, on the whole the IMF has maintained the greatest number and intensity of direct civil society contacts with economic research bodies. Next to university departments, think-tanks, and consultants in the area of economics, the IMF has pursued its most substantial contacts in civil society with business associations.[68] The number of involved public interest NGOs has remained quite small. The activity has mainly come from a handful of specialised bureaux, the debt campaigns, and certain development and environmental NGOs.[69]

General coordination of IMF relations with civil society organizations occurs through the IMF's External Relations Department. External Relations gathers information relating to IMF activities and summarizes events, papers, and discussions relevant to civil society organizations in a quarterly newsletter, which is sent (by e-mail and mail) to subscribers and published on the IMF website.[70]

IV. Practice of WTO Engagement with NGOs

There is often a marked difference between, on the one hand, the forms of NGO involvement provided for in the constituent and/or secondary legal instruments of an international organization and, on the other hand, the practice of NGO involvement in the activities of that international organization or the engagement of that organization with NGOs. As discussed above, a prime example of such difference is the engagement of the IMF with NGOs. As noted above, this engagement is not provided for in any legal instrument, and yet this engagement is—albeit limited—a reality. Additionally, the involvement of NGOs in the activities of the United Nations goes beyond what is provided for in ECOSOC Resolution 1996/31 and as a practice has evolved to allow for a certain degree of informal participation by NGOs in the work of the General Assembly's main committees and several of its subsidiary bodies, as well as in special sessions of the Assembly.[71]

In practice, the principal forms of WTO engagement with NGOs at present are attendance of the formal plenary meetings of the Ministerial Conference; public symposia and forums on WTO-related issues; access to WTO information; regular informal briefings of NGOs; opportunities for information exchange; informal meetings with NGO; the Informal NGO Advisory Body; and involvement in dispute settlement.

A. Attendance of the Plenary Meetings of the Ministerial Conference

While its 1996 Guidelines did not provide for this, the General Council decided in the run-up to the first session of the WTO's Ministerial Conference in Singapore in December 1996 that NGOs would be invited to attend the formal plenary meetings of the Ministerial Conference. It was also decided that an NGO Centre with facilities for organizing meetings and workshops would be set up alongside the official Conference Centre in Singapore. The 108 NGOs that attended the first session of the Ministerial Conference, did, however, not have observer or consultative status; they were not allowed to make any oral statements at, or submit written statements to, the meetings they could attend. Since the Singapore Session, the number of NGOs attending the formal plenary meetings of the Ministerial Conference has increased with each session, with the exception of the Doha Session in 2001, when limited local facilities (and other restrictions) did not allow a large number of NGOs to participate. For the Hong Kong Session of the Ministerial Conference in 2005, the number of 'accredited' NGOs had reached 1,065, of which 836 actually attended.

Trend in NGO Representation at Sessions of the Ministerial Conference[72]

	Number of 'accredited' NGOs	NGOs attended
Singapore 1996	159	108
Geneva 1998	153	128
Seattle 1999	776	686
Doha 2001	651	370
Cancún 2003	961	795
Hong Kong 2005	1,065	836

Although the attendance of the formal plenary meetings of the Ministerial Conference has now become a well-established practice, there is currently no standing legal arrangement for the participation of NGOs in these meetings. For each session of the Ministerial Conference, the General Council has to agree on NGO attendance and determine the modalities of this attendance.[73] As for the previous sessions, attendance by NGOs of meetings of the Ministerial Conference at the Hong Kong Session in December 2005—the last session to date—was limited to the formal plenary meeting of the Ministerial Conference. However, these meetings involve little more than the reading of prepared remarks by heads of government or trade ministers, which are often of a general nature. As already noted, NGOs have not been allowed to make any statements, whether orally or in writing, to the Ministerial Conference. The fact that the formal plenary meetings of the Ministerial Conference were web-cast makes the right of NGOs to attend them even less meaningful. Access to all other meetings, including negotiating sessions, has been denied. As at previous sessions, NGOs at the Hong Kong Session were provided with an NGO Centre, equipped with office and media facilities, and briefed about the conference developments by WTO Secretariat officials. In Hong Kong, for the first time in WTO history, with the aim of improving transparency and inclusiveness, NGOs were accommodated under the same roof as the delegates of the WTO Members.[74]

B. Public Symposia and Forums

As provided for by the 1996 Guidelines, a number of symposia for NGOs and delegations of Members on specific issues was organized by the WTO Secretariat in the late 1990s. Three of these symposia concerned the issue of trade and the environment, one the issue of trade and development, and one the issue of trade facilitation.[75] These first symposia were organized in the form of plenary sessions with hundreds of participants gathered in one room. This format was criticized as ineffective because it resulted in poorly focused discussions and overly general conclusions.[76]

In reaction to this criticism, in 2000, the WTO changed the format of symposia and turned them into annual two- or three-day events featuring a variety of separate workshops and seminars in which panellists and interested participants discuss a broad range of topical WTO-related issues. These annual symposia are financed from extra-budgetary sources, in particular from voluntary contributions of individual WTO Members.

As of 2005, the WTO no longer exercises control over the issues to be discussed or the selection of speakers, panellists, or other participants. The symposia—or forums (as they are now called)—are organized through a "bottom-up" or—as WTO Director-General Pascal Lamy, calls it—a 'grassroots' process.[77] The WTO's role in the organization of the symposia is now confined to matters such as arranging for rooms, interpretation, and financial support to speakers from developing countries. Themes of seminars and workshops are suggested by NGOs themselves (and other organizers such as academic institutions). Any NGO may approach the WTO Secretariat with a suggestion to organize a workshop on a particular issue of interest to it. The NGO itself then determines the speaker(s) and/or the panellists. The WTO does not interfere with this process. As up to five or six workshops can take place simultaneously, this setup creates a refreshing competitive atmosphere between NGOs (and other organizers), who are all competing for the attention of the participants at the symposium.

Breakdown by category of the on-line registered participants for the 2006 Public Forum[79]

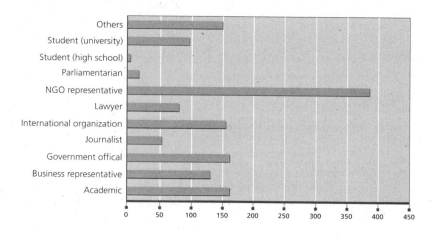

At the WTO Public Symposium of May 2004 called 'Multilateralism at the Crossroads', there were almost 1,200 registered participants and 150 speakers. This three-day event featured a total of 29 workshops on the agricultural negotiations; prospects for developing countries after the failure of the Cancún Session of the Ministerial Conference; trade liberalization and sustainable development; the environment and biodiversity; South-South cooperation; and the challenges presented by regional trade agreements.[78]

At the WTO Public Symposium of April 2005, 'WTO After 10 Years: Global Problems and Multilateral Solutions', most of the discussions focused on the Doha Development Round negotiations, with much attention devoted to agricultural trade. Twenty-three workshops were held on a wide variety of themes, with between five and six concurrent sessions held each morning or afternoon. At the WTO Public Forum of September 2006, 'What WTO for the XXIst Century?', there were 1,532 registered participants, among which were many NGO representatives but also academics, business representatives, and officials of international organizations.

The 2007 WTO Public Forum titled 'How Can the WTO Help Harness Globalization?' was held at the WTO in Geneva on 4 and 5 October 2007.[80] In his opening remarks, Director-General Pascal Lamy stated:

> Today, I am proud to announce that 1750 participants from across the globe have registered for this Forum—in and of itself an indicator of the extent of globalization! This number testifies to the relevance of the WTO to the wider world, and

it is precisely for this reason that the WTO must continue to consult that wider world on how best it can meet its needs and aspirations. Registered today are various types of non-governmental organizations—from environmental, to human rights, to labour rights groups; numerous parliamentarians; various academic institutions; members of the business community; journalists; lawyers; representatives of other international organizations; and students. It is precisely this very broad spectrum of society that the WTO was hoping to tap into. So thank you all for coming in such record numbers, and thank you for helping us make this year's event successful.[81]

The topics on the agenda of the 2007 Public Forum that civil society selected (the grassroots approach) fell into four broad categories: (1) global governance; (2) coherence between the national and international levels of policy-making and between different multilateral institutions; (3) economic growth and the role of trade as a vehicle for development; and (4) sustainable development. The 2008 WTO Public Forum, 'Trading into the Future', was held on 24 and 25 September 2008.[82]

The public symposia or—as they have been re-baptized in 2006—'public forums' do not lead to any specific outcomes, such as, for example, a civil society statement to the WTO Ministerial Conference or General Council. While in the context of other international organizations, similar meetings of representatives of NGOs have in the past led to civil society statements, this is not the ambition of the WTO public symposia and forums. Their aims have been more modest, namely to facilitate the exchange of views and perspectives on WTO issues in a frank and open way and to allow participants to network and establish contacts. In view of these aims, the lukewarm participation of diplomats and other government officials of WTO Members has been a source of frustration for NGOs as well as the organizers.

C. Access to WTO Information

In the absence of a right to attend meetings of WTO bodies, the right to access documents produced in the course of, and in relation to, these meetings becomes essential for NGOs that wish to keep WTO activities under scrutiny. In parallel with the 1996 Guidelines, the General Council adopted procedures for the de-restriction and circulation of WTO documents, establishing the basic principle that most documents would be immediately circulated as unrestricted. However, this principle was, at the time, still subject to important exceptions. In particular, working documents, minutes of WTO meetings, WTO Secretariat background papers, and Ministerial Conference summary records were commonly only de-restricted, and thus made available to the public, eight to nine months after circulation. In 2002, after years of discussion, the General Council reached a decision to accelerate de-restriction of official WTO documents, cutting the time period in which most documents are made publicly available to six to twelve weeks.[83] The General Council also significantly reduced the number of exceptions to the principle of public availability of WTO documents.[84] Therefore, today, most WTO documents are immediately made available to NGOs and the public at large, and those documents that are initially restricted are de-restricted much faster. All unrestricted WTO documents are made available online, in all three official WTO languages (English, French, and Spanish).

Further, since 1998, the External Relations Division of the WTO Secretariat—now the Information and External Relations Division—has been organizing briefings for NGOs on meetings of WTO bodies. Normally, NGO briefings are held after meetings of the General Council and of the Trade Negotiations Committee. Usually between twenty and thirty NGOs attend these briefings. They are mostly NGOs with offices in Geneva.[85] The WTO Secretariat informs Geneva-based NGOs about the briefings by e-mail. If there are other NGOs that would like to attend, they have to send a request to the Information and External Relations Division.[86] During the meeting of ministers in Geneva in July 2008, the WTO Secretariat briefed both visiting and Geneva-based NGOs on a daily basis. Briefings were held in the building of the World Meteorological Organization across the road from the WTO building. Over 300 representatives from business and non-business groups were in Geneva at the end of July. Approximately 100 attended the daily briefings.

On the access for civil society to online information about the WTO, One World Trust, a British NGO, reported in its Global Accountability Report 2003:

> Information on the WTO's trade activities is excellent. The WTO provides access to the legal texts of its agreements by topic, alongside a full, non-technical description of the law. This is very important given the technical nature of much of the work it covers. The public are able to review the extent to which members have implemented agreements and view the process and documentation surrounding any decisions taken by the disputes panel. The information available from the committees is standardized. Each committee produces an annual report of its work for the General Council outlining its activities.[87]

However, in its Global Accountability Report 2006, One World Trust noted that the WTO's 'transparency capabilities are the weakest' in its accountability dimension.[88]

D. Opportunities for Information Exchange

Since 1998, the WTO website has included an NGO page.[89] This page contains specific information on NGO-related WTO activities (such as the public symposia and forums) and on NGO participation in past (and future) sessions of the Ministerial Conference (including announcements of registration procedures and deadlines).

Furthermore, the WTO Secretariat, and in particular the Information and External Relations Division, has, since 1998, compiled a monthly list of position papers it receives from NGOs. This list is circulated to WTO Members. A copy of any of these NGO position papers can be obtained from the WTO Secretariat. All NGO position papers received are also posted on the NGO page of the WTO website and can be easily downloaded. The WTO Secretariat includes in the monthly list, and posts on the NGO page, only position papers relating to WTO issues and activities.[90] The 2008 list includes position papers on subjects such as fisheries subsidies and the Information Technology Agreement (ITA).[91] The WTO Secretariat reserves the full right not to include on the list material that, in its opinion, does not relate to WTO issues or activities.

E. Informal Meetings with NGOs

The 1996 Guidelines envisaged the possibility for chairpersons of WTO councils and committees to meet with NGOs. There are no written procedures that govern such meetings. They take place at the initiative of either NGOs or the relevant chairperson. The information about upcoming meetings is rarely published; it is circulated within NGO networks informally. In practice, the NGOs invited and attending are the Geneva-based NGOs that are also invited to and attend the regular briefings organized by the Secretariat. Usually during the informal meetings with the chairpersons of relevant WTO councils or committees NGOs and chairpersons exchange information and views, mostly in relation to ongoing negotiations. Not surprisingly, the interest of NGOs in such meetings is considerable when negotiations enter a crucial phase and/or important new proposals are tabled and discussed for the first time. Due to the informal nature of the meetings, it is uncommon for reports on these meetings to be issued.

Similar informal meetings take place between NGOs and WTO Secretariat staff from various divisions. These may be devoted to negotiations or cover technical issues of interest to NGOs. There is no schedule for these meetings; they are organized on an ad hoc basis, but normally some WTO–NGO interaction of this nature occurs almost every week.

Additionally, three to four times a year, the WTO Secretariat organizes presentations of NGO studies or publications. These presentations are primarily organized for the benefit of delegates of WTO Members. However, whether due to the busy agenda of these delegates or other factors, they have aroused limited interest to date.

Building on its efforts to have regular briefings for NGOs on specific issues, in 2007, the WTO Secretariat started a series of issue-specific dialogues with civil society. These dialogues offer an opportunity to Geneva-based NGOs, WTO Members, and Secretariat staff to exchange—in an informal manner and off the record—information and views on specific issues. The first dialogue in this series took place in April 2007 and related to the development component of the Doha Development Round.[92] To date, the second dialogue has not yet taken place.

Finally, while not specifically aimed at NGOs, the WTO Secretariat will, during and at the end of important meetings, hold briefings to keep the press and the public at large abreast of the progress made in the negotiations. During the meeting of Ministers in Geneva from 21 to 29 July 2008 to achieve a breakthrough in the Doha Development Round negotiations, Keith Rockwell, the WTO spokesperson, briefed the press daily on the progress made. These press briefings were also web-cast.

F. Informal NGO Advisory Body

Unlike some other international organizations, such as the United Nations Development Program (UNDP) and the World Bank, the WTO does not have a permanent body through which a formal 'dialogue' between the WTO Members and civil society, including NGOs, can take place. Suggestions to establish such consultative bodies have received little support from WTO Members. However, in 2003, the then WTO Director-General, Dr. Supachai Panitchpakdi, took a personal initiative to establish the Informal NGO Advisory Body and the Informal Business Advisory Body. Both advisory bodies were established as informal bodies because under the 1996 Guidelines, the Director-General does not have a mandate to formally institutionalize relations with NGOs in such a manner.

The Informal NGO Advisory Body, made up of ten high-level representatives from NGOs, was designed to provide a platform for dialogue between the WTO Director-General (not the WTO Members) and NGOs from around the world.[93] The main function of the Informal NGO Advisory Body was to advise the WTO Director-General on WTO-related matters and to channel the positions and concerns of civil society on international trade to the WTO membership. The Informal NGO Advisory Body last met in January 2004. The Informal NGO Advisory Body in fact existed only during the term in office of Supachai

Panitchpakdi. Supachai's successor, Pascal Lamy, decided to discontinue the Informal NGO Advisory Body (as well as the Informal Business Advisory Body).

G. Involvement in WTO Dispute Settlement

The settlement of trade disputes between WTO Members is one of the most important and successful functions of the WTO. Both developed and developing Members make extensive use of the WTO dispute settlement system. A significant number of the disputes dealt with to date by the WTO dispute settlement panels and the Appellate Body concerned national environmental legislation (*US—Gasoline*; *US—Shrimp*; *Brazil—Retreaded Tyres*), public health legislation (*EC—Hormones*; *EC—Asbestos*; *EC—Approval and Marketing of Biotech Products*; *Canada—Continued Suspension* and *US—Continued Suspension*) and other legislation of particular interest to NGOs (*EC—Bananas III* and *EC—Tariff Preferences*).[94] Not surprisingly, NGOs have looked for ways to make their voices heard by panels and the Appellate Body. This is not self-evident since WTO proceedings are usually closed to the public. Consultations, panel proceedings, and appellate review proceedings are—as a rule—confidential. WTO proceedings differ sharply in this respect from the proceedings before the International Court of Justice and other international courts and tribunals such as the International Tribunal for the Law of the Sea.[95]

The 2004 Sutherland Report noted that 'the degree of confidentiality of the current [WTO] dispute settlement proceedings can be seen as damaging to the WTO as an institution'.[96] The Sutherland Report therefore recommended that, as a matter of course, panel meetings and Appellate Body hearings should generally be open to the public.[97] Certain WTO Members share this view, as evidenced by the recent opening to the general public of a few panel meetings and one oral hearing of the Appellate Body in disputes involving the European Communities, the United States, Canada, Australia, and New Zealand.[98] For the first time in September and October 2006, the panel in *Canada—Continued Suspension* and *US-Continued Suspension*[99] authorized—at the request of the parties (the United States, Canada, and the European Communities)—the simultaneous closed-circuit television broadcast of its meeting with experts and its second meeting with the parties.[100] These meetings were broadcast to a separate viewing room at WTO Headquarters in Geneva with about 200 places, which were allocated on a 'first-come, first-served' basis (on receipt of an application form).[101] However, despite the frequent calls by NGOs for increased transparency of dispute settlement proceedings, few actually 'attended' and the enthusiasm of those attending waned considerably after the first few hours (after the novelty had worn off).[102]

In July 2007, the panel in *EC and Certain Member States—Large Civil Aircraft* was more cautious than the panel in *US/Canada—Continued Suspension* (because of concerns regarding the protection of confidential business information) and merely allowed its second meeting with the parties to be video-taped and broadcast in an edited version two days later in Geneva.[103] In November 2007, the panel in *EC—Bananas III (Article 21.5—United States)* decided to allow the delegates of WTO Members and the general public to actually observe the panel's meeting with the parties from the public gallery above the meeting room. As only a limited number of places were available, prior registration with the WTO Secretariat or either party in this dispute, the United States or the European Communities, was required to secure a seat.[104] Most recently, in August 2008, the panel in *Australia—Apples* decided at the request of the parties (New Zealand and Australia) to open its first meeting with the parties to the public.[105] This meeting was held in September 2008, and del-egates of WTO Members and members of general public were able to attend the hearing from the public gallery.

While controversial and objected to by most developing country Members, the decision of the panels in *Canada—Continued Suspension* and *US—Continued Suspension, EC and Certain Member States—Large Civil Aircraft, EC—Bananas III (Article 21.5—United States),* and *Australia—Apples* to 'open' up (to different degrees) their meetings to the public is on solid legal ground. The provision con-cerning the confidentiality of panel meetings is contained in the Working Pro-cedures for the panel set out in Appendix 3 of the WTO Understanding on the Rules and Procedures for the Settlement of Disputes (the DSU). Article 12.1 of the DSU explicitly authorizes panels to deviate, after consulting the parties, from the rules set out in Appendix 3.[106] This is what the panels in the above-men-tioned cases have done.[107] In July 2008, in the appeals in *Canada—Continued Sus-pension* and *US—Continued Suspension,* the Appellate Body for the first time opened up its oral hearing. This was a less obvious step for the Appellate Body than it had been for panels. Article 17.10 of the DSU states that the proceedings of the Appellate Body are confidential, and in adopting additional procedural rules in a specific appeal pursuant to Rule 16.1 of the *Working Procedures for Appel-late Review,* the Appellate Body cannot deviate from procedural rules set out in the DSU (such as Article 17.10). In support of its decision to allow the simulta-neous closed-circuit television broadcast of its oral hearing in *Canada—Con-tinued Suspension* and *US—Continued Suspension,* the Appellate Body argued that

> the DSU does not specifically provide for an oral hearing at the appellate stage. The oral hearing was instituted by the Appellate Body in its *Working Procedures,* which were drawn up pursuant to Article 17.9 of the DSU. The conduct and organization

of the oral hearing falls within the authority of the Appellate Body (*compétence de la compétence*) pursuant to Rule 27 of the *Working Procedures*. Thus, the Appellate Body has the power to exercise control over the conduct of the oral hearing, including authorizing the lifting of confidentiality at the joint request of the participants as long as this does not adversely affect the rights and interests of the third participants or the integrity of the appellate process.[108]

The Appellate Body was satisfied that the lifting of the confidentiality of the oral hearing would not adversely affect the integrity of the appellate process. To avoid the rights and interests of the third participants being adversely affected, the oral statements and responses to questions by those third participants that objected to the lifting of the confidentiality (Brazil, India, China, and Mexico) were not subject to observation by the public. The broadcast of the oral hearing was interrupted when these third participants contributed to the oral hearing. A total of 80 individuals registered to observe the oral hearing in *Canada—Continued Suspension* and *US—Continued Suspension*.

At the request of Ecuador, the European Communities, and the United States, the oral hearing of the Appellate Body in the appeals *EC—Bananas III (Second Recourse to Article 21.5 by Ecuador)* and *EC—Bananas III (Recourse to Article 21.5 by the United States)* on 16 and 17 October 2008 were also opened up to the public. Again, public observation took place via simultaneous closed circuit television broadcast to a separate room.[109] In December 2008, the Appellate Body opened up its oral hearing in *US—Continued Suspension*. It is clear that by opening up its oral hearings to the public, albeit via closed-circuit television broadcast, the Appellate Body is aligning itself more to the practice of the International Court of Justice and other international courts and tribunals regarding access by the general public to hearings.

In a number of disputes, environmental and human rights NGOs, labour unions, and industry associations have attempted to make themselves heard and influence the outcome of disputes by submitting unsolicited written briefs, commonly referred to as *amicus curiae* briefs ('friend of the court' briefs) to panels or the Appellate Body.[110] Such briefs have either been attached to parties' or third parties' submissions or have been submitted independently. They can serve at least three different functions: (1) providing legal analysis and interpretation; (2) providing factual analysis as well as evidence; and (3) placing the trade dispute into a broader political and social context.[111] NGOs can advance arguments WTO Members fear using because they are concerned that later, in other disputes, those arguments may be used against them.[112] The acceptance by panels and the Appellate Body of *amicus curiae* briefs, and, in particular, those that are submitted independently from parties or third parties, has been very controversial and criticised by most WTO Members.

In *US—Shrimp*, the Appellate Body came to the conclusion—on the basis of Articles 13, 12, and 11 of the DSU[113]—that panels have the authority to accept and consider *amicus curiae* briefs.[114] While NGOs or other friends of the court do not have a right to have their briefs accepted or considered, it is the right of a panel to accept such briefs if it considers it useful to decide a case. A few panels in later disputes did, on the basis of this ruling of the Appellate Body in *US—Shrimp*, accept and consider *amicus curiae* briefs. However, in most instances, panels have refused to accept and consider *amicus curiae* briefs submitted to them.[115] In *US—Lead and Bismuth II*, the Appellate Body ruled with respect to its own authority to accept and consider *amicus curiae* briefs submitted in appellate review proceedings. It concluded—on the basis of Article 17.9 of the DSU and Rule 16.1 of the *Working Procedures for Appellate Review*[116]— that it had the legal authority to accept and consider any information that it believed to be pertinent and useful in rendering its decision. However, in this particular case, the Appellate Body did not find the two *amicus curiae* briefs filed by industry associations (American Iron and Steel Institute and the Specialty Steel Industry of North America) to be useful.[117] In October 2000, the Appellate Body Division hearing the appeal in *EC—Asbestos* adopted an additional procedure, to deal with the 'avalanche' of *amicus curiae* briefs that the Appellate Body expected to receive in that dispute.[118] It adopted this additional procedure in the 'interests of fairness and orderly procedure'.[119] The procedure required applicants to file for leave to submit a brief. The application had to respond to a set of questions, including questions on the objectives and financing of the applicant and on how the proposed brief would make a contribution that is not likely to be repetitive of what the parties in the dispute have already said. While eventually the Appellate Body did not grant any applicant leave to submit its *amicus curiae* briefs,[120] most WTO Members were infuriated by the Appellate Body's adoption of the additional procedure and its apparent willingness to accept and consider *amicus curiae* briefs. At a tumultuous Special Meeting of the General Council in November 2000, most Members expressed the opinion that since there was no specific provision in WTO law allowing for the acceptance and consideration of *amicus curiae* briefs, such briefs should not be accepted and considered. In his concluding remarks, the chair of the General Council stated that 'in the light of the views expressed and in the absence of clear rules, [he] believed that the Appellate Body should *exercise extreme caution* in future cases until Members had considered what rules were needed'.[121] To date, WTO Members have been unable to adopt any rules on *amicus curiae* briefs. The Appellate Body has repeatedly confirmed its case law on the authority of panels and the Appellate Body to accept and consider such briefs. However, in no proceedings to date has the Appellate Body accepted and considered *amicus curiae* briefs.

The Warwick Commission in its 2007 Report, 'The Multilateral Trade Regime: Which Way Forward?', urged panels and the Appellate Body to be more open to the consideration of *amicus curiae* briefs submitted by NGOs. According to the Warwick Commission, permitting NGOs to participate in this way has

> the benefit of enriching the nature and quality of information that panelists have when considering disputes and of contributing to the transparency of dispute resolution processes.[122]

This is, according to the Warwick Commission, particularly true in disputes that involve conflicts between economic and non-economic values. With regard to the fear of some WTO Members that the dispute settlement process could be 'overwhelmed by *amicus* submissions', the Warwick Commission pointed out that 'experience over the past decade suggests that this fear can be easily overstated'.[123]

It is useful to note that the International Court of Justice (ICJ) also does not have rules on the formal acceptance and consideration of *amicus curiae* briefs submitted by individuals or non-governmental organizations.[124] However, a practice direction adopted by the ICJ in 2001 deals specifically with 'a document or written statement' submitted by an 'international non-governmental organization' on its own initiative, but it is limited to advisory opinion cases. Practice Direction XII provides that 'such statement and/or document is not to be considered as part of the case file'. At the same time, the practice direction stipulates that 'such statements and/or documents shall be treated as publications readily available and may accordingly be referred to by States and intergovernmental organizations presenting written and/or oral statements in the case in the same manner as publications in the public domain.' Practice Direction XII also requires the ICJ to make those written statements and/or documents available to the states and intergovernmental organizations that are involved in the same advisory proceeding.[125]

Other international courts and tribunals, such as the International Tribunal for the Law of the Sea and the European Court of Justice, have been equally hesitant to accept and consider *amicus curiae* briefs submitted by individuals and NGOs in interstate disputes.[126] However, international criminal courts and regional human rights courts are generally empowered to invite or grant leave to any state, organization, or person to appear before them and to make submissions on any issue specified by the court.[127]

Two additional observations with regard to a possible involvement of NGOs in WTO dispute settlement should be made. First, pursuant to Article 13 of the DSU, a panel has the right to seek information and technical advice from any individual or body it deems appropriate. Panels could thus call on NGOs for information and technical advice. However, the requirements of the *Rules of Conduct* for WTO dispute settlement and, in particular, the requirements of independence and impartiality also apply to all those a panel calls on for expert information and advice.[128] Second, it has been accepted since the Appellate Body ruling in *EC—Bananas III*, that parties and third parties are free to determine for themselves the composition of their delegation at hearings of panels and the Appellate Body.[129] It is, therefore, possible for a party or a third party to include NGO representatives in its delegation. The panel in *Korea— Certain Paper* thus rejected the objections of Korea against the presence of representatives of the Indonesian paper industry in the delegation of Indonesia at the panel meetings.[130]

V. Rules and Procedures for the Accreditation of NGOs

Ever more NGOs wish to be involved in the policy-making, policy implementation, compliance monitoring, and dispute settlement activities of international organizations. For good reason, international organizations want to keep the number of NGOs involved in their activities 'manageable' and also want to avoid the involvement of NGOs that could potentially harm them in their efforts to achieve their objectives. Therefore, selecting among various NGOs is a necessity. Selection is needed to ensure that only NGOs that 'add value' to the policy-making, policy implementation, compliance monitoring, and dispute settlement activities 'enjoy' specific forms of involvement and associated rights. To this end, a number of international organizations, and most prominently the United Nations, have elaborated rules on NGO accreditation. These rules include substantive rules setting out the requirements that a NGO must meet to be accredited and procedural rules for taking decisions regarding accreditation and the subsequent monitoring of accredited NGOs.

A. NGO Accreditation by the UN ECOSOC

ECOSOC Resolution 1996/31, the 'Consultative Relationship between the United Nations and Non-Governmental Organizations', already discussed above, is quite specific about the requirements that NGOs must meet in order to be accredited and thus conferred consultative status. Pursuant to Resolution 1996/31, the NGO must, first, be concerned with matters falling within the (very broad) competence of the council and its subsidiary bodies.[131] It must be able to demonstrate that its program of work is of direct relevance and can contribute to the mission of the United Nations.[132] The aims and purposes of the NGO must be in conformity with the spirit, purposes, and principles of the

UN Charter.[133] Second, the NGO must also have recognized standing within its field of competence.[134] Third, the NGO must have an established headquarters with an executive officer;[135] a democratically adopted constitution;[136] a representative and accountable inner structure;[137] and the authority to speak for its members.[138] Fourth, as regards the funding of the NGO, the basic resources must be derived from either national affiliates or from individual members.[139] Finally, the NGO must attest that it has been in existence for at least two years at the date of receipt of its application for consultative status.[140]

As explicitly stated in Resolution 1996/31, decisions regarding arrangements for consultation should be guided by the principle that they are made, *on the one hand*, for the purpose of enabling the council or one of its subsidiary bodies to secure expert information or advice from NGOs having special competence in the relevant subjects, and *on the other hand*, to enable international, regional, sub-regional, and national NGOs that represent important elements of public opinion to express their views.[141] Therefore, the arrangements for consultation made with each NGO should relate to the subjects in which that NGO has special competence and in which it has a special interest.[142] Consequently, the decisive factor in which form of consultative status will be granted (general, special, or roster) is the scope of the NGO's activities and competence. For the general status, it must be as broad as, or at least comparable to, that of ECOSOC; for special status, the NGO's scope must cover a few relevant fields; for roster status, a narrower scope is permitted. Finally, in selecting NGOs, ECOSOC must to the extent possible encourage the participation of NGOs from developing countries, in order to help achieve a just, balanced, effective, and genuine involvement of NGOs from all regions and areas of the world.[143]

As set out in ECOSOC Resolution 1996/31, an NGO must submit an application to obtain consultative status with ECOSOC and/or its subsidiary bodies, which is then reviewed by ECOSOC's Committee on NGOs (NGO Committee). The NGO Committee consists of 19 UN Member States that are elected every four years by the council on the basis of equitable geographical representation.[144] The committee, which meets twice each year, in practice discusses all new applications during informal meetings prior to its formal sessions. NGO applications are grouped into two lists. List 1 includes 'unproblematic' NGOs; List 2 features those NGOs that gave rise to questions from one or more delegations.[145] These questions are sent to the NGO concerned so that it may respond before the beginning of the formal session of the NGO Committee at which its application will be discussed.[146] If Member States are not satisfied with answers received from a particular NGO, its application is deferred and additional questions are posed. After deliberations on each NGO, the chairperson of the committee usually suggests recommending special consultative status, and if there are no objections or proposals to change the type of status (into general or roster) from Member States, this recommendation will be transmitted to ECOSOC for final approval. In difficult cases, the NGO Committee may turn to voting before submitting its recommendation. The final decision on granting consultative status is taken by ECOSOC itself.

An NGO granted general or special consultative status by ECOSOC is under an obligation to submit a report on its activities every four years.[147] This report, commonly referred to as the quadrennial report, allows the NGO Committee to review whether the NGO concerned continues to satisfy the substantive criteria of consultative status as set out above. If the committee is of the opinion that this is not the case, it can recommend to ECOSOC the reclassification, the suspension (for up to three years), or withdrawal of the NGO's consultative status.[148] To date, ECOSOC has suspended or withdrawn the consultative status of only a few NGOs.

B. NGO Accreditation by WIPO

With regard to the rules on NGO accreditation applied by WIPO, it should be noted that Article 13(2) of the WIPO Constitution does not contain any guidance as to which NGOs can be accredited to WIPO. It only provides that both international and national organizations may be granted observer status. In fact, accreditation criteria have been explicitly established—in 2002—only for national NGOs applying for permanent observer status.[149] As for international NGOs, the WIPO website lists only the documents and information that it requires applicant NGOs to submit but does not spell out the criteria against which it will assess whether international NGOs will be granted permanent observer status. However, such criteria for granting international NGOs permanent observer status do exist; they have been developed through actual practice and the experience of the WIPO Secretariat since the 1970s, but have not been officially formalised.[150] In particular, these criteria include the following:[151]

- The NGO must be international. In determining, whether a particular NGO is international, WIPO pays attention to whether the NGO has offices in more than one country, whether it has national NGOs as members, and whether there are persons of different nationalities among the NGO's officers.
- The competence and activities of the NGO must be relevant to those of WIPO. This does not mean that the NGO's competence has to cover all intellectual property rights; one or two aspects (for example, copyright issues or industrial property alone) are sufficient. The proof of relevant

activities usually includes studies, position papers, newsletters, and other publications produced by the NGO, as well as workshops, seminars, and other events organized by the NGO.

- The NGO must be non-profit, which follows from the generally recognized definition of an NGO.
- The NGO must be independent from the government, including financially, which also follows from its nature as a *non-governmental* organization.
- The NGO must have a statute or bylaw on the basis of which it functions and must be duly registered in the country where it has its headquarters.

International NGOs are required to provide the WIPO Secretariat with the following documents or information:

- a text of its constituent instrument (articles of incorporation, bylaws, etc.);
- the date and place where it was established;
- a list of its officers (showing their nationality);
- a complete list of its national groups or members (showing their country of origin);
- a description of the composition of the members of its governing body or bodies (including their geographical distribution);
- a statement of its objectives; and
- an indication of the field or fields of intellectual property (e.g., copyright and related rights) of interest to it.[152]

This information helps to establish that applicant NGOs meet the accreditation criteria applied by WIPO. The Secretariat may employ additional tools to ensure that the criteria are satisfied; in particular, it may do Internet-based research and consult NGO databases.[153]

In relation to *national* NGOs applying for a permanent observer status, the WIPO website lists a number of criteria ('principles') that have to be satisfied.[154] They are these:

- The NGO shall be essentially concerned with intellectual property matters falling within the competence of WIPO and shall, in the view of the Director General, be able to offer constructive, substantive contributions to the deliberations of the assemblies of WIPO.
- The aims and purposes of the NGO shall be in conformity with the spirit, purposes, and principles of WIPO and the United Nations.
- The NGO shall have an established headquarters. It shall have democratically adopted statutes, adopted in conformity with the legislation of the Member State from which the NGO originates.

- The NGO shall have authority to speak for its members through its authorized representatives and in accordance with the rules governing observer status.
- The admission of national NGOs to observer status shall be the subject of prior consultations between Member States and the Secretariat.[155]

These criteria are quite typical for international organizations that have a system of NGO accreditation. They ensure the relevance of accredited NGOs to the WIPO's matters of competence, exclude NGOs of extremist or violent character, and ascertain the legality and observance of basic democratic principles by NGOs.[156]

The criteria for ad hoc accreditation have also not been formalized. However, the criteria applied by the WIPO in practice are essentially the same criteria as those for the permanent observer status but are applied in a 'less strict manner'.[157] The principal criterion for obtaining ad hoc accreditation is the relevance of the concerned NGO's activities to the subject matter of a WIPO body or of an event that accreditation is requested for.[158]

The power to accredit NGOs lies with WIPO's intergovernmental bodies. It is provided in Rule 8(2) of the WIPO General Rules of Procedure that 'each body shall decide, in a general way or for any particular session or meeting, which … organizations shall be invited to be represented by observers'. Permanent observer status is granted by WIPO assemblies. Ad hoc observer status admitting NGOs to meetings of particular WIPO bodies is granted by the WIPO bodies concerned.

The procedure for obtaining permanent observer status is not described on the WIPO website or in any other public source. In practice, it follows the principal steps described below.[159]

- An NGO mails to the WIPO Director-General its request for permanent observer status. In this request the NGO briefly describes its international or national character, objectives, and activities, and indicates the place and date of its establishment.
- NGO requests are forwarded to the WIPO Office of Legal Counsel for consideration. The latter informs the applicant NGO about the documents that it must provide for its application to be considered.
- The NGO submits the documents required by the Office of Legal Counsel. If the NGO fails to do this, its application remains pending for two to three years, with the Secretariat sending occasional reminders to the NGO, and then it is dropped from the list of applicants.
- On the basis of the complete set of documents received from the NGO, the Office of Legal Counsel verifies whether the NGO satisfies the criteria for

accreditation reviewed above. The application is rejected at this stage only if there is a 'manifest inconsistency' with one or more of the criteria.

- The Office of Legal Counsel prepares a 'resumé' of the NGO, which features its date of establishment and headquarters, objectives, governance structure, and membership. The NGO's name is then included in the memorandum of the Director-General for consideration of the upcoming WIPO assemblies, and the NGO's resumé is included in an annex to the said memorandum.[160] This memorandum usually lists several NGOs that have applied during the year preceding the session of the assemblies. The Office of Legal Counsel does not make a recommendation to the assemblies as to whether particular NGOs should or should not be accredited. NGOs are notified that their candidature has been submitted to the consideration of the WIPO assemblies.

- Admission of observers is one of the agenda items of the WIPO assemblies. The assemblies consider all listed NGOs together, and unless there is an objection to a particular NGO, they are passed en bloc. In the case of objections, the matter can be decided by voting. So far, there has been no case when a government objected to the admission of a particular NGO. NGOs whose applications are being considered cannot attend the meeting, as they have yet to gain observer status.

- The WIPO assemblies' decisions on whether to grant permanent observer status to particular NGOs are contained in the General Report.[161] The WIPO Director-General sends accredited NGOs an official letter in which it confirms the grant of permanent observer status and states that, from now on, they will receive invitations to all WIPO meetings where NGO attendance is possible.

The deadline for submission of requests from NGOs is usually set in May, whereas the WIPO assemblies are convened from late September to early October. Thus the whole procedure takes no less than six months. There is no possibility of appeal in case the NGO request for permanent observer status is declined, but the NGO can re-apply later.

As is the case with the procedure for obtaining permanent observer status, the procedure applicable in requesting ad hoc observer status is not set out on the WIPO website or any publicly available document. However, this procedure follows the basic steps of the procedure for obtaining permanent observer status, with two 'deviations':

- It is not the WIPO Office of Legal Counsel that reviews the NGO application for ad hoc accreditation. This is a task of a secretarial unit serving a WIPO body to which the ad hoc accreditation is being requested.

- It is not the WIPO assemblies that grant accreditation but a particular WIPO body to which the ad hoc accreditation is being requested.[162]

As with permanent observer status, so far there has not been a case where admission of ad hoc observer NGOs was blocked by a government. In case of a refusal, there is no appeal procedure but the NGO can re-apply later.

Unlike the ECOSOC, WIPO does not have rules for monitoring of accredited NGOs, such as requiring them to submit annual or other reports. Also, there is no rule that would empower WIPO, or prevent it from, withdrawing or suspending permanent or ad hoc observer status from an NGO. So far, no such problems have arisen.[163] As a matter of practice, NGOs can be deleted from the list of permanent observers if they cease to exist as a result of dissolution or merger with another NGO. In most instances, NGOs themselves inform WIPO that they are closing down or merging. Exclusion from the list of permanent observers can also happen if the WIPO Secretariat loses contact with the NGO—in particular, when all invitations for WIPO meetings are returned to WIPO with a note that the addressee has moved out.[164]

C. NGO Accreditation by the IMF

With regard to the accreditation rules and procedures applied by the IMF, a distinction should be made between accreditation to the IMF-World Bank annual and spring meetings and other IMF meetings with civil society. In order to attend the IMF-World Bank annual and spring meetings as well as the activities running parallel, and in connection with, these meetings, civil society organizations must be accredited.[165] This accreditation is ad hoc—a particular civil society organization has to request accreditation for each particular meeting. Accreditation criteria and procedures applied by the IMF and the World Bank have not been legally established but exist rather as a matter of practice of both institutions. According to the World Bank website, to be accredited NGOs have to engage with the World Bank and the IMF on a broad range of development operations and in policy dialogue at the local, national, and global levels.[166] As a matter of practice, the World Bank and the IMF do not require that civil society organizations *engage* with either of the institutions but only satisfy themselves that the civil society organizations' activities concern development policy or other issues relevant to either of the two institutions.[167] There are no requirements concerning the organizational or governance structure of civil society organizations, their decision-making processes, funding, length of existence, or other criteria applied by other international organizations. These lax requirements of the World Bank and IMF can perhaps be explained by the fact that NGOs are not able to influence the course of the meetings as they do not enjoy any important participatory rights.

Since 2005, requests for accreditation are submitted online. NGOs may also check the status of their applications through the World Bank's or IMF's website. All requests are reviewed by the External Affairs Department of the Bank and the External Relations Department of the IMF. Working in coordination, these two departments make an assessment of whether applying civil society organizations are bona fide (not fictitious) and whether they meet the accreditation criterion. As no documents are required from NGOs for accreditation, this assessment is made on the basis of previous contacts and knowledge about the organization and the individuals concerned; in case of doubt, World Bank and IMF officials may conduct Internet searches, contact the World Bank's relevant country office, or contact the organization directly. The External Affairs Department and the External Relations Department automatically recommend accreditation for those civil society organization representatives that were accredited to previous annual or spring meetings.[168] Accreditation is denied for individuals or organizations whom the External Affairs Department and the External Relations Department are unable to identify and/or contact and to those who do not meet the accreditation criterion.

The External Affairs Department and the External Relations Department make a joint decision on each of the applicants and e-mail, on a weekly basis, the names and organizations of individuals who have applied to the executive director's office that represents the country from which the request originated, with the proposed action (clearance or denial) on each particular application. In the absence of any objection from the executive director, the decision is deemed approved on a lapse-of-time basis after eight working days. If the executive director objects to the accreditation of a particular civil society organization, he/she is expected to give reasons for his/her opinion. This opinion is not subject to review or appeal, although it may be subject to negotiations.[169]

For the 2005 annual meetings, the number of accredited civil society organizations equalled 274 (1 refusal), out of which 180 representatives actually attended. For the 2004 annual meetings, 328 civil society organizations were accredited (5 refusals of accreditation), out of which only 151 civil society organization representatives were present. Spring meetings attract less attention, with only 80 civil society organizations accredited for the 2005 spring meetings (no refusals).[170]

With respect to other IMF meetings with civil society, the rules on the selection criteria for civil society organizations and relevant procedures remain to a large degree not formalized. The IMF's broad policy as to which civil society organizations to engage with is built on the following points:

- Engage with different sectors of civil society;
- Aim to alternate the IMF's contacts between different civil society organizations, rather than always and only meeting the same organizations;

- Contact locally based associations as well as the local offices of transnational civil society organizations (in particular, staff should not rely on North-based groups to speak on behalf of South-based stakeholders);
- Meet with civil society organizations across the political spectrum (include critics as well as supporters of the IMF and/or of the current government of a country); and
- Reach out beyond civil society circles that look familiar.[171]

These points do not serve as criteria determining which civil society organizations can be consulted and which cannot. Rather, they help to divide the multitude of civil society actors into groups that should be represented and given a voice in the IMF's outreach to civil society. To engage with the IMF, civil society organizations can be international, regional, national, or local. As mentioned above, civil society organizations with offices in Washington find themselves in a privileged position.

Additionally, the *Guide for Staff Relations with Civil Society Organizations* sets out another set of (non-binding) guidelines for selection of civil society organizations for cooperation. The offered criteria are designed to ensure that selected civil society organizations have the necessary legitimacy. The *Guide* suggests considering the following features of civil society organizations:

(a) Legality—i.e., whether they are officially recognized and registered;
(b) Morality—i.e., whether they pursue a noble and right cause;
(c) Efficacy—i.e., whether they perform competently;
(d) Membership base; and
(e) Governance—i.e., whether they operate in a participatory, tolerant, transparent, and accountable manner.[172]

According to competent IMF officials, they do not check whether NGOs that apply for meetings with the IMF staff satisfy each of these criteria. The criteria serve as very general guidelines, rather than as a mandatory checklist applied in every situation. Relevant IMF officials already know most of the NGOs that have an interest in the Fund activities, so these do not require any additional verification.[173] Additionally, most of these criteria are quite imprecise and leave it to relevant IMF officials to determine, for example, which cause is 'right and noble', whether the civil society organization membership base is sufficiently broad, or whether the civil society organization performs competently enough. This does not necessarily mean, however, that IMF officials use their discretion to limit the number of NGOs that they interact with, or to close access to NGOs considered 'undesirable'. On the contrary, according to IMF officials, the flexibility of the selection criteria allows the IMF to avoid the long and cumbersome bureaucratic accreditation/selection procedures that exist in some other international organizations, and to maintain an 'open door policy' in relation to NGOs.[174] However, the negative side of the loose legal regulation and the broad discretion is that they may one day lead to an easy substitution of the 'open door policy' by a 'closed door policy'. Possibly to prevent this, the *Guide* suggests that, in general, the IMF should seek to apply an inclusive approach to civil society organization involvement and should deny a civil society organization access only with good reason (for example, if the organization has malicious intent or presents a seriously distorted account of itself).[175] However, this provision can hardly be an effective safeguard because of the non-binding nature of the *Guide*.

The *Guide* does not enumerate documents or information that civil society organizations are required to submit to demonstrate that they meet the set requirements (for example, proof of registration, statutes, by-laws, annual reports, etc.). The *Guide* only names the sources that could be consulted in order to assess whether a particular civil society organization meets the set standards. These sources include the following:

- the IMF's own records of civil society contacts;
- government officials;
- bilateral donor agencies;
- embassies;
- local staff in IMF resident representative offices;
- staff of the World Bank and other multilateral institutions (especially their civil society specialists where these exist);
- apex civil society bodies;
- relevant academic specialists; and
- other professional consultants.[176]

To request a meeting, NGOs may contact the IMF External Relations Department, a relevant geographic area, or functional department or the IMF resident representative in a particular country. Although a relevant geographic area/functional department does not need an authorization from the External Relations Department to hold meetings with civil society organizations, in most cases, it is the External Relations Department that will be involved in organizing a meeting, at least as far as logistics is concerned.[177]

The *Guide* also makes clear that the IMF should be sensitive to the opinions of national governments in relation to particular civil society organizations. It provides that if a government raises objections to IMF relations with certain, or all, civil society organizations, staff should first try to explain the rationale for such contacts. If the difference of views persists, staff should refrain from the contacts and refer the disagreement to headquarters for possible follow-up with the government concerned.[178] However, in practice, at least at the head-quarter level, governments (represented by executive directors) do not exercise any control over meetings held by IMF staff with civil society organizations.[179]

In sum, the (non-binding) rules concerning the criteria and procedures for selection of civil society organizations that are common to all interactions with civil society organizations leave a large number of matters unsettled—for example, which organ makes a decision on civil society organization selection, which documents and information it can request from civil society organizations, whether it considers civil society organizations aside from the one that has shown interest in a particular meeting, what are the time limits, what may be grounds for refusal, etc. Thus the relevant rules and practices cannot be uniform and consistent; they vary across the institution and depend on the context of particular meetings.

D. NGO Accreditation by the WTO

In sharp contrast with the elaborate substantive and procedural rules on accreditation applied by ECOSOC and to the lesser extent WIPO, the WTO, much like the IMF, is subject to virtually no explicit, legally binding rules to ensure that it engages only with NGOs that 'add value' to its policy-making, policy implementation, compliance monitoring, and dispute settlement activities. Article V:2 of the WTO Agreement merely states that the WTO should restrict its engagement to NGOs *concerned with matters related to those of the WTO*'. The 1996 Guidelines do not provide for any further accreditation requirements or selection criteria. There are also no specific procedural rules for the decisions on accreditation.

When the WTO was first confronted with the problem of accrediting NGOs on the occasion of the first session of the Ministerial Conference in Singapore in December 1996, the WTO Secretariat accredited *all* non-profit NGOs that could point to activities related to those of the WTO. The applicant-NGOs were not submitted to any further examination of their objectives, membership, institutional structure, or financing.[180] Apart from the criterion of 'WTO-related activities', the only additional accreditation criterion applied at the time was the '*non-profit character*' of the NGO. Private companies and law firms were refused accreditation on this basis.

This practice continued at subsequent sessions of the Ministerial Conference. The WTO Secretariat merely checked the WTO-related nature of the activities of the applicant NGO and its non-profit character.[181] Rather than a system of selection and accreditation of NGOs, the WTO applies a simple system of ad hoc registration for *one* event, namely the biannual session of the

Ministerial Conference. This registration/accreditation system of NGOs for the biannual sessions of the Ministerial Conference is left to the discretion of the WTO Secretariat, although the WTO General Council can address any issue concerning accreditation/registration that may arise in the run-up to a session of the Ministerial Conference.[182] Despite these rather lax criteria for accreditation/registration, only 1,065 NGOs out of roughly 1,630 applicants were accredited for the 2005 Hong Kong Session of the Ministerial Conference. Of those *not* accredited, about 220 requests for accreditation were not processed because of lack of further response or information from the NGOs concerned. The remaining requests were refused because of insufficient evidence of WTO-related activities or of the non-profit character. Due to the high number of requests for registration for the Hong Kong Session of the Ministerial Conference, the WTO was stricter in screening applications than was customary for earlier sessions. Reportedly, applications from purely research institutions or student associations, which do not have any advocacy functions, or similar features that usually characterize NGOs, were refused.

While the general absence of WTO rules and procedures for the selection of NGOs should be noted with concern, it could be argued that as long as NGO involvement in WTO activities remains as modest as it currently is, there is little use for elaborate accreditation rules and procedures. The 2004 Sutherland Report, 'The Future of the World Trade Organization', noted in this respect that while a formal system of accreditation might have 'attractions' (for example, ensuring that 'responsible NGOs get the advantage of a closer relationship with the WTO'), it would impose a continuing bureaucratic burden to receive, sieve, and make judgments about candidate NGOs.[183] As long as NGOs have no consultative status with the WTO (i.e., not allowed to participate in the meetings of WTO bodies), it is indeed doubtful whether a formal system of accreditation is 'a worthy investment for a small organization with a limited budget'.[184]

VI. Conclusion

When one compares the extent of current WTO engagement with NGOs to that of the GATT or early WTO engagement with NGOs, it is clear that significant strides have been made. Largely due to the efforts of the WTO Secretariat, the relations between the WTO and NGOs are currently more meaningful, more constructive, and less antagonistic than ever before. The involvement of NGOs in the policy-making, policy implementation, compliance monitoring, and dispute settlement activities of the WTO remains, however, quite modest. The potential of Article V:2 of the *WTO Agreement* has definitely not been exploited by WTO Members to date. As stated in the 1996 Guidelines, it was and still is not 'possible for NGOs to be directly involved in the work of the WTO or its meetings'.[185] With the exception of the formal plenary meeting of the Ministerial Conference and the limited exception (when all parties agree) of WTO panels meetings and Appellate Body oral hearings, NGOs are not allowed to attend—let alone actively participate in—any meetings of WTO bodies.

When addressing the question of whether there is a need and/or scope for more NGO involvement in the activities of the WTO, the 2004 Sutherland Report, 'The Future of the World Trade Organization', first noted (in line with the view held by most—if not all—WTO Members) that the primary responsibility for engaging civil society in trade policy matters rests not with the WTO, but with its Members.[186] The Sutherland Report also noted that while all international organizations share common objectives in the pursuit of transparency, each organization's particular mandate and structure might call for specific objectives, forms of involvement, and the choice of civil society organizations with whom to collaborate.[187] The Sutherland Report pointed out that the WTO is founded on contractual commitments negotiated among governments, and for that reason there are limits to how much further the WTO can go in involving NGOs in its deliberations and processes.[188] The Sutherland Report called on WTO Members to develop a new set of clearer guidelines for the relations of the WTO Secretariat with NGOs and to scale up the administrative capacity and financial resources of the WTO Secretariat.[189] The Sutherland Report referred to new 'systematic and in-depth relations' between the WTO Secretariat and NGOs but was silent about the types of activities that such relations could comprise.[190] In fact, the Sutherland Report did not suggest any substantial improvements in the degree of the WTO's engagement with NGOs. Rather, it called for streamlining and further developing the existing forms of engagement, with an emphasis on the Secretariat's (as opposed to WTO Members') relations with NGOs.

While appreciating the wisdom of the authors of the Sutherland Report of limiting proposals for reform to 'realizable' reforms, the Sutherland Report shows a regrettable lack of ambition in the area of dialogue with civil society. It could be argued that the WTO can, and should, engage with NGOs, and allow for NGO involvement, more than it currently does. Why can (selected) NGOs not have observer/consultative status in WTO bodies? In the United Nations, UNCTAD, the ILO, WIPO, and other international organizations that deal with economic matters, NGOs have such status and participate in the meetings of the bodies of these organizations. Why is this not possible in the WTO? Does the intergovernmental character of the WTO prevent granting NGOs observer/consultative status? Would further engagement with NGOs, in particular, by allowing (selected) NGOs to participate in formal meetings of its bodies, be counterproductive to the conduct of negotiations within the WTO? A more open and engaged dialogue with civil society will make the WTO a more transparent and responsive organization, enjoying greater support among the general public in developed as well as developing country Members. Justified concerns about the legitimacy, the accountability, and the 'politics' of NGOs can be eliminated, or at least mitigated, by introducing a system of accreditation in the WTO, modelled on the system applied by the UN ECOSOC. While NGO involvement in the WTO definitely has its limits, the involvement of NGOs in other international organizations, in particular in the United Nations and WIPO, suggests that these limits have not yet been reached.

Notes

* The author also thanks Vydyanathan Lakshmanan, Willemijn Noordhoek, Stéphanie Cartier, Bas Megens, and Nina Buttgen for their able assistance. A shorter version of this article, focusing on the WTO and the United Nations, appeared as Peter Van den Bossche, 'NGO Involvement in the WTO: A Comparative Perspective', 11 Journal of International Economic Law 717 (2008). This article also incorporates findings and conclusions on NGO involvement in WIPO and the IMF, previously published in Sergey Ripinsky and Peter Van den Bossche, *NGO Involvement in International Organizations: A Legal Analysis* (British Institute of International and Comparative Law, 2007).

1 Kal Raustiala, 'The "Participatory Revolution" in International Environmental Law', 21 Harvard Environmental Law Review 537 (1997), at 539.

2 See Karsten Nowrot, 'Symposium, The Rule of Law in the Era of Globalization: Legal Consequences of Globalization: The Status of Non-Governmental Organizations under International Law', 6 Indiana Journal of Global Legal Studies 579 (1999), at 586–87.

3 Report of the Panel of Eminent Persons on United Nations-Civil Society Relations, *We the People, Civil Society, the United Nations and Global Governance* (Cardoso Report), A/58/817, dated 11 June 2004, para 13, http://daccessdds.un.org/doc/UNDOC/GEN/ N04/376/41/PDF/ N0437641.pdf?OpenElement (visited 16 January 2009).

4 Guy de Jonquières, 'The WTO's Capacity to Arouse Controversy Highlights a Growing Public Awareness of its Role', *Financial Times,* 24 September 1999.

5 See Daniel Esty, 'Non-Governmental Organizations at the World Trade Organization: Cooperation, Competition, or Exclusion', 1 Journal of International Economic Law 136 (1998).

6 See Markus Krajewski, 'Democratic Legitimacy and Constitutional Perspectives of WTO Law', 35 Journal of World Trade 167 (2001), at 167–86.'

7 See Jeffrey L. Dunoff, 'The Misguided Debate over NGO Participation at the WTO', 1 Journal of International Economic Law 437 (1998).

8 Gary P. Sampson, 'Overview', in Gary P Sampson (ed), *The Role of the World Trade Organization in Global Governance* (Tokyo: United Nations University Press, 2001) 11.

9 *UN System and Civil Society: An Inventory and Analysis of Practices,* Background Paper for the Secretary-General's Panel of Eminent Persons on United Nations Relations with Civil Society, Introduction, May 2003, http://www.un.org/reform/civilsociety/ practices.shtml (visited 16 January 2009).

10 Ibid.

11 WTO, *The Results of the Uruguay Round of Multilateral Trade Negotiations, the Legal Texts* (Geneva: WTO, 2003) 3.

12 See Article III:5 of the Agreement Establishing the World Trade Organization (WTO Agreement).

13 Both the World Bank and the IMF take the position that engagement with NGOs is permissible as long as the general provisions of their Articles of Agreement are observed.

14 See Article 87(2) of the Havana Charter on the International Trade Organization.

15 See for a detailed analysis in this regard, Steve Charnovitz, 'Opening the WTO to Non-Governmental Interests', 24 Fordham International Law Journal 173 (2000). Charnovitz points out that it was only the International Chamber of Commerce (ICC) that participated (and that too occasionally) in the GATT organs. No other NGO seems to have had any role during the early days of the GATT. See also, Changrok Soh, 'The Role of NGOs in International Economic Organizations: Critical Theory Perspectives', http://www.koreagsis.ac.kr/research/journal/vol7/7-02-Changrok%20Soh.pdf, 28, (noting that "the GATT [...] failed to establish any formal linkages with NGOs or social movements in its forty-seven-year history ... ").

16 NGOs as such were not invited to Marrakesh; those NGOs present were registered as members of the press.

17 Decision by the General Council, Guidelines for Arrangements on Relations with Non-Governmental Organizations, WT/L/162, dated 23 July 1996.

18 Ibid, at paras II and IV.

19 Ibid, at paras IV and V.

20 Ibid, at para VI.

21 Ibid, at para VI.

22 Article V:2 of the WTO Agreement: 'make appropriate arrangements for consultations and cooperation with non-governmental organizations concerned with matters ... '; and Article 71 of the UN Charter: 'may make suitable arrangements for consultation with non-governmental organizations which are concerned with matters... '.

23 UN Economic and Social Council, Consultative Relationship between the United Nations and Non-Governmental Organizations' (ECOSOC Resolution 1996/312), UN Document E/1996/312, 5 July 1996, http://www.un.org/documents/ecosoc/res/1996/eres1996-31.htm. Resolution 1996/312 updated the arrangements previously set out in Resolution 1296 (XLIV) of 23 May 1968.

24 The 'roster' is a list of NGOs that have neither general nor special consultative status but with which ECOSOC nevertheless maintains a relationship.

25 ECOSOC Resolution 1996/312, above n 23, at paras 27–28.

26 Ibid, at para 32 (b).

27 Ibid, at paras 29 and 35.

28 Ibid, at para 30.

29 Ibid, at para32 (a).

30 They are informed of the provisional agenda of the council (ibid, at para 27); they may sit as observers at public meetings of the council and its subsidiary bodies (ibid, at paras 29 and 35); and they may submit written statements with a maximum of 500 words for circulation to the members of the council (ibid, at para 31 [e]).

31 Ibid, at para 38 (a).

32 Ibid, at para 32 (a).

33 Ibid, at paras 27 and 29.

34 Ibid, para 24.

35 Such consultations may be conducted upon the request of the NGO or upon the request of the secretary-general (ibid, at para 65). Also, the UN secretary-general may request an accredited NGO to carry out specific studies or prepare specific papers (ibid, at para 66).

36 Ibid, at para 67.

37 (WIPO Convention), done at Stockholm, 14 July 1967, http://www.wipo.int/treaties/en/convention/trtdocs_wo029.html (visited 9 April 2009).

38 NGOs also participate in WIPO technical cooperation activities with developing countries. In particular, NGOs possessing expertise on specific intellectual property matters are frequently invited to share their knowledge at regional meetings and capacity-building seminars for countries-recipients of technical assistance. No rules govern these forms of NGO involvement; relevant WIPO officials appear to have unchecked discretion when dealing with these matters. See Sergey Ripinsky and Peter Van den Bossche, *NGO Involvement in International Organizations: A Legal Analysis* (British Institute of International and Comparative Law, 2007) 86, referring to an interview with Ms. Joëlle Rogé, Director-Advisor on Non-Governmental Organizations, WIPO Sector of External Relations, 23 November 2005.

39 Ibid.

40 Ibid, at 87.

41 Ibid.

42 Note that in recent years there has been a rise in the number of NGOs applying for permanent observer status at WIPO. For example, in 2005 alone, 40 NGOs (22 international and 18 national) were granted permanent observer status.

43 Ripinsky and Van den Bossche, above n 38, at 87.

44 Ibid, at 88.

45 WIPO, Admission of Observers—Memorandum by the Director-General, A/37/8, dated 19 August 2002, at para. 10. This rule also applies to national NGOs. See Ripinsky and Van den Bossche, ibid, at 88, referring to an interview with an official from the WIPO Office of the Legal Counsel, 21 November 2005.

46 Ripinsky and Van den Bossche, ibid, at 88–89.

47 Ibid, at 89.

48 In addition to NGOs, civil society organizations include business forums, faith-based associations, labour movements, local community groups, philanthropic foundations, and think-tanks. Civil society does not include parliamentarians, political parties, subnational authorities, individual businesses, or the mass media. In the late 1990s, it was suggested that the Articles of Agreement be amended in order to give a legal basis to the IMF's engagement with civil society organizations, but no such amendment was made. See Ripinsky and Van den Bossche, above n 38, at 178.

49 IMF, 'Guide for Staff Relations with Civil Society Organizations' (10 October 2003), at para II.2, http://www.imf.org/external/np/cso/eng/2003/ 101003.htm (visited 28 December 2008).

50 The *Guide* is not mandatory and does not apply in all situations; it is intended to 'supplement, not replace, sound judgment and experience' of IMF staff. Ibid, at para I.2.

51 IMF, 'The IMF and Civil Society Organizations: A Factsheet' (September 2008), http://www.imf.org/external/np/exr/facts/civ.htm (visited 16 January 2009).

52 T. Dawson and G. Bhatt, 'The IMF and Civil Society Organizations: Striking a Balance', IMF policy discussion paper, PDP/01/2 (September 2001), at 2, http://www.imf.org/external/pubs/ft/pdp/2001/pdp02.pdf (visited 16 January 2009); Jan Aart Scholte, 'Civil Society Voices and the International Monetary Fund' (Ottawa: North-South Institute, 2002) at 8, www.nsi-ins.ca/english/pdf/Int_Mon_Fund.pdf (visited 9 April 2009).

53 See Ripinsky and Van den Bossche, above n 38, at 179; IMF, above n 49, section V.A.

54 Ripinsky and Van den Bossche, ibid, 179–80, referring to IMF External Relations Department, 'A Review of the Fund's External Communication Strategy' (13 February 2003), at 97 (Annex III), http://www.imf.org/external/np/exr/docs/2003/021303.pdf (visited 9 April 2009).

55 IMF, above n 51. For the results of the IMF-conducted survey on country-level outreach to civil society, see IMF External Relations Department, ibid, at 88 (Annex II).

56 See Ripinsky and Van den Bossche, above n 38, at 180, referring to an interview with Ms. Simonetta Nardin and Ms. Jennifer Bisping, IMF External Relations Department, 24 January 2006.

57 IMF, above n 49, at para V.G.3.

58 IMF External Relations Department, above n 54, at 96.

59 Ibid.

60 Dawson and Bhatt, above n 52, at 3.

61 IMF External Relations Department, above n 54, at 96.

62 R.E. Kelly, "A Micro-View of Global Governance: The Spring and Annual Meetings of the Bretton Woods Institutions," Transnational Associations 203 (2003/4), at 205.

63 Dawson and Bhatt, above n 52, at 21.

64 See Ripinsky and Van den Bossche, above n 38, at 181, referring to data obtained from Ms. Simonetta Nardin and Ms. Jennifer Bisping, IMF External Relations Department, 24 January 2006. These data reflect only those meetings that the IMF External Relations Department was aware of or involved in. Other meetings between IMF officials and civil society representatives might occur without the External Relations Department's knowledge.

65 IMF, 'Civil Society Engagement at the 2008 Annual Meetings', (23 October 2008), http://www.imf.org/external/np/exr/cs/news/2008/102308.htm (visited 16 January 2009).

66 See Ripinsky and Van den Bossche, above n 38, at 181–82, referring to an interview with Ms. Simonetta Nardin and Ms. Jennifer Bisping, IMF External Relations Department, 24 January 2006.

67 IMF, above n 49, at para IV.C.2 and Annex para A.2.

68 Scholte, above n 52, at 22.

69 Ibid, 16. Some examples include the Fifty Years Is Enough coalition; the Bretton Woods Project; the European Network on Debt and Development; Oxfam; Friends of the Earth; and World Economy, Environment and Development. See ibid, 14–16.

70 See IMF, 'IMF Civil Society Newsletter', http://www.imf.org/external/np/exr/cs/eng/index.asp (visited 28 December 2008).

71 UN Office of the President of the Millennium Assembly, 'Reference document on the participation of civil society in United Nations conferences and special sessions of the General Assembly during the 1990s', 1 August 2001, at paras 13–20, http://www.un.org/ga/president/55/speech/civilsociety1.htm (visited 17 August 2008).

72 See WTO, 'NGO Participation in Ministerial Conference Was Largest Ever', 6 October 2003, http://www.wto.org/english/news_e/news03_e/ngo_minconf_6oct03_e.htm (visited 8 February 2004); WTO, 'NGO Attendance to the WTO Sixth Ministerial Conference', http://www.wto.org/english/thewto_e/minist_e/min05_e/list_ngo_hk05_e.pdf (visited 12 October 2006).

73 For the latest of these decisions, see WTO Ministerial Conference, 'Procedures Regarding Registration and Attendance of Non-Governmental Organizations at the Sixth Session of the Ministerial Conference', WT/MIN(05)/INF/6, Adopted 1 June 2005.

74 The NGOs were provided with an entire floor with support staff and copying equipment, a computer room, and about 10 meeting rooms for purposes of their lobbying activities and meetings. NGOs were also provided with an information hall, where the WTO proceedings and briefings as well as the daily NGO meetings program were on video-display throughout the day, and where relevant NGO literature could be displayed and made available on a continuous basis. The information hall was visited by hundreds of delegates during the conference proceedings. See Esmé D. du Plessis, Co-Chair Committee Q94, 'Report to AIPPI' (February 2006), at 7, http://www2.aippi.org/ reports/q94/ report_wto_6th_ministerialconf.pdf (visited 16 January 2009).

75 See WTO, 'Relations with Non-Governmental Organizations/Civil Society', http://www.wto.org/english/forums_e/ngo_e/intro_e.htm (visited 16 January 2009).

76 See Charnovitz, above n 15, at 191, 214; Gabrielle Marceau and Peter N. Pedersen, 'The World Trade Organization and Civil Society', 33 Journal of World Trade 5 (1999) 18.

77 Pascal Lamy, 'Keynote Address to the WTO Public Forum', 4 October 2007, http://www.wto.org/english/news_e/sppl_e/sppl73_e.htm (visited 16 January 2009).

78 Alex Lofthouse and Florencia Jubany, 'Multilateralism at the Crossroads', Report for International Trade Canada on WTO Public Symposium (June 2004), http:// www.international.gc.ca/trade-agreements-accords-commerciaux/assets/pdfs/ CCC-FOCALREPORT22-07-04-en.pdf (visited 16 January 2009).

79 See WTO, 'WTO Public Forum 2006', http://www.wto.org/english/forums_e/ public_forum_e/forum06_e.htm (visited 16 October 2006). Note that 1,396 participants registered online for the 2006 Public Forum, and 136 people were registered manually after the expiry date of the online registration.

80 See WTO, 'WTO Public Forum 2007', http://www.wto.org/english/forums_e/ public_forum2007_e/programme_e.htm (visited 20 November 2007).

81 See WTO, 'Lamy: Civil Society Is Influencing the WTO Agenda', 4 October 2007, www.wto.org/english/news_e/sppl_e/sppl73_e.htm (visited 49 April 2009).

82 See WTO, 'WTO Public Forum 2008: "Trading into the Future"', http://www.wto.org/ english/forums_e/ngo_e/forum08_background_e.htm (visited 9 April 2009).

83 Decision of the General Council, 'Procedures for the Circulation and De-restriction of WTO Documents', WT/L/452, dated 16 May 2002. For a discussion of the timelines for de-restriction of documents, such as submissions by members, Secretariat documents, Accession Working Party documents, minutes of meetings, and Schedules Renegotiation documents, see 'Explanatory Report of Old and New Procedures', http://www.wto.org/ english/forums_e/ngo_e/derestr_explane_e.htm (visited 17 August 2008).

84 Ibid.

85 The WTO does not provide an official list of the NGOs who are invited to these meetings. However, an exhaustive list of NGOs based in Geneva is available at http:// hec-executive.ch/iomba/www/?pid=316 (visited 17 August 2008).

86 Having satisfied itself that the applicant is indeed an NGO, the External Relations Division includes it on the list of participants.

87 Hetty Kovach, Caroline Neligan, and Simon Burall, *Power Without Accountability: The Global Accountability Report 2003* (London: One World Trust, 2003) 15.

88 See Robert Lloyd, Jeffrey Oatham, and Michael Hammer, *2007 Global Accountability Report* (London: One World Trust 2007), http://www.oneworldtrust.org/documents/OWT_GAR_07_colour_lo-res.pdf (visited 17 August 2008).

89 See WTO, 'For NGOs', http://www.wto.org/english/forums_e/ngo_e/ngo_e.htm (visited 17 August 2008).

90 Newsletters, brochures, and announcements will not be included in the list.

91 For a complete list of all NGO position papers made available and posted by the WTO Secretariat to date, see http://www.wto.org/english/ forums_e/ngo_e/pospap_e.htm (visited 17 August 2008).

92 See WTO, 'First Series of Issue-specific Dialogues with Civil Society Organized by the WTO Secretariat', http://www.wto.org/english/forums_e/ngo_e/ngo_dialogue_e.htm (visited 16 January 2009).

93 To form the Informal NGO Advisory Body, Director-General Supachai Panitchpakdi selected, on a discretionary basis, those NGOs that he considered to be influential and broadly representative, and seeking, where possible, to maintain regional balance and balance between NGOs from developed and developing countries. Interestingly, some NGOs, including Friends of the Earth International and Oxfam International, rejected their invitations to become members, arguably fearing criticism from their peers and potential bad publicity. Perhaps for the same reason, the NGOs that agreed to participate asked the Director-General to abstain from publicizing the existence of the Advisory Body. That is why the WTO website did not include any information on the composition or the activities of the Informal NGO Advisory Body. Members of the informal NGO Advisory Body included Consumers International, Consumer Unity and Trust Society, the International Federation of Agricultural Producers, World Wide Fund for Nature (WWF) International, Third World Network, Christian Aid, the International Confederation of Free Trade Unions, Public Services International, the International Center for Trade and Sustainable Development, and the International Institute for Sustainable Development. See WTO Reporter, 'WTO Chief Sets Up Advisory Bodies With Business, NGOs to Boost Dialogue', 17 June 2003, http://www.tradeobservatory.org/headlines.cfm?refID =18358 (visited 16 January 2009).

94 See, *United States—Standards for Reformulated & Conventional Gasoline* (*US—Gasoline*), WT/DS2; *United States—Import Prohibition of Certain Shrimp & Shrimp Products* (*US—Shrimp*), WT/DS58; *Brazil—Measures Affecting Imports of Retreated Tyres* (*Brazil—Retreaded Tyres*), WT/DS332; *European Communities—Measures Concerning Meat and Meat Hormones* (*EC—Hormones*), WT/DS26; *European Communities—Measures Affecting Asbestos & Asbestos-Containing Products* (*EC—Asbestos*), WT/DS135; *European Communities—Measures Affecting the Approval and Marketing of Biotech Products* (*EC—Approval & Marketing of Biotech Products*), WT/DS291; *Canada—Continued Suspension of Obligations in the EC—Hormones Dispute* (*Canada—Continued Suspension*), WT/DS321; *United States—Continued Suspension of Obligations in the EC—Hormones Dispute* (*US—Continued Suspension*), WT/DS320; *European Communities—Regime for the Importation, Sale & Distribution of Bananas* (*EC—Bananas III*), WT/DS27, and *European Communities—Conditions for the Granting of Tariff Preferences to Developing Countries* (*EC—Tariff Preferences*), WT/DS246.

95 See, for instance, Article 46 of the Statute of the International Court of Justice, which states: 'The hearing in Court shall be public, unless the Court shall decide otherwise, or unless the parties demand that the public be not admitted'; and Article 26(2) of the Statute of the International Tribunal for the Law of the Sea, which states: 'The hearing shall be public, unless the Tribunal decides otherwise or unless the parties demand that the public be not admitted.'

96 Consultative Board to Director-General Supachai Panitchpakdi, *The Future of the WTO: Addressing Institutional Challenges in the New Millennium* (Sutherland Report) (Geneva: WTO, 2004) para 261 (emphasis omitted).

97 Ibid., at para 262. See also Warwick Commission, *The Multilateral Trade Regime: Which Way Forward?*, Report of the First Warwick Commission (Coventry: University of Warwick, 2007) 34.

98 Note that in 1999 in *United States—Imposition of Countervailing Duties on Certain Hot-Rolled Lead & Bismuth Carbon Steel Products Originating in the United Kingdom* (*US—Lead and Bismuth II*), a dispute involving the United States and the European Communities, the United States requested that the panel allow observers into the panel meetings. In response to this request, the panel held: 'Since it is up to each party to decide whether or not it chooses to forego its right to confidentiality for its written and oral submissions to a panel, we are obliged to seek the agreement of each party before implementing Working Procedures that might undermine the confidentiality of a party's written and oral submissions. By its 14 June response to the US request of 11 June 1999, the EC effectively withheld such agreement. As a result, we are not in a position to develop any Working Procedures that might jeopardize the confidentiality of the EC written and oral submissions to the Panel. Accordingly, we are unable to grant the US request to open this meeting to observers.' See Panel Report, *US—Lead and Bismuth II*, WT/DS138/R and Corr. 2, adopted 7 June 2000, para 6.2. Note also that, in the ongoing negotiations on DSU reform, both the EC and Canada have proposed allowing panel and Appellate Body meetings to be open to the public, provided that the parties to the dispute agree, in order to enhance the transparency of the dispute settlement system. See Communication from the European Communities, TN/DS/W/1, dated 13 March 2003, at 6; and Communication from Canada, TN/DS/W/42, dated 24 January 2003, at 5.

99 These cases were brought by the European Communities to secure the lifting of retaliation measures applied by the United States and Canada in the *EC—Hormones* dispute.

100 The meeting with the experts took place on 27–28 September and with the parties on 2–3 October 2006. See Communication from the Chairman of the Panels, *EC—Hormones (Article 21.5) II*, WT/DS320/8, WT/DS321/8, dated 2 August 2005. See also WTO, 'Hormones Panels to Open Proceedings with Parties to the Public', dated 4 August 2005, see www.wto.org/english/news_e/news05_e/ news05_e.htm (visited 16 January 2009).

101 See WTO, ibid.

102 See also Francis Williams, 'WTO Opens Hearing to Public', *Financial Times*, 13 September 2005.

103 See United States Trade Representative, 'Notice of Public Meeting in the WTO Dispute: European Communities and Certain Member States—Measures Affecting Trade in Large Civil Aircraft (DS316)', http://www.ustr.gov/assets/Trade_Agreements/Monitoring_Enforcement/WTO_Airbus_Case/asset_upload_file81_13158.pdf

(visited 16 January 2009). The delayed broadcasting allowed the panel to verify that no confidential business information would be inadvertently disclosed in showing the videotape.

104 WTO, 'WTO Hearings on Banana Dispute Opened to the Public', 29 October 2007, http://www.wto.org/english/news_e/news07_e/dispu_banana_7nov07_e.htm (visited 9 April 2009).

105 See WTO, 'WTO Hearings on Apple Dispute Opened to the Public', 11 August 2008, http://www.wto.org/english/news_e/news08_e/hearing_11aug08_e.htm (visited 17 August 2008).

106 See for example, Panel Report, *EC—Bananas III (Article 21.5—US)*, WT/DS27/RW/USA and Corr.1, adopted 22 December 2008, para 1.11; Panel Report, *Canada—Continued Suspension*, WT/DS321/R, adopted 14 November 2008, paras 7.1–7.52.

107 Note that in *Brazil—Retreaded Tyres*, the Centre for International Environmental Law (CIEL) requested the panel to allow the web-casting of the first meeting of the panel with the parties. After consultations with the parties (Brazil and the European Communities) and in light of the views expressed by them, the panel informed CIEL that its meetings with the parties would be held in closed sessions in accordance with the Working Procedures adopted by the panel at the beginning of the proceedings. See Panel Report, *Brazil—Retreaded Tyres*, WT/DS332/R, adopted 17 December 2007, para. 1.9.

108 See, for example, Appellate Body Report, *US—Continued Suspension*, WT/DS320/AB/R, adopted 14 November 2008, Annex IV (Procedural Ruling of 10 July to Allow Public Observation of the Oral Hearing, para 7).

109 Note, however, that no third participant requested that its oral statements and responses to questions remain confidential and not subject to public observation.

110 According to M. Jeffords, in the period between 1998 and 2003, more than 70 NGOs have submitted *amicus curiae* briefs either to panels or the Appellate Body. See Maura Jeffords, 'Turning the Protester into a Partner for Development: The Need for Effective Consultation Between The WTO and NGOs', 28 Brooklyn Journal of International Law 937 (2003) 961. A further 22 *amicus* briefs have been received by panels or the Appellate Body since 2003. Note that this count does not include briefs considered by the Appellate Body that were already before the panel. Such briefs have been counted only once.

111 Lise Johnson and Elisabeth Tuerk, 'CIEL's Experience in WTO Dispute Settlement: Challenges and Complexities from a Practical Point of View' in Tullio Treves, Marco Frigessi di Rattalma, Attila Tanzi, Alessandro Fodella, Cesare Pitea, and Chiara Ragni (eds), *Civil Society, International Courts and Compliance Bodies* (T.M.C. Asser Press: The Hague, 2005) 243–60 at 249.

112 Steve Charnovitz, 'Participation of Non-Governmental Organizations in the World Trade Organization', 17 University of Pennsylvania Journal of International Economic Law 331 (1996), at 353.

113 Article 13 of the DSU states in a relevant part: 'Each panel shall have the right to seek information and technical advice from any individual or body which it deems appropriate.' Article 12.1 of the DSU states: 'Panels shall follow the Working Procedures in Appendix 3 unless the panel decides otherwise after consulting the parties to the dispute.' Article 11 of the DSU provides that it is the function of panels to make an objective assessment of the matter before them.

114 See Appellate Body Report, *US—Shrimp*, WT/DS58/AB/R, adopted 6 November 1998, paras 104, 105, and 106.

115 Note that the acceptance and consideration of *amicus curiae* briefs attached to the submissions of parties and third parties to the panel or the Appellate Body are not controversial (anymore). These brief are considered to be an integral part of the submissions they are attached to.

116 Article 17.9 of the DSU states: 'Working procedures shall be drawn up by the Appellate Body in consultation with the Chairman of the DSB and the Director-General, and communicated to the Members for their information.' Rule 16.1 of the Working Procedures for Appellate Review, to which the Appellate Body in *US—Lead and Bismuth II*, referred only in footnote, states in the relevant part: 'In the interests of fairness and orderly procedure in the conduct of an appeal, where a procedural question arises that is not covered by these Rules, a division may adopt an appropriate procedure for the purposes of that appeal only, provided that it is not inconsistent with the DSU, the other covered agreements and these Rules.'

117 Appellate Body Report, *US—Lead and Bismuth II*, WT/DS138/AB/R, adopted 7 June 2000, paras 39 and 42.

118 See Appellate Body Report, *EC—Asbestos*, WT/DS135/AB/R, adopted 5 April 2001, paras 51–52.

119 Ibid.

120 In response to the form-letter rejections, several NGOs issued a critical press statement. The statement complained that the Appellate Body gave no reason for the rejections. Among the signatories to the statement were two large environmental NGOs, the WWF and Greenpeace International. See Charnovitz, above n 15, at 189.

121 Emphasis added. See Minutes of the General Council Meeting of 22 November 2000, WT/GC/M/60, Adopted 23 January 2001, para 120.

122 Warwick Commission, above note 97, at 33.

123 Ibid, at 33–34.

124 See Article 34 (on the participation of international organizations) and Article 62 (on third-party interventions) of the Statute of the International Court of Justice and Rules 62 and 63 (on expert evidence) of the Rules of Court of the International Court of Justice.

125 International Court of Justice, 'Practice Direction XII', http://www.icj-cij.org/documents/index.php?p1=4&p2=4&p3=0 (visited 16 January 2009).

126 The Rules of the International Tribunal for the Law of the Sea (ITLOS/8), as amended on 15 March and 21 September 2001, provide that the tribunal can request further documents from the parties and expert opinions (Rules 77 to 81), and the tribunal can also request any additional information from 'intergovernmental organizations' (Rule 82). See also Article 40 of the Statute of the European Court of Justice (March 2008), http://curia.europa.eu/en/instit/txtdocfr/index.htm (visited 9 April 2009).

127 As for international criminal courts and tribunals, see, for instance, Rule 103 of the Rules of Procedure and Evidence of the International Criminal Court; Rule 74 of the Rules of Procedure and Evidence of the International Criminal Tribunal for the Former Yugoslavia; Rule 74 of the Rules of Procedure and Evidence of the International Criminal Tribunal for Rwanda, Rule 74 of the Rules of Procedure and Evidence of the Special Tribunal for Sierra Leone. As for regional human rights courts, see Rule 44(2) on third-party intervention of the Rules of Court of the European Court of Human Rights (July 2007), which provides that 'any member State which is not a party to the

proceedings, or any person concerned who is not the applicant may submit written comments or, in exceptional cases, take part in a hearing'. Finally, consider Rule 63(3) of the Rules of Procedure of the Inter-American Court of Human Rights, reprinted in Basic Documents Pertaining to Human Rights in the Inter-American System, OEA/Ser.L/V/I.4 rev.9 (2003), which stipulates that '[t]he President [of the Inter-American Court of Human Rights] may invite or authorize any interested party to submit a written opinion on the issues covered by the request'. On the relation of international courts and tribunals with civil society, see also Tullio Treves Marco Frigessi di Rattalma, Attila Tanzi, Alessandro Fodella, Cesare Pitea, and Chiara Ragni (eds), *Civil Society, International Courts and Compliance Bodies* (Cambridge: Cambridge University Press, 2004).

128 See WTO, 'Rules of Conduct for the Understanding on Rules and Procedures Governing the Settlement of Disputes', WT/DSB/RC/1, Adopted 11 December 1996, Rule 4(1).

129 See Appellate Body Report, *EC—Bananas III*, WT/DS27/AB/R, adopted 25 September 1997, para. 10. The ruling in *EC—Bananas III* concerned only the freedom of parties to decide on the composition of their delegations at hearings of the Appellate Body. However, the reasoning underlying this ruling also applied to the composition of delegations at panel meetings. The latter was explicitly stated in Panel Report, *Indonesia—Certain Measures Affecting the Automobile Industry*, WT/DS54/R, WT/DS55/R, WT/DS59/R, WT/DS64/R and Corr.1 and 2, adopted 23 July 1998, para 14.1.

130 See Panel Report, *Korea—Anti-Dumping Duties on Imports of Certain Paper from Korea* (*Korea—Certain Paper*), WT/DS312/R, adopted 28 November 2005, paras 7.10, 7.11.

131 ECOSOC Resolution 1996/312, above n 23, at para 1.

132 Ibid, at paras 3 and 8.

133 Ibid, at para 2. This requirement may be used to exclude NGOs that advocate violence, racial discrimination, or disrespect for human rights.

134 Ibid, at para 9.

135 Ibid, at para 10.

136 Ibid.

137 Ibid, at para 12.

138 Ibid, at para 11.

139 Ibid, at para 13. This requirement may be waived if an NGO provides a satisfactory explanation in accordance with paragraph 13.

140 Ibid, at para 61(h).

141 Ibid, at para 20.

142 Ibid.

143 Ibid, at para 5.

144 Ibid, para 60.

145 At its session in January 2006, the NGO Committee considered applications for consultative status from 99 NGOs. It recommended that 60 were put on List 1 and 39 on List 2.

146 In many instances, these questions have little to do with the compliance of the NGO with the established accreditation criteria, but have to do more with political sensitivities of particular UN member states. To give just one example, at the January 2006 session of the NGO Committee, Cuba posed a question to an NGO that focused on human rights violations 'in the Global South': did this NGO consider that there were no human rights violations 'in the Global North'? Although this NGO eventually was granted special consultative status, the example is illustrative.

147 ECOSOC Resolution 1996/312, above n 23, at para 61(c). Under 'exceptional circumstances', the NGO Committee can ask for a report between the regular reporting dates. The committee may ask for such special reports when it is informed of an act or a pattern of acts of the NGO concerned that could lead to suspension or withdrawal of the consultative status. See ibid.

148 There are three cases in which the consultative status of an NGO may be suspended for up to three years or withdrawn:
   (1) if an NGO clearly abuses its status by engaging in a pattern of acts contrary to the purposes and principles of the UN Charter, including unsubstantiated or politically motivated acts against Member States of the United Nations incompatible with Charter's purposes and principles;
   (2) if there exists substantiated evidence of influence from proceeds resulting from internationally recognized criminal activities such as illicit drugs trade, money-laundering, or illegal arms trade;
   (3) if, within the preceding three years an organization did not make any positive or effective contributions to the work of the United Nations and, in particular, to the work of ECOSOC or its subsidiary organs (ibid, para 57).

149 For the first time they were listed in WIPO, above n 45, at para 16.

150 See Ripinsky and Van den Bossche, above n 38, at 90, referring to an interview with an official from the WIPO Office of the Legal Counsel, 21 November 2005.

151 These criteria were enumerated in an interview by an official from the WIPO Office of the Legal Counsel, 21 November 2005.

152 These documents have to be provided, whenever possible, in English, French, and Spanish.

153 See Ripinsky and Van den Bossche, above n 38, at 91, referring to an interview with an official from the WIPO Office of the Legal Counsel, 21 November 2005.

154 See WIPO, 'Observers, NGOs, IGOs', http://www.wipo.int/members/en/admission/observers.html (visited 16 January 2009). These criteria were originally set out in WIPO, above n 45, at para 16.

155 As a matter of practice, member states are not consulted by the WIPO Office of Legal Counsel when it reviews the application from a national NGO. A member state is assumed to be able to raise its objections, if any, at the meetings of the assemblies that will consider granting of permanent observer status.

156 The documents and information required by WIPO from national NGOs applying for observer status are nearly identical to those required from international NGOs.

157 See Ripinsky and Van den Bossche, above n 38, at 92, referring to an interview with an official from the WIPO Office of the Legal Counsel, 21 November 2005.

158 Ibid. There is no official list of documents and information that NGOs applying for ad hoc accreditation must submit. Typically, NGOs will send a request for accreditation without enclosing any additional documents. It is then for a secretarial unit reviewing the application to decide which documents and information it would like to request. Normally, the list of required information does not go beyond the list established for NGOs requesting permanent observer status. See ibid.

159 Ibid, at 93. The procedure is set out as described in an interview by an official from the WIPO Office of the Legal Counsel, 21 November 2005.

160 See, for example, WIPO, 'Admission of Observers—Memorandum of the Director General', A/41/8, 15 August 2005, http://www.wipo.int/edocs/mdocs/govbody/en/a_41/a_41_8.pdf (visited 16 January 2009).

161 See, for example, WIPO, 'General Report adopted by the Assemblies', A/40/7, 5 October 2004, paras180–81.

162 See Ripinksy Van den Bossche, above n 38, at 94–95, referring to an interview with an official from the WIPO Office of the Legal Counsel, 21 November 2005.

163 Ibid, at 95.

164 Ibid. The Office of Legal Counsel, and not the assemblies, decides whether to remove the NGO from the list of permanent observers.

165 Formally, for participation in the dialogues, no accreditation is required on days prior to when the official meetings begin and security measures are increased, but civil society organizations benefit from accreditation to have easier access to the IMF and the World Bank buildings. See ibid, at 161, referring to an interview with Ms. Simonetta Nardin and Ms. Jennifer Bisping, IMF External Relations Department, 24 January 2006.

166 See World Bank, 'Dialogue with Civil Society', http://web.worldbank.org/WBSITE/EXTERNAL/TOPICS/CSO/0,,contentMDK:20094167~menuPK:283025~pagePK:220503~piPK:220476~theSitePK:228717,00.html (visited 28 December 2008).

167 See Ripinsky and Van den Bossche, above n 38, at 161, referring to an interview with Ms. Simonetta Nardin and Ms. Jennifer Bisping, IMF External Relations Department, 24 January 2006.

168 Ibid.

169 Ibid, at 163.

170 Ibid.

171 See IMF, above n 49, at para IV.C.2.

172 Ibid, at paras V.F.1 and 2.

173 See Ripinsky and Van den Bossche, above n 38, at 185, referring to an interview with Ms. Simonetta Nardin and Ms. Jennifer Bisping, IMF External Relations Department, 24 January 2006.

174 Ibid.

175 IMF, above n 49, at Annex para A. 3.

176 Ibid, at paras V.F.3 and 5.

177 See Ripinsky and Van den Bossche, above n 38, at 186, referring to an interview with Ms. Simonetta Nardin and Ms. Jennifer Bisping, IMF External Relations Department, 24 January 2006.

178 IMF, above n 49, at para V. B.3.

179 Except for the annual and spring meetings, when all civil society organizations (as well as all other 'visitors') wishing to obtain accreditation require approval of the executive director concerned.

180 It has been suggested that such examination was beyond the resources of the WTO Secretariat.

181 To prove its non-profit character, an NGO is required to produce registration documents or a charter pointing to the aims of the organization. If these are not available, the WTO requires at least production of documents that would prove the organization formally exists. Strictly speaking, the non-profit character is not a criterion for selection *among* NGOs but rather a feature characteristic of all NGOs that distinguishes them from other types of organizations.

182 Note that for the Hong Kong Session of the Ministerial Conference, the accreditation procedure is waived for those NGOs that were duly registered for at least two previous sessions of the Ministerial Conference. See WTO Ministerial Conference, Procedures Regarding Registration and Attendance of Non-Governmental Organizations at the Sixth Session of the Ministerial Conference, WT/MIN(05)/INF/6, dated 1 June 2005.

183 Sutherland Report, above n 96, at para 207.

184 Ibid, at para 208. The report did, however, suggest formalizing the 'criteria to be employed in selecting those civil society organizations with which the Secretariat might develop more systematic and in-depth relations'.

185 See above n 17, at para VI.

186 Sutherland Report, above n 96, at para 212.

187 Ibid, at paras 186 and 212.

188 Ibid, at paras 179 and 206.

189 Ibid, at para 212.

190 Such activities could arguably include joint WTO Secretariat-NGO research projects and NGO involvement in WTO training and technical assistance programs.

PART VI

Regional Trade Agreements and the WTO

Accommodating Developing Countries in the WTO: From Mega-Debates to Economic Partnership Agreements

GERHARD ERASMUS

I. Introduction

The debate about accommodating developing countries in international organizations is an old one. International trade arrangements have achieved some success in this regard, such as the recognition of least developed countries (LDCs) as a special category and the adoption of the Everything but Arms program. Developing countries also enjoy flexibility when it comes to compliance with many of the standard rules applicable to Members of the World Trade Organization (WTO).[1]

The concept of special and differential treatment has been built into many provisions of WTO law. During the Kennedy Round, Part IV of the GATT 1947 was adopted, requiring developed countries to accord high priority to the reduction of trade barriers to products exported from developing countries. It also introduced the concept of non-reciprocity for less developed contracting parties. The special efforts of the United Nations Conference on Trade and Development (UNCTAD) resulted in the launching of the Generalized System of Preferences (GSP) in 1968. It has been observed that the 'single undertaking' approach of the Uruguay Round did not put an end to the granting of special and differential treatment and that there are no fewer than 145 such provisions.[2]

There remain a number of unresolved issues and new complications with respect to the accommodation of LDCs. The special preferences have not worked as intended. Specifically, they have not solved the problem of the marginalization of developing countries. Special preferences have produced some negative economic consequences, and certain economists argue that 'little benefit has in fact accrued to developing countries' through preferential schemes.[3]

Many developing countries have become trapped by preferential schemes, often resulting in failures to implement domestic reforms. In addition, GSP schemes are unilateral, grantor states determine the product coverage (developed country lobby groups are not inactive), and preferences have become dependent on other conditions. The Sutherland Report makes the valid point that 'recipient countries have been burdened with obligations unrelated to trade, which are expressed as conditions to receiving preferences. Thus, it can be argued, that preferences are no longer unreciprocated'.[4]

Preferential treatment has also caused or contributed to structural conditions and legal arrangements that work against the integration of many developing countries into the global economy. The African, Caribbean, and Pacific (ACP) countries are an obvious example. Practically all ACP countries have continued to trade with their main trading partner, the European Union (EU), outside of normal rules. The special arrangements concluded for this purpose (the Cotonou Agreement and its predecessors) required WTO waivers. These waivers have now expired, and the majority of these states are not prepared for the 'normal' rules-based system. Catching up becomes tougher. The rules of the game introduced by the establishment of the WTO can fully apply only to the players inside the system. The ACP countries have largely traded in arrangements outside this system. Although most of them are Members of the WTO, they have also been 'outsiders'.[5]

This chapter endeavours to contribute to the discussion by making three points. The first is that the mega debates about trade and development have produced limited success. It would be more constructive to address smaller or more focused sets of problems. The WTO could, for example, allow the Economic Partnership Agreements (EPAs), currently being negotiated between the European Union and the ACP countries, to include a development-promoting dimension by applying less strict rules regarding WTO compatibility of regional trade arrangements. The EPAs have to comply with Article XXIV GATT and Article V GATS. This challenges the WTO to link development aims to regional integration issues. Will the WTO allow these free trade agreements (which will not be based on the Enabling Clause)[6] enough flexibility when they have to comply with the rules for regional trade arrangements?

The second point made in this chapter is that technical assistance and 'implementation assistance' are not necessarily the same thing. The latter allows for technical assistance directed at the needs of a specific developing country (or groups of them) with regard to the implementation of particular obligations or specific regional arrangement. This approach should focus on domestic requirements, including legal and institutional reforms and capacity building aimed at specific outcomes. International assistance programs will show better results if undertaken in smaller, focused contexts. It is not practical to attempt to reform a whole state or groups of states at once or to build capacity across the whole range of public needs.

Many international organizations implement specialized development assistance programs and claim that success depends on domestic responses and local absorption capacity. Problems with delivery continue. Were the EPAs to have well-designed implementation chapters, which run in tandem with what other international organizations do, the results would be better. New regional integration arrangements foreseen under the EPAs will be launched on a firmer footing if accompanied by a proper focus on implementation.

The third and final point is related to the previous one and maintains that regional integration initiatives have the potential to serve as development and capacity-advancing mechanisms. This point must be qualified. The track record of existing regional trade arrangements among ACP countries, and in Africa in particular, is not reassuring. They tend to be over-ambitious and with a focus on grand schemes.[7] The EPAs should be more realistic and focus on local capacity needs for promoting regional trade and should develop technical expertise in that context. Ineffective institutions and weak enforcement mechanisms in developing countries are a sign of deeper institutional deficiencies that hamper development and integration into the multilateral trade system. And it is not getting better. Thus far, obligations in trade agreements and technical assistance programs have had limited success in developing sustainable remedies for these institutional weaknesses.[8] The EPAs should do better if they are to accomplish what they have taken on.

II. Why Focus on the Economic Partnership Agreements?

The focus on the EPAs is justified because these agreements can directly assist in the belated introduction of the ACP countries into the rules-based system of multilateral trade. Notwithstanding the creation of the WTO in 1995, ACP countries remain largely outside the global trading system. Furthermore, these countries are still not fully prepared for WTO membership. The EPAs have, by implication, a deeper agenda: to be platforms for reform and assistance measures to equip the ACP countries for meaningful WTO membership. Integration into the global economy, one of the expressly stated objectives of the EPA negotiations, is not possible without attention to this aspect.

The EPAs will have implications for how ACP states will trade with the European Union and with each other, how they will pursue their plans for regional integration, and how the challenges of development, technical capacity deficits, and domestic implementation of international obligations will be tackled. The implementation of the EPAs will require follow-up measures and focused technical assistance, as well as new domestic and regional institutions and laws. The necessary technical and institutional capacity is still lacking and undermines efforts to comply with WTO obligations.

The EPAs should target domestic reforms and assist these countries generally in coping with the legal and technical demands of trade under the multilateral system. This becomes more urgent as the preferences of the WTO waivers have fallen away and WTO compatibility of regional trade arrangements becomes unavoidable.

The current chapter uses the Southern African Development Community (SADC) EPA as a basis for discussion. It is a poignant illustration of how difficult it has become to gain trade concessions from the developed world, despite promises by the developed world under WTO law to act in a pro-development manner. The issues and the outcomes of the negotiations of the SADC EPA to date will be discussed in order to determine the general direction of the debate. Are there indications that the EPAs will live up to the hopes and expectations stated above? Will the ACP countries subsequently be better positioned with regard to WTO participation?

The SADC EPA also provides a realistic context. Trade between the European Union and Southern Africa displays areas of competition. These offensive interests make for tough negotiations. There are additional complications in the form of challenges to square the EPA for this region with an existing customs union. This will especially test the resolve of the European Union to support the pursuit of deeper regional integration in the developing world. The SADC EPA includes the oldest African regional trade arrangement: the Southern African Customs Union (SACU).[9] It will be very difficult to manage the common external tariff of SACU and to protect the union's integrity if this EPA excludes South Africa (which is not a member of the ACP group). The present EU position is to exclude South Africa from the market access benefits offered to the other SADC members. South Africa is the strongest economy in SACU (and in sub-Saharan Africa), and if it has to trade with the European Union in a separate bilateral arrangement there will be several negative consequences for SACU and for Southern Africa's own plans for deeper integration. Regional as well as global integration will become tougher, and the very existence of SACU could be jeopardized.

The consequences could be more far-reaching in light of the fact that SACU has a unique arrangement in the form of a common revenue pool. Customs and excise duties (of which more than 90 percent are generated by South African duties) are paid into this common pool and later shared. The sharing occurs by means of a formula based on the value of intra-SACU trade, not the source of the duties.[10] This is highly beneficial to the other four SACU members. South Africa, however, claims that it is actually transferring large amounts of its own resources to the other members, a transfer they object to.[11] If SACU ceases to exist and the common revenue pool disappears, the consequences for SACU members, especially Lesotho and Swaziland, would be calamitous.[12]

III. EPAs In the Context of the Global Trading System

The negotiations to conclude Economic Partnership Agreements are taking place against the background of a bigger debate. This debate is contemplating changes in the architecture of the multilateral trade system and the implications of the increase in regional trade arrangements.[13] How does this context affect the EPA negotiation process?

Developing countries see the EPAs as a *sui generis* form of regional trade agreement, with a development objective and purpose. What are the prospects of their being recognized as a special category of 'development' free trade agreements? The Doha Round has, by implication, this issue on its agenda in the context of discussions with respect to the implementation of GATT Article XXIV. A failed Doha Round might mean a lost opportunity for changing and updating those rules.

When and if the Doha talks meaningfully resume, the world will be a different place. This is true not only because of the growing muscle of the emerging economies. There will be many more regional agreements, and it is into this environment that the EPAs will have to fit. The mushrooming of regional agreements may make it more difficult to accept the EPAs as falling into a special category of development-promoting trade agreements.

Another matter to consider is the recent efforts by African governments to adopt an all-Africa approach to EPA negotiations and to link the process to their own schemes for regional integration in the continent.[14] The development of an African template for these negotiations may have the benefit of elucidating complicated issues but comes too late to redirect the EPA outcomes in a fundamentally different way. Five separate African EPAs are currently being contemplated.[15] It is difficult to see them being conflated into one single arrangement.

IV. Developing Countries and the WTO: From Mega Debates to Lesser Expectations

There is general agreement that developing countries should be more actively and constructively involved in the WTO. These nations cannot prosper in isolation. Many commentators will go further and call for WTO reforms so that development needs can be better accommodated. Others point to larger systemic benefits for developing countries (e.g., more clout in trade negotiations) and the fact that the system will become more legitimate with increased participation by developing countries. John Jackson has observed, while commenting on the WTO dispute settlement system, that the 'participation of developing countries in this system is, in the opinion of many, vital to the long-term durability and effectiveness of the WTO dispute settlement system, and therefore, probably the WTO itself'.[16]

The realpolitik undertone in Jackson's observation serves as a reminder that international organizations function best in stable and 'legitimate' environments. It is neither desirable nor practical that large parts of the world are absent from multilateral arrangements. Lasting solutions for global problems cannot be worked out by the selected few, as the protection of the environment and the debate about security issues have demonstrated. Globalization has caused quicker spillover effects into more and more areas, while the jurisdictional boundaries of international organizations tend to become softer. The concerns about the effects of poverty on the international system straddle many agendas. Multilateral organizations are required to respond.

Developing countries will claim that the multilateral trade system is not geared to the accommodation of their needs. Then the debate about goals, definitions, graduation, and responsibilities starts all over again. The fact that the WTO is a 'member-driven' organization and a forum for trade negotiations between sovereign states means that the emphasis is on consensually derived rules for international trade. Underdevelopment may (or may not), from time to time, be on the agenda but it is not the WTO's raison d'être. The WTO Agreements are not about development assistance in the sense of providing funds or technical assistance to solve infrastructural problems. These agreements focus on the movement of goods and services across borders. The WTO rules provide the benefits of certainty, predictability, transparency, and information about conditions in export markets.

The accepted wisdom is that the WTO is not a 'development organization'. This raises further questions. Does it imply that the development challenge is compartmentalized and is the purview of specifically designed bodies where a big-bang solution will be found? We know that the totality of the challenges is too complex to expect specialized institutions such as the World Bank to deal with them by means of recipes such as domestic reconstruction plans or a Washington consensus, valid as such plans might have been at certain times and under specific conditions.

The Sutherland Report points out that certain prerequisites and conditions must be in place for developing countries to benefit from the WTO regime. These nations must have the 'capacity to participate', they must put in place 'an environment offering security, institutional integrity and administrative efficiency without which their exporters can never be competitive and investors will never show interest'.[17] They should abandon failed policies of protectionism and their political leadership must 'respond to the opportunities presented by the WTO'.[18] In meeting this challenge, developing countries still face an uphill struggle.

The suspension of the Doha Development Round in July 2008 has challenged expectations that WTO mega-debates (in the sense of trade rounds) can achieve comprehensive solutions for development problems. It also confirms many of the caveats about how to deal (or not to deal) with the challenge posed by issues clustered under the 'development' rubric. The Doha talks did not fail because certain developing countries demanded special safeguards for agricultural products. 'Development' cannot provide the ratio for a WTO trade negotiation round. The development problem the Doha Round has to tackle does not fit into the logic and procedures of a trade round. The pursuit of pro-development outcomes has become lost in the detail, demands for concessions, and a timetable beyond control. In the words of a negotiator from a developing country:

> The current impasse in the Doha Round negotiations arises fundamentally, in my view, from a displacement as the priority matters of developmental issues by commercial demands of interest groups in the developed world. The WTO negotiation process has been described as a schmorgasbord, where one puts something into the pot in order to take something out. Only the naïve would imagine that in such a process there would not be some payment for the reforms and demands sought by the developing world.[19]

The very cause of the impasse as identified in this observation is also the reason that it is unlikely that the Doha Round can be revived as a 'development round'. Trade rounds are about concessions. The accommodation of development needs within the multilateral trade order requires a different approach. The required political will (and domestic support is a precondition) must first exist to pursue this particular objective (development) and to agree on outcomes capable of solving the problem at hand. The WTO is not geared toward generating this type of consensus. Rather, the WTO is the overseer of the system for rules-based, multilateral trade liberalization. The current international financial crisis and the signs of economic nationalism are additional reasons why the revival of the Doha Round (with the expectation that it will bring about real benefits for the poor countries) becomes increasingly unlikely.

Power relationships among WTO Members have changed but have not resulted in a reorientation of priorities to the benefit of poorer nations. China,

India, and Brazil have become dealmakers but they are not, despite the political rhetoric, 'developing countries'. Their objectives in WTO deliberations are to secure their new status and protect their rights of market access into rich economies. It would be unrealistic to expect otherwise. The Doha Round has not and cannot produce a clear set of principles on which all nations loosely described as developing countries are in agreement. The development discourse has in fact become more nuanced and more difficult.

Where does this leave us with regard to the discussion suggested in the title of this chapter? When it comes to addressing underdevelopment and poverty in the international system, there are mega-debates and those that focus on specific sets of challenges. The mega-debates fulfil a useful political function, and developing countries insist on having them. Such occasions are viewed as evidence that the multilateral community cares for and recognizes the validity of their concerns. This chapter addresses the accommodation of developing countries in a more limited context, focusing on the EPAs as new agreements to replace the regime governing trade between the European Union and the ACP countries. The previous EU–ACP regime existed alongside the WTO order.

Will the EPA negotiations result in fundamentally different outcomes for the ACP countries? Will the negotiations be more difficult for the developing countries engaged in these talks because they are negotiating in small groups? Answers to these questions are tentative because these negotiations are ongoing[20] and the EPA negotiations are being conducted among different configurations of developing nations. The EPAs could, in principle, produce positive outcomes and tailor-made results, but that is not yet evident. There are, in the mean time, enough facts to merit a discussion and to support certain conclusions.

V. Economic Partnership Agreements: Origins, Intentions, and Realities

The origins of the EPA negotiations go back to the Lomé Convention of 1975, which granted ACP goods tariff-free access into the European Union, while also providing for aid flows and export-earning guarantee schemes. The Cotonou Agreement, concluded in June 2000, extended this regime until the end of 2007. After 1995, the ACP countries continued to trade with the European Union, their biggest trading partner, pursuant to a WTO waiver permitting exceptional and preferential treatment.[21] That waiver expired at the end of 2007.

The European Union's non-reciprocal preferences for goods imported from former colonies gradually became an awkward and WTO-incompatible remnant of a former era. The object of the current EPA negotiations is to replace the previous preferential trade arrangement with a more modern and

WTO-compatible regime. EPA negotiations currently concern the European Union and the 79 ACP countries. There will be several separate EPAs. They will be rules-based agreements covering trade in goods and, according to the European Commission, also services and investment. The EPAs must also address long-standing developmental challenges and promote deeper regional integration among ACP nations.

To date, the European Union has not successfully concluded any EPAs with African states. However, some states have initialled interim EPAs. The negotiations about services and investment are continuing, and the European Union hopes that they will be completed by the end of 2009, a goal that is unlikely to be reached.

EPA negotiations between the European Union and Caribbean states were completed in 2007. Thirteen Caribbean Forum member states and the European Union signed the 'full' Caribbean Forum–European Community Economic Partnership Agreement in early October 2008. Guyana signed a few days later. The Government of Haiti requested more time to review this EPA.[22] Negotiations to conclude a single EPA for the Pacific region are also continuing, though several issues remain outstanding. Ministers from these states agreed that a comprehensive EPA might include provisions relating to intellectual property rights with obligations not going beyond those contained in the Cotonou Agreement.[23]

The collapse of the Doha Development Round in July 2008 was a major setback to the EPA negotiation process. The game plan for the EPAs (the Cotonou Agreement) has been linked to certain expectations about these multilateral talks. It was hoped that the Doha Round's emphasis on 'development' would create space to accommodate the special needs of the ACP countries, such as more 'flexibility' with regard to the requirements of Article XXIV GATT. New rules on safeguards in services trade were also expected. These outcomes have not, as yet, materialized. The result is that WTO compatibility of the EPAs as regional trade arrangements will be measured by rules designed in 1947, with the added qualification that the EPAs will now be justiciable.

EPA negotiations have been tough, and the ACP countries have found it increasingly difficult to carve out 'development-friendly' arrangements. The world has changed since the time when the Cotonou Agreement was adopted. Brussels' new 'Global Europe' strategy emphasizes

> a more results-oriented approach that focuses on concrete problems that EU businesses face in third country markets.... A strong market access policy is a key function of the common commercial policy, and a key area in which the EU can deliver real economic benefits for its Member States. When it comes to taking action against trade barriers, we need to identify ways to improve the use of the existing tools and—where possible—to develop new ones.[24]

Civil society organizations have joined the debate about the EPAs and the WTO rules to be met. Most are critical of the approach and the proposals of the European Commission. One criticism has been that the EPAs go beyond WTO requirements and thus would increase the burden to implement new obligations. Others point to the tough legal commitments demanded of the European Union by ACP states, unfair benefits for European firms (reciprocity is part and parcel of the new arrangements), and failure of the European Union to deliver on promised development assistance. African regional integration plans, it is argued, will be derailed by the different EPA configurations and concomitant WTO requirements.

For its part, the European Union denies these claims. The European Union view is that aid, provided by other programs, must be used effectively[25] and that 'the success of the regional integration process also requires national public institutions to be strengthened and involved more in a climate of democratic governance'. For the European Union, regional integration is an ongoing process to boost the underlying logic of development:

> [In] harmonised markets, the free movement of goods, services, capital and people permits economies of scale, stimulates investment and boosts economic growth and South-South trade. But, in the light of past experience, policies of this kind yield the best results when combined, supported and generally backed up with the simultaneous implementation of sectoral policies agreed at national and regional level aimed at increasing productive capacity, improving the competitiveness of the ACP economies and promoting sustainable social and environmental development in partner countries and regions.[26]

Articles 36–38 of the Cotonou Agreement reveal the original intention of the EPA scheme:

- The EPAs must be WTO-compatible and be introduced gradually.
- Non-reciprocal trade preferences will be maintained during a transition phase.
- The parties reaffirmed the importance of the commodity protocols.
- The original target date for the entry into force of EPAs was 1 January 2008.
- The preparatory phase had to be used for capacity building, in the public and private sectors of the ACP countries, with 'appropriate assistance to budgetary adjustment and fiscal reform, as well as for infrastructure upgrading and development, and for investment promotion'. The ACP countries claim that this objective has been moved to the back burner.
- Duty-free access for products from all least developed countries had to be assured.

- There had to be a timetable for the progressive removal of trade barriers, in accordance with the relevant WTO rules.
- Negotiations had to take account of the level of development and the socio-economic impact of trade measures on ACP countries and their capacity to adapt and adjust their economies to the liberalization process. 'Negotiations will therefore be as flexible as possible in establishing the duration of a sufficient transitional period, the final product coverage, taking into account sensitive sectors, and the degree of asymmetry in terms of [a] time table for tariff dismantlement, while remaining in conformity with WTO rules then prevailing.' The parties undertook to collaborate in the WTO to defend the arrangements reached, in particular with regard to the degree of flexibility available.
- A joint ACP–European Union Trade Committee was established to pay special attention to ongoing multilateral trade negotiations, with a view to preserve the benefits for the ACP–European Union trading arrangements.

There were several rounds of negotiations in 2007 to conclude 'interim' EPAs before the WTO waiver expired at the end of that year. Some interim benefits have been achieved. Since the beginning of 2008, goods from ACP countries have enjoyed duty-free and quota-free access to European markets. The European Commission, which negotiates on behalf of the European Union, insists that these advantages will become permanent only once the EPAs have been signed. If these discussions fail and no new agreements are concluded, the ACP countries outside the EPA system will trade with the European Union on the basis of the Generalized System of Preferences, with LDCs qualifying for the Everything but Arms scheme. This will bring disadvantages for specific countries with regard to coverage and conditions. For example, Namibia's main export, beef, is not included in the GSP. In this regard, the European Union has stated:

> The European Union qualified its offer by undertaking that it would not be tied to the requirement of equivalent openness from the ACP countries. The EPAs are not free trade agreements in the classic sense. Flexibility under WTO rules means that ACP counties will have to offer market access, but this will phase in over many years. The ACP will also retain the right to protect sensitive products where the removal of import duties could threaten local producers.[27]

So what happened? The membership of the various EPA configurations in Africa became, from the outset, a major problem. African countries had to propose their own configurations to negotiate with the EC. What they came up with did not always match their existing regional arrangements. Some African states have blamed the EC for the choices made, an allegation that Brussels denies.

Some peculiar and complicated EPA configurations have emerged, and future integration schemes in Africa will face new complications as a result. The SADC EPA is not an EPA for the Southern African Development Community. The 15 SADC member states are negotiating their EPAs in about five different configurations.[28] Tanzania remained part of the SADC EPA group for a long time, despite being a founding member of the East African Community (EAC).[29] It later decided to rejoin the EAC EPA.

The 2007 negotiations were largely conducted on the basis of EC proposals, with detailed provisions on *inter alia* rules of origin, trade remedies, non-tariff measures, customs and trade facilitation, technical barriers to trade, SPS measures, dispute settlement, and development cooperation. The second round of negotiations will address services and investment.

The fact that the expected WTO flexibility for free trade agreements with developing members has not materialized has been a major stumbling block. The promise in the Cotonou Agreement that the EPAs would not be 'free trade agreements in the classic sense' has remained an elusive goal. There are no new rules on flexibility, and one will have to wait and see how other WTO Members will respond once the EPAs are notified and whether there will be a WTO regime for 'development-oriented' trade agreements via the EPAs.

VI. The SADC EPA and the Challenges of Regional Integration

The Interim SADC Economic Partnership Agreement (IEPA) between the European Union, and the members of the Southern African Customs Union (SACU) and Mozambique (but excluding South Africa) was finally initialled at the end of 2007. Angola is part of this group but has not initialled the IEPA. This interim document covers trade in goods only.

The initialling of the text of the interim agreement proved, in the end, to be quite a diplomatic challenge. This can partly be explained by the fact that the SADC EPA is a complex arrangement. Obligations due to existing structures had to be taken into account and there are new legal and institutional challenges. The failure to develop internal integration policies for SADC beforehand created additional complications.

The implications for SACU may be even more serious. The membership of this organization is divided over further negotiations with the European Union and the implementation of the interim arrangements for the trade in goods will pose considerable challenges.[30] The five SACU states are all members of SADC but they have not agreed on strategies for promoting regional integration or ensuring that both SACU and SADC pursue the same game plan.

SADC proclaimed itself a free trade agreement in July 2008 (including all 15 members) and wants to be a customs union by 2010. This has to be followed by a common market. This time frame is unrealistic and the general aim is over-ambitious. An even grander scheme has subsequently been added in the form of a decision in October 2008 to launch a tripartite FTA consisting of all the members of the Common Market for Eastern and Southern Africa, the EAC, and SADC. There is overlapping membership between these organizations and all three of them have plans to become customs unions.

The exclusion of South Africa from the SADC EPA, the fact that Mozambique (not a member of SACU) is a party, the different policy decisions of SACU's members regarding the second phase of negotiations (on services and investment), and the reservations by Namibia before it initialled the SADC IEPA text are some of the problem areas still to be addressed. Namibia refused to initial the text together with Botswana, Lesotho, and Swaziland, and on 23 November 2003 Mozambique entered certain reservations. Angola will apparently join the process when ready. Accession at a later date is possible.[31] South Africa and Namibia decided not to participate in the second phase, where trade in services and investment will be negotiated with the EC.

Article 31(3) of the SACU agreement remains another obstacle. It requires the consent of all members before new trade agreements with third parties can be entered into. Before the SADC EPA can enter into force this issue will have to be resolved, and South Africa holds the key, at least with regard to the letter of the law. There is no procedure as to how Article 31 consent can be demonstrated. This is a problem that a common negotiating mechanism, which Article 31 also calls for, could have solved. SACU has as yet no common negotiating mechanism.

When Namibia initialled the SADC IEPA late in 2007, it noted several concerns that needed to be resolved before negotiations could continue. South Africa and Angola share Namibia's concerns and have raised additional ones. They point to the detrimental effects of the IEPA on regional integration among the SADC EPA states, including diminished space for national development policies, inconsistency with WTO obligations, and tension with the entitlements in the Cotonou Agreement. There are also complaints about the objectives of the IEPA text.[32]

The most-favoured-nation clause in the SADC EPA text constitutes a particular problem. Article 28 of the SADC IEPA deals with future free trade agreements and states that

> the SADC EPA States shall accord to the EC Party any more favourable treatment applicable as a result of the SADC EPA States or any Signatory SADC EPA State becoming party to a free trade agreement with any major trading country after the signature of this Agreement.

A 'major trading economy' is defined as

> any developed country, or any country accounting for a share of world merchandise exports above 1 percent in the year before the entry into force of the economic integration agreement referred to in paragraph 2, or any group of countries acting individually, collectively or through an economic integration agreement accounting collectively for a share of world merchandise exports above 1.5 percent in the year before the entry into force of the economic integration agreement referred to in paragraph 2.

It is true that the EPAs offer duty-free and quote-free access for ACP goods and that in this regard there cannot be an advantage to be lost. The concern is, however, about lost bargaining space when negotiating new free trade agreements with other parties, particularly when third parties know in advance that offers between them and the ACP countries will automatically benefit the EU. Future free trade agreements between developing countries and third parties may, in addition, contain provisions on other types of preferences and measures not granted by the EPAs. The EU would then be able to demand the same.

Brazil has raised its concern about how this regional most-favoured-nation provision will undermine the possibility in the Enabling Clause for developing countries to meet less severe standards when concluding regional agreements *inter se*. The EPAs will also operate *ex nunc,* and previous advantages already granted in other free trade agreements concluded by the EU are excluded.

Export taxes and levies are another concern. They are introduced by Article 24 of the interim SADC EPA, dealing with 'duties, taxes or other fees and charges on exports'. It prohibits 'new customs duties on exports or charges having equivalent effect… '. Namibia claims that this provision hampers its freedom to adopt domestic policies in areas such as beneficiation in the mining industry. Namibia is further concerned about the provision on infant industry protection and the refusal by the EC to accommodate its proposal to insert a clause along the lines found in existing regional agreements binding on the SADC EPA states.

Article 27 of the interim SADC EPA regulates the free movement of goods. It provides that 'customs duties shall be levied only once for goods originating in the EC Party or in the SADC EPA States in the territory of the other Party.' The SADC EPA states are not a homogenous block and belong to organizations with overlapping membership. SACU is a customs union, with a single customs territory and common external tariff. Mozambique and Angola are not members of this customs union, though they are members of SADC and administer their own customs territories. The implementation of this provision will require special and new legal arrangements between Mozambique (and later Angola) on the one hand and SACU (or some of its members) on the other. This will undermine the administration of SACU's common external tariff. Trade facilitation measures will be another casualty and there is the additional danger of trade deflection. These concerns are still on the negotiating agenda.

VII. GATT Article XXIV and the SADC EPA

Article XXIV determines how WTO compatibility of regional trade agreements is to be achieved. They must be notified to the Committee on Regional Trade Agreements (CRTA). CRTA reports can be adopted (on the basis of consensus) without necessarily deciding the question of consistency. Express decisions that a notified scheme is inconsistent with the rules are rare.[33] Many regional trade arrangements have not been notified and most existing ones 'have not received an affirmative consensus decision that they are GATT-consistent'.[34] The consistency of a customs union or free trade agreement with WTO rules can be challenged in disputes between WTO Members under the Dispute Settlement Understanding. But as one commentary notes after having analyzed WTO practice and case law: 'As a result, except for some obvious cases, we simply cannot tell whether the numerous plurilateral trade agreements currently in practice are GATT consistent or not.'[35]

There are no legal instruments specifically designed for regional trade agreements between developed countries, on the one hand, and developing countries and LDCs, on the other. The rules of Article XXIV cannot be discerned with sufficient clarity, and even if they could, they should not, according to the Cotonou Agreement, be applied *stricto jure*; flexibility had to be built in. The extent of the flexibility cannot be determined in advance because there is no formula for flexibility.

Flexibility should find its application in asymmetry and in formulations recognizing the needs (i.e., the development component) of the developing countries and the LDCs in the EPAs. Flexibility is also about a specific approach to a negotiated outcome. In this instance, the challenge is to develop offers and to agree on outcomes (this goal must be shared by all parties) that will demonstrate an honest effort to comply with the general concerns underpinning GATT Article XXIV, while striving to accommodate the needs of developing countries and specifically LDCs. It is not an open-ended approach, but neither is it a case of adhering to strict rules; there are no such rules. It must be possible to eventually justify the negotiated outcome by demonstrating approximation with the general requirements of GATT Article XXIV.

Most ACP countries have complained about the lack of flexibility on the part of the EC, including neglect of the 'development dimension'. This is a demonstration of how difficult it has become to accommodate development needs through standard WTO arrangements. Article XXIV was negotiated as part of the 1947 GATT. No specific attention was then given to the needs of developing countries. It is, therefore, in its pure form, not suitable for evaluating the EPAs for the purpose of determining WTO compatibility.

The Enabling Clause came later in the life of GATT but cannot accommodate the needs of the SADC EPA because the latter is not strictly speaking about a free trade agreement between developing countries. It does, however, provide indications of how the development dimension has been accommodated, and in particular that it must be done flexibly.

The substantially all-trade requirement in GATT Article XXIV poses another problem. Two types of measurement approaches have developed: quantitative and qualitative. The first uses a statistical benchmark to indicate the percentage of trade and the other refers to the notion that no sector or major sector should be excluded.[36] In the Doha Negotiating Group on Rules, it has been observed that the 'percentage of trade method has been traditionally favoured as an indication of regional trade agreement coverage… '.[37] However, there is a willingness to explore how to supplement 'a benchmark based on coverage by trade with an assessment of trade coverage measured by number of tariff lines'.[38] This may result in a combined average threshold. Substantially all trade also refers to other trade restrictions. Duties are a self-interpreting term. This is not the case with respect to substantially all trade. One commentator quotes from the working Party Report on *EC—Agreement with Portugal* and concludes that there 'is no exact definition of the expression referring to the term "substantially all trade"'.[39]

The literature discusses a number of working reports and cases but provides no examples of how an EPA-type arrangement has been dealt with. This leaves negotiators with the challenge to be innovative, while endeavouring to approximate their offers to the general principles underpinning Article XXIV as well as accommodating the development dimension.

VIII. Where Do Services and Investment Fit In?

It has been argued that the Cotonou Agreement contains no clear obligation to negotiate services as part of the EPAs. Article 41 of the Cotonou Agreement confirms 'the growing importance of services in international trade and their major contribution to economic and social development'. The only undertaking appears in Article 41(4):

The Parties further agree on the objective of extending under the economic partnership agreements, and after they have acquired some experience in applying the Most Favoured Nation (MFN) treatment under GATS, their partnership to encompass the liberalisation of services in accordance with the provisions of GATS and particularly those relating to the participation of developing countries in liberalisation agreements.

It is not particularly useful to base decisions about trade in services on arguments about the extent of legal obligations. Are services necessary for development and regional and global integration? The evidence is that they are and that, therefore, they should be included in new negotiations.[40] Services represent about two-thirds of the global GDP and the share of value added by services in GDP tends to rise with national income.[41] Economists emphasize the links between services and competitiveness when it comes to trade in goods. The ACP economies cannot be integrated into the global economy unless trade in services is given the necessary attention. It is unfortunate that South Africa and Namibia have decided to exclude themselves from these EPA negotiations. They argue that they are not yet ready and that they will pursue liberalization in services under the GATS.

Article 67 of the Interim SADC EPA provides that the parties will complete negotiations on services liberalisation on the basis of a liberalisation schedule for each participating SADC EPA State, including a commitment to a standstill as specified in Article V.1.b(ii) GATS for all services sectors andagreement to negotiate progressive liberalization with substantial sectoral coverage within a period of three years following the conclusion of the full EPA. It was also agreed 'to support capacity building aimed at strengthening the regulatory framework of the participating SADC EPA States.'

The parties have further agreed to adopt an investment chapter, 'taking into account the relevant provisions of the SADC Protocol on Finance and Investment, no later than 31 December 2008'. However, the SADC Finance and Investment Protocol has not yet been finalized, and a general Services Protocol for SADC is an even more remote prospect. Namibia and South Africa, although not included in the SADC EPA services negotiations, are involved (as SADC members) in the negotiations for this SADC Protocol and will in all likelihood be parties thereto.

A study by Fink and Jansen makes important points about the economic effects of services in regional trade agreements.[42] Multilateral liberalization generally yields greater welfare gains. However, there are additional gains from preferential trade, associated with greater economies of scale and knowledge transfer. If 'learning by doing' effects are important, preferential liberalization may enable domestic service suppliers to become more efficient, as they face some competition within the free trade agreement territory but are not yet exposed to global competition. This rationale applies mainly to agreements among developing countries, where firms operate below best-practice productivity levels.[43]

The issue of regional most-favoured-nation provisions also appears in services provisions of regional trade agreements. Most regional trade agreements negotiated by EFTA, Japan, and the United States have incorporated them.[44] They are also included in the EPAs. Fink and Jansen discuss the reasons for including non-party most-favoured-nation clauses in regional trade agreements:

> The inclusion of a non-party in a MFN clause in a services RTA [regional trade agreement] or BIT [bilateral investment treaty]is best explained by bargaining considerations. To begin with, for any given RTA each party has an incentive to ask its trading partner for MFN treatment and it ensures that domestic services benefits from current and future trade preferences are extended to non-parties. However, a country bound by many non-party MFN obligations faces a less favourable bargaining situation in future RTAs. A new RTA partner knows that any negotiated preferences will be extended automatically to others. Thus, service importers and investors from that partner will not have access to the domestic market, reducing the value of a future RTA commitment. Consequently, the willingness of a new RTA partner to 'pay' for additional market opening may be reduced. On balance, a country with liberal trade policies in services has a stronger interest in a non-party MFN clause than a country that maintains substantial trade restrictions under a RTA. The former has few preferences left to grant and can only benefit from the extension of future market opening measures by RTA partners. The latter may be more cautious about widening the scope of any future liberalization undertaken and may not want to weaken its bargaining position with trade to other parties. It is thus not surprising that RTAs involving developed countries typically feature a non-party MFN obligation, whereas agreements between developing countries do not always incorporate such a discipline.[45]

Regional trade agreements dealing with services do not, unlike the regional arrangements for trade in goods, give rise to the 'spaghetti bowl' concern of overlapping membership and difficult rules of origin. In services, rules of origin primarily deal with the origin of service providers rather than the origin of the traded services. This point brings Fink and Jansen to observe that 'a world of barrier-free service RTAs will indeed approximate free multilateral trade'.[46] They are of the belief that

> only time will tell whether the current wave of RTAs proves to be helpful or harmful for the WTO. A multitude of political economy forces are pushing in different directions. In the specific case of services, however, there are reasons to believe

that preferential agreements are more likely to be building blocks than stumbling stones. The main grounds for this more optimistic outlook are the weakly discriminatory nature of services RTAs and the web of non-party MFN clauses to which many countries are already bound in existing agreements. There is some concern about preferential market opening of mode 4 and regulatory cooperation agreements, which are inherently more discriminatory. However, it is not clear to what extent full multilateral progress in these areas will ever be feasible.[47]

The main source of discrimination in regional services liberalization lies in the preferential regulatory cooperation agreements that may accompany regional trade agreements. This is an unknown factor that may not be of primary importance in the case of such agreements between developing countries. Their growing regional integration will, however, increase the use of such implicit regulatory barriers, as will, in principle, also happen in the EPAs. The GATS endeavours to discipline the use of regulatory measures in Article VI(4), which states:

> With a view to ensuring that measures relating to qualification requirements and procedures, technical standards and licensing requirements do not constitute unnecessary barriers to trade in services, the Council for Trade in Services shall, through appropriate bodies it may establish, develop any necessary disciplines.

Work has started to develop disciplines for the accounting sector, and the Working Party on Professional Services has been renamed the Working Party on Domestic Regulation, focusing on the extension of these disciplines to other professions.[48]

What are the prospects for regulating trade in services among ACP countries and within their own regional organizations? This is a neglected topic. Most ACP nations invoke arguments about capacity constraints and are hesitant to commit to new services obligations. The SADC states have only recently started a debate about trade in services as part of their integration plans but the process is limited to the financial sector. The SACU agreement does not cover services.[49] South Africa has consistently refused to discuss services with the EC in the context of the SADC EPA. This does not mean that trade in services (involving South African firms) does not take place. They are important suppliers of many services (such as telecoms, construction, retail, and energy) in sub-Saharan Africa. The tourism sector is important for African countries generally and most of the ACP countries, in the context of the EPA, seem ready to negotiate with respect to this sector.

IX. Conclusion

As it becomes more difficult to make substantive progress in multilateral trade negotiations, the limits as to what mega-trade debates can generate (and under what circumstances) have become more obvious. Mega-outcomes to mega-debates depend on, among others, the right mix of conditions. The conclusion of the Uruguay Round is an example. More and more commentators have been calling for plurilateralism in international trade negotiations, which would allow the willing few to move forward. Such a development will not be without its dangers for the WTO.[50]

The conditions conducive to a successful mega-trade deal do not currently exist. So what are the implications for the EPA negotiations? Would it, nevertheless, be possible to get them accepted in the WTO as a special category of free trade agreement? This depends on a variety of factors, such as the political resolve to design and notify them as such.

Do the EPAs have the right architecture and the necessary political support? The current evidence is not reassuring. The European Union and the African ACP countries have adopted different approaches. The EC has offered broad access for goods but, in exchange, insists on the inclusion of new generation issues and firm rules. African states want special assistance for domestic needs and enough time to develop their own policies and regulations. They are not keen on binding international legal instruments, formal dispute resolution, and new disciplines. The debate is not really about the design of a new genre of free trade agreements within the WTO system but rather about immediate bargains.

What about implementation assistance? The EPAs have been and are being negotiated in different configurations, which create opportunities for tailor-made answers to local problems. However, a proper 'implementation assistance' dimension will come about only if the EPAs generate a new philosophy about development and accept firm disciplines about implementation. Outcomes should be monitored and be measurable. Such plans should be linked to national and regional programs in ACP countries directed toward the same goals and should be co-owned by the European Union.

The outcomes depend on what the negotiators finally settle on, the membership structures of the EPAs, and how ACP countries will pursue domestic and regional reforms. Currently, the European Union does not offer special or new development assistance packages; existing programs should suffice. The African governments are also not very clear as to how new development formulas should look. The notion of 'implementation assistance', which requires a different design and specific commitments, is not really on the table. New obligations are never popular, but for implementation assistance to be acceptable and achievable, commitments about national and regional reforms should be included in the texts of new agreements. That would have the additional benefit of clarifying regional integration issues in Africa, which currently look rather confused.

The potential of the EPAs to promote regional integration in Africa is uncertain. There are in fact two debates and two sets of integration initiatives proceeding concurrently: the EPAs and the African Union debates. These two discourses do not share the same conception and potential outcomes of integration. The EPA process is also not synchronised with Africa's home-grown integration plans. The result is lack of focus regarding an important aspect of the structural framework for development, which regional integration can provide.

The idea that the EPAs should result in a new and *sui generis* type of free trade agreement with ACP countries has brought larger systemic issues concerning regional integration into sharper focus. The linear approach to integration (to move from a free trade agreement to a customs union and common market within a tight time frame) generally being pursued in Africa must be questioned. Grand schemes and rapid progress under tight time frames have resulted in many missed deadlines and scant respect for legal obligations.[51]

Integration is not an end in itself. Configurations should make sense and should be designed on the basis of achievable goals, realistic membership choices, a serious commitment to implement and respect rules, sound institutions, and the potential to promote trade. Regional trade arrangements require a carefully designed architecture and attention to local needs. Current plans for regional integration in Africa will not escape the dangers of the 'spaghetti bowl', which is caused by duplication and overlapping membership. A parallel stream of new integration initiatives via the EPAs may complicate matters further. The integration debate requires a new start and a single, integrated focus. The EPA negotiations have not generated the right debate and are not asking the critical questions.

Many of the current problems have their origin in old issues. Negotiations on the SADC EPA have focused attention more sharply on the unconsolidated nature of SACU under its new agreement. This is an old customs union but is burdened by a specific legacy with an emphasis on revenue sharing. Although the new SACU Agreement emphasizes the importance of 'common policies and common institutions', the actual focus is still on revenue sharing, rather than on the adoption of policies to promote deeper integration, common trade negotiations, or joint industrial development.

What do these developments and tendencies imply for developing country participation in the WTO? It will be an uphill battle to sell the EPAs as development-friendly free trade agreements. The WTO framework for doing so is absent as the multilateral system was designed for a different fabric and at a time when regional trade did not figure as prominently as they now do. The rules contained in Article XXIV have not been designed for the current explosion of regional trade agreements. Article V GATS is still very much untested terrain. In the words of a recent study:

> Whatever else the GATT/WTO has achieved over the six decades of its existence— and many would agree that these achievements have been significant—the fact remains that to all intents and purposes, the WTO has been something of a passive observer as regionalism has exploded.[52]

The regional most-favoured nation clause in the EPAs constitutes a controversial feature. They generate an inherent multiplier that cannot be ignored by developed countries (or the likes of China, India, and Brazil) when they have to decide whether to conclude new trade agreements, be they regional or bilateral, with states already locked into the obligations of the EPAs.

Developing countries in Africa struggle with the rules-based dimension of international trade, whether with regard to their WTO membership or in the context of regional trade arrangements. Once the EPAs are in place, it will no longer to possible to invoke waivers or unilateral preferences, neither in Brussels nor in the capitals of the ACP countries. Other WTO Members will monitor compliance and may decide to raise disputes when they consider their rights to be violated.

This predicament will become more acute. In most instances, national trade laws and procedures in ACP countries are not WTO compliant, and the private sector cannot reap the benefits of WTO membership. These countries need a considerable amount of technical assistance (together with their own efforts), which must focus on domestic reforms and capacity building to implement and adhere to WTO disciplines and the new rules associated with the EPAs.

There is no template for solving these problems. Patience, dedication, and well-focused efforts are necessary and must be backed up by technical assistance, financial support, and realistic legal and institutional arrangements within developing countries and their regional trade arrangements. National governments, civil society, and the private sector must be part of the answer. They must 'own' development programs, while solutions must be developed to address particular local needs.

The mega-debate regarding the accommodation of developing countries in the WTO will continue. It will be a difficult debate and the usefulness of a 'Development Round' as the way forward is doubtful. As some have argued, it requires a new approach within the WTO:

As for the issue of development, which has largely caused the negotiation process of the WTO to become stalled, it remains the most important issue on the WTO agenda and it will be negotiated again although not necessarily in the same manner as pursued in the Doha Round. Development is clearly a bigger issue than the machinery (trade negotiation) by which it has been addressed in the Doha Round. It will be necessary to rethink what the WTO can accomplish in economic development that is still consistent with the inherent capabilities and constraints of the trade negotiating process. Then, too, it may be necessary to rethink the hoary construct of 'developing country', and to question whether this construct as it is currently employed in WTO negotiations is conducive to dealing with the problems of underdevelopment and poverty in the international system. Developing countries are an economic diverse group in the WTO, and the most destabilizing dimension of this diversity is, in fact, economic development. It may be necessary to determine what about 'developing country' can be effectively addressed in a multilateral trade negotiation, and what about 'developing country' needs to be addressed by other policy tools.[53]

Notes

1   For examples of such flexibilities in the context of the dispute settlement system of the WTO, see Peter van den Bossche, *The Law and Policy of the World Trade Organization*, 2nd ed. (New York: Cambridge University Press, 2008) 231 ff.

2   Hunter Nottage, 'Trade and Development' in Daniel Bethlehem, Donald McRae, Rondey Nuefeld, and Isabelle Van Damme (eds), *The Oxford Handbook of International Trade Law* (Oxford University Press, 2009) 488.

3   Consultative Board to the Director-General Supachai Panitchpakdi, *The Future of the WTO: Addressing Institutional Challenges in the New Millennium* (Sutherland Report) (Geneva: WTO, 2004) 24 (discussing special and differential treatment).

4   Ibid, at 24. The Sutherland Report also notes that the Appellate Body report in *European Communities—Conditions for the Granting of Tariff Preferences to Developing Countries*, WT/DS246/AB/R, adopted 20 April 2004, indicates that there are limits to what developed countries can demand as conditions for preferences.

5   African governments have practically never been involved in proper dispute settlement proceedings before the WTO. This is owing in large part to the relatively small amount of trade flows from and within Africa.

6   The EPAs include the developed countries of the European Union and, therefore, cannot be based on the more flexible rules for regional trade arrangements allowed by the Enabling Clause.

7   The decision of a tripartite summit in October 2008 in Kampala to establish a new free trade area encompassing the 26 members of Common Market for Eastern and Southern Africa, the East African Community, and Southern Africa Development Community is a case in point. Seventeen of these countries are either in an existing customs union and negotiating an alternative one, or are in the process of negotiating separate customs unions.

8 Carsten Fink, 'Enforcing Intellectual Property Rights: An Economic Perspectives' in ICTSD (ed),
  The Global Debate on the Enforcement of Intellectual Property Rights and Developing Countries (Geneva, ICTSD IPRs and Sustainable Development Programme, Issue Paper No. 22, 2009), http://ictsd.net/downloads/2009/03/fink-correa-web.pdf (visited 2 April 2009).

9 It was established in 1910, and it is claimed that this is the world's oldest customs union. A new agreement was signed in 2002 and entered into force in 2004, replacing the 1969 agreement. The member states are Botswana, Lesotho, Namibia, South Africa, and Swaziland.

10 Annex I of the Southern African Customs Union (SACU) Agreement, done at Gaborone, Botswana, 21 October 2002, http://www.sacu.int/main.php?include=docs/legislation/2002-agreement/main.html (visited 2 April 2009).

11 South Africa manages the common external tariff on behalf of the union. The other members claim the high SACU tariffs are caused by South African policies, while they suffer the consequences.

12 Lesotho obtains more than 60 percent of its public revenue from this pool. For Swaziland it is more than 50 percent. The tax base of these countries is very small and practically no alternative sources can be tapped.

13 There are 350 of these agreements in existence. For a discussion of the implications of regional trade agreements, see Richard Baldwin and Patrick Low (eds), *Multilateralizing Regionalism—Challenges for the Global Trading System* (Cambridge: Cambridge University Press 2009).

14 See the report by the United Nations Economic Commission for Africa, *North-South FTAs After All? A Comprehensive and Critical Analysis of the Interim Economic Partnership Agreements*, June 2008, http://www.acp-eu-trade.org/library/files/ECA_EN_0408_Commonwealth_North-South-FTAs-after-all.pdf (visited 2 April 2009).

15 For the SADC region, for Eastern and Southern Africa, for the East African Community, for Central Africa, and for Western Africa. These EPA configurations and even the ultimate number of EPAs have yet to be finalized. Some countries (e.g., oil-exporting Nigeria) have opted not to sign EPAs and to trade under the GSP. LDCs have the safety net of Everything but Arms. In 2000 South Africa concluded a bilateral trade agreement (the Trade, Development and Cooperation Agreement) with the European Union.

16 John Jackson, 'Perceptions about the WTO Trade Institutions', 1 World Trade Law Review 101 (2002) at 111 (Keynote Address on the occasion of the inauguration of the Advisory Centre for WTO Law on 5 October 2001).

17 Sutherland Report, above n 3, at para 47.

18 Ibid.

19 Dr. Rob Davies, Deputy Minister of Trade and Industry, South Africa, 'Reclaiming the Development Dimension of the Multilateral Trading System', Geneva Lectures on Global Economic Governance, Graduate Institute of International and Development Studies, University of Geneva and the Global Economic Governance Programme University College, Oxford, 2 March 2009, http://www.globaleconomicgovernance.org/wp-content/uploads/davies-oxford-geneva-university-lecture.pdf (visited 2 April 2002).

20 An interesting political development occurred in Brussels at the end of 2008 when a new EU trade commissioner and a new chief negotiator were appointed. Those involved in the first negotiations with them in early 2009 spoke of new progress and positive developments.

21 WTO Doha Ministerial Conference, European Communities—The ACP-EU Partnership Agreement, WT/MIN(01)15, adopted 21 November 2001.
22 For a discussion of the Caribbean Forum EPA, see Sanoussi Bilal, 'To Sign or not to Sign? The Caribbean Dilemma', 7(8) Trade Negotiations Insights 1 (2008), http://ictsd.net/downloads/tni/tni_en_7-8.pdf (visited 2 April 2009).
23 Melissa Julian, 'EPA Negotiations Update', 7(9) Trade Negotiations Insights 14 (2008), http://ictsd.net/downloads/tni/tni_en_7-9.pdf (visited 2 April 2009).
24 European Commission, 'Global Europe: A Stronger Partnership to deliver Market Access for European Exporters' (18 April 2007), http://trade.ec.europa.eu/doclib/docs/2007/april/tradoc_134507.pdf (visited 2 April 2009).
25 The Council of the European Union recently pointed out 'the imminent adoption of the regional indicative programmes of the 10th EDF and the fact that they devote nearly 75% of their allocations to support for regional economic integration'. Those programs 'will form a central element of regional packages and of the accompaniment component of the EPAs, but ... they should still be coordinated with aid for trade from the Member States and other donors, in particular in the partner countries, in order to better meet the needs expressed by the ACP countries': see Council of the European Union, 'Council Conclusions on Regional Integration and the Economic Partnership Agreements for Development in the ACP Countries', 2902nd General Affairs Council Meeting, Brussels, 10 November 2008, http://www.consilium.europa.eu/ueDocs/newsWord/en/gena/103969.doc (visited 2 April 2009).
26 Ibid, at para 4.
27 European Union Delegation to the United States, 'Press Statement: EU Offers Full Market Access to Africa, Caribbean and Pacific Regions in EPA Negotiations', 4 April 2007, http://www.eurunion.org/eu/index.php?option=com_content&task=view&id=134 (visited 2 April 2009).
28 Some of the configurations are changing but the following EPAs had SADC states at one stage or another: SADC, ESA (Eastern and Southern Africa), EAC, and CEMAC (Central Africa). South Africa trades with the European Union under the TDCA.
29 The EAC members are Tanzania, Kenya, Uganda, Rwanda, and Burundi.
30 The five members trade with third parties via a common external tariff. If some of them are excluded from the SADC EPA, there will not be a common external tariff with the European Union. SACU's new agreement was signed in 2002 and provides for a Tariff Board to manage the common external tariff. This institution has not yet been established.
31 Articles 110 and 111 of the SADC IEPA.
32 These objectives are listed in Article 1 of the SADC IEPA.
33 Petros C. Mavroidis, *The General Agreement on Tariffs and Trade: A Commentary* (Oxford: Oxford University Press, 2005) 230.
34 Ibid, at 231.
35 Mitsuo Matsushita, Thomas J. Schoenbaum, and Petros C. Mavroidis, *The World Trade Organization*, 2nd ed. (Oxford: Oxford University Press, 2006) 578.
36 Systemic issues in the CRTA are discussed in James H. Mathis, *Regional Trade Agreements in the GATT/WTO* (The Hague: Asser Press, 2002) 227 *et seq.*
37 WTO, Committee on Regional Trade Agreements, Coverage, Liberalization Process and Transitional Provisions in Regional Trade Agreements, WT/REG/W/46, 2 April 2002, at para 11, http://docsonline.wto.org/DDFDocuments/t/WT/REG/W46.doc (visited 2 April 2009).

38 WTO, Negotiating Group on Rules, Submission on Regional Trade Agreements by the European Communities, TN/RL/W/179, 12 May 2005, at para 8, http://trade.ec.europa.eu/doclib/docs/2008/september/tradoc_140500.pdf (visited 2 April 2002).

39 See Mavroidis, above n 33, at 236.

40 Ninety percent of new employment opportunities in OECD countries come from services. Data from African countries are difficult to obtain but all indications are that services and agriculture are the major sources of employment.

41 Carsten Fink and Marion Jansen, 'Services Provision in Regional Trade Agreements: Stumbling or Building Blocks for Multilateral Liberalization?', Paper presented at the Conference on Multilateralising Regionalism, sponsored by the WTO/HEI, 10–12 September 2007, Geneva, http://www.wto.org/english/tratop_e/region_e/con_sep07_e/fink_jansen_e.pdf (visited 2 April 200).

42 Ibid.

43 Ibid, at 6.

44 Ibid, at 12.

45 Ibid, at 17.

46 Ibid, at 20.

47 Ibid, at 21.

48 WTO, Working Party on Professional Services, 'Report to the Council for Trade in Services on the Development of Disciplines on Domestic Regulation in the Accountancy Sector', S/WPPS/W/21 (Draft), 27 November 1998.

49 Implied exceptions are areas such as transport.

50 See, for example, the discussion in the Sutherland Report, above n 3, at 82. It notes that the GATS scheduling approach might be one avenue for pursuing plurilateralism.

51 See further Colin McCarthy, 'Is African Economic Integration in Need of a Paradigm Shift?' in Anton Boesl, Willie Breytenbach, Trudi Hartzenberg, Colin McCarthy, and Klaus Schade Boesl (eds), *Monitoring Regional Integration,* 2007 ed. (Stellenbosch: Trade Law Centre for Southern Africa, 2007), 6–43, http://www.nepru.org.na/fileadmin/download/books/MRIY_07_total_book.pdf (visited 2 April 2009).

52 Richard Baldwin and Patrick Low (eds), *Multilateralizing Regionalism—Challenges for the Global Trading System* (Cambridge: Cambridge University Press, 2009) 3.

53 Gilbert R. Winham, 'The Evolution of the World Trading System—The Economic and Policy Context', in Daniel Bethlehem, Donald McRae, Rodney Nuefeld, and Isabelle Van Damme (eds), *The Oxford Handbook of International Trade Law* (Oxford: Oxford University Press, 2009) 28.

꘡ ꘡ ꘡ **14**

Saving the WTO from the Risk of Irrelevance: The WTO Dispute Settlement Mechanism as a 'Common Good' for RTA Disputes

HENRY GAO AND CHIN LENG LIM*

I. Introduction

Over the past few decades, Regional Trade Agreements (RTAs)[1] have mushroomed worldwide.[2] The consensus in trade circles now is that 'regionalism is here to stay',[3] 'will [not] disappear',[4] and that 'little can be done to prevent ... [the] ... spread of [RTAs]'.[5] Such proliferation of RTAs has created a renewed sense of urgency for the World Trade Organization (WTO). The WTO must act to avoid the fate of being eclipsed into irrelevance. There are a number of options for the WTO today.

The first option sees the WTO as an RTA *'terminator'*. Theoretically speaking, the best approach would be to heighten the level of ambition in global trade talks to reduce all trade barriers to zero so that the discriminatory effect created by RTAs could be reduced or even eliminated.[6] In reality, however, Members would probably never adopt such an approach. First, while an RTA, by reducing the tariffs of its members to zero at the regional level, increases the incentive for non-RTA members to urge WTO Members to reduce tariffs to zero at the WTO, it will also increase the incentive for the RTA members not to extend zero tariffs to non-RTA members for fear of erosion of their RTA preferences.[7] As the decision whether to reduce tariffs is to be taken by RTA members, it is highly unlikely that they will choose to harm their own interests. Second, even if assuming, *arguendo*, that somehow the members to an RTA could overcome their fear of preference erosion and offer to non-RTA members in the WTO the same tariff concessions they can offer to their fellow members, it would be irrational to assume that they would be willing to offer more than what they are willing to give each other at the regional level. As several studies have shown, many RTAs have carved out certain sectors, with agriculture being the most well-known example, from the tariff reduction schedules.[8] Thus, at least with regard to those sectors, the RTA has entrenched trade protectionism and made it more difficult, rather than easier, for RTA members to agree to further reduce tariffs at the WTO. Third, while history is filled with examples of the ebb and flow of regional trade deals followed by major breakthroughs in multilateral trade negotiations, thus far it has not been possible for multilateral economic integration to reach the same level and depth of liberalization as regional economic integration. While the increased technical complexity of trade negotiations together with the increased number of participants is one explanation, a more plausible explanation is that regional integration is rarely about trade alone; instead, most RTAs, if not all, are driven more by the need to trade small economic losses for major political and strategic gains.[9] Offering zero tariffs to everyone at the WTO, however, would not score any political gains for most countries, as the WTO has become so large that it includes the friends and rivals of almost every country.

The second option sees the WTO as an RTA '*confessor*'.[10] If preferential treatment is regarded as a cardinal sin in the religion of free trade, the 'terminator' would wipe out those sins by eliminating the preferences. Under the second option, countries might seek, through 'confession', to alleviate their guilt even if they cannot wipe out their sins. According to this view, the WTO could, first, provide objective research to help better understand the impact of RTAs on non-members; second, set up a negotiating forum for the coordination, standardization, and harmonization of rules of origin;[11] and, third, draft 'best practices' or model RTAs[12] to minimize the effect of further fragmentation created by different breeds of RTAs. However, there are several reasons that this approach is not entirely satisfactory.

First, while the authors agree that the WTO would be the best institution to examine the pros and cons of different RTAs in the general sense, critical findings on particular RTAs would make the WTO (Secretariat) vulnerable to criticisms of infringing upon Member's rights to conclude RTAs under Article XXIV, and allegations of breaching the impartiality of the WTO and the Secretariat. Moreover, as it will be politically incorrect for the WTO to outsource such research to external researchers, the WTO most likely would assign the work to its Trade Policies Review Division[13] or the Economic Research and Statistics Division.[14] Even though these two are the largest divisions among all the functional divisions in the WTO,[15] their resources are still limited if the task to be performed is considered, i.e., examining the complex web of 400 RTAs[16] that currently involve all but one WTO Member.

Second, using the WTO to harmonize rules of origin is also difficult to achieve. First of all, since many preferential rules of origin are intentionally designed as devices to deny non-RTA members preferences, it is doubtful whether WTO Members would be willing to get rid of these carefully crafted devices. Second, even if assuming such reluctance can be overcome in most sectors, it would still be nearly impossible to streamline rules of origin for some politically sensitive sectors.[17] Third, even if the rules of origin can be harmonized in general, the application of such standardized rules of origin to particular products could still create problems An example of this would be a product that is manufactured with a 20 percent value-added in each of the five countries to an RTA, while the WTO adopts a uniform 30 percent value-added rule of origin for all RTAs with no provision for cumulation rules.

Third, with regard to the role of the WTO as an authoritative source of 'best practices' for RTAs or a model RTA, the problems are that first, as each country brings its unique blessings and predicaments to the RTA negotiating table, a 'one-size-fits-all' approach might not work. One possible solution to this is to draft 'best practices' or a model RTA in such a way that different options for a given rule are provided for potential RTAs to choose from. The danger, however, is that a country would simply choose the worst possible combinations, resulting in a 'Franken-stein' RTA to defeat the very purpose of having such best practices in the first place.

Yet another option offered is to turn the WTO into an '*inquisitor*' by strengthening the existing WTO monitoring system. The 2006 rules on transparency is a recent example of this.[18] Unfortunately, because the Committee on Regional Trade Agreements (CRTA) is hamstrung by the consensus rule, merely having heightened monitoring rules would not be of much practical use here.

This chapter discusses a fourth option: to make the WTO an '*enforcer*' by using the WTO dispute settlement mechanism as a venue for resolving at least some disputes among RTA parties, and possibly even disputes between RTA and non-RTA WTO Members. In a certain sense, this option complements rather than replaces the previous options. The rationale underlying this initiative is that, by using the WTO dispute settlement system for some RTA disputes, the Members will be able to develop, albeit gradually, incrementally, and pragmatically, a body of 'common law' on RTAs. Such a body of common principles could form the basis of multilateral rules on RTAs or harmonize RTA rules. This could minimize the harmful effect of RTAs.

In order to use the WTO dispute settlement system as a 'common good' for RTAs, three further questions must be addressed:

- Can the WTO dispute settlement system be used to adjudicate at least some RTA disputes?

- Which rules can the WTO apply in RTA disputes?
- How can the WTO machinery be equipped to deal with RTA disputes?

This chapter provides some preliminary thinking on these matters in the hope that our suggestions will trigger greater discussion about how the WTO could become more relevant given the current invasion of RTAs.

II. Panel and Appellate Body Jurisdiction

Can the WTO dispute settlement system be used to address disputes arising from RTAs? Consider two scenarios. The first concerns the power of the WTO Dispute Settlement Body (DSB) to adjudicate disputes that involve general requirements imposed on the formation of RTAs under the relevant WTO agreements. These include,[19] for example, whether an RTA satisfies the 'substantially all trade' requirement in GATT Article XXIV.8.b or the 'substantial sectoral coverage' requirement under GATS Article V, whether an interim agreement exceeds the 'reasonable length of time' as provided for under GATT Article XXIV.5.c, whether particular trade policy instruments constitute 'other restrictive regulations of commerce' under GATT Article XXIV.8.a.i, whether 'the duties and other regulation of commerce' for non-members are 'higher or more restrictive' than the pre-RTA level under GATT Article XXIV.5, or how to determine if particular products are 'products originating in such territories [of RTA Members]', etc. Most of these are preconditions that an RTA must satisfy before its Members could invoke GATT Article XXIV or GATS Article V to justify its deviation from the MFN obligation. As the CRTA was given an explicit mandate to examine individual regional agreements,[20] there used to be doubt about whether the WTO Panel and Appellate Body could conduct an examination themselves. In the *Turkey—Textile* case, however, the Appellate Body made it clear that the panel does have the necessary jurisdiction to examine the consistency of an RTA with the requirements under GATT Article XXIV.[21]

While the Appellate Body's ruling on this issue has been subject to the criticism that it upsets the institutional balance between the WTO's political and judicial organs,[22] this is probably the only practical solution. Otherwise Article XXIV could be used to justify all kinds of violations of GATT obligations. Moreover, the Dispute Settlement Understanding (DSU) specifically mandates a panel to 'address the relevant provisions in any covered agreement or agreements cited by the parties to the dispute'[23] and make 'an objective assessment of ... the applicability of and conformity with the relevant covered agreements'.[24] It seems then that a panel could be in breach of its obligations under the DSU if it fails to address the consistency of an RTA with the requirements under GATT Article XXIV. After all, Article XXIV itself is a provision in the 'covered agreements'. This is further confirmed by the Understanding on the Interpretation of Article XXIV of the GATT 1994. It provides that 'any matters arising from the application of those provisions of Article XXIV' shall be subject to the normal dispute settlement procedure under the DSU.

The second issue concerns the power of the WTO DSB to adjudicate disputes on substantive rules in individual RTAs. In order to fully discuss this question, a few preliminary observations are required.

First, according to a number of DSU articles, including Articles 1.1, 3.2, 7.1, and 11, the jurisdiction of WTO panels is limited to claims under the WTO covered agreements.[25]

Second, while a panel is obliged to 'address the relevant provisions in any covered agreement or agreements cited by the parties to the dispute'[26] and make 'an objective assessment of ... the applicability of and conformity with the relevant covered agreements',[27] there is no *obligation* for a panel to address provisions that are not part of a 'covered agreement'. On the other hand, just like a judicial organ or arbitral body, the panel has inherent jurisdictional *powers*. Pauwelyn characterized such powers as powers of 'incidental or implied jurisdiction', and he took this to mean the jurisdiction (1) 'to interpret the submissions of the parties' in order to 'isolate the real issue in the case and to identify the object of the claim'; (2) to determine whether one has substantive jurisdiction to decide a matter (the principle of *la compétence de la compétence*); (3) to decide whether one should refrain from exercising validly established substantive jurisdiction;[28] and (4) to decide all matters linked to the exercise of substantive jurisdiction and inherent in the judicial function (such as claims under rules on the burden of proof, due process, and other general international law rules on the judicial settlement of disputes or state responsibility, including the power to order cessation, assurances of non-repetition, and reparations).[29]

Thus, where a substantive rule is provided for under only the RTA but not under any WTO agreement, it can provide the basis for a claim only under the RTA but not the WTO. This also means that a WTO panel will apparently have no jurisdiction in such a case. One example would be an RTA that, for example, contains national treatment obligations for the legal services sector. If none of the RTA members have scheduled such an obligation in their GATS schedule in the WTO, disputes arising from the RTA commitment can be brought only under the RTA's dispute settlement system. Another example occurs when an RTA contains an investment chapter akin to NAFTA Chapter 11, and it provides for an investor-state dispute settlement mechanism. Such disputes typically cannot be brought before the WTO.[30] Note that in the example given, the reason the dispute cannot be brought before the WTO is that the substantive obligations do not arise from the WTO 'covered agreements', not because the RTA has its own dispute settlement mechanism or that the RTA mechanism is meant to be exclusive. This issue will be addressed below.

The most problematic situation, however, occurs when both the RTA and the WTO contain overlapping substantive obligations, thus a claim is possible under either regime. This would be a situation of 'true conflict' or jurisdictional overlap. An example would be the national treatment obligation for goods, something that can be found under both the WTO and many RTAs. In such cases, as the obligation arises from the 'covered agreements' of the WTO, the WTO dispute settlement system clearly has jurisdiction over the claim. The more difficult question, however, is whether that jurisdiction should be exclusive. DSU Article 23 seems to suggest that this is the case, where it states that[31]

> [w]hen Members seek the redress of a violation of obligations or other nullification or impairment of benefits under the covered agreements or an impediment to the attainment of any objective of the covered agreements, *they shall have recourse to, and abide by, the rules and procedures of this Understanding.*

> In such cases, *Members shall … not make a determination* to the effect that a violation has occurred, that benefits have been nullified or impaired or that the attainment of any objective of the covered agreements has been impeded, *except through recourse to dispute settlement in accordance with the rules and procedures of this Understanding*, and shall make any such determination consistent with the findings contained in the panel or Appellate Body report adopted by the DSB or an arbitration award rendered under this Understanding.…

This view (i.e., of exclusive WTO jurisdiction) would be uncontroversial in the following kinds of cases:

1. Where the RTA does not include any dispute settlement provision, or
2. Where an RTA provides applicable rules to resolve jurisdictional conflicts between the RTA and the WTO, and where such provisions explicitly make the WTO the forum of choice in case of conflict. This might be referred to as the 'exclusive forum selection clause' scenario. An example is the EC–Chile Interim Agreement,[32] which provides in Article 189.4.(c) that:

> [u]nless the Parties otherwise agree, when a Party seeks redress of a violation of an obligation under this Part of the Agreement which is equivalent in substance to an obligation under the WTO, it shall have recourse to the relevant rules and procedures of the WTO Agreement, which apply notwithstanding the provisions of this Agreement.[33]

To sum up, the WTO *definitely* has exclusive jurisdiction in cases regarding the general requirements for RTAs under the relevant WTO agreements, but does not have jurisdiction in cases concerning substantive rules that are provided for only in the RTA. Beyond these two scenarios are relatively uncharted waters.

III. WTO–RTA Jurisdictional Conflicts

Short of simply saying that DSU Article 23.2.(a) means that WTO Members have no recourse but to submit to WTO dispute settlement whenever there is a question involving the violation of an obligation under a covered agreement of the WTO, the exclusivity of WTO jurisdiction may be called into question in situations involving the following:

1. An exclusive forum selection clause, electing RTA dispute settlement: The most obvious example occurs when there exists an exclusive forum selection clause choosing the RTA as the exclusive forum for all disputes or a certain class of disputes.
2. A non-exclusive forum selection clause: The RTA provides for an alternative dispute settlement system in addition to the one available under the WTO and gives the Members the choice to resort to either system even if the matter falls within the jurisdiction of the WTO. This method may be found, for example, in Article 56(2) of the EFTA–Singapore FTA.[34] Another example is Article 1 of MERCOSUR's Olivos Protocol.[35]
3. The *Lis Alibi Pendens* Approach: Another model, which is tagged on to the EFTA–Singapore FTA and Olivos Protocol model above, requires the dispute to be brought exclusively within the RTA's dispute settlement procedure where the dispute is first submitted under that procedure (i.e., as opposed to WTO dispute settlement). Under such a '*lis pendens*' clause approach, it could also work the other way. A dispute brought before WTO dispute settlement could preclude the same dispute being brought under the RTA. In addition to the two examples above, the most famous example of this sort of forum selection clause is Article 2005.6 of the North American Free Trade Agreement (NAFTA),[36] which states that:

[o]nce dispute settlement procedures have been initiated under Article 2007 or dispute settlement proceedings have been initiated under the GATT, the forum selected shall be used to the exclusion of the other, unless a Party makes a request pursuant to paragraph 3 or 4.

As can be seen, that example also contains an exception to the rule. Another interesting feature is that unlike the post-WTO RTAs, NAFTA Article 2005.6 as with its predecessor rule, Article 1801 of the

Canada–U.S. FTA, is *lex priori* and therefore may be said to be subject to the later rule in Article 23 of the DSU.[37] The same cannot be said of post-WTO RTAs.

4. The *Res Judicata* or Collateral Estoppel Approach:[38] Another variant is to eschew the *lis alibi pendens* approach in favour of a *res judicata* or collateral estoppel approach. An example would be Article 26 of MERCOSUR's Olivos Protocol. Notwithstanding the Olivos Protocol, Brazil still argued in the *Argentina—Poultry* case that the *res judicata* rule did not apply as it was bringing a fresh dispute on a different legal basis before WTO dispute settlement.[39]

5. The Comity Approach: Comity is a principle whereby a court declines to exercise jurisdiction over matters that would be more appropriately heard by another tribunal. In a recent article,[40] Henckels argues that, following the examples set by other international tribunals such as the International Court of Justice (ICJ) and the arbitral tribunal under the United Nations Convention on the Law of the Sea, the WTO should use its 'inherent power to apply comity' and decline to exercise jurisdiction in appropriate cases of competing jurisdiction.[41] However, there are several problems with this approach, the most notable one being that there is no textual basis in the DSU for this.[42] Henckels argues, however, that '[t]he inherent power to find no jurisdiction *in limine litis* or to decline to exercise jurisdiction arises notwithstanding the text of the DSU, unless these inherent powers are specifically extinguished or modified in the text'.[43] One difficulty with this approach is that if a panel were to apply comity and decline jurisdiction in a particular case, it may be accused of having breached its obligation under the DSU not to 'add to or diminish the rights and obligations provided in the covered agreements'[44] and violated the rights of WTO Members to 'have recourse to ... the rules and procedures of [the DSU]'.[45] Indeed, as Henckels concedes, this is how the WTO Panel and Appellate Body have approached the issue in *Mexico—Soft Drinks* and *Argentina—Poultry*, two cases where, according to Henckel's theory, the WTO should have applied the comity principle.[46] There seems to be a reluctance, at the very least, on the WTO's side to press the comity argument too far.

6. Further complexities arise when the RTA includes a provision not to invoke the WTO dispute settlement system between the parties. This could mean that the dispute should be referred to the RTA tribunal or that there is no dispute settlement system at all and all disputes shall be settled by consultations and negotiations among the parties. An example for the latter case is Article 19.5 of the Closer Economic Partnership

Arrangement (CEPA) between Mainland China and Hong Kong, which provides that 'any problems arising from the interpretation or implementation of the CEPA' shall be resolved 'through consultation in the spirit of friendship and cooperation'.[47]

While these cases all differ from each other in some ways, the key legal issue involved in all of them is the same, i.e., whether a party can challenge the jurisdiction of the panel in a case by resorting to non-WTO law and whether in turn the panel can decline to exercise jurisdiction by resorting to non-WTO law.

The Appellate Body's jurisprudence is equivocal at best on this point. Perhaps the most basic assumption is that RTAs form an exception to the WTO system. Based on this assumption, the impression created is that any overlap between RTA and WTO dispute settlement is the exception, not the rule. This is based on the view that RTAs are themselves the exception, at the very least to the MFN doctrine, under GATT Article XXIV and GATS Article V. Therefore, while the DSU includes GATT and GATS as covered agreements, RTAs emerge as 'uncovered' agreements and therefore fall into a dispute settlement vacuum. Whether this is true remains contestable. Currently, controversy continues as to the extent to which GATT Article XXIV provides an exception to WTO obligations other than the MFN principle. The issue has arisen in relation to safeguards, for example.[48] Similar arguments may also be offered in relation to RTA dispute settlement mechanisms.

Is the assumption that RTAs form an exception to the WTO system—in other words that they fall into a 'black hole'—justified? The suggestion receives some support from the Appellate Body's ruling in *Mexico—Soft Drinks*, where the Appellate Body seems to have considered that NAFTA disputes are 'non-WTO disputes' and that it is not the function of panels and the Appellate Body to adjudicate on such non-WTO disputes.[49] Before *Mexico—Soft Drinks*, the panel ruling in *Argentina—Poultry* had, quite sensibly, suggested that a WTO panel may construe an RTA in relation to a provision therein governing the relationship between the RTA and WTO dispute settlement.[50] The decision of the Appellate Body in *Mexico—Soft Drinks*, however, seems to have cast some doubt on the panel's decision in *Argentina—Poultry*.

The Appellate Body in *Mexico—Soft Drinks* also went on to suggest that an overlap with RTA regulation will not necessarily prevent a WTO dispute settlement as panels and the Appellate Body do not have a discretion to decline to rule in cases brought before them absent special circumstances. But the Appellate Body appears also to have confined itself specifically to 'the case ... before it'.[51] One possible reading is that the Appellate Body would not rule on non-WTO disputes and would usually not decline jurisdiction because, absent 'other circumstances', it would not have the discretion to do so.[52]

Exercising judicial economy, however, the Appellate Body did not further explain what might constitute such 'special' or 'other' circumstances.

Can *Mexico—Soft Drinks* be read to suggest that in exceptional circumstances at least WTO panels or the Appellate Body may decline their own jurisdiction in favour of RTA dispute settlement? If so, might this also be taken to suggest that having separate RTA dispute settlement procedures is not *per se* violative of DSU Article 23? Is a conflicting RTA provision a ground for invoking such exceptional circumstances—what the Appellate Body in *Mexico—Soft Drinks* referred to blandly as 'other circumstances' in a highly couched ruling? Does *Mexico—Soft Drinks* mean that RTA dispute settlement clauses could, in exceptional or special circumstances, *prevail* over a WTO dispute settlement?

Even if the answer to all the questions above is yes, it would still be worthwhile to consider, or even to make, the WTO at least an *optional* forum for the RTA parties for the reasons suggested later in this chapter. If the WTO were to serve such a function, the current DSU may however require amendment so that the jurisdiction of a WTO panel and Appellate Body would not be limited, at least in some cases, to 'covered agreements'. This is especially important where no general rule of international law may be relied on to resolve the problem by way of some interpretative or jurisdictional rule.

The largest question here would have to do with when the WTO should have the jurisdictional authority to develop RTA rules. Should the WTO confine itself to resolving situations of conflict only, or should it play a larger role? This jurisdictional problem will be addressed after dealing with the question of applicable law below.

IV. Applicable Law

The problem here is related to but not exactly the same as the first question. Can a WTO panel and Appellate Body apply non-WTO rules in a WTO dispute? It is important to note the difference between the two sorts of question from the outset. Clearly, some questions, on the basis of the *Mexico—Soft Drinks* doctrine, cannot be adjudicated by WTO dispute settlement. But it raises the question of what rules panels and the Appellate Body can and cannot apply, or in an even further refinement, when it has jurisdiction over the parties to the dispute, and when such jurisdiction is precluded over certain subject matter involving the rules to be applied. Here, the distinction between 'jurisdiction' and 'applicable law' is made for the sake of simplicity.[53] Put slightly differently, a principal difference is that while the jurisdictional question is mainly concerned with the jurisdictional basis for a *claim* in a dispute, the question of applicable law is about what *arguments* you may use to support your own claim or to defend yourself against claims made by others. As the Appellate Body stated in *EC—Hormones*, even though '[p]anels are inhibited from addressing legal claims falling outside their terms of reference', 'nothing in the DSU limits the faculty of a panel freely to use arguments submitted by any of the parties—or to develop its own legal reasoning—to support its own findings and conclusions on the matter under its consideration'.[54] Thus, the inquiry on applicable law could be totally independent of the jurisdictional question.

While perhaps no WTO scholar would seriously disagree that the DSU limits the jurisdiction of the panel to claims brought under WTO-covered agreements,[55] the real question is whether, in examining such claims, non-WTO norms could be brought into play. Generally speaking, non-WTO rules might be introduced in the WTO dispute settlement process under three different circumstances.

The first is to use non-WTO rules, mostly general principles of law, to solve procedural issues that have not been clearly spelled out in WTO rules.[56] Examples include the participation of private lawyers in panel proceedings, the admissibility of amicus briefs in panel and Appellate Body proceedings,[57] treatment of domestic law as questions of law or facts, etc. Even though neither the DSU nor the other WTO agreements have explicitly provided the power to apply these rules to panels or the Appellate Body,[58] the issue has largely been uncontroversial because these are widely regarded as implied powers of a tribunal, and it would have been very difficult for the panels or the Appellate Body to carry out their job without such powers.[59]

The second is to use rules of treaty interpretation to interpret certain provisions in the covered agreements. This relates mainly to the treaty interpretation rules under the Vienna Convention on the Law of Treaties (VCLT),[60] especially Articles 31 and 32. While there might be some uncertainty as to whether the panels and the Appellate Body had such a power during the early days of the existence of the WTO, such doubt has since dissipated, especially since the Appellate Body made the resounding warning that WTO rules shall not be read 'in clinical isolation' from public international law in the *US–Gasoline* case.[61] That pronouncement rests on the explicit reference to 'customary rules of interpretation of public international law' in the DSU as tools for clarifying WTO provisions.[62]

The third is to apply non-WTO rules as norms that create substantive, rather than procedural, rights and obligations. As discussed earlier, under the current WTO regime, non-WTO norms cannot be invoked as a basis for staking out claims in a dispute. Instead, their only possible substantive use would be as defence against claims of violation or justification for adopting measures that are inconsistent with WTO obligations. This is the hardest of the three scenarios, and it is also where the real controversy lies.

This third scenario can be analyzed at two levels: first, whether such non-WTO norms could be invoked by parties and applied by panels at all; second, even if they could be invoked despite running against WTO norms (which would typically be the case as otherwise the party invoking them would have relied on some WTO provision instead), whether they may prevail against WTO norms.[63]

To some commentators, the answer to the first question is yes. Pauwelyn, for example, has urged that 'the fact that the substantive jurisdiction of WTO panels is limited to claims under WTO covered agreements does not mean that the applicable law available to a WTO panel is necessarily limited to WTO covered agreements'.[64] He offers the following reasons:

First, WTO panels and the Appellate Body have not limited themselves to the four corners of WTO covered agreements: they have referred to general principles of law and customary international law, such as the VCLT.[65] In this sense, rules other than the WTO's treaty rules can be applied in WTO proceedings.

A key assumption underlying Pauwelyn's argument is that there is no legal basis in 'the four corners of WTO covered agreements' for the application of the VCLT. A closer examination of the Appellate Body's famous statement in *US—Gasoline* reveals, however, that the reference to general principles of law and customary international law or even the VCLT by the panel and the Appellate Body is made exactly pursuant to the mandate within 'the four corners of WTO covered agreements' as the Appellate Body clearly based its decision on the requirement under Article 3.2 of the DSU that the panel and the Appellate Body shall 'clarify the existing provisions of those agreements in accordance with customary rules of interpretation of public international law'.[66] Moreover, the mere fact that panels and the Appellate Body have referred to rules of interpretation to help *clarify* the meaning of the substantive obligations in the covered agreements does not necessarily mean that they can refer to other non-WTO rules to *change* the substantive obligations under the WTO covered agreements.

Secondly, Pauwelyn notes that among those 'customary rules of interpretation of public international law' referred to in DSU Article 3.2 lies Article 31.3 of the VCLT. It states that the treaty interpreter shall take into account not only the treaty itself but also 'any subsequent agreement between the parties regarding the interpretation of the treaty or the application of its provisions'.[67] In this further sense, he argues that 'non-WTO law' can and should be applied in WTO cases.

Unfortunately, this is, again, a misreading. First of all, while Article 31 states that a treaty shall be interpreted '*in accordance with* the ordinary meaning to be given to the terms of the treaty', the 'subsequent agreement' and 'relevant rules of international law' are only to be '*taken into account*, together with the context' (emphasis added). This means that, while the terms of the treaty at issue shall be *directly* applied, the other relevant agreements and rules shall only be used to *supplement* the interpretation based on the context and may not be applied directly. Second, the scope of such agreements is not as expansive as Pauwelyn may have suggested. Instead, only subsequent agreements that are concluded '*between the parties regarding the interpretation* of the treaty *or the application* of its provisions' (emphasis added) could be used as a supplementary interpretive tool. It means that the only agreements that can be invoked are those that are *both* made between exactly the same parties to the original agreement *and* regarding the interpretation of the treaty or the application of its provisions specifically. It is easy to see that most RTAs would not satisfy either requirement, because first, RTAs are, by definition, limited to a subset of WTO Members; and second, they are mainly concerned with establishing obligations beyond those agreed in the WTO rather than the interpretation or application of WTO obligations. For these reasons, RTA rules should not be applicable in WTO disputes.

Third, according to Pauwelyn, the WTO agreement is a treaty and therefore is part of public international law. Thus, 'even without the explicit confirmation in DSU Article 3.2, the WTO agreement cannot … be applied in isolation from other rules of international law'.[68] To illustrate his point, Pauwelyn draws an analogy between contract law and international law:[69]

> Just as private contracts are automatically born into a system of domestic law, so treaties are automatically born into the system of international law. Much the way private contracts do not need to list all the relevant legislative and administrative provisions of domestic law for them to be applicable to the contract, so treaties need not explicitly set out rules of general international law for them to be applicable to the treaty.

However, this argument is probably not as strong as it might at first appear. An initial objection may be dealt with swiftly. First, the basic assumption underlying Pauwelyn's analogy has to do with the degree of similarity between domestic and international legal systems. The analogy is not altogether unproblematic. As Philip Allott puts it, the international legal system still lacks 'most of the essential characteristics of their national legal systems'.[70] Assuming however that such an analogy is sustainable in the current case, the real reason behind the parties' decision to enter into private contracts is not because they want to incorporate general contract rules, but because they want to vary the default rules between them absent explicit provisions in each individual contract.[71] Thus to say that general international law applies even when the WTO Members have decided to establish some specific rights and obligations in the covered agreements ignores the purpose of WTO Members in taking the trouble to negotiate WTO agreements in the first place. At the very least it raises the question of what general, background international rights and obligations the Members have sought to vary and which they have sought to leave intact. One example is the extent to which the WTO's dispute settlement rules have been intended to replace the classic international law rule that self-help might be resorted to in the face of a breach of an international treaty obligation.[72] The usual answer is that this is the whole point of the DSU. Yet what this chapter tries to show is that the answer is not as simple as it seems. There may yet be further trade obligations undertaken outside the WTO that are subject to rules concerning their breach and the consequences of such breach that stand in uneasy relation to the WTO rules on dispute settlement. Third, even accepting that 'treaties are automatically born into the system of international law' just like private contracts,[73] it does not necessarily follow that the WTO Dispute Settlement Body must necessarily apply non-WTO norms in WTO disputes. Again the question here is related to jurisdiction: the WTO dispute settlement panel is not a tribunal of general jurisdiction; instead its jurisdiction is limited only to claims founded on WTO rules.[74] Fourth, notwithstanding our previous analysis, even if Pauwelyn's argument that WTO norms 'are automatically born into the system of international law' were accepted, and that international law should simply be applied in WTO disputes without further qualification, it will not be of any help to the argument that RTA rules should be applied by panels and the Appellate Body in WTO disputes. The reason is simply that most RTAs did not even exist when the GATT or the WTO was established. Thus it's more accurate to state that the RTA rules are born into a system of WTO rules that in its relation with general international law is properly considered to be *lex specialis*.

Fourth, while Pauwelyn recognizes that Article 3.2 specifies that WTO panels or the Appellate Body cannot 'change' the WTO treaty, he argues that this does not limit the extent to which WTO Members may conclude or have concluded other treaties that can influence their mutual WTO rights and obligations.[75] Thus, Pauwelyn concludes:

> As important as the distinction is between Panel jurisdiction (WTO claims only) and applicable law (potentially all international law), so too is the distinction between interpreting WTO rules (and the prohibition to add or detract from those rules in the process) and examining WTO claims in the context of other applicable international law (where the expression of state consent and conflict rules of international law must decide the outcome).[76]

As Pauwelyn does not provide further illustration on this point in his article, it is not always clear what exactly he means by this. One logical interpretation of the argument seems to be this:

> Even though the Panel and the Appellate Body have no power to change the rights and obligations of the Members, the Members themselves can always conclude other treaties (such as RTAs) to change their rights and obligations under the WTO. To give effect to these treaties, the panel and the Appellate Body shall have the power to apply them in WTO disputes as well. Otherwise, the power of Members to conclude other treaties would be diminished.

While Article 30.3 of the VCLT seems to confirm Pauwelyn's argument by stating that '[w]hen all the parties to the earlier treaty are parties also to the later treaty …, the earlier treaty applies only to the extent that its provisions are compatible with those of the later treaty', anyone who rushes to the conclusion that the VCLT is applicable here would fail to appreciate the crucial differences between the rights and obligations established under WTO agreements and those under the garden variety of multilateral treaties. First, for concessions on trade in goods, while most of the tariff negotiations today are formula based, the GATT/WTO regime has a long history of negotiating tariffs based on other approaches. Moreover, even today, not all negotiations on goods are based on formulae as there are special rules for tariff cuts by developing countries or sensitive products by certain countries. This is more so with trade in services, which has been dominated by a bilateral request-offer approach.[77] This means that, when two countries negotiate an RTA and cut all tariffs to zero, not only are they making concessions on the products that they themselves are most interested in, they are also extending concessions on products that do not interest the other party. Yet, through the operation of the MFN principle, it will affect the interests of a third country that has a keen export interest in such products. This is wholly different from the case of, say, a treaty between three countries to solve their border disputes. Now suppose two of the three countries later on make another treaty to change a boundary on their mutual border but this does not affect the border of the third country; of course the second treaty would not have affected the interests of the third country. In contrast, because of the MFN rule, the multilateral, even the plurilateral, obligations of the WTO are not merely 'bilateral obligations multiplied'.[78] They have a very far-reaching effect.

Second, the legal effect of an RTA is only to create new rights and obligations for the members under the RTA regime, rather than changing the rights and obligations under the 'covered agreements' of the WTO. The reason for this, as argued by Trachtman, is that since the WTO Agreement provides exclusive procedures to be followed in amending the obligations under the 'covered agreements', any amendment must follow such prescribed procedures before it could change the content of the 'covered agreements' under the WTO.[79] Of course, this does not mean that WTO Members cannot change their trade obligations outside of the WTO framework. However, even if such non-WTO rules are agreed between the parties, such modifications would not usually be applicable law in WTO dispute settlement.[80]

This leads to the third point, that is, for those RTAs that either do not provide for formal dispute settlement or do provide a dispute settlement system that is, however, not compulsory, the very fact that members to such RTAs intentionally chose to shun the WTO dispute settlement system, or any dispute settlement system for that matter, probably means that they never intended to make such an agreement enforceable through the WTO dispute settlement system. If, however, a panel follows Pauwelyn's advice and decides to drag a Member into a formal WTO dispute settlement proceeding, that is clearly an infringement on the sovereign rights of a Member that never intended to be held to account in the WTO for breaches of its obligations under these non-WTO treaties.

Assuming, *arguendo*, that the RTA rules could be invoked in WTO disputes, should such rules, to the extent that they are inconsistent with WTO norms, prevail over WTO rules? For many public international lawyers, the answer seems to be yes when one applies the two familiar rules for resolving treaty conflicts, that is, *lex posterior derogat priori* and *lex specialis derogat generali*.[81] The arguments are that, first, because the RTAs are concluded after the WTO agreements have been concluded, they are later rules and must prevail over prior rules; second, because the RTAs are special rules that are created on top of the general rules under the WTO agreements, the RTA rules must prevail as well. Again, however, the issues are not that simple. First of all, WTO rules are not carved in stone. Both the general rules for the WTO and the specific concessions of individual Members are periodically modified in successive rounds of trade negotiations. Thus, even if an RTA that was concluded in 2000 prevails over the WTO agreements concluded in 1994, should whatever results Members manage to reach in the Doha Round, say in 2010, also prevail over all RTAs among WTO Members between 1994 and 2010? Second, even though most RTAs are concluded after the WTO came into being, there are some RTAs, such as NAFTA, that were concluded before the WTO agreements entered into force. If the *lex posterior* rule is applicable here, does it mean that these RTAs have been effectively rendered useless by the establishment of the WTO? At the very least, an attempt to resolve the issue by resorting to the *lex posteriori* rule would produce arbitrary solutions each time. It would amount to nothing more than checkerboard justice.[82] Third, to the extent that the *lex posterior* and *lex specialis* rules are applicable, they can be applied only among laws that are of the same hierarchy. That is why the Marrakesh Agreement states in Article XVI.3 that '[i]n the event of a conflict between a provision of this Agreement and a provision of any of the Multilateral Trade Agreements, the provision of [the Marrakesh] Agreement shall prevail to the extent of the conflict'. Thus, to the extent that a WTO obligation may be said to be situated higher in the hierarchy of norms than RTA rules, it cannot be overruled simply because of an RTA obligation.

In sum, under the current WTO legal framework, RTA rules can be applied only under limited circumstances, just as there may be practical or doctrinal limits to what may be brought under WTO dispute settlement. New thinking is needed if the WTO dispute settlement system is to apply RTA rules and generate a body of 'common law' for RTAs—what might be tentatively called the 'public international law of trade'.

In this regard, it would be worthwhile as a practical matter to make the WTO at least an *optional* forum for the RTA parties so that the WTO *could* contribute to the development of such a body of 'common law', and that in this way, under the stewardship of the Appellate Body, the law will in time work itself pure.[83] But if the WTO were to serve such a function, the current DSU may require amendment so that the jurisdiction of the WTO Panel and Appellate Body would not be limited, at least in some cases, to 'covered agreements'. Alternatively, even if they would not be limited in all cases, amendment would provide much needed certainty and clarity. Coupled with the jurisdictional problem discussed earlier above, DSU Article 23.2.(a) may yet be taken to mean that WTO Members have no recourse but to submit to WTO dispute settlement where there is a question involving the violation of a WTO covered agreement obligation.

V. 'Farming Out' the WTO Dispute Settlement Procedure for RTA Disputes: The 'Best Forum' Argument

The idea that there are multiple options to the compulsory settlement of international disputes is hardly novel.

The traditional difficulty with subjecting diplomatic dispute over various subjects to compulsory dispute settlement was the principle of sovereign choice. Sovereigns chose how they would have their disputes resolved. But one option that had been revived from antiquity during the nineteenth century is international arbitration. The commission established under the 1794 Jay Treaty was one such example,[84] and arbitration was given renewed impetus with the

Alabama Claims (or *'Geneva'*) arbitration.[85] The idea of compulsory jurisdiction may be traced to this but at present has been muddled with the idea of exclusive jurisdiction.

Exclusive compulsory dispute settlement is only a subset. That the WTO dispute settlement procedure may provide for the compulsory settlement of trade disputes today is nothing new. But does it mean that the WTO's jurisdiction is exclusive? The option of electing WTO dispute settlement in some RTA provisions is only the latest manifestation of a far more established doctrine; namely, that of the free choice of means of settling sovereign disputes.[86] Of course, the immediate retort to this is that DSU Article 23 is meant to foreclose the doctrine of sovereign choice. Is that true?

Viewed carefully, the difficulty in the modern RTA context involves conflicts of jurisdiction, not a failure of compulsory dispute settlement. True, the problem is particularly acute in light of the widespread appreciation post–Uruguay Round that trade disputes would be semi-automatically submitted to WTO dispute settlement. In other words, the problem arises because RTAs threaten to undermine the WTO dispute settlement process. But unless an uncompromising stance is taken in the name of WTO law, there is no clear prohibition of a future treaty prevailing over an earlier treaty, at least with regard to international law doctrine. The same applies in the case of a more specific treaty rule prevailing over a general rule.

It might be thought that the *practical* problem arises because arbitrators tasked with settling an RTA dispute might not recognize the WTO's jurisdiction as prevailing over their own. This has some legal justification in arbitration law. The doctrine of *kompetenz-kompetenz* had been established for far longer than it has been in WTO jurisprudence.[87] Arbitrators are liable to fail to comprehend why WTO dispute settlement should somehow constitute an exception to a well-known arbitral doctrine. Put differently, if arbitrators can rely on the *kompetenz-kompetenz* doctrine against national courts, why would they be precluded from doing so against WTO dispute settlement?

One neat solution may be to channel the actual handling of WTO disputes to the WTO dispute settlement process itself. In cases where it is particularly unclear whether a WTO or RTA rule controls the dispute, the idea of having the choice of court process settled in advance of the choice of law issue seems particularly attractive. Practical wisdom might also suggest that if you put the issue before the right 'forum', the 'right' choice of law would be more likely to follow.[88] In other words, *some* RTA disputes might best be resolved by those persons who have some knowledge, familiarity, or professional credibility in applying WTO rules. This would also ensure the harmonization of rules, particularly those rules dealing with WTO-RTA jurisdictional conflicts.

The fundamental problem here seems to be this. Had parties really wished to have *all* their trade disputes resolved at the WTO they would have said so. So the question should ideally be taken back to be resolved in Geneva's multilateral setting. There are other advantages to a multilateral solution in Geneva. Aside from the obvious psychological advantage in favour of a multilateral solution, virtually all the active RTA-pursuing countries and all WTO Members would be present. This allows the question of whether a WTO mandated solution should be preferred to be pursued but without sacrificing bilateral consultations between WTO Members.

To help the WTO carry out this task, the following is suggested as a possible starting point for deeper reflection on the issues:

1. The DSU should be amended to provide the possibility for RTA Members to use the WTO dispute settlement system to resolve their RTA disputes. To provide the legal basis for this, Members to an RTA *should* insert the following clause on dispute settlement in their RTAs:

   The Parties agree to refer all relevant disputes under this agreement to the WTO dispute settlement body. The WTO dispute settlement body shall have the exclusive competence to decide whether a dispute constitutes a relevant dispute for the purposes of the present provision. A ruling on a relevant dispute by the WTO dispute settlement body shall be considered binding before any arbitral or other dispute settlement body or procedure established pursuant to the present Agreement.

Correspondingly, Appendix 1 of the DSU could be amended to include the following:

(D) Regional Trade Agreements

The applicability of this Understanding to the Regional Trade Agreements of Members ('the individual agreement') shall be subject to the adoption of a decision by the parties to the individual agreement setting out the terms for the application of this Understanding to such agreements, including any special or additional rules or procedures for inclusion in Appendix 2, as notified to the DSB.

2. In order to facilitate the adjudication of RTA disputes by the panel or the WTO Appellate Body, any RTA that adopts the WTO dispute settlement system should also grant the panel and Appellate Body the powers to decide on the following two issues: First, whether the RTA fully complies with the requirements under GATT Article XXIV or GATS Article V. To the extent that an RTA cannot be justified, the Members will not be allowed to invoke the RTA as a defence against non-compliance

of their relevant WTO obligations. Second, whether or not the RTA affects the interests of non-Members. To the extent that it does, such non-Member shall be given the opportunity to join in the dispute as well.

VI. Institutional Design

One last question has to do with what kind of institutional framework might be adopted for the adjudication of RTA disputes at the WTO. Should the normal rules for the constitution and operation of WTO panels be retained, or should the institutional framework under individual RTAs be adopted? In other words, should it be more akin to ad hoc arbitration or the kind of institutional arbitration that simply resorts to institutional arbitration rules for the convenience they might afford?[89] What, in other words, should be the *lex arbitri*?[90] In our view, to maintain the integrity of the WTO dispute settlement system, the current procedural rules and practices under the DSU should be adopted to the furthest extent possible, while providing the possibility for the panel to adopt different procedures. If so, a further clause should also be inserted into the RTA stating this. With regard to the specific procedural issues, our suggestions are as follows:

1. Parties to the dispute: Generally speaking, only parties to a specific dispute can be parties of a case. In cases involving substantive rules in the RTA that affect all members of the RTA, the other RTA members that are not parties to the dispute should have the right to join in the dispute settlement proceeding. Even in cases that involve only the substantive rights of the parties to the particular dispute, non-party members can join as third parties if the main parties to the dispute agree. In cases involving the substantive rights of non-RTA members, such non-RTA members should also have the right to join in the dispute settlement proceeding. Even in cases that involve only the substantive rights of RTA members, non-RTA members can join as third parties if *all* the members of the RTA agree. Such an arrangement will ensure that the interests of all parties, RTA members and non-members alike, are adequately represented in such dispute settlement proceedings. This will ensure not only the highest degree of support among all parties who might have an interest in such cases, but also the highest degree of uniformity between different cases as well.

2. Composition of a panel: While panellists should have a sufficient understanding of the particular issues facing the members of an RTA, because RTAs are tolerated in the multilateral trading system only because they are perceived as 'building blocks' that contribute to the ultimate goal of

global trade liberalization through the gradual expansion of regional economic integration, the idiosyncrasies in particular RTAs should not be used as an excuse to upset the carefully negotiated balance of rights and obligations in the WTO as a whole. Therefore, of the three panellists to each panel, at least one should be someone who is not chosen by one of the RTA parties. This should be a person of recognized authority, with demonstrated expertise in law, international trade, and the subject matter of the covered agreements generally. The other two would be nominated respectively by the two principal parties to the dispute. In case of disagreement among the two panellists nominated by the RTA members, the ruling of the third panellist shall prevail. Such arrangement is intended to ensure not only that the panel has the necessary expertise to solve the dispute at hand, but also consistency with WTO jurisprudence would be maintained.

3. Generally, the proceedings of the panel may be kept confidential and limited only to the disputing parties. If all the parties to the dispute agree, however, or if the RTA whose provisions are called into question provides expressly for public hearings, then the proceedings may be open to the general public. The reports of a panel should, however, be generally made available to WTO Members so that such reports can gradually build up the 'common law' of RTA.

4. The meetings of the panel may be held either in Geneva or at another mutually agreed location, such as in the territory of an RTA member or in a third country. To the extent possible, both the WTO Secretariat and the secretariat for the RTA shall provide the necessary legal and administrative support to the panel.

5. While the particular findings and recommendations of the panel in a particular dispute shall be binding only on the parties to the dispute, the analysis by the panel on substantive rules in an RTA should ideally also apply to future cases between members of the same RTA, while the analysis by the panel of general WTO provisions shall also be of persuasive value for future disputes involving similar provisions between the members of other RTAs.

6. If a party to a dispute is not satisfied with the ruling of a panel, it shall have a right to appeal the report to the Appellate Body.

7. To avoid the diversion of resources from the current responsibilities and functions of WTO panels and the Appellate Body, the expenses for a case from an RTA should be funded by the RTA members involved in such dispute. Special and differential treatment could be provided to RTA members that are developing countries.

VII. Conclusion

This chapter has addressed the possibility of using the WTO dispute settlement system as a common good for RTA disputes. In answering this question, the doctrinal analysis has been separated from recommendations for reform, that is, what *could* be done to use the WTO dispute settlement system as a common good for RTA disputes under the WTO legal framework as it stands, versus how the current WTO legal framework *should* be changed to make it more useful. While it is desirable to use the WTO dispute settlement system to resolve RTA disputes, there are significant uncertainties under the current WTO legal framework. Ideally, that framework should be amended. By confronting the conflict between the current WTO dispute settlement rules and RTA disputes in a direct manner, the temptation to twist the current rules to achieve such results has been avoided. Such shortcuts create false hope for those who believe that the WTO dispute settlement system has a role to play in RTA disputes. It also threatens the integrity and legitimacy of the WTO dispute settlement system as a whole by trying to feed it with something that it cannot readily digest, resulting in congestion and possibly a great combustion of the WTO dispute settlement system.

While we recommend that a new treaty rule should be undertaken on a plurilateral basis, WTO Members which might encounter difficulty in signing on to the new regime should nonetheless be allowed to bring their RTA conflicts to WTO dispute settlement by way of special agreement instead. This additional flexibility has in any case proven extremely useful in the context of disputes before the ICJ.[91]

Notes

1   For the sake of consistency and clarity, we use the term 'Regional Trade Agreements' in this paper to refer to both free trade agreements (FTA) and customs unions (CU) under GATT Article XXIV, as well as economic integration agreements under GATS Article V. The word 'regional' carries no geographical connotations, and agreements between parties that are geographically remote from each other (such as the United States and Singapore) are also included.

2   First Warwick Commission. *The Multilateral Trade Regime: Which Way Forward? The Report of the First Warwick Commission* (Coventry: University of Warwick, 2007) 45.

3   Richard Baldwin, 'Multilateralising Regionalism: Spaghetti Bowls as Building Blocs on the Path to Global Free Trade', 29 (11) The World Economy 1451 (2006), at 1508.

4   First Warwick Commission, above n 2, at 53.

5   Consultative Board to the Director-General Supachai Panitchpakdi, *The Future of the WTO: Addressing Institutional Challenges in the New Millennium* (Geneva: WTO, 2005) para 103.

6 Consultative Board, ibid, para 104; First Warwick Commission, above n 2, at 51.

7 Consultative Board, ibid, at para 104.

8 See, for example, WTO, *World Trade Report 2007* (Geneva: WTO, 2007) 309–10, www.wto.org/english/res_e/booksp_e/anrep_e/world_trade_report07_e.pdf (visited 25 April 2009), which quotes a WTO Secretariat study in 2002 and a study by the Inter-American Development Bank (IADB) in 2006.

9 For a discussion of the main motives for countries to enter RTA negotiations in the Asia Pacific Region, see Henry Gao, 'Synthesis Report', in Asia-Pacific Economic Cooperation (APEC) Secretariat, *The New International Architecture in Trade and Investment: Current Status and Implications* (Singapore: APEC, 2007) 10–13.

10 According to the *Shorter Oxford English Dictionary*, 5th ed. (Oxford: Oxford University Press, 2002), a confessor is '[a] priest who heard confessions'. By the power granted by Christ, confessors, i.e., ministers with proper qualifications, could forgive sins of believers. See *Catholic Encyclopedia: Sacrament of Penance*, http://www.newadvent.org/cathen/11618c.htm (visited 18 September 2008).

11 Baldwin, above n 3, at 1509–11.

12 See First Warwick Commission, above n 2, at 52. See also C.L. Lim, 'Free Trade Agreements in Asia and Some Common Legal Problems', in Yasuhei Taniguchi, Alan Yanovich, and Jan Bohanes (eds), *The WTO in the Twenty-First Century: Dispute Settlement, Negotiations, and Regionalism in Asia* (Cambridge: Cambridge University Press, 2007) 434, 445–46, 454–55.

13 In addition to its main task of supporting the Trade Policy Review Body, the Trade Policy Review Division also supports the work of the Committee on Regional Trade Agreements. See http://www.wto.org/english/thewto_e/secre_e/div_e.htm (visited 18 September 2008).

14 The functions of the Economic Research and Statistics Division are to provide 'economic analysis and research in support of the WTO's operational activities, including monitoring and reporting on current economic news and developments', as well as supporting 'WTO Members and the Secretariat with quantitative information in relation to economic and trade policy issues'. See http://www.wto.org/english/thewto_e/secre_e/div_e.htm (visited 18 September 2008).

15 The Economic Research and Statistics Division currently has 50 staff members, while the Trade Policy Review Division currently has about 39 staff members. See http://www.wto.org/english/thewto_e/secre_e/intro_e.htm (visited 18 September 2008).

16 According to the WTO Secretariat, close to 400 RTAs are scheduled to be implemented by 2010 if 'we take into account RTAs which are in force but have not been notified, those signed but not yet in force, those currently being negotiated, and those in the proposal stage'. See http://www.wto.org/english/tratop_e/region_e/region_e.htm (visited 18 September 2008).

17 Baldwin, above n 3, at 1511.

18 First Warwick Commission, above n 2, at 52.

19 For a summary of the legal issues involved in the interpretation of the relevant WTO provisions, see WTO, Synopsis of 'Systemic' Issues Related to Regional Trade Agreements: Note by the Secretariat, WT/REG/W/37, 2 March 2000. For an empirical rather than normative analysis of these issues, see WTO, above n 8, at 307 ff.

20 WTO General Council, Decision to establish a Committee on Regional Trade Agreements, WT/L/127, adopted on 7 February 1996.

21 See Lim, above n 12, at 434.

22 Frieder Roessler, 'The Institutional Balance Between the Judicial and Political Organs of the WTO', in Marco Bronckers and Reinhard Quick (eds), *New Directions in International Economic Law* (Kluwer Law International, 2000) 325–45.

23 Article 7.1 of the Understanding on Rules and Procedures Governing the Settlement of Disputes (DSU), Article 7.1, in World Trade Organization. *The Legal Texts. The Results of the Uruguay Round of Multilateral Trade Negotiations* (Cambridge: Cambridge University Press, 1999.

24 Article 11 of the DSU.

25 Joost Pauwelyn, 'The Role of Public International Law in the WTO: How Far Can We Go?' 95 (3) American Journal of International Law 535 (2001) 554. See also Joost Pauwelyn, *Conflict of Norms in Public International Law: How WTO Law Relates to Other Rules of International Law* (Cambridge: Cambridge University Press, 2003) 440–86.

26 Article 7.1 of the DSU

27 Article 11 of the DSU.

28 This chapter disagrees with this statement. See discussion below.

29 Pauwelyn, 'The Role of Public International Law', above n 26, at 555–56.

30 One more obvious exception may relate to services trade via mode-3 (commercial presence); see Lim, above n 12.

31 Article 23 of the DSU (emphasis added).

32 Agreement establishing an association between the European Community and its Member States, of the one part, and the Republic of Chile, of the other part, done at Brussels, 18 November 2002. Available online at http://www .worldtradelaw.net/fta/agreements/ecchilfta.pdf (visited 18 September 2008).

33 Of course, critics might point out that it is difficult to say whether the negotiators considered that such a clause was required under WTO law, or that it was simply preferable. The phrase 'unless the Parties otherwise agree' may be interpreted to mean that the parties never considered this a WTO legal requirement.

34 EFTA-Singapore Free Trade Agreement, 26 June 2002.

35 The Protocol of Olivos for the Settlement of Disputes in MERCOSUR, 18 February 2002.

36 http://www.nafta-sec-alena.org/DefaultSite/index_e.aspx?DetailID=78 (visited 18 September 2008).

37 Michael J. Trebilcock and Robert Howse, *The Regulation of International Trade* (London: Routledge, 2005) 149.

38 This chapter does not seek to distinguish clearly between these two concepts. Put simply, in the case of collateral estoppel there does not have to be a litigation on the same claims for the doctrine to operate. See further *Hunt v. B.P. Exploration Co. (Libya) Ltd.*, 492 F. Supp. 885 (1980) (United States District Court, Northern District of Texas). See further Adrian Briggs, *Conflict of Laws* (Oxford: Oxford University Press, 2002) 132 ff on the (English) common law distinction between 'recognition' and 'enforcement' in private international law.

39 Panel Report, *Argentina—Definitive Anti-Dumping Duties on Poultry from Brazil (Argentina—Poultry)*, WT/DS241/R, adopted 19 May 2003, at para 7.22.

40 Caroline Henckels, 'Overcoming Jurisdictional Isolationism at the WTO FTA Nexus: A Potential Approach for the WTO', 19 European Journal of International Law 571 (2008).

41 Ibid, at 584 ff.

42 Ibid, at 593–94.

43 Ibid, at 594.

44 Article 3.2 of the DSU.

45 Article 3.2 of the DSU.

46 In *Mexico—Soft Drinks*, for example, the Appellate Body not only did not adopt the comity principle, but also explained in detail how the principle is inconsistent with several key DSU provisions, including Articles 3.2, 7.1, 7.2, 11, 19.2, and 23. See Appellate Body Report, *Mexico—Tax Measures on Soft Drinks and Other Beverages (Mexico—Soft Drinks)*, WT/DS308/AB/R, adopted 24 March 2006, paras 47–57.

47 http://www.tid.gov.hk/english/cepa/legaltext/fulltext.html (visited 18 September 2008).

48 See, for example, Joost Pauwelyn, 'The Puzzle of WTO Safeguards and Regional Trade Agreements', 7 Journal of International Economic Law 109 (2004).

49 Appellate Body Report, *Mexico—Soft Drinks*, above n 47, paras 56, 78.

50 Panel Report, *Argentina—Poultry*, above n 40, para 7.27. There, the panel had gone on to interpret the Protocol of Brasilia, ruling that on its proper construction the Brasilia Protocol does not limit the right of the parties to bring WTO Panel proceedings in relation to a measure that is already the subject of a dispute under that protocol.

51 Appellate Body Report, *Mexico—Soft Drinks*, above n 47, paras 54, 57.

52 Ibid, at para 54.

53 Part of the difficulty has to do with the highly undeveloped categories of jurisdiction *ratione personae*, jurisdiction *ratione materiae,* and choice of law known elsewhere in both private and public international law thinking. It might be said that these categories do not apply to our current question because WTO jurisdiction *ratione personae* is given in the case of a WTO Member. But this raises another question. Is that jurisdiction given in the case of WTO membership or in the case of WTO membership in the absence of a competing RTA rule? In the usual context in which that distinction operates, a sovereign may be immune *ratione personae* from the jurisdiction of a domestic court, whereas even if such immunity is defeated in exceptional situations, a domestic court may not have jurisdiction over the attachment or execution of the property of a foreign sovereign. See, for example, C.L. Lim, 'Non-Recognition of Putative Foreign States (Taiwan) under Singapore's State Immunity Act' 11 Asian Yearbook of International Law 3 (2003–04), at 18 ff. Likewise, in private international law, the distinction, loosely speaking, between personal jurisdiction and the prescriptive, legislative, and subject-matter jurisdiction is generally well known and established in common law countries even if the details may differ significantly from jurisdiction to jurisdiction—for example, personal jurisdiction has a constitutional dimension in the United States, whereas the distinction between personal and subject-matter jurisdiction may not be so clear or may not even exist under a civilian system that may tailor jurisdictional questions to factors such as the place of the characteristic performance

of the contract or the place of the commission of the tort, thus emphasizing the connection with the claim as opposed to the defendant, for example. See, for example, Ralph H. Folsom et al., *International Business Transactions: A Problem Oriented Coursebook,* 9th ed. (St. Paul Minnesota: Thomson/West, 2006)1192. These issues and their attendant complexities need not detain this analysis. However, it has been suggested that similar notions of judicial comity should be applied where there are conflicts between international tribunals. See our discussion of the comity principle in this chapter. See also the discussion of the MOX Plant dispute in Lim, above n 12, at 453.

54 Appellate Body Report, *EC Measures Concerning Meat and Meat Products (EC—Hormones)*, WT/DS26/AB/R, WT/DS48/AB/R, adopted 13 February 1998, at para 156.

55 Article 1.1. of the DSU. See, for example, Joost Pauwelyn, 'How to Win a WTO Dispute Based on Non-WTO Law: Questions of Jurisdiction and Merits', 37 Journal of World Trade 997 (2003), at 1000; Pauwelyn, *Conflict of Norms*, above n 25, at 443–45.

56 For such resorting to such "non-consensual" general principles in the public international law field, see O.A. Elias and C.L. Lim, 'General Principles of Law, "Soft" Law and the Identification of International Law', 28 Netherlands Yearbook of International Law 3 (1997), at 4–44.

57 Even though some WTO Members argue that the admissibility of amicus briefs affect their substantive rights, there remains a strong body of opinion among members that the issue is mainly procedural in nature. See further, C.L. Lim, 'The Amicus Brief Issue at the WTO', 4 Chinese Journal of International Law 85 (2005), at 99, 105, 108, 109–10 for a survey of these differing opinions among the several delegations in Geneva.

58 Of course, one may argue that the statement in Article 11 of the DSU that the panel shall 'make *such other findings* as will assist the DSB in making the recommendations or in giving the rulings provided for in the covered agreements' (emphasis added) implicitly grants such powers to the panel, while the Appellate Body has been explicitly granted the powers to draft working procedures for appellate review by Article 17.9.

59 See also Hersch Lauterpacht, *Private Law Sources and Analogies of International Law: With Special Reference to International Arbitration* (London: Longmans, 1927) 215–96.

60 Done at Vienna on 23 May 1969. Entered into force on 27 January 1980, 1155 U.N.T.S. 331.

61 Appellate Body Report, *United States—Standards for Reformulated and Conventional Gasoline (US—Gasoline)*, WT/DS2/AB/R, adopted 20 May 1996, DSR 1996:I, 3, at 17.

62 See further, C.L. Lim, 'Law and Diplomacy in World Trade Disputes', 6 Singapore Journal of International & Comparative Law 436 (2002), at 470–71.

63 Some of the issues discussed here were explored in a different context in Henry Gao, 'The Mighty Pen, the Almighty Dollar, and the Holy Hammer and Sickle: An Examination of the Conflict Between Trade Liberalization and Domestic Cultural Policy with Special Regard to the Recent Dispute Between the US and China on Restrictions on Certain Cultural Products', 2 Asian Journal of WTO and International Health Law and Policy 313 (2007), at 333–36.

64 Pauwelyn, 'The Role of Public International Law', above n 25, at 560. See also Pauwelyn, *Conflict of Norms,* above n 25, at 460 ff.

65 Pauwelyn, above n 55, at 1001.

66 Appellate Body Report, *US—Gasoline,* above n 61, at 17.

67 Pauwelyn, above n 55, at 1001.

68 Appellate Body Report, *US—Gasoline,* above n 61, at 17.

69 Pauwelyn, above n 55, at 1001.

70 Philip Allott, 'The Concept of International Law', 10 European Journal of International Law 31 (1999) 35.

71 Put differently, treaties are 'more individualistic' than customary or general international law; see O.A. Elias and C.L. Lim, *The Paradox of Consensualism in International Law* (The Hague: Kluwer, 1998), 183. See further, H.L.A. Hart, *The Concept of Law,* 2nd ed. (Oxford: Clarendon, 1992), Chapter 3.

72 What trade lawyers see as unilateral retaliation, international lawyers might view as lawful countermeasures instead, and they would have a long line of international legal authorities that might also suggest that the power to modify the law of countermeasures is limited. See further, the *Case Concerning the Gabcikovo-Nagymaros Project (Hungary v. Slovakia),* ICJ, 25 September 1997, ICJ Reports 1997; *Case Concerning the Air Services Agreement of 27 March 1946,* US–France Arbitral Tribunal, 9 December 1978, RIAA Vol. XVIII.

73 The 'contract model' does in fact inform much of McNair's classic *Law of Treaties* (Oxford: Clarendon, 1961) but is beside the point. The debate came to the fore in the context of the succession of newly independent states to colonial treaty obligations, see R.P. Anand, *New States and International Law* (Delhi: Vikas, 1972); S. Prakash Sinha, 'Perspective of the Newly Independent States on the Binding Quality of International Law', 14 International & Comparative Law Quarterly 128 (1965); Georges Abi-Saab, 'The Newly Independent States and the Rules of International Law', 8 Howard Law Journal 95 (1962).

74 Joel Trachtman, 'Book Review: Conflict of Norms in Public International Law by Joost Pauwelyn', 98 American Journal of International Law 855 (2004), at 858.

75 Pauwelyn, above n 58, at 1002–03.

76 Ibid, at 1003.

77 See Henry Gao, 'Evaluating Alternative Approaches to GATS: Negotiations: Sectoral, Formulae and Other Alternatives', in Pierre Sauvé, Marion Panizzon, and Nicole Pohl (eds), *GATS and the Regulation of International Trade in Services* (Cambridge: Cambridge University Press, 2008) 183–208.

78 Even if strictly they are because the MFN rule is agreed between each WTO Member with the other in what might be viewed as an accumulation of bilateral relationships. It is in this sense that the MFN rule has the magical effect of being a 'tariff accelerator'.

79 Trachtman, above n 74, at 859.

80 Ibid.

81 See further, Michael Akehurst 'The Hierarchy of Sources of International Law', 47 British Yearbook of International Law 273 (1974–75).

82 See Ronald Dworkin, *Law's Empire* (Cambridge, Mass.: Belknap, 1996) 178–84.

83 '[A]nd adapts itself to the needs of a new day.' The phrase is Lord Mansfield's. Cited in Lon Fuller, *The Law in Quest of Itself* (Chicago: Foundation Press, 1940) 140.

84 Opened for signature 19 November 1794, UK–US, 12 Bevans 13 (entered into force 24 June 1795).

85 John Bassett Moore, *History and Digest of the International Arbitrations to Which the United States Has Been a Party* (Washington: Government Printing Office, 1898) vol. 1, at 495–682.

86 See, for example, C.L. Lim, 'The Uses of Pacific Settlement Techniques in Malaysia-Singapore Relations', 6 Melbourne Journal of International Law 313 (2005) (discussing the continued salience of the sovereign choice doctrine among Southeast Asian nations).

87 A question arises concerning the extent to which an inter-party dispute in a modern FTA (as opposed, for example, to an investor-state dispute) may be said to result in an arbitral award, and more to the point is to be considered 'arbitration' in the first place. It might be argued that they are no more 'arbitration' than the WTO dispute settlement procedure.

88 For the theoretical argument, see Adrian Briggs, 'Conflict of Laws: Postponing the Future?', 9 Oxford Journal of Legal Studies 251 (1989), at 253 ff.

89 See further, Alan Redfern and Martin Hunter et al., *Law and Practice of International Commercial Arbitration,* 4th ed. (London: Thomson Sweet & Maxwell, 2004) paras 1.99 ff.

90 Ibid, at paras 2.08–2.11. For the distinction between the arbitration rules and the *lex arbitri* (the law governing the arbitration), see ibid, at paras. 2.12–2.13.

91 For persuasive arguments in favour of the special agreement procedure in the context of the International Court of Justice, see, for example, Gary L. Scott and Craig L. Carr, 'The ICJ and Compulsory Jurisdiction: The Case for Closing the Clause', 81 American Journal of International Law 57 (1987).

Regional Agreements and the WTO:
The Gyrating Gears of Interdependence

PABLO HEIDRICH AND DIANA TUSSIE

I. Introduction

In order to map a route it first helps to know where you are going. Before delving into the challenges posed by proliferating regional and preferential trade agreements, it is necessary to outline some central assumptions that underlie this chapter. This chapter does not treat regionalism and multilateralism as opposites, but rather as interdependent phenomena. Interdependence here is defined as mutual dependence.[1] Interdependence refers to situations characterized by reciprocal, though not necessarily symmetrical, effects. The term 'effect' is crucial: interactions that have no significant effects are simply interconnections. Interdependence involves costs. There is no guarantee that interdependence will lead to mutual benefit at all times and tensions are bound to arise over such issues. There may be joint gains and losses, and there may, at the same time, be relative gains and distributional losses. This distinction is vital to this chapter's discussion of how multilateralism interacts with regionalism and how each contributes to the other's existence over different time periods. Not only are national policies affected by international considerations, but each country makes demands on the international system that in turn contribute to shaping it. In this vein, the ties of interdependence fall into two categories: (1) issues of systemic relevance; and (2) issues of relevance to the individual members of regional trade agreements.

This chapter focuses on both forms of interdependence as seen through the lens of south-south regionalism. Developing countries, once a blind spot in the General Agreement on Tariffs and Trade (GATT), have become the fastest-growing constituency inside the World Trade Organization (WTO).

Simultaneously, from a mere trickle, the number of south-south arrangements has increased dramatically.

This chapter proceeds in four sections. First, the perceived interaction between regional and multilateral agreements is canvassed. Second, the systemic issues at stake are considered. Third, the WTO surveillance procedures that apply, in particular to south-south regional trade agreements, are reviewed. Fourth, this chapter highlights how countries actively involved in regional agreements also remain active in and make use of WTO-specific services. A case study of the disputes raised by Latin American regional agreements in the WTO, and a comparison with the trends in the use of regional arbitration mechanisms, is presented.

Disputes regarding regional trade arrangements and their discriminatory effects on third parties have been precedent setting and attracted attention for good reasons. However, such disputes have arisen rather infrequently. The most prominent of these wide-ranging disputes has been the so-called banana dispute. In April 1993, five Latin American countries filed a complaint before the GATT concerning the European Union's (EU) banana import regime under the Lomé Convention (now the Cotonou Agreement). The central issue was whether the Lomé Convention fell under the category of free trade area as defined in GATT Article XXIV and thus could not discriminate against banana imports from non-Lomé signatories. The panel concluded that the Lomé Convention was a non-reciprocal agreement and hence did not meet the GATT Article XXIV definition of a free trade area.[2]

A second significant dispute concerns India's request for the establishment of a WTO Panel in 2003 to review the European Union's special tariff preferences under a program for drug eradication that benefited only 12 developing countries. Much like the banana dispute, the panel found the European Union's arrangement to be inconsistent with WTO obligations because it discriminated against other developing countries.[3] Neither of these schemes, which benefited limited groups of developing countries, met the criteria stipulated in GATT Article XXIV and hence were deemed to require a waiver from WTO rules. These precedent-setting cases have been the subject of significant academic attention. This chapter does not seek to revisit these cases but rather to evaluate some of the subtle undercurrents that were present in them.

The WTO Dispute Settlement Understanding has been used with striking frequency to address regional trade relations. Neither GATT Article XXIV nor GATS Article V exert much discipline on the workings of regional trade agreements. In any case, discipline is exerted after rather than before the event. This *ex post facto* reliance suggests that it is the underlying assurance of the WTO itself as an enforcer of last resort that makes these regional agreements possible. In this form of cooperation and interdependence, the judicial function of the WTO acquires much greater relevance, while the legislative functions recede to the background.

II. The Interface Between Regional Trade Agreements and the Multilateral Trading System

Hirschman's case study of Germany and Bulgaria remains the classic case of how commercial relations can be tied to national political power where there is a significant difference in size and market power of the countries involved.[4] In 1938, the bilateral trade between the two countries represented 52 and 59 percent of Bulgaria's total imports and exports respectively. However, for Germany, trade with Bulgaria represented less than 2 percent of its total trade for both imports and exports. While the trade between the two was balanced (i.e., no trade deficit), Hirschman suggested that 'it will be much more difficult for Bulgaria to shift her trade with Germany to other countries than it will be for Germany to replace Bulgaria as a selling market and a source of supplies'.[5]

This notion of asymmetry as a function of territory and market size remains evident in commercial diplomacy and perhaps more so today where countries are engaging in numerous regional trade agreements. As noted by Hirschman, the ability to credibly threaten the termination of trade was once at the core of trade policy. The establishment of a most-favoured-nation clause in international trade as a global policing mechanism was meant to curb the ability of the more powerful market to create political dependence on the trade concessions.

It is well known that the GATT system was conceived as a means of preventing the resurgence of the competing economic blocs that had prevailed prior to World War II. The GATT, therefore, adopted non-discrimination as a pillar. Most-favoured-nation was viewed as a means of eroding imperial preferences, while at the same time protecting the interests of smaller and weaker territories. Most-favoured-nation can also been viewed as an instrument favouring larger-producing interests since it guarantees them a right of access on an equal footing with all others. Both conceptions have always been in tension in the historical justifications for most-favoured-nation.

The Draft Charter for the International Trade Organization (ITO), which was put forward by the U.S. government in 1946, recognized only customs unions as exceptions to the most-favoured-nation rule.[6] It was at the drafting conference that the original concept of free trade areas appeared. In 1947, developing countries introduced the initial concept of free trade areas where 'two or more developing countries might be prepared to abolish all trade barriers among themselves, though not wishing to construct a common tariff towards the rest of the world'.[7] Developing countries thought that non-discrimination principles did not always benefit them and a certain degree of preferential treatment would be necessary in order to promote their economic development. Moreover, they regarded customs unions as poor mechanisms for utilizing preferential treatment owing to their strict conditions.[8] The concept of a free trade area received support from many participants in the drafting session, especially from European countries, and it was successfully incorporated into the draft agreement. European countries regarded the concept of free trade areas as an extension of the bilateral preferential trade arrangements that had been a common practice in Europe before World War II. Most of the GATT founding Contracting Parties had in effect taken the position that some discrimination would help to promote trade liberalization and that not all discrimination was bad.[9]

During the ITO drafting session, the United States had intended that preferences should ultimately be eliminated. Yet the U.S. government also desired any agreement to apply as widely as possible in order to enhance its reach and effectiveness. As a result, the United States compromised on the issue of including new preferences and accepted free trade areas as an exception to the unconditional most-favoured-nation rule. While the exception, articulated in GATT Article XXIV, is not the only exception in the trading rules to most-favoured-nation, it is probably the most important. The increasing number of regional trade agreements brings into question the extent to which free trade areas are truly an exception and what core functions the WTO actually retains. In effect, the interface between regional trade agreements and the WTO defines the role and functioning of the system itself. This relationship is usually understood by examining both the substantive rules and institutional controls that are provided to secure it. In any case, dispute settlement presents an opportunity to resolve issues not addressed in negotiations, though few cases concerning regional trade agreements have been brought to the WTO.

The erosion of most-favoured-nation has gone hand in hand with deep tariff cuts. Tariffs are now so low they no longer constitute, as in the 1930s, a source of effective discrimination. If the early post–World War II mind-frame was marked by a fear of the re-emergence of warring economic blocs, the GATT of the 1960s and 1970s was dominated by the structural contraposition between developed and developing countries. This focus on north-south trade, however, needs to be reshaped, with a new emphasis on south-south trade relations. History marches on. As developing countries become the fastest-growing constituency in the WTO, old mind-frames need to be reshaped and new issues are raised, namely that of intra-south relations. In today's circumstances, the relationship between regionalism and multilateralism must be recast in a novel light: how do regional trade agreements use WTO services, and how are these services increasingly required and currently provided, especially with regard to ordering the interstices among regional members themselves rather than with third parties. These latter types of issues are infrequently a point of controversy. In this light, when considering rule enforcement there are two sets of issues that need to be addressed: (1) issues of systemic relevance, and (2) issues of relevance to the members of regional trade agreements taken individually. These two issues will be canvassed over the following four sections.

III. General Systemic Issues in Regional Trade Agreements

Systemic issues in regional trade agreements relate to the potential and actual costs that can be incurred by third parties. The work program of the current Doha Round of multilateral trade negotiations includes a provision dealing with these systemic implications of GATT Article XXIV. Paragraph 29 of the Doha Declaration states:

> We also agree to negotiations aimed at clarifying and improving disciplines and procedures under the existing WTO provisions applying to regional trade agreements. The negotiations shall take into account the developmental aspects of regional trade agreements.[10]

Work on systemic issues in regional trade agreements has proceeded in the Negotiating Group on Rules, which reports to the Trade Negotiations Committee (TNC). There have been lengthy and unwieldy discussions on the issue of coverage. The concept of coverage requires that duties and other restrictive regulations of commerce must be eliminated on 'substantially all the trade' between the constituent territories of a customs union or a free trade area. Because of its imprecision, the term 'substantially all trade' is at the centre of the debate and has produced submissions proposing qualitative and quantitative indicators that could be used to clarify the concept. Progress in this debate has been grim, and there appears to be little hope for consensus on a more specific test for trade coverage.

One area that has begun to see some progress is the improvement of transparency and reporting requirements vis-à-vis regional trade agreements. In this regard, a draft with the title of 'Transparency Mechanism for Regional Trade Agreements' was forwarded by the Negotiating Rules Committee in the summer of 2006 and adopted by a decision of the General Council in December of 2006.[11] This decision has important implications for the functioning of the regional trade agreements, including the following:

- Early announcement provisions upon commencement of negotiations and signature of a regional trade agreement;

- Formal notification of regional trade agreements to the WTO no later than directly following the parties' ratification of the regional trade agreement or any party's decision on application of the relevant parts of an agreement, and before the application of preferential treatment between the parties;
- Preparation of a report concerning notified regional trade agreements by the WTO Secretariat on the basis of the data submitted. This report must refrain from value judgments on the questions of consistency with rules and cannot be used as a basis for dispute resolution;
- A formal review meeting will be conducted to consider each notified regional trade agreement;
- At the end of the implementation period, the parties to a regional trade agreement shall submit to the WTO a short written report on the realization of the liberalization commitments originally notified; and
- Any Member may, at any time, bring to the attention of the committee any regional trade agreement that it considers ought to have been submitted or notified.

Despite the considerable energy expended in the negotiation of these provisions, it represents modest progress. The legacy of vague and incomplete rules has not been addressed and the important issue of rules of origin remains untouched. However, as noted by the Warwick Commission, 'transparency is typically a precondition for progress in improving the policy environment'.[12] To this end, added transparency may assist in addressing structural issues in respect of regional trade agreements.

A central issue during negotiations of the decision was whether regional trade agreements between developing countries notified according to the Enabling Clause[13] would be covered at all by the transparency provisions under the decision. If so, another issue then became which committee within the WTO would be entrusted with reviewing such regional trade agreements. The compromise reached was that the Committee on Trade and Development would remain responsible for agreements notified under the Enabling Clause. Additional developing country issues raised in the discussions were the degree of reciprocity between a developed and developing country for the elimination of tariffs, and the different period of time for implementation (i.e., whether a developing country can be entitled to a longer implementation period). Both these issues raise the possibility of including special and differential treatment (S&D) considerations into the text of GATT Article XXIV.

Despite a flurry of activity, negotiators have been unable to resolve these questions. Negotiators are attempting to balance constraining discrimination with retaining flexibility in the pursuit of new preferential agreements. For the time being, negotiations do not seem to be slowing down, and the multilateral system and regional trade agreements remain intertwined. The complexities of this relationship are especially profound for developing countries, which on one hand have access to a two-track notification system, and on the other have made active use of the dispute settlement mechanism to resolve their disputes over regional trade agreements.

IV. Notification of South-South Agreements: Living with Inchoate Systemic Certification

Both the Enabling Clause and GATT Article XXIV allow for deviations from the guiding principle of non-discrimination. However the necessary conditions for regional trade agreements negotiated under the rules differ considerably as between the Enabling Clause and the GATT. The criteria stipulated in GATT Article XXIV are much stricter than those of the Enabling Clause. This dualistic legal framework leaves room to conclude that developing countries can be exempt from equal liberalization when they negotiate their trading agreements. Developing countries have come to demand that their regional agreements should be allowed to proceed even when they fall short of the conditions stipulated in GATT Article XXIV.

The regular practice with respect to notification of developing country regional trade agreements, including customs unions, to the WTO has been to present them under the Enabling Clause rather than Article XXIV and subsequently to notify the agreements to the Committee on Trade and Development (CTD). The mandate of the CTD contemplates review of all matters relating to the Enabling Clause[14] and has been extended to responsibility for reporting and transparency issues related to developing country regional preferential arrangements for trade in goods. There have been several occasions in which developing countries have contemplated the creation of a legal entity that falls within the criteria and definitions of GATT Article XXIV. The legal consequences of the differences between the Enabling Clause and GATT Article XXIV, including the allocation of supervision of south-south regional trade agreements, has yet to be resolved under the DSU.

The question of the allocation of supervision is more relevant for the transparency and reporting requirements than for the process of review itself. This is because the CRTA appears to adopt the review procedures of the CTD when it examines developing country preferential arrangements that also fall within the terms of GATT Article XXIV. Early in Doha Round negotiations concerning GATT Article XXIV, opinion was split among Members on the question of whether any new transparency and reporting requirements should also apply to the south-south agreements notified according to the Enabling Clause. Following the adoption of the Transparency Mechanism in 2006, the debate appears to have been resolved in favour of equivalent transparency for all agreements, including GATT Article XXIV, GATS Article V, and Enabling Clause arrangements.

The difference between the review carried out by the CTD and the CRTA is potentially more important. This is particularly true if a proposed regional trade agreement seeks to be defined under the lower trade coverage requirement of the Enabling Clause as opposed to the customs union definition in GATT Article XXIV. This issue can also arise in the notification of free trade areas under the Enabling Clause, though the formation of a customs union will potentially provoke stronger reactions by third parties. This is because customs unions often involve a modification of most-favoured-nation tariff rates applicable to other WTO Members. This in turn affects established export interests and could provoke third party claims under GATT Articles I and II.

The only example to date of how a customs union among developing countries has been treated is that of the MERCOSUR. MERCUSOR predated the Uruguay Round Understanding on Article XXIV and the creation of the CRTA. Nevertheless, the MERCOSUR case is illuminating given that the Council for Trade in Goods decided to examine MERCOSUR under both the Enabling Clause and the provisions of GATT Article XXIV. The terms of reference for that examination reveal a striking duality:

> To examine the Southern Common Market Agreement (MERCOSUR) in the light of the relevant provisions of the Enabling Clause and of the GATT 1994, including Article XXIV, and to transmit a report and recommendations to the Committee on Trade and Development for submission to the General Council, with a copy of the report transmitted as well to the Council for Trade in Goods. The examination in the Working Party will be based on a complete notification and on written questions and answers.[15]

Both committees have remained involved in subsequent reviews of MERCOSUR, with the CTD being responsible for the reporting function. This duality of review reveals the overlapping terms of reference for both the committees whereby the CTD retains the prerogative to review all arrangements under the Enabling Clause and the CRTA examines arrangements under GATT Article XXIV and GATS Article V. But there has been no clarity as to whether the application of the Enabling Clause overrides the substantive requirements for customs union formation under GATT Article XXIV(8), especially as it relates to the issue of coverage.

Subsequent customs unions have yet to generate a dualistic approach similar to MERCUSOR. Table 1 outlines the customs unions that have been notified to date.

Table 1: Notification of South–South Agreements

Agreement	Date of entry into force	Date of notification	Related provision	Type of agreement	Status
Andean Community	25 May 88	1 Oct 90	Enabling Clause	Customs union	No report
COMESA	8 Dec 94	29 Jun 95	Enabling Clause	Preferential arrangement	Examination not requested
MERCOSUR	29 Nov 91	5 Mar 92	Enabling Clause	Customs union	Factual examination concluded
CARICOM	1 Aug 73	14 Oct 74	GATT Art. XXIV	Customs union	Report adopted
WAEMU	1 Jan 00	3 Feb 00	Enabling Clause	Preferential arrangement	Examination not requested
ECOWAS	1993	26 Sep 05	Enabling Clause	Preferential arrangement	Examination not requested

Source: www.wto.org, 'Regional Trade Agreements Notified to the GATT/WTO and in Force by GATT/WTO Related Provision', in *Regional Trade Agreements gateway* (accessed 8 December 8, 2008).

Both the Caribbean Community and Common Market (CARICOM) and MERCOSUR were notified as customs unions while the Economic Community of Western Africa (ECOWAS), the Common Market of East and South Africa (COMESA), and the Western Africa Monetary Union (WAEMU) were notified as preferential arrangements. Such a difference in the stated ambition of the arrangement might result in the applications of stricter review criteria. The 1977 Working Party Report on CARICOM treated this arrangement as an interim agreement leading to the formation of a customs union. However, that review also predated the 1979 Enabling Clause.[16]

A more recent example is the Framework Agreement on Comprehensive Economic Cooperation between the Association of South East Asian Nations and the People's Republic of China. This agreement was notified in December 2004 under the Enabling Clause as a preferential arrangement. To complicate matters, the Framework Agreement takes a phased approach to trade liberalization. The Framework Agreement triggered a first partial scope agreement and will lead to a second-step commitment to a future free trade area.[17] The uncertainty between each of the steps was raised by some WTO Members. After losing both the banana and drug-related preferences disputes, the EU raised noted that

> the recently concluded FTA in goods should have been notified under GATT Article XXIV and be referred to the WTO Committee on Regional Trade Agreements. The EC strongly encourages the parties of the FTA to take the necessary steps towards this end.[18]

Was the EU looking to settle an old score, or was this mere formality? If the latter, why do parties to an arrangement simply avoid drawing attention to the uncertainty and drop either the reference to Article XXIV or the term 'free trade area'? At the same time, if the terms of the Enabling Clause are so vague that they allow any arrangement between developing countries, what difference does it make what the Members want to call their arrangements or what trade coverage they include or even what sectors they wish to exclude?

Some countries have attempted to structure their arrangements so as to avoid this definitional conundrum. For example, the Cotonou Agreement between the EU and the group of African, Caribbean, and Pacific states proclaims that the agreement's trade provisions are 'WTO compatible trading arrangements, removing progressively barriers to trade between them and enhancing cooperation in all areas relevant to trade.'[19] To provide a stronger legal footing, the preferences under the Cotonou Agreement will not be notified under the Enabling Clause. When completed, the trade preferences will be treated under WTO law by a notification to the Council on trade in goods and for services, and then referred to the CRTA for examination under GATT Article XXIV and GATS Article V.[20]

The above discussion of how review and supervision are treated in the proliferating regional trade agreements under the WTO is illustrative of the tensions and contradictions in the global trading system.. Supervision is plagued with ambiguity and a number of loopholes. Since its inception, the Enabling Clause removed the 'substantially all trade' requirement for customs unions or free trade agreements among developing countries. The Doha Round is not addressing the Enabling Clause requirements for south-south agreements, though arguably this may not be within the Doha Round's work program. Rules are more often the result of power relations than they are the causes of its limitation. Restrained or unrestrained, south-south regional trade agreements, especially between the larger and rapidly growing developing countries, are likely to be created. What is emerging is a gap between the member-driven political system of 'mutual indulgence'[21] and the strongly legalistic Dispute Settlement Understanding (DSU), on which members of regional trade agreements rely to fill in gaps and provide interpretations.

While there is wide consensus that the proliferation of regional trade agreements is a threat to the WTO system, there is another *realpolitik* view suggesting that it is the underlying assurances of the WTO itself that makes these regional agreements possible. If regional trade agreements are generating trade benefits for their members, so the argument goes, and this is the vehicle of choice for realizing the trade objectives of countries, then so be it. In this scenario the judicial function of the WTO acquires greater relevance while the legislative functions recede. Making the WTO an 'enforcer' among regional trade agreement parties and between regional trade agreement and non-regional trade agreement WTO Members would create an opportunity for the incremental development of a body of common law of regional trade agreements that could eventually form the basis of multilateral rules on regional trade agreements. This could turn regional trade agreements from stumbling blocks into building blocks of the multilateral trading system.[22] In fact, many developing countries have made wide use of the dispute resolution process within the WTO framework to address disagreements of interpretation. The traditional systemic contribution of the WTO to the global most favoured nation governance of trade pale in relation to its specific contribution to the partners tied by regional trade agreements. Latin America is a case in point.

V. Use of the DSU: The Case of Latin America

Since 1995, Latin American countries have been frequent participants in cases brought under the DSU. Five Latin American countries (Colombia, Costa Rica, Guatemala, Nicaragua, and Venezuela), first excluded from the banana regime under the Lomé Convention and then from the Cotonou arrangements, have requested panels that clarified the interpretation of the Enabling Clause as applicable to north-south agreements. Perhaps surprising is that, despite Latin American countries accounting for only 5 percent of global trade, 23 percent of all the disputes brought to the WTO have involved these countries. Nearly 12.5 percent of all disputes brought to the WTO have involved disagreements between Latin American Members. Again, this is surprising given that intra-regional trade accounts for barely 20 percent of total trade. Based on this, it is fair to say that Latin American trade appears to generate a disproportionate number of WTO cases.

Table 2 outlines the cases brought by or against Latin American countries under the DSU. Interestingly, despite being a major regional political force, Brazil has been a party to only five disputes.

In relation to regional trade agreements, the consultation requests made by Latin American WTO Members is quite telling. There are essentially three kinds of preferential trade arrangements in the region. The first are those that are under the old Latin American Integration Association (LAIA) system of 1980, covered by the Enabling Clause and based on a philosophy of gradual and partial trade liberalization. Second, free trade agreements, roughly comparable to others done in the rest of the developing world, have developed. Third are the more ambitious integration schemes, such as those of MERCOSUR, the Central American Common Market, and the Andean Community. The a

Table 2: Participation of Latin America in the DSU

Country	Complainant	Respondent	Total
Argentina	7	3	10
Brazil	4	1	5
Chile	6	8	14
Colombia	3	2	5
Costa Rica	1	0	1
Guatemala	3	2	5
Honduras	3	0	3
Mexico	5	5	10
Nicaragua	1	2	3
Panama	2	1	3
Dominican Rep.	0	3	3
Ecuador	0	3	3
Peru	0	4	4
Uruguay	0	1	1

Source: Economic Commission for Latin America and the Caribbean, op cit, footnote 10.

priori expectation would be that those agreements pursing ambitious integration would produce more instances of intra-Latin American litigation at the WTO, particularly given the known problems of institution-building and rule-enforcement in most trade integration initiatives among developing countries.[23]

The reality tells a different story. As Tables 3 to 6 demonstrate, more ambitious Latin American integration schemes have not stirred up much WTO activity. To date, just four cases have arisen out of the region's customs unions, despite the fact that these integration schemes implicated 75 percent of the region's trade in 2007. Free trade agreements signed among Latin American countries have accounted for ten of the cases considered at the DSU. Countries that have the most superficial form of integration via the Economic Cooperation Agreements in the LAIA accounted for 14 other cases. The remaining 7 cases of intra–Latin American WTO disputes have been among countries that do not have any sort of treaty signed for preferential trade.[24]

The most notorious Economic Cooperation Agreement is between Argentina and Chile. These two countries have sought repeated consultations on policies related to the agricultural and agro-industrial exports sectors. Argentina sought consultations in respect of countervailing duties applied by Chile through its

Table 3: Cases Arising from Deeper Integration Schemes (MERCOSUR, Andean Pact, Central American Free Trade Agreement)

Complainant	Respondent	Grouping	Year
Honduras	Nicaragua	CACM	2000
Argentina	Brazil	MERCOSUR	2006
Brazil	Argentina	MERCOSUR	2001
Brazil	Argentina	MERCOSUR	2000

Table 4: Cases Arising from Latin American FTAs

Complainant	Respondent	Grouping	Year
Chile	Mexico	FTA 1998	2001
Costa Rica	Dominican Republic	FTA 1998	2005
Honduras	Dominican Republic	FTA 1998	2003
Honduras	Dominican Republic	FTA 1998	2003
Nicaragua	Mexico	FTA 1998	2003
Guatemala	Chile	FTA 1999	2001
Guatemala	Mexico	Northern Triangle FTA 2000	2005
Guatemala	Mexico	Northern Triangle FTA 2000	2003
Mexico	Guatemala	Northern Triangle FTA 2000	1999
Mexico	Guatemala	Northern Triangle FTA 2000	1996

Table 5: Cases Arising from Economic Cooperation Agreements Groupings

Complainant	Respondent	Grouping	Year
Colombia	Chile	ECA 1994	2001
Colombia	Chile	ECA 1994	2001
Chile	Ecuador	ECA 1995	2003
Argentina	Chile	ECA 1996	2006
Argentina	Chile	ECA 1996	2006
Argentina	Chile	ECA 1996	2002
Argentina	Chile	ECA 1996	2001
Argentina	Chile	ECA 1996	2000
Chile	Uruguay	ECA 1996	2002
Chile	Argentina	ECA 1996	2001
Chile	Peru	ECA 1998	2002
Chile	Peru	ECA 1998	2001
Argentina	Peru	ECA 2003	2002
Brazil	Peru	ECA 2003	1997

Table 6: Cases between Countries without Bilateral Trade Agreements

Complainant	Respondent	Year
Brazil	Mexico	2000
Colombia	Nicaragua	2000
Mexico	Panama	2005
Mexico	Ecuador	2000
Mexico	Ecuador	1999
Panama	Colombia	2007
Panama	Colombia	2006

policy to maintain price bands on agricultural goods, such as vegetable oils, and fructose.[25] The full implementation of the WTO ruling in favour of Argentina[26] remains an outstanding issues. Chile sought consultations over imposition of duties on its exports of processed peaches and eventually obtained a favourable panel ruling.[27] Colombia and Guatemala have also taken Chile to the WTO concerning alleged protectionist agricultural policies.[28]

Tables 7 and 8 canvass the products and the types of measures at issue in WTO cases between Latin American Members. The prevailing measures challenged among trade partners have been anti-dumping and safeguard measures, both applied to provide temporary relief from imports. Combining the information on the products and the type of measure, it can be concluded that cases are brought to the WTO to protect or support industries often characterized by strong concentration in domestic markets or a strong regional export propensity, a feature that is particularly present in the region because of the relatively high volume of competitive intra-regional trade.

WTO disputes between Latin American Members have tended to involve sectors with larger businesses present in the market. For example, in the cases brought between Chile and Argentina, the companies on the complainant side were strong players, such as the Argentine oil seeds crushers, dairy exporters, and the Chilean peach exporters.[29] For those involving Mexico and Guatemala, it was the large (by most standards monopolistic) cement companies that sought action through their governments. Disputes between Guatemala, Venezuela, Mexico, and Argentina concerning steel pipes and tubes were also

Table 7: WTO Cases between Latin American Members by Product

Sector	Number of cases	Examples
Agricultural	2	black beans, fresh fruits, wheat
Agro-industrial	12	edible oils, dairy products, pasta, flour, poultry, fructose
Commodities	8	cement, sugar
Manufactures	12	cigarettes, buses, steel pipes, textiles, shoes, matches, electric transformers
All goods	3	custom values, import financing
No data	1	
Total	38	

Table 8: WTO Cases between Latin American Members by Measures Challenged

Type of measure	Number of cases
Anti-dumping	12
Customs procedures	4
Domestic taxation	4
Exchange rate fee	1
Modification of tariff lines	1
Safeguard measures	12
SPS	1
Tariff by origin	2
No data	1
Total	38

litigated in support of large exporting national producers[30] that still compete intensely with each other and have not yet come under merger pressure.

As in most other regional agreements, intra–Latin American trade agreements have opened markets to large regional business interests. However, these agreements have not been accompanied by regional production agreements or common industrial policies, such as those adopted in early stages of the European Economic Community or the European steel restructuring plans of the 1970s. Neither have intra–Latin American trade agreements required parties to eliminate or curtail their use of trade remedies. The combined result has been use of the DSU by Latin American trading partners to resolve sensitive disputes that have not been amenable to bilateral or multilateral negotiation.

VI. Comparison of Latin American Regional Trade Dispute Mechanisms and the WTO DSU

The main reason for the extensive use of the WTO DSU by Latin American countries has been a lack of comparable and enforceable regional dispute settlement mechanisms, particularly among least developed preferential trade agreements in the region. However, some of the region's more advanced agreements such as MERCUSOR and the Andean Pact[31] do provide for dispute settlement. A comparison between these regional dispute mechanisms and the WTO DSU can help locate areas of common interest and assist in evaluating the place of regional trading systems in the WTO context.[32]

A. Usage of the MERCOSUR Dispute Mechanism

Since its formation in 1991, MERCOSUR has handled 542 disputes. Most of these disputes (some 53 percent) have involved Argentina and Brazil. The bulk of the disputes (85 percent) arose between 1995 and 2001. This period coincided with economic crises in Argentina and Brazil, including a devaluation in Brazil in 1999 that altered trade flows inside MERCOSUR. Furthermore, this period coincided with the implementation of free trade within the customs union. The fact that no provision had been made with regard to remedial trade measures in the original MERCOSUR agreement likely played a role in the significant increase in disputes between 1995 and 2001. Table 9 reviews all disputes between 1991 and 2007.

Table 9: Mercosur Dispute Cases

Complainant	Respondent					
	Argentina	Brazil	Paraguay	Uruguay	Multiple parties	Total
Argentina		167	14	43	4	228
Brazil	122		16	26	2	166
Paraguay	31	25		12	0	68
Uruguay	24	23	5		4	56
Multiple parties	5	7	3	9		24
Total	182	222	38	90	10	542

B. Usage of the Andean Pact Dispute Mechanisms

The Andean Pact has a long history of institutional development, including one of the oldest regional schemes to address trade disputes. The secretariat of the Andean Pact has its own juridical identity, enabling it to open cases against any or even all the members when alleged non-compliance with common legislation arises. Furthermore, individuals and firms can file cases in the dispute arbitration mechanism of the Andean Pact against those government policies that fall under its jurisdiction (i.e., trade and investment).

Table 10 outlines the number of disputes and the parties to disputes under the Andean Pact. One item of note is that over half the cases have been initiated by the Andean Pact's Secretariat. This power of initiation may explain why Andean Pact members have not initiated as many cases. Among individual members, Colombia has initiated the single largest number of cases, an unsurprising fact given its larger economic size inside this integration initiative and, thus, larger economic interests. The private sector has also participated often, accounting for almost 15 percent of all complaints.

Table 10: Disputes under the Andean Pact

Complainant	Respondent							
	Bolivia	Colombia	Ecuador	Peru	Venezuela	Multiple parties	Private sector	Total
Secretariat	13	40	65	39	44			201
Bolivia		1	1	2	1	2	1	8
Colombia	0		14	9	16	22		61
Ecuador	0	5		1	2	12		20
Peru	3	3	3		5	11		25
Venezuela	0	4	3	1		5		13
Multiple parties								0
Private sector	2	14	5	6	9	7	4	47
Total	18	67	91	58	77	59	5	375

Table 11: Issues Submitted to the WTO and Regional DSU

Type of measure	WTO intra–Latin American (1995–2007)	MERCOSUR (1993–2007)	Andean Pact (1974–2007)
Anti-dumping	12	113	30
Competition policies	0	40	29
Customs procedures	4	105	15
Domestic taxation	4	93	92
Exchange rate fee	1	0	0
Modified tariff lines	1	89	56
Safeguard measures	12	3	81
SPS	1	59	35
Tariff by origin	2	23	5
No data / Others	1	17	32
Total	38	542	375

C. Comparing Usage of the Regional Dispute Mechanisms and of the WTO DSU

The types of disputes brought before the WTO, MERCOSUR, and Andean Pact tend to be strikingly similar. For example, the topics most often raised at the WTO DSU are those related to anti-dumping and safeguards. Anti-dumping has also frequently been the cause of regional disputes. Interestingly, MERCOSUR and the Andean Pact have been preferred by countries in the region to resolve differences over sanitary and phyto-sanitary (SPS) issues, even though there is a specific WTO agreement on this topic.

A sectoral analysis shows that most disputes within both MERCOSUR and the Andean Community relate to the agro-industrial complex, which explains the recurrence of SPS in regional disputes. Other disputes have focused on non-agricultural commodities and manufactured exports. These similarities naturally correspond to the particularities of intra-regional trade, but also point to the areas where lessons are being learned, with regional agreements advancing beyond the WTO.

Table 12: Sectors Making Use of WTO and Regional DSU

	WTO intra–Latin America (1995–2007)	MERCOSUR (1995–2007)	Andean Pact (1974–2007)
Agricultural	2	6	11
Agro-industrial	12	180	115
Commodities	8	50	46
Manufactures	12	62	64
All goods	3	126	97
Others	1	115	47
Total	38	542	375

VII. Conclusions: Multilateral Relevance Anew

The wheels connecting regionalism with multilateralism seem to be turning ever faster as trading grounds and linkages become more crowded and intense. They do not stop for a moment. Because the pattern defies rationalization into tidy cells does not mean that we must view it through an ominous lens. The fact that the *ex ante* disciplines are not clear, after the 13 years of the WTO's life, perhaps tells a more relevant story about the convenience or *realpolitik* interests of regionalism of the more powerful countries inside the WTO decision-making process. The fuzziness that has characterized the reporting process for regional trade agreements is only one part of an otherwise normal trade cooperation picture.

The chapter has examined a group of developing countries that trade quite intensely with each other and are particularly litigious. These countries resort to the WTO DSU in order to settle high-stakes trade disputes that seem almost too big to be resolved by regional agreements or are of a precedent-setting nature, such as bilateral FTAs or the more limited economic complementary agreements. The WTO might be highlighting the main shortcomings of those regional trade deals, such as lack of adjustment or remedial measures, and the inability to manage the ambitious schedules of liberalization. The fact that most conflicts in the Latin American example are coming from the shallow integration initiatives, as opposed to the deeper agreements such as MERCOSUR, the Andean Pact, and CACM, might indicate that the WTO has attained by default a role of tutor or marker to assist some types of regional objectives.

The establishment of a general most-favoured-nation clause in international trade was seen as a global policing mechanism to curb the ability of the more powerful markets to threaten the suspension of concessions, therefore effectively switching suppliers. While most-favoured-nation attempted to provide equal treatment, erosion of most-favoured-nation demands new attention from broader multilateral institutions to address problems of asymmetric interdependence, especially in circumstances where countries are engaging in numerous regional trade agreements with a multitude of partners of all sizes and colours. The notion of asymmetry remains alive even in south-south commercial diplomacy.

The multilateral lever is being used to clarify lacunae arising within and among regional trade agreements. At the same time, enhanced transparency will gradually lead to the strengthening of notification and a more systematic examination of regional trade agreements. Overly strict multilateral monitoring of regional trade agreements could impede regional endeavours, without necessarily guaranteeing a renewed emphasis on multilateralism. Yet one would expect that as the process of cooperation advances, agreed-upon benchmarks for new regional trade agreements can and will emerge.

Notes

1 Robert Keohane and Joseph Nye, *Power and Interdependence: World Politics in Transition*, 2nd ed. (Boston: Little, Brown and Co., 1977).

2 GATT Panel Report, *EEC—Import Regime for Bananas*, DS38/R, 11 February 1994, unadopted.

3 WTO Appellate Body Report, *European Communities—Conditions for the Granting of Tariff Preferences to Developing Countries*, WT/DS246/AB/R, adopted 20 April 2004.

4 Albert Hirschman, 'Devaluation and the Trade Balance: A Note', 31 (1) The Review of Economics and Statistics 50 (1949).

5 Ibid, at 68.

6 In March 1948, the ITO Charter was adopted at the United Nations Conference on Trade and Employment in Havana. Since only two countries ratified the Charter, the plan to establish the ITO lost momentum. However, in order to enforce the results of the round, parts of the ITO Charter were selected to form the core of the General Agreement on Tariffs and Trade.

7 Frank A. Haight, 'Customs Unions and Free-Trade Areas under GATT: A Reappraisal', 6 (4) Journal of World Trade Law 391 (1972).

8 In order for a preferential arrangement to constitute a customs union, at least three requirements should be met: elimination of duties among parties; the setup of common external tariffs; and the harmonization of foreign trade regulations.

9 Robert Hudec and James Southwick, 'Regionalism and WTO Rules', in Miguel Rodríguez Mendoza, Patrick Low, and Barbara Kotschwar (eds), *Trade Rules in the Making* (Washington, D.C.: OAS and Brookings, 1999) 47–80.

10 Doha Ministerial Declaration, WT/MIN(01)/DEC/1, Adopted on 21 November 2001, http://www.wto.org/english/thewto_e/minist_e/min01_e/mindecl_e.htm (visited 4 April 2009).

11 WTO General Council, Transparency Mechanism for Regional Trade Agreements, WT/L/671, Adopt 18 December 2006.

12 Warwick Commission, *The Multilateral Trade Regime: Which Way Forward?* (Coventry: University of Warwick. Commission Report, 2007), http://www2.warwick.ac.uk/research/warwickcommission/archive/worldtrade/ (visited 4 April 2009).

13 Adopted in 1979, it allowed developed countries to discriminate between different categories of trading partner according to the latter's development level, providing legal grounds for the maintenance of the North-South Generalized System of Preferences and preferences among developing countries.

14 In 1979, as part of the Tokyo Round of the GATT, the Enabling Clause was adopted in order to permit trading preferences targeted at developing and least developed countries that would otherwise violate GATT Article I.

15 WTO Committee on Regional Trade Agreements, Note on the Meeting of 26 and 26 July 2005, WT/REG/M/40, Adopted 31 August 2005. See also Legal Note on Regional Trade Arrangements Under the Enabling Clause, WT/COMTD/W/114, Adopted 13 May 2003.

16 James Mathis, *Regional Trade Agreements in the GATT/WTO: Article XXIV and the Internal Trade Requirement* (Boston: Cambridge University Press, 2002); Robert Scollay, *Substantially All Trade: Which Definitions Are Fulfilled in Practice? An Empirical Investigation* (London: Commonwealth Secretariat, 2005).

17 Roberto Fiorentino, Luis Verdeja, and Christelle Toqueboeuf, 'The Changing Landscape of RTAs' (WTO Discussion Paper No. 12, 2007), http://doc.abhatoo.net.ma/doc/IMG/pdf/Changing_Landscape_RTA_2006.pdf (visited 4 April 2009).

18 WTO Committee on Trade and Development, Framework Agreement on Comprehensive Economic Cooperation Between the Association of South East Asians Nations and the People's Republic of China, WT/COMTD/51/Add.2, Adopted 8 February 2006.

19 Article 36 of the ACP–EU Partnership Agreement (Cotonou Agreement), done at Cotonou, Benin on 23 June 2000, http://ec.europa.eu/development/geographical/cotonouintro_en.cfm (visited 4 April 2009).

20 Gerhard Erasmus, 'Accommodating Developing Countries in the WTO: From Mega-Debates to Economic Partnership Agreements', which can be found in this volume.

21 Warwick Commission, above n 12.

22 Henry Gao and Lim Chin Leng, 'Saving the WTO from the Risk of Irrelevance: WTO Dispute Settlement as a Common Good for RTAs,' which can be found in this volume.

23 Mikio Kuwayama, José Durán, and Verónica Silva, *Bilateralism and Regionalism: Reestablishing the Primacy of Multilateralism: A Latin American and Caribbean Perspective* (New York: United Nations, 2006).

24 All data for the Latin American disputes brought to the WTO or solved inside the region by its different trade integration schemes were obtained from the Economic Commission for Latin American and the Caribbean's Integrated Database of Trade Disputes for Latin American and the Caribbean, found at http://idatd.eclac.cl.

25 Diana Tussie and Valentina Delich, 'Dispute Settlement Between Developing Countries: Argentina and Chilean Price Bands', in Peter Gallagher, Patrick Low, and Andrew Stoler (eds), *Managing the Challenges of WTO Participation: 45 Case Studies* (Cambridge: Cambridge University Press, 2005) 23–47.

26 WTO Appellate Body Report, *Chile—Price Band System and Safeguard Measures Relating to Certain Agricultural Products*, WT/DS207/AB/R, adopted 23 October 2002.

27 WTO Panel Report, *Argentina—Definitive Safeguard Measure on Imports of Preserved Peaches*, WT/DS238/R, adopted 15 April 2003.

28 WTO, Chile—Price Band System and Safeguard Measures Relating to Certain Agricultural Products, Request for Consultations by Guatemala, WT/DS220/1, 10 January 2001 (note that this dispute did not proceed to the panel stage).

29 See Tussie and Delich, above n 25, at 12.

30 On the manner in which these partnerships work, see Gregory Shaffer, 'How to Make the WTO Dispute Settlement Work for Developing Countries: Some Proactive Developing Country Strategies' in 'Towards a Development-Supportive Dispute Settlement System in the WTO' (ICTSD Resource Paper No. 5, Geneva, 2003).

31 The Central American Common Market is also a fully functional trade integration initiative but it has only recently developed a dispute settlement mechanism. The few cases brought up so far are listed in the general comparative table at the end of this section.

32 Much of the analysis in the proceeding section draws from Sáez, Sebastián, *Las controversias en el marco de la Organización Mundial de Comercio: de dónde vienen, en dónde están, a dónde van* (Santiago: CEPAL, 2006).

﷽ ﷽ ﷽ Bibliography

Monographs

Alexandroff, Alan S., ed. *Trends in World Trade: Essays in Honor of Sylvia Ostry* (Durham, NC: Carolina Academic Press, 2007).

Alexandroff, Alan S., Sylvia Ostry, & Rafael Gomez, eds. *China and the Long March to Global Trade: The Accession of China to the World Trade Organization* (London: Routledge, 2002).

Barton, John H. *et al.*, eds. *The Evolution of the Trade Regime: Politics, Law, and Economics of the GATT and the WTO* (Princeton: Princeton University Press, 2006).

Blagescu, Monica, & Robert Lloyd. *2006 Global Accountability Report. Holding Power to Account* (One World Trust, 2006), online: One World Trust <http://www .oneworldtrust.org/index.php?option=com_docman&task=cat_view&gid=83& Itemid=55>.

Boughton, James M. *Silent Revolution. The International Monetary Fund 1979–1989* (Washington: International Monetary Fund, 2001).

Bradford Jr., Colin I., & Johannes F. Linn. *Global Governance Reform: Breaking the Stalemate* (Washington, D.C.: Brookings Institution Press, 2007).

Broude, Tomer. *International Governance in the WTO: Judicial Boundaries and Political Capitulation* (London: Cameron May, 2004).

Byers, Michael, ed. *The Role of Law in International Politics: Essays in International Relations and International Law* (Oxford: Oxford University Press, 2000).

Carin, Barry, & Angela Wood, eds. *Accountability of the International Monetary Fund*, (Ottawa: International Development Research Centre, 2005).

Cass, Deborah. *The Constitutionalization of the World Trade Organization: Legitimacy, Democracy, and Community in the International Trading System* (Oxford: Oxford University Press, 2005).

Chase, Kerry A. *Trading Blocs: States, Firms, and Regions in the World Economy* (Ann Arbor: University of Michigan Press, 2006).

Cottier, Thomas, & Petros Mavroidis, eds. *The Role of the Judge: Lessons for the WTO* (Ann Arbor: University of Michigan Press, 2003).

Crocker, Chester A., Fen Osler Hampson, & Pamela Aall, eds. *Leashing the Dogs of War: Conflict Management in a Divided World* (Washington, D.C.: United States Institute of Peace Press, 2003).

Croome, John. *Reshaping the World Trading System: A History of the Uruguay Round* (Boston: Kluwer Law International, 1999).

De Cooker, Chris, ed. *Accountability, Investigation and Due Process in International Organizations* (Leiden/Boston: Martinus Nijhoff Publishers, 2005).

de Vries, Margaret G. *The International Monetary Fund 1972–1978. Cooperation on Trial* (Washington, D.C.: International Monetary Fund, 1985).

de Vries, Margaret G., & J. Keith Hosefield, eds. *The International Monetary Fund 1945–1965* (Washington, D.C.: International Monetary Fund, 1969).

Drezner, Daniel. *All Politics Is Global: Explaining International Regulatory Regimes* (Princeton: Princeton University Press, 2007).

Footer, Mary E. *An Institutional and Normative Analysis of the World Trade Organization* (Leiden: Martinus Nijhoff Publishers, 2006).

Franck, Thomas M. *Fairness in International Law and Institutions* (Oxford: Oxford University Press, 1996).

Grasso, Patrick G., Sulaiman S. Wasty, & Rachel V. Weaving, eds. *World Bank, Operations Evaluation Department: The First 30 Years* (Washington, D.C.: World Bank, 2003).

Griller, Stefan, ed. *At Crossroads: The World Trading System and the Doha Round* (New York: Springer Wien, 2008).

Gruber, Lloyd. *Ruling the World: Power Politics and the Rise of Supranational Institutions* (Princeton: Princeton University Press, 2000).

Held, David, & Mathias Koenig-Archibugi, eds. *Taming Globalization: Frontiers of Governance* (Cambridge: Blackwell Publishing, 2003).

Hoekman, Bernard, & Michel Kostecki. *The Political Economy of the World Trading System: The WTO and Beyond*, 2nd ed. (Oxford: Oxford University Press, 2001).

Horsefield, J. Keith. *The International Monetary Fund 1945–1965* (Washington, D.C.: International Monetary Fund, 1969).

Hudec, Robert E. *Enforcing International Trade Law: The Evolution of the Modern GATT Legal System* (Salem: Butterworths, 1993).

Jackson, John H. *Restructuring the GATT System* (London: Pinter Publishers, 1990).

——. *World Trade and the Law of GATT* (Indianapolis: Bobbs-Merrill, 1969).

Joerges, Christian, & Ernst-Ulrich Petersmann, eds. *Constitutionalism, Multilevel Trade Governance and Social Regulation* (Oxford: Hart Publishing, 2006).

Kahler, Miles, & David A. Lake, eds. *Governance in a Global Economy* (Princeton: Princeton University Press, 2003).

Kapur, Devesh, John P. Lewis, & Richard Webb. *The World Bank: Its First Half Century*, (Washington, D.C.: Brookings Institution, 1997) 2 vols.

Kenen, Peter B. *Reform of the International Monetary Fund* (Council on Foreign Relations, 2007), online: <http://www.cfr.org/content/publications/attachments/IMF_CSR29.pdf>.

Keohane, Robert, ed. *Power and Governance in a Partially Globalized World* (New York: Routledge, 2002).

Kirton, John J., & Peter Hajnal, eds. *Sustainability, Civil Society and International Governance* (Aldershot: Ashgate Publishing, 2006).

Kruger, Anne. *The WTO as an International Organization* (Chicago: University of Chicago Press, 1998).

Mason, Edward S., & Robert E. Asher. *The World Bank Since Bretton Woods* (Washington, D.C.: Brookings Institution, 1973).

Matsushita, Mitsuo, Thomas J. Schoenbaum, & Petros C. Mavroidis. *The World Trade Organization: Law, Practice and Policy*, 2nd ed. (Oxford: Oxford University Press, 2006).

Mitchell, Andrew, ed. *Challenges and Prospects for the WTO* (London: Cameron May Publishers, 2005).

Narlikar, Amrita. *International Trade and Developing Countries: Coalitions in the GATT and WTO* (London: Routledge, 2003).

Nye, Jr., Joseph S. *The Paradox of American Power: Why the World's Only Superpower Can't Go Alone* (New York: Oxford University Press, 2002).

Nye Jr., Joseph S., & John D. Donahue, eds. *Governance in a Globalizing World* (Washington, D.C.: Brookings Institution Press, 2000).

Nye Jr., Joseph S. *et al. The 'Democracy Deficit' in the Global Economy: Enhancing the Legitimacy and Accountability of Global Institutions* (Trilateral Commission, 2003).

Odell, John. *Negotiating Trade: Developing Countries in the WTO and NAFTA* (Cambridge, UK: Cambridge University Press, 2006).

———. *Negotiating the World Economy* (Ithaca: Cornell University Press, 2000).

Pagem, Sheila. *Developing Countries: Victims or Participants: Their Changing Role in International Negotiations* (London: Overseas Development Institute, 2003).

Petersmann, Ernst-Ulrich, ed. *Reforming the World Trading System: Legitimacy, Efficiency and Democratic Governance* (Oxford: Oxford University Press, 2005).

Pincus, Jonathan R., & Jeffrey A. Winters, eds. *Reinventing the World Bank* (Ithaca: Cornell University Press, 2002).

Porter, Roger B. *et al*, eds. *Efficiency, Equity, and Legitimacy: The Multilateral Trading System at the Millennium* (Washington, D.C.: Brookings Institution Press, 2001)

Ripinsky, Sergey, & Peter Van den Bossche. *NGO Involvement in International* (British Institute of International and Comparative Law, 2007).

Shaffer, Gregory C. *Defending Interests: Public-Private Partnerships in WTO Litigation* (Washington, D.C.: Brookings Institution Press, 2003).

Shihata, Ibrahim F. I. *The World Bank Inspection Panel: In Practice*, 2nd ed. (Oxford: Oxford University Press, 2000).

Steger, Debra P. *Peace Through Trade: Building the World Trade Organization* (London: Cameron May, 2004).

Stiglitz, Joseph E. *Globalization and Its Discontents* (New York: W.W. Norton, 2003).

Stiglitz, Joseph E., & Andrew Charlton. *Fair Trade for All: How Trade Can Promote Development* (Oxford: Oxford University Press, 2005).

Trachtman, Joel P. *International Economic Law Revolution & the Right to Regulate* (London: Cameron May Publishers, 2006).

Truman, Edwin M., ed. *Reforming the IMF for the 21st Century* (Washington, D.C.: Institute for International Economics, 2006).

van Houtven, Leo. *Governance of the IMF: Decision-Making, Institutional Oversight, Transparency, and Accountability* (Washington, D.C.: International Monetary Fund, 2002).

Winham, Gilbert. *International Trade and the Tokyo Round Negotiation* (Princeton: Princeton University Press, 1986).

Wolfrum, Rüdiger, Peter-Tobais Stoll, & Karen Kaiser, eds. *WTO: Institutions and Dispute Settlement* (Leiden/Boston: Martinus Nijhoff, 2006).

Xu, Yi-chong, & Patrick Weller. *The Governance of World Trade: International Civil Servants and the GATT/WTO* (Cheltenham, UK: Edward Elgar, 2004).

Articles

Abbott, Frederick M. 'A New Dominant Trade Species Emerges: Is Bilateralism a Threat?' (2007) 10 Journal of International Economic Law 571.

——. 'Distributed Governance at the WTO-WIPO: An Evolving Model for Open-Architecture Integrated Governance' (2000) 3 Journal of International Economic Law 63.

Ala'i, Padideh. 'The Multilateral Trading System and Transparency', in Alan S. Alexandroff, ed, *Trends in World Trade: Essays in Honor of Sylvia Ostry* (Durham, N.C.: Carolina Academic Press, 2007).

——. 'Free Trade or Sustainable Development? An Analysis of the WTO Appellate Body's Shift to a More Balanced Approach to Trade Liberalization' (1998) 14 American University International Law Review 1129.

Alvarez, José E. 'International Organizations: Then and Now' (2006) 100 The American Journal of International Law 324.

Antkiewicz, Agata, & John Whalley. 'BRICSAM and the Non-WTO' (2006) 1 The Review of International Organizations 237.

Arie Reich, 'The Threat of Politicization of the World Trade Organization' (2005) 26 University of Pennsylvania Journal of International Economic Law 779.

Arup, Christopher. 'The State of Play of Dispute Settlement "Law" at the World Trade Organization' (2003) 37 Journal of World Trade 897.

Bacchus, James. 'A Few Thoughts on Legitimacy, Democracy, and the WTO' (2004) 7 Journal of International Economic Law 667.

Barr, Michael S., & Geoffrey P. Miller. ' Global Administrative Law: The View from Basel' (2006) 17 European Journal of International Law 15.

Bellemann, Christophe, & Richard Gerster. 'Accountability in the World Trade Organization' (1996) 30 Journal of World Trade 31.

Bercero, Ignacio G. 'Functioning of the WTO System: Elements for Possible Institutional Reform' (2000) 6 International Trade Law and Regulation 103.

Berman, Nathaniel. 'Intervention in a "Divided World": Axes of Legitimacy' (2006) 17 European Journal of International Law 743.

Blackhurst, Richard. 'The Future of the WTO: Some Comments on the Sutherland Report' (2005) 4(3) World Trade Review 379.

———. 'The Capacity of the WTO to Fulfill Its Mandate', in Anne Krueger, ed, *The WTO as an International Organization* (Chicago: University of Chicago Press, 1998) 31.

Blackhurst, Richard, & David Hartridge. 'Improving the Capacity of WTO Institutions to Fulfill Their Mandate', in E.U. Petersmann and James Harrison, eds, *Reforming the World Trading System: Legitimacy, Efficiency and Democratic Governance* (Oxford: Oxford University Press, 2005).

Bradford, Colin I., & Johannes F. Linn. 'The G20 Summit: Could the Financial Crisis Push Global Governance Reform?' (24 October 2008), online: Brookings Institution <http://www.brookings.edu/opinions/2008/1024_g20_summit_linn.aspx?p=1>.

Bradlow, Daniel D. 'The Governance of the IMF: The Need for Comprehensive Reform' (Presentation given at the meeting of the G24 Technical Committee, September 2006).

Bronckers, Marco. 'More Power to the WTO?' (2001) 4 Journal of International Economic Law 41.

———. 'Better Rules for a New Millennium: A Warning Against Undemocratic Developments in the WTO' (1999) 2 Journal of International Economic Law 547.

Broude, Tomer. 'The Rule(s) of Trade and the Rhetos of Development: Reflections on the Functional and Aspirational Legitimacy of the WTO' (2006) 45 Columbia Journal of Transnational Law 221.

Buchanan, Allen, & Robert O. Keohane. 'The Legitimacy of Global Governance Institutions' (2006) 20 Ethics and International Affairs 405.

Carmody, Chios. 'WTO Obligations as Collective' (2006) 17 The European Journal of International Law 419.

———. 'Beyond the Proposals: Public Participation in International Economic Law' (2000) 15 American University International Law Review 1321.

Cass, Deborah Z. 'The "Constitutionalization" of International Trade Law: Judicial Norm-Generation as the Engine of Constitutional Development in International Trade' (2001) 12 The European Journal of International Law 39.

Chang, Seung W. 'WTO for Trade and Development Post-Doha' (2007) 10 Journal of International Economic Law 553.

Charnovitz, Steve. 'A Close Look at a Few Points' (2005) 8 Journal of International Economic Law 311.

——. 'The World Trade Organization in 2020' (2005) 1 Journal of International Law and International Relations 167.

——. 'Transparency and Participation in the World Trade Organization' (2004) 56 Rutgers Law Review 927.

——. 'The WTO and Cosmopolitics' (2004) 7 Journal of International Economic Law 675.

——. 'Triangulating the World Trade Organization' (2002) 96 The American Journal of International Law 28.

——. 'Opening the WTO to Nongovernmental Interests' (2000) 24 Fordham International Law Journal 173.

Chelsky, Jeff. 'The Role and Evolution of Executive Board Standing Committees in IMF Corporate Governance' (Independent Evaluation Office of the International Monetary Fund, BP/08/04, April 2008), online: IMF <http://www.ieo-imf.org/eval/complete/pdf/05212008/CG_background7.pdf>.

Chimni, B.S. 'The World Trade Organization, Democracy and Development: A View from the South' (2006) 40 Journal of World Trade 5.

Cooper, Andrew F., & John English. 'Introduction: Reforming the International System from the Top—A Leaders' 20 Summit', in John English, Ramesh Thakur, & Andrew F. Cooper, eds, *Reforming From the Top—A Leaders' 20 Summit* (Tokyo: United Nations University Press, 2005) 1.

Cortell, Andrew, and Susan Peterson. 'Dutiful Agents, Rogue Actors, or Both? Staffing, Voting Rules, and Slack in the WHO and WTO', in Darren G. Hawkins *et al*, eds, *Delegation and Agency in International Organizations* (Cambridge: Cambridge University Press, 2006) 255.

Cottier, Thomas. 'Preparing for Structural Reform in the WTO' (2007) 10 Journal of International Economic Law 497.

Cottier, Thomas, & Satoko Takenoshita. 'The Balance of Power in WTO Decision-Making: Towards Weighted Voting in Legislative Response' (2003) 58(2) Aussenwirtschaft 171.

Davey, William J. 'The Sutherland Report on Dispute Settlement: A Comment' (2005) 8 Journal of International Economic Law 321.

de Rato, Rodrigo. 'The IMF View on IMF Reform', in Edwin M. Truman, ed, *Reforming the IMF for the 21st Century* (Washington, D.C.: Institute for International Economics, 2006) 127.

de Vries, Margaret. 'The Process of Policy Making', in Margaret G. de Vries and J. Keith Hosefield, eds, *The International Monetary Fund 1945–1965* (Washington, D.C.: International Monetary Fund, 1969) vol. 2.

de Wet, Erika. 'The International Constitutional Order' (2006) 55 International and Comparative Law Quarterly 51.

Denters, Erik. 'The Sutherland Report' (2005) 18 Leiden Journal of International Law 887.

Drache, Daniel, & Sylvia Ostry, 'From Doha to Kananaskis: The Future of the World Trading System and the Crisis of Governance', in John M. Curtis and Dan Ciuriak, eds, *Trade Policy Research 2002* (Ottawa: Public Works and Government Services Canada, 2002).

Dunoff, Jeffrey. 'Constitutional Conceits: The WTO's Constitution and the Discipline of International Law' (2006) 17(3) European Journal of International Law 647.

——. 'The Post-Doha Trade Agenda: Questions about Constituents, Competence and Coherence', in R.P. Buckley, ed, *The WTO and the Doha Round: The Changing Face of World Trade* (The Hague: Kluwer Law International, 2003) 59.

——. 'The Death of the Trade Regime' (1999) 10 European Journal of International Law 733.

——. 'The Misguided Debate over NGO Participation at the WTO' (1998) 1 Journal of International Economic Law 433.

Ehlermann, Claus-Dieter, & Lothar Ehring. 'The Authoritative Interpretation under Article IX:2 of the Agreement Establishing the World Trade Organization: Current Law, Practice, and Possible Improvements' (2005) 8 Journal of International Economic Law 803.

——. 'Decision-Making in the World Trade Organization' (2005) 8(1) Journal of International Economic Law 51.

Elsig, Manfred. 'Agency Theory and the WTO: Complex Agency and "Missing Delegation"?' (2007), online: <http://www.cis.ethz.ch/events/pastevents/PEIO/Elsig_PAWTO>.

——. 'The World Trade Organization's Bureaucrats: Runaway Agents or Masters' Servants?', NCCR Trade Regulation Working Paper 19 (March 2007), www.nccrtrade.org/images/stories/publications/IP2/MElsig_NCCRWP_Agency.pdf (visited 4 April 2009).

——. 'The World Trade Organization's Legitimacy Crisis: What Does the Beast Look Like?' (2007) 41 Journal of World Trade 75.

——. 'Different Facets of Power in Decision-making in the WTO' (Paper delivered at the 2006 Annual Meeting of the American Political Science Association, Philadelphia, Pennsylvania, 31 August 2006), online: SSRN < http://papers.ssrn.com/sol3/papers.cfm?abstract_id=1090146>.

Esty, Daniel C. 'Good Governance at the World Trade Organization: Building a Foundation of Administrative Law' (2007) 10 Journal of International Economic Law 509.

——. 'Good Governance at the Supranational Scale: Globalizing Administrative Law' (2006) 115 Yale Law Journal 1490.

——. 'The World Trade Organization's Legitimacy Crisis' (2002) 1 World Trade Review 7.

——. 'Non-Governmental Organizations at the World Trade Organization: Cooperation, Competition, or Exclusion' (1998) 1 Journal of International Economic Law 123.

Finger, J. Michael. 'The Future of the World Trade Organization: Addressing Institutional Challenges in the New Millennium Report by the Consultative Board to the Director General Supachai Panitchpakdi: A Review' (2005) 39 Journal of World Trade 795.

Frey, Bruno S., & Alois Stutzer. 'Strengthening the Citizens' Role in International Organizations' (2006) 1 The Review of International Organizations 27.

Garcia, Frank J. 'Global Justice and the Bretton Woods Institutions' (2007) 10 Journal of International Economic Law 461.

Gazzini, Tarcisio. 'The Legal Nature of WTO Obligations and the Consequences of Their Violation' (2006) 17 The European Journal of International Law 723.

Gold, J. 'Developments in the Law and Institutions of International Economic Relations—Weighted Voting Power: Some Limits and Some Problems' (1974) 68 American Journal of International Law 687.

Goodhart, Michael. 'Democracy, Globalization, and the Problem of the State' (2001) 33 Polity 527.

Griffith-Jones, Stephany. 'Governance of the World Bank' (undated), online: <http:/stephany.acrewoods.net/_documents/Governance_of_the_World_Ban._Paper_prepared_for_DFID.pdf>.

Grosse Ruse-Khan, Henning M. 'The Role of Chairman's Statements in the WTO' (2007) 41 Journal of World Trade 475.

Guzman, Andrew T. 'Global Governance and the WTO' (2004) 45 Harvard International Law Journal 303.

———. 'Trade, Labor, Legitimacy' (2003) 91 California Law Review 885.

Heiskanen, Veijo. 'The Regulatory Philosophy of International Trade Law' (2004) 38 Journal of World Trade 1.

Hoekman, Bernard. 'Strengthening the Global Trade Architecture for Development: The Post-Doha Agenda' (2002) 1 World Trade Review 23.

Howse, Robert, & Kalypso Nicolaidis. 'Enhancing WTO Legitimacy: Constitutionalization or Global Subsidiarity?' (2003) 16 Governance 73.

Howse, Robert, & Kalypso Nicolaïdis. 'Legitimacy and Global Governance: Why Constitutionalizing the WTO Is a Step Too Far', in Roger B. Porter *et al*, eds, *Efficiency, Equity, and Legitimacy: The Multilateral Trading System at the Millennium* (Washington, D.C.: Brookings Institution Press, 2001).

Howse, Robert. 'How to Begin to Think about the "Democratic Deficit"', in Robert Howse, ed, *The WTO System* (London: Cameron May, 2007) 57.

———. 'WTO Governance and the Doha Round' (2005) 5(4) Global Economy Journal 16.

———. 'From Politics to Technocracy—and Back Again: The Fate of the Multilateral Trading Regime' (2002) 96 American Journal of International Law 94.

———. 'The Legitimacy of the WTO', in J. Coicaud and V. Heiskanen, eds, *The Legitimacy of International Organizations* (Tokyo: United Nations University Press, 2001) 355.

Hudec, Robert E. 'The New WTO Dispute Settlement Procedure: An Overview of the First Three Years' (1999) 8 Minnesota Journal of Global Trade 1.

——. 'The Role of the GATT Secretariat in the Evolution of the WTO Dispute Settlement Procedure', in Jagdish Bhagwati & Mathias Hirsch, eds, *The Uruguay Round and Beyond: Essays in Honour of Arthur Dunkel* (Springer-Verlag, 1998) 101.

Hufbauer, Gary C. 'Inconsistency Between Diagnosis and Treatment' (2005) 8 Journal of International Economic Law 29.

Jackson, John H. 'International Economic Law: Complexity and Puzzles' (2007) 10 Journal of International Economic Law 3.

——. 'The World Trade Organization after Ten Years: The Role of the WTO in a Globalized World', in Jane Holder *et al*, eds, *Current Legal Problems 2006*, vol. 59. (Oxford: Oxford University Press, 2007) 427.

——. 'The Changing Fundamentals of International Law and Ten Years of the WTO' (2005) 8 Journal of International Economic Law 3.

——. 'The Varied Policies of International Juridical Bodies—Reflections on Theory and Practice' (2004) 25 Michigan Journal of International Law 869.

——. 'The WTO Institution and Constitution: Evolution and Prospects', in Mitsuo Matsushita & Dukgeun Ahn, eds, *In WTO and East Asia* (London: Cameron May, 2004) 13.

——. 'Sovereignty-Modern: A New Approach to an Outdated Concept' (2003) 97 The American Journal of International Law 782.

——. 'The WTO "Constitution" and Proposed Reforms: Seven "Mantras" Revisited' (2001) 4 Journal of International Economic Law 67.

——. 'International Economic Law in Times That Are Interesting' (2000) 3 Journal of International Economic Law 3.

——. 'Global Economics and International Economic Law' (1998) 1 Journal of International Economic Law 1.

Kuijper, Pieter Jan. 'WTO Institutional Aspects', in Daniel Bethlehem *et al*, eds, *Oxford Handbook of International Trade Law* (Oxford: Oxford University Press, 2009) 79.

Kapur, Devesh. 'The Changing Anatomy of Governance of the World Bank', in Jonathan R. Pincus & Jeffrey A. Winters, eds, *Reinventing the World Bank* (Ithaca: Cornell University Press, 2002) 54.

Keohane, Robert O., & Joseph S. Nye. 'The Club Model of Multilateral Cooperation and the World Trade Organization: Problems of Democratic Legitimacy', in Roger B. Porter *et al*, eds, *Efficiency, Equity, and Legitimacy: The Multilateral Trading System at the Millennium* (Washington, D.C.: Brookings Institution Press, 2001) 264.

——. 'Between Centralization and Fragmentation: The Club Model of Multilateral Cooperation and Problems of Democratic Legitimacy' (Paper prepared for the American Political Science Convention, Washington, D.C., 31 August–3

September 2000), online: <http://ksgnotes1.harvard.edu/research/wpaper.nsf/
rwp/RWP01-004/$File/rwp01_004_nye_rev1.pdf>.

Köpp, H. Eberhard. 'Promoting Professional and Personal Trust in OED', in Patrick G. Grasso, Sulaiman S. Wasty, & Rachel V. Weaving, eds, *World Bank, Operations Evaluation Department: The First 30 Years* (Washington, D.C.: World Bank, 2003) 55.

Krajewski, Marcus. 'Democratic Legitimacy and Constitutional Perspectives of WTO Law' (2001) 35 Journal of World Trade 167.

Lang, Andrew T.F. 'Reconstructing Embedded Liberalism: John Gerard Ruggie and Constructivist Approaches to the Study of the International Trade Regime' (2006) 9 Journal of International Economic Law 81.

Lawrence, Robert Z. 'Rulemaking Amidst Growing Diversity: A Club-of-Clubs Approach to WTO Reform and New Issue Selection' (2006) 9(4) Journal of International Economic Law 823.

Mann, Erika. 'A Parliamentary Dimension to the WTO—More Than Just a Vision?!' (2004) 7 Journal of International Economic Law 659.

Mao, Norbert. 'Experiences with the Parliamentary Network on the World Bank: A View from the Inside', in Barry Carin & Angela Wood, eds, *Accountability of the International Monetary Fund* (Ottawa: International Development Research Centre, 2005) 62.

Marceau, Gabrielle, & Peter N. Pedersen. 'Is the WTO Open and Transparent?' (1999) 33 Journal of World Trade 44.

Masserli, Thomas. 'The WTO as Decision-Making System—Business Interests and the Dynamics of Trade Policy' NCCR Trade Regulation, Working Paper No 2007/21 (May 2007).

Mattoo, Aaditya, & Arvind Subramanian. 'What Would a Development-Friendly WTO Really Look Like?' IMF Working Paper WP/03/153 (2003), online: <http://www.imf.org/external/pubs/ft/wp/2003/wp03153.pdf>.

McGinnis, John O., & Mark L. Movsesian. 'The World Trade Constitution' (2000) 114 Harvard Law Review 511.

Messerlin, Patrick A. 'Three Variations on "The Future of the WTO"' (2005) 8 Journal of International Economic Law 299.

Narlikar, Amrita. 'Fairness in International Trade Negotiations: Developing Countries in the GATT and WTO' (2006) 29 The World Economy 1005.

——. 'The Ministerial Process and Power Dynamics in the WTO: Understanding Failure from Seattle to Cancun' (2004) 9(3) New Political Economy 413.

——. 'WTO Institutional Reform—A Role for G20 Leaders?' (Breaking the Deadlock in Agricultural Trade Reform and Development Conference, Oxford, 8–9 June 2004, Centre for International Governance Innovation), online:<http://www.igloo.org/library/edocuments?id={2B7128BF-202E-4B3A-B686-B6AC42E04358}&view=full>.

——. 'WTO Decision-Making and Developing Countries' South Centre TRADE Working Paper, No. 11 (November 2001), online: <http://www.southcentre.org/index.php?option=com_content&task=view&id=367&Itemid=67>.

Narlikar, Amrita, & John Odell. 'The Strict Distributive Strategy for a Bargaining Coalition: The Like Minded Group in the World Trade Organization, 1998-2001' (Paper presented at Research Conference, Developing Countries and the Trade Negotiation Process, 6-7 November, 2003, UNCTAD, Palais des Nations, Geneva).

Narlikar, Amrita, & Diana Tussie. 'The G20 at the Cancun Ministerial: Developing Countries and Their Evolving Coalitions in the WTO' (2004) 27 The World Economy 947.

Nordstrom, Hakan. 'The World Trade Organization Secretariat in a Changing World' (2005) 39 Journal of World Trade 819.

Nye, Jr., Joseph S. 'The Place of Soft Power in State-Based Conflict Management', in Chester A. Crocker, Fen Osler Hampson, & Pamela Aall, eds, *Leashing the Dogs of War: Conflict Management in a Divided World* (Washington, D.C.: United States Institute of Peace Press, 2003) 389.

Odell, John. 'Chairing a WTO Negotiation' (2005) 8(2) Journal of International Economic Law 425.

——. 'Making and Breaking Impasses in International Regimes: the WTO, Seattle and Doha' (Paper presented at the Conference on Gaining Leverage in International Negotiations, Yonsei University Seoul, 14–15 June 2002).

Ostry, Sylvia. 'The World Trade Organization: NGOs, New Bargaining Coalitions, and a System under Stress' Munk Centre for International Studies MCIS, Controversies in Global Politics and Societies, Occasional Paper No. IV (2006).

——. 'The World Trading System: In the Fog of Uncertainty' (2006) 1 The Review of International Organizations 99.

——. 'The Multilateral Agenda: Moving Trade Negotiations Forward', Munk Centre for International Studies MCIS Briefings (November 2005).

——. 'The Post Doha Trading System' (Paper presented at the Pre-G8 Academic Conference, University of Glasgow, 29–30 June 2005), online: <http://www.utoronto.ca/cis/ostry/>.

——. 'Summitry and Trade: What Sea Islands Could Do for Doha', in Michele Fratianni et al, eds, *New Perspectives on Global Governance: Why America Needs the G8* (Aldershot: Ashgate Publishing, 2005) 205.

——. 'What Are the Necessary Ingredients for the World Trading Order?', in Horst Siebert, ed, *Global Governance: An Architecture for the World Economy* (New York: Springer, 2003).

——. 'The World Trading System: In Dire Need of Reform' (2003) 17 Temple International & Comparative Law Journal 109.

———. 'Article X and the Concept of Transparency in the GATT/WTO', in Alan S. Alexandroff, Sylvia Ostry, & Rafael Gomez, eds, *China and the Long March to Global Trade: The Accession of China to the World Trade Organization* (London: Routledge, 2002) 123.

———. 'The Uruguay Round North-South Grand Bargain: Implications for Future Negotiations', in Daniel L.M. Kennedy & James D. Southwick, eds, *The Political Economy of International Trade Law: Essays in Honor of Robert E. Hudec* (Cambridge: Cambridge University Press, 2002) 285.

———. 'Global Integration: Currents and Counter-Currents' (Walter Gordon Lecture, Massey College, University of Toronto, 23 May 2001), online: <http://www.utoronto.ca/cis/ostry/docs_pdf/GlobalIntegration.pdf>.

———. 'World Trade Organization: Institutional Design for Better Governance', in Roger B. Porter *et al*, eds, *Efficiency, Equity, and Legitimacy: The Multilateral Trading System at the Millennium* (Washington, D.C.: Brookings Institution Press, 2001) 361.

———. 'The WTO and International Governance', in Klaus Gunter Deutsh & Bernhard Speyer, eds, *The World Trade Organization Millennium Round* (Oxford: Routledge, 2001) 285.

———. 'Looking Back to Look Forward: The Multilateral Trading System after 50 years', in *From GATT to the WTO: The Multilateral Trading System in the New Millennium* (Geneva: World Trade Organization, 2000).

———. 'The Changing Scenario in International Governance', in Gilles Paquet & David M. Hayne, eds, *Governance in the 21st Century* (Toronto: University of Toronto Press, 1999) 23.

———. 'The Future of the World Trade Organization', in Susan M. Collins & Robert Z. Lawrence, eds, *Brookings Trade Forum 1999* (Washington, D.C.: Brookings Institution Press, 1999) 167.

———. 'China and the WTO: The Transparency Issue' (1998) 3 UCLA Journal of International Law and Foreign Affairs 1.

———. 'Globalization: What Does It Mean?' (Speech given at the G-78 Annual Conference, Econiche House, Ottawa, Ontario, October 1999), online: <http://www.utoronto.ca/cis/ostry/docs_pdf/G78CONF.pdf>.

Pauwelyn, Joost. 'The Sutherland Report: A Missed Opportunity for Genuine Debate on Trade, Globalization and the Reform of the WTO' (2005) 8 Journal of International Economic 329.

———. 'The Transformation of World Trade' (2005) 104 Michigan Law Review 1.

Petersmann, Ernst-Ulrich. 'Multilevel Judicial Governance of International Trade Requires a Common Conception of Rule of Law and Justice' (2007) 10 Journal of International Economic Law 529.

———. 'Addressing Institutional Challenges to the WTO in the New Millennium: A Longer-Term Perspective' (2005) 8 Journal of International Economic Law 647.

——. 'Challenges to the Legitimacy and Efficiency of the World Trade System: Democratic Governance and Competition Culture in the WTO' (2004) 7 Journal of International Economic Law 585.

Picciotto, Robert. 'The Logic of Renewal: Evaluation at the World Bank, 1992–2002', in Patrick G. Grasso, Sulaiman S. Wasty, & Rachel V. Weaving, eds, *World Bank, Operations Evaluation Department. The First 30 Years* (Washington, D.C.: World Bank, 2003) 61.

Qin, Julia Y. '"WTO-Plus" Obligations and Their Implications for the World Trade Organization Legal System: An Appraisal of the China Accession Protocol' (2003) 37 Journal of World Trade 483.

Raustiala, Kal. 'Rethinking the Sovereignty Debate in International Economic Law' (2003) 6 Journal of International Economic Law 841.

Rugman, Alan M. 'Regional Multinationals and Regional Trade Policy: The End of Multilateralism', in Michele Fratianni, Paolo Savona, & John J. Kirton, eds, *Corporate, Public and Global Governance The G8 Contribution* (Aldershot: Ashgate Publishing Limited, 2007) 77.

Schaefer, Matthew. 'Ensuring That Regional Trade Agreements Complement the WTO System: US Unilateralism a Supplement to WTO Initiatives?' (2007) 10 Journal of International Economic Law 585.

Shaffer, Gregory. 'Can WTO Technical Assistance and Capacity Building Serve Developing Countries?' (2006) 23 Wisconsin International Law Journal 643.

——. 'The Challenges of WTO Law: Developing Country Strategies for Adaptation' (2006) 5 World Trade Review 177.

——. 'Power, Nested Governance and the WTO: A Comparative Institutional Approach', in Michael Barnett & Raymond Duvall, eds, *Power and Global Governance* (Cambridge: Cambridge University Press, 2005) 130.

——. 'The Role of the WTO Director-General and Secretariat' (2005) 4 World Trade Review 429.

——. 'Parliamentary Oversight of WTO Rule-Making: The Political, Normative, and Practical Contexts' (2004) 7 Journal of International Economic Law 629.

——. 'The World Trade Organization under Challenge: Democracy and the Law and Politics of the WTO's Treatment of Trade and Environment Matters' (2001) 25 Harvard Environmental Law Review 1.

Skaggs, David E. 'How Can Parliamentary Participation in WTO Rule-Making and Democratic Control Be Made More Effective in the WTO?: A United States Congressional Perspective' (2004) 7 Journal of International Economic Law 655.

Slaughter, Anne-Marie. 'Governing the Global Economy through Government Networks', in Michael Byers, ed, *The Role of Law in International Politics: Essays in International Relations and International Law* (Oxford: Oxford University Press, 2000) 177.

Steger, Debra P. 'The Culture of the WTO: Why It Needs to Change' (2007) 10 Journal of International Economic Law 483.

——. 'Commentary on the Doha Round: Institutional Issues' (2005) 5 Global Economy Journal Article 17, online: < http://www.bepress.com/gej/vol5/iss4/17/>.

——. 'The Appellate Body and Its Contribution to WTO Dispute Settlement', in D. Kennedy & J. Southwick, eds, *The Political Economy o f International Trade Law: Essays in Honour of Robert E. Hudec* (Cambridge: Cambridge University Press, 2002) 482.

——. 'The World Trade Organization: A New Constitution for the Trading System', in Marco Bronckers & Reinhard Quick, eds, *New Directions in International Economic Law: Essays in Honour of John H. Jackson* (The Hague: Kluwer Law International, 2000) 153.

Steger, Debra P., & Susan M. Hainsworth, 'World Trade Organization Dispute Settlement: The First Three Years' (1998) 1 Journal of International Economic Law 199.

Stein, Eric. 'International Integration and Democracy: No Love at First Sight' (2001) 95 The American Journal of International Law 489.

Steinberg, Richard. 'Judicial Lawmaking at the WTO: Discursive, Constitutional and Political Constraints' (2004) 98 American Journal of International Law 247.

——. 'In the Shadow of Law or Power? Consensus Based Bargaining in the GATT/WTO' (2002) 56(2) International Organization 339.

Stoler, Andrew. 'Globalisation Gains and Strains in 2005' (2006) 31 The New Zealand International Review 2.

Sureda, Andres Rigo. 'Informality and Effectiveness in the Operation of the International Bank for Reconstruction and Development' (2003) 6 Journal of International Economic Law 565.

Sutherland, Peter. 'The Doha Development Agenda: Political Challenges to the World Trading System—A Cosmopolitan Perspective' (2005) 8 Journal of International Economic Law 363.

Sutherland, Peter, John Sewell, & D. Weiner. 'Challenges Facing the WTO and Policies to Address Global Governance', in Gary P. Sampson, ed, *The Role of the World Trade Organization in Global Governance* (Tokyo: United Nations University Press, 2001) 81.

Thompson, Alexander, & Duncan Snidal. 'Guarding the Equilibrium: Regime Management and the WTO' (Paper presented at the Annual Meeting of the American Political Science Association in Washington, D.C., 3 September 2005).

Tietje, Christian. 'Global·Governance and Inter-Agency Co-operation in International Economic Law' (2002) 36 Journal of World Trade 501.

Trachtman, Joel P. 'Regulatory Jurisdiction and the WTO' (2007) 10 Journal of International Economic Law 631.

——. 'The Constitutions of the WTO' (2006) 17 European Journal of International Law 623.

Trondal, Jarle, Martin Marcussen, & Frode Veggeland. 'International Executives: Transformative Bureaucracies or Westphalian Orders?' (2004) 8 European Integration Online Papers, online: <http://eiop.or.at/eiop/pdf/2004-004.pdf>.

Tussie, Diana, & Miguel F. Lengyel. 'Developing Countries: Turning Participation into Influence', in Bernard Hoekman, Aaditya Mattoo, & Philip English, eds, *Development, Trade and the WTO: A Handbook* (Washington, D.C.: World Bank, 2002) 485.

Ullrich, Heidi. 'Toward Accountability? The G8, the World Trade Organization and Global Governance', in Michele Fratianni, Paolo Savona and John J. Kirton, eds, *Corporate, Public and Global Governance: The G8 Contribution* (Aldershot: Ashgate Publishing Limited, 2007) 99.

Van den Bossche, Peter. 'Radical Overhaul or Pragmatic Change? The Need and Scope for Reform of Decision-Making in the World Trade Organization', in Agata Fijalkowski, ed, *International Institutional Reform Provides an Overview of the 7th Hague Joint Conference in 2005* (Cambridge University Press, 2007) 6.

——. 'Debating the Future of the World Trade Organization: Divergent Views on the 2005 Sutherland Report' (2005) 8 Journal of International Economic Law 759.

Van den Bossche, Peter, & Iveta Alexovicová. 'Effective Global Economic Governance by the World Trade Organization' (2005) 8 Journal of International Economic Law 667.

von Bogdandy, Armin. 'Legitimacy of International Economic Governance: Interpretative Approaches to WTO Law and the Prospects of Its Proceduralization', in Stefan Griller, ed, *International Economic Governance and Non-Economic Concerns: New Challenges for the International Legal Order* (New York: Springer, 2003) 103.

Wade, Robert. 'Greening the World Bank: The Struggle over the Environment, 1970–1995', in Devesh Kapur, John P. Lewis, & Richard Webb, *The World Bank: Its First Half Century* (Washington, D.C.: Brookings Institution, 1997) vol. 2, 611.

Weiler, J.H.H. 'The Rule of Lawyers and the Ethos of Diplomats: Reflections on the Internal and External Legitimacy of WTO Dispute Settlement' (2001) 35 Journal of World Trade 191.

Weiss, Friedl. 'Transparency as an Element of Good Governance in the Practices of the EU and the WTO' (2007) 30 Fordham International Law Journal 1545.

Wilkinson, Rorden. 'The WTO in Crisis: Exploring the Dimensions of Institutional Inertia' (2001) 35 Journal of World Trade 397.

Winham, Gilbert R. 'An Institutional Theory of WTO Decision-Making: Why Negotiation in the WTO Resembles Law-Making in the U.S. Congress', Munk Centre for International Studies, Controversies in Global Politics & Societies, Occasional Paper No. II (2006).

Wolfe, Robert. 'Can the Trading System Be Governed? Institutional Implications of the WTO's Suspended Animation', in Alan S. Alexandroff, ed, *Can the World Be Governed? Possibilities for Effective Multilateralism* (Waterloo: Wilfrid Laurier University Press, 2008) 289–352.

Wolfe, Robert. 'New Groups in the WTO Agricultural Trade Negotiations: Power, Learning and Institutional Design' (Canadian Agricultural Trade Policy Research Network, CP 2006-2).

——. 'Decision-Making and Transparency in the "Medieval" WTO: Does the Suther-land Report Have the Right Prescription?' (2005) 8 Journal of International Economic Law 631.

Woods, Ngaire. 'Power Shift. Do we need better global economic institutions?' Institute for Public Policy Research (January 2007), online: http://www.ippr.org.uk/members/download.asp?f=%2Fecomm%2Ffiles%2Fpower%5Fshift%2Epdf.

——. 'The Globalizers in Search of a Future: Four Reasons Why the IMF and the World Bank Must Change, and Four Ways They Can' (Center for Global Development, 2006).

Yenkong, Ngangjoh H. 'World Trade Organization Dispute Settlement Retaliatory Regime at the Tenth Anniversary of the Organization: Reshaping the "Last Resort" Against Non-compliance' (2006) 40 Journal of World Trade 365.

——. 'Third Party Rights and the Concept of Legal Interest in World Trade Organization Dispute Settlement: Extending Participatory Rights to Enforcement Rights' (2004) 38 Journal of World Trade 757.

Zamora, Stephan. 'Voting in International Economic Organizations' (1980) 74 American Journal of International Law 566.

Zampetti, Americo B. 'Democratic Legitimacy in the World Trade Organization: The Justice Dimension' (2003) 37 Journal of World Trade 105.

——. 'A Rough Map of Challenges to the Multilateral Trading System at the Millennium', in Roger B. Porter et al, eds, Efficiency, Equity, and Legitimacy: The Multilateral Trading System at the Millennium (Washington, D.C.: Brookings Institution Press, 2001) 34.

Ziegler, Andreas R., & Yves Bonzon. 'How to Reform WTO Decision-making? An Analysis of the Current Functioning of the Organization from the Perspectives of Efficiency and Legitimacy', NCCR Trade Regulation, Working Paper No 2007/23 (May 2007).

Zoellner, Carl-Sebastian. 'Transparency: An Analysis of an Evolving Fundamental Principle in International Economic Law' (2006) 27 Michigan Journal of International Law 579.

Background Papers, Reports, and Multilateral Documents

Berg, Peter, & Gerald J. Schmitz. 'Strengthening Parliamentary Oversight of International Trade Policies and Negotiations: Recent Developments in Canada and Internationally', Library of Parliament, Parliamentary Information and Research Service, PRB 05-68E (9 February 2006), online: <http://www.parl.gc.ca/information/library/PRBpubs/prb0568-e.pdf>.

Committee of Eminent Persons on IMF Governance Reform. Final Report (International Monetary Fund, 2009), online: <http://www.imf.org/external/np/omd/2009/govref/032409.pdf>.

Consultative Board to the Director-General Supachai Panitchpakdi, *The Future of the WTO: Addressing Institutional Challenges in the New Millennium* (Geneva: WTO, 2004), online: WTO <http://www.wto.org/english/thewto_e/10anniv_e/future_wto_e.htm>.

First Warwick Commission. *The Multilateral Trade Regime: Which Way Forward? The Report of the First Warwick Commission* (Coventry: University of Warwick, 2007), online: <http://www2.warwick.ac.uk/research/warwickcommission/archive/worldtrade/report/>.

GATT. Group of Negotiations on Goods, Negotiating Group on the Functioning of the GATT System, *Proposal by the United States*, GATT Doc. MTN.GNG/NG14/W/45 (1990), online: WTO <http://docsonline.wto.org>.

——. *Consultative Group of Eighteen: Note by the Director-General*, GATT Doc. L/4189 (1975), online: GATT Digital Library <http://gatt.stanford.edu>.

——. *Management of GATT: Note by the Secretariat*, GATT Doc. L/4048 (1974), online: GATT Digital Library <http://gatt.stanford.edu>.

International Monetary Fund. 'Transparency at the IMF. A Factsheet' (March 2009), online: IMF <http://www.imf.org/external/np/exr/facts/trans.htm>.

——. *The IMF's Communication Strategy, External Relations Department* (29 May 2007), online: IMF <http://www.imf.org/external/np/pp/2007/eng/052907.pdf>.

——. 'Report of the Executive Board to the Board of Governors—Quota and Voice Reform—Progress Since the 2006 Annual Meetings', online: IMF <http://www.imf.org/external/np/pp/2007/eng/101607.pdf>.

——. *Report of the Working Group of IMF Executive Directors on Enhancing Communication with National Legislators* (15 January 2004), online: IMF <http://www.imf.org/external/np/ed/2004/ecnl/index.htm>.

——. *Good Governance: The IMF's Role* (August 1997), online: <http://www.gdrc.org/u-gov/doc-govern.pdf>.

International Monetary Fund, Independent Evaluation Office. *Aspects of IMF Corporate Governance—Including the Role of the Executive Board* (April 2008), online: <http://www.ieo-imf.org/eval/complete/pdf/05212008/CG_main.pdf>.

——. *Governance of the IMF: An Evaluation* (Washington, D.C.: International Monetary Fund, 2008) 4, and online: <http://www.ieo-imf.org/eval/complete/pdf/05212008/CG_main.pdf>.

——. *Evaluation Report. The IMF and Argentina, 1991 – 2001* (2004).

——. *Annual Report 2003* (Washington, D.C., 2003), online: IMF <http://www.imf.org/external/np/ieo/2003/ar/Report.pdf>.

International Monetary Fund, Legal Department. 'Selected Decisions and Selected Documents of the IMF, Thirtieth Issue. Transparency and Fund Policies. Publication Policies' (30 June 2006), online: IMF <http://www.imf.org/external/pubs/ft/sd/index.asp?decision=13564-(05/85)>.

Joint Ministerial Committee of the Board of Governors of the Bank and the Fund on the Transfer or Real Resources to Developing Countries. 'Voice and Participation of Developing and Transition Countries in Decision Making at the

World Bank' (DC2007-0024, 11 October 2007), online: <http://siteresources.
worldbank.org/DEVCOMMINT/Documentation/21510673/DC2007-0024
(E)Voice.pdf>.

Peretz, David. 'The Process for Selecting and Appointing the Managing Director and
First Deputy Managing Director of the IMF' (Independent Evaluation Office
of the International Monetary Fund, July 2007), online: <http://www.ieo-imf.org/
pub/background/pdf/BP071.pdf>.

UN Commission on Human Rights. *Role of Good Governance in the Promotion of
Human Rights*, U.N. Doc. E/CN.4/RES/2000/64 (2000).

World Bank. *Issues and Options for Improving Engagement Between the World Bank
and Civil Society Organizations* (Washington, D.C., 2005), online: <http://web.
worldbank.org/WBSITE/EXTERNAL/TOPICS/CSO/0,contentMDK:
20413156~pagePK:220503~piPK:220476~theSitePK:228717,00.html>.

———. *Accountability at the World Bank: The Inspection Panel. 10 Years On* (Washington, D.C., 2003).

———. *The World Bank Policy on Disclosure of Information* (Washington, D.C., 2002)
http://siteresources.worldbank.org/OPSMANUAL/Resources/DisclosurePolicy.
pdf at 2. (visited 11 August 2008).

World Trade Organization General Council, *Decision on Transparency Mechanism for
Regional Trade Agreements Adopted on 14 December 2006*, WTO doc. WT/L/671
(2006), online: WTO <http//docsonline.wto.org>.

———. Council for Trade in Goods, *Waiver Concerning Kimberley Process Certification
Scheme for Rough Diamonds*, WTO doc. WT/L/518 (2003), online: WTO
<http://docsonline.wto.org>.

———. General Council, *Guidelines for Arrangements on Relations with Non-governmental
Organizations*, WTO Doc. WT/L/162 (1996), online: WTO <http:docsonline
.wto.org>.

———. Ministerial Conference, *Ministerial Declaration Adopted on 14 November 2001*,
WTO doc. WT/MIN(01)/Dec/1 (2001), online: WTO <http://docsonline.wto.org>.

———. Ministerial Conference, *Ministerial Declaration on the TRIPS Agreement and
Public Health Adopted on 14 November 2001*, WTO doc. WT/MIN(01)/DEC/2
(2001), online: WTO <http://docsonline.wto.org>.

———. *The Legal Texts. The Results of the Uruguay Round of Multilateral Trade Negotiations*, (Cambridge: Cambridge University Press, 1999).

———. Ministerial Conference, *Ministerial Declaration on Trade in Information Technology Products Adopted on 13 December 1996*, WTO doc. WT/MIN(96)/
16 (1996), online: WTO <http://docsonline.wto.org>.

———. *Rules of Procedure for Sessions of the Ministerial Conference and Meetings of
the General Council*, WTO doc. WT/L/161 (1996), online: WTO <http://
docsonline.wto.org>.

———. *GATT Analytical Index: Guide to GATT Law and Practice*, 6th ed. 2 vol. (Geneva:
World Trade Organization, 1995).

🏮 🏮 🏮 Contributors

PADIDEH ALA'I is Professor of Law at Washington College of Law, American University in Washington, D.C., where she specializes in areas of international trade law, development, and comparative legal traditions. She teaches World Trade Organization law and writes in the areas of history and free trade, international efforts to combat corruption, and trade and good governance. She received her J.D. from Harvard Law School in 1988 and was in private legal practice with the law firms of Jones Day and Reichler, Milton and Medel prior to joining the American University in 1997. From 2003 to 2005, she was the Co-Chair of the International Economic Law Group of the American Society of International Law.

ALBERTO ALVAREZ-JIMÉNEZ is a Colombian lawyer and holds a Doctor of Laws from the Faculty of Law, University of Ottawa. He is a former Research Fellow of the EDGE Network and now serves as a consultant and law professor. He has lectured in North America, Latin America, and Europe, and his articles on international trade law and foreign investment law have been published in a number of leading international journals.

LJILJANA BIUKOVIÇ is Associate Professor at the Faculty of Law, University of British Columbia, Canada. She teaches Contracts, European Union Law, External Relations of the European Union, and Global Law. Her current research interests are in the areas of international trade, in particular on the adaptation of international legal norms by national governments and the impact of regionalism on multilateral trade negotiations, as well as the development of European Union law. She is an Associate of the Institute for European Studies at UBC. She recently received the Farris Award to examine the interface between commercial arbitration and the courts in Canada.

YVES BONZON is a doctoral student at the Faculty of Law, University of Lausanne in Switzerland. In 2007–08, he was a Visiting Researcher at the Georgetown University Law Center, Washington, D.C., and in 2005–06 a researcher for the NCCR Trade Regulations project based at the World Trade Institute in Bern, Switzerland. He is now completing a doctoral thesis on the regulation of non-state actors' participation in WTO decision-making.

THOMAS COTTIER is Managing Director of the World Trade Institute, Professor of European and International Economics Law, and Dean of the Faculty of Law, University of Bern, Switzerland. He directs a national research program on trade law and policy—NCCR-Trade. He was a Visiting Professor at the Graduate Institute, Geneva, and currently teaches also at the Europa Institut Saarbrücken, Germany, and at Wuhan University, China. Professor Cottier has had a long-standing involvement in GATT/WTO activities. He served on the Swiss negotiating team of the Uruguay Round from 1986 to 1993, first as chief negotiator on dispute settlement and subsidies for Switzerland, and subsequently as chief negotiator on TRIPs. He has held several positions in the Swiss External Economic Affairs Department and was the Deputy-Director General of the Swiss Intellectual Property Office. He has also served as a panel member in a number of disputes in the WTO.

CAROLYN DEERE BIRKBECK is the Director of the Global Trade Governance Project in the Global Economic Governance Programme, University College, Oxford. She is also a Senior Research Associate at Oxford University's Centre for International Studies and a Resident Scholar at the International Centre for Trade and Sustainable Development (ICTSD) in Geneva, Switzerland.

MANFRED ELSIG is a Senior Research Fellow at the World Trade Institute in Bern, Switzerland, and a Visiting Lecturer at the Graduate Institute of International and Development Studies in Geneva. From 1997 to 1999, he worked at the Swiss Federal Office for Foreign Economic Affairs. He later joined the Institute of Political Science of the University of Zurich and received his Ph.D. in 2002. After working as a personal advisor to the Minister of Economy in Zurich, he taught at the London School of Economics and Political Science in 2004–05. His research focuses primarily on the international political economy of trade, European Union trade policy, international organizations, and private actors in global politics.

GERHARD ERASMUS is an Associate with the Trade Law Centre for Southern Africa (TRALAC), in Stellenbosch, South Africa, which he founded in 2002 with the initial financial assistance of the Swiss Government. He is also Professor Emeritus at the Faculty of Law, University of Stellenbosch. He has been involved in the drafting of new constitutions in Namibia, Malawi, and South Africa and has worked on regional water law projects in southern Africa. He holds an LL.B from the University of the Free State, South Africa, a Master's degree from the Fletcher School of Law and Diplomacy in Boston, Massachusetts, and an LL.D from the University of Leiden in the Netherlands. He is an Advocate of the Supreme Court of South Africa and serves on the editorial boards of a number of African Law Journals.

Henry Gao is currently on leave from the Faculty of Law, University of Hong Kong, and is Associate Professor of Law at Singapore Management University. He has published widely on issues relating to China and WTO. He has spoken at conferences around the world and trained hundreds of government officials on WTO issues. A consultant to several national governments and international organizations, including the WTO, the World Bank, and the APEC, he is also a frequent commentator in major international media such as the Wall Street Journal, CNN, and Bloomberg.

Pablo Heidrich is Senior Researcher, Trade and Development, with the North-South Institute in Ottawa, Canada. Previously, he worked for the Facultad Latinoamericana de Ciencias Sociales (FLACSO) and the Latin American Trade Network (LATN) in Argentina, where his research focused on issues of regionalism, energy integration, and infrastructure. He studied political economy and public policy at the University of Southern California, focusing on the links between financial crises and trade policy in the developing world. He holds a Master's degree in International Political Economy from the University of Tsukuba in Japan.

Julio Lacarte Muró was the first Chairman of the WTO Appellate Body and Chair of the Uruguay Round negotiations on the establishment of the WTO and the dispute settlement understanding. He was Delegate or Head Delegate to numerous international conferences, including the United Nations, World Bank, International Monetary Fund, International Labour Organisation, UNCTAD, UNESCO, the Organization of American States, Latin American Free Trade Association, the River Plate Basin, Economic Commission of the United Nations for Latin America and the Caribbean, Inter-American Development Bank, Group of 77, Latin American Economic System, the Food and Agriculture Organisation, Non-Aligned Nations, UN Economic Commission for Africa, and the WTO. He has had a long and distinguished career as a diplomat, including as Uruguay's ambassador to Argentina, Germany, Japan, and the United States, as well as ambassador to the Organization of American States, the United Nations (Geneva) and the GATT. He served as Minister of

Trade and Industry in Uruguay, as well as President of the Uruguayan Chamber of Commerce and Services. He has been a frequent panellist and Chair in WTO dispute settlement proceedings as well as in disputes under NAFTA and MERCOSUR. Decorated by the governments of Argentina, Bolivia, Ecuador, and Germany, he received the Medal of the Uruguayan Foreign Service. The author of numerous books and articles, he has also been a lecturer at the International Faculty for Comparative Law in Strasbourg as well as ORT University and Artigas Foreign Service Institute in Montevideo.

CHIN LENG LIM is currently Academic Dean and Professor of Law at the Hong Kong University Law School. Following an academic career in England, he left London University's Queen Mary & Westfield College in 1998 to join the United Nations Secretariat in Geneva, where he worked on Gulf War reparations. Subsequently, he was an international lawyer in the Singapore Attorney-General's Chambers and counsel to the Government of Singapore in its free trade agreement negotiations. He also has been a member of the law school at the National University of Singapore.

SEEMA SAPRA is a practising lawyer in New Delhi, India, and has several years of private practice experience, having worked in commercial law firms as well as with the office of the Attorney General of India. She works and writes on trade and WTO issues. She has served as a Visiting Fellow at the Indian Council for Research on International Economic Relations (ICRIER) and was the Director of Trade and Policy at the law firm of Amarchand Mangaldas in New Delhi. She has also been a visiting fellow at the Institute of International Economic Law, Georgetown University Law Centre, Washington, D.C. Ms. Sapra is also a contributor to the "India in the WTO" blog,

NATALIA SHPILKOVSKAYA is currently Editor of the "Bridges" project at the International Centre for Trade and Sustainable Development (ICTSD), Geneva. Previously, she was First Secretary – Legal Adviser in the Permanent Mission of the Russian Federation to the United Nations Office and other international organizations in Geneva (2002 to 2006). She holds an LL.B. from Moscow State Academy of Law and an LL.M. from the University of Ottawa.

DEBRA STEGER is Professor at the University of Ottawa, Faculty of Law, where she teaches in the fields of international trade, international investment, dispute settlement, and governance of international institutions. She is also the leader of the EDGE Network project on global economic governance. Previously, she served as the first Director of the Appellate Body Secretariat of the World Trade Organization in Geneva. Recently, she was Chair of a WTO dispute settlement panel. During the Uruguay Round, she was the Senior Negotiator for Canada on Dispute Settlement and the Establishment of the World Trade Organization as well as the Principal Counsel to the Government of Canada for all of the Uruguay Round agreements. From 1991 to 1995, she was General Counsel of the Canadian International Trade Tribunal. She serves on the Editorial Advisory Board of the Journal of International Economic Law, as well as in executive capacities in several international law organizations.

DIANA TUSSIE is Head of the Department of International Relations at FLACSO/Argentina and is the founding Director of the Latin American Trade Network (LATN). She has served as junior secretary for trade negotiations in the Government of Argentina, and was a member of the International Trade Commission in Argentina. She is a current member of the Committee for Development Policy of the United Nations and serves on the editorial boards of several international journals. In 2007, she joined colleagues from Canada and India in the external evaluation of the WTO's technical assistance program.

PETER VAN DEN BOSSCHE is Professor of International Economic Law, Head of the Department of International and European Law, and Academic Director of the Institute for Globalisation and International Regulation at Maastricht University in the Netherlands. He holds an LL.M. from the University of Michigan and a Ph.D. in law from the European University Institute, Florence. From 1997 to 2001, he was Counsellor in the Appellate Body Secretariat of the World Trade Organization, Geneva. In 2001, he served as Acting Director of the Appellate Body Secretariat.

HENG WANG is Associate Professor at Southwest University of Political Science and Law, China. He is a member of Executive Council of the Society of International Economic Law and of the Organizing and Selection Committee of the Asian International Economic Law Network. He has lectured at nearly 30 universities in North America and Europe, including Northwestern University, London School of Economics and Political Science, University College London, and University of Paris I. He has conducted research at the WTO Secretariat and been a Visiting Professor at the Faculty of Law, University of Ottawa. Most recently, he served as a Visiting Professor at Yokohama National University.

꠵ ꠵ ꠵ Index